PENGUIN BOOKS

CRIME OF THE CENTURY

Ludovic Kennedy is one of Britain's foremost journalists and broadcasters. Born in Edinburgh, Scotland, he was educated at Eton College and Oxford University before becoming a newscaster of British television programs. In addition to his long and widely acclaimed career in broadcast journalism (which includes the documentary *Who Killed the Lindbergh Baby?*, shown on PBS), he was a columnist for *Newsweek International* as well as writing for other newspapers and magazines. In 1994, Kennedy was knighted by the Queen, and in 1995 he was elected President of England's Voluntary Euthanasia Society. He lives in England with his wife, Moira Shearer.

The author of several recent books of non-fiction, including *In Bed with an Elephant: A Journey Through Scotland's Past and Present*, and *Euthanasia: The Good Death*, Kennedy is perhaps best known for three works which have resulted in the vindication of innocent people falsely convicted of murder: *10 Rillington Place*, *A Presumption of Innocence*, and *Wicked Beyond Belief*. He has also published a volume of collected writings, *Truth to Tell*, and an autobiography, *On My Way to the Club*.

Ludovic Kennedy

CRIME OF THE CENTURY

The Lindbergh Kidnapping and the Framing of Richard Hauptmann

PENGUIN BOOKS

PENGUIN BOOKS
Published by the Penguin Group
Penguin Books USA Inc., 375 Hudson Street, New York, New York 10014, U.S.A.
Penguin Books Ltd, 27 Wrights Lane, London W8 5TZ, England
Penguin Books Australia Ltd, Ringwood, Victoria, Australia
Penguin Books Canada Ltd, 10 Alcorn Avenue, Toronto, Ontario, Canada M4V 3B2
Penguin Books (N.Z.) Ltd, 182–190 Wairau Road, Auckland 10, New Zealand

Penguin Books Ltd, Registered Offices: Harmondsworth, Middlesex, England

First published in the United States of America as *The Airman and the Carpenter*
by Viking Penguin Inc. 1985
Published in Penguin Books 1986
This edition with a new introduction published in Penguin Books 1996

1   3   5   7   9   10   8   6   4   2

Grateful acknowledgment is made to the following
for permission to reprint copyrighted material:
Curtis Brown Ltd., London: A passage from *A Reasonable Doubt*,
by Julian Symons. Copyright © 1960 by Julian Symons.
Harcourt Brace Jovanovich, Inc.: Excerpts from *Hour of Gold, Hour of Lead* and
Locked Rooms and Open Doors, by Anne Morrow Lindbergh, and also to *Chatto and
Windus Ltd.* for the selections from *Bring Me a Unicorn*, by Anne Morrow Lindbergh.
Copyright © 1974, 1973, 1972, 1971 by Anne Morrow Lindbergh.
Liberty Library Corporation: Excerpts from articles by Harold Hoffman published in
Liberty Magazine during 1938. Copyright 1938 by McFadden Publications, Inc.
Nigel Nicolson and William Collins, Sons & Co. Ltd.: Excerpts from *Harold Nicolson
Diaries and Letters, 1930–1939*.
Pantheon Books, a Division of Random House, Inc.: Excerpt from *Gift from the Sea*,
by Anne Morrow Lindbergh. Copyright © 1955 by Anne Morrow Lindbergh.
Anthony Scaduto: Excerpts from *Scapegoat*, by Anthony Scaduto.

LIBRARY OF CONGRESS CATALOGING IN PUBLICATION DATA
Kennedy, Ludovic Henry Coverley.
The airman and the carpenter.
Bibliography: p.
Includes index.
1. Lindbergh, Charles A. (Charles Augustus), 1902–1974.   2. Hauptmann, Bruno
Richard, 1899–1936.   3. Kidnapping—New Jersey—Case studies.
4. Trials (Kidnapping)—New Jersey.   I. Title.
HV6603.L5K46   1986   364.1′54′0926   86–830
ISBN 0 14 02.5812 4

Printed in the United States of America
Set in Sabon

FOR FIONA WITH LOVE

'As flies to wanton boys are we to the gods. They kill us for their sport.'

(Shakespeare. *King Lear*, IV, 1)

'At a trial events are often seen in a distorted perspective. A violent event has taken place, and we work backwards from it, considering primarily the evidence bearing on that event. If we work forwards in a natural sequence, from a natural starting point, this evidence may wear a very different appearance.'

(Julian Symons. *A Reasonable Doubt*)

'They think when I die, the case will die. They think it will be like a book I close. But the book, it will never close.'

(Richard Hauptmann)

Contents

Illustrations

News = NY Daily News Photo; AP = Associated Press Photo; Life = Life Picture Service; Frost = The John Frost Historical Newspaper service; UPI = UPI/Bettmann Archive; NJ = New Jersey State Police Files.

Text Illustrations

Introduction

The events described in this book belong to a certain place and time, for the conviction and execution of Bruno Richard Hauptmann for the murder of the Lindbergh baby were the product of conditions that were then current in America and are less evident today.

In the Western world the 1920s and 1930s was a period split between people's overwhelming relief that the horrors of the Great War (the war to end all wars) were over and increasing fears that another would soon be upon them. It was the age of jazz and speakeasies, free love and an uninhibited free press. America saw the regular lynchings of Southern blacks, gangsters like Capone and Dillinger on the rampage, and weekly kidnappings. The Depression was just round the corner.

Upon this tawdry scene stepped without warning a knight in shining armour in the shape of Charles Augustus Lindbergh, whose solo flight from New York to Paris stunned the world by its daring, prophesied the shape of things to come, and made him overnight the number one hero of America – a position which was strengthened first by his marriage to the beautiful, cultured daughter of the banker and politician Dwight Morrow, and later by the birth of 'Little Lindy', their blue-eyed, golden-haired son.

Yet if Lindbergh was the standard-bearer for both the spirit of exploration and the new technology which would be his country's great contribution to the twentieth century, Hauptmann was no less a part of the American scene; for it was those like him, the poor and tempest-tossed who, finding in their own countries (as he did in postwar Germany) destitution and unemployment, felt impelled to seek a new future for themselves across the sea.

In the climate of those times, in the minds of the jury who tried him and of the American people whom that jury represented, there could be no real choice between the word of the airman and that of the carpenter, between that of the public hero and the illegal im-

migrant. Yet there were two institutions which might and should
have afforded Hauptmann protection, and neither of which did.

The first was the law, which, as practiced in the courtroom at
Flemington, New Jersey, was a travesty of what the law should be:
leading questions were asked, hearsay evidence admitted, testimony offered and accepted without corroboration or proof, and,
worst of all, a whole mass of evidence which would have cleared
Hauptmann ruthlessly suppressed or destroyed. Such abuses would
not be permitted today, at least not on that scale.

The conduct of the press was, if anything, worse. With no judicial curbs on them, the newspapers branded Hauptmann as the
Lindbergh baby's kidnapper and murderer from the moment of his
arrest, so that almost no one in America was given the opportunity
to consider a contrary view; and they continued to assert his guilt
until the day of his execution, embellishing their stories with either
inventions or, more often, downright lies. Today, I am told, the
American newspapers are more disciplined in their reporting of
current cases (though not yet as disciplined as in England and not,
American friends tell me post-O.J. Simpson, disciplined enough).

For me the story began in September 1981, in a hotel room in
New York, where I had gone on a BBC assignment. One morning
early, while awaiting the arrival of orange juice and coffee, I was
flicking through the various television channels when my attention
was held by an item on the NBC *Today* show: an elderly lady with
a German accent declaring with passion to her interviewer, Tom
Brokaw, that her husband was innocent of the crime for which he
had been executed. As the interview progressed, I realised I was
looking at Anna Hauptmann, widow of Richard Hauptmann, the
convicted kidnapper and killer of the Lindbergh baby, and whose
haggard, anguished face had filled the front pages of British
tabloid newspapers the day after his arrest in 1934 and had been
one of my earliest and most vivid childhood memories.

The longer I listened to Anna Hauptmann, the more I was convinced that she was telling the truth. It was clear that she and her
husband had been very close, and had she known him to have
been the kidnapper and murderer a New Jersey jury had declared
him to be, it was unlikely that fifty years later and at the age of
eighty-three she would have wanted to appear in public vehe-
mently to assert her belief in his innocence. Nor, I was certain, was
she acting: such intensity of feeling was beyond contrivance.

My interest in what she was saying was in no way casual; for all my life I have believed that to be deprived of life or liberty for something one hasn't done is one of the most agonising things that can happen to one; and to that end I had written several books in Britain to correct miscarriages of justice. The most notorious case was that of Timothy Evans, who had been hanged for a murder committed by another, and after my book on the case[1] was published was granted by the Queen what was quaintly called a posthumous free pardon; two other books helped to persuade the authorities to release from prison three men who had already served many years of life sentences for murders of which they were entirely innocent.

Although I had decided some time before coming to New York that I would call a halt to correcting any more miscarriages of justice (there were so many I could have filled my time doing nothing else), the plea of Anna Hauptmann for her husband's case to be reconsidered was a challenge I found impossible to resist. NBC put me in touch with her lawyer, whose action in persuading the New Jersey police to open up the Hauptmann case archives at Trenton under the Freedom of Information Act was the peg for the television interview. I also read two of the most important books on the case, *Kidnap,* by George Waller and *Scapegoat* by Anthony Scaduto; and as a first step I contracted with the BBC to make an hour-long television documentary film.

In the spring of 1982 I returned to the United States with producer Sue Crowther and a camera team, and we visited the main locations associated with the case: the former nursery at Hopewell (the Lindbergh house in the Sourland hills of New Jersey and now a home for delinquent boys) from which little Charlie Lindbergh had been snatched; the two cemeteries in the Bronx where the ransom money had been negotiated and handed over; the courthouse in Flemington where Hauptmann had been tried; the Union Hotel, where jury and visiting journalists had stayed; the death cell in the state prison at Trenton where Governor Hoffman had visited Hauptmann, and the chamber next to it where he had been electrocuted; and the archive room at police headquarters where the original ransom notes, the famous ladder, and thousands of documents could be inspected.

So long after the event, it was surprising to find so many participants still alive; David Wilentz, New Jersey's former attorney gen-

[1] *Ten Rillington Place:* Victor Gollancz, London, 1961; Simon and Schuster, New York, 1985

eral and the chief prosecutor of Hauptmann at his trial; Lewis
Bornmann, the detective who had claimed that part of the kidnap
ladder had come from a piece of flooring in Hauptmann's attic;
Betty Gow, the Scottish nursemaid who had been the first to find
the baby missing; Ethel Stockton, last surviving member of the
jury that had found Hauptmann guilty of first-degree murder;
Hauptmann's best friend, Hans Kloppenburg, and another close
friend, Henry Uhlig. Many of these people gave us useful information, and most appeared in the completed film. We were also lucky
to find thousands of feet of archive film about the case, including
statements to camera from most of the principal participants, and
long synchronised sound sequences of the trial itself (it was said
that these were obtained covertly, but when you consider how
bulky cameras were in those days and the extra lights they needed,
one must conclude that Judge Trenchard turned a blind eye).

The film, called *Who Killed the Lindbergh Baby?*, was shown
on BBC Television and on PBS in the United States at the end of
1982 to favourable reviews. But while television can always stimulate interest in a subject, its ephemerality can rarely do it proper
justice; the seven thousand words of commentary that is about all
that an hour-long documentary allows are quite inadequate for a
case as complex and controversial as that of Hauptmann. So in the
summer of 1982 I revisited America with my wife to prepare material for a book. We spent a week in New Jersey, staying at the delightful Lambertville House on the Delaware, equally convenient
for Hopewell, Flemington, and Trenton; and a further week in
New York to visit the Woodlawn and St Raymond's cemeteries,
the beach at Hunter's Island where Hauptmann spent so many
weekends and his former apartment at 222nd Street in the Bronx.
With the film out of the way I began writing; the manuscript was
delivered in the summer of 1984, and this book was published for
the first time in 1985. It did not cause a great stir but it sold reasonably well and most reviews said I had proved my case. However, the American people as a whole had believed so long and so
emphatically in Hauptmann's guilt that on a promotional tour I
found a great reluctance to have that belief disturbed.

In treatment and structure the book follows the same pattern as
my books on British miscarriages of justice, the nub of which is en-
shrined in the quotation from Julian Symons's *A Reasonable
Doubt* which appears on the frontispiece of all of them. 'At a trial
events are often seen in a distorted perspective. A violent event has

taken place, and we work backwards from it, considering primarily the evidence bearing on that event. If we work forwards in a natural sequence, from a natural starting point, this evidence may wear a very different appearance.'

For me the starting point has always been some time long before any crime has been committed, when it is possible to assess without prejudice the character, attitudes and behaviour patterns of the person who later falls victim to the miscarriage; for the only way to discover whether a convicted person found guilty is innocent is first to assume his innocence and then (because in life one event often leads to another) to tell his story chronologically. If the person in question is truly guilty, the assumption will not take one very far, but if he is innocent things which proved puzzling before will then be seen to fit into place; and events which seem unfavourable to the convicted man in isolation may take on an unrealised significance when viewed sequentially.

To give an example, consider the documents in the Hauptmann case which show (a) his claim to have been beaten up by the New York police within a day or two of his arrest, (b) the report of the two New York City police doctors who examined him and found nothing wrong and then (c) the report of a private doctor who also examined him and stated that his body bore the marks of a severe beating-up. At first sight these claims would seem to be mutually contradictory and to cast doubts on whether he *was* beaten up (i.e., if the police doctors' report was true, perhaps the private doctor's report was faked). But told sequentially we can see that after the New York City police had questioned Hauptmann all day on September 20, 1934, without obtaining the confession they expected, they resolved on rougher methods; and to safeguard themselves from charges that might subsequently be made against them, they had the police doctors examine him *just before* the beating-up to declare that they found him in good shape. The beating-up followed, and five days later the private doctor's report confirmed it. Similarly Hauptmann's story of his friend Isidor Fisch giving him a shoe-box which was later found to contain marked ransom bills becomes much more convincing if we get to know of Fisch's many crooked activities before the handing over of the shoe-box rather than after it.

Other questions which troubled commentators at the time – the biggest and longest-running being Hauptmann's steadfast refusal to 'confess' and which seemed unanswerable on the assumption of his guilt—wither away in the light of his innocence. But public prejudice then was so strong, the desire for a scapegoat so universal, that people were blinded. Lindbergh (the man for whom New Jersey police chief Norman Schwarzkopf said he would willingly break any oath) was the hero who could do no wrong, Hauptmann the illegal immigrant with a criminal record. Today we see them rather differently: airman and carpenter caught up in a human tragedy which was beyond the understanding of either. In death they are more equal than in life; within the confines of the trial Hauptmann, who told the truth, emerges as a more creditable figure than Lindbergh, who, unintentionally, bore him false witness.

Another advantage of the chronological approach is that it helps to simplify what has become for many a very confusing story. In the last analysis, belief in Hauptmann's innocence depends entirely on one's view of why he hid the ransom money in his garage. Everything else flows from it. Was it, as people at the time believed and wanted to believe, because he was a principal participant in the crime? Or was it, as he always claimed, because he found the money in the shoe-box left by Fisch and, Fisch being dead and owing him money, he was going to use it himself – money moreover which being in banned gold certificates (that is, only redeemable against gold) he could not deposit in a bank. Was he speaking the simple truth when he said, 'I had no more idea it was Lindbergh ransom money than the man in the moon'? Was that the phraseology of a guilty man?

If it was difficult at the time for people to believe in Hauptmann's innocence, it is impossible now to sustain a belief in his guilt. For not only do we know that the most essential pieces of evidence against him were faked, but if he *was* guilty, if with his own hands he kidnapped and murdered Charlie, wrote the ransom notes, received all the ransom money, it seems inconceivable that he would (a) have agreed so readily to copy out for the New York City police parts of the ransom notes with their uniquely peculiar mis-spellings, (b) told the gas station attendant to whom he handed one of the ransom money bills that he had a hundred more at home and (c) and most convincing of all, continued to deny until death that he had played any part in the crime, despite being promised by the Governor and Attorney General of New Jersey that in return for a full confession they would commute his sentence to life imprisonment, and later when there was to be no reprieve, being promised by a New York newspaper that in return for a similar confession they would make provision of $90,000 for his wife and son (now destitute) after his execution. Hauptmann told Anna he had seriously considered inventing some cock-and-bull story of involvement to save his life, but knew he would not be able to sustain it.

After first publication of this book, I had not expected any further life for it. So I was all the more surprised and pleased when my agent Norman North telephoned me to say that a film company called Astoria Productions was interested in acquiring the film rights. The leading light of this company was the delightful Barbara Broccoli, whose father, the late Cubby Broccoli, was responsible for the James Bond films; and when I met her and her partner Amanda Schiff in London and discovered their enthusiasm for the project, readily agreed to grant their company an option. This was renewed from year to year, and then Astoria Productions made an offer for the film rights which on Norman's advice I accepted. By this time the company had commissioned Bill Nicholson, the author of the brilliant *Shadowlands* and *Life Story* (about the discovery of DNA) screenplays, to write a script based on the book and this turned out to be everything I could have wished, true to the book and at times very moving.

After this there were no further developments for a bit and I began to have doubts (in fact I had had them all along) that the film would ever be made. Then, only last year (1995), came the news that Astoria had made a deal with the prestigious American cable television company Home Box Office for a film to be called *The Crime of the Century* (what the press called it at the time), to be made in 1996. The distinguished director Mark Rydell of *On Golden Pond* fame would direct and two European actors – Isabella Rossellini, daughter of Roberto Rossellini and Ingrid Bergman, and the Irishman Stephen Rea – would play the parts of Anna and Richard Hauptmann.

The film was shot in California in early 1996 and although at the time of writing I haven't yet had an opportunity of seeing a rough cut, I am told that HBO and the production team are well pleased. Whereas the book has been and will be read by thousands, the film will be seen by millions, and I have every hope that it will convince the American people once and for all of the dreadful miscarriage of justice that was done in their name. I hope too that the Governor and Board of Pardons of New Jersey will do at

last what they have declined to do before, exonerate Hauptmann's
name officially, much as Governor Dukakis of Massachusetts did
in the equally notorious case of Sacco and Vanzetti.

In the whole affair I have only one regret. It is that Anna Hauptmann, whose marvellous stoicism enabled her and her son, Manfred, to survive the years of hardship after Richard's death, did not
live long enough to see the film clear his name, dying in October
1994 at the age of ninety-six. During my researches in New Jersey
and New York, my wife and I came to know her well and to admire and indeed love her. She was a woman of the greatest rectitude and courage, and we shall always treasure the Christmas and
Easter cards which she used to send us every year. I am also sorry
that Manfred does not seem to have the same interest in the case
as his mother nor in the efforts of those of us whose object is to re-
habilitate his father's reputation.

Are there any lessons to be learned from this tragic story? I believe so, even though Hauptmann was executed sixty years ago
this year, even though it may cause resentment that an outsider
should voice an opinion on American criminal law (in extenuation
I plead what John Donne said three centuries ago, 'Any man's
death diminishes me, because I am involved in mankind'). It is
worth recalling that no European nation, from which most of today's Americans are descended, any longer retains the death
penalty for homicide. But the US Supreme Court, having once
abolished it as 'cruel and unusual' and therefore unconstitutional,
thought fit to restore it, and executions are once again legal in a
majority of states.

And yet what a trail of anguish and deprivation, now and yesterday, capital punishment has left in its wake. It is a fact and not
an opinion, as former Supreme Court Justice Lewis R. Powell says,
that the death penalty does nothing to deter violent crime (the only
true deterrent is the certainty of being apprehended, which no per-
petrator of violent crime thinks, and with reason, he ever will be).
It is a fact and not an opinion that, on average, states that exercise
the death penalty have higher homicide rates than those that have
abolished it; and it is a fact and not an opinion that after an execution the homicide rate in that state often increases. Violence
would seem to breed violence.

It is also a fact and not an opinion that once a state or society
has legitimised capital punishment, then over a period of time a

proportion of those convicted and a proportion of those executed will be found to have been innocent. A few years ago Hugh Bedau, Professor of Philosophy at Tufts University, in Massachusetts, together with Michael Radelet, Associate Professor of Sociology at the University of Florida, and the writer Constance E. Putnam produced a horrifying book called *In Spite of Innocence*,[1] in which they listed more than four hundred cases since 1900 of innocent men (including Hauptmann) having been convicted and many executed by hanging, strangling, shooting, gassing, electrocution or lethal injection. Such miscarriages continue to this day (the Johnson, Tafero and Salazar cases are the latest I know of), a situation which penal reformers on both sides of the Atlantic consider to be a blot on the good name of America, one of the most technologically and sociologically advanced countries in the world. Of all the arguments against retaining the death penalty which are put forward, I find its irrevocability the most cogent; in Britain the Timothy Evans case was a powerful factor in determining the abolition of the death penalty there. Could not the Hauptmann case, along with those of all the other executed innocents, do the same for America?

It would seem not. But why not? 'You used to have a saying in England', a New York lawyer once said to me, 'that it's better for twelve guilty men to go free than for one innocent man to be executed. Here, it's the other way round. We're told we're still a frontier society, believing that Indians and outlaws are waiting to attack us, and that we have to have guns ready to defend ourselves. Well, we're not a frontier society anymore – anyone can see that – but making it easy for people to buy guns allows us to think we are'.

I would endorse that and hope also that before long, American politicians of every party would join together to stand up to the gun lobby and so in time help bring about the climate for a less violent society; and, at the same time, for the Supreme Court to reassert its former beliefs that killing transgressors in cold blood is cruel, unusual and unconstitutional. Only then will innocents like Hauptmann be enabled, as is their due, to continue to enjoy life, liberty and the pursuit of happiness.

July 3, 1996

[1]Northeastern University Press, Boston, 1992.

Prologue

In the early fall of 1934, which was Roosevelt's second year of office, the airman and his wife were staying with her sister Elisabeth and Elisabeth's English husband at Will Rogers' ranch in Beverly Hills, California. In the evening the telephone rang. It was Colonel Norman Schwarzkopf, the head of the New Jersey State Police. For two and a half years his energies had been channeled into hunting for the kidnapper and murderer of the airman's baby son. And now, as he saw it, the long search was over.

'Great news, Colonel!' he said. 'We arrested a guy in the Bronx this morning, German carpenter by the name of Hauptmann. A ransom note he passed to a gas station was traced back to him, and when we picked him up, we found another in his wallet. No doubt of it, he's the guy we've been looking for.'

The airman's wife, who earlier had lived through what no woman should ever have to live through, said, 'Oh, God, it's starting all over again.'

The airman said, 'Yes, but they've got him at last.'

And next day and for a long time after, and without a particle of evidence to link the carpenter to either the kidnapping or the murder, few Americans doubted that they had got whom they were looking for at last. 'LINDBERGH KIDNAPER JAILED' said the *New York Daily News* next day in headlines two inches high, and a week later the airman's wife was writing to his mother, '. . . this man you read about in the papers is beyond doubt one of the right people'.

One must emphasize this at the outset, for it determined almost everything to come.

Book I

CAUSE

Book 1

CAUSE

PART ONE

THE AIRMAN

'He was such a gay, lordly, assured little boy and
had lived always loved and a king in our hearts.'

(Anne Morrow Lindbergh.
Hour of Gold, Hour of Lead)

1

Who was this man whose baby son had been taken from his crib
and murdered? What were the forces that had shaped him? The
world knew him as the aviator who had flown alone from New
York to Paris in 1927, and by it changed the history and geography
of the world. Yet how to explain the impact he made, the mystery
not just of what he did but of who he was, the oddest, shyest,
steeliest, most seemingly un-American hero there has ever been?

The child is father to the man, and there was a pattern to Lindbergh's life that is constant. The flight to Paris was but the last in
a series of heroic inner challenges to which he had responded. But
not impulsively: before accepting he prepared the ground carefully,
and he never smoked or drank, not even coffee or Coca-Cola, for
fear they might affect his judgment. He took decisions alone, not
with others; and while in matters of aviation his judgment was
seldom wrong, elsewhere, as we shall see, it could be faulty.

His boyhood was spent on a homestead on the banks of the
Upper Mississippi in Little Falls, Minnesota, among the woods and
lakes and fields that his grandfather and other Swedish immigrants
chose for their resemblance to those at home. With his Congressman father as guide, he learnt to hunt and fish, row a boat, swim
in the creek, chase butterflies, study woodcraft, collect turtles.

When he was six he was given his first rifle, at seven a shotgun
with which he knocked down ducks in flight, and at nine this
enterprising lad built himself a pair of stilts, a raft for the river and

a garden hut. But the event that transformed him was when his father bought a Model T Ford. At eleven, he found that his legs were just long enough to reach the pedals. It was as well, for his parents had little in the way of driving skills. Peering between the spokes of the wheel, Charles took his mother on expeditions into the countryside, later chauffered his father in his campaign for the Congress in the 1914 elections. Controlling a powered machine, he found, making it do what you wanted, gave him an almost ecstatic pleasure. It also afforded him glimpses – the first of many – of worlds elsewhere.

In his daydreams he went further. Lying on his back in the fields, he would spend hours watching the clouds drift overhead. 'It was a different world up there,' he wrote. 'How wonderful it would be, I'd thought, if I had an airplane – wings with which I could fly up to the clouds and explore their caves and canyons – wings like that hawk circling above me. Then I would ride on the wind and be part of the sky . . .'

In 1916, when he was fourteen, his parents parted. It distressed him at the time, but it brought him closer to his mother. That year he planned a trip with her to California in a new car, a Saxon Six. He overhauled the engine thoroughly, then in dreadful weather on dreadful roads drove his mother and uncle all of the 1500 miles to the coast; the journey took them forty days.

Back home a new challenge awaited him; taking over from his father the man's role in the house. Previous winters had been spent with the Congressman in Washington, so now it was Charles who made the house stormproof and installed a pump and pressure tank in the basement, doing all the plumbing himself. At his father's suggestion and because of wartime shortages, he consulted with local farmers about livestock to buy for the spring. He bought a tractor. He exercised his dog Wahgoosh. He went to school, hating it. He slept on the porch, often in temperatures of 40° below, so that he could see the stars; perhaps even then he sensed his destiny would depend on them. And he was reading a serial in *Everybody's Weekly* called 'Tam o' the Scoots' by the British writer Edgar Wallace. It was about a young Scottish fighter pilot on the Western Front. When I am a little older, he thought, that is what I would like to be.

Early in 1918, when Charles was sixteen, it was announced that pupils wishing to leave school to do farm work would be granted academic credits during their absence. Thankfully he left, never to return, and threw himself into the life of the farm, milking, lambing, ploughing, sowing and reaping, building and mending fences, going to market and performing all the other perennial and often boring chores that are part of a farmer's life. It kept him busy all day, and with his mother's company at meals and after work, he was content. Had the War not ended when it did, he might have made farming his career.

The War did end however, and his mother, to whose advice he always listened, thought he might benefit from college. So they let the farm to a tenant and went to Madison, Wisconsin, where Charles enrolled as an engineering student in the University of Wisconsin. There was a challenge of sorts here, to major in engineering after a three-year course, but it was not one to which he responded. Recently head of his household and managing a farm, he found the regulations irksome. 'They treat you like a baby,' he said. The classes bored him and he found himself out of tune with the tastes of his fellow students. They liked drinking, smoking, the movies, girls. He cared for none of them. In three semesters he never once dated a girl. He thought his classmates frivolous; they found him a prude.

His only outlet was riding the motorbike he had brought with him from Little Falls. He and two friends with bikes would go on cross-country scrambles, careering over bluffs, tearing through scrub, gunning along dried-up river beds. He used the bike to meet the next big challenge of his life, testing his courage to the limit, meeting fear head-on, courting danger so as to eliminate it. The wish to fly was now never far from his mind, and riding the bike was the nearest thing to it. He once told a friend he had fantasies of taking the bike to the top of the college ski-jump, flying through the air on it and landing, hopefully still upright, on the ice of Lake Mendota.

College ended sooner rather than later. In 1922, when he was twenty, he told his mother that he had written to a company in Lincoln, Nebraska, that advertised flying instruction, and had been accepted.

'It all but broke my heart,' she said, but she knew that it had to be. The company, which had its own problems, reneged on the flying instructions before he could go solo; but every day, hanging about the workshops and talking to the pilots, he learnt the rudiments of his craft; and when a barnstormer by the name of Erold Bahl showed up to buy a company plane, Lindbergh went along with him on a tour of the Midwest for the price of his board and keep.

It was with barnstormers that Lindbergh spent the next two years; with each pilot or group he joined he tested his courage a little further. He used to have nightmares about falling from heights, and to overcome these he suggested to Erold Bahl that when they were flying low over some new town, he should climb out on the wing and wave to the people in the streets to attract their attention. He hated doing it, but it paid off handsomely.

When a husband and wife parachuting team came to Lincoln, he told them he wanted to make his first drop a double one – opening the first chute, cutting it away, free-falling, then opening the second chute. They told him that no novice had ever done this before. But he did it, and afterwards found that his nightmares had left him. He learned the trick of appearing to hang from a wing by his teeth; also of standing upright on the wing, attached to the plane by straps, while the pilot looped the loop. He made parachute jumps all over the Midwest and was billed as DARE-DEVIL LINDBERGH on the posters.

In the spring of 1923, with a bank loan guaranteed by his father, Lindbergh went south to Georgia where the army was selling off surplus planes, and bought an old crock of a Curtiss Jenny for $500. But how to take it away? He hadn't flown in six months, he had only ever had eight hours' instruction, he had *never* soloed; and this was a strange plane with unfamiliar instruments.

A helpful pilot who had noticed his hesitant taxi-ing across the field took him on a couple of circuits to get the feel of the plane, then Lindbergh was on his own. The take-off was shaky, but once airborne he felt at home. He climbed steadily upwards until it seemed half America was at his feet, and then he knew that heady amalgam of exhilaration and power which airmen pursue and are pursued by all their lives: an addiction as compelling as sex to the libertine or alcohol to the boozer; entry into a world of stunning purity and total isolation, where time and space have lost their hold, and the infinite and eternal seem within measurable grasp.

For the next year he barnstormed himself, diving with a hook fixed to the undercarriage to snatch flags from the tops of trees, scattering leaflets for his father's unsuccessful campaign to win nomination for a seat in the Senate, once landing in the middle of a Texan town, and having his fair share of minor crashes. But as summer ended, so did the demand for barnstormers; when on a visit to some air races at Lambert Field, St Louis, he was made an offer for his plane, he accepted.

But now what to do? An acquaintance who had noted his dilemma said, 'Why don't you join the army as an air cadet? That's what I did. You'll learn all the flying you ever need, and what's more they pay you for it. And when you've got your commission, you can either stay in or get out.'

So Lindbergh joined the army as one of the 104 cadets who reported to Brooks Field in Texas in the spring of 1924, and was one of only eighteen survivors who passed out as second lieutenants a year later. He learnt about aerodynamics and meteorology, radio operating and military law. He was taught aerial navigation, how to swing a compass and lay a course. He practised formation flying, photography, observation, pursuit. He made more parachute jumps, one involuntary when his plane and another crashed in mid-air. He studied late into the night and at weekends; and when it was all over, he came out top in oral tests, written tests and flying.

It was during his army time that Lindbergh first showed one of his least attractive traits, that of practical joker. His revenge on a group who had tried to throw him into a pond was to put itching powder into the pyjamas of four of them and a live snake into the bed of the ringleader. When a sergeant who snored too loudly returned to the dormitory one night, he found that Lindbergh had removed his bed to the roof. On another occasion he let loose a skunk in a classroom.

On leaving the army (he put in for a permanent commission but never received a reply) Lindbergh did another short spell of barnstorming, this time working out of Denver, Colorado, where he met and accepted another flying challenge — that of night landings and take-offs to give firework displays over towns. It was a hazardous business, operating from farmers' fields and with only car headlamps to see him off and guide him down, but the experience was invaluable and as usual his luck held.

After this he returned to Lambert Field to join a small aircraft company which had just won the airmail contract for the St Louis to Chicago run, and wanted Lindbergh, at twenty-four, to be their chief pilot. He chose as assistants two pilots who had been with him in the army, and after staking out a route with emergency landing fields, took off on the inaugural flight in April 1926, making a two-way journey via Peoria and Springfield, Illinois.

Summer flying was unexacting and enjoyable, but the winter brought new challenges. There was snow to contend with, and ice and fog. Twice Lindbergh was unable to see his way down and had to bale out in the darkness, once in a snowstorm from 13,000 feet. Both times he managed to land safely, find the crashed planes, salvage the mail and send it to Chicago by train. Sometimes, having force-landed, he stayed awake all night to keep the engine turning over, prevent it from seizing up with cold. He seemed impervious to the cold, though his fellow pilots complained bitterly. Once on a trip to Chicago his fellow passenger, the station manager, fearing he was about to freeze to death, forced Lindbergh to land.

As if this wasn't enough, he went barnstorming on days off, took a newsman from a St Louis paper through the night to Florida to report on the latest hurricane, flew passengers to other Missouri cities. During the St Louis motorboat races on the Mississippi he delighted the crowds by stunting, gliding riverwards, skimming his undercarriage through the water like an osprey, then with full throttle soaring up.

What made him do it, continue to court danger day after day when in the past four years he had seen the deaths of so many of his fellow pilots? He gave the answer himself. 'I love the sky and flying more than anything else on earth. Of course there's danger; but a certain amount of danger is essential to the quality of life. I don't believe in taking foolish chances, but nothing can be accomplished without taking any chance at all.' Admiral Nelson had said the same 130 years before.

Outside flying he still had no private life: no bars, no dances, no girls. It was strange because he was extremely personable: tall and lithe ('Slim' was his nickname), with strong blue eyes and aristocratic good looks that men were later to admire and women to find magnetic. Yet when one of his pilots, Philip Love, telephoned a girl in Lindbergh's presence, it was to the accompaniment of childish yahoos.

The practical jokes continued, rather nastier than before. Returning from an evening with a girl, Philip Love would find his bed alive with frogs and lizards. When he failed to respond to the alarm clock in the morning, he was woken by Lindbergh pouring ice-cold water over him. And when his old friend from Lincoln days, Bud Gurney, arrived back one hot and sticky evening and took a swig from his water jug, he felt a terrible burning in his throat and stomach. Lindbergh had filled the jug with kerosene. Gurney was rushed to hospital and in time recovered. Oddly he bore Lindbergh no ill will.

It was in a Chicago movie-house in September 1926, on the day after one of his forced parachute jumps, that an event occurred that was to take Lindbergh to his greatest challenge yet. He was making a rare visit to the movies to see the film *What Price Glory?* about war on the Western Front. Yet it was less this that held his attention than a newsreel sequence of a huge three-engined plane built by Igor Sikorsky, and in which a Frenchman named René Fonck was about to enter for the Orteig Prize of $25,000, to be awarded to the first flier or group of fliers to make a trip direct from New York to France or vice-versa.

Lindbergh sat up. Often in the cockpit, as he reeled off the miles between St Louis and Chicago, he had mentally pushed himself beyond existing horizons. It was what he had done all his life, first imagining, then acting out each flight of fancy: as a small boy exploring the upper reaches of the river; as a bigger boy prospecting with his mother the by-ways of Minnesota and California; as a barnstormer writing his own map of the United States. Already his mind was stretching beyond the route from St Louis to Chicago. A Bellanca airplane, he knew, could carry enough fuel to cross the Atlantic. In his mind's eye he saw himself crossing the Atlantic. Now that dream could become reality too; for here, in the Orteig Prize, was his invitation card.

But how to organize and finance it? He would find a way because whenever he wanted to do something badly enough, he invariably did it. With a lack of shyness that may have surprised even him, he approached a number of St Louis businessmen, some of whom he had taken flying, and persuaded them to put up $15,000 to back the venture. The owner of the only Bellanca available refused to sell it unless he could choose his own pilot, so he commissioned a small and comparatively unknown aircraft company in California and its designer Donald Hall to build a monoplane to his own specifications. By early 1927 it was ready. It was now a race against time, for other competitors were already lining up.

On 10 May he left California in the aptly named *Spirit of St Louis* and headed east towards Missouri. Only two days earlier he had heard that the Frenchmen Coli and Nungesser had taken off from Le Bourget, Paris, westbound, and feared he was going to be beaten at the post; but by now they were overdue and presumed lost. He flew through the night, crossing the Rockies in darkness, and landed at St Louis in the morning. The trip had taken fourteen and a half hours and had been an excellent proving flight. A round of entertainments was awaiting him, but he told his backers he couldn't wait, and within twenty-four hours was on his way to New York.

His arrival there marked the death of Lindbergh the private man and saw the birth of Lindbergh the public figure. It was a transition he had neither foreseen nor desired, and was to be a source of discomfort for years. The tabloid press annoyed him most. He was happy to talk about the flight to anyone who would listen, but their reporters asked questions he found impertinent and irrelevant. What did he think about girls? Did he have a sweetheart? What was his favorite pie? It made no difference what he said, they printed what they fancied – at best inaccuracies, at worst inventions. They got the facts of his early life wrong, they said he was called Lucky and that he landed and took off by periscope.

Photographers marched into his bedroom without knocking and demanded pictures of him in his pyjamas, shaving. When his mother visited him, and he refused to kiss her for the cameras, one paper pasted pictures of their heads over those of a couple embracing and printed that. After a practise flight he was reported as saying, 'Boys, she's ready and rarin' to go.' Another paper referred to him as 'the lanky demon from the wide open spaces'.

What sickened Lindbergh was less the vulgarity than the inaccuracies, and he became contemptuous of those who themselves showed such contempt for the truth. Accuracy, he wrote, 'means something to me. It's vital to my sense of values. I've learned not to trust people who are inaccurate. Every aviator knows that if mechanics are inaccurate, aircraft crash. If pilots are inaccurate, they get lost – sometimes killed. In my profession life itself depends on accuracy.' From these early encounters Lindbergh developed a distaste for the popular press that was to last his lifetime.

On the evening of May 20, 1927 Lindbergh was on his way to Broadway with some publicity people to see a musical. Before entering the theatre, one of the party telephoned the weather bureau and was told that conditions over the Atlantic, which had been thick for the last few days, were now clearing. At once Lindbergh returned to the field to make preparations for a dawn departure. All night the weather over the field remained poor – overcast with drizzle; this held no worries for a seasoned airmail pilot like himself but he hoped it would be enough to deter his two rivals, Commander Byrd of North Pole fame in his three-engined Fokker and Clarence Chamberlin in the Bellanca he had been refused. He snatched a couple of hours' sleep, then supervised the towing of the plane from Curtiss Field across to Roosevelt Field, which had a longer runway. The hangars housing the planes of Byrd and Chamberlin were, he noted with relief, closed.

When dawn came it was still drizzling. The runway was sodden, the plane was carrying a thousand pounds more than ever before, the moisture on the fuselage made it even heavier, the engine was running below maximum revolutions because of the damp, and as he reached the start of the runway the wind changed direction from ahead to behind. It was going to be touch and go but, as he said, nothing could be accomplished without taking a chance. He signaled the chocks away and started off down the runway, the wheels sluggish on the waterlogged ground. Halfway along, the wheels became airborne briefly, dropped back into the wet, lifted again, dropped again, lifted a third time, rose a little higher and a little more and cleared the telephone wires at the end of the runway by twenty feet. It would be 3500 miles and thirty-three hours later when they touched land again, in the heart of the French capital.

No need to retell the story of the flight, for no one has done it better than he.[1] It was an epic on many levels. First the boldness of it, the sheer effrontery of this boy of twenty-five who looked eighteen, relying on his skills and the endurance of his frail craft to take him where no one had been before. It was an odyssey like that of the heroes of antiquity, a voyage into the uncharted – into a tunnel of darkness and storm, cold and turbulence, hallucinations and exhaustion – all of which he overcame to emerge into a daylight that was both real and metaphorical, purified and strengthened by the ordeal.

Of course he wasn't the first to fly the Atlantic. The British airmen Alcock and Brown had done it in their twin-engined bomber eight years earlier. But they could prod each other into wakefulness, and in any case had traveled only half Lindbergh's distance, taking off from St John's, Newfoundland and crash-landing in a bog in Ireland. When Lindbergh passed over Newfoundland he had already been airborne *ten hours*.

To win the Orteig Prize Lindbergh didn't have to fly to Paris. The rules said the shores of France, and nobody would have

[1] *The Spirit of St Louis* by Charles A. Lindbergh

thought any the less of him if, after two days and a night in the air, he had put his plane down before dark in some convenient field in Normandy or Brittany.

But he knew it had to be Paris. It was where the crowds were, and where he was expected; a night landing at Le Bourget among cheering crowds would be – and in the event was – a dramatic end to the most dramatic of journeys. Psychologically it was right too that an emissary of the New World should make his touchdown in the capital of the Old, the continent from whose loins America was formed, the matrix of her people. So the journey was as much into the past as the future; home-leaving and home-coming at one and the same time.

It was right too that it should have been an American and not a European to blaze this particular trail. Europe had had its fair share of pioneering explorers: Stanley and Burton, Scott and Amundsen, Nobile and Andrée, Eckener and Blériot. Now an American could join their company. And the craft in which he had done it symbolized, more than any other, the new technology with which America was soon to lead the world.

And finally there was the realization, by only a handful then, but later by increasing numbers, that the flight had altered irrevocably the way people looked at the map. Abroad, at one stroke, seemed no longer unattainable and mysterious, the province of sailors and adventurers, writers and the rich. Abroad was at hand, or soon would be: soon, it was said, no place on earth would be further from any other by more than a matter of hours.

No wonder America, and Europe too, took Lindbergh to their hearts. In an age of hedonistic materialism he had shown courage and self-denial of a high order; in an age of corporations and committees he had acted alone. From afar people worshipped him for having done and been what they would have liked to do and be and never would, and so made of him a kind of god. The gangling mechanic from the backwoods of Minnesota had gone for ever. Henceforth he would walk in glory and sup with presidents and kings.

The honors, the first of scores, began almost at once. The French President decorated him with the Cross of the Légion d'Honneur, the Mayor of Paris with the city's Gold Medal. He addressed the French Assembly, and at a dinner given by the French Aero Club met Louis Blériot,[1] whom he called his 'mentor'. The French,

---

[1] The first man to fly the English Channel.

who had half expected a hick cowboy, were at first amazed, then disarmed, by his blend of modesty and self-possession.

He flew to England where a vast, excited crowd welcomed him at Croydon Airport. At Buckingham Palace the King asked him how on the flight he had managed to pee, and Lindbergh said in an aluminium container which he had ditched before landing. But by now the American people were growing impatient to honor him themselves, and President Coolidge sent an admiral in a cruiser to fetch him.

In Chesapeake Bay the cruiser was met by four destroyers, two army dirigibles and a fly-past of planes from all three services. In Washington there was a parade and a ceremony at which the President decorated Lindbergh with the Distinguished Flying Cross. Congress voted him the United States Medal of Honor (the first time it had awarded this for a civilian achievement); the entire Cabinet entertained him to dinner, and the Secretary for War promoted him to the rank of Colonel in the US Army Air Corps Reserve – and he was still only twenty-five!

Then it was the turn of New York and a ticker-tape parade watched by three to four million people, and a speech by the Mayor which concluded, 'Colonel Lindbergh, New York City is yours – I give it to you.' After that he flew down to St Louis to thank and celebrate with his backers. The first of two million fan letters started coming his way, and presents of all kinds from all over the world. He could have done without any of it. 'I was so filled up with this hero stuff,' he told a friend later, 'I could have shouted murder.'

One vocal relic of all these tributes survives. It is part of a speech he gave to the Washington Press Club, and listening to it today, to the high, nasal, rather flat intonation, one marvels once again at the young man's self-assurance, the ease and wit with which he addressed those tough newspapermen, and the sense of timing of which any seasoned after-dinner speaker would have been proud.

'When I landed at Le Bourget a few weeks ago, I landed with the expectancy and hope of being able to see Europe. [Pause. Laughter and clapping.] It was the first time I'd ever been abroad [laughter] . . . I'd only been gone from America for two days or a little less and I wasn't in any hurry to get back. [Pause. Prolonged laughter and clapping.] But by the time I'd been in France a week and Belgium a day and England two or three days, by the time I'd opened several cables from America, and. I'd talked to three ambassadors and their attachés, I found it didn't make much difference whether I wanted to stay over there or not [laughter and clapping] and I was informed that while it wasn't an *order* to come back home, there'd be a battleship waiting for me . . .' [Loud laughter, clapping and cheers].

*   *   *

Lindbergh had already demonstrated to the world his skill as an airman. Now he was showing another, quite unexpected quality: that when he spoke, people listened; that he had an outstanding natural authority. From now on people of all sorts would recognize and respond to it; yet, as will be seen, it would not always be to his advantage.

In the summer of that year, and under the sponsorship of the millionaire Harry Guggenheim, head of the Foundation for Aeronautical Research, Lindbergh set off in the *Spirit of St Louis* on a four-month tour of the United States to promote the idea of air travel. It was a grueling trip, during which he covered over 20,000 miles, spent at least one night in each of the forty-eight states, missed only one engagement despite indifferent weather, and led a parade in no less than eighty-two different cities. The flying side of it he loved; with the social side he was less happy. Hysterical crowds, star-struck girls, tireless autograph hunters, cameramen who suggested ridiculous poses, reporters who asked inane questions, greeted him wherever he went. The more he showed women that he was a bachelor who preferred the company of men, the more frenzied their claims on him; the more importunate the demands of everybody, the more aloof and withdrawn he became.

It was nevertheless a highly successful trip, and one which made him richer by $50,000. With promotional fees from firms whose products he had used on the trip, payment for a series of articles in the *New York Times* and advance royalties for a book on the Atlantic trip, Lindbergh was well on his way to leaving money worries behind him.

The crowds and their adulation had become a problem, however, and when Harry Guggenheim offered him the use of a suite at Falaise, his baronial mansion at Port Washington on the north shore of Long Island, Lindbergh accepted gladly. Here he found the privacy he needed to complete his first book on the flight, subsequently published as *We*. Here too he met some of the leading figures of American public life, millionaires like John D. Rockefeller Jr and Dwight Morrow, airline pioneers like Juan Trippe and Orville Wright, politicians like Herbert Hoover and Theodore Roosevelt Jr. It had been Guggenheim's intention to take Lindbergh under his wing, teach him the social graces and see that he matched up to what he called his 'new status as a public figure'. But Lindbergh did not need to be taught these things; he took to them naturally and effortlessly. And Guggenheim and his friends found him 'remarkably mature in his judgments'.

At the end of the year Lindbergh received an intriguing invitation, and one which was to change his life as surely as the flight to Paris. The banker Dwight Morrow, a small, rather shambly man who had started life in an obscure Pittsburgh lawyer's office and had risen to become a senior partner in J. P. Morgan, had recently been appointed Ambassador to Mexico. Relations between that country and the United States were not good at the time, and Morrow asked Lindbergh if he would consider a flying goodwill visit to Mexico City before Christmas.

Lindbergh accepted. The invitation, from President Calles of Mexico, arrived soon after and on December 13, 1927 the airman took off from Washington in the *Spirit of St Louis*. Although he could have made the trip in easy hops, he thought it important to show once again his airplane's paces: he left Bolling Field early in the afternoon, flew through the night, and landed at Mexico City early the following afternoon. It was another first, for no one had made the flight non-stop before. He found that a huge grandstand had been erected for him, and that President Calles, at the head of a vast crowd, had come to greet him personally and hand him the keys of Mexico City.

Lindbergh and Morrow drove in a motorcade through cheering spectators (already the visit was doing more to improve US–Mexican relations than months of diplomacy) to the American Embassy. Here Lindbergh met Morrow's wife, Elizabeth, and Constance, the youngest of his three daughters.

Elisabeth, the eldest daughter, and the middle one, Anne, then studying at Smith College, Massachusetts, would be arriving for Christmas in a week's time.

2

The world in which Anne Morrow grew up could hardly have been more different to that of Charles Lindbergh. Although Dwight Morrow had come from modest beginnings, he had since prospered, especially as senior partner in J.P. Morgan, the international bankers. He kept a house and staff at Englewood, New Jersey, just across the river from New York; he had a summer home, Deacon Brown's Point, on North Haven Island off the coast of Maine, and an apartment in New York.

The prosperity of the Morrows was tempered by a strong vein of Puritanism, for her as well as him, a belief in God, the work ethic and the value of education. Dwight Morrow had had to scrape his way through Amherst College by tutoring and borrowing, but the experience, Anne said, had been a release for his mind and spirit. Similarly her mother's years at Smith College 'were a rich and liberating experience that marked her life and in turn marked ours'. From her parents Anne inherited a love of books and music and the gift of an inquiring mind.

They were a close-knit family: all three girls and their mother corresponded regularly, and when Dwight went abroad on banking or government business, he would take the family with him; then a careful programme of sightseeing would be arranged, to Tintern Abbey or Grasmere, Chartres or Mont St Michel. At Thanksgiving and Christmas aunts, uncles and cousins were invited to Englewood for family parties. Although Anne's letters and diary entries that touch on the family are sometimes almost cloying in their affectionate intensity, those with less close ties may read them with envy. 'We are so happy in ourselves, our family,' she wrote to her Grandmother Cutter on her eighty-first birthday. 'Mother and Daddy have done it of course. But you have done it through Mother . . . So many things we love are you . . . so much of our reading and thinking – so many of our sweet customs and so much of our . . . well, our religion. It is all *you*. I hadn't realized it before.'

Looking back on her childhood Anne was surprised, despite the travelling and the reading, how isolated she had been from what she called 'the real world'. This was partly because in those days events in other countries seemed too remote to be real, partly because of the strong, all-embracing family bonds. Although, as she said, she grew up in the age of Prohibition, speakeasies, free love, flappers and the Charleston, 'the wave of these intoxicating possibilities never lapped the shores of our serene and respectable island'.

In the year that Lindbergh flew the Atlantic Anne was twenty-one, though she looked younger. She was, according to one biographer,[1] 'a tiny brunette with an elfin figure and an air of shy fragility which was apt to bring out the protective instincts of everyone who met her, men and women alike . . . It was a joke in the family that though she presented herself as a timid mouse to the outside world, in fact she had the courage of a tigress, plus a dogged determination that was not prepared to let anything or anyone stand in her way when she wanted something badly enough.' She had oval features, a high forehead and a warm, generous mouth that was not without a hint of self-mockery.

She was then in her third year at university, having followed in her mother's footsteps to Smith College at Northampton, Massachusetts. The year had opened badly with 'wretched' exam results which had brought on guilt and self-reproach; and socially things were little better. 'It is "Spring" dance weekend. There are many boys . . . I am *so* sick of mediocre boys – I mean nice boys who don't interest me very much . . . It seems to me that I have seen one every weekend for ages. I *am* so tired of them.' At Groton where she partnered her brother Dwight for the Washington's Birthday dance, she stayed with Mrs Tuttle, wife of an English teacher, and envied her lot. 'She is young and charming,' she wrote to her sister Elisabeth, 'and has an enchanting house – lots of prints and flowers and a great many rare and beautiful books – *and* a baby, an enchanting baby!'

'Don't you often wish,' she went on, and without an inkling of what the future held, 'this marrying business was all over? I would be willing to sacrifice "falling in love" and all that – honeymoon, etc. – if I could just jump into an everyday life like hers . . . everything settled and everyday, no romance but a kind of humdrum divinity.'

The historic date of May 21 does not appear in her diary, and absorbed as she was in books and music and college life generally, it is clear that the flight made little impact. She spent the summer vacation at North Haven, swimming, sailing, reading, writing

[1]*Lindbergh* by Leonard Mosley.

observations on flowers, birds, the weather. She read Chekhov, Proust, Plato, and visited her neighbor Helen Choate to hear her play Brahms and César Franck. And yet she was dissatisfied. 'I want to write – I want to write – I want to write, and I never, never will. I know it and I am so unhappy and it seems as though nothing else mattered . . . I wish someone would tell me brutally, "You can *never* write *anything*. Take up home gardening." '

Yet without knowing it she was already tentatively shaping a style. In mid July John Pierpont Morgan's vast yacht *Corsair* anchored in the bay: here is her account of going on board for dinner. 'We were transported very swiftly in a closed-in motorboat to the great steamer – portholes sending out flickering lines of light. We stepped out onto the steps, the gangplank, and at the top stood Mr Morgan – great, gruff, cordial, always with his superb manner, large smile, large gestures, large hearty "How do you do?" – his round, full voice, English accent.' After the simplicity of life at Deacon Brown's Point, she likened the *Corsair* to suddenly being transported to Paris or Biarritz. At dinner there was 'music in the distance, lights, candles, lights on the plate and glasses, smoke, the low murmur and laughter of men's voices.'

Anne was secure enough to take this sort of evening in her stride; but back at Smith in the fall she showed her true feelings.

Today I was having my clothes fitted by sweet, bright-eyed little Miss A. She was so rushed. A chance word of sympathy, and she was sitting down on the couch wiping her eyes and telling me everything. I was so appalled. She is twenty-one – my age – her father dead, her mother having slaved for them. An older sister (dreamer) a boy (thoughtless and egotistical) and Miss A working for all of them ever since four-teen . . .

Finally striking out alone, helped by one friend. She had to take all work, at lower price, work every night, she and her mother; work badly done by helpers. She undid it rather than scold them, and redid it herself, late at night, so tired . . . Thoughtlessness of college girls, leaving it Thursday, must have it by Friday, and then don't come for it.

The winter semester passed quickly. In October her mother came to see her before leaving with her father for Mexico City ('How happy your visit made me,' Anne told her, and cried when she left.) Then a week before Christmas, she and Elisabeth also left for Mexico and for Anne's date with destiny.

*   *   *

Her first diary entry in Mexico is a preparation for what is to come. 'This was to be an objective diary. It stops here! I don't care how much I rave, if only I could get down to keep a little the feeling of what has happened in the last week. I wish to heavens I had written it down as it happened, but I was too moved – and too ashamed of my emotion.' Still in a state of turmoil a week later, she tried to recreate her reactions as they occurred.

The train had reached Mexico City in the evening, and she and Elisabeth were met by their father and Constance. He told them of Lindbergh's arrival. Anne was a little annoyed – 'all this public hero stuff breaking into our family party . . . a nice man, perhaps, but not at all "intellectual" and not of my world at all, so I wouldn't be interested. I certainly was *not* going to worship "Lindy" (that *odious* name) anyway.'

At the embassy a red carpet had been rolled out, with officers at attention lining the steps and her mother and a group of people at the top. She heard her mother say, 'Colonel Lindbergh, this is my eldest daughter Elisabeth,' and looked, and saw 'a tall, slim boy in evening dress – so much slimmer, so much taller, so much more poised than I expected. A very refined face, not at all like those grinning 'Lindy' pictures – a firm mouth, clear, straight blue eyes, fair hair and nice color. Then I went down the line, very confused and overwhelmed by it all. He did not smile – just bowed and shook hands.'

She was just as confused later that evening when her father returned with Lindbergh from a dinner engagement, and invited her and Elisabeth into the small sitting room. 'We sat around the fire stiffly. Colonel L. stood awkwardly by the desk, shifting from one foot to another.' Elisabeth, at ease, talked – so that Anne had to ask herself, 'Why is it that attractive men stimulate Elisabeth to her best and always terrify me and put me at my worst?'

She was in love already. 'He is very, very young and was terribly shy – looked straight ahead and talked in short direct sentences which came out abruptly and clipped. You could not meet his sentences – they were statements of fact, presented with such honest directness; not trying to please, just bare simple answers and statements, not trying to help a conversation along. It was amazing – breathtaking. I could not speak. What kind of boy was this?'

Next afternoon they all went to the airfield to meet Lindbergh's mother. She arrived in a big three-engined Ford, accompanied by five escort planes. Anne, who had never looked at a plane in her life before, felt 'the thrill, the tremendous excitement as of a strong electric current' at the sound of their engines. 'I felt – almost – I could die for this.'

That evening they went to a reception at the Residence of the Counsellor, and during dinner heard the sounds of a vast crowd chanting for Lindbergh outside. Anne found it 'ominous and terrifying', like the crowds of the French Revolution. When they went on to the balcony after dinner a great press of people surged forward, some singing, some waving, most shouting '*Viva Lindbergh!*' Beneath the balcony, boys were climbing trees to get nearer to him. The cheering and shouting went on and on, as they had done in Paris and London and New York. 'Who has moved like that before,' Anne asked, 'not with a speech, not intentionally, not trying to move them by any means – just standing there, just existing?' And what did *he* think about it? How did he explain it to himself? Did he think it was just his flight across the ocean that had done it? No, he was too clear-headed to think that. Then how *did* he explain it? The answer, she realized, was that he had no answer, he just accepted it.

But the ice remained unbroken. 'Con,' she wrote next day, 'says he has stiffened up terribly since we came. He avoids us – at least me – as much as I do him, for I *can't* treat him as an ordinary person (and *will* not treat him as an extraordinary one), so I just avoid him as much as possible.' Sitting next to him at lunch on Christmas Day, she remained tongue-tied. 'Anything I might say would be trivial and superficial like pink frosting flowers. I felt my whole world before this to be frivolous, superficial, ephemeral, and I was so young, so fuddled, so ignorant.' She envied Elisabeth's and Con's ease of manner with him, and felt she was of no use, no value – 'I had nothing to give him or *anyone* and I envied those who had.' How could she know that it was because of her reticence that Lindbergh was noticing her the most?

They made an expedition to the floating gardens at Xochimilco in the afternoon, but for Anne the highlight of the week came when Lindbergh took them up in the three-engined Ford. She was now as much in love with his planes as with him, and on the way to the field, aware that she was about to fly with the most famous flier in the world, she kept saying to herself, 'God, let me be *conscious* of it. Let me be conscious of *what* is happening *while* it is happening.' Her mother, Elisabeth, Con, herself and two others climbed in and settled themselves in the wicker chairs. Lindbergh, 'in his everyday suit and grey felt hat', strode across from the hangars, made his way to the pilot's seat and started the engines. The quiver they sent through her body made Anne feel exalted.

When they were well up, the three sisters came forward and sat just behind the cockpit. 'Then we were happy – so terribly and ecstatically happy, alone and together and able to watch him.' They flew over fields which looked like braided cloth and watched their shadow, like that of a great bird, tearing along beneath them; they flew over the city and looked down at 'the black motes' of people in the street; and sometimes Anne let her eyes rest on him – 'looking clearly and calmly ahead, every movement quiet, ordered, easy – and *completely* harmonious . . . he moved so *very* little and yet you felt the harmony of it'. And when they came down, 'it was a complete and intense experience. I will not be happy till it happens again.'

But it wouldn't happen again for many months. At 5.30 the next morning they drove through darkened streets to the airfield to see him leave. 'The engine roared, a cloud of dust and blank grey darkness, then above our heads wings dipping in salute.' When he had gone she wrote, 'The idea of this clear, direct, straight boy – how it has swept out of sight all other men I have ever known, all the pseudo-intellectuals, the sophisticates, the posers – all the "arty" people. All my life, in fact my world – my little embroidery-beribboned world is smashed.' She believed she would never see him again, and that he had not noticed her, but she felt exultant joy that such a person should exist, and that she was on earth to know it. Henceforth she would look at clouds and stars and birds in a quite different way. 'I must have been walking with my head down looking at the puddles for twenty years.'

*   *   *

Back at Smith for her last semester she was preoccupied with other things. Her friend Frances Smith committed suicide, and she blamed herself dreadfully for not being at hand when she was needed. Her old flame 'P' shocked her by announcing his engagement, and another suitor, 'Y', was too ardent and had to be checked. As usual she read extensively – Virginia Woolf, Flecker, Coleridge, Robert Frost, T. S. Eliot – and was persuaded by her tutors to enter for the Jordan Prize for the most original literary work in prose or verse, and for the Montagu Prize for an essay on a woman, historical or fictional, of the eighteenth century. In neither did she rate her chances highly.

But the Colonel was never far away. At the dentist, the sound of the drill reminded her of airplane engines. When she saw a plane in the sky, her heart leapt. She bought a technical book called *Airmen and Aircraft*, and found it 'so incomprehensible that it gives me a tremendous thrill to comprehend the smallest glimmer of it'. With a friend she went to the local airfield, and persuaded a pilot there to take them up. 'It was intense pleasure, and *real, so real*! . . . a new sense that it gives you – a fifth dimension, a shock of revelation, as if one suddenly saw the world upside down.'

And yet, despite a successful last semester in which to her delight she carried off both the Jordan and Montagu Prizes, the sky was clouded. The Colonel had promised to fly up to North Haven that summer, but never came. Worse, Anne heard that he was seeing Elisabeth in New York, and she had always known that Elisabeth had more in common with him than she. To lessen the hurt she and Con fantasized about a Lindbergh–Elisabeth wedding. 'There would be cartoons about it and popular songs and a special number of *Life* . . . Think of Mrs Lindbergh and Mother in the front pew!' She consoled herself by repeating over and over that Lindbergh's world was not her world and vice versa. 'I am nearer to the man who digs ditches, or the man who sells papers, or the fruit-store man or my Italian dressmaker . . . than I am to Colonel L.' She had recurring moods of melancholia and feelings of uselessness at the thought that both her sisters were more self-confident and socially at ease than she. 'I want to be married, but I never, never will.'

Her sun, however, was about to rise. Back at Englewood in the fall, the telephone rang. The boy Colonel was about to re-enter her life.

*   *   *

For him the nine months since Mexico City had been arduous. He had taken the *Spirit of St Louis* on a good will mission to other South American countries, at times pushing himself and his craft to the limits in order to arrive on schedule. On return he flew to Washington to receive his Medal of Honor from President Coolidge, and spent part of his week there giving free trips to Congressmen (some of whom had known his father) and their wives. Crowds and the press still followed him everywhere, making him feel increasingly hemmed in. People touched him to obtain virtue; the yellow press harassed him with embarrassing, personal questions. He became so paranoid in his relations with the media that once, on a flight from Detroit to New York, he was reported overdue because he would not allow officials to announce his safe arrival.

In the summer he took the *Spirit of St Louis* on a last flight from St Louis to Washington, where he presented it to the Smithsonian. It hangs there today, suspended from the ceiling like a toy mobile; a source of wonder to both children and adults, who find it hard to believe that something so small and flimsy could, even today, remain airborne from New York to Paris. Then he joined Transcontinental Air Transport (later Trans World Airlines) as technical director.

All that time the thought of Ambassador Morrow's second daughter can never have been far from his mind. Her reticence and shyness, in contrast to the giggling, star-struck girls he usually met, were like his own; and there was an added challenge in that she came from a world that, socially and culturally, was a cut above his. Perhaps all he knew at the time was that he wanted to know her better; perhaps at a deeper level she represented to him as great a challenge as the Atlantic, a different sort of prize. He remembered the sisters asking him in Mexico City if they could learn to fly, and that he had promised Anne (who had seemed more serious about it than the others) that when he came East he would take her on a flight.

So now on this October day he put it to her on the telephone and she, hardly able to believe that she was talking to him, stammered and stuttered that she would love to if he wasn't too busy. Of course he wasn't too busy, and he proposed coming over to discuss it. She was ready for him a quarter of an hour early. ('I knew the doorbell would make me die of paralysis,' she told Con.) He arrived late, but looking much the same ('his hair is so fair and he grins such a lot') and asked her what sort of plane she wanted to go up in. An open plane, she said, and where would they go from? 'Well,' he said, 'we can't go to any of the fields, or we'd be engaged the next day.' And it was hard to know which of them blushed the more.

So they met at a friend's apartment in New York, and he drove her in his Franklin sedan to see the Guggenheims at Falaise, and she was amazed by how much at home he seemed to be there, 'pushing open the great carved door without knocking, picking up his mail casually, introducing me with the most complete poise . . .' It was upper-crust, Ivy League Anne who felt ill at ease, having to sit down to a formal lunch (which he had never mentioned) in clothes – riding trousers, high-heeled shoes, golf stockings and hat – which she realized were wildly unsuitable.

He left for Roosevelt Field to fetch the plane while the Guggenheims horrified her with tales of 'Slim's' practical jokes. Presently a silver-winged biplane skimmed over the trees and landed in a field. He showed her how to operate the controls, and then they were up, and she tried to fly a little and couldn't and loved every moment of it. And on the way home she found what she had found that morning, that she could now be quite natural with him, that she didn't feel afraid of him or worship him any more, that he was no longer a Norse god but a dear, gentle, considerate man.

After that it was a question of time. There were more flights and more visits to Englewood, and exchanges of views on a thousand things, some of which she confided to her diary or in letters to Con. 'He was very cautious,' she told an interviewer years later, 'and sometimes it was very irritating. Even in a car he'd check all the instruments and the tires. You felt he was over-careful, but then I remembered that in the air he had to be.' And then the press (who had earlier reported the Colonel engaged to Elisabeth) found out, and the family had to be more secretive than ever, referring to him in their letters as Boyd (a character in a magazine short story based on him). There were also moments of doubt. 'He never opens a book, does he?' she wrote to Con. 'How that separates him from our world. Oh, I am afraid, terribly afraid. I do not want to see him again. It is terribly upsetting, liking someone so utterly opposed to you.' In fact it was the wish of each to explore and understand each other's world that became the core of their relationship.

He joined her in Mexico in November. They flew only once, but for Anne it was an unforgettable experience; a journey far into the interior, over pine forests and green gorges and rivers, meeting the snows on the western side of Popocatepetl and spiralling up to 17,000 feet to peer down at the smoking crater on top. This was what flying gave you, a passport to the secret places of the earth, to a world as far removed from the pages of Proust and T. S. Eliot and Virginia Woolf as you could imagine. She was aware too of what cross-country train travelers experience on a lesser scale, 'the immeasurable chasm between *us* and *it* . . . the contrast of being so perilously near and so impossibly far away at the same time'.

And doubts were melting day by day. In a letter to the frail Elisabeth, convalescing on Long Island from the heart condition from which she would never fully recover, she wrote: 'He is much more like us than you could imagine . . . amazingly understanding, sees far outside of his world, even into ours.' And she admitted frankly, 'As you can see, I am completely upset. He is the biggest, most absorbing person I've ever met . . .'

She was home for Christmas and for the huge New Year party for nearly a thousand guests to celebrate the move into Next Day Hill, their new fifty-acre Englewood home, with its pine paneling, pile carpets, Hoppners and Raeburns. And early in the New Year she was writing to her old friend Corliss Lamont, son of her father's partner in J. P. Morgan, Thomas Lamont, 'Apparently I am going to marry Colonel Lindbergh . . .'

3

The engagement was formally announced from the American Embassy in Mexico City on February 12, 1929. Before it, said Anne, her father had spoken about Lindbergh in glowing terms. 'He said, "Look at this young man. He doesn't smoke, he doesn't drink, he doesn't go around with women." He was promoting him – until we got engaged, and then he said, "What do we know about this young man Lindbergh?" '

Now, like her fiancé before her, Anne had to say goodbye to the private life she had always cherished and become part of the public life of her future husband. It was an ordeal she had not foreseen. Each day the press waited at the embassy gates for the pair to appear and then set off in pursuit, even as far as the Ambassador's weekend residence in Cuernavaca where, in search of scoop pictures, they climbed like monkeys onto roofs and miradors. To avoid them the fugitives used back doors, changed cars, put on disguise. The only true escape was flying; after posing on the airfield, they took off into the blue, shook the crowds and dust from them, then landed on some deserted plain to enjoy a picnic with no one else within miles.

Knowing that the publicity accompanying their wedding would be almost unbearable, they agreed to marry privately and without warning. On 27 May a few close friends and relatives were invited to a reception for Anne at the new house in Englewood. On arrival they were told the truth. Anne, radiant, appeared in a wedding dress and Brussels cap made by the local seamstress (who had been sworn to secrecy) and carrying a bouquet picked by Elisabeth from the garden. There were no photographers (a photographer might have let the news out in advance). Afterwards Anne lay on the floor of a borrowed car while her husband drove past the pressmen at the gate. That evening they boarded a cabin-cruiser in Long Island Sound and headed north towards Maine.

If they had cherished the idea of an undisturbed honeymoon, they were in for a shock. Two days later, while refuelling at Block Island, they were recognized. Lindbergh took the boat out to sea, but they were pursued relentlessly and had to spend the night anchored far out on the fishing banks in dreadful weather, unable to lie comfortably in their bunks and with china crashing about them. 'They found us again in the morning,' Anne wrote to her mother. 'That terrifying drone of a plane hunting you, and boats.' She felt like an escaped convict. For seven hours one cameraman circled the boat, bawling for them to come and pose on deck. She recalled what bliss it had been earlier, being a nobody, free to go anywhere without being followed, stared at, shouted at. 'Fame,' she concluded later, 'is a kind of death.'

But the marriage itself was a source of ever growing security. 'The sheer fact of finding myself loved was unbelievable,' she wrote, 'and changed my world, my life and myself. I was given confidence, strength and almost a new character.' Another door to self-liberation was in flying, for it was no part of her husband's plans that his wife should stay dutifully at home. Wherever he flew, she would fly with him, not as a passenger but as a properly trained radio operator and navigator. With her bluestocking background she might well not have wanted this; in the event she welcomed it. 'From being earth-bound and provincial, I was given limitless horizons. From the cloistered atmosphere of books, writing and introspection, I was freed to action.' And when there was a lull in the action, flying gave her peace 'to sink down into oneself, to think, to learn poetry'.

Hardly had the honeymoon ended when they were up and away across the United States to survey a route for Transcontinental Air

Transport, a journey which was to be a combination of train and plane. It meant staying in Harvey Houses or small hotels in places like Columbus, Ohio; Clovis, New Mexico; Waynoka, Oklahoma; Winslow, Arizona. As well as the hazards of flying (thick fog over the Alleghenies) they had to contend with tiresome people; importunate autograph hunters in Columbus, a couple in a Kansas City hotel who said they'd been mistaken for Anne and 'Lindy' and wanted to drop by and say hello; boring, garrulous women everywhere. But there were compensations: diving down from twilight through grey-blue clouds to land in night-time St Louis, glimpsing through the darkness the confluence of the Mississippi and Missouri glistening below; flying over the Grand Canyon and Death Valley and the Indian adobe huts; a weekend in a log cabin in the Californian Redwoods. 'Really,' Anne wrote to Con, 'this is much more fun than I imagined.'

The only major snag was in having to adopt a *persona* all the time, rarely being able to relax and be herself. Early in their married life Charles had said, 'Never say anything you wouldn't want shouted from the housetops, and never write anything you wouldn't mind seeing on the front page of a newspaper.' For a girl who liked sharing her enthusiasms and reservations, who had said at college that the most exciting thing in life was communication, the advice was dampening. Yet she did her best to keep to it, and for the first three years of married life gave up her diary. The worst aspect was being polite to strangers without saying anything personal, knowing that anything she did say might be repeated and made into a story. 'I have to keep *so* reserved and taut and on edge for pitfalls'; she found the strain 'rather terrific'.

They were back in the East in August, staying a weekend with the Hoovers at the White House, dropping into Cleveland to attend the air races and visit Cutter relations. But the seemingly endless to-ing and fro-ing was making Anne desperately homesick for her family, all now on summer vacation at Deacon Brown's Point. 'Oh, I long, *long* to be with you. I dream about North Haven every night,' she told her mother, and there were letters to Elisabeth and Con in the same vein. About to go there, they had to switch abruptly to Albuquerque, New Mexico to investigate the disappearance of a TAT passenger plane, later found crashed on a mountain with no survivors. When they took off for St Louis her father's sad voice – 'You can't get up here *at all*?' – was ringing in her ears, and Anne confessed that never in her life had she been so disappointed.

They did manage a few days in North Haven on return, then were off again, this time in a tri-motored Fokker on a survey flight of the West Indies and Central America for Pan-Am: they were accompanied by Juan Trippe, the founder and President of Pan-Am, and his wife. Also by a bagful of books, Forster's *Aspects of the Novel*, Meredith's *The Egoist*, David Garnett's *No Love*, and *Crime and Punishment*. They flew from Miami to Cuba, Haiti, Puerto Rico, Dutch Guiana, Trinidad, Venezuela, Colombia, Panama, British Honduras, and back to Miami. They were greeted ecstatically, entertained royally and listened to bands playing 'Lucky Lindy' wherever they went. They rose before dawn and flew until dusk; they looked down on green mountains, palm-fringed beaches, lavender and turquoise seas.

In Puerto Rico they changed from the land-based Fokker to two amphibian S.38s, and took off and landed in harbours big and small. In Haiti Anne found the black government ministers 'condescending' in a way that American blacks, however well educated, could never be. At St Thomas the British Governor begged them not to land at St Kitts until after Sunday morning church service. At Government House, Trinidad, they drank to the King and danced to the gramophone. In Caracas the President took Charles's hands in his and said of him in Spanish, 'What a straight stick of a man!' By the time they reached Panama Anne was exhausted by the round of teas, dinners and receptions and 'wild, wild' to get home; but she claimed that the actual flying had been the loveliest she had ever had.

For the first five months of their marriage the Lindberghs had been on the go almost continuously, never staying more than a few days in any one place, living out of suitcases. Now it was time to find a home, somewhere accessible from New York and as secluded as possible. But Anne was worried about the publicity that would surround the move, and in a rare but understandable burst of emotion she told her mother,

I have gotten utterly bitter about it. I have no patience, no understanding, no sympathy with the people who stare and follow and giggle at us ... Oh, Mother, it is so wearing. I wonder if it will ever slacken ... It is like being born with no nose, or deformed – everyone on the streets looks at you once and then *again*; always looks *back* – that second look, the *leer*. No one else gets that. President Hoover doesn't get it; Daddy doesn't get it; they get a dignified curiosity. But that look, as though we were a public amusement, monkeys in a cage. There are

so few people in the world who treat us *naturally* . . . And then it
works both ways; if *they* aren't natural, I can't be.

There was another reason why she longed for a place of her
own: not only as a shield against the giggles and leers of the
uncomprehending, but to fulfil herself as a woman. She was going
to have a baby. At the end of October she told her mother she was
feeling wretched, but 'Tell Elisabeth not to start making bibs with
rabbits until we are sure.' A week later Dr Foster confirmed it. The
sickness continued, so she breakfasted in bed in the suite that
she and Charles now had at Englewood, and read the letters of
Katherine Mansfield and Chekhov.

By New Year 1930 she was well enough to leave with Charles
for Los Angeles to fetch a brand new Lockheed Sirius and in it
attempt the west to east transcontinental record. They made the
journey there in an open Falcon in easy stages, flying only in the
mornings. Resting in hotel rooms in the afternoon Anne learnt a
poem or two 'to help amuse me when flying, when it's cold and
dreary to look out'. A favourite was Sir John Beaumont on the
death of his son Gervase, aged seven. 'I think the first four lines
are perfect and compact and heartrending,' she wrote to her
mother.

> Dear Lord, receive my son, whose winning love
> To me was like a friendship, far above
> The course of nature or his tender age;
> Whose looks could all my bitter griefs assuage . . .

Later she would look back and recognize the cruelly prophetic ring
to it.

In California they visited Douglas Fairbanks and Mary Pickford
at 'Pickfair' (a name they found so absurd they joked about calling
their own home 'Spengustus' after their middle names of Spencer
and Augustus) and met Will Rogers and Amelia Earheart, the first
woman to fly the Atlantic, the year after Lindbergh. Amelia, almost
as tall and spare as Charles, impressed Anne greatly. 'She is the
most amazing person – just as tremendous as C, I think. It startles
me how much alike they are in breadth.' For her part Amelia took
the opportunity to disassociate herself from the 'Lady Lindy' tag
bestowed on her by the popular press. ('The title was given me, I
believe, probably because one of us wasn't a swarthy runt.')

She thought Lindbergh an odd fish, however, and was a witness to one of his tiresome practical jokes. Standing behind his wife one evening at a friend's house, he let fall drops of water from his glass on to her blue silk dress where it covered her shoulder. Anne put up with it for a while, then rose and stood with her back to the others, her head resting on her arm. Amelia thought she was going to cry. Then Anne turned and emptied her glass of buttermilk over Charles's blue suit. His reaction was first amazement, then 'he threw up his head and shouted with laughter'. For Anne the action was out of character, but in the circumstances probably the best she could do.

On Easter Sunday 1930, with Anne as navigator, the Lockheed flew from Los Angeles to New York in 14 hours and 45 minutes, breaking the transcontinental record. But to avoid bad weather Lindbergh had to take the plane above ten thousand feet (one of the objects of the flight was to show how commercial airplanes could get through whatever the weather). There was no oxygen, with the result that Anne, now seven months pregnant, had a rough and painful ride, and had to be carried from the plane on landing. It was typical of Lindbergh to assume that because he was impervious to physical discomfort, others would be the same; and typical of Anne to suffer in silence rather than jeopardize the success of the trip.

Being young and strong she soon recovered, and now her thoughts were concentrated on the baby's birth. Because of the press, she told her mother-in-law, they had agreed to make no announcement of it until after formal registration. But to let his mother know of it Charles had devised 'a very business-sounding telegram'. If she received a message from Reuben Lloyd saying 'Advise accepting terms of contract', it would mean it was a girl, while 'Advise purchasing property' would mean a boy. Would Mrs Lindbergh be terribly disappointed if it wasn't a boy? 'I'm afraid C will, though he is discreet and won't say so . . .' They were looking for land on the Palisades to build a house. 'I'm a little afraid the baby will roll off into the Hudson, but C says being a Lindbergh it will have more sense than that.'

Their son was born at Englewood on 22 June, his mother's twenty-fourth birthday, and, in the American fashion, named Charles Augustus after his father and grandfather. 'When I first saw it,' Anne told Mrs Lindbergh, 'I thought, "Oh dear, it's going to look like me – dark hair and a nose all over its face." But then I discovered what I think is Charles's mouth, *and the unmistakable cleft in his chin.*' A month later she was writing to Elisabeth of her great happiness and of how Charles had been 'understanding, patient, dear beyond words'. The baby was 'such fun now' and gaining weight. 'Every day I hold him once or twice and talk to him, and his eyes — very big and blue — look at me and then he smiles and opens up his face as Charles does.' In August she was reading baby-care books which advised against over-fondling. 'I don't want to "fondle" him at all,' she told her mother, 'so perhaps there's something wrong with me . . . And he doesn't like "fondling" but kicks and knocks his fists about, so perhaps there's something wrong with him! But he enjoys being talked to and he is curious and attentive.'

By the end of September, after much searching, she and Charles bought a piece of land on which to build a house. It lay on a hill a few miles from Hopewell in the Sourland Mountains of New Jersey, twenty minutes by car from Princeton and two hours from New York. It was surrounded by woods — oak and sassifras and dogwood — had a fine rolling view, and there was a field in front on which to land a plane. Meanwhile they rented a small farmhouse with white palings five minutes from Princeton from which they could supervise the building of the house and Charles could commute to New York by train. Anne was thrilled. 'Our own home — imagine it!' she wrote to her mother-in-law, and asked advice on how to run a house.

By November they were into the Princeton House, with an English couple — Olly and Elsie Whately — to cook (though *not*, the Colonel insisted, to wait at table), a Canadian trained nurse, Miss Cummings, to look after the baby, and invitations to Con and Charles's mother to come and stay in the one guest room. 'It's real country and quiet, and there's a great big fireplace.' In the garden she was planting bulbs, red and yellow tulips, and 'little upstart crocuses'. Moreover, she found a bookshop in Princeton where the owner, she told Con, was as gaga about Katherine Mansfield as they were.

But thoughts of the baby were paramount. 'It almost breaks my heart,' she wrote to Con, 'when I get back from the city late, after six, and from the far corner of the main road I have watched for the light in his window to see if he is still awake, and I see that it is dark, and I know he has been put to bed and I will not get one of those eyes-squeezed-up smiles until ten o'clock.' And she finished another letter to her sister, 'I must go and get my fat lamb, who is sleeping in the barn . . . He has a blue sweater suit on and lifts his arms for you to pick up, and laughs when C takes him ceiling flying.'

This idyll could not last for ever, and in the New Year of 1931 Charles (now working in New York as a technical consultant to TAT and on medical research with the French biologist, Alexis Carrel) was planning another trip, this time to California in the spring. Naturally Anne was worried about leaving the baby, for although in their new life the oglers had been kept at bay, they had not entirely disappeared. One day a woman whom Anne described as 'a little bit off' arrived at the door saying she *must* see the baby – 'a matter of life and death'. Then at Englewood a car with sightseers had driven fast into the front court, knocked down and killed her beloved West Highland terrier Daffin, and sped away.

Would Anne's staff of the Whatelys and Betty Gow – an attractive Scots girl of twenty-seven who in February had taken the place of Miss Cummings – be able to cope with reporters and publicity? 'The baby,' she wrote to Con, 'is not quite in the same position as most other babies . . . The house is rather unprotected. The baby sleeps outside. Unless he is watched every second, anyone could walk in and photograph him, etc.' (A year later she could have looked back and said that if photography was all that people were after, they could have had all the pictures they desired.) 'I would feel a lot happier,' she wrote to Mrs Lindbergh from Princeton, 'if you were here. I know you could deal with any situation like that.' And she concluded, 'My, how I hate to leave that baby! I suppose that's it, at the bottom.'

In the end the Californian trip was cancelled, but later that year, and while the house at Hopewell was completing, she and Charles made preparations for another epic flight – this time to explore for commercial purposes the Great Circle route to China via Hudson's Bay, Alaska, Siberia and Japan. They would be away at least three months. To ease the burden on her husband Anne not only did a full radio operator's course (the little squeak when she first pressed the key on a practise set, she said, 'brought four dogs and the baby scrambling into the room') but, at a country club on Long Island, learnt to fly solo as well. 'We were there every night for supper,' she told Mrs Lindbergh; 'some good days, some bad days, some scoldings, etc. You know how it is.'

There was still the problem of where to send the baby, whose claims on their affections were growing day by day. Everyone was agreed that he was looking more and more like his father, though his eyes were more his mother's. His hair was curlier and lighter, too, and he scrambled out of the room after people, pulling himself up by chairs and tables and his father's knees. He was beginning to understand a few words like 'more' and 'no' and the names of the two dogs, Skean and a black and white terrier called Wahgoosh, a present from the Colonel's mother, to take the place of the murdered Daffin.

In the end it was decided to send the baby and Betty Gow to join the rest of the Morrows on vacation at Deacon Brown's Point, and a drawing room in the Bar Harbour Express was reserved in the names of Betty and Mary. 'I am very anxious,' Anne told her mother, 'for no one to know, to get him up there quietly.' She was overjoyed that her mother would be with the boy as it meant he would be safe and happy and loved. 'Will you keep some kind of record of his actions and take a picture about once a month? Don't let Betty give him too many toys . . . and don't let people fuss over him or pay attention to his little falls and mistakes, will you? I'm sure you'll do it all just right – I'm not worrying.'

On 29 July Charles and Anne in their Lockheed Sirius float-plane landed in the North Haven harbour on the first leg of their trip. It was a fleeting visit but for Anne an important one, not only to see her son happily settled into his new quarters, but to satisfy a childhood need to touch home base (as she put it) before starting out on a new race. For once she enjoyed the crowds who came to watch them land; they were neighbors and fellow islanders who had known her all her life. She walked through every room of the white clapboard house, lingering over loved objects like the Audubon prints and the Toby in the dining room. Then, in the morning, they were gone, heading north-west for Ottawa and points beyond. For Anne it had been a visit 'of supreme joy'.

From Ottawa they flew to Moose Factory and along the northern rim of Canada, over perilous seas and faery lands forlorn. They battled with fog and the radio, and landed in tiny settlements where lived Eskimos and Indians, American traders and Scots missionaries, few of whom had ever seen a plane before. At Petropavlovsk in Siberia, a hotel they were staying in caught fire. Off Ketoi Island they force-landed in a fog and were saved from the rocks by singing Japanese sailors. In Osaka they found a stowaway in the baggage compartment. In Tokyo Lindbergh was given a welcome to rival those of Paris and New York.

Yet amidst all these distractions Anne's son was never far from her mind. 'I dream about the baby every night almost . . .' she wrote, and at Osaka was thrilled to get a letter from her mother with news of him (exploring Mrs Morrow's room while she wrote, dancing with her at night, his curls coming out from under his blue cap – 'All just what I want to hear'). On Karaginski Island two Russian women, a blonde zoologist and an interpreter, shyly asked to see pictures of Charles, and Anne was happy to oblige. 'They were gay and sweet,' she wrote, 'spreading them all on the table. And when I left, my boy seemed nearer to me because they had seen his picture and talked of him.'

From Japan they flew to China where rivers had burst their banks and hundreds of thousands of square miles of countryside were under flood. Told that the Sirius was the only plane in the country with sufficient range, they surveyed the flooded area for the Chinese Government, and ferried doctors and medical supplies to isolated habitations. In Shanghai disaster struck. They had accepted the invitation of Captain Maclean of the British aircraft carrier *Hermes*, at anchor in the Yangtse, to haul the Sirius on board each night. One morning in the course of its being lowered with Charles and Anne aboard, the swollen current swept the floats sideways and began to tip the plane over. Charles and Anne had to swim for it, and after rescue were revived with Royal Navy Bovril and castor oil to kill the Yangtse's germs. But the plane would need more than on-the-spot repair, and when on 5 October they received word that Dwight Morrow had died (thus dashing the hopes of many Republicans that he might be the party's next Presidential nominee), Lindbergh decided to cancel the rest of the trip and return home immediately by sea.

In mid October Betty Gow and the baby moved from North Haven to Next Day Hill, and it was here on 27 October that parents and son were reunited. Anne found him what contemporary photographs confirm: 'a strong, independent boy swaggering around on his little firm legs', not recognizing his parents after so long an absence, yet not afraid of them either. She sometimes took to referring to him as Charlie to avoid confusion with his father. His father adored him, gave him tit-bits of cornflakes and jam from the breakfast table, tossed him playfully in the air which the boy enjoyed so much he came running to his father with outstretched arms, crying 'Den!' (Again!) Every night he took his grandmother Lindbergh's toy lamb or pussycat to bed with him, hid it under the bedclothes, then like some artful conjuror pulled it out with shouts of glee. He was less certain about a duck which quacked when pulled: he laughed at the noise but shied away from pulling it himself.

At this time Elisabeth Morrow was running a school at Englewood for very small children, and persuaded her sister to allow Charlie to join it, although at eighteen months he was six months younger than the youngest child there. For him it was an opening to a ruder world. On his first morning all the other children made a great fuss of him; then a little boy called Donald, who had made as much fuss as anybody, punched him in the back. Utterly bewildered, Charlie sat down and cried. 'That anyone should hurt him *purposely*,' Anne wrote, 'that hadn't entered his life before.'

The rest of his initiation showed little improvement. As soon as Charlie stopped crying, Donald hit him again, took away his shovel and pulled his hair. His mother saw this happen five times. The girls were fascinated by his curls. One little girl tried to scrape them off with a trowel. 'Consequently,' wrote Anne, 'Charlie cried most of the first three days.'

When Anne suggested, a little diffidently, that Charlie was really too young for school, the whole staff rallied round and volunteered to give Charlie individual attention. A Dr Mitchell, the little people's consulting psychologist, was called in, and gave his opinion that Charlie should play alone in the sandbox until he had gotten accustomed to his environment and was able to make social adjustments. (No suggestion that the others might make social adjustments to him!) This seems to have worked. 'Charlie,' wrote his mother, 'is perfectly happy playing in the sandbox or rustling in the leaves, completely . . . unconscious of his social obligations.'

The house at Hopewell was almost complete and soon after her return from the East Anne took her mother, Elisabeth and Charlie to spend a night there. Inviting Mrs Lindbergh to stay, she wrote, 'We're not going to make much of Christmas, except for the boy.' The doctor had said he needed a haircut – 'but I don't want to cut his curls off till you see him'. She added: 'He has great fun with his father. C says, "Hi, Buster!" to him whenever he sees him, so the other day when Charles came into the room, the baby looked up and said, "Hi! Hi!" and . . . when C left the room, the baby said, "Hi all gone!" ' And he could now say 'P'ease' for 'Please' and 'Da-da' for 'Thank you'.

Early in the New Year of 1932 they began to use Hopewell regularly for weekend visiting, although some of the furniture was borrowed and temporary, and there were no curtains to the windows. This meant that at night, until the shutters were drawn, anyone could approach the house through the woods and observe what was happening inside; and the location and development of 'the eagle's eyrie' had been well publicized in the press.

Set in five hundred acres of woodland and meadow, the house was approached from a narrow country road by a half-mile winding drive. It was a modest establishment, one oblong central section flanked by two small wings and made of fieldstone with a whitewash finish; from it there was a pleasant view across open country to the south.

The interior was fussy and a little gloomy; many small rooms and a plethora of doors and closets. Betty Gow never liked it, and the wife of the warden of the boys' home in residence there now thinks it must have been a brute to decorate. On the ground floor from west to east were the servants' quarters, the dining room, the living room and Lindbergh's study, all with interconnecting doors. Above the servants' quarters and dining room were two guest rooms, above the living room the Lindberghs' bedroom and bathroom, and above Lindbergh's study, Charlie's nursery. There were stairs at either end of the house, then uncarpeted. Visiting the place today one is struck by how small-scale everything is.

The nursery, for instance, measured 15 by 13 feet, although it had three windows: a long one facing south and two smaller ones with square panes facing east. The wallpaper was of toy trees, a church, a man with a dog, while between the two east windows was a fireplace with Dutch tiles (still there today) of a fisherman, a windmill, an elephant and a boy with a hoop. On the mantelpiece and beneath the two sconces (also there today) stood a large ornamental clock. Against the wall opposite was Charlie's crib with its tapered wooden bars – what they called a fourposter cot; beside it, to keep out draughts, was a pink and green screen with pictures of farmyard animals.

During the week the Lindberghs continued to live in their suite at Next Day Hill, convenient for Charles's visits to New York and ideal for Anne not only to answer the hundreds of letters of sympathy on her father's death, but to begin writing her first book: an account of the 'magical' trip to the East which, under the title *North to the Orient*, would eventually become a minor aviation classic. The writing was going slowly, she told her mother, but she was pleased with the chapter on the stopover at Deacon Brown's Point – the last glimpse of Charlie for three months and the last sight of her father ever.

She also found she was pregnant again, and when she received three baby blankets from Mrs Lindbergh, she was uncertain whether they were for Charlie or the baby to come. Charlie continued to call his father 'Hi'. When a car ran into the back of theirs in New York, smashed the tail-light and mudguard and sent the luggage flying, Charlie seemed unconcerned. But when his father got out to remonstrate with the other driver, Charlie 'in a calm, high voice' said, 'Hi all gone.'

Despite the inconvenience, Anne loved the weekends at Hopewell, for there she looked after Charlie herself, leaving Betty Gow at Next Day Hill. 'It's such a joy,' she wrote to Mrs Lindbergh from Hopewell on 7 February, 'to hear him calling for "Mummy" instead of "Betty"! And she understands just how I feel about it, and helps me.' News of Charlie's doings filled the letter. He and the dog Wahgoosh played wildly, chasing each other round the room. Charlie had had a pillow fight with his father: he was knocked down, didn't cry (which made his father very proud) and tried to throw the pillow back.[1] He could now wind up the music-box himself. His favorite toy was the elephant, but he preferred to take the pussycat with the flat tail to bed at night. At the time of writing he was trying to stand on his head and look at his mother upside down through his legs.

And that was to be the last happy news of Charlie, indeed almost the last news of him at all; for in three weeks' time he would have disappeared.

*   *   *

On the last weekend of February the Lindberghs were at Hopewell again. They were due to return to Englewood on the Monday (Anne knew how much her mother dreaded Mondays, the day her father had died), but as Charlie had a nasty cold, Anne chose to stay over at Hopewell until Tuesday, March 1. By the Tuesday Charlie's cold was no better, so she decided to stay that night too,

---

[1] Will Rogers, visiting the family at Englewood a week later, noticed much the same thing. 'His mother sat on the floor in the sun parlor among all of us and played blocks with him for an hour. His dad was pitching a soft sofa pillow at him as he was toddling around. The weight of it would knock him over ... After about the fourth time of being knocked over, he did the cutest thing. He dropped of his own accord when he saw it coming.'

and rang Englewood for Betty Gow to be sent over by car to help her look after him. This decision was taken on the spur of the moment. Charlie had never spent a Tuesday night at Hopewell before.

Tuesday was bleak and cold, and for most of the day the rain swept steadily across the Sourland Mountains. Beyond the house the dogwood trees in winter white looked like an army of dripping, ragged ghosts. It cleared a little in the afternoon, and Anne went for a walk. On return she stood outside Charlie's nursery window and threw a pebble against it to attract his attention. Betty Gow came to the window holding Charlie, and when he saw his mother he waved and she waved back.

In the evening the rain stopped altogether, but then the wind rose and it blew most of the night. Betty took Charlie down to the living room to play with his mother, while she went to the staff sitting room for tea. Later Anne would write how glad she was that she had spoiled him that weekend when he was sick, had taken him on her lap and had rocked and sung to him.

Shortly before six Betty took him back upstairs. She read to him, then gave him his supper, a plate of cereal which he ate at a little maple table, surrounded by his toys. When Anne came in the two women prepared him for bed. Betty put drops in his nose and Vick's ointment on his chest, and wrapped him in a little flannel shirt stitched with blue Silko thread that she had run up specially to keep out the cold. On top of this was put a sleeveless wool shirt, diapers and rubber pants and, to cover everything, a Dr Denton's one-piece sleeping-suit. It seems a lot of clothing for so small a child, but they were anxious to protect him from further cold.

For the same reason, having put him in the crib, they fastened two large safety pins through the sheets, blankets and mattress at the head of the bed, to prevent him kicking off his bedclothes during the night. They placed the pink and green draught screen at the head of the bed, but opened the south window a little to let in fresh air. They closed the two east windows, also two of the three green lattice shutters – but the shutters outside the window to the right of the fireplace had become so warped they would not shut. They were the only warped shutters in the house, and had been that way for at least three weeks; no one had thought to have them fixed.

As Charlie dozed off, Anne went down to the living room to write while Betty moved to the bathroom next door to wash some of his clothes. At eight she returned to the nursery and satisfied herself that Charlie was sleeping peacefully; then she went to the staff sitting room for supper. At about 8.35 the Colonel arrived from New York (having forgotten a speaking engagement) and, after hearing from Betty as he passed through the house that his son was better, joined his wife in the living room.

Between 8.35 and 9.10, said Anne, she and Charles were having dinner in the dining room. They then went into the living room for five or ten minutes, and while there Charles heard, above the moaning of the wind, a sharp crack, like (as he described it later) 'the top slats of an orange-box falling off a chair' and which he presumed came from the kitchen. Then they went upstairs to run baths. By this time Betty Gow and Elsie Whately were also upstairs in Elsie's room, looking at her new dress. Ollie Whately and the dog Wahgoosh remained in the staff sitting room; after his bath Lindbergh went down to his study to read.

At ten Betty broke off her discussion with Elsie to take Charlie on his final visit to the bathroom. On entering the nursery she did not switch on the light, so as not to startle him, but she closed the south window and turned on a heater to take the chill from the room. Standing in the dark and warming her hands, she began to sense that something was amiss. She could no longer hear Charlie's regular breathing. 'I thought that something had happened to him, that perhaps the clothes had got over his head. In the half-light I saw he wasn't there, and felt all over the bed for him.'

Puzzled and concerned, Betty knocked at the bedroom next door to ask Anne Lindbergh, then preparing for bed, if the baby was with her. No, said Anne, surprised. 'Perhaps the Colonel has him,' said Betty, praying yet doubting he had, and ran down to the study to ask. No, he said in even greater surprise, he didn't have the baby; and he ran upstairs to join Anne in the nursery.

With the light on they saw that the two big safety pins were in their place, and that the bedclothes and pillow still bore the imprint of Charlie's small body. Husband and wife stared at the empty crib with incredulity, having to think the unthinkable, to register an event of such hideous and shocking enormity that the mind instinctively recoiled from it.

The Colonel was the first to accept it.

'Anne,' he said, 'they've stolen our baby.'

Outside in the darkness the wind howled like a dog, as if to articulate their anguish.

'Oh, my God!' said Anne.

PART TWO

THE CARPENTER

' "God, I thank you!" These were my first words
as I trod the pavements of the New World.'

(Richard Hauptmann)

4

Now it is time to turn to the carpenter, for although he does not
appear on the scene until later, he was a contemporary of the
airman, being only two years older. His origins and background
were as different from the airman's as the airman's had been from
those of his wife; but, in the context of the whole, of equal
importance.

Bruno Richard Hauptmann was born on November 26, 1899
in Saxony, some seventy miles south of Berlin and not far from
Dresden and the Czechoslovak border. Kamenz, which lies on the
banks of the Schwarze Elster, was then a town of some ten thousand
people, most of whom were employed in light industry.

Richard (as he liked to be called) was the youngest of the five
children of Herman Hauptmann, a stone-mason, and his wife
Paulina: he had three elder brothers, Herman, Max and Fritz,
and an elder sister Emma. They owned and lived in No. 64
Bautzenerstrasse, a two-storey brick house, occupying the ground
floor and renting out the upper one. As the family grew, the kitchen
was turned into another bedroom, and the cooking was done on
a stove in the living room; a bench round the stove became the
center for family gossip. At the back of the house was a small
garden with pear and apple trees, and in the back yard two sheds
which housed pigs and goats.

When Richard was very small his mother used to dress him in
girl's clothes, and his earliest memory – he thinks he must have
been three – was of saying to her, 'Mama, I don't want to wear a

dress any more. I don't want to be a girl any more, I want to be a boy.' Once in boy's clothes he felt happier, but later wondered what had motivated his mother. Was it because she had hoped for another girl rather than a fourth boy?

The family rented a couple of fields on the outskirts of the town to grow vegetables and provide hay, and in later life Richard looked back on the trips there with pleasure. They took the family wagon which his brothers pulled, his mother and sister pushed, and he rode in. While they were harvesting, his mother allowed him to explore, pick wild flowers, do what he liked. 'I believe it was during this period,' he wrote, 'that I acquired my passion for nature.' It was a passion that was to last throughout his life.

When he was six, his mother filled a knapsack with a slate, a sponge and his lunch and sent him to join his brothers and sister at the local school, with its stern exhortation engraved above the entrance: 'Learn wisdom, practise virtue.' On their first day new children were given a bag of sweets, ostensibly from the school, to lull their fears, but handed in secretly by their parents. At first Richard was unhappy because of a speech impediment which made pronunciation difficult, and for which he was teased. A sympathetic teacher helped him overcome it, and being of an inquiring disposition and anxious to improve himself, he grew to enjoy school.

Richard's father was not a church-goer, but his mother took the children every Sunday. Richard was always impressed by church, by the grandeur and scope of it, the fact that it was God's house, by the way its eight huge pillars 'held up the sky'. On Sunday afternoons in winter there was sledding in the snow: in summer there would be a family walk through the woods to a beer garden where the children would be given a glass of sweet beer and a sandwich, and a ride on the beer garden merry-go-round.

But always in Richard's mind were thoughts of the woods and fields that lay beyond the town, the haunts of birds and animals, where a boy might run free. His second brother, Max, first took him there when sent by their mother to look for herbal leaves and mushrooms, and berries to preserve for winter use. The mushrooms they sold for a good price. 'In this way,' said Richard, 'I earned the money for my clothes and shoes, and was very proud.'

One day they strayed further and stayed longer than they meant, and when a storm broke they made a bed of branches and lay down and slept. It was morning when they woke, and having washed in a brook and breakfasted on fresh huckleberries, they slowly made their way home. Naturally they found their mother frantic with worry, and had to promise never to stay out at night again. On this trip Richard found two baby rabbits which he brought home and succoured, but when they began to refuse food he returned them to the forest.

When Richard was nine, his father became superintendent of a quarry, and sometimes the boy would take him his lunch there, then pick camomile and coltsfoot and look for blindworms under the stones. But now his father began drinking heavily and staying late in beer halls, long after the time for family dinner. Often Richard was sent to fetch him, his mother hoping that the father's love for his youngest son might persuade him to return. Sometimes this was successful. 'But once,' said Richard, 'when I said, "Papa, come home, Mama and we are waiting for you, we want to eat," he struck me in front of everyone. At that moment something in me died . . . from that day I could never again say Papa, only Father.'

And so the years went by, with their customary seasonal celebrations. In August there was the Kamenz Forest Festival, in which a thousand children dressed in white and marched in procession through the town, carrying wreaths of oak-leaves and flowers. At Christmas there was nightly carol singing in the market square, in which Richard liked to join; and his mother made up a little basket for him to take to the needy, for 'although we were poor, she never forgot there were those even poorer'. Sometimes the army would arrive in the town, and the soldiers would be billeted in the houses. 'Then,' said Richard, 'I could hardly sleep for excitement.' He and his friends marched with the soldiers down the street, watched fascinated while they cleaned their rifles in the evenings and took pride in being permitted to polish their boots.

Now, as the elder children left home to seek work, the family began to break up. Herman was the first to go, then Emma and a girlfriend left to seek a new life in America. Richard and Fritz picked a box of apples for them as a farewell present, then Fritz left to take up an apprenticeship in tailoring. 'Now I was alone with mother. I could no longer look up to my father with childish love. I was always afraid when I had to speak to him . . . so my mother became everything to me.' In the evenings, when his father was in the beer hall, they sat together in the living room, she telling him of her own family, of her father who had been blind for forty years, he not only of his deeds and misdeeds but of his innermost thoughts and feelings. 'There was nothing in my life, good or bad, that I did not tell her . . . Here on the bench round the stove, the twilight hours passed on wings.'

Richard was beginning to stretch his own wings, too. His enthusiasm for outdoor life found a fruitful outlet in an organization called the *Pfadfinderbund*, or Pathfinders, similar to the Boy Scouts but with an emphasis on nature (and which twenty years later was to form the core of the Hitler Youth). On summer weekends they camped in the woods, swam and ran races, cooked meals over log fires, practised field crafts, and on Sunday evenings marched home singing. Being German, there was an army officer in charge, and what Richard called 'a military slant' to the exercises. He soon became a troop leader and remained in the organization three years; on his first trip away from home his group took part in a regional rally at Magdeburg where they were quartered in the military barracks. They exercised in the Harz mountains, and Richard's youthful imagination was stirred by the legend of Kaiser Barbarossa, frozen in the subterranean castle beneath the Kyffhauser mountain, only to be awakened by the mountain's guardian ravens.

At other times, fired by reading *The Last of the Mohicans* and *The Trapper*, he and his friends dressed up as Indians and trappers and set off for the Deutschbaselitz dam and the woods above it. Here they launched crude rafts of branches and reeds which they propelled by hand, swam underwater, and caught trout with their hands and pike with snares. Once Richard found a baby hawk which he took home and fed on mice caught by the cat. But, like the baby rabbits, the hawk soon pined, so he took it to the door and let it go. It flew onto the roof, stared at him, screamed and flew away. 'Now we were both happy.'

At Easter 1913, when he was fourteen, Richard was confirmed in the Lutheran Church; although like most children he had found the confirmation classes dull as well as difficult, he admitted to approaching his first communion with trepidation. Then, having collected his attendance certificates and said goodbye to his teachers, it was time to leave what he called 'the golden freedom' of schooldays and apply himself to a trade.

For someone who loved the woods, carpentry seemed a natural choice. His mother took him to an old carpenter she knew to advise him on tools, and having followed his advice to buy his axe from a smithy and not a factory, he and four others joined the old

carpenter as apprentices. His first job was to grade boards from
the sawmill, put aside those suitable for building and cut up the
rest for firewood. Here, and later at a trade school, he mastered
the rudiments of his craft. 'I learnt the strength and carrying power
of different types of wood, and what to take along for each type
of construction.'

The war put an end to the carpentry apprenticeships. Most
of his fellow apprentices were dismissed outright, while he was
transferred to office work. But as his contract had specified learning
carpentry, he left in 1915 and tried to join the army. Being only
sixteen (though he claimed to be eighteen) he was not taken on,
so he went home and was lucky to be accepted for another
apprenticeship, this time in mechanical engineering. His mother
had to pay fifty marks a year for this, but the manager was so
pleased with his progress that he waived the fee and gave him three
marks a week pocket money. With his father's health deteriorating
and his three brothers all at the front – Herman in France, Max
in Russia, Fritz in Rumania – the work of feeding the pigs and
goats and tending the crops in the fields fell on Richard and his
mother. Five thousand miles away, on the banks of the Mississippi,
fourteen-year-old Charles Lindbergh and his mother were doing
much the same.

In 1916, when he was seventeen, he began to take an interest in
girls. At first he refused to join his friends in dancing lessons,
preferring to be out in the countryside, but when his mother told
him that he would be a laughing-stock at dances standing around
like a piece of wood, he succumbed. 'I never became much of a
dancer,' he said, 'but I learned to be at ease among the ladies.'
Noticing this, his mother said she hoped he would do nothing that
would shame the family.

In 1917 Richard received his calling-up papers for the artillery,
but was told he could continue his apprenticeship for the moment.
One evening he returned home to find his mother in tears. 'She
could not speak but pointed to the telegram on the table.' Herman,
her favourite son, had been killed in action. His father remained
very silent, but she wept every day for several weeks. Then, one
afternoon at work, Richard received word to go home immediately,
as his mother had received another telegram. Max had also been
killed in action. 'Mother and I sat for a long time hand in hand on
our bench.' In the same year came news that Fritz was missing.
'How my mother felt after all this, only a mother can understand.

My father's heart was broken, and although he did not show it, I could see how he suffered.'

In 1918 Richard Hauptmann was called up at last, not to the artillery but to the 103rd Infantry Replacement Regiment, and found himself billeted in the requisitioned dance hall in Kamenz where he had been such a tentative patron. He and his fellow conscripts were issued with uniforms which were mostly too large or too small. One day a new, rather pompous officer asked him his name. '*Hauptmann, Herr Hauptmann*,' ('Captain, Mr Captain') he replied. The officer, thinking his leg was being pulled, kept repeating the question to Hauptmann – and to others – and, always receiving the same reply, became apoplectic with rage.

In early summer while at nearby Königsbruck for training with the 12th Machine Gun Company, he heard that his father had died. 'In spite of the fact that we had not understood one another, I was deeply moved. Latterly I had always tried to get close to my father, but in vain.'

There was a comic opera touch to their embarkation for the Western Front. Expecting an issue of army underwear, they were given ladies' nightgowns instead. 'We asked if these were for our girl-friends, but the sergeant explained there was a shortage of underwear. He said he felt very tenderly towards us and we should be honored to wear such beautiful things.' They were cut low front and back with lace at the top and little bows on the shoulders, and offered what Hauptmann called 'plenty of movement'. Passing through Thuringia they sat on the roof of the train wearing these and waving, to the astonishment of the local inhabitants.

They passed through Kaiserlautern and Metz and detrained in pouring rain in some woods near St Mihiel on the Meuse. Here Hauptmann began his brief war, sleeping the first night on a piece of wire netting slung between two trees. In charge of a machine gun, he was in action with American troops a few days later, but afterwards his company withdrew.

Hauptmann's memories of his first weeks at the Front were those of discomfort rather than fear. Noticing a nipping sensation all over his body, he was told by an old soldier that he had lice. 'I was so ashamed,' he said, 'but was told that all of us were blessed with the little creatures.' Hunger was permanent. In a vineyard in the Moselle they stuffed themselves with unripe grapes and suffered severe stomach pains. In an abandoned village they found a cat, chased it for two days and ate it. Resting in Luxembourg one night they enjoyed a roast, allegedly goat but in fact an officer's dog, seized by one soldier as a birthday present for another. During the meal the officer came in and asked if anyone had seen his dog. No one had, but he was offered a portion of goat. He declined at first, said Hauptmann, but later sent over his orderly with a plate and was given a generous portion.

Returning to the Front at night along duckboards laid across a quagmire of mud and water, Hauptmann set up his machine gun in a nest made of railway ties on a hillside within sight of Verdun. 'There were wild roses on the roof,' he said, 'which gave us natural protection. It must have been an idyllic place in summer.' He was slightly wounded in an artillery barrage and the post was abandoned. Sent by night to another part of the Front to relieve the 177th Company, he remained in a shell hole until dawn, exhausted by the weight of his machine gun and its ammunition. Later, on a hillside, he endured another artillery barrage, was again slightly wounded and sent back to a field hospital. He was there when the war ended.

It wasn't until January 1919 that Hauptmann was released from the army and along with Fritz returned to Kamenz, to their mother's inexpressible joy. Their home town however, like many others in Germany, had been badly affected by the war: few families could not claim a relative dead or wounded, food and clothing were scarce, and work almost impossible to obtain. And how had the war affected Hauptmann? 'I thought that I was no different when I returned, but I deceived myself. My moral point of view was no longer the same.' His mother had instilled in him high principles, but army life had taught him otherwise: that other people's property was no longer sacred; that – as in the incidents of the grapes or the officer's dog – stealing from necessity was not really stealing at all. 'Although I knew I was doing wrong,' he wrote, 'I quieted my conscience with the words, "Oh, well, others do it too." '

His first piece of wrong-doing occurred soon after his return. Having searched for work unsuccessfully in Kamenz and the surrounding villages, he eventually obtained employment as a repair machinist on night shift at the Wiednitz coal mine. It lay several miles away and he travelled there by afternoon train. It was the custom of the work force, when coming off shift, to put a few pieces of coal into their knapsacks to take home; but on reaching the station one morning Hauptmann found a group of colliery officials waiting to inspect their knapsacks and then read a lesson on stealing. 'I never thought,' he wrote, 'that people who had an abundance could be so small as to take away a few pieces of coal from a poor devil.' Ten years earlier he would have known that taking coal was stealing it; ten years later the colliery officials would probably have condoned it; the time was out of joint.

Soon after this Hauptmann missed his train, reported late for work and was dismissed. Back in Kamenz he looked for work everywhere without success. Leaving the last of several places of employment that had rejected him, he noticed a flock of geese in the yard. On an impulse, and still smarting from being refused work again, he picked up the nearest goose and walked out of the yard with it. But what to do with it? He could hardly take it to his mother. 'Making some excuse, I gave it to a man who happened to be passing by.'

Worse was to follow. He met a pre-war friend, Fritz Petzold, a locksmith who had also been in the army, and together they looked for work everywhere, but again without result. They were cold (for they did not have enough clothes) and hungry, and neither of them had any money.

> How we came to think of stealing, or what gave us the impulse to do this, I can no longer remember. I know that before I entered the army, I never had such a thought, even though I often had to forgo pleasures which required just a little money.
>
> I cannot say that my friend had a bad influence on me because he too had had the same good upbringing as I. We both started down a road which we loathed and regretted, but when we came to realize this it was too late.
>
> I no longer remember where we committed our first burglary. There were three occasions altogether. Two of them occurred in the neighboring villages and one in Kamenz. We were familiar with all these places and knew just where to go.

The German records show that all three burglaries took place within a period of only six days – March 14 to 20, 1919. It was as though all the normal, conventional restraints which had hitherto held them in check were suddenly in abeyance, as though pent-up feelings of deprivation, resentment and despair had been released like water from a burst pipe, in one brief uncontrollable flood. They first broke into a house in the village of Rackelwitz on the night of March 14 and stole from a desk in the living room 400 marks in cash, a watch and a gold-plated chain. The next night they went to another village, Bernbruch, climbed through an open window in the house of Herr Schierach, the Mayor, forced open a desk with a crowbar and stole some 250 marks and a silver pocket watch.

Then, five days later, they committed a crime which would come to haunt Hauptmann for ever afterwards and play a powerful part in determining his ultimate fate; a crime negligible in cash terms but despicable in human ones and which Hauptmann was later to call 'the greatest shame of my life'. At 10 a.m. on the morning of March 20 he and Petzold, to whom he had given his army pistol, accosted two women wheeling pushcarts laden with foodstuffs on the road from Tesa to Nebelschutz. At first the women refused to stop but then Petzold pointed the pistol at them and threatened to shoot. From the pushcarts they took nine bread rolls, eight food ration cards and a pocketbook containing three marks. The same night in Kamenz, flushed with success, they broke into No. 62 Bautzenerstrasse, only three doors away from Hauptmann's home, and from yet another writing-desk, the property of a leather merchant named Scheumann, they stole a further 200 marks and another watch. Six days later they were arrested.

Writing years later of the offense against the two women, Hauptmann claimed that they committed it because they were hungry. But it is difficult to reconcile this with the fact that less than a week earlier they had stolen more than 800 marks[1] with which they could surely have bought some food, even without ration cards. It looks as though all their crimes, and the frenzied pace at which they carried them out, were prompted more by a compulsion to assert their identity, to hit back at a society which had for so long rejected them in protest against the continued emptiness and frustration of their lives.

The two were kept in Kamenz Jail for a month, then put in a prison wagon to go for trial to the regional center of Bautzen, fifteen miles away. At a place called Bischofswerda, Hauptmann escaped and made his way home. Next day, no doubt at his mother's insistence, he gave himself up and was taken under escort to Bautzen.

On June 3, 1919 at the Country Court in Bautzen both men were sentenced to two and a half years' imprisonment on the larceny charges, and on June 17 before a different judge to a further two and a half years on the highway robbery charge. For first

---

[1] Worth then about $15 or £3.50.

offenders it was a harsh punishment but lawlessness due to unemployment and food shortages was rife in Germany then, and deterrent sentences were thought necessary.

In prison Hauptmann came to his senses, recognized the shame that his actions had brought on the family, especially his mother, and the embarrassment he had caused his friends. 'Everything was forfeited,' he wrote, 'and for the first time in my life I cursed the day I was born. Why did my brothers have to die and I remain? What would happen to my life?' His conduct however, and that of Petzold, were exemplary, and they were soon put in positions of trust, supervising others. Hauptmann sang in the choir, learnt to accompany himself on the mandolin and in the prison library read all the travel books he could find. 'I made the acquaintance of strange people, strange customs and the natural beauties of other countries. The books took the place of all the things I wanted to do.' He and Petzold used to walk in the garden together, 'but we never talked about our past, we were too ashamed of it'.

After nearly four years they were released on three years' probation (which meant that if convicted of a further offence within three years they would have to serve the remaining year in addition to any other sentence imposed on them) and on a fine spring day of 1923 Hauptmann took the train to Kamenz. On the journey his eyes lingered on the forests and meadows which had given him such pleasure in his youth. 'As I walked from the station to our house, I had a feeling that all eyes were watching me. I could no longer hold my head high, as I had done before.' But his mother's love for him was steadfast, and friends called round as though nothing had happened. He was angry when his mother received a bill for his board and lodging in prison on the grounds that she owned her house and that one day her son would inherit a share of it. Outraged (for he had worked hard in prison), Richard begged her not to pay the bill but she insisted, even though it meant borrowing.

Once again he began the seemingly endless round in search of work, both in Kamenz and the neighborhood, and once again he drew a blank. 'It was not that people did not want to employ me,' he said. 'They really had no work.' So he decided to go further afield, to southern Germany where the prospects might be brighter. He took his knapsack, two pots for cooking, and soldering equipment to earn a little money from repair jobs along the way. From Leipzig he walked south towards Bayreuth and Nürnberg, staying in 'nature' cabins where he could, otherwise in the open, seeking work and not finding it. *En route* he met three other young Saxons, two sculptors and a painter on their way to Italy, and from them he learnt and put to good use an ancient law whereby anyone homeless in a strange village could claim a free bed from the local Mayor.

At the youth hostel in Nürnberg he met young men from the south on their way to find work in the north, and realized the futility of continuing his journey. So, having spent a fruitless day in Nürnberg searching for work, and another in Chemnitz where there were many machine factories, he reached home footsore, penniless and utterly frustrated.

It was soon after his return to Kamenz in June 1923 that he once again succumbed to the temptation of trying to obtain something for nothing. The German record states that on the night of June 7 leather drive belts were stolen from three separate locations in Kamenz – a pottery, a sawmill and a machine factory – and that Hauptmann was suspected of complicity in all three thefts: certainly as an apprentice carpenter and machinist he would have had knowledge of at least two of the locations. His own story was rather different: that a machinist friend who had recently fitted new drive belts to some machinery had kept the old ones instead of returning them to their owner, and – even old leather being then of value – had asked Hauptmann to sell them. ('We all did that,' he said, 'and no one considered it as stealing.') Whatever the truth of the matter, Hauptmann was apprehended with the drive belts on him (in Dresden where, he claimed, he had gone to sell them), arrested, and taken to prison.

In prison again he took stock of his position. 'Even if I was acquitted of any charge, I knew I would have to go back and serve the last year of my previous sentence. I also knew I would be lost if ever again I found myself behind prison walls. So I decided to run away. I saw the gate open and no guard in the yard. Providence could not have made it any easier for me. I simply walked out and went through the nearby fields to the woods. No one followed me.'

In the woods Hauptmann came to a decision, one that he had been contemplating for some time. It was clear there was no future for him in Germany. No one had tried harder or failed more completely to obtain employment; even if he found it now, the prospect of a further stretch of imprisonment would for ever be hanging over him. For a long time his sister's letters from America and the books on America that he had read in Bautzen Jail had fired him with the desire to go there and begin a new life: there was work in America and there was freedom. He had been unable to go before because he had no money for the fare (he had written to ask his sister to advance him the fare money, but she was unable to). Now necessity would take him there without the fare. He would go as a stowaway.

He went home to tell his mother of his intention to emigrate and she 'with a heavy heart' agreed, helping to pack his knapsack and giving him a packet of food and what money she could spare for the journey to Hamburg. On parting he gave her a solemn promise that he would never do anything seriously wrong again, no matter what the circumstances. It was a promise which, many people would say, he kept.

From Hamburg he traveled to Bremerhaven, and found the North German Lloyd liner *York* in harbor, preparing to sail for the United States. There were no problems in going aboard her, and after several days' search he found a suitable hiding-place beneath one of the boilers. Here he curled up with his knapsack, a loaf of bread and a bottle of water, and awaited the ship's departure. When he felt the vibration of the engines he knew they were on their way. It was an emotional moment. 'Farewell, my homeland. Farewell, my mother.' Exhausted by nervous and physical tension he fell asleep.

When he awoke he found his hiding-place had become uncomfortably hot and that the movement of the ship was making him seasick. He picked up his knapsack and made his way to the crew's bathroom where he washed and changed. Then he went on deck where the wind and rain revived him. He asked where they were and was told the English Channel. He spent that night on deck, walking up and down or dozing in a sheltered position behind one of the funnels.

Next day he was in luck. He spent the morning browsing undetected in the ship's library, then, hearing the sound of a mandolin, struck up a friendship with its owner and fellow-player who invited him to join his table. The problem of food was now solved, and the problem of a billet was also solved when he found an unoccupied cabin.

It looked now like a smooth passage to New York. But the next day his luck ran out. A ship's officer approached him on deck and, probably noticing his shabby clothes, asked to see his ticket. He confessed he had none, was taken before the captain and sent to the crew's quarters for the rest of the voyage. But he was given no work and spent each day sun-bathing on the upper deck, watching the passengers playing games and gossiping, wondering what would happen to him in New York.

From the crew he learnt that there were half a dozen other stowaways on board, still undetected, and that on approaching New York he would probably be put in a cabin before being sent to the Immigration Center on Ellis Island. He decided to find some opportunity of jumping overboard and swimming to the shore for, having come so far, he was determined to succeed. On the voyage he had learnt what English words to use when looking for work and how to recognize the sign 'Dishwasher wanted'. After Germany the thought of work exhilarated him. 'I did not mind what I did. I wanted to get a start and learn the language. That was more important than the kind of work or amount of wages.'

After quarantine and an examination by the Immigration doctor he was locked in a cabin while the *York* sailed up river and docked at Hoboken. Out of the cabin window he saw the tall buildings glide by, so near he could almost touch them, so distant they could have been a dream; then the ship stopped and he heard the sounds of disembarkation. He and others were put on board a small steamer bound for Ellis Island; as it prepared to leave the pier, he jumped over the side.

He knew that to be seen swimming fully clothed towards the land would be to invite certain arrest, and that to escape detection he would have to wait until dark. It was then only midday so he stayed shivering on a beam under the end of the pier, his legs dangling in the water, until 9 p.m.; then, exhausted and frozen, he swam the length of the pier until he came to a flight of steps. He managed to crawl to the top and was about to try and stand up when he was seized by a pier security guard.

The guard and his colleagues treated him kindly, took him to their quarters, gave him a hot bath, a meal, a night's rest and even made a collection for him before sending him to Ellis Island. He stayed two weeks there, looking with longing at the skyline of Manhattan, then was put on board the German ship *Seydlitz* bound for Bremerhaven. He and another man shared a comfortable cabin on the upper deck, once again he was given no work and (since far from being discouraged by what had happened, he could hardly wait to try again) he spent much of the voyage learning English.

Back in Germany, he joined up with a friend with the idea of emigrating to South Africa, but they traveled no further than the occupied Rhineland where they were apprehended for trespass. Back on the east side of the river they looked for work everywhere without result but scraped up enough money to reach Bremen. Here Hauptmann sold his field glasses to enable them to travel to Bremerhaven. They suffered extreme poverty and hunger there, sharing the same bed in a small room, selling their watches and even Hauptmann's good shirt to survive; his weight was down to 126 pounds. 'But,' he claimed, 'I remembered my promise to my mother, and no one could say that I even stole an apple.' He might have added that with a year of his original sentence still to serve for having violated his probation, in addition to any further sentences connected with the drive belts and his escaping from prison, it was hardly worth the risk. When a food parcel of bread, bacon and lard arrived from his mother it proved too much for empty stomachs, and both friends retired to bed with severe colic.

But now the North German Lloyd liner *Derflinger*, a sister ship of the *York*, was preparing for sea after refit, and they went aboard her. Hauptmann found himself in luck from the start. 'I soon discovered a couple of Saxons, told them I was a stowaway and asked if I could sleep on the floor of their cabin. They were willing and also found me a place at their table.' For nine days Hauptmann lived in untramelled comfort. Then, while approaching New York, and as he was walking down a narrow passageway, a cabin door opened and out stepped the same officer who had asked him for his ticket on the previous voyage. 'At first we were both so surprised, we burst out laughing.' The officer asked the question again, and Hauptmann had to give the same reply. The officer took him before *the same captain*. This time Hauptmann was sent to the mailroom where he found several other detected stowaways, including a young man making his seventh unsuccessful attempt. They were taken to Ellis Island and sent home on the next boat. Hauptmann's friend was not among them, so he assumed he must have reached New York.

It says much for Hauptmann's determination to make something of his life that, despite two unsuccessful attempts, his first thought on reaching Bremerhaven was to try again. But he had learnt some lessons: not to mix with the passengers, and thus avoid contact with the officers; and to choose an American ship rather than a German one. So he traveled to Hamburg where the American

Line's *Washington* was taking passengers on board, and after a thorough inspection below decks, made his way to the coal bunkers, put on overalls and dug himself a hiding-place in the coal.

Twelve hours out and feeling cramped and hungry, he heard a noise, looked up and saw a man approaching. At first he thought the man was looking for stowaways, then to his astonishment he saw him crawl over the coal towards him and, on reaching his hole, hold out a chicken and a bottle of coffee. Gratefully Hauptmann took them, even more gratefully ate them. But who was his benefactor? The answer came as he prepared to sleep, when a noise close by revealed the intended recipients of the food, a nest of three stowaways. Apologizing, he offered them his bread and water; but far from feeling resentment they invited him to move over and share their nest and further supplies of food which, said Hauptmann, came down with extreme regularity.

Here they passed the time companionably enough, being able, despite the discomfort, to appreciate the absurdity of their situation. 'We were all so black with coal dust that we could only see the whites of our eyes.' On the third day out they found a nest of three more stowaways, making seven of them in all. They took it in turn to keep an eye on the hatchway, and one day two men came down with flashlights; but by closing their eyes and remaining quite still, they avoided detection. They were no further alarms after this, although as more and more coal was used up, they had to keep digging new nests further along the bunkers.

They were still in the bunkers when the ship docked at Hoboken.

'Now we made our way to the bathroom, just like the crew, and gave ourselves a thorough cleaning. The passengers had already left the boat while I was still shaving.

'Now I too walked down the gangplank without being stopped. I reached the pier and from there went into the street. "God, I thank you." These were my first words as I trod the pavements of the New World.'

It was the state of New Jersey (in which Hoboken lies) that welcomed Hauptmann to his new life. Twelve years later it would help to usher him out of it.

5

Alone in a strange land, knowing no more than a word or two of English, understanding even less, and with only a few cents in his pocket, Hauptmann might have been excused for feeling disoriented and apprehensive; the more so when, having crossed in the ferry to Manhattan and walked from 23rd Street to 86th Street to see his only contact in New York, a friend called Albert Diebig, he found that Albert had moved to an unknown address. But to be alive and free, with the prospect of work and of earning and saving money, was exhilarating. 'I was so happy I wanted to sing. I was in the best of health and had recovered my inner peace.'

It was to be a new beginning in every way. 'I thought no more about my past. I had locked it behind me.' As in Germany, there was one good practical reason for not transgressing again: he was an illegal immigrant, and any entanglement with the law would lead to deportation back home and, once there, a return to prison. But in fairness it should be said that never again would he face the dreadful living conditions which had precipitated him into wrongdoing in the first place.

Although he had failed to find Albert, a young German who had overheard his inquiries invited Hauptmann to stay at his parents' home until he could find work and a place of his own. His name was Fred Aldinger and his mother, Lena, was a washerwoman. From this base Hauptmann set out on foot and by subway in search of the magic sesame sign, 'Dishwasher wanted'; within a few days he spotted it in the window of a lunchroom in Greenwich Village.

'My heart beat somewhat faster as I walked up and down past the window. I rehearsed my English several times. At first softly and then louder and louder I said to myself, "I am a dishwasher." '

At last he took his courage in both hands and, as he put it, 'stormed into the lunchroom'. As the owner approached and was about to say something, Hauptmann almost shouted at him, 'I am a dishwasher.' The owner looked startled and attempted to reply. 'To everything he said to me,' declared Hauptmann, 'I answered "Yes" and sometimes by way of variety, "All right." Naturally I had not the slightest idea of what he was saying.' The cook, who had overheard what was going on and understood German, came to the rescue. 'The boss says you can start work right away and he will give you $15 a week.' Hauptmann was overjoyed. 'Oh, God, what a surprise. I had no idea it would happen so quickly.'

He worked in the lunchroom from eight to four, and in the evenings and at weekends, and with the help of the Aldingers improved his English and learnt American customs and idiosyncrasies. Mistakes were inevitable, and one that Hauptmann always remembered was seeing a car at a street corner and a man in the passenger seat looking at him with outstretched arm. Thinking this was some acquaintance from the *York* or *Derflinger* he went over and warmly shook his hand. The man looked astonished. He had put out his hand to indicate a turn to the right.

After a few weeks' dishwashing, he had saved enough money to buy a set of machine tools: with these he obtained work as a repair locksmith at a wire factory on the East River, and later as a lathe operator in Brooklyn, for which he received $26 a week. But working with machines was a dirty business, and he decided to take up the other trade for which he had been trained – that of carpenter. 'I bought the cheapest tools I could find, because I did not know if I would be competent after not working at it for so long.' He need not have worried. He was taken on by a firm on 44th Street which specialized in repair work and paid $44 a week. When this fell through he found work on a new construction in Parkway Gardens. 'The boss was German, and as I was alone, I learned very much from him.'

Among those for whom Lena Aldinger did washing was a well-to-do Jewish couple called Rosenbaum who lived on Riverside Drive. They employed a German maid called Anna Schoeffler, and when Lena was at the Rosenbaums she often spoke to Anna of Richard, whom she described as 'the quiet young man who is like another son to me'. Lena, who came from the same part of Germany as Anna, often invited her home in the evenings, but Anna was shy and took some time to accept. On her first visit she met Richard. 'We talked and listened to the radio. Richard and another friend sang. It was like our home in Germany. I enjoyed myself very much.' At the end of the evening Richard walked her to the subway.

One Sunday Lena and Anna visited Coney Island, then a popular New York seaside resort. 'All my life I had heard of Coney Island,' said Anna, 'and was anxious to go.' When they arrived, they saw Hauptmann sitting on the sand. 'He joined us,' she said, 'we made the round of all the amusements and had a fine time.' They began seeing each other regularly, so that later Hauptmann could write, 'During that summer of 1924 I knew that I had found my dear wife.'

Anna was then twenty-six, a year older than her future husband, red-haired, handsome rather than pretty, with a charming smile and the same moral principles as those of her future mother-in-law. 'An upright Christian woman,' Hauptmann once called her, 'to whom truth is sacred'; and all those who have known her would agree. She came from Markgröningen, not far from Stuttgart, in the Württemberg-Baden area of Germany and, like Richard, had followed a sister across the Atlantic to find work. During the war she had been employed at the Bosch factory in Feuezbach and walked to and from home each day, a distance of six miles. After the war she worked occasionally as a maid, including some time with a Russian family in Switzerland who were so mean to their servants, she said, that they were each given part of a loaf to last a week, and when they wanted a bath had to take a galvanized tin bath into the garden.

Richard and Anna came to know each other on walks in the evening when he picked her up after work on Riverside Drive. During those long summer nights they might stroll along the Hudson watching the river traffic, count the cars as the freight trains rolled by, feed the squirrels in the park. 'He loved nature,' she said, 'and all kinds of animals and birds.' They talked of their homes and families in Germany (Anna noted with what love he spoke of his mother), and of their hopes for the future. And, painful though it was, Richard told her about his past. 'I must say,' he declared with honesty, 'that I passed over everything as superficially as I could, for I was afraid that I might lose her love.' But Anna accepted it. 'It was not hard to understand,' she wrote, 'if you were in Germany after the war. Food was scarce and there was no money. It was hard to live.' She told him, 'That is all behind you now, and will not affect our happiness and love.'

Their courtship lasted more than a year, for they wanted to save as much as possible. Meanwhile Hauptmann's friend Diebig showed up: together they took an apartment and spent their spare time learning English. In October 1924 they were employed in the construction of a bungalow in Lakewood, New Jersey, and lived in the town. Richard spent the evenings fashioning a handsome, inlaid veneered box which was his Christmas present for Anna when they returned to New York: a similar one made two years later today remains one of her proudest possessions.

In the spring and summer of 1925 Richard and Anna continued to save, so that by the time they were married on October 10, 1925 at the home of a cousin of Anna's in Brooklyn, they had put by some $1600; in addition, and without telling Anna, Richard had set aside a further $1000 to go towards the purchase of a house, on which, she told him, she had set her heart. They intended spending their honeymoon motoring to Los Angeles where Richard's sister Emma Gloeckner now lived, and exploring the wonders of America on the way. Richard would take his tools with him so that if work became available in California they would make their home there. With the proceeds from the sale of his furniture Hauptmann bought a secondhand car for $300, and they set off west, but within a few blocks of leaving the car broke down and had to be abandoned. Had the Hauptmanns succeeded in reaching California, it is unlikely the world would ever have heard of them.

During the next four years Richard and Anna prospered. They lived at first in a furnished room, then moved to an apartment on Park Avenue near 118th Street, which they furnished themselves. Hauptmann had regular work with a Swedish contractor named Herman Olsen in the well-to-do Riverdale area of the Bronx, and also took on contract work of his own for the construction of houses. By 1926 he had become so skilled at his trade that he applied for and was granted membership of the Carpenters' Union.

Anna too was making money, as an assistant in a bakery; first an Italian one on 183rd Street and later at Fredericksen's Bakery and Café in Dyre Avenue. Here, in addition to free meals during working hours, she was given food from the kitchen to take home at night. Between them they were often earning more than $100 a week and saving most of it. A further economy was noted by Anna's friend from Markgröningen, Louise Wollenberg, wife of a barber: Hauptmann, she said, was very tight with money and always let the other fellow pay for the beer.

So, by hard work and thrift, the impoverished ex-soldier of Kamenz now found himself with money to spare. To several friends he lent it at 6 per cent interest (Rheinhold Haberland, a fellow carpenter to whom he advanced $700 in 1926, repaid it in 1928). He bought a lunchroom for $800 with Albert Diebig and sold his share in it at a profit of $400 a month later. On the Monday after the Wall Street crash of October 24, 1929, he withdrew

$2800 from his savings account and began buying stocks. Initially this was a smart move as the market had nowhere to go but up. There is also evidence, with the banks crashing all over the country (Hauptmann himself lost $90 in an ancillary account), that he was putting a fair proportion of his assets into a trunk at his home. By 1931 he and Anna were telling their friends that they were worth $10,000–12,000[1] and he had advanced a friend a $3750 mortgage for a house, on which he was receiving $224 a year interest.

In 1928 Anna Hauptmann was able to afford a trip to Germany to see her ageing parents. She also visited her mother-in-law in Kamenz, bearing Richard's love and his hopes of soon being able to visit her himself. In that same year she and Richard moved north, to Needham Avenue in the Bronx. The Bronx, for those who do not know it, is an area of some 40 square miles that lies between the Hudson river on the west and Long Island Sound on the east, Yonkers on the north and Manhattan on the south; it then had a population of some one and a half million. It was named after the Danish merchant Jonas Bronk who in the mid seventeenth century bought 500 acres of it from the Weckquaskeck Indians for two kettles, two guns, two adzes, two cows, a barrel of cider, six pieces of silver and two shirts.

For two hundred years it was mostly farming land, but in the second half of the nineteenth century when successive waves of immigrants – at first Irish, Italians and Jews, later blacks and Puerto Ricans – were causing eastside Manhattan to burst at the seams, cheap housing on a massive scale began going up in the Bronx. And what the New York City Planning Commission said of it in 1969 was broadly true of it in 1928. 'The Bronx is a paradox. It is the home of some of the wealthiest and most notable citizens as well as of hordes of the poorest and most anonymous. Some of the city's finest and most spacious parks are here, yet there are crowded districts that boast little or no space except for their teeming streets and junk-strewn vacant lots.'

It was not the choicest area in which to live, yet Richard and Anna were content. 'We worked hard but we were happy . . . our future looked rosy,' he said, and echoing him Anna said, 'He was always whistling and singing – when he came home I heard him whistling coming up the stairs.' Louise Wollenberg found him a handy man about the house, making coffee and setting the table

[1] Worth $60,000–70,000 today (1984).

and (Anna told her) sometimes doing the washing and ironing. Hauptmann's friend Hans Kloppenburg, then a bachelor and a frequent visitor, spoke of the happy atmosphere in the apartment as well as his enjoyment of Mrs Hauptmann's cooking. Other regular visitors were Anna's niece Maria Müller and her husband Hans, a waiter.

Most evenings they stayed at home, listening to the wireless and going to bed early, as in the morning Richard would take Anna to the bakery before going to work himself. On Tuesdays when Anna worked late, Richard would go to fetch her, being given a free meal in return for helping to wash the dishes. On the first Saturday of each month they held musical evenings. Hauptmann played and sang to the mandolin, Hans Kloppenburg played the guitar and another German friend the zither. 'With singing and playing and a little home-made wine,' said Hauptmann, 'we passed some very enjoyable evenings.' Looking back on those years Anna would say, 'I never had an unpleasant day. He was kind and thoughtful and did his best to make me happy.' What they lacked was what they both badly wanted – a baby; but, they consoled themselves, one would arrive in God's time.

For a man who loved the outdoor life as much as Hauptmann, whose happiest boyhood memories were of the Harz Mountains and the forests and meadows of Saxony, life in the concrete jungle of the Bronx had its limitations. But there were compensations. Some four miles east of Hauptmann's apartment on 222nd Street lies a 2000-acre conservation and picnic area known as Pelham Park: it has seven miles of foreshore on Long Island Sound, including the 500-acre promontory of Hunter's Island and, connected to it by a pencil of land known as Rodman's Neck, the smaller City Island, famous for boat-building and seafood restaurants.

It was to Hunter's Island (once the property of a John Hunter) that Hauptmann went nearly every weekend in winter and summer. Here he met many other friends in the community of German immigrants: Otto Wollenberg the barber, Henry Lempke and Emil Muller, both bakers, Carl Henkel, a painter who shared lodgings with Kloppenburg, Ludwig Kübisch, a butcher, Harold Zint who worked in the kitchens of the Savoy Plaza Hotel, and many others. 'We enjoyed a wonderful outdoor life there,' said Hauptmann. In the winter they played football; in summer (when often their wives came too) they swam, boated, fished, sunbathed, cooked meals and in the evening gathered round the dying fire to play music and sing songs that reminded them of home. It was like life in the *Pfadfinderbund*, only better. Anna had given him a pair of field glasses to observe the bird life and later he bought a canoe in which to fish and paddle around the bay. 'Everyone seemed to know Hauptmann,' said Louise Wollenberg. 'And,' said Kloppenburg, 'everyone liked him.'

In 1930 Hauptmann's work with Herman Olsen ended, and he worked for a number of contractors, a cabinet-maker called Lollenbeck on 72nd Street, a general contractor called Griccil who had premises in Manhattan and the Bronx; then after a spell with a builder called Langinracher also on 72nd Street he went back again to Griccil. He also took on individual jobs, purchasing wood from the National Millwork and Lumber Company at 3541 White Plains Road. He tried to keep up with the stock market and opened an account with a broker, but, as he admitted, he was not very successful. 'In the first place I understood nothing about it and so listened too much to others. At the same time I was working, and so did not have time to watch the market.' However his total losses between 1929 and the early part of 1932 amounted to no more than $500.

In 1931 there was a slump: demands for carpenters fell away, and the stock market was in the doldrums. But Hauptmann still had considerable funds, so now was the time to act on the idea that he had never abandoned – that of exploring America by motor car and visiting his sister Emma in California. Anna was enthusiastic, but first they had to find a car. One evening they saw in a showroom window a dark blue Dodge sedan which was going for $737. At Fredericksen's a little later Richard asked Anna to come outside. There was the car. 'Go ahead, sit in it,' he said. 'It's ours.'

When Hauptmann told Hans Kloppenburg about the trip, Hans asked if he might come and share the expenses as he too had a sister living in California. And so it was agreed, and they made two trunks (one for the rear of the car and the other on the running-board) for clothes, camping gear, cooking utensils and tools in case they found work along the way. Richard would take his field glasses and camera, a small pistol for protection while sleeping in the open, his mandolin and Hans's guitar; the tent they were going to share would be strapped to the roof. They aimed to be away three months. Hans would subscribe half the running costs of the car and a third of the food.

At this time Hans Kloppenburg was a tall (6 foot 2), striking-looking man with gray eyes, a darkish complexion and thinning hair. He must have looked older than he was, for when Richard's sister first met him she thought he was forty-three, when he was, like Richard, thirty-two. She noticed how heavily accented his English was, and said that Richard had told her that because of his slowness Hans sometimes found it difficult to hold down a job. Hans was devoted to Richard and Anna, and they to him. 'We were like brothers,' he said of Richard. 'He was the nicest fellow, and the best friend I ever had.'

In June 1931 Hauptmann removed the $4000 he was keeping at home in the trunk, put it in a locked satchel and gave it to Anna's Uncle Gleiforst[1] in Brooklyn for safekeeping. Then he cleared everything out of Needham Avenue and put the furniture in store; and at the beginning of July, at about the time that the Lindberghs were preparing for their trip to the Orient, the green Dodge sedan and its three occupants left New York in pouring rain and headed west. They gaped at the Niagara Falls, camped on the shores of Lake Erie, and crossed the Mississippi at Davenport – an evocative moment for Hauptmann, to see the legendary river made vivid by his boyhood reading. From Omaha they followed the old covered wagon trail down the Platte Valley through Nebraska, where at one camp, while Richard was observing some unusual birds, Hans and Anna, washing dishes, toppled into a river.

The further west they went, the more entranced they were; overcome by the grandeur of the Rockies, they camped for a whole day in the foothills, beside a stream where the water was so soft they needed no soap for washing clothes. 'An entire new world was opened to us here, and we saw animal life we had never seen before.'

They crossed the Rockies by the Falls River Pass, and in Yellowstone Park met Richard's sister Emma, her Austrian husband Charles, and their teenage daughter Mildred, who had motored up from Los Angeles. For brother and sister it was an emotional event, for they had not seen each other for twenty-two years. 'Even if I had not known she was my sister,' said Hauptmann, 'I would still have recognized her, for she was the picture of my mother.' His brother-in-law said he was a chauffeur and during the past five

[1] He had married Anna's father's sister.

years had been chauffeur to several film stars including Joan Crawford and Lew Cody.

They spent a few days sightseeing in Yellowstone Park, then took the two cars north on a trip to Montana, Washington and Oregon, camping each night, having sing-songs round the fire, taking pictures of each other picnicking and making music. The three easterners were dazzled by each new sight; their first glimpse of the Pacific through a gap in the clouds, the beauty of the Columbia River, the cool of the Redwoods. Hauptmann liked the Redwoods best. 'I could have stayed here for ever, because I love forests. But my brother-in-law had to get back to Los Angeles.'

They traveled by the coast road from San Francisco and stayed at the Gloeckners' for two weeks. It was a happy time. They made picnic trips into the San Bernadino mountains, swam at Santa Monica or in the sulphur springs, and at a local air circus Hauptmann took a ten-minute flip – the nearest he would ever get to the world of Charles Lindbergh. Before leaving he told his sister about his losses on the stock market, and made her promise that she would not tell their mother. Then it was time to go. 'It was very difficult for both of us. Although we tried not to show our feelings, we could not keep back the tears. The first day of our return trip, we were all very sad.'

They traveled north again to see Kloppenburg's sister at Willows, then took the classic tourist route east – Death Valley, Las Vegas, the Grand Canyon, the Meteorite Crater and the Petrified Forest, the Carlsbad Caverns in New Mexico. 'I could never have believed,' said Hauptmann, 'that nature could hold such wonders if I had not seen them for myself.' They went south to El Paso, along the Mexican border to New Orleans and across to Florida, where they would have stayed longer but for the mosquitoes. Their last, and as it turned out happiest, camping place was beside the ocean at Tybee near Savannah, Georgia, where they made friends with the owner of a lunchstand, Robert Schneider and his wife, were lent his boat to go fishing, caught a turtle and cooked it, swam every day and postponed their departure twice. On their last evening the Schneiders called in some neighbors; with the beer flowing they sat under the palms on the edge of the ocean, and with Richard playing the mandolin and Hans the guitar, sang English and German songs far into the night. 'It was two before the guests departed,' said Richard. 'It was an evening none of us would ever forget.'

And so, by way of Washington and Philadelphia, they arrived back in New York at the end of September after journeying more than fourteen thousand miles in which the Dodge had never once let them down. The whole trip had cost the Hauptmanns $500, Kloppenburg $300. All three had been bowled over by what they had seen. 'After the beauties of America,' wrote Richard, 'I cannot understand why so many people go to Europe to see nature.' He wrote a long account of his trip and sent it to his niece Mildred.

On 15 October, 1931 the Hauptmanns moved into a new apartment, the upper floor of a two-storey house at 1279 East 222nd Street. It consisted of a sitting room, two small bedrooms, kitchen and bath and was reached by a door and staircase leading from the front hallway of the house. The rent was $50 a month (or $48 a month for every two months they guaranteed to stay) and the landlord, a Mr Rauch, lived with his mother on the ground floor. There was no garage for the Dodge, but room for it on an adjoining plot. Mr Rauch said that if Hauptmann was prepared to build a garage, he would supply the wood for it and let him have it rent-free. Hauptmann, who also wanted the garage for a workbench and to store tools, agreed.

To save money for a trip to Germany she was planning for her mother's seventieth birthday, Anna returned to her old job at Fredericksen's Bakery. Richard would take her there in the Dodge each morning, and on Tuesdays and Fridays, when she worked until nine, come to fetch her. Mr Fredericksen would give him supper and afterwards, waiting for Anna to finish, he would sometimes take the Fredericksens' German Shepherd dog for a walk.

He himself found steady employment difficult and filled in with temporary work, obtaining wood from the National Millwork and Lumber Company (only a five-minute ride from home) and doing contract jobs for them. 'Sometimes they gave me too much work,' he said, 'and sometimes too little.' One of his contracts was a new luncheon counter for Fredericksen's Bakery. He retrieved the $4000 from his uncle in Brooklyn and put it back in the trunk which he now kept in a closet in the front room. On the first Saturday of the month he resumed the musical evenings with Kloppenburg and others, and on Sundays when the weather was fine, the expeditions to Hunter's Island.

This then was the pattern of the Hauptmanns' lives during the fall and winter of 1931–2, the time, it will be recalled, when the

Lindberghs were beginning to use their new estate at Hopewell for weekend visits.

One morning in mid February 1932, Hauptmann met a customer in the bakery to whom Anna served breakfast every day, and who worked at the Reliant Employment Agency on 6th Avenue. Hauptmann asked him about prospects for work, and the man suggested he go down to the agency and inquire. There a Mr E. V. Pescia told him there was a likelihood of steady employment for a skilled carpenter in the near future. 'In order not to miss an opportunity,' said Hauptmann, 'I went to the agency every day from then on, either in the morning or afternoon.' In America as in Germany, no one could accuse Hauptmann of not exerting himself to find work whenever there was the least chance of it.

Pescia's records show that towards the end of February he informed Hauptmann that there would soon be a vacancy for a skilled carpenter at the Majestic Apartments – a big block on 72nd Street and Central Park West then in the course of completion; and that having received from Hauptmann a $10 booking fee, he instructed him and another carpenter called Gus Kassens to report to the construction supervisor at the Majestic, one Joseph M. Furcht. Hauptmann reported on Saturday, February 27 and was told to start work on Tuesday, March 1 (the day of the Lindbergh kidnapping) at $100 a month.

Later on that Saturday Hauptmann and Hans Kloppenburg visited Hunter's Island in the car, arriving between 1 and 2 p.m., playing soccer with Emil Müller and others, and going home when it became dark. On the Sunday morning Hauptmann sharpened his tools and in the afternoon again visited Hunter's Island and again played football with Emil Müller, Müller's friend Ludwig Kübisch and a score of others. It was blowing so hard that evening that Müller and Kübisch, who had hired a boat from the mainland, were unable to row it back, and spent the night there. On the Monday morning, February 29, Hauptmann took his tools to the Majestic Apartments and left them in the carpenters' shop in the cellar. In the afternoon he returned to Hunter's Island where he met Müller and Kübisch, still weather-bound, and in conversation told them he was starting on a new job next day. Müller saw Hauptmann leave the island at around 5 p.m.

'On 1 March, 1932, at 8 a.m.,' declared Mr Furcht, 'Bruno Richard Hauptmann and Gus Kassens reported for work at the Majestic Apartments and worked throughout that entire day until five o'clock ... Hauptmann was a skilled carpenter who much against my wishes I was forced to put on maintenance work which is ordinary work instead of skilled carpenter work.' Kassens later recalled having met Hauptmann that day.

After work, it being a Tuesday and Anna's late night at the bakery, Hauptmann drove there at around 8 p.m. to fetch her, so that she would not have to come home through deserted streets alone.

The news of the Lindbergh baby's kidnapping that night, like the news of the assassination of President Kennedy thirty-one years later, was an event so shocking and traumatic that long afterwards people could remember where they were when they heard it. Later, as will be shown, this enabled two people to recall that they had seen Hauptmann that evening, and in circumstances in which one encounter independently confirmed the other.

Anna first heard the news at the bakery next morning, after Richard had dropped her there at 7 a.m. 'I went inside, put on my uniform, and went behind the counter. There was a customer there having his breakfast. A steady customer. And he got up to pay me and went to the counter and he held up a *Times* and said, Honey did you see that? And I looked at it, and I see a baby and I read "Kidnapping". And I said, what is that, does that mean somebody *stole a baby*? And he said Yes. I said, Oh my God!' It was what Anne Lindbergh had said the night before. Hauptmann heard the news when buying a paper at the 225th Street subway on White Plains Avenue, on his way to work at the Majestic Apartments. That evening he and Anna talked about it; there was no one in America who didn't.

Mr Furcht said that for the rest of that week Hauptmann worked at the Majestic Apartments from eight to five every day.

PART THREE

THE KIDNAPPERS

'We have prepared this a very long time.'

(Ransom note)

6

The Colonel told Whately to call the police at Hopewell, then seized his rifle and went out into the wild night, down the drive and into the road. But he had no flashlight; he could see nothing but the dim shapes of trees, hear nothing but the wind soughing and sighing in the tops. Whately joined him in the car, and shone the headlights either side of the road. But the kidnappers had had too long a start. Telling Whately to go into Hopewell and procure a flashlight, Lindbergh returned to the house, telephoned the New Jersey State Police, and his lawyer Colonel Henry Breckinridge[1] in New York.

Anne, Betty Gow and Elsie Whately meanwhile had made a fruitless search of all rooms and closets. Now with nothing to occupy them they had gathered disconsolately in the living room. Elsie was sobbing quietly, Anne and Betty sat in stunned silence. They were thinking the same thoughts – wondering where and in whose alien hands little Charlie was now, and if he was being properly cared for. Betty longed to say something to comfort Anne, but could think of nothing adequate. Then the police arrived, Chief Wolfe and Assistant Chief Williamson from Hopewell. Whately was just behind them, having met them on the road and been told they had flashlights.

Lindbergh took the two officers up to the empty nursery. He told them there was an envelope lying on the radiator grill beneath the window on the right of the fireplace; and assuming charge,

---

[1] US Assistant Secretary for War, 1913–16.

told them what they might have been expected to tell him – not to touch it or anything else until the fingerprint expert arrived. The window itself was closed; beyond it the left-hand shutter was closed and the right-hand one open. On the carpet and on top of a suitcase which rested on a chest close to the window were small particles of yellow clay.

They took their flashlights and went outside. In the wet soil beneath the nursery window they found two holes which looked as though made by the uprights of a ladder; and leading away from this, and in the dirt area between the house and scrub some 60 or 70 feet away (which in summer would become a lawn), footprints. Flashing their torches they followed the footprints across the dirt area to the edge of the scrub, and found three sections of a home-made collapsible ladder, the two bottom sections together, the top section some 12 feet away. The rungs were set much further apart than on a normal ladder, and the uprights of the bottom section, near the join to the middle section, had broken and split – a possible explanation, it was thought, for the noise that Lindbergh had heard. Nearby they also found a thirty-year-old Buck's chisel with a ¾-inch blade and a wooden handle.

They returned to the house and joined the three women and Ollie Whately in the living room. The officers questioned them briefly but, said Williamson, 'did not learn anything of value in relation to the kidnappers'. He added, 'My observations of all those present were that the Colonel was collected, Mrs Lindbergh very nervous and restless, the butler depressed and nervous, and his wife was crying; the nursemaid appeared to me to be the coolest of the lot.' But Whately in his statement said that Betty was 'genuinely upset and crying'.

By now other officers were appearing on the scene, alerted by a flash put out by the New Jersey State Police: State Troopers Wolf and Cain from Lambertville; State Troopers de Gaetano and Bornmann from the Training School at Wilburtha; State Trooper Kelly, the fingerprint expert, from Morristown Barracks; Captain Lamb and Lieutenant Keaton; Major Schoeffel, deputy to Colonel Schwarzkopf, head of the New Jersey State Police and, in time, the dapper Colonel Schwarzkopf himself. Wolf, who was one of the first to arrive, went out to look for footprints and subsequently reported: 'The kidnappers consisted apparently of a party of at least two or more persons ... Apparently two members of the party proceeded on foot to the east side of the Lindbergh residence and assembled a three-piece home-made extension ladder ... Two sets of fresh footprints led off in a south-east direction ... Kidnappers arrived in a car which was left parked some distance from the house either in Lindbergh's private lane or a rough road known as Featherbed Lane.' Trooper de Gaetano confirmed this. 'We traced rubber boots or overshoe impressions from the ladder down an old road towards the chicken coop. The footprints went across the road and appeared to stop alongside impressions from an auto.' One very clear footprint lay in the dirt beneath the nursery window, and so anxious was de Gaetano to obtain an impression of this before it was obliterated that, instead of borrowing a tape measure from the Whatelys or Betty Gow, he measured the length with his flashlight and the width with the palm of his hand, concluding that it was 12 to $12\frac{1}{8}$ inches long and 4 to $4\frac{1}{4}$ inches wide.

Naturally everyone was agog to know what was in the envelope that had been left on the nursery radiator grill. With the arrival of Trooper Frank Kelly, soon after midnight, their curiosity was satisfied. 'I put on a pair of gloves,' said Kelly, 'picked the letter up by the edges, and brought it over to a small table in the center of the room where I conducted a latent print examination on the outside surface of the envelope. Black powder was used in an effort to obtain any possible prints, but without results. I then opened the letter with a nail file and powdered the note and the inside of the envelope for possible prints, but none were obtained.'

The letter was written in pencil in a very uneven hand, one clearly designed to disguise the writer's normal hand:

> Dear Sir!
> Have 50.000 $ redy 25 000 $ in
> 20 $ bills 1.5000 $ in 10 $ bills and
> 10000 $ in 5 $ bills. After 2–4 days
> we will inform you were to deliver
> the Mony.
> We warn you for making
> anyding public or for notify the Police
> the chld is in gute care.
> Indication for all letters are
> singnature
> and 3 holds.
> [SYMBOL – see plate 13]

The symbol consisted of two interlocking circles, and within the interlock an oval. The circles were colored blue, the oval red, and at the center of each in a horizontal line were square holes.

The flash put out by the New Jersey State Police had been picked up by the local radio stations, and as the night wore on a stream of reporters and photographers arrived at the house to join the swelling numbers of policemen. With little for the police to do (except try, unsuccessfully, to keep the press from milling around on the dirt lawn and obliterating the footprints), they were sent out in groups to search houses, barns and sheds in the immediate vicinity. That night, and in the course of the next few weeks, they interviewed literally thousands of people: all residents living within a radius of five miles from the house; every one of the 120 construction workers who had helped to build the house and the drive leading to it; the staffs of local bus stations, railroad depots, car-hire firms and airfields who might furnish information about unusual or suspicious travelers; and the telephone exchange operators at Hopewell for a record of all recent, listed calls to the Lindbergh house.

Nor were these searches confined to the immediate neighborhood. In New York the City Police sealed off the Washington Bridge and other entrances to the city from New Jersey, and made a systematic search of all inward-bound cars. At ports along the eastern seaboard customs officials and waterfront police boarded boats large and small. All over the country people were so outraged by what had happened that on their own initiative they searched lonely huts and empty houses in case the boy had been taken there. All over the country the police were called on to investigate reports of people sighting him with strangers, and subsequently found themselves facing angry, bona-fide parents. Houses reported anonymously to the police as containing the boy were found to be (for this was the time of Prohibition) the liquor dumps of rival bootleggers. A motorist driving to California with New Jersey license plates was stopped a dozen times.

The press were no less active. Lindbergh was news, kidnappings were news; the two together were explosive. When Inspector Harry Walsh of the New Jersey City Police arrived at the house at noon next day he found no less than four hundred press and picture people. They included the entire staff of the International News Photo Service who had fitted two ambulances with developing equipment, and whose screaming sirens would ensure a fast passage to New York. The Associated Press had sent six representatives in four cars, the International Press five in three cars, the United Press six in three cars, the *New York Daily Mirror* twelve men and women, the *New York American* twenty including its President, William Randolph Hearst, and the papers of Philadelphia twenty-two reporters and photographers. Other representation was on a similar scale.

There were so many in fact that for fear of jeopardizing contact with the kidnappers Lindbergh persuaded most to move down to Trenton, the state capital and headquarters of the State Police. Some stayed in Hopewell where they took over the local hotel and kept it open night and day, paid inflated sums for beds in private houses, filled the waiting rooms in the railroad station with copying and transmitting equipment, obliged the telephone exchange to treble its capacity, trampled over private gardens, drove recklessly down the village street, and asked impertinent questions of anyone likely to provide the most trivial copy.

Silas Bent, who wrote an account of press activities in *Outlaw* magazine said that the actual news the papers had would have filled a thimble. Yet for days afterwards the story drove all others off the front page, eclipsing news of the Chinese–Japanese war, the doings of Hitler, an important tax Bill being considered by Congress. The International News Service sent out fifty thousand words (equivalent to a short novel) the first day, thirty thousand the second; the staid Associated Press delivered ten thousand words daily. They were mostly balderdash, said Bent, wild invented tales such as that local applejack distillers had kidnapped the boy to frighten his parents from the district or that a representative of J. P. Morgan was about to fly to Detroit with $250,000; also patronizing stories about local 'hillbillies' – Hopewell's oldest inhabitant, the man who ran the grocery store, and Lindbergh's mailman – and 'posed' pictures of a minister of religion at prayer, and a farmer milking his cow while listening to the latest news on a portable radio supplied by the paper's photographer. But it worked: people were avid for news, any news, and in the weeks after the kidnapping there was an overall rise in circulation of between 15 and 20 per cent.

America and the world were deeply shocked. Lindbergh's great odyssey had given him the status of a god, his subsequent aloofness the mystery and mystique of a god; as with primitive tribes the violation of some appurtenance of the god was sacrilege of the most abhorrent kind. In a thousand newspapers leader-writers reflected their readers' outrage and disgust; in a thousand places of worship, prayers were offered for the boy's return. The President of the United States, the King of England, the Presidents of France and Mexico were among those who sent messages of condolence or condemnation; the Governor of New York State, Franklin D. Roosevelt, put his entire police force at Colonel Schwarzkopf's disposal; the Governor of New Jersey called a conference of police chiefs of the main eastern cities and J. Edgar Hoover, the head of the FBI. As the days went by without further news people felt increasingly angry, frustrated, helpless, burning for revenge yet without the means of attaining it. A newsreel commentator, speaking over shots of posters featuring a blown-up photograph of the boy, then being pasted up all over the country, expressed the mood of many. 'I know what I'd like to do to that kidnapper if I could get my hands on him for just four minutes.'

At this time kidnapping was a state, not a federal, offence, which meant that J. Edgar Hoover and the FBI, with their unique knowledge and experience of large-scale crime detection, had no authority in the case. This was unfortunate, as the New Jersey State Police was more a quasi-military force than an agency of crime detection. Its chief was 37-year-old Colonel Norman Schwarzkopf, a First World War veteran, now in his third term of office and described by one writer as 'a handsome young man with a crew haircut and waxed blond moustache who, between graduating from West Point and embracing crime detection, had served a hitch as a floor-walker at Bamberger's Department Store in Newark'. Schwarzkopf had never patrolled a beat or arrested a criminal; a case as formidable and far-reaching as this was beyond anything in his previous experience. Nevertheless he was determined to solve it without help from the FBI; and the day after the kidnapping he transformed the Lindbergh garage (at the other end of the house from the nursery) into a kind of staff headquarters with a switchboard and twenty telephone lines. It also became the clearing-house for the letters from well-wishers, Lindbergh haters, soothsayers, amateur sleuths, dreamers, poets and others that were arriving by the thousand every day.

There were several flaws in the State Police's detection methods, the most glaring being the inability of the fingerprint man, Trooper Kelly, to find any latent prints on the ransom letter and envelope, on the ladder, the chisel, the window, the windowsill, the crib or

Charlie's toys. When this news reached the ears of a former Justice of the New Jersey Supreme Court, James F. Minturn, he made contact with his friend Dr Erastus Mead Hudson who, as an amateur, had been experimenting successfully with a silver nitrate process for years. Hudson was invited down to Hopewell and in the presence of Kelly and Schwarzkopf used his method to produce hundreds of prints on the ladder as well as several of Charlie's on his books and toys. Kelly photographed most of these, and Captain Snook of the New Jersey State Police informed Dr Hudson that at least thirty to forty of the ladder prints were other than those of troopers known to have handled it. Hudson suggested these be sent to Washington for comparison with the FBI's huge fingerprint collection of known criminals, the most comprehensive in the country. Schwarzkopf refused; and later also refused Dr Hudson's proposal to subject the ransom note to a special new iodine-gas process he had invented.

The ladder was an enigma, a ramshackle affair composed, according to one police report, of 'old, nondescript lumber which has been lying around for some time'. Fully extended it was just over 20 feet long, tapering from a width of 14 inches on the bottom section to 11 inches at the top, each section being joined by dowel pins. It was also unusual in that the gaps between the rungs were either 18 or 19 inches instead of the standard 12 inches. With three sections the ladder stretched from the two holes in the soil to some way above the right of the nursery window; with two sections it ended 30 inches below and 6 inches to the right of the window sill. As the bottom half of the window when fully opened was (and by my measurements still is) only 30½ by 26 inches, the intruder would have found it virtually impossible when leaving to have gained a foothold on the top rung of the ladder and taken a few steps down it while carrying a 30-pound baby; and when you further consider that he needed a free hand to close the window before descending, it becomes clear that whoever took the baby from the crib did not also take him down the ladder. Most probably he handed the baby (possibly in a bag, both for convenience and to stifle any cries) to an accomplice waiting halfway up the ladder. This could also explain how the ladder came to split.[1]

What puzzled the police most was the uncanny intelligence the kidnappers seemed to have had about Charlie's movements. He

[1] See Appendix 1

had never stayed at the house on a Tuesday night before, and he was only there that Tuesday because of the decision taken by his mother that morning. The kidnappers not only knew exactly where his room was, but had chosen a time to remove him when (to guard against spoiling) his father had given instructions that he was not to be disturbed.

All this pointed to inside information, and in particular to the Lindbergh servants. Chief suspect was Betty Gow; not only was she nearest to the baby but before leaving Next Day Hill she had left a message for her boy-friend, Henry ('Red') Johnsen, a Norwegian sailor she had met on the Lamont's yacht at North Haven, that she must cancel their date that evening, and to ring her at Hopewell. He did ring her there just before 9 p.m. When the police inquired for him, they were told that he had left by car to stay with his brother in Hartford, Connecticut. The Hartford police ran him to earth and, finding a milk bottle in the back of his car (a feed for the baby?), clapped him in jail. Suspicions grew when he admitted to taking lodgings in Englewood to be near Betty and, on three occasions, to driving her from Next Day Hill to Hopewell to visit the Whatelys. Further interrogation however showed Johnsen to be no more than an illegal immigrant who happened to be fond of Betty Gow and of milk; in due course he was taken to Ellis Island and deported.

Betty Gow's devotion to Charlie had long since been proved (on his first birthday she had written a poem about him which began 'I know a darling, darling thing/Who's one year old today' and put it on Anne's dressing table) and she was distraught by what had happened, feeling in some way responsible. 'I just feel numbed and terribly lost without that darling,' she wrote to her mother the next day; 'I love him so.' Eventually, after lengthy and often quite rigorous interrogations, Trooper Bornmann was able to report: 'The consensus of opinion is that she is a highly sensitive girl of good morals ... above being in any way connected with the persons responsible for the kidnapping of the baby.'

Having also cleared the Whatelys, the police turned their attention to the twenty-nine servants at Next Day Hill, some of whom knew of the Lindberghs being at Hopewell on the Tuesday, and dug out some choice old skeletons in the Morrow household cupboard. The English butler, Septimus Banks, whose previous employers had included Lord Islington and Andrew Carnegie, had been fired often for drunkenness ('on several occasions he has had to be loaded into a taxi and taken home') but always reinstated. Mrs Grimes-Graeme, the English housekeeper, forty-five and with dyed hair, fallen on hard times since the death of her husband in the war, and whose Evelyn Waugh-ish name was no doubt devised to increase her status, had fixed herself lucrative backhanders with the local tradespeople. George Cowe, the gardener, filched estate petrol for his own use and Ellison, the second chauffeur, entertained at the pool when the Morrows were away.

But the only person to be remotely suspected was another English servant, Violet Sharpe, who was what the English then called 'a house parlor-maid' and the American press 'a home waitress'. It was she who had taken the call from Anne Lindbergh on the Tuesday morning asking for Betty to be sent over. Described variously as 'shy and retiring' and 'moody and highly-strung', she was reported to have had an abortion as a result of an affair with Banks the butler, with whom she was in love, though he was not with her. She had also been married briefly in England in 1929, to a Mr George Payne. Asked about her movements on the night of the kidnapping she first said she was at a cinema, but later admitted to visiting a road house with a man who had picked her up, and another couple. The police thought it unlikely she was part of any kidnap plan but made a note to interview her again later.

If none of the servants was implicated and it wasn't an inside job, how had the kidnappers come to know when and where to strike? They themselves were to give the answer to this question. No less than five times – three times in writing and twice verbally – they later emphasized the planning they had done. 'We have been preparing this,' they said (in different words) 'for a very long time.'

If this was so – and there seems no reason to doubt it – they would have first read and seen pictures in the newspapers of the construction of the Hopewell house, the lay-out of the rooms and who was to occupy them. They would have got to know that the house was visited by the family only at weekends, and that a man posted in the trees near the single entrance could see undisturbed their comings and goings; indeed the very isolation which the Colonel had sought for his own protection was ideal for their purpose in being able to approach unobserved.

Yet not even they could have foreseen the stroke of luck they were to have in that there were as yet no curtains to the windows, so that day and night they could see who was in what room – either directly or, after dark, through the cracks in the shutters.

And during the week, after the Whatelys had gone to bed at the far end of the house, they had ample time and opportunity to put a ladder against the windows (it is unlikely that the Whatelys closed the shutters of unoccupied rooms), shine a flashlight through and observe the lay-out — perhaps even climb in to see for themselves. And was it just an extraordinary coincidence that in this brand-new house the only faulty shutters were those guarding the window through which one of the gang was to climb? Or had they made the shutters faulty as part of their careful preparations?

Some have expressed surprise that the kidnappers did not wait until the household had gone to bed when the boy, once taken, would not be missed until morning. But it would have been too risky. The nursery was separated from Anne's bedroom by a bathroom, from Betty's room by a small landing. With the likelihood of doors being left open in case Charlie wanted something in the night, any intruder would almost certainly be heard — especially if the boy was to cry out when being taken from his crib. They may also have considered that if a hue and cry was raised in the small hours of the night and the police were after them, their getaway car would be one of the few still on the road. Far safer to strike between 8 p.m. and 10 p.m. when past observation had told them that the baby was left undisturbed and they could see all the members of the household fully occupied downstairs. Yet when every explanation has been made, the act and the successful execution of it remain a piece of astonishing effrontery.

One last conundrum, which has puzzled many. Why did the kidnappers wait until the Tuesday night when they had no reason to suppose the boy would still be there? Statements by Anne Lindbergh on March 11 and by Betty Gow on March 10 supply the answer. On the previous three nights, said Anne, she had kept the light burning in the bathroom between the nursery and her room until after Charlie was lifted at 10 p.m.; in addition, on Saturday night, there was a light burning in Betty's room, then occupied by a guest. Seeing these lights, and not knowing if the rooms were occupied, the kidnappers would not have dared to attempt entry.

But on the Tuesday night, said Betty, after seeing that Charlie was asleep at 8 p.m., 'I put out the bathroom light and put out the light in my room, and went downstairs.' Turning off lights in unoccupied rooms is what all British, and particularly Scottish, people are taught to do. For the kidnappers though, standing in the darkness outside, it was an indication that the coast was clear. They saw their opportunity, and they took it.

*   *   *

'The history of America,' wrote Edward Dean Sullivan in *The Snatch Rackets*, 'is the history of lawlessness,' and he estimated that in the three years up to 1932 there had been at least 2500 kidnappings. On the day after Charlie was taken, eleven-year-old James de Jute was kidnapped in Niles, Ohio, and on the same day in New York three men were sentenced to life imprisonment for kidnapping a butcher; altogether that March no less than sixteen kidnappers were given prison sentences. Kidnappings in Missouri and Illinois where the penalty was death were always above average. Some of the nationwide victims were children, some adults; some were released unharmed, some murdered, some exchanged for ransom money, some disappeared.

The threat of kidnapping had brushed the Morrow family before. On April 24, 1929 Anne's younger sister Constance, then fifteen and at Milton Academy, Dedham, Massachusetts, received a letter telling her on pain of death to write to her father for $50,000. In three weeks' time a further letter instructed her to put the money in a package behind the wall of an estate in Westwood, Mass. An actress impersonating Constance left an empty package there a few days later. Two cars were observed by detectives to drive slowly past the spot, but they did not stop and nothing further happened. Constance was sent home to Next Day Hill but later, for safety's sake, Lindbergh flew her, Anne and Elisabeth to North Haven.

The case which interested Lindbergh most was that of the rich and beautiful Nell Donnelly, owner of the Donnelly Garment Works of Kansas City, Missouri, who just before Christmas had been kidnapped with her black chauffeur. From the house where they were held she wrote a letter to her lawyer James Taylor asking him to pay $75,000. Her lawyer's partner was the Missouri senator James Reed, who issued a statement that the gang could have their $75,000 but that if they harmed a hair of Nell Donnelly's head, he would see they were brought to justice. Because Reed was an immensely influential figure in Kansas City politics and because the city's known hoodlums and gangsters were beginning to wince under the pressure of police inquiries, a northside political boss offered to help. As a result a rival gang stormed the house where the victims were being held, beat up the kidnappers and released Nell and the chauffeur.

This scenario – in which the release of someone rich and famous had been brought about by gangland pressure – was one with which Lindbergh at once identified; he lost no time in impressing on Colonel Schwarzkopf that nothing should be allowed to jeopardize the retrieval of the baby and the payment of the ransom. This attitude, understandable as it was, was in direct conflict with Schwarzkopf's duty as a policeman to catch criminals, but he was so mesmerized by Lindbergh's *persona* ('I would do anything he asked of me,' he once said) that he was powerless to challenge it. Lindbergh, his wife admitted to Eric Sevareid fifty years later, was not a leader; but because of the deference with which everyone treated him, he was led to believe he was. Part of his genius, and part of his failure, said Anne, was that he never listened to advice from anyone. 'He was inner-directed . . . he listened to himself. If he had listened to people, he would never have flown to Paris. It was a characteristic that worked for him and against him.'

And so instructions went out, not only to the New Jersey Police but to forces all over the country that the objective of any search was to be the return of the baby. 'The arrest of the kidnappers,' ran General Order No. 18 of the District of Columbia Police Department, 'is a subordinate consideration, and any member of the Force is authorized to enter into personal and confidential negotiations for the safe return of the infant without responsibility for the detection or arrest of the kidnappers.' This may have been contrary to police practise and ethics, but it reflected the wishes of most American people.

Each day at Hopewell a committee of four colonels – Lindbergh, Schwarzkopf, the long, lean Breckinridge and 'Wild Bill' Donovan (then preparing to run for Governor of New York) sat down under their host's chairmanship to direct his campaign. 'C now a general,' Anne wrote to her mother-in-law, 'managing his forces with terrific discipline but great judgment.' On March 2 they issued a message to the kidnappers about the baby's diet (a half cup of orange juice on waking, the yolk of one egg daily, a half cup of prune juice after the afternoon nap, etc.) which appeared on the front page of every newspaper on March 3. That day a further statement was issued in which Lindbergh declared that any representatives of his whom the kidnappers found 'suitable' would be prepared to meet their representatives 'at any time and at any place they may designate'. All arrangements would be kept strictly confidential, 'and we further pledge ourselves that we will not try to injure in any way those connected with the return of the child'. When Colonel Breckinridge handed the statement to the press, he added that Lindbergh himself would be prepared to meet the kidnappers, 'under any conditions they may wish to lay down'. All this was rather too much for New Jersey's Attorney General, William A. Stevens, who himself issued a statement that neither Lindbergh nor the New Jersey State Police had the authority to grant the kidnappers immunity from prosecution, and that if the Lindberghs were not prepared to prosecute, the State of New Jersey was.

To Lindbergh and his committee there were already signs that the underworld would be prepared – as in the case of Nell Donnelly – to help in the return of the baby. The famous gangster Al Capone, then languishing in jail for income tax evasion, declared that if released, he would engineer the boy's return within days. 'I know,' he added genteelly, 'how Mrs Capone and I would feel if our son was kidnapped.' And gangs in New York and other eastern cities were becoming increasingly harassed and would continue to be harassed by the police in their efforts to find the child: they were therefore as keen as anyone to see the baby returned, and if it needed a thief to catch a thief they would gladly co-operate.

In Colonel Donovan's law office was a thirty-year-old lawyer called Robert Thayer, married to a Standard Oil heiress, a patron of speakeasies and gambling joints, in the jargon of the 1930s 'a sportsman'. One of his clients was little Morris (Mickey) Rosner, said to possess the key to many doors into New York's underworld; and when Thayer put forward his name as one likely to make contact with the kidnappers, the committee agreed to take him on. In fact kidnapping the Lindbergh baby was just about the last thing that New York's professional underworld would have contemplated.

Rosner came out to Hopewell and stated his terms: $2500 for expenses; not to be followed by the police or secret service; and to be given a generally free hand, reporting only to Colonel Breckinridge or Thayer. To these extravagant terms the committee agreed. Rosner then returned to New York with a copy of the first ransom note, and later showed it to an underworld friend by the name of Owney Madden.

Two days later came a second letter from the kidnappers, written in the same semi-legible hand, with the same symbol of interlocking circles. Far from being shaken by the publicity the case was receiving, they were extremely angry. 'We have warned you note [sic] to make anyding Public also notify the Police now you have to take the consequences . . .' They would now have to keep the baby until everything had quietened down, so the ransom demand would be increased to $70,000. Lindbergh would be told later where to deliver the money, but not 'until the Police is out of ths (*sic*) case and the Pappers are quiet'. The baby was being cared for night and day, would be fed according to the diet and would be sent back in good health. A psychiatrist, Dr Dudley Shoenfeld, commented that the ransom notes were unusual in that they did not threaten the victim with death if their demands were not met. The explanation for this was not to become clear until later.

With Lindbergh's permission Rosner (since returned to Hopewell) took the second ransom note to Colonel Breckinridge's office in New York where it was read by the Colonel and Owney Madden. That evening Rosner contacted two other underworld chums by the name of Salvy Spitale and Irving Bitz, and next day after meeting them Lindbergh issued a statement appointing them as go-betweens.

When New York's Police Commissioner Mulrooney heard this, he was outraged. Press inquiries revealed that Rosner, who had described himself as a former government agent, was under indictment for grand larceny in a stock-selling promotion in which the public had lost more than $2 million; that Spitale was a bootlegger and speakeasy owner who had started off as a bouncer in a Williamsburg dance hall; and that Bitz, another bootlegger and speakeasy boss, had done time in Atlanta for peddling dope. Soon after Lindbergh appointed them, they were charged with landing a cargo of liquor at a beach in Brooklyn, but in the light of their newfound status were acquitted.

Newspaper editors and ministers of religion deplored their involvement. Father Charles E. Coughlin, a Michigan priest whose demographic radio broadcasts reached millions, spoke for many when he said: 'Do you know who these men are? They are unlawful. They are racketeers. They are the new Almighty we have in the United States . . . And that is what Prohibition has done for us – Prohibition that has not made the country safe for democracy but instead has made it safe for the bootleggers, the gangsters, the thugs. Such are the people Colonel Lindbergh felt it necessary to appoint.'

Nor were their activities in the least fruitful. They made various secretive journeys to centres of gangsterdom (including one to Montreal where Bitz, it was said, concluded a satisfactory rum-running deal) but returned emptyhanded. By March 11, with press and public clamoring for results, Rosner felt it necessary to show evidence of progress. The baby was alive, he said, and would soon be returned to its parents. 'My statement,' he added, 'does not represent my *opinion*, but is based on what I actually *know*.' Everyone waited breathless for further developments, but none came. Eventually Spitale called a press conference to admit defeat. 'If it was someone I knew,' he declared, 'I'd be God-damned if I didn't name him. But I been in touch all round, and I come to the conclusion this one was pulled by an independent.' He meant that the kidnapping was the work of amateurs not professionals, and by now this was the view of most.

Spitale and Bitz had failed to reach the kidnappers, although considered by some most likely to succeed. The man who did succeed would have been considered by most to have been among the least likely. For whereas Lindbergh had chosen Spitale and Bitz because they were crooks, the kidnappers' choice was someone of assumed rectitude.

7

His name was Dr John F. Condon, a 72-year-old retired teacher and athletics coach who lived at 2974 Decatur Avenue, a three-storey wooden frame house in the Bronx, and who still taught twice weekly at nearby Fordham University. He was 6 foot 2, weighed 200 pounds and was a physical fitness buff. He had a white mane of hair, a large white walrus moustache, and wore a black derby or bowler hat, like any English city gent. He thought and never tired of saying that America was the finest country in the world and the Bronx the most beautiful borough in it. 'Every Fourth of July,' wrote one observer, 'he hit the outdoor festival circuit and, sweating in a dark winter suit, sang "The Star-Spangled Banner".' Many adjectives have been used to describe Dr Condon: chauvinistic, sentimental, garrulous, sycophantic, histrionic, patronizing, pseudo-humble; above all anxious to see himself and be seen by others in the best possible light.

It was Condon's love of the Bronx that brought him and the kidnappers together. For many years he had been a regular contributor to the *Bronx Home News* (circulation 100,000) with poems and occasional pieces signed P. A. Triot, J. U. Stice, L. O. Nestar, etc., the sort of whimsy its readers found agreeable. As outraged as anybody by the kidnapping, Condon sent a letter to the editor that he would not only be prepared to act as intermediary between Lindbergh and the kidnappers (and promise never to testify against them) but would add his savings of $1000 to the ransom demand; and the editor printed the offer as a front-page article.

To most people – even to Condon – it seemed unlikely that the kidnappers would either read the article or, if they did, pay any attention to it. On both counts they were wrong. Concerned as the kidnappers must have been by the much-publicized antics of Spitale and Bitz, and with time and the ransom money beginning to slip away from them, they saw in Dr Condon their best hope yet. The article was published in the edition of March 8. The next evening, after returning from a lecture at about 10 p.m., Condon found an envelope waiting for him, addressed to 'Mr Doctor John F. Condon'. Inside was a note and another envelope.

The note said:

Dear Sir: If you are willing to act as go-between in Lindbergh cace please follow stricly instruction. Handel incloced letter *personaly* to Mr Lindbergh. It will explan everyding. Don't tell anyone about it. As son we find out the Press or Police is notifyd everyding are cansell and it will be a further delay. Afffter you gett the money from Mr Lindbergh put these 3 words in the *New York American*

Mony is redy

After that we will give you further instruction. Don't be affrait we are not out fore your 1000 $ keep it. Only act stricly. Be at home every night between 6–12 by this time you will hear from us.

Despite instructions not to tell anyone, Condon felt he needed advice, so took a streetcar to Max Rosenhain's restaurant on 188th Street and Grand Concourse to confer with his friend Al Reich, a former professional boxer. Reich wasn't there, but he showed the letter to Rosenhain and another friend, Milton Gaglio, a clothing salesman, who advised him to call Hopewell immediately. He did so and the telephone was answered by Robert Thayer. Here accounts of what followed differ. Thayer is emphatic that he and he alone spoke with Condon. Condon says that he insisted on speaking with Lindbergh personally and that eventually he did so: Lindbergh categorically denied it. Condon, as we shall see, had an almost unrivalled capacity for embroidery, self-dramatization and even invention.

Condon read out the letter, then Thayer asked him to open and read what was in the accompanying envelope.

Dear Sir, [Condon read] Mr Condon may act as go-between. You may give him the 70,000 $ make one packet. the size will bee about [here Condon explained there was a drawing of a box with its dimensions – seven by six by fourteen inches – printed alongside] we have notifyt you allredy in what kind of bills. We warn you not to set any trapp in any way. If you or someone els will notify the Police ther will be a further delay. affter we have the mony in hand we will tell you where to find your boy. You may have a airplane redy it is about 150 mil awy. But befor telling you the adr. a delay of 8 houers will be between.

'I took this letter down on pencil and paper as he read it to me,' said Thayer, 'and it was apparent to me from the first few words that this letter was from the same people that had left the ransom note. This was confirmed when I asked him to give me a vague idea of the signature . . . I then told him to get into a car as quickly as he could and come down to Hopewell bringing the letter with him.'[1]

It was after 2 a.m. when Condon, accompanied by Max Rosenhain and Milton Gaglio, reached Hopewell. They were welcomed by Breckinridge and Lindbergh, who studied the notes and believed them to be genuine. Then, as it was so late, Condon accepted Lindbergh's offer to stay the night; Gaglio and Rosenhain returned to the Bronx by car.

Of this adventure and others to come Condon later wrote a book; so that the reader may catch a whiff of his strange personality and attitudes, here are some extracts of what he wrote about the rest of that night.

---

[1] Condon's invented version was that, after he had read the letter, Lindbergh asked in a tired voice if that was all, but that when he mentioned the interlocking circles, Lindbergh said he would come to see him at once. 'No,' Condon had said, 'you have anguish enough and you are needed at home. I will come to you.' And Lindbergh had said, 'It is kind of you.' This, of course, is what Condon would have *liked* to have happened.

'If I might,' he claims to have said to Lindbergh, 'I would like to meet Mrs Lindbergh.'

As it was now past three in the morning, it was a strange request. What made him think she wasn't asleep? Why not wait anyway until morning? However, Lindbergh seemed happy to oblige and took Condon into Anne's bedroom where he saw 'a tiny, childlike, pretty creature, sitting on the edge of the bed . . . dressed in a simple dark frock of some sort'.

After they had been introduced,

she stretched out her arms towards me instinctively in the age-old appeal of motherhood.

'Will you help me get back my baby?'

'I shall do everything in my power to bring him back to you.'

As I came closer to her I saw the gleam of tears in her soft dark eyes. . . . I smiled at her, shook a thick reproving forefinger at her. With mock brusqueness I threatened Anne Lindbergh:

'If one of those tears drops, I shall go off the case immediately.'

She brushed away the tears. When her hands left her face, she was smiling, sweetly, bravely.

'You see, Doctor, I am not crying.'

'That is better,' I said. 'That is much, much better.'

Did this encounter, one wonders, with its *Woman's Own* dialogue, ever take place? Or was it a scenario etched by Condon to portray himself as the father figure in whom all might trust, the humble teacher who would bring peace and comfort to the nation's hero and his anguished wife? Condon was so great a self-deluder that neither then nor now can one believe without confirmation anything he says.

With Colonel Breckinridge and Mrs Morrow occupying the two spare beds, Lindbergh could only offer Condon a makeshift bed of army blankets on the nursery floor, saying 'These are my own. No one else has ever used them.' Before Lindbergh left, Condon felt the need to address him.

' "Colonel," I told him, "I want to tell you that, from this moment on, my one steadfast purpose will be to serve you. Nothing that you may wish to ask of me will be too much. My very life — it has not too long to run — is at your disposal." '

Lindbergh, said Condon, patted his arm and left. Condon looked round the room, at the empty crib with the two big safety pins still attached to the bedclothes, at the window through which one of the kidnappers had climbed, and whom perhaps he would be meeting face to face. He undressed and snuggled down into the blankets: there he heard voices.

'Condon?'
'Yes.'
'Don't you need help?'
'Yes.'
I got out from beneath the warm blankets. I put my hands around the rung of the Lone Eaglet's crib. On my knees I prayed . . .

Brimful with initiative, Condon came down to breakfast next morning with the two safety pins and some toys of Charlie's which, he said, might come in useful for identification purposes. If Lindbergh and Breckinridge were surprised, they did not show it. They said they were prepared to accept him as intermediary, and gave him a signed statement to that effect. Breckinridge said he would take the 'Money is Ready' ad. to the *New York American* that afternoon, but to avoid using Condon's own name (and resulting press invasion) a nom-de-plume was necessary. Condon suggested 'Jafsie', the sound of his initials 'J.F.C.' when run together; the kidnappers would recognize this, but no one else.

After lunch, Breckinridge drove Condon to the Bronx. Because neither he nor Lindbergh were entirely sure that this weird, garrulous old man was strictly on the level, Breckinridge asked if he might stay as his houseguest until negotiations were concluded. Condon said he would be delighted. And he was. Playing host to Lindbergh's lawyer was the next best thing to playing host to Lindbergh himself.

Events moved fairly quickly from now on. The 'Money is Ready – Jafsie' ad. appeared in the *New York American* the next day (March 11) and at noon the same day Dr Condon's telephone rang. He was away at Fordham, and Breckinridge was at his law office, so it was answered by Mrs Condon. The caller, in what she described as 'a thick, deep, guttural accent', asked for her husband. Told he was out but would be back at six, the caller said he would telephone again at seven and advised Dr Condon to stay in.

He did telephone again and spoke to Condon. In his verbatim account of the conversation to the police, Condon stated that the caller, speaking with a Scandinavian or German accent, first asked Condon if he had 'gotted' their note, then told him to stay in from six to twelve for the rest of the week when he would receive another

note and should act accordingly. Then, said Condon, he heard
Italian voices in the background and a man shouting '*Statti zitto!*'
which he recognized as the Italian for 'Shut up!'

At 8.30 the following night the doorbell rang. It was a taxi-driver
with an envelope for Dr Condon. Recognizing the printed letters,
Condon showed the driver to the front parlor and asked him to
wait. Then he opened the envelope and with Colonel Breckinridge
read the contents. Condon was to drive to the last subway station
from Jerome Avenue. A hundred feet from this station on the left
hand side was an empty frankfurter stand with a big open porch
round it. Under a stone in the center of the porch Condon would
find further instructions. The letter was full of the usual mis-
spellings: 'this notise will tell you were to find uss. act accordingly.
after ¾ of a houer be on the place. bring the mony with you.'

Although the money was not yet ready, Condon thought he
should keep the rendezvous to show willingness and make initial
contact, and that Al Reich, who had called in a short while ago
with Milton Gaglio, should go with him. In the front parlor they
spoke with the taxi-driver, one Joseph Perrone. He had a small
round face and pebble glasses which gave him the appearance of
a marmoset. He said he'd been hailed by a man on the corner of
Knox Place and Gun Hill Road (this was about a mile away, quite
near to Jerome Avenue and the frankfurter stand mentioned in the
note), where he was given a dollar and told to deliver the envelope.
The man had been wearing a brown topcoat and brown felt hat,
and had taken Perrone's license number before leaving. Gaglio
asked to see Perrone's badge number, checked it with the ID card
in the cab and made a note of the cab's licence number. Only then
was a somewhat bemused Perrone allowed to leave.

A few minutes later Condon and Reich embarked in Reich's car
to follow the kidnappers' instructions. When they reached the
last subway station in Jerome Avenue, they spotted the deserted
frankfurter stand a hundred feet away on the other side of the
road. 'A typical summer refreshment stand,' commented Condon,
'it looked gloomy and forbidding on this bitterly cold night.' Al
Reich parked the car beside it.

Condon alighted, went to the center of the porch, lifted up a big
stone and found an envelope. In it was a further message telling
him to cross the road and follow the fence to 233rd Street. The
fence in question bounded the west side of the 400-acre Woodlawn
Cemetery, scene of a battle between British and Revolutionary

troops, and where such native sons as F. W. Woolworth, Jay Gould, William Whitney, Admiral Farragut, Charles Scribner, Joseph Pulitzer and Herman Melville lie buried; the fence runs in an unbroken line to the cemetery's main entrance, half a mile away, at 233rd Street. As they motored there, Al Reich joked to Condon: 'When they shoot you tonight, they won't have to carry you too far to bury you.'

The Woodlawn main gates lie a little way back from the Jerome Avenue and 233rd Street intersection, forming a crescent across the right-angle made by the two streets. Reich parked the car short of the intersection and switched off the engine. A man whom Condon thought was a look-out walked by: Italian-looking, short and swarthy, wearing a cap and with a handkerchief over his face. Condon climbed out and waited in the triangle between the road and the cemetery gates. Nothing happened. After ten minutes, he returned to the car. Al Reich wanted to go with Condon and grab the kidnapper but Condon, like Lindbergh, was determined to play it straight. He returned to the gates and presently saw a white handkerchief being waved inside the cemetery.

> 'I see you,' I said.
> I walked over to the gate. In the shadows, three feet behind the gate, stood a man. He wore a dark overcoat and a soft, felt hat, its brim pulled down. He held the handkerchief before his face.
> He spoke, and I recognized at once the guttural voice that had talked to me over the telephone the night before.
> 'Did you *gottit* my note?' he asked.
> 'Yes, I got it.'
> 'Have you *gottit* the money with you?'
> 'No,' I replied, 'I could not bring the money until I saw the baby . . .'

At this point, said Condon, there was the snap of a broken twig and, turning, the man saw a cemetery guard approaching: he shinned up the gate, swung himself over, dropped down at Condon's feet and ran across the road into Van Cortlandt Park. Condon, despite his seventy-two years, followed shouting (if we are to believe him), 'Hey, come back here. Don't be so cowardly,' and – if we are still to believe him – finally coming close enough to grip his left arm, just above the elbow. 'I bawled him out unmercifully . . . "You should be ashamed of yourself," I scolded. "Here you are, my guest. No one will hurt you." ' With the man allowing Condon to keep a grip on his arm, Condon led him to a park bench. ' "Sit down there," I commanded, "I'll have a look round and make sure we're entirely alone." ' Having satisfied himself on that score, Condon returned to the bench, resumed his grip, and said, 'You shouldn't have run as you did. Don't ever do that again.'

The above is taken from Condon's book, *Jafsie Tells All*, which was written years later and, as the reader will have observed, endeavors to portray Condon in an admirable light, brave and forceful, dominating the situation. He is equally unconvincing when later in the conversation he adopts a Good-Samaritan role. When the man (who says his name is John) coughs, Condon says, 'Your coat is too thin for this time of the year. Take my coat. I have another at home.' And when John refuses, Condon says, 'Come with me then, and I will get you something for your cough.'

A few weeks later Condon was asked by Lieutenant James Finn of the New York City Police to describe John. This was difficult as although they were together for nearly an hour, they were in the dark. The man had his hat pulled down and, as Condon admitted, he only once saw his face for a fleeting moment. However he thought he was about 5 foot 8 to 10, aged thirty to thirty-five, weighing 158 to 165 pounds, with fair to chestnut hair (how could he tell if John never took his hat off?) and almond-shaped eyes like those of a Japanese or Chinaman. Elaborating further, he said that John had a 'fleshy lump at the base of the left thumb', a husky voice and a hacking cough. John had told him he was a sailor by profession and came from north of Boston. He spoke with a marked accent, pronouncing his 't's as 'd's and 'c's as 'g's. Condon asked him in German if he was German ('*Bist du Deutsch?*') and when the man, not understanding, didn't reply, Condon repeated it in English, to which he said no, he was Scandinavian.

John, said Condon, told him there were six of them in the gang, including two women who were looking after the baby in a boat which was six hours away and had two white cloths on the masts. The ransom money would now be $70,000 because Lindbergh had called the police: of this the leader would get $20,000, the others $10,000 each. Twice John said what had already been said twice in the ransom notes – that they had been preparing for a long time. Then he added:

'Would I burn if the baby is dead?'

Condon, confused, replied he didn't know the facts.

'Would I burn,' said John, '*if I did not kill it?*'

Condon was sufficiently disturbed by this to ask how the baby was, and was relieved to be told that he was in good health and being given the diet published in the papers. John added that they would not be sending any more letters with the signature, but to prove they were holding the baby they would shortly be sending his sleeping-suit. And Condon must agree to putting an ad. in next Sunday's *Bronx Home News* saying 'Baby is Alive and Well. Money is Ready' to prove to his friends that they had met and that the deal was on. Condon agreed, and the man slipped away into the darkness of the park, where it was clear, said Condon, that another of the gang was waiting.

It was 10.45 before Condon returned to the car to find Al Reich half frozen and fuming with frustration. 'You've no idea,' he told Condon, 'how close I came to following you. I wanted to hit that fellow.'

It is a wry thought in the light of what we know now that if Reich had grabbed John as he wanted to on arrival at Woodlawn or, better still, if John had been followed and picked up by the police, a case which has baffled people for fifty years might have been cleared up and the principals apprehended within days.

The 'Money is Ready' ad. appeared in the *Bronx Home News* on Sunday March 13, and a similar one on the Monday. On the Wednesday a bulky package was delivered to Condon's house which he knew must be the baby's sleeping-suit. He called Breckinridge who called Lindbergh who said that Hopewell was surrounded by reporters but that he would come when he could. He arrived in disguise (amber-colored glasses and a tourist cap) at 1.30 the next morning and was greeted by Condon ('I was proud that this slender, clean-cut youngster who was America's national hero ... was a guest in my humble home.') The package was opened and found to contain a newly-washed Dr Denton's No. 2 baby's sleeping-suit. Lindbergh examined it carefully, particularly the number of buttons and flaps, and declared unequivocally that it was the suit Charlie had been wearing on the night he was taken.

A note was attached to the sleeping-suit, with the familiar red and blue circular symbol. The baby was well and being given the diet. They would not allow their man to attend any more conferences. The ransom would be $70,000 without sight of the baby first. If agreed, an ad. should be put in the *New York American* saying 'I accept Mony is redy.' The note ended: 'After 8 houers we have the money receivd we will notify you where to find the baby. If thers is any trapp you will be responsible what will follows.'

Lindbergh and Breckinridge (and Schwarzkopf too when told) were now convinced that they were dealing with the genuine kidnappers and not, as some had suggested, with a different lot of extortionists. The similarity of the latest ransom note to the previous ones, the repetition of the statement that the gang had been preparing the kidnap 'for a year already', and finally the identification of the sleeping-suit, all confirmed it.

Lindbergh accepted the terms of the note and proposed that the ransom money should be handed over. There were two reasons why he wanted things concluded: firstly, he, and Anne even more so, were beginning to feel the strain, and secondly, although they had been lucky so far in keeping Condon's participation from the press (apart from two or three senior *Bronx Home News* staff who had been sworn to secrecy), every day that passed increased the risk of discovery – and with it, inevitably, the end of negotiations.

Condon felt strongly that it would be wrong to hand over the money without proof that the kidnappers had the baby, and he prepared an ad. proposing that money and baby be exchanged simultaneously. Lindbergh vetoed it: any more prevarication and the kidnappers might lose patience. This view was understandable, and yet there was one simple way in which the kidnappers could have furnished proof of the baby without risk to themselves. Both Schwarzkopf and Lindbergh knew that Dr Mead Hudson had raised several of Charlie's fingerprints from his nursery toys: all the kidnappers had to do was to take a fresh set of his prints and forward them to Lindbergh for comparison. It is incredible that this was not insisted on.

A further example of Lindbergh's faith in the kidnappers was his order to those putting together the ransom money at J. P. Morgan to make no record of the serial numbers of the notes. But when he enlisted the help of the US Treasury's chief law enforcement officer, Elmer Irey, Irey declared that the Treasury would play no part in helping kidnappers to escape the law and insisted not only on the serial numbers of the notes being recorded, but on the bulk of them being gold certificate bills, easier to trace. Accordingly two bundles were prepared, one of $50,000 of which $35,000 in fives, tens and twenties were gold certificates, and a second package of $20,000 consisting of four hundred $50 bills, all in gold certificates – 5150 separate bills in all.

There were further exchanges with the kidnappers. Two of their letters were postmarked in a particular New York area, and Commissioner Mulrooney suggested watching every letter dropped there, and apprehending the sender of any further letters addressed to Lindbergh or Condon. The scheme might have worked, for another letter was dropped, but predictably Lindbergh refused to approve it.

One of these notes again stressed that the case had been prepared for a year, 'so the Police won't have any look to find us'. Twice on March 15 Italian door salesmen (a needle seller and a scissors grinder) called at Condon's house, and went away without calling at any other house; at a charity bazaar on March 19 Condon said he was approached by what he described as an Italian-looking woman who asked him to be at the Tuckahoe railroad depot at 5 on Wednesday 23rd when she would give him an important message.[1] Condon showed up, but not the woman. Earlier, it will be recalled, when telephoned by one of the gang, Condon had heard a voice say in Italian '*Statti zitto!*' ('Shut up!'), and waiting at Woodlawn Cemetery he had spotted what he thought was an Italian look-out. Were the kidnappers Italians; or non-Italians trying to lay a false scent?

On Thursday March 31 Condon's ad. 'I accept. Money is Ready. Jafsie' appeared in the *New York American*, and next day he received a letter for Lindbergh that the money must be ready by the following (Saturday) evening; further instructions would follow as to where and how to deliver it. Eight hours after receiving the money he would be given the baby's address. Acknowledgement should be made by an ad. in Saturday's *New York American*.

On the Saturday morning the ad. ('Yes. Everything OK Jafsie') duly appeared, and that evening Condon, Al Reich, Breckinridge and Lindbergh gathered in the Decatur Avenue living room with the money to wait for the kidnappers' final instructions. Earlier Lindbergh had told Condon that the handing over of the money could be dangerous, and offered him the opportunity to withdraw. Condon declined. Lindbergh also told Condon that instead of Al Reich driving him to the rendezvous at Woodlawn, he would drive him there himself. What he did not tell him was that by this time he and Breckinridge had their suspicions about Condon and wanted to keep an eye on him. Al Reich suggested that Lindbergh drive

[1] Later Condon denied that this meeting ever took place (see Harold Hoffmann, *Liberty Magazine*).

his car (which the kidnappers knew from the previous occasion)
rather than take his own, and Lindbergh accepted. Condon noticed
that beneath his jacket Lindbergh had strapped on a gun.

At 7.45 p.m. the doorbell rang. Condon's daughter Myra went
to answer it. A taxi-driver handed her an envelope, then returned
to his cab and drove away before Condon could stop him. With
Lindbergh and Breckinridge standing either side of him, Condon
opened the envelope and read:

> Dear Sir: take a car and follow
> tremont Ave to the east
> until you reach the number
> 3225 east tremont Ave.
>
> It is a nursery
>
> Bergen
>
> Greenhauses florist
>
> there is a table standing
> outside right on the door, you
> find a letter undernead the table
> covert with a stone, read and
> follow instruction.

There followed the familiar signature with the three interlocking
circles; and then this:

> don't speak to anyone on
> the way. If there is a ratio [radio]
> alarm for policecar, we
> warn you, we have the same
> equipment. have the money
> in one bundle.
> We give you ¾ of a houer to
> reach the place.

The old man and the young one took the two packages containing the money, climbed into Al Reich's car, and set off east in the
direction of Long Island Sound. The New York Police had had
strict orders not to follow them. When they reached 3225 Tremont
Avenue they found a greenhouse and florist's shop marked J. A.
Bergen, and on the other side of the road the dark recesses of St
Raymond's Cemetery, built on reclaimed swampland in 1877 and
now the burial ground of Bronx political families like the Bradys,
O'Tooles and Sullivans. It was an ideal place for handing over

ransom money: no one about, very dark, and plenty of cover in the way of tombstones, mausoleums and trees to avoid, or attack, a pursuer.

They parked the car on the same side as the florist's facing west. Condon alighted, went to the table outside the shop and saw the stone. Under the stone was an envelope. He took it to the car and with Lindbergh read the contents with a flashlight:

> cross the street and
> walk to the next corner
> and follow Whittemore Ave
> to the soud
> take the money with
> you. come alone
> and walk
> I will meet you.

Condon stood by the car while reading the note so that any look-out might have time to identify him. It proved a sensible precaution, for just then Lindbergh saw a man coming along the sidewalk towards him. 'He was wearing a brown suit and a brown felt hat. His hat was pulled down over his eyes. As he passed the car he covered his mouth and the lower part of his face with a handkerchief and looked at Dr Condon and me. He continued along Tremont and passed out of sight.'

Lindbergh opened the car door to follow the kidnapper's instructions, but Condon stopped him. On the way Condon had been fretting about Lindbergh's gun and the possibility that if confronted by a man, or associate of a man, who had kidnapped his son, he would use it. Now the note gave him the excuse he needed to ask Lindbergh to stay put. 'It says to come alone,' he said. Lindbergh handed him the bigger of the two packages but Condon was in no mind to wander around in the dark with $50,000 without first establishing where Whittemore Avenue was and if anyone had showed up to meet him. 'I'll come back for it,' he said.

He crossed the street and followed Tremont Avenue to the east. Presently he came to Whittemore Avenue, a narrow, unlighted dirt road that intersects the cemetery to the south. To walk into the darkness there seemed a recipe for disaster, so he continued along Tremont to the cemetery's main gate, peering among the tombstones as he went. Then he retraced his steps and at the top of Whittemore Avenue shouted to Lindbergh in the car, 'I guess there's no one here. We'd better go back.' Almost immediately a voice from inside the cemetery shouted 'Hey, Doc!' so that Lindbergh in the car some 80 to 100 yards away heard it.

Condon turned and saw a man walking among the tombstones to his left, parallel to Whittemore Avenue. If he was to keep up with him, there was nothing for it but to plunge into Whittemore Avenue himself. Wary of an ambush, he kept to the center of the road until he reached a lane leading into the cemetery on the left. Here the man jumped over a high wall, crossed the lane and crouched behind a hedge. Condon approached him, and claims to have said, 'What are you doing here? Stand up if you want to talk to me.' According to Condon the man stood up. He was wearing a fedora hat with the brim pulled down, and a dark suit. Condon said he recognized him as Cemetery John.

John asked Condon if he had the money, and Condon said no, it was in the car with Colonel Lindbergh, and asked for a written note as to where the baby was. John said he didn't have it with him but would fetch it and be back in ten minutes. Condon, anxious to do Lindbergh a favour, told John that Lindbergh hadn't been able to raise the extra $20,000 but he could have the $50,000 now. John, by now no doubt as anxious as Lindbergh to see the matter concluded, did not demur.

Fifteen minutes later both men were back at the hedge. Condon handed John the box with the money at the same time as John handed Condon the note. John opened the box, handled the tightly packed bills and expressed satisfaction. 'The gang says your work is perfect,' said John. 'Everyone of them drust you.' He told Condon that the baby was 'on a boad called *Nelly*' up at Gay Head, but that the note containing the information was not to be opened for six hours. Condon says he told John that if he found he was double-crossing him, he'd follow him to Australia. Then they parted.

When Condon reached the car Lindbergh related how a few minutes earlier the man in the brown suit with the handkerchief had come running down the other side of the street from the direction of Whittemore Avenue. 'As he passed the car, he covered his face with the handkerchief and blew his nose so loudly that it could be distinctly heard across the street . . . I had no direct view of his face, he removed the handkerchief and with a quick motion threw it down with his left hand into an open lot opposite the florist's shop.'

A mile from the cemetery Lindbergh and Condon opened the envelope and saw for the last time the familiar handwriting. This is what they read:

> the boy is on Boad Nelly
> it is a small Boad 28 feet
> long, two person are on the
> Boad, the are innosent.
> you will find the Boad between
> Horseneck Beach and gay Head
> near Elizabeth Island.

Relieved, they drove back to Decatur Avenue and gave the expectant and anxious little party there – Breckinridge and Al Reich, Mrs Condon, Myra and Myra's husband Ralph Hacker – news of the successful transaction. Then Condon accompanied Lindbergh and Breckinridge downtown to the Morrow apartment at 2 East 72nd Street. They were in lighthearted mood; the mission had been accomplished without violence or mishap and they believed that within a day or two Charlie would be restored to his mother. At the apartment Elmer Irey and Frank Wilson of the US Treasury were waiting, and Irey's face fell when Condon told him how he had saved Lindbergh $20,000 by keeping back the second package, for the $50 gold bills in it would have been the easiest of all to trace. Condon brightened when Irey spoke of the possibility of obtaining a footprint where John had jumped down from the cemetery wall. Later he and his son-in-law Ralph Hacker did find a footprint there. Hacker made a plastic mould, and it was found to be size 8–8½.

Next day Lindbergh set off by plane from Bridgeport, Connecticut, to search the waters round the Elizabeth Islands between Martha's Vineyard and Cape Cod. But neither on that day nor on any that followed, as he swept up and down the New England coast, did he find the slightest trace of a boat called *Nelly*, or of his son. Disconsolate and depressed at having been so easily and ruthlessly duped, Lindbergh returned to Hopewell and his pregnant wife.

8

During the entire period of Condon's negotiations with the kidnappers and the payment of the ransom money, all police forces which might have been of help were rendered impotent. At Hopewell Colonel Schwarzkopf knew what was going on in New York, but had promised Lindbergh and Breckinridge not to interfere; in New York the City Police had promised the same.

The FBI, which had no jurisdiction in the case but whose experience in criminal matters was unrivalled, was not even called on to advise in a consultative capacity. Just how far they were kept in the dark is revealed in a recently released report from Special Agent J. M. Keith to the Director, J. Edgar Hoover, dated April 9, 1932.

The day after the kidnapping Special Agent Wayne Merrick arrived at Hopewell to offer his services to Schwarzkopf. Schwarzkopf however 'did not show him the ransom note, nor did he give him any intimate basic details upon which this Bureau could conduct an intelligent inquiry'. On March 5 Merrick and another Special Agent, E. J. Connelley, found Lindbergh equally unco-operative. 'Connelley,' reported Keith, 'does not even know for certain that there was a ransom note,' but thought there was because of something said by Lindbergh's aviator friend Thomas Lanphier, in whom Lindbergh had confided. Yet at a press conference on March 7 the New Jersey Police flatly denied there had been any ransom note.

Lanphier would seem to have been as much perturbed by Lindbergh's attitude as the FBI, and on March 23 he persuaded Lindbergh to let Connelley come to Hopewell again. It proved fruitless, however. 'Connelley was not furnished with specific information contained in the ransom note nor with details as to the contacts attempted or consummated with the kidnappers.' Lindbergh gave Lanphier and Connelley a ride back to New York, where he was attending a conference with Breckinridge and two officers of the Special Intelligence Unit of the Internal Revenue Bureau, Frank Wilson and Arthur Madden. 'Connelley,' reported Keith, 'was never furnished with any information as to the results of this conference.' It was not surprising; the object of the conference was to decide on how the ransom money was to be made up to make the tracing of it easier. And yet, said Keith, 'Lanphier later told Connelley that Lindbergh did not trust Wilson and Madden, and had given them no information concerning the kidnapping . . .'

By this time Connelley had won Lanphier's confidence, and when, on March 28, an FBI lead came up that Connelley thought important, Lanphier persuaded Breckinridge to let Connelley tell him about it. 'Breckinridge,' reported Keith, 'was reached by Lanphier at an address in the Bronx' (i.e. Condon's house), but not wishing to invite Connelley there, met him elsewhere and then sat in his car for two hours. The lead led nowhere, but Breckinridge, although described by Connelley as 'very cagey', opened up a little for the first time. He admitted that contact with the kidnappers had been established; that a representative of the Lindberghs had met them recently in a graveyard; that they appeared to be of German or similar foreign extraction; and that they would return the baby a few hours after payment of the ransom money. But Breckinridge would not discuss with Connelley the contents of the ransom 'note' (sic) nor the manner in which communications with the kidnappers had been established.

On the last day of March Lanphier told Connelley that the original ransom demand of $50,000 had been increased to $70,000, and that the Lindberghs' go-between was Dr John Condon of Fordham University and 2974 Decatur Avenue; and that the 'Jafsie' notices that had been appearing in the *New York American* were his.

On hearing this Connelley did two things: made inquiries at Fordham about Condon's past history (and learnt that 'young attorneys' from Breckinridge's law firm had recently been doing the same); and put a mail cover on 2974 Decatur Avenue. This produced an immediate result, the tracing of a letter delivered to that address on April 1, 1932, as follows: 'Mr Dr John Condon, 2974 Decatur Avenue, New York City'. The letter was the kidnappers' instructions to put the 'Yes. Everything OK.' ad. in the *New York American* the next morning, and to be prepared to deliver the money the same evening. The handwriting on the envelope, said Keith, suggested the writer was probably German, as did the complimentary title, 'Mr Doctor' (German, *'Herr Doktor'*).

In addition, and at the request of Lanphier (who clearly sensed that events were reaching a climax), Connelley placed Special Agent Lackey in a room opposite Condon's house, and two other agents in a room a block away, 'to be reached by Connelley on the telephone should any sudden emergency require their presence'.

They were just two weeks too late. Although Lackey got some of his times and facts wrong, he seems to have observed Lindbergh and Condon return from St Raymond's on the night of April 2 with two black bags, and a little later leave with Breckinridge, presumably to meet Irey at the Morrow apartment. Two days later Special Agent Merrick at Hopewell observed Lindbergh and Breckinridge drive into the Lindbergh estate. 'They had with them the two black bags heretofore mentioned, and appeared dejected.'

This watching brief was the total extent of FBI involvement at this stage of the Lindbergh case. Had they ever gained Lindbergh's confidence and learnt what they did earlier rather than later, the outcome might have been very different.

*   *   *

And what of she whose agony in this affair was greatest, who passed her days and nights out of the public eye, and whom the policeman Lewis Bornmann sometimes observed 'flitting from room to room like some distracted ghost'? In all these weeks of hope and disappointment, how was Anne Lindbergh?

We know partly, because of the letters she sent daily, sometimes twice daily, to her mother-in-law, Evangeline Lindbergh, in Detroit. On the day after the kidnapping she wrote a remarkably controlled account of what had happened, concluding, '. . . the detectives are very optimistic though they think it will take time and patience.' News of her husband varied. At first he was being 'marvellous – calm, clear, alert and observing'. But this was less than half the truth, for she later admitted: 'The first two days he looked like a desperate man – I could not speak to him. I was afraid to.' Betty Gow, too, had never seen him so changed. But (as he had proved in the *Spirit of St Louis*) he had remarkable powers of recovery; and – as Lewis Bornmann observed – whatever his mood, he never lost his huge appetite.

Bornmann was one of a score of state troopers now camping in the house. 'Bedlam,' Anne called it; 'hundreds of men stamping in and out, sitting everywhere, on the stairs, on the pantry sink. The telephone goes all day and night. People sleep all over the floors on newspapers and blankets. I have never seen such self-sacrifice and energy.' And later: 'Mattresses all over the dining room and other rooms at night. At any time I may be routed out of my bed so that a group of detectives may have a conference in the room.

It is so terrifically unreal that I do not feel anything.'

But she was thankful that the press had moved out, as they could now go for walks. 'Wahgoosh follows C around the grounds and I think it distracts and pleases him.' As to why Wahgoosh hadn't barked that night: 'he was at the other end of the house and couldn't have heard anything through the howling wind'. ('He has been barking ever since,' she added.) The Whatelys and Betty Gow were a great help. 'Betty was terribly pleased by a note from you this morning. It came just at the right time, for she has had so much grilling and criticism, and is such a loyal girl.'

The dominant theme of all Anne's letters was hope, for hope was what everyone – 'friends, advisers, detectives, police' – was feeding her; they knew it was all she had to live on. On March 5, after receipt of the second ransom note and an encouraging word from Charles, she told her mother-in-law, 'We seem to have pretty tangible word that the baby is safe and well cared for.' The entry of Spitale and Bitz – whom she called 'the two underworld kings' – raised hopes further. And wasn't it strange, she added, that they showed more sincerity in their sympathy than a lot of politicians who'd been there?

Hoping and waiting and being unable to help – this was the pattern of her days and the pattern of her letters to Mrs Lindbergh.

> C and Col Henry continue very hopeful and active . . . All have faith in the ultimate success . . . In a survey of 400 cities, 2000 kidnapped children returned . . . Never in the history of crime has there been a case of a gang bargaining over a dead person . . . It is a very hard time because there is nothing to do, but the men do not feel less hopeful . . . They keep assuring me the baby is safe and will be returned . . . There really is definite progress.

Daily she was buoyed up by encouragement and love: from her husband who throughout proved a rampart of strength; from the knowledge of the new life quickening within her; from the presence of her mother, who had been at Hopewell since the day after the kidnapping. 'She has been so wonderful,' Anne wrote to her sister Elisabeth, 'never trying to comfort me when I felt I might cry. Always here, always understanding C and the situation. And of course knowing I'm tired before I do.' She found comfort too in 'the sympathy and indignation of hundreds of people all over the country as shown by the thousands of letters, the newspapers and the editorials . . .' And in a letter to Mrs Lindbergh she wrote:

'Did you hear that in Madison Square Garden last night they . . . asked everyone to stand for three minutes and pray for the safe return of the baby? I think it thrilling to have so many people moved by one thought.'

The letters that Anne referred to had been arriving at Hopewell at the rate of more than a thousand a day, where they were screened and sorted by the New Jersey Police. By early April, when the rate had dwindled to less than a hundred, they lay waist-high along one side of the garage wall. There were 38,000 of which 12,000 recounted dreams, 11,500 expressed sympathy, 9500 offered suggestions and 5000 were from cranks. 'Isn't it surprising,' Anne wrote to her mother-in-law, 'the number of people who have written their dreams to us?' Among the cranks were demands for money in exchange for the child, and which she found 'very shocking'.

Nor, despite the protection of the police, were they entirely free from cranks in the flesh. One lunatic, having persuaded guards and family that he had important information which he could only deliver to Anne personally, declaimed to her 'To be or not to be'. Betty Gow was woken one night by Lindbergh and told that a woman had arrived who swore that she could identify Betty as a member of a gang. Betty had never seen her in her life.

The worst of the cranks was a nut called Murray Garrson, allegedly from the Washington office of the Secretary for Labour, who had been checking residences around Hopewell for information as to aliens. At 3 a.m. on a morning in late March, he and his followers arrived at the Hopewell house, where he not only demanded entry as a Federal official, but announced that he would break the case within the next forty-eight hours. His subsequent behavior was recorded in Special Agent Keith's report to the Director of the FBI.

> . . . he caused all servants to be aroused, and began a nonsensical, pompous interrogation of members of the Lindbergh household; openly interviewed the nurse, Betty Gow, and during the course of his asinine interrogation of her called her 'a damned liar' and 'a monkey' and other uncomplimentary phrases; ordered Mrs Lindbergh, in her present delicate condition, to go upstairs and walk around in the nursery in order that he might determine whether her footsteps could be heard.

According to the FBI Anne Lindbergh complied with the request, but

Garrson was so busy interrogating others he forgot to listen for her footsteps and later caused her to return to the nursery for the same purpose. Garrson then ordered Mrs Lindbergh to show him the furnace, accompanied her to the cellar, and in her presence began poking around in the ashes to see if he could discover any remains of the child, thereby leaving the plain inference that the Lindberghs themselves had killed the youngster and burned the body.

Although Anne knew of the handing over of the ransom money on April 2, and of Charles's fruitless search for the boat *Nelly*, she didn't mention them to her mother-in-law on April 6. 'We have had some very disappointing setbacks,' was as far as she would go, 'but the consensus is that the child is still safe and well.' She expressed the same optimism on April 8, but by the 10th, when she wrote again, the news had broken in the papers. The reason they had handed over the money first, she said, was on the best advice of criminologists, detectives, etc: 'If we had not done that . . . we would have blamed ourselves for ever for not trying what works in most cases.' The worst aspect was the 'leak' in the papers that the serial numbers of the ransom bills had been noted and would be used to track the kidnappers. 'Of course the publicity makes it almost impossible for them to get the baby to us. There will probably be terrific delay.' Neither Charles nor anyone else thought the baby had been killed. 'They say it is harder to dispose of a dead baby than a live one.'

Throughout April Anne remained optimistic, believing they might be called on to make a double pay-off (Charles had met some parents to whom this had happened), hearing also of a little boy of two or three who had been returned in good shape after four months. And then a new lead came up, that of a Norfolk boat-builder called John Hughes Curtis who, with the support of two acquaintances of Lindbergh – an English clergyman called Dobson-Peacock and Admiral Guy Burrage, who had brought him home from France in the cruiser *Memphis* – persuaded Lindbergh that he was in touch with the kidnap gang. What attracted Lindbergh to this lead was Curtis's apparent knowledge that negotiations were in progress (though nothing of Condon's activities had appeared in the press) and his later saying that the baby was on a boat called the *Mary B. Moss* off the Jersey coast. The 'other' kidnappers had indicated a boat called *Nelly*. Perhaps there was a link – had the name *Nelly* been changed to *Mary B. Moss*? It was worth investigating – anything was worth investigating to bring the boy back – and with Curtis he began organizing a search for the *Mary B. Moss* by air and later in the yacht *Cachalot*. Anne told Mrs Lindbergh that everyone she respected thought this lead 'a lot of hooey, a waste of time', and that the sooner Charles got clear of it, the better. Inwardly perhaps Charles felt it too, but it appeased his restlessness, gave him something to do.

April gave way to May. Charles, in the *Cachalot*, continued looking for the *Mary B. Moss*. Anne and her mother went for walks on the estate, around the house among the pink and white dogwood, in the woods full of violets, in the fields where grew the apple and wild cherry. 'The place looks so beautiful now . . . I wish C were here to see it with me . . . Perhaps we will all still be here together in the spring sometime – and happy.'

But for Anne now any thoughts of happiness came abruptly to an end. On the late afternoon of May 12 her mother came to her, where and when we do not know, but, we can be sure, at a place and time of wise choosing. 'The baby is with Daddy,' she said. It must have taken Anne a moment to absorb the full import of those words, ones which afterwards she would never forget. Yet horrifying as they were, they at least put an end to the uncertainty and unreality of the past nine weeks; and in the diary which after three years abstinence she had resumed only the day before, she wrote:

> I feel strangely a sense of peace – not peace but an end to restlessness, a finality, as though I were sleeping in a grave.
> It is a relief to know that he did not live beyond that night. I kept him intact somehow by that. He was with me the last weekend and left loving me better than anyone. But that is merely selfish and small.
> To know anything definitely is a relief. If you can say 'then he was living', 'then he was dead', it is final and finalities can be accepted.

Charlie's body (less his sleeping-suit) had been found by a truck driver in woods 30 yards off the Hopewell-Princeton Road, a mile from Hopewell and some 4½ miles from the Lindbergh house. The remains, lying face downwards in a shallow ditch and half covered in leaves beside a burlap bag, were in an advanced state of decomposition: the left leg was missing from the knee down, so were the left hand and right arm, and all the major organs except the heart and liver; yet enough of the features remained for Sergeant Zapolsky, the first police officer to reach the scene, to recognize them from a photograph he had as those of the Lindbergh baby.

Lindbergh and the *Cachalot* were contacted off Cape May[1] and next day at the morgue in Trenton Lindbergh and Betty Gow formally identified the body: by his hair (found by chemical analysis to match a lock kept by Anne), by his sixteen teeth (of which the four eye-teeth had just begun to show through the gums), by the inward-curling and overlapping little toes (the result, Betty Gow says, of his shoes being too tight), by the shape of the nose and formation of the toenails, by the little flannel shirt with the blue Silko thread which Betty had run up and put on him the evening he was taken, and by the sleeveless shirt marked 'B. Altman Co., New York' put on over that. There were traces, too, in the fatty substance found on the undershirt, of the Vick ointment that Betty had rubbed on his chest to keep out the cold. Dr Mitchell's post-mortem findings were that death had occurred some two or three months previously and was the result of a fractured skull.[2]

How and when Charlie died has been a subject for speculation ever since. One theory is that having been snatched from his crib he was put in the burlap bag, both to stifle his cries and as a means of getting him easily to the ground; that the ladder broke and fell over under the combined weight of Charlie and the man carrying him, and the bag fell and Charlie's head hit the cement windowsill; and that when the kidnappers realized he was dead, they disposed of his body as soon as possible. Another theory is that Charlie was alive and well when they left the estate, but that the kidnappers had got behind schedule and on reaching Hopewell and seeing behind them the house ablaze with lights (or else passing a police car with screaming sirens) they became panic-stricken, killed the baby, and fled. A third theory is that there was envy and hatred in the hearts of the kidnappers for so god-like a figure as Lindbergh, and to hit where it would most hurt, they killed his son deliberately.[3]

Whatever the truth, the action of the kidnappers in continuing to negotiate as though Charlie was alive when they knew he was not, stripping the sleeping-suit from his dead body to indicate they

[1] Curtis was at first thought to have been a hoaxer, attempting to extort money from Lindbergh because of financial troubles; and after some rough handling by the New Jersey police, he signed a statement to that effect. Later the authorities and his own counsel came round to the view that he had in fact been in touch with the kidnappers. Charged with obstructing the course of justice, he was fined $1000 and given a one year's suspended prison sentence.

[2] See Appendix II.

[3] The fracture to the baby's skull was so severe and extensive that one inclines to the belief that he was killed purposely and not accidentally.

still had him, <u>seems unbelievably calculating and callous</u>. Yet, dead or alive, what difference did it make to men such as these? What they wanted was the money. It has also been said that it was bold of them to enter into negotiations with Condon, knowing the baby's body might at any time be found. But the risk was small; this being America, news of the discovery of the body would become public knowledge almost at once.

Years later, when Anne re-read the letters she had sent to her mother-in-law after the kidnapping, she expressed shock and bewilderment. 'How could I have been so self-controlled, so calm, so factual, in the midst of horror and suspense?' She had hinted at the reasons in her March 18 letter to Elisabeth. 'Time has not continued since that Tuesday night. It is as if we just stepped off into one long night. And I have a sustained feeling – like a high note on an organ that has got stuck – inside me.' The unreality had paralyzed her. There was also the feeling that she must not let the side down. 'Not only was I surrounded by hopeful people, I was surrounded by disciplined people. The tradition of self-control and self-discipline was strong in my own family and also in that of my husband. The people around me were courageous and I was upheld by their courage.'

Now she could however confide her deepest thoughts to her diary; and some of the entries after the discovery of Charlie's body, although more than fifty years old, are almost unbearably poignant.

May 13th. He has already been dead a hundred years. A long, sleepless night but calm with C sitting beside me every hour, and I could see it all from a great distance . . .
  Then a long day when everything personal flooded back over me, a personal physical loss, my little boy – no control over tears, no control over the hundred little incidents I had jammed out of sight when I was bargaining for my control . . .
  Impossible to talk without crying.

May 15th. I hope he was killed immediately and did not struggle and cry for help – for me.

May 16th. I dreamed . . . I was walking down a suburban street seeing other people's children and I stopped to see one in a carriage and I thought it was a sweet child, but I was looking for *my* child in his face. And I realized, in the dream, that I would do that forever. And I went on walking heavy and sad and woke heavy and sad.

May 17th. C's grief is different from mine and, perhaps, more funda-mental, as it is not based on the small physical remembrances. There is something very deep in a man's feeling for his son, it reaches further into the future. My grief is for the small intimate everyday person. How much of it is physical and can be allayed by another child?

May 18th. I thought I would lead him and teach him and now he has gone first into the biggest experience in life. He is ahead of me. Perhaps when I have to go through it I will think of him – my gay and arrogant child going into it – and it will not seem so terrifying, so awesome, a *little* door.

May 21st. Last night I went into his closet, opened the door, a flood of warmth. His blue coat on a hook, his red tam, his blue Dutch suit, the little cobweb scarf we tied round his neck. I opened the suitcase and went over each suit. His two wrappers hung on a hook and a pair of white shoes and his bunny bedroom boots. In the pockets of his blue coat I found a shell, a 'tee', and his red mittens. It was like touching his hand. In the drawers I found the Hansel and Gretel set he played with that last day and the little pussycat I pushed in and out of a little toy house for him. It delighted him so. It gave me a pang of happiness to find it again.

On this day, the fifth anniversary of Lindbergh's epic flight, Amelia Earhart flew from Newfoundland to Ireland – the first woman to cross the Atlantic alone. In the afternoon the family left Hopewell. Mrs Morrow and Elisabeth went to Englewood, Charles and Anne to the Guggenheims at Falaise where, long ago, he had first encouraged her to fly. It was still and cool there, she wrote, dark with lilacs, rain on the terrace and on the pearl-gray sea.

'The smell of wet ground, of the tide, and the quiet sound of waves. C and I might be coming back from our honeymoon three years ago. It is so peaceful, like that evening – only I am old, old, and I understand nothing any more.'

*   *   *

And now the coda to the life of poor Violet Sharpe, the Morrow maid who had told the New Jersey State Police conflicting statements about her movements on March 1, and whom Inspector Walsh had made a note to interview again. She does seem to have been a very strange girl. At her first interview Walsh found her 'a cold, abrupt, defiant and surly individual, who frequently grinned at a question regardless of its importance concerning the investigation of the kidnapping'.

Walsh interviewed her again at Hopewell on May 21, after she had been discharged from hospital following a tonsils and adenoid operation, and when it had become known that the baby was dead; and while she was at Hopewell, other officers went to Next Day Hill and made a thorough search of her room. The interview lasted only six minutes, 'she being a total physical wreck: It is impossible for me or anyone else to mimic her condition. Her entire body shook and she could not talk coherently. She maintained also the same cold, sullen and defiant bearing that she had exhibited at Englewood.'

During the six minutes, however (and before a doctor was called to advise that the interview be discontinued), Violet Sharpe had made further conflicting statements, as a result of which Walsh later made another attempt to interview her. Her condition being no better, this interview lasted only three minutes.

But now Walsh's blood was up. If Violet was as innocent as she claimed, why had she lied to him, not once but again and again? On the morning of June 10 he telephoned Englewood and left word that a police car would soon be arriving to take Violet Sharpe to police headquarters at Alpine (up the Hudson from Englewood) for further investigation. A doctor would be present in case she felt unwell.

But, doctor or no doctor, Violet had had enough of Inspector Walsh, his searching of her room and his endless questions, all designed, it seemed, to saddle her with some responsibility for the crime. She went upstairs, dissolved in water some crystals of cyanide chloride she used for cleaning silver, and drained it. Within a few minutes she was dead.

Despite exhaustive police inquiries, no connection between Violet Sharpe and Charlie's kidnappers was ever made. But that is not to say there was no connection. She was after all one of only a handful of people who knew of the sudden decision for Charlie to stay over at Hopewell on March 1, and the kidnappers' uncanny knowledge of knowing just when and where to act does tend to suggest inside information. That Violet was an associate of the gang can, I am sure, be dismissed: from all accounts a role of that sort would have been beyond her. But is it possible that on that Tuesday, being a naïve and gullible person, she passed on information to someone quite unthinkingly; that after the kidnapping she recognized what she had done and lied to Inspector Walsh in panic; and that after the discovery of the body and in a state of depression following her discharge from hospital she killed herself because of the guilt she now felt for the baby's death; a guilt which she knew she would sooner or later be forced to admit to Inspector Walsh and the world? It is of course possible that she was one of those unfortunately neurotic people who in certain circumstances find it impossible to tell the truth, and who because of their neurosis are more prone to suicide than others. But she was a vivacious girl with most of her life before her, and a deeper explanation for such a sudden and irrevocable act is surely needed.

Schwarzkopf and Walsh however, with the baby dead, the ransom money paid and nothing to show for it, had no doubts about the matter at all. 'The suicide of Violet Sharpe,' Schwarzkopf told the press, 'strongly tends to confirm the suspicions of the investigating authorities concerning her guilty knowledge of the crime against Charles Lindbergh Junior.'

Adding his own chirrup Walsh said: 'I am convinced that Violet Sharpe deceived us and that she did so deliberately. I am convinced that she was the informant and agent for the kidnappers.'

The kidnappers however had vanished into thin air leaving Schwarzkopf and Walsh whistling in the dark, and the New Jersey State Police, the New York City Police, the FBI and the committee of colonels no further on than when they started.

PART FOUR

INTERLUDE 1932-4

'If I live to be a hundred, I shall love you more each year.'

(Letter from Richard to Anna Hauptmann, Summer 1932.)

9

The year wore on; with no further developments in what had come to be called the Crime of the Century, news editors were obliged to fall back on more staple fare: the Sino-Japanese war, the civil disobedience campaign of Mahatma Gandhi, the rise of Hitler, the nomination and election of Franklin Roosevelt as President of the United States.

Violent crime in 1932 was as widespread as today, though, while punishments were everywhere more savage. Throughout America kidnappings and, in the South, lynchings of young blacks for real or imagined attacks on whites occurred with depressing regularity. During the year 140 convicted murderers were sent to the electric chair. In May President Doumer of France was assassinated (as was Premier Ki Inukai of Japan) and in September his murderer, Dr Paul Gorguloff, was publicly guillotined before a crowd of fifty thousand people.

The same month the *New York Times* announced the death in the State Prison at Bridgwater, Mass., of a 69-year-old man called Jesse Harding Pomeroy. Described as 'a degenerate', Pomeroy had been found guilty and sentenced to be hanged at the age of thirteen for mutilating and killing two children. Today he would have been sent to a mental institution for young offenders; then, although the death sentence was commuted, he was detained in solitary confinement for the next forty-one years, being allowed to mix with other prisoners for only the last fifteen years of his life.

Some deaths that year were more comic than tragic. The hunting

season in Pennsylvania accounted for fifty-four thousand deer and
seven sportsmen (excluding deaths from heart attacks), while in a
hotel in Mobile a Mr J. R. Goodman was drowned by firemen
trying to put out a fire.

Other news was the cold of the European winter ('Fifteen waifs
freeze to death in Lisbon' – 'Canals in Venice ice over'); the election
of Eamonn de Valera as President of Ireland; the decision of
Congress to move the inauguration date of the Presidency from
March 4 to January 24; the suicide of Ivar Kreuger, the Swedish
match-king; and of George Eastman, inventor of Eastmancolor
('To my friends,' he wrote, 'my work is done. Why wait?')

On the show-biz front it was the year of *Grand Hotel* with
its all-star cast of the Barrymores, Garbo, Joan Crawford; *The
Red-Headed Woman* in which Jean Harlow debunked the Holly-
wood myth that sin didn't pay; and *The Champ* with Wallace
Beery and Jackie Cooper. From Tin Pan Alley came 'Night and
Day', 'How Deep is the Ocean?' and the song that epitomized the
times, 'Buddy, Can you Spare a Dime?'

*   *   *

If there was no further hard news in the Lindbergh case, there was
no doubting the sense of outrage and eagerness to find and punish
the perpetrators of the crime that still possessed the American
people. The day after the discovery of Charlie's body President
Hoover announced: 'I have directed the law enforcement agencies
and the several secret services of the Federal Government to make
the kidnapping and murder of the Lindbergh baby a live and
never-to-be-forgotten case, never to be relaxed until the criminals
are brought to justice . . . its agencies will be unceasingly alert to
assist the New Jersey Police in every possible way until this end
has been accomplished.' Later that month the New Jersey State
Legislature authorized the Governor to offer a reward of $25,000
leading to the kidnappers' arrest and conviction, and in June
Congress passed a bill making kidnapping a federal offense.

Until the discovery of Charlie's body the law enforcement agencies had concentrated their efforts on finding the boy alive and
restoring him to his parents. Now that he was dead, they could
shift attention to the pursuit and arrest of the kidnappers. The
scope of their efforts was astonishing. In New York they collected
the names of all those who were renting safe-deposit boxes in New
York State in March and April, together with photostated copies

of their signatures. They investigated thousands of income-tax returns. They checked on the origins and background of every unclaimed corpse found in New York after payment of the ransom on the grounds that, Condon being considered likely to identify Cemetery John, John might have been bumped off by the rest of the gang. They checked out individually *all* the former pupils of the school where Condon had been headmaster for twenty-five years to see if any with criminal records might have responded to his letter to the *Bronx Home News* because of this link.

More specifically the police had two available sets of clues: artifacts such as the ransom letters and the ladder; and the two witnesses who had been in contact with members of the gang, John Condon and the taxi-driver, Joseph Perrone.

Perrone, asked to describe a man of whom he had had only a fleeting glimpse in the dark a month before, was of no help at all. Shown hundreds of photographs from various rogues' galleries, he was unable to identify any. Was there any physical characteristic about the man, he was asked, that was noticeable?

'No,' he replied, 'I didn't pay any attention to anything.'

'Is there anything about this man that fixes itself in your mind?'

'No.'

'Would you know him if you saw him?'

Perrone gave the only answer he could.

'No, sir,' he said.

Condon was another matter, for he had seen and talked with one of the kidnappers on two occasions – the first for nearly an hour. Also, since the failure of his mission, his status had dramatically changed. During negotiations he had assumed the mantle of a saviour, but after the discovery of the body and the disclosure of his strange role in the affair, he seemed to many a likely suspect. There was only his word he was on the level. Who was to say that his letter to the *Bronx Home News* and the kidnappers' reply was not part of a prearranged plot leading to the handing over of the money?

One officer who thought so was Inspector Harry Walsh, and soon after the suicide of Violet Sharpe, he had Condon brought across the river to New Jersey, ostensibly to view a rogues' gallery at Paterson, in reality to be given a thorough grilling at police headquarters at Alpine. The grilling lasted four hours ('You're going to stay here until you confess, Condon!') and was followed by a walk along the Palisades with Condon positioned between

Walsh and the terrifying drop to the Hudson. 'Don't you feel like jumping down there?' said Walsh threateningly, and Condon said, no, he didn't. Eventually he was allowed to go, but remained a police suspect: they searched his house for secret panels, dug up the ground around his summer shack on City Island, tapped his telephone and monitored his mail.

Yet if Condon managed partly to clear his own name, he was no help at all in identifying Cemetery John – hardly surprising as both his encounters were in the dark. Despite visiting half a dozen East Coast cities, including Pennsylvania and Boston, to view men behind bars and thousands of rogues' gallery photographs, he either drew a blank or picked out people who couldn't have been there. The police, for instance, having learnt that a Czechoslovak criminal called Simek who had since been deported might have been involved in the kidnapping, showed pictures of him to Condon. 'Boys!' said Condon. 'You are hot. I want to see that man.' Subsequent inquiries showed that Simek was in Santo Domingo at the time of the kidnapping.

Another time – and perhaps punch-drunk from looking at so many photographs – he pointed to another picture and declared excitedly to Schwarzkopf, Lamb and Keaton that this was Cemetery John, there was no question or doubt about it. The man was duly investigated and proved not to have been in New Jersey when the crime occurred, and not in New York when the ransom was handed over. Later Condon was shown more pictures of the same man *including the original photograph*, and declared unequivocally that none of them looked anything like John. In addition, he made further statements about his meetings with John which contradicted his original statement. From now on the New Jersey Police 'placed no reliance at all in Dr Condon'. Lieutenant Finn of the New York City Police called him 'a screwball' and Lieutenant Keaton thought him 'whacky – if not guilty then mentally deranged'.

Nor, at this juncture, did the ransom notes and ladder reveal any information of significance. After the New Jersey State Police had taken the ladder apart and put it together again, Frank Kelly took it down to Washington DC, where it was examined by two representatives of the Forest Service of the Department of Agriculture, Mr Brush and Mr Betts. They found that the sides or rails of the three sections were made of either southern pine or Douglas fir, the cleats were made of Ponderosa pine and the dowel pins that held the sections together were of birch. They noted that some of the sides had nail holes, suggesting they had previously been used for some other purpose. Because of the different kinds of wood in the ladder and the variety of thicknesses, they concluded that the material had not been obtained from a lumber yard, but assembled from 'a miscellaneous accumulation of pieces'; and that the lack of moisture in the wood implied it had been under cover for some time. But as to where it had come from and what sort of person had put it together, they had no suggestions to offer.

The ransom notes were a little more helpful. They had all been posted or delivered in the New York area, and from the fact that the writer had spotted Condon's letter to the *Bronx Home News* and was clearly well-acquainted with Woodlawn and St Raymond's Cemeteries, it was reasonable to assume that he lived in or near the Bronx. The wording and phraseology of the notes suggested he was German or Austrian – '*gute*' and '*haus*' had been used in place of 'good' and 'house', the construction of sentences was that of a man thinking in German and writing in English: words unhyphenated in German were spelt unhyphenated in English, e.g. 'sleepingsuit' (German '*schlafrock*' or '*schlafanzug*'); while the formation of some letters such as 't', 'g', 'a' and 'x' were typical of German script. Some of the spelling mistakes like 'nihgt' and 'singnature' were what you would expect of a German not well versed in English, though the fact that the author seemed to have had no trouble with more difficult words like 'instructions', 'arrangements', 'go-between', and at times wrote in a forceful and fluent style led some people to the view that the mistakes were deliberate, and/or that the letters had been composed by one person and written by another.

Some useful additional comments on the ransom notes came from a trip to Europe made by Schwarzkopf's deputy, Major Charles H. Schoeffel. Aware of his own force's limitations and lack of experience yet wanting to steer clear of the FBI, Schwarzkopf hoped that the legendary Scotland Yard and/or the German police might throw new light on the case. Schoeffel sailed in the *Mauretania* on March 28 – the week before the ransom money was handed over – taking with him enlarged photographs of all ransom letters received so far. The British Press got wind of his arrival, but he was able to avoid them by shifting to another hotel where he registered in the name of John Condon (not after the doctor, he assured Schwarzkopf, but because that was the name of his wife's brother).

Scotland Yard ('who apparently,' said Schoeffel, 'do not think much of American police methods') considered the kidnappers were not professional criminals: the ransom letters were 'far too wordy and too solicitous . . . with phraseology not used by criminals'. They thought that one person had written all the letters, but that the whole of the first letter and the first four lines of the second had been written with the left hand. They agreed they were probably written by a German or Austrian (and were definitely not written by a Frenchman or Italian).

A visit to Berlin proved a waste of time, as it coincided with the Presidential elections when offices and shops were closed because of anticipated trouble from 'the Hitler party'. In addition Kriminal-kommissar Dr Trettin, the head of the Criminal Investigation Division, proved to be an old windbag who boasted that if he could visit America, he would soon return the baby to his father. ('I had quite a time,' reported Schoeffel, 'in making Dr Trettin understand the object of my visit.')

In Vienna however he found a sympathetic listener in the American Minister, Gilchrist Stockton, who was not only familiar with letters from Germans written in English, but whose hobby was the study of handwriting. 'His immediate reaction was that the handwriting was that of a southern German or Austrian, and definitely *not* that of a German from the north or west or Prussia, and to prove his point he had a clerk bring a number of letters from the files, which were from Austrians but written in English, applying for positions with the American Embassy.' On studying these, Schoeffel found 'a great deal of similarity in the various characteristics between the writing of the notes and the writing he displayed'. Stockton suggested that Schoeffel leave behind one of the ransom letter photographs with which he would compare the writing of every south German and Austrian who had successfully applied to their American consulates for emigration documents during the previous ten years (in Vienna alone there were some thirteen thousand).

While it was obviously helpful in narrowing the area of search to have established that the writer of the ransom letters – and presumably the rest of the gang – were among the many thousands of Germans and Austrians who had made their homes in the Bronx and Upper Manhattan, it did not take matters very much further. The best hope for Schwarzkopf and his men now was for the marked ransom bills to start showing up in the city's banks, all of which had been supplied with a list of their serial numbers.

At first it looked as though this might produce results, for on April 4 – only two days after the handover – a $20 ransom bill was spotted by a teller in the East River Savings Bank at 96th Street and Amsterdam Avenue. It had been deposited by a Mr David Marcus, himself on the level but unable to recall where he had acquired it. Unfortunately a few days later a teller in Newark, New Jersey, broke the confidentiality enjoined on banks to keep the serial numbers secret, by informing a local newspaper; the story was picked up by every paper in America. As a result no further $20 bills – the easiest of the denominations to trace – turned up for a considerable time.

Some of the $5 bills however soon began appearing, and continued to do so at irregular intervals. Many more must have been passed and lost without trace, for with some 700,000 separate bills worth $5 million being deposited in New York banks daily, the odds against discovery were enormous. Nor was the task of the tellers made any easier by the serial numbers being listed in a 57-page booklet which made ready reference impossible, and was therefore often ignored (later the numbers were printed on a single sheet measuring 17 by 28 inches).

Finally, there was a time lag of between two and three days between a ransom bill being deposited in a bank and the tracing of it back to the depositor. Most of the depositors were chain stores, cigar and candy shops, cafés and restaurants, whose customers were to be numbered in hundreds if not thousands a day. Occasionally a waitress or shop assistant would try to recall the person who had handed over the bill ('an Italian', 'a German six feet tall', 'a man in shabby clothes who looked like a taxi-driver') but even if these had been apprehended, it was unlikely they would have been able to remember where they had acquired the bills. Some of the bills were found to have come from banks, showing how easily they had escaped the attention of the tellers taking deposits. In all only twenty-seven ransom bills (twenty-one of $5, four of $10 and two of $20) were found in the eight months from the handing over of the money on April 2 to the end of 1932.

*   *   *

It will be recalled that Mr Joseph Furcht, the construction supervisor at the Majestic Apartments, had had to shift Hauptmann from the skilled carpentry work which he had been promised on to maintenance work, having a full quota of skilled men. This was a disappointment to Hauptmann, for not only did maintenance work make small demands on his time and talents, but his wage of $100 a month was about half of what he had been earning in the days before the Depression, and indeed in weekly terms ($25) was less than what Anna was earning at the bakery, with tips.

So, on Saturday April 2, he gave in his notice after work, collected his tools and went home. That evening, four miles away in St Raymond's Cemetery, Dr Condon handed over the $50,000 ransom money to Cemetery John. The same evening, it being the first Saturday of the month, Hauptmann and Hans Kloppenburg had their regular musical get-together. On the Monday Hauptmann made the long journey back to the Majestic Apartments to collect his two days' April wages, amounting to $6.67, but he was told that payments were made only twice a month, and he must wait until April 15.

It was said later that from this time on Hauptmann never worked again. But this was not so. He had no regular job because work was scarce and there was a glut of labour on the market. But he did continue to do contract work for the lumber yard and on his own account, whenever an opportunity arose. He and Kloppenburg, for instance, worked together that summer on a contract job for merchandize display stands. But he did have more time on his hands than before, and increasingly found himself heading in the direction of Steiner, Rouse & Co. to play the stock market.

Financially he and Anna were reasonably cushioned from the Depression. He had the $4000 worth of cash in the trunk, more than $1000 worth of gold coins and gold certificates as a hedge against inflation, the mortgage for $3750 which he had taken out in 1927, and several thousand dollars in the bank – the last two of which were bringing in a healthy interest – in all some $12,000–15,000. In addition Anna was earning up to $30 a week in the bakery. Their living expenses were small – $10.50 a week on rent and $30 a week on housekeeping. At the end of the year Hauptmann took most of the money in the trunk to invest in a second mortgage of $3750, and handed the cash to the Trustees at the Bank of Manhattan (whose manager, Mr McCron, said it was in regular bills, not gold certificates).

On Hunter's Island and elsewhere the Hauptmanns maintained their links with relations and friends. On Easter Sunday they visited Anna's niece, Maria Müller, and her waiter husband Hans, then very poor, and brought a present of two dresses for Maria's little girl, Ruth. There was some talk of the Lindbergh kidnapping, and Maria said how upset she had been and how she had cried. They went on to Brooklyn with presents for Anna's Uncle Gleiforst, who had looked after the satchel containing the $4000 during the trip to California.

They were also seeing Otto Wollenberg and his wife Louise. Anna and Louise, it will be recalled, were both from Markgrön-ingen, and one Saturday evening in May, after finishing a carpentry job, Hauptmann drove the two of them to Philadelphia to spend the weekend with a third Markgröningen childhood friend, a Mrs Blessing. Anna had been saving for another trip to Germany that summer to see her mother, and no doubt the object of this visit was for her to take letters and messages to the families of the other two. Later the Wollenbergs came to dinner with the Hauptmanns and admired their Stromberg-Carlson radio (bought at one third discount because the model had gone out of production). Anna's brother, Ernst Schoeffler, and his wife were there, and after dinner they all went for a drive in the Bronx Park.

Anna had booked a third-class ticket sailing on the *Europa* in June, and she and Louise spent the day of embarkation together. Anna confided to Louise that she had lost $50 while buying her ticket and did not want Richard to know of it. Richard was there when the boat sailed and felt quite emotional. While she was away, he wrote to Anna almost every day. On his return home that night, 'If the waves could talk, they would tell you how much I already miss you.' Another time, 'If I live to be a hundred I will love you more each year.' He had a formal 10 by 8 portrait taken at a photographer's in Yorktown and sent it to Markgröningen 'so I can be with you'. And he was delighted when the photographer thought so well of it that he put a copy in the display window.

Anna would be away until early September and during that long, hot summer Hauptmann divided his time between visits to Steiner, Rouse, occasional carpentry work, and trips to Hunter's Island at weekends and in the evenings. Twice, because he was on his own, the Wollenbergs had him to stay on a Saturday night; and he drove them to the island on the Sunday morning, with a picnic prepared by Louise. Hauptmann remained popular with the Hunter's Island crowd, both on his own account and, as one of the very few with a car, in taking people in the evening to the subway station, otherwise an hour's walk. He was pleased with the canoe he had bought at Macy's and kept at Dixon's Boatyard on nearby City Island. In it he took Louise, Anita Lutzenberg, and other friends for trips round the bay, and caught fish including eels which he cooked over the open fire. (If only, he must have thought, he had had a boat like this as a boy on the Deutschbaselitz dam.)

If one had to pinpoint the time and place that began the chain of events that were to alter so drastically the course of Hauptmann's life — and eventually to end it — it was here at Hunter's Island in the summer of 1932. Although there is no evidence that Richard was ever unfaithful to Anna, there is no doubt that he was a man attractive to and attracted by other women. With Anna in Europe, it was inevitable that he would be more susceptible than usual; and among the crowd of carefree and lightly dressed German girls who frequented Hunter's Island, his eye fell on Gerta Henkel, the blonde wife of Carl Henkel, the painter. He had known of them for some time, for they had two rooms in the same lodging house as Hans Kloppenburg (Mrs Selma Kohl's establishment at 149 East 127th Street). Within a few days Gerta invited Hauptmann back for coffee, and soon hardly a day passed when he was not dropping in for coffee and a chat on his way to Steiner, Rouse. Tongues might have wagged had not, as one neighbor remarked, 'he seemed just as happy seeing her when Carl was there as not', and in his letters to Anna he said how much he looked forward to her meeting his new friends the Henkels.

One day when he was with Gerta and Carl, the door opened and in came a small, skinny-looking German Jew whom Hauptmann had already met casually on Hunter's Island, and whom Carl now formally introduced as Isidor Fisch, another of Mrs Kohl's lodgers. Before his marriage, Carl said, he used to share rooms with Mr Fisch and another friend, Henry Uhlig, who were both in the fur trade. Fisch and Hauptmann seem to have got on well, and Fisch accepted Hauptmann's invitation to visit his home and see the souvenirs he had collected on his California trip. Thus began a relationship, the stark consequences of which neither could have foreseen.

Another woman attracted to Hauptmann was Louise Wollenberg. Before Anna left, Louise volunteered to keep their apartment clean, but Anna, no fool, said that Richard was perfectly capable of doing that himself. However Louise did come and clean the apartment towards the end of July, and again at Richard's request a few days before Anna's return at the end of August. She spent three days over it, scrubbing the woodwork and cleaning the windows; but if she was hoping for anything else, she was to be disappointed. Richard fetched and took her home, but in between times went off to Steiner, Rouse and Gerta. Louise noticed that while he had bought a plant for $16 and other flowers for Anna's return, there was no present for her. Perhaps Richard felt that a payment might be misunderstood; or that taking Otto and Louise to Hunter's Island in the car was payment enough; or that a labor of love needed no payment.

For Germans in New York that summer was one of high excitement, for there was to be a return title fight between Max Schmeling, the German heavyweight champion, and Jack Sharkey, the former American champion of the world, whom Schmeling had defeated on a foul in 1930. The venue was the Madison Square Garden Bowl, and Hauptmann went along with the Henkels and Otto Wollenberg. The result was a disappointment, for Sharkey beat Schmeling on points. An added annoyance for Hauptmann was having the Zeiss glasses Anna had given him stolen from his car. Before her return he bought another pair, since if she had known, 'I am sure she would have taken it badly.'

Anna arrived in New York on a Sunday in early September and was met by Richard and Louise: at dinner at the Franziskaner Restaurant she gave them the latest news of Markgröningen and Kamenz. She had discovered that Richard was free to return to Germany legally whenever he wanted, and he planned to go there in 1935 for his mother's seventieth birthday.

The Hauptmanns resumed their old life at 1279 East 222nd Street, though Anna did not return to her work at the bakery until October and then only briefly. 'We were as happy as previously,' said Richard, and Anna agreed. 'I was as happy as anyone on earth . . . I cared little for anything but my home and we enjoyed being at home together.' Some Sundays they went to the Lutheran Church of St Paul's on 156th Street. Richard introduced Anna to the Henkels, whom she liked, and from now on the four met regularly.

In the fall he had an accident in the Dodge, knocking down Alexander Begg, a pedestrian who, he claimed, was crossing against the lights, and breaking his leg. Reading Hauptmann's account of the accident on the official form, and also a letter he wrote to Mrs Begg, one is struck by how fluently he expressed himself in English (though he still thought in German and was to do so until he died) and how well he spelt English words. After the accident, concerned that there might be a large claim against him, he transferred most of his assets into the name of his wife. In the event he settled with Mr Begg for $300.

Dec. 9. 1933

Dear Madam!

I received your letter and I am very sorry Mr. Begg is not well. If I had more, I would have send you the money long ago. But I try to send you ten or twenty dollars befor Christmas.

My wife has a baby since five weeks and so the few dollars I made I needed badly. As soon as I am able to. I will send you the rest of the money

I wish Mr. Begg will get better soon

Yours truly
Richard Hauptmann

Letter to Mrs Begg.

In the fall he went on two hunting trips with Carl Henkel, one to Garfield, New Jersey, where they saw nothing, another to Maine. This was more successful: they were away three weeks and managed to bag a deer.

On New Year's Eve the Hauptmanns gave a small party to which they invited all those they knew from Mrs Kohl's establishment (the Henkels, Hans Kloppenburg, Isidor Fisch) as well as the Wollenbergs and one or two other old friends. During the evening Otto Wollenberg, rather the worse for drink, pointed at Fisch and said, 'Who is that little shrimp over there?' He said it loud enough for Hauptmann to hear. 'That guy,' said Hauptmann heatedly, 'is worth thirty thousand dollars. He is my partner in furs and the stock market. We have an agreement to go half and half on everything.'

                              *   *   *

Of all the diverse characters who people the Lindbergh kidnapping story, the most mysterious, the most enigmatic, the most sinister is undoubtedly Isidor Fisch.

His family came from Poland, where he was born in 1905, but they settled in Leipzig soon after. His father, Salomon Fisch, ran a store, and he had an elder brother Pinkus and a sister Hanna. He went to school in Leipzig until he was seventeen when he was apprenticed to the firm of R. Schwarze and Co, furriers, where he stayed for three years. There he met Henry Uhlig, another apprentice, who became his lifelong friend. The foreman who taught them their craft was a man called Hermann Kirsten.

Before Fisch and Uhlig had completed their apprenticeships, Kirsten emigrated to New York with his wife and two daughters, Gerta and Erica, and because of conditions in Germany encouraged them to follow when they could. 'Like everybody else in the country,' said Uhlig, 'we were working in the black market at the time, and the money that we saved, we put aside for the fare to America.' When they had saved enough for one passage, Uhlig crossed and stayed with the Kirstens, managed to find work, and presently sent Fisch the money to come over too. When Fisch arrived, he was disappointed that Kirsten had not found work for him, as he had promised, but by now Kirsten had given up furs for bootlegging, an altogether more profitable trade. However Fisch managed to find work as a cutter in the fur trade, then established in midtown Manhattan on the west side, and he and Uhlig shared an apartment. For a time Fisch seems to have prospered, earning first $50, later $100 a week, perfecting his English at night school, sending money regularly to his parents. When Uhlig met a German woman who cooked for a rich family, Mrs Augusta Hile, she asked if he and Fisch would have room in their apartment for her son, Carl Henkel, who wanted to come over from Germany, and they agreed. So Carl (who like Richard Hauptmann was a native of Kamenz) joined them, and through them met the Kirstens and his future wife, Gerta.

Fisch at this time was 5 foot 5½ inches tall, under 150 pounds in weight, had brown hair and eyes, a pair of outsize ears and a persistent, hacking cough – the first signs of the tuberculosis that was eventually to kill him; not a very prepossessing appearance. Uhlig was the opposite: a big man with blond hair and gray eyes whom Hans Kloppenburg called 'a chubby, happy sort of fellow, always making jokes'. When they went out together, 'Fisch said little, but Uhlig was always the life and soul of the party'.

Reports of Fisch at the time he met Hauptmann vary. Most agree that he had no women friends and was not a conspicuous dresser (though one witness said she had always seen him in a green hat and green gabardine suit), and he is said to have spoken with a slight Jewish-German accent. A Mrs Kuntz spoke of him having dancing lessons and becoming so good at it ('he was very adept at the tango') that he became an instructor at the place where he had learnt – a thought so strange that one wonders if she was not muddling him with someone else. To his friends he never appeared to have any money. At Mrs Kohl's he had the cheapest room in the house, right up in the attic, for which he paid only $3.50 a week – and even then, said Mrs Kohl, he was often behind with the rent. Henkel told Kloppenburg he thought Fisch was 'poor as a church mouse', and members of the Chrzanower Society, the Young Men's Jewish Society to which he belonged, thought he was destitute.

But there was another side to Fisch of which his friends were ignorant. Because working for long hours in chilled fur storage rooms was not helpful to his damaged lungs, he looked around for some more congenial activity; and in the process found he had a remarkable gift for persuading people to invest money in dubious enterprises. In short he became a con man. In 1930 he told Mrs Kuntz that he needed $3000 to invest in the Long Sign Company and she gave him $500 which she never saw again. The next year he was involved in an implausible scheme for showing movies in the parks in daytime. To this he got Alois Motzer to stump up $1000. Wisely, Motzer had insisted on collateral (a piece of real estate Fisch had purchased on Long Island), so that when the scheme fell through, his money was repaid.

But Fisch's biggest con was an outfit called The Knickerbocker Pie Company, a pie-making business at 61 Downing Street, New York City. Early in 1931, when it was already on its last legs, it was being run by two crooks called Charles Schleser and Joe DeGrasi. Schleser was a professional gambler who had served a prison sentence for grand larceny, and DeGrasi was a gangster who had robbed a woman of $5000 in 1931 and fled to his native Italy. (He returned clandestinely to New York where he was seen in April 1932, and later people said he bore a resemblance to the

Italianate look-out observed by Reich at the Woodlawn Cemetery.) That Fisch knew Schleser and DeGrasi at this time shows that he was already associating with proven criminals. At any rate they persuaded Fisch to invest $1000 in the Knickerbocker Pie Company and become its president.

In a desperate attempt to keep the company afloat, Fisch persuaded Carl Henkel's mother, Mrs Hile, to invest $1250, and William and Mary Schaefer, the parents of a young friend, Eric Schaefer, to part with $2500. But the Knickerbocker Pie Company was beyond salvation. In July 1931, with the gas cut off due to non-payment of bills and money owing to sundry creditors including the landlords, it finally went bankrupt.[1]

Having developed an addiction for winkling money out of the unsuspecting, Fisch was reluctant to discontinue it. From now on, and long after the Knickerbocker Pie Company had closed its doors, he sang its praises to anyone who would listen; he also persuaded people to part with money for investment in furs. The results were gratifying. Mrs Kirsten, Gerta's mother, gave him $4000, Mrs Hile a further $2850, Max Falek $800, Henry Uhlig $400, Ottilia Hoerber $250, Gerta's sister Erica, Anna Stotz and others further undisclosed sums. Uhlig reckoned that Fisch must have raked in more than $13,000, but according to Fisch's brother Pinkus it was nearer $17,000. Apart from Carl Henkel not a single investor saw his or her money again.

What Fisch did with this money is a mystery. We know he did not spend it on high living, for his mode of existence continued to be as frugal as before. He boasted to Hauptmann that he was trading successfully in furs, and though he may have been, there is little evidence to support it. Hauptmann boasted to him that he was doing well on the stock market. With each wanting to benefit from the know-how of the other, it seemed logical to join forces. But there would be this difference: whereas Hauptmann's business dealings with Fisch were always on the level, Fisch was preparing to con Hauptmann, just as he had conned all the others.

It seems strange that Hauptmann remained in ignorance of Fisch's tendencies. He had had a warning of the kind of world in which Fisch moved when at one of their earliest meetings, Fisch

[1] In a letter dated November 1, 1932, months after the Knickerbocker Pie Company had folded, Fisch was writing to Mr Schaefer: 'Allow me at the present time to use the capital further until such time that I can develop my plans further, about which I think every day.' He added, 'Please do not lose your trust in me and I will prove to you I am an honest man.'

said – to Hauptmann's astonishment – that he was aware that Hauptmann had entered the country illegally, and that he knew someone who could fix citizenship papers for $200. Then there were Gerta's relations – her mother Mrs Kirsten, her mother-in-law Mrs Hile and her sister Erica – all of whom had fallen victims to Fisch's blandishments. Could not Gerta have warned him? Perhaps she didn't know. Perhaps, like a good con man, Fisch was still holding out to these ladies promises of future dividends.[1] Also, like a good con man, he stressed to those who gave him money the importance of keeping things to themselves. 'It's nobody's business but ours,' he told Mrs Hile; and Uhlig said, 'He incited his acquaintances against each other, so that they did not speak to each other about their private affairs, and so it was possible for him to borrow money from each . . .'

Thus, in the late fall of 1932, began the business venture between Richard Hauptmann and Isidor Fisch that was to lead to Hauptmann's undoing.

10

At Falaise for a few days Anne found a kind of temporary peace. 'Mrs Guggenheim is gentle and calm. Her faith is whole, like a child's, and soothing. This place is beautiful and untouched and quiet as a cloister. I have come back from the war.' Back at Englewood the memories came flooding back. She slipped upstairs to Charlie's room when she thought no one was looking, and shut out the world among his things, the toys, the Johnson's baby powder, the pictures she had tacked on the wall for him, the blue knitted jacket he wore when he came down to play every night. 'Just the familiarity of my hand on the crib seemed to put him back there. What is this thing that is presence and yet not presence? I went down crying but more satisfied. I did not click the nursery gate – afraid.'

There was added anguish in a new medical examination of Elisabeth which showed that her early rheumatic fever had caused irreversible damage to the heart valve; in those days that meant only a short time to live.

[1] No doubt they were impressed that when Henkel, who had invested $200 in the Pie Company, asked for repayment, Fisch promptly gave it to him plus $100 'interest'.

Visions of Charlie ebbed and flowed. She would go to bed each night thinking of him – 'so vividly I almost see him' – and he would come to her in dreams. In one dream he had been condemned to die. '. . . saw him running, hair all tangled and curly and I said, "Betty, I cannot remember how you combed his hair." Then I was raging like an animal against the people who were going to take his life.' Strangely the dream stayed with her all day, 'warm and delicious like a remembered tune'. Yet ten days later she was writing, '. . . by day he is getting further and further away – even the clothes, now I have looked at them three or four times, have lost his presence.'

The next day reality returned with the news of Violet Sharpe's suicide, in the very house where she was staying. 'Oh, what a terrible train of misery and sorrow this crime has pulled behind it. Will the consequences never cease?' One consequence was that reporters and photographers were once more at their heels and they woke to find their pictures 'smeared all over the front pages'. To escape further harassment they escaped, sad and bruised, to Falaise where Harry Guggenheim gave them some tough advice on the subject of press publicity.

It was no good, he said, being always on the defensive. 'You will have to meet it, you can't get away from it. The only thing to do is to change your whole attitude. Conquer it inside of you, get so you don't mind. You've got to stop fighting it, stop trying to get away from it.'

But, said Anne, suppose we do give in to it, stop fighting it, throw open our doors to them, *will we have peace then*?

'No,' said their host, 'not unless you're willing to live in vegetating oblivion. And you never will be.'

They knew they would have to return to Hopewell one day, if only to decide on its future. Meanwhile Englewood suited them well, with Lindbergh commuting into New York to work with Dr Carrel each day, and Anne writing *North to the Orient* and awaiting the birth of her second child. Only a few miles away across the river in the same damp heat, tellers in a hundred banks continued to search for Lindbergh ransom bills, Dr Condon scrutinized another hundred rogues' gallery photographs, as well as posing in a Bronx store beside a replica ladder, and out at Hunter's Island in his canoe Hauptmann, sustained by Gerta and Louise, looked forward to Anna's return.

The question of the Hopewell visit was taken out of their hands when Lindbergh was summoned as a witness to the trial of John Hughes Curtis for obstruction of justice, then about to begin at Flemington. 'I dread going to Hopewell,' Anne wrote, 'to live there in no hope, where I lived so long *just* on that.'

They drove there with Betty Gow (now Anne's lady's maid) on a hot Sunday, and Anne's initial response was favorable. 'The house gleams fresh and white after the Whately's work. It is cool and peaceful, a home again . . .' She even found the nursery 'the same secure intimate room it was in that other world'. But an evening drive to Princeton was a nightmare, as it meant following the route of the kidnappers ('they went this way with the body of my boy, looking for a place to hide it') and they were chased by a car containing youths who had recognized them. 'C hot and nervous, I bitter and angry.' Next day she wrote, 'I don't believe I can ever live in this house in freedom and sanity . . . I shall always be trying to know just what happened in terror and curiosity and misery.'

And yet after a few days both she and Charles found themselves falling in love with it again. Charles called it 'a wonderful house' and she wrote: 'We really don't see how we can leave it. It was so perfect and lovely, I wonder if we can ever make it so again.' And they began planning new schemes for house and grounds.

In the end they decided against it, and before the year was out offered it to the State of New Jersey as a boys' home, which it is today. But when he still believed in the idea, Lindbergh said they *could* live there so long as they had a good guard dog. So they went to Princeton and chose a huge, fierce German Shepherd which bared its teeth and snarled at them. 'That's fine,' said Charles, 'I want a dog who won't make friends with strangers.'

Its trainer brought the dog out in a van, put it in the garage with wire covering one door, and told Lindbergh not to go near it for several days: he would be back to feed it in the morning. But when the dog knocked over its water bowl, Lindbergh with his usual courage went inside, righted the water bowl and filled it, put the dog on a leash and took him for a walk. By evening the dog had been released from the garage and was enjoying wild games with Wahgoosh. When the trainer arrived in the morning, he could hardly believe his eyes.

They christened the dog Thor and took it back to Englewood where it terrified the terriers Skean and Bogey and roamed about like a panther. Soon it began following Anne everywhere, 'his big soft, heavy paws like socks of sand padding behind me': she found it 'quite thrilling, like having a new beau'.

Yet however courageous Lindbergh had been in taming Thor, there was another, meaner side to him. Having hitched Thor to Skean and Bogey to let them get used to him, he urged Thor into the swimming pool: inevitably one of the little dogs went under and Lindbergh had to dive in to save it from drowning. He must have known this might happen and how frightened they would be. Another time, and perhaps because of the heat, he shaved Skean down to his skin and for some days the dog ran about with his tail between his legs, whimpering. This was like some of his practical jokes and the persistence with which he had knocked Charlie over with soft cushions – to see how much anyone, human or dog, could take. Always seeking new ways of testing his own courage, he saw nothing wrong in trying out that of others.

For privacy Anne planned to have the new baby in the Morrow apartment in New York, where there were porters and liftmen to keep away the press. The labor pains started at Englewood at midnight, and she was in the apartment by dawn, with Dr Hawks, who had delivered Charlie, and an anaesthetist in attendance. The pains were quite severe and in the later stages she needed whiffs of gas.

The baby was 'perfect', a fine, healthy 7 pound 14 ounce boy whom they called Jon, and Anne could hardly believe that there was not a flaw or blemish on him. Later she wrote:

> I felt I had given birth to more than a baby: to a new life in myself, in C, in Mother. C, a teasing boy again; Mother, gently, softly gay as she used to be with Charlie. And I felt as if a great burden had fallen off me. I could not imagine the baby would do this for me, but I felt life given back to me, a door to life opened.

Inevitably Charlie kept breaking through. Her first thought on being told she had a boy was how lovely it would have been for Charlie to have had a brother. Sometimes she and her mother called the baby 'Charlie' by mistake – 'it slipped out so naturally'. But as the days passed the reality and joy of the one and the memory and sadness of the other sorted themselves out in her mind. In September Lindbergh flew her to North Haven to join the rest of the family. It was the first time she had flown for months, and she was overwhelmed both by the ecstasy of flying (as she always had been) and the beauty of the sea and land below. Her mother was there, and her sisters and brother: for a few weeks the ghosts of her father and Charlie were in abeyance. There were family picnics and jokes, tennis and golf and sailing: it was a healing time. Back in Englewood in the winter Elisabeth announced her engagement to a Welshman called Aubrey Morgan, and on December 28 in a simple ceremony at Next Day Hill she married him, looking so lovely and assured, said Anne, as to make her want to cry. Triumphantly life went on.

*　　*　　*

On the world stage the events of 1933 were to shape its history for the next decade. Japan temporarily ended her long war with China, enabling her to plan long-term aggression elsewhere. In Germany Hitler became Chancellor, the Reichstag was set on fire, opposition parties were proscribed. German Jews felt the pricks of persecution, and while their co-religionists in New York marched in protest, Hitler's portly, hedonistic Minister of the Interior, Hermann Goering, banned nudism as 'a grave danger to German culture and morals'. In Palestine there were Arab riots against Jewish immigration; and in India the British Raj imprisoned Gandhi again, thus knocking another nail in its own coffin.

In America Prohibition, with its corrupting, criminal consequences, was repealed in December: the day after, New Yorkers celebrated by downing a hundred thousand bottles of Scotch and running entirely out of stock. In the deep south the lynchings of blacks continued. In St Joseph, Missouri, Lloyd Warner, aged nineteen, who had confessed to attacking a white girl, was seized from the jail by the mob, hanged on the court-house lawn and set alight with rags soaked in gasoline. In Nashville, Tennessee, Cord Cheek, aged eighteen, whom a Grand Jury had refused to indict for attacking a white girl, was taken from his home by an armed gang and also hanged.

There were half a dozen major kidnappings, some fatal; on one occasion the kidnappers were lynched. Two men called Thurmond and Holmes kidnapped a merchant by the name of Brooke L. Hart in San José, California, took him to the San Mateo Bridge, shot him, wired and weighted him and dumped the body in San Francisco Bay. In the course of demanding $40,000 ransom money from his father, they were arrested and taken to San José Jail. The people there were so enraged they broke down the jail doors, took out

the men and hanged them from nearby trees. 'A good job,' was
the comment of California's Governor Rolph. 'An example to
every state in the union.'

On a lighter note, the New York Customs seized reproductions
of frescoes from the Sistine Chapel as being obscene, in Richmond
Hill a cat was ransomed for $10 and in Portugal a galaxy of
shooting stars caused people to scream and pray to Heaven. The
most memorable films that year were the legendary *42nd Street*,
with Dick Powell, Warner Baxter and Ruby Keeler, *King Kong*,
the story of the great ape, Wallace Beery's *Tugboat Annie*, and Noel
Coward's mawkish extravaganza of twentieth-century Britain,
Cavalcade. It was a rich year for songs too: Berlin's 'Easter Parade',
Carmichael's 'Lazy Bones', Kern's 'Smoke Gets in Your Eyes'.

*   *   *

Throughout the year the law enforcement agencies continued their
inquiries, chasing leads all over the United States and further
afield, taking statements from scores of people, arresting some on
suspicion, letting them go when nothing could be proved against
them.

During the first three months of the year not a single ransom
bill showed up – though some, perhaps many, may have been
passed. After eight months of checking that had led nowhere, the
tellers had lost their initial enthusiasm. It could take up to a minute
to check the number of a single bill against the numbers on their
list, so that checking became random and arbitrary; and most
tellers now considered it a waste of time.

Measures were therefore taken to re-stimulate interest. It was
decided to establish a fund of $100 from which any teller finding
a ransom bill would be rewarded with $2, to continue until the
$100 ran out; neither the New Jersey nor New York Police having
funds for this purpose, Lindbergh provided the money himself. In
addition the New York Police secured an appropriation of $1500
to print a hundred thousand circulars listing the serial numbers of
the ransom bills, to be placed in retail stores and the pari-mutuel
departments at racing tracks: these not only proclaimed the
$25,000 reward for information leading to the arrest of the kidnap-
pers offered by the State of New Jersey, but promised a $10 reward
to anyone finding any of the next hundred ransom bills, and a $5
reward to the finder of any of the hundred after that. Lieutenants
Keaton and Finn called on every press agency and newspaper editor

in New York asking them not to disclose this information, and none did.

Only one ransom bill turned up in March, but in April came a flood. In line with other countries at this time, America was going off the gold standard, and on March 9 Congress authorized the President to call in all gold coins and gold certificate bills by April 5 – later extended to May 1. Since after this date no individual could legally hold more than $100 worth of gold coin or gold certificates, it was expected that the kidnappers would trade in the bulk of the $35,000 gold certificate ransom money, and instructions went out to banks in New York and New Jersey to keep a sharp look-out.

How many of the ransom gold certificates *were* exchanged for regular currency is impossible to say because of the sheer volume of traffic – $30 million worth in New York alone, $500 million throughout the country. But almost $4000 worth of ransom gold certificate bills was found. On or about April 27 three separate exchanges were made within a few blocks of each other in Manhattan: a package of fifty $10 bills at the Manufacturers' Trust Company at 149 Broadway, another package of fifty $10 bills at the Chemical National Bank at Cortlandt Street and Broadway, and then on May 1 a package of 296 $10 bills together with a single $20 bill at the Federal Reserve Bank at Liberty and Nassau – a total of $3980. Neither of the tellers who had handled the two packages of $500 could recall who had presented them. The depositor of the $2980 had signed a slip giving his name as J. J. Faulkner of 537 West 149th Street, New York City. This set hopes alight everywhere; but despite exhaustive inquiries at 537 West 149th Street and far beyond, the depositor was never found.

Four more bills turned up in June, none in July, August, September (Kidnappers on vacation? Tellers wilting in the heat?) and only another six during the rest of the year. Of the twenty-two deposits of ransom bills made at banks during the year, all but three were in midtown or downtown Manhattan. One was in Brooklyn and two in the Bronx.

*   *   *

The only other lead the police were working on at this time was the enigmatic kidnap ladder, which so far had failed to reveal any clues that might identify its origins or builder. Now a new source of information opened up in the shape of a balding, middle-aged government servant by the name of Arthur Koehler. Arthur Koehler was head of the Forest Service Laboratory of the US Department of Agriculture at Madison, Wisconsin, and it was to him, soon after the kidnapping, that slivers of wood from the ladder had been sent for identification. When Schwarzkopf proposed to Major Robert Stuart, the chief of the Forest Service, that Koehler might

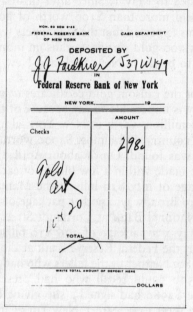

The deposit note for $2980 ransom money
in gold certificates.

examine the ladder *in toto*, Stuart was enthusiastic. Koehler, he said, was the leading authority in the country on wood identification and wood construction; his expertise had been of great use to the courts and once his evidence had led an arsonist to confess.

So Koehler journeyed to Trenton and on to the New Jersey Police's Training School at Wilburtha where the ladder had been sent after its examination in Washington. Koehler spent four days at Wilburtha. His work was meticulous. First he gave numbers to each part for easy reference: the rungs were numbered 1 to 11 from the bottom up, while the side-rails of the three sections were, from left to right, 12 and 13 (bottom section), 14 and 15 (middle section) and 16 and 17 (top section). He spent hours examining each section under a microscope, and on March 4, 1933 he wrote his report and conclusions.

First, the constitution of the ladder in detail. Rails, 12, 13 and 16 were of North Carolina yellow pine which grows in North Carolina and neighboring states. Rails 14, 15 and 17 were Douglas fir which grows in the west. The first ten rungs (which he called cleats as they were not recessed securely into the side-rails) were Ponderosa pine, which also grows in the west, but the eleventh was Douglas fir. The dowel pins for joining the sections together were white birch from the north-east.

Next, the ladder as a whole. 'The construction in general is very crude, showing poor judgment in the selection of the lumber and in the design of the ladder, and poor workmanship . . . very little skill or care in the use of carpenter tools.' The rungs were widely spaced, indicating it was not intended for general use, and they showed no wear, indicating no previous usage. A sharp chisel had been used for making the mortises for the rungs, but it was not possible to determine the width of the chisel used – a view already expressed by Dr Souder when he examined the ladder and abandoned ¾-inch Buck's chisel in May 1932.

Rails 12 and 13 of yellow pine contained no nail holes, indicating no previous usage. All three Douglas fir rails (14, 15 and 17) contained one to three nail holes made by round nails and the yellow pine Rail 16 contained four slanting nail holes made by old-fashioned square nails. When these rails were boards, said Koehler, they had probably been in storage or 'in the interior of a crude building, possibly an attic, shop, warehouse, or barn', but the spacing of the nail holes gave no indication as to what the boards had been used for. As there was no evidence of the nails having been pulled out with a claw or nail puller (which would have left a mark), he concluded that the boards must have been prised off whatever they were fastened to and the nails driven out from the other side. The nails in Rail 16, he added, must have come out easily, otherwise the nail heads would have left marks as they were pulled towards the holes.

Rail 16, indeed, was the odd man out. All other five rails consisted of standard 1- by 4-inch dressed strips, but Rail 16 had been crudely planed down from something wider. It was a much poorer grade of lumber than the two other yellow pine rails and had three knots in it of between ¾ and 1 inch diameter. It was slightly narrower than the other rails and had different machine-planing on the face from Rails 12 and 13. And the fact that there were no rust marks in its four nail holes indicated that as a board it had been nailed down in the interior of a building, or used briefly outside and then stored under cover.

Under the microscope Koehler discovered something else about the ladder: that the yellow pine Rails 12 and 13 had tiny grooves in both the edges and the flat surface that showed that at the lumber mill which had processed them, the eight knives that had dressed the surface contained one defective knife, and the six knives that had dressed the edges contained another defective knife; and that the distance between the cuts made by these defective knives showed that the lumber had gone through the planer at 0.9 inch per revolution on the surface and 0.86 inch per revolution on the edges.

Koehler knew that there could be only one lumber mill in the United States with a planer that had had these unique character-istics. If he could find out where it was, how much lumber had been dressed by it and where the lumber had been shipped to, then the search for where the ladder had been assembled might be narrowed considerably. It was, he realized, a very long shot, because North Carolina yellow pine is one of the commonest woods used in construction. He took down his reference book of lumber mills handling yellow pine and found there were 1598 of them. With the help of Detective Lewis Bornmann, whom Schwartzkopf had detailed to assist him, he made arrangements for a cyclostyled letter of inquiry to be sent simultaneously to each one.

This was clearly going to be a long haul, so on April 13, 1933 Bornmann sent a memo to Schwartzkopf:

> It is the opinion of the undersigned that the services of Mr Arthur Koehler . . . can be dispensed with for the time being, or until such time as information of importance is received which involves technicalities which we would not be able to work out.

But he remembered what Koehler had said about Rail 16 having probably been fastened to something in a barn or attic, shop or warehouse.

*   *   *

In mid January 1933, with the weather in New York at its coldest, Richard and Anna Hauptmann climbed into the Dodge and headed south in search of Florida sun. On the way they stopped for an afternoon and night with the Schneiders beside the ocean at Tybee Island, Georgia, where they had spent such a happy time camping with Hans Kloppenburg eighteen months before. In Florida they stayed for four weeks in a cabin at the Federal Holiday camp at Diana, paying $7 a week rent and doing their own cooking. When about to return, they heard a weather report forecasting heavy snow, so drove the 1400 miles back to New York without a stopover. It must have been at Diana that Anna Hauptmann conceived, for a few weeks later, 'my dear wife imparted to me the sweet secret that there would soon be three in our family'. Richard was overjoyed. 'Is there a greater happiness for any man than that?' In answer to Roosevelt's first proclamation calling in gold, he dutifully exchanged the $750 in gold certificates and $500 in gold coin that he was keeping as a hedge against inflation. (He retained $120 in gold coin, $20 more than the personal limit.)

Hauptmann was now seeing Isidor Fisch almost daily, either at Steiner, Rouse where Fisch often accompanied him, or at Mrs Kohl's (where there was also the opportunity of seeing Gerta)[1] or at Hauptmann's own apartment. Neither of the two people closest to Hauptmann cared for him. 'He was a mystery man,' said Anna. 'One moment at Hunter's Island you'd be talking with him, the next moment he'd disappeared,' while Kloppenburg called Fisch 'a sneaky, foxy sort of guy, you never knew where you were with him. When they were at Richard's place and wanted to talk business, they went into the bedroom and shut the door.' Fisch asked Hauptmann not to discuss their business dealings with Uhlig. Uhlig, also in the fur trade, would have known when Fisch was telling lies.

Initially the two partners seem to have prospered. Hauptmann said he was 'astonished' at the large amount of profits coming from the furs – during 1933 more than $6000 – though whether all these were genuine profits or the fruits of some shady business which Fisch was giving to Hauptmann in exchange for having a

[1] 'Isidor got on my nerves,' said Gerta, 'pacing up and down the floor and looking out of the window to see if Hauptmann come or not. He was always there until about half past nine in the morning. He would go away with Hauptmann, but sometimes Hauptmann didn't come and he go away alone. I said "Where you go, working or what?" He said he go down to the stock market.' (Scaduto, p. 355)

foothold in the stock market, it is impossible to say. Hauptmann's dealings on the stock market prospered too, with profits from such shares as Curtis Wright which he bought for $850 in February 1933 and sold for $1456 in May, Penn Railroad bought for $1887 in April and sold for $2045 four days later, and Dominion bought for $1612 on April 25 and sold for $1978 on May 17.

Later, said Hauptmann, Fisch started choosing his own stocks and lost heavily. Later too the partnership lost – over the next two years $4000–5000. How much these were Hauptmann's losses and how much Fisch's it is impossible to say, for while Hauptmann kept a ledger in which he listed all his stock transactions (and which later the FBI found to be extremely accurate) he does not specify how much belonged to Fisch and how much to him. Again, entries in the ledger showing cash deposits do not itemize whether they represent investment money from Fisch, profits from furs, or monies from other sources.

In the summer of 1933 Hauptmann and Hans Kloppenburg spent ten days at Freehold, near Lakewood, New Jersey, helping their friend Henry Lempke build a chicken house. They took with them mandolin and guitar and in the evenings had sing-songs with Lempke, Nostersky and others – though not before Hauptmann had gone into town each day to buy a paper showing the closing prices. Back in New York, Hauptmann and Fisch entered into a more formal business arrangement in furs and stocks, of which the basis on paper was an investment of $17,500 by Hauptmann and $17,000 by Fisch. But once again the details of it were never spelt out, and Hans Müller chided his uncle Richard for such unprofessional ways. Why did Fisch have no place of business, he asked? Why had they not employed a notary public to draw up a proper agreement between them. Why had they not opened a partnership bank account? And where did Fisch keep his furs?

'I ask him one time, I said, "Richard, if you go in storage business and you buy so much furs, don't you have to have storage or loft?" He said, No, that is not done in business like this . . .'

The absence of these facilities gave Fisch the conditions he needed to fleece the naïve Hauptmann. In June Pinkus Fisch sent his brother a shipment of cat skins worth $84. Fisch sold these to a firm called Fishbein and Klar and the proceeds, which he should have sent to Pinkus, he pocketed. The name gave Fisch the idea of inventing a bogus firm which he called Klar and Millar, ordering up stationery with the name printed on it, and arranging for a stenographer he knew, Louisa Helfert, to type out a list of non-existent furs which he then valued at two to three times their actual worth. It was because Fisch had invested so heavily in these furs, Hauptmann believed, that he was unable to pay into the stock account the balance of $5000 which he owed to it. Hauptmann was left with the impression that the partnership owned more than $20,000 worth of furs, and that his $5000 would be realized when the furs were sold.

Whether it was at this time or earlier that Fisch, in addition to all his other crooked activities, began acquiring 'hot' money is not certain. But evidence that hot money, including Lindbergh ransom money, was being offered for sale at discount and that Fisch had a part in it, comes from several sources. Early in 1936 a man called Oscar J. Bruchman told his lawyer and the *New York Times* that Fisch had asked his help in disposing of hot money; and Fisch's friend Henry Uhlig was informed by a private detective that Fisch had been seen exchanging money in a pool room at 86th Street and 3rd Avenue. Also in 1936 a convict named Stephen Spitz produced $1000 of Lindbergh ransom money and said he had bought it in New York at forty cents in the dollar. And in a deposition quoted in Anthony Scaduto's book *Scapegoat*, a friend of Fisch by the name of Arthur H. Trost tells of meeting Fisch frequently in the same pool room at 86th and 3rd from the summer of 1931 onwards. After February 1932 (just before the kidnapping) he did not see him there again until the summer. His deposition ends:

> I have been acquainted since March or April 1931 with a man who is also a painter and who I know only by the name of Fritz . . . In June or July 1932 I met Fritz at a restaurant at 1603 2nd Avenue at which time he asked me if I wished to buy some 'hot money' for fifty cents on the dollar from a friend of his. I told him that I would go with him to see the people who had it for sale and he then took me to the same billiard parlor, and when we arrived there he started to introduce me to Isidor Fisch. I then told Fritz that I was already acquainted with Isidor Fisch and needed no introduction to him. I also told Fritz that Fisch was already indebted to me for borrowed money, and that I could not believe any of Fisch's stories. I was led to believe that this 'hot money' was in the possession of Fisch and that Fisch had it for sale.

* * *

Although the new baby, Jon, was a source of increasing happiness to Anne, the memory of the other was always there. On New Year's Day 1933 she recalled being at Rosedale the New Year before, which made her think 'with sudden heartsickness that I will never never be as happy again as I was in that house . . . We had him.' A few days later, looking at the vacant faces in the subway, she was more bitter. 'All these people – listless, tired, already dead . . . Horrible, horrible-looking people. I wanted to say, "And which one of you killed my boy?"'

One reason for her preoccupation with the crime was its coming anniversary. Mrs Lindbergh sent her roses and her mother a cable, and these gave her comfort because, as she told each, 'we were both thinking of the same thing'. The anniversary, she said, seemed to take the boy further away from her, for she would now no longer be able to say, 'This time last year I still had him.'

In fact the inability to say this any more marked a kind of turning-point for her, the beginning of looking forward and (almost) the end of harking back. Years later she told a television interviewer, 'I've always felt about tragedies that one dies – but the wonderful thing about life is that you're born again. You are born many times in life, and that is, I think, what happened to us.'

So, as if to emphasize this rebirth, that very evening of the anniversary she and Charles put on disguises and went out on the town. Charles put black wash on his hair, she wore the highest of high heels to make him look shorter, a bang on her prominent forehead and a 'schoolmarm' hat; and both wore glasses. 'We walked down Broadway together and went to a show – entirely without stares. It was perfectly thrilling! I felt as though we were thieves about to be nabbed at any moment . . . the excitement of having passers-by look at you and then look away was too exhilarating.'

For some time they had been planning a short motoring holiday in disguise ('C says it's the only kind of vacation he wants, away from himself, that is the publicity self') and the success of the Broadway foray encouraged them to start. A week later, with Betty Gow in charge of Jon at Englewood and with the State Police guarding the grounds, they left New York by car to see Anne's Cutter grandmother in Cleveland and to stay with Mrs Lindbergh in Detroit. At hotels and cafés they went entirely unrecognized. 'We said we were from Hackensack and gave a false name . . . It was such fun.' They came home refreshed ('C felt entirely free for

Lindbergh and Hauptmann

1. Lindbergh and his mother beside the tiny plane in which in 1927 he flew non-stop to Paris from New York. 'It was an odyssey like that of the heroes of antiquity . . . and altered irrevocably the way people looked at the map.'

2. Hauptmann in the Kaiser's army. 'I thought that I was no different when I returned from the war. But I deceived myself.'

Marriages

3. Richard and Anna Hauptmann. 'During that summer of 1924 I knew that I had found my dear wife. . . . We worked hard but we were happy.'

4. Charles and Anne Lindbergh. 'The sheer fact of finding myself loved was unbelievable, and changed my world, my life and myself.'

The Summer of 1931

5. Charles and Anne Lindbergh take off for the Orient. Leaving her son with her mother, Anne wrote: 'Will you keep some record of his actions and take a picture about once a month?'

6. Charles Augustus Lindbergh, Junior.

7. Betty Gow wheeling Charlie and Wahgoosh. Taken at North Haven the day the Lindberghs left for the Orient.

8. Charles and Anne with Elizabeth and Dwight Morrow.

9. On holiday in California. *From left to right:* Anna Hauptmann, Emma Gloeckner (Richard's sister), Richard, Hans Kloppenburg, Mildred Gloeckner, Karl Gloeckner.

8

9

10

11

The Kidnap

10. The Lindbergh house at Hopewell, with a ladder up against the window of the nursery from which Charlie was abducted. 'The kidnappers . . . saw their opportunity and they took it.'

11. Charlie's nursery, showing the window through which one of the kidnappers entered, and the windowsill on which the first ransom note was found.

12. The empty crib. 'Beside it, to keep out draughts, a pink and green screen with pictures of farmyard animals.'

13. The first ransom note. For text see page 83.

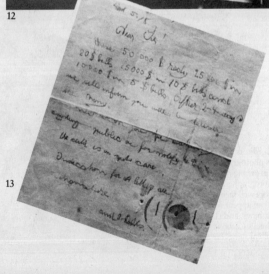

12

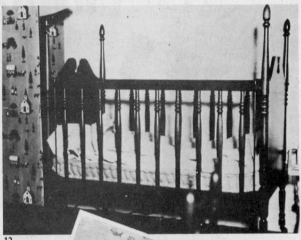

13

The News Breaks

14. News of the kidnapping breaks – one of thousands of headlines that appeared on March 2, 1932 in the world's press.

15. Poster announcing the disappearance of Charlie, given nationwide publicity. The height of 29 inches is a misprint for 2 feet 9 inches, and was soon after corrected.

WEATHER FORECAST
Nebraska—Generally fair, slightly colder today; tomorrow cloudy.
Iowa—Mostly cloudy, rain or snow in the north today; tomorrow partly cloudy.

Ōma

VOL. LXVII.—No. 132.

OMAH

LINDBERG

15

WANTED
INFORMATION AS TO THE
WHEREABOUTS OF

CHAS. A. LINDBERGH, Jr.
OF HOPEWELL, N. J.
SON OF COL. CHAS. A. LINDBERGH
World-Famous Aviator

This child was kidnaped from his home
in Hopewell, N. J., between 8 and 10 p.m.
on Tuesday, March 1, 1932.

DESCRIPTION:

Age, 20 months   Hair, blond, curly
Weight, 27 to 30 lbs.   Eyes, dark blue
Height, 29 inches   Complexion, light
Deep dimple in center of chin
Dressed in one-piece coverall night suit

ADDRESS ALL COMMUNICATIONS TO
COL. H. N. SCHWARZKOPF, TRENTON, N. J., or
COL. CHAS. A. LINDBERGH, HOPEWELL, N. J.

ALL COMMUNICATIONS WILL BE TREATED IN CONFIDENCE

COL. H. NORMAN SCHWARZKOPF,
Supt. New Jersey State Police, Trenton, N. J.

JAPANESE CLAIM
CHINESE TROOPS
IN FULL RETREAT

Defenders Are
in North and
Kiangwan.

ACTIVE

More News Coverage
in The World-Herald

Beginning March 1, The
World-Herald added to its special news service the foreign staff of the Chicago Daily News. This trained corps of newspaper men, widely scattered over the world, now contributes to the leased wire and mail news of the Consolidated Press association which serves The World-Herald exclusively for Nebraska and Iowa readers. This in addition to the full Chicago Tribune-leased wire and the 24-hour service of the Associated Press affords Omaha's home newspaper superior coverage in the news field everywhere.

FEDERAL GRAND JURY
QUIZZES MRS. KUBIK

South Side Sportsman

NEW TAX M
DRAFT UP
COMMITTEE

Increased Le
Expected to
Least $1,100,

SPEED IS S

Washington, D. C.,
—The first complete
new revenue bill com
structures, sales and
will be laid before t
ways and means com
row by Acting Chair
A subcommittee
mously approved a 2 p
structures sales tax
mated yield of 525 m
and excise levies to
high million dollars

16/17. With editors clamoring for copy, press photographers were shameless in arranging posed pictures. (16) the photographer places a radio beside a Hopewell farmer milking a cow, so he can appear to be listening to the latest news, and (17) children at the St Michael's Catholic Orphanage in Hopewell 'praying' for the return of Charlie.

16

World-Herald
Morning

WEDNESDAY, MARCH 2, 1932—TWENTY-TWO PAGES.   THREE CENTS

BABY KIDNAPED

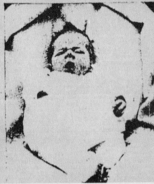

TAKEN ASLEEP
FROM FAMILY
HOME IN N. J.

Note, Contents Kept
Secret, Is Found on
Window Sill.

ROADS WATCHED

Child Was One of
the Most Carefully
Guarded in World.

New York, March 1.—
Charles A. Lindbergh, Jr., baby

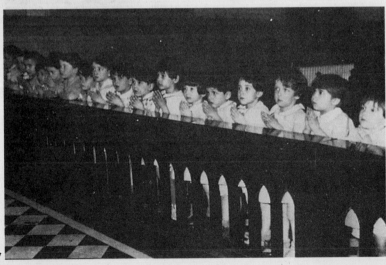

18

19

20

21

Extortion, Murder and Suicide

18. Joseph Perrone, the taxi-driver engaged by the kidnappers to take one of the ransom notes to Dr Condon. According to Colonel Schwarzkopf 'a totally unreliable witness'.

19, 20, 21. Some of the ransom notes. Compare the handwriting with that of Hauptmann's pre-arrest handwriting on page 133.

22. Dr John F. Condon. 'Chauvinistic, sentimental, garrulous, sycophantic, histrionic, patronizing, pseudo-humble … anxious to see himself and be seen by others in the best possible light.'

23

THE LINDBERGH BABY SLAIN

BALTIMORE, FRIDAY, MAY 13, 1932

Dr. Condon And Curtis Are Held By New Jersey Police

HOOVER PUTS FORWARD HIS RELIEF PLAN

BROKER TELLS OF $26,635 GIFT TO WALKER

BLOWS FRACTURING SKULL CAUSED DEATH OF INFANT ABOUT TWO MONTHS AGO

Physicians Say Flyer's Son Might Have Been Hurled From Car Night Of Kidnapping From Parents' Estate

NEGRO MAKES DISCOVERY FIVE MILES FROM HOPEWELL

23. The headlines of May 13, 1932 announcing the discovery of Charlie's body.

24. The Morrow maid who killed herself: Violet Sharpe (seated) with her sister. 'One of only a handful of people who knew of the sudden decision for Charlie to stay over at Hopewell on the Tuesday ... is it possible that she passed on information unthinkingly?'

24

25

THE UNITED STATES OF

TO BE FORWARDED TO
THE BUREAU OF NATURALIZATION

Petition No. 95765

Personal description of holder as of date of naturalization: Age 26 color of hair
complexion DARK   color of eyes BROWN   none   Hobb
weight 130 pounds; visible distinctive marks   race
marital status SINGLE   I certify that the description above given is true, and the

STATE OF NE
COUNTY OF
Be it know
then residing a
having petition
a term of the

the court h
United Sta
States in
ordered

day

The Mysterious Mr Fisch

25. The enigmatic Isidor Fisch
(right) with his friend Henry
Uhlig. 'I believe,' Uhlig wrote his
parents, 'that Isidor bought this
Lindbergh money from some
vagabond (as he knew many)
with the money he had
borrowed from his friends.'

26. Petition of Isidor Fisch for US citizenship.

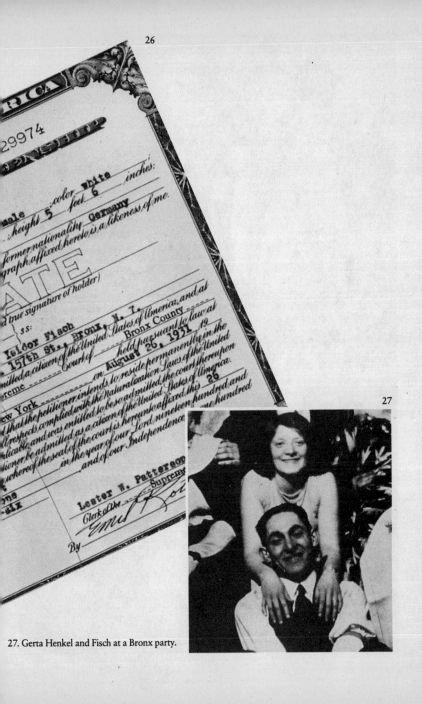

RICA

29974

male   color white   inches:

height 5 feet 6   inches:

former nationality Germany

graph affixed hereto is a likeness of me.

ATE

a true signature of holder)

ss:

Isidor Fisch   N. Y.
157th St., Bronx, N. Y.
                     Bronx County
                     held pursuant to law at
mitted a citizen of the United States of America, and at
reme
ew York   on August 26, 1931   19
that the petitioner intends to reside permanently in the
l respects, complied with the Naturalization Laws of the United
plicable and was entitled to be so admitted the court thereupon
tioner be admitted as a citizen of the United States of America.
whereof the seal of the court is hereunto affixed this 26
              in the year of our Lord nineteen hundred and
              and of our Independence   one hundred

Lester W. Patterson
Clerk of the   Supreme
                                 Emil

By

27

27. Gerta Henkel and Fisch at a Bronx party.

28

Hunter's Island

28. Hauptmann (*seated*) with Anita Lutzenberg (*left*) and Hans Kloppenburg (*top right*).

29. *Rear:* Henry Lempke, Hans Kloppenburg, Anna Hauptmann; *Front:* Richard Hauptmann, Albert Diebig.

30. Richard Hauptmann with his son Manfred.

29

LINDBERGH KIDNAPER JAILED

,750 NSOM ONEY FOUND

32

32

The Arrest

31. Hauptmann's guilt already assumed on the news of his arrest.

32. Hauptmann being fingerprinted after his arrest.

the first time in six years'). She was overjoyed to see Jon again (looking strangely like Charlie) and believed that she could now 'shake off the terrible winter pre-occupation with the crime' and think of Charlie as belonging to spring.

In April they flew to California to bring back the Lockheed Sirius which had been undergoing refitment after the accident in the Yangtse the year before, and was now needed for the proving flight to Europe they had agreed to make for Pan Am. At St Louis on the way out there was a happy reunion with Phil Love, Lindbergh's former fellow pilot and butt of his practical jokes. On the return journey near Las Vegas they were caught in a dust-storm and Anne believed she would be killed. But, as always, Lindbergh found a way through, and on hitting Kansas City a day later, was told that three planes had been up looking for them and people had been seriously worried.

They set off on the proving flight at the beginning of July by way of North Haven and Deacon Brown's Point where their mothers, Jon, Betty Gow and the butler Banks were settled in for the summer. The trip would take them five months and they would travel by way of Labrador, Greenland, Iceland, the Faeroes and Shetlands to Scandinavia, and back by way of England, France, Spain, West Africa, Brazil and Trinidad. The idea was to study the feasibility of future commercial flight-paths between Europe and America.

As a public relations exercise the trip was a huge success, with Anne playing a full part as radio operator and navigator. Yet one wonders if Lindbergh ever realized to what strains and stresses he was subjecting her. In Labrador and Greenland, and later in West Africa, they had to live rough, eating whatever food was available, often sleeping in the tiny, cramped baggage compartment of the plane while it rode uneasily at anchor. There were many times when Anne was frightened – in a fog off the Dutch coast, landing at night on the Seine – but always Lindbergh bore a charmed life, crushing the elements to convince millions that flying was safe. He often told Anne that he was too occupied to be frightened. She, less occupied, would have welcomed a nod of reassurance, a smile, but he was not that kind of man; and perhaps in the end she was glad of it.

They were entertained by royalty and rulers in several European countries (in Oslo the King, in Denmark the King and Queen, in Sweden the Crown Prince, in England the Prime Minister) but when it came to accepting the adulation of the crowds, it was a different story. There was an acutely embarrassing moment in Copenhagen when they were told by the amiable Commander Dam, who had looked after them in Greenland, that he had arranged a reception followed by a drive through the streets ('One half hour and then you are left alone'). Lindbergh refused point-blank. Dam and the reception committee were crestfallen, Anne mortified and intensely unhappy ('I wish we had never come'). One understands Lindbergh's deep reluctance to allow himself to be idolized, yet after the homage of the great, could he not have extended the same courtesy, however briefly, to the common people? He always made this rigid dividing-line between public and private.

In Sweden (which reminded Anne of Maine and Charles of Minnesota) they visited the Lindbergh family homestead in Skåne. In Russia they toured a score of art galleries and museums and, like thousands of westerners before and since, were bored rigid by having these explained to them in social rather than aesthetic terms. In Scotland they were told to look out for the Loch Ness Monster. In Wales they stayed with Anne's sister Elisabeth, now living with her husband Aubrey in a rented house in Glamorgan, but about to leave for a year in California after suffering another heart attack. Anne was amused at how quickly Elisabeth had adapted to British lady-of-the-manor ways ('Michael, will you tell Cook I want to see her about the dinner?').

By way of Amsterdam, Geneva, Lisbon, Madeira and Porto Praia they arrived at Bathhurst, Gambia at the end of November, and after waiting a week for wind, took off across the Atlantic for Brazil. They arrived safely after an uneventful flight of 1875 miles in sixteen hours (Anne was thrilled to make radio contact with a station in Massachusetts), and then flew 1000 miles up the Amazon to Manaos. It was here, after months of keeping a diary without reference to Charlie, that on a visit to the rubber factory, 'a stupid American blurted out excitedly, "You know, we were the first to hear of the kidnapping here" . . . It suddenly turned everything quite black. That thing – it happened here too. I had thought in this faraway place it had not happened.'

Their journey ended at Flushing Bay, Long Island, on December 19 and they were home at Englewood for Christmas. Just thirteen days earlier another of the principal characters of this story had also left America for Europe: Isidor Fisch, racked by coughing and with his weight down to 120 pounds, embarked with his friend Henry Uhlig for Germany. Uhlig would return, but Fisch had quitted the United States for ever, leaving a legacy that, before another year was out, was to stun the world.

11

Throughout the summer and fall of 1933 Richard and Anna were much occupied with thoughts of their coming baby, an event which they had long hoped for. 'Richard was very kind to me during the months just before the baby arrived,' Anna wrote. 'He was always doing some little thing that he knew would make me happy.' He brought her flowers and candy, and once, when her engagement ring was lost or stolen and she was much distressed, he bought another and slipped it on her finger when she was asleep. On November 3 Anna was delivered of a healthy boy at the Misericordia Hospital on 86th Street. At the suggestion of Maria Müller, Anna's niece, they called the child Manfred, and Maria became his godmother. After ten days Hauptmann went to fetch them in the Dodge. 'My wife and child!' he wrote. 'My heaven on earth!' For the next three weeks, while Anna was nursing the child, Maria came to the apartment to do the cooking and cleaning.

Some time before this, at the beginning of August, Fisch had informed Hauptmann that he intended to return to Leipzig for Christmas and with his brother Pinkus to set up the German end of an import-export business in furs; on August 18 he went to the steamship office of Mr George Steinweg on East 86th Street and paid a deposit for a third-class cabin for himself and Henry Uhlig, who also wanted to go home to Leipzig for Christmas, on the SS *Manhattan*, leaving for Hamburg on December 6.

On the morning of November 14 Fisch returned to Mr Steinweg's office to pay the balance of the two tickets amounting to $410 and to buy $650 of traveler's checks ($500 for himself and $150 for Uhlig) – a total of more than $1000. There are two accounts of the transaction, both quoted in *Scapegoat*. The first is the report of an interview by a private detective with the ticket agent, George Steinweg:

Fisch paid for the German money and the tickets with gold certificates of ten and twenty dollar denominations. Steinweg told me that Fisch paid for his tickets in Lindbergh ransom notes.

> The agent Steinweg remembered the transaction perfectly well for several reasons. First, he had been rather surprised to see so much money come out of the pocket of a fur cutter who had never looked as though he was very prosperous. Secondly he remembered the gold certificates and saved most of them because they were nice and crisp and he wanted to give some of them to his wife on her birthday. But before this happened, a friend of his, a Mr Gartner, who also went to Germany, asked him for some of these bills and he paid by check for the amount. But when this man went to the Federal Reserve Bank to pass some of the bills, he was arrested on the suspicion he was J. J. Faulkner, and he had to write his own and Faulkner's name a good many times to convince the police that he was not this man nor the kidnapper of the Lindbergh baby ...

This account is similar to that of the United Press reporter Sidney Whipple in his book _The Lindbergh Crime_. Confirming that Fisch had paid for tickets and traveler's checks in $10 and $20 gold certificates, Whipple wrote:

> George Steinweg, the steamship agent, remembered the transaction perfectly for many reasons. First, he had been rather surprised at seeing so much cash come out of the pocket of a fur cutter who had never appeared to be over-prosperous. Second, he remembered the gold certificates. Third, it appeared to him that Fisch was financing his friend Uhlig's trip abroad.
>
> When Steinweg therefore read in the newspapers that Fisch's name had been brought into the case, he went to the police and divulged what he knew about the transaction. And after that, going back to the flutter of gold notes over his agency counter he went to his own bankers and asked if they had a record of a deposit in such certificates, on or about November 14, 1933.
>
> The bank officials also remembered the matter very well. They had discovered, upon checking over the certificates, that they were a part of the Lindbergh ransom money. But at that time they had no means of tracing them back to the depositor, and although the federal government was notified, the trail was lost.[1]

Never willing to pay for anything himself that he could persuade others to pay for him, Fisch approached Hauptmann later that day and (without telling him he had already paid for his tickets and traveler's checks) asked if he would advance him $2000 from their joint stock account for his fare and living expenses in Germany: he said he did not want to have to sell any of the investments tied

[1] These two statements must be treated with caution, as no notification of receipt of this money at the federal bank appears in the long list of Lindbergh ransom money found in New York.

up in their joint fur account. Hauptmann, unaware that the fur account existed only on paper and believing it would produce more profits, agreed and wrote Fisch a check. The two of them then hurried to Hauptmann's bank where Fisch managed to cash the check just before the bank closed.

During this period Fisch seems to have continued to lead an extraordinary double life. To his friends in the Chrzanower Society he seemed as penniless as ever. One member, observing his general condition and how scantily he was dressed, gave him a sweater to keep him warm. Others slipped him the odd dollar; and when he met Charlie Schleser, his former partner in the Knickerbocker Pie Company, and told him he wanted to go home to Germany for Christmas but couldn't afford it, Schleser and another friend gave him $34 towards the fare. One way and another Fisch's steamship ticket was proving quite profitable.

Anna was too busy nursing Manfred to celebrate her own birthday on November 19, but they invited Fisch along on Richard's birthday on November 26. In mid afternoon an old school friend of Anna's, Paul Vetterle, arrived unexpectedly, having just been to Markgröningen, and Anna persuaded him to stay on. Maria was also in the apartment, and Paul was able to give her a present from her mother of a knitted dress and a *kleine hausmutter* (a little medallion with her mother's picture in it) which he had brought from Markgröningen. Presently Richard arrived from Hunter's Island, and later Fisch with a present of a pen. They stayed talking (Vetterle and Fisch in High German) and playing the radio until around ten, when Hauptmann drove Fisch and Vetterle to the subway.

A few days later, on December 2, the Hauptmanns gave a farewell party for Fisch who, flush with the $2000 he had recently conned from his host, very sportingly provided the drinks. The Wollenbergs came, Mr and Mrs Heyne from Kamenz and New Jersey, Hans Kloppenburg, the Schoefflers, Maria Müller and Mr Schüssler from the back quarters downstairs. When Fisch came he brought a package wrapped in paper and tied with string which Kloppenburg, who was standing by the door, described as a shoe-box. Fisch asked if Hauptmann would look after the package while he was away (he had already left two valises and some furs) and Hauptmann readily agreed. Fisch said to keep it in a dry place. 'I asked if it had papers in it . . . but I no longer remember his reply . . . I stuck the package on the top shelf of the kitchen closet and soon forgot about it.' It seems to have been a good party, with much music-making and drinking and conversation, and didn't break up until after one. Louise Wollenberg stayed the night.

On the eve of his departure Fisch visited the Hauptmanns again. Mrs Fredericksen from the bakery was also there, and at the end of the evening she drove Fisch to the subway. Fisch seems to have been in uncharacteristically uproarious form, flourishing dollar bills, said Mrs Fredericksen, and suggesting they go downtown and 'raise the roof'. Mrs Fredericksen had no wish to raise the roof and dropped Fisch off at Pelham Station.

At 9 a.m. the next day Hauptmann collected Fisch and Henry Uhlig in the Dodge and took them to the boat. For this kindness Fisch ungraciously said when they reached the boat that as he had other friends coming to say goodbye and as Hauptmann didn't know them, perhaps he'd better go home. Later Gerta Henkel told Hauptmann that she and her mother, Mrs Kirsten, had also gone to the boat to say goodbye, and that Fisch had sent them away for the same reason. But then Fisch had always been a man who didn't want his right hand to know what his left hand was doing.

*   *   *

Time marched on. 1933 gave way to 1934. This was the year of Hitler becoming President as well as Chancellor, of the Night of the Long Knives and the end of the Brownshirts, of Germany leaving the League of Nations and Russia joining it. It was the year when the Chicago stockyards were destroyed by fire, when the Dionne quintuplets were born in Canada, when Bonnie and Clyde met a sticky end in Arcadia, Louisiana, and when Irving Bitz, Lindbergh's original bootlegging intermediary, was sent to prison for jumping bail on a pistol-carrying charge. In Libya snow fell for the first time in living memory, in Tibet General Kusho Lungshar had his eyes put out for plotting against the government, in Belgium King Albert tumbled over a cliff and died, in the Caribbean the officers of the *Mauretania* spotted a sea serpent sixty feet long. It was the year of *The Barretts of Wimpole Street* and *The Children's Hour*, of 'Anything Goes' and 'Blue Moon', of cute little Shirley Temple belting out the joys of the good ship Lollipop.

Lindbergh was in the news again too, publicly protesting against Roosevelt's decision to cancel airmail contracts (because of widespread graft involving airline companies and government officials) and to hand over deliveries of mail to the army air force. After nine army pilots had been killed, the decision was negated and a committee that included Orville Wright was set up to look into the matter: Lindbergh, angry at what he considered equally unfair treatment to airline and army pilots (and he had been both), refused to serve on it, and a rift opened between him and the President that was never healed.

Otherwise, for him and Anne, it was a quiet time. They rented an apartment in New York and lived there with Jon and Betty Gow and Elsie Whately (Ollie had died the year before) and Skean and Wahgoosh and Thor (which made it a trifle overcrowded). Anne's diary and letters are full of the activities of Jon: Jon shouting with glee on his slide or throwing his spinach around the room. In July they went to North Haven for a holiday, in August when the rent of the apartment was raised they moved back to Englewood, in September they took delivery of a new monoplane and flew out west to join the ailing Elisabeth and her husband Aubrey at Will Rogers' ranch near Los Angeles. 'This is a heavenly place,' Anne wrote to her mother, 'way up on a hill overlooking the sea . . . It reminds us both of Cuernavaca . . . No one knows we are here.'

The officers of no less than three law enforcement agencies were now working on the Lindbergh case, the New Jersey and New York police forces having at last been joined in October 1933 by the FBI under its formidable chief, J. Edgar Hoover; and because the vast majority of ransom bills had been surfacing in New York, an FBI divisional office was established at 370 Lexington Avenue with fifteen men under the direction of Special Agent Thomas Sisk. This news was widely welcomed, for ever since kidnapping had become a federal offense the FBI had had a remarkable record in securing convictions. In twelve major cases listed by the *Philadelphia Record* as occurring between March 1933 and April 1944 there were convictions in eleven, and in the twelfth Verne Nankey, kidnapper of Charles Boettcher II, committed suicide.

The New Jersey State Police, however, were less enchanted. Schwartzkopf publicly welcomed the move, but told Sisk he did not intend to open his files to him. More hostile were the attitudes of his two chief subordinates, Lieutenant Keaton and Captain Lamb. For nearly two years these officers had devoted to the case not only all their time and energies but a kind of manic and often useless thoroughness. They had checked out on every person released from a US penitentiary or sanitorium prior to the kidnapping, contacted every taxi firm in New York to try and trace the driver who had brought Condon the St Raymond's note, been through the records of every cemetery employee in New Jersey, read and assessed some hundred thousand letters that purported to give a lead. Their having to co-operate with Captain Oliver and Lieutenant Finn of the New York Police was bad enough, but now, they asked themselves, were all their efforts to be set at naught by what they scathingly called 'the educated investigators'? Were the FBI about to succeed where they themselves had signally failed?

The fact was that both Keaton and Lamb were third-raters; Lamb in particular (whose red face one writer likened to an angry tomato) was none too bright. Here is Sisk's account of them to Hoover:

> ... this agent had a conversation with them on one occasion during which they spent considerable time criticizing Scotland Yard. After exhausting this subject, they launched upon a tirade against the Northwest Mounted Police, then the New York Police, the Department of Labor Investigators, Post Office Inspectors and the Treasury Department ...
>
> On several occasions Lieutenant Keaton and Captain Lamb have openly bragged about the fact that their men have orders not to give the New York police officers or the Division [FBI] agents any information whatsoever. It is a practise of Captain Lamb to frequently criticize the New York Police, particularly Lieutenant Finn, who is characterized by Lamb as 'a nitwit', Captain Oliver as 'a sugar man' and Commissioner O'Ryan as 'an old broken-down General'.

Keaton also told Sisk that 'Roosevelt and his gang' were dangerous Communists, and that when the Republicans were elected, 'Hoover goes out and Schwartzkopf goes in.'

Lieutenant Finn, meanwhile, with the amiable assistance of Corporal Horn of the New Jersey State Police and the FBI's Special Agent Seery, continued plotting on a large map the location of ransom money as it turned up. Earlier in the year it had been appearing at irregular intervals and almost entirely in $5 greenbacks, four in January, one in February, forty-one in March, fifteen in April, fourteen in May, and a total of only seventeen in June, July and August; one or two had been found in places as far away as Troy, Utica, Minneapolis and even Chicago, all the rest in New York. All these bills had made their way to the Federal Bank via large department stores, transportation depots, restaurants, etc, which made the depositors impossible to trace.

But early in September one or two bills began appearing on the

East Side between 84th and 103rd Street, which showed an entirely different pattern. These were not $5 greenbacks passed through big organizations, but $10 and $20 gold certificates (now only rarely seen) handed in at smaller shops and stores, mostly for very small purchases; and the first breakthrough came when a $10 gold bill was traced to Boccanfuso's fruit and vegetable store on Third Avenue and 89th Street. A clerk named Levantino recalled the transaction because the customer had given the $10 bill for a ten cent purchase, and he was able to give a description of him. Two more $10 gold bills were traced to food stores in the same district and a $20 gold bill to the Exquisite Shoe Corporation at 226 East Fordham Road in the Bronx. Albert Shirkes, an assistant there, remembered the man who had passed the bill in payment for a pair of lady's suede slippers; and his description matched that of Levantino's.

With a mounting sense of excitement and a belief that two and a half years' work was about to come to fruition, representatives of the three law enforcement agencies met to decide on a concerted plan of action. A number of plain clothes officers had already been planted in the general area where the bills were being passed, and now Sisk proposed putting in more. This was too much for Lamb, whose resentment against the FBI and the New York Police had been simmering all summer, and who sensed an imminent arrest in which he might play no part. 'Sisk,' said Lamb, 'you and your outfit want to run this thing. You make me sick. You're darn poor sports and you jump around like a bunch of fleas.' Sisk replied, 'What did you ever contribute to this case except to knock everybody and everything? You do nothing but sit around and try to make everybody think you're smart.' Lamb shouted, 'Don't you talk to me like that,' and Inspector Lyons and Lieutenant Keaton shouted 'Shut up, Lamb,' and then Lamb said he guessed he had the jitters and apologized.

Earlier in the year the newspapers had been reporting when and where ransom bills had shown up, but at the request of the police they no longer did so, in order not to alarm the kidnappers. Finn and Seery prayed that this self-denying ordinance would continue. But at home at Neponsit, Long Island, on the evening of Sunday September 16, Finn was horrified to hear the broadcaster and columnist Walter Winchell declare in his regular weekly radio programme that Lindbergh money was again being exchanged in the Bronx and Manhattan. 'Boys,' he said, addressing the city's tellers, 'if you weren't such a bunch of saps and yaps, you'd have already captured the Lindbergh kidnappers.' But Finn need not have worried. Within two days another bill had surfaced (showing that the money was being passed by someone who had not heard Winchell or, if he had, was ignorant of the bill's origins).

This latest one, a $10 gold certificate, was found at the Corn Exchange Bank at 125th Street and Park Avenue. The assistant manager there telephoned Sisk, Sisk telephoned Seery, and Seery, Finn and Horn went along to examine it. At first it seemed like any other bill, but when Horn turned it over, he saw that some figures had been lightly penciled on the back: 4U13.41. It looked like a vehicle license number, perhaps jotted down by an attendant at a filling station. The teller who had accepted the bill, Miran Ozmec, was summoned and said Yes, the pack had contained deposits from three filling stations. He gave the names, of which one, a Warner-Quinlan station, was only a few blocks away at Lexington and 127th Street.

At the station they showed the bill to the manager, Walter Lyle. Did he remember who had passed it?

'Sure,' he said, 'a guy driving a 1931 Dodge sedan. Nicely dressed. Spoke with an accent.'

'Why did you write down his number?'

'I didn't know the banks were taking gold notes any more. I didn't want to get stuck.'

'Did he say anything about it?'

'Yeah. I said, you don't see these around much any more, and he said, "I have only about a hundred of them left." '

Finn went to the telephone and dialled his friend Gus in the Bureau of Motor Vehicles. 'Gus,' he said, 'I got a number for you. 4U13.41.'

'Right away, Lieutenant,' said Gus.

It had been a long haul, but it looked as though they had got there at last.

*   *   *

A legend has grown up that by the beginning of 1934 Hauptmann had long ceased to do any kind of carpentry work. While it is true that since 1932 he had not been on any regular payroll, he still continued to work freelance. In January 1934 the Retail Credit Company reported:

Richard Hauptmann . . . has a small jobbing business of his own. He works for small property owners in the Bronx and has been receiving a fair amount of work in spite of generally slack conditions in the building trade. He is a hard-working and industrious type of individual and he is able to get along on his income at the present time, though in the past good years he has earned much more than he is now. They [the Hauptmanns] lead a normal home life, and have the name among their neighbors of meeting their local bills when due.

The bulk of Richard's time however was spent playing the stock market. With Fisch away in Germany Hauptmann, unaware of Fisch's crookedness, was resolute in protecting his interests. At the brokerage house one day a Mr Alexander Singer gave him a tip about a stock. Hauptmann bought some of the stock but when Mr Singer asked if he would also buy some for him on credit, Hauptmann said that he could do nothing without the consent of his partner who was abroad.

Hauptmann kept his partner posted about the movements of their stocks which at first he bought and sold profitably, later at a loss. He had to sell his Eitington-Schild stocks, he told Fisch, as the stock exchange was no longer quoting them. He received a few letters and cards in reply but was disappointed that Fisch had not been able to visit his mother, as promised. Fisch also wrote to Schaefer to keep him sweet regarding the $2500 Fisch owed him, and in reply Schaefer hoped that matters would soon be settled 'to your and my satisfaction'. Fisch had told Hauptmann that he intended to be away only six weeks, but when February gave way to March and there was no sign of him, nor any further letters, Hauptmann was puzzled as to what he was doing.

The answer was that years of latent tuberculosis combined with his extraordinary lifestyle (not giving himself enough to wear or eat, working in refrigerated storerooms, playing the con man) had at last caught up with him. Since the middle of 1933 he had been sweating profusely at nights and coughing up green bile. On Thursday March 22 he began coughing blood and had trouble with his breathing. He was taken to St Georg Hospital, Leipzig, where he was found to be undernourished and 'giving out a hollow sound when breathing'. His condition deteriorated. His family came to his bedside and in his last moments of consciousness he said there was something he wanted Hauptmann to know, but was too weak to tell it. On March 29, at two in the afternoon, he died.

Hauptmann received the news at the end of April from Fisch's brother Pinkus. Pinkus told Hauptmann that Isidor had often spoken about him and their business associations in stocks and furs, and he mentioned the possibility of a will and other papers in a New York bank safety deposit box. Isidor, he said, 'advised us that the stocks and merchandise would amount to quite a lot of money', and he hoped that Hauptmann would help him realize his brother's estate.

On receipt of this letter Hauptmann began looking into Fisch's affairs. His first shock came when, at the request of Mrs Kirsten, Mrs Hile and Erica Kirsten, he inquired into the state of the Knickerbocker Pie Company. 'For the past few days,' he wrote to Pinkus on May 4, 'I have been running around trying to locate this bakery, but all I could learn was that the bakery went bankrupt about two years ago. I can hardly believe it because Isidor had told me, just before he left on the boat, that everything was all right.' Perhaps, he added hopefully, Isidor's papers in his bank box would explain everything.

In the same letter he listed the business arrangements regarding Fisch and himself, the monies invested in stocks and furs and the shares of each. He added that (in addition to the $2000 that he had given Isidor for his steamship fare and living expenses) he had also given him $5500 from his private account. This was not exactly true, but since Fisch owed him this amount and he had nothing in writing to show for it, he obviously thought that this gave him a better chance of redeeming the money when it came to the sale of the furs. After all, he alone had been bearing the recent losses in their joint stock account.

But where were the $20,000 of furs? 'Would it be possible,' Hauptmann asked Pinkus, 'for you to . . . send the address of the warehouse where the furs are stored, and also the address of the bank?'[1] Although Pinkus thought it 'very mysterious' that a man who claimed to be his brother's business partner should not know where their jointly owned goods were stored, he replied on June 3, giving the addresses of various warehouses and the address of the bank. He also said he was giving Henry Uhlig a letter of authority which he hoped would lead to the opening of Isidor's safety deposit box.

---

[1] He was not the only one to inquire. On May 2 Fisch's friend Erich Schaefer wrote to Pinkus asking what arrangements for repayments of debts Isidor had made, and concluding, 'You must always think of him as he was, upright and honest, loyal and true to his ideals . . .' which, as time went by, even Pinkus must have found hard to swallow.

When Uhlig reached New York he and Hauptmann joined forces
in a search for Fisch's assets. First, they opened the two valises he
had left with Hauptmann and found they contained nothing but
clothes and papers. Next they set off for the bogus firm of Klar
and Miller on whose bogus writing paper Fisch had made a list of
non-existent and over-valued furs. 'When we reached the address,'
said Hauptmann, 'we found there was no such firm.' They toured
every fur warehouse and storage depot in New York and apart
from one place where Fisch had stored some skins a year before,
no one knew anything about him. Would his safety deposit box
reveal all? At first, having no receipts or papers of authorization,
they were unable to secure permission to examine it. Then they
met Max Falek who, Pinkus had told Uhlig, owed Isidor $2000
for a business investment. Falek greeted this news with laughter.
Far from owing Isidor anything, he said, Isidor owed him $800
for his investment in the Knickerbocker Pie Company, and he had
a receipt to show for it. With this receipt and a copy of Fisch's
death certificate Falek obtained a court order to examine
Fisch's safety deposit box. On June 5 Falek, Hauptmann and Uhlig
gathered hopefully round. The box was opened but, said Uhlig,
'There was nothing in it but dust.'

At long last Hauptmann realized the extent to which Fisch had
deceived him. He was particularly disillusioned because, as he had
said in his first letter to Pinkus, 'our business was built up in
trusting each other'. 'I think,' he told Hans Kloppenburg, 'that
Fisch is the biggest crook I ever met,' and even Fisch's friend Uhlig
had to admit that Isidor had 'behaved like a swine'. (Those whom
Fisch had borrowed money from, he told his family, now all
wanted to tear him to pieces.) Another person to be grievously
disappointed by Fisch's lack of assets was Pinkus, and when he
saw the letters Uhlig had written to his family in Leipzig about
Isidor's crooked ways and shady connections, he couldn't resist
having a crack at him. 'I would like to question Mr Uhlig who the
shady friends are who are associated with my brother . . . as the
friendship between Uhlig and my brother was so great . . . Uhlig
must have associated with the same friends and must know them
well.' In fact Fisch had never introduced Uhlig to his shady friends.

During that summer, when not in pursuit of imaginary Fisch
assets, Hauptmann resumed the old Hunter's Island life, now
sometimes in the company of Uhlig. Uhlig remembers Hauptmann
going out in his canoe to set the eel traps and on the next visit

hauling them in, full of eels and other fish. He was struck by Hauptmann's popularity ('he was always included when there was a little party going on'), and on visits to 222nd Street noticed how devoted Hauptmann was to his baby son. 'I always felt he never wanted to let him out of his sight. He liked to take care of him and play with him and march him around and carry him on his shoulder.' (In Manhattan Lindbergh was doing much the same with Jon.) Mrs Rauch, the landlord's wife, noticed that he had constructed a crib, a high chair and a rocking chair for Manfred and painted them green and yellow. And sometimes in the evenings, before Manfred went to sleep, his father would play the mandolin and sing to him, especially Brahms's cradle song.

In July the Hauptmanns made several trips out of town: once with Manfred to visit an old Kamenz acquaintance, Otto Heyne and his wife in Elizabeth, New Jersey; and again to New Jersey to visit the chicken farm of a Mr Blank, father of a new friend, Joseph Blank, in order to buy fresh eggs for the baby. This farm was close to the town of Flemington, which Hauptmann was to see again in very different circumstances.

Let Hauptmann now describe the next thing that happened in his life, the event on which turns the central nub of this story:

It was about this time, in the middle of August 1934 on a rainy Sunday, when we did not go out because the weather was too bad for the child. Late in the afternoon I had transplanted some flowers, and some soil had fallen on the floor. I went to the kitchen closet to get the broom. In taking out the broom I touched the things on the top shelf with it. As I looked up to see if I had knocked anything over, I saw the little package which Mr Fisch had given me to keep for him when he left. I had broken through the wrapping which was soaked with water, and . . . I saw the yellow shine of money.

When Fisch had given him the package, Hauptmann hadn't attached any importance to it, and since then had forgotten it. Had he remembered it and, after Fisch's death, had the slightest suspicion that it contained money, there can be little doubt he would have opened it. (Indeed, had he discovered the money earlier it is unlikely he would have written to Pinkus on May 4 saying that Isidor owed him $5500.)

He put the package in a bucket and took the bucket to the garage. Here he opened the package and found it crammed full of $10 and $20 gold certificate bills. The notes were so wet and glued together that when he tried to separate them, they tore. So he put them in a basket to dry and when they had dried he counted them. They came to $14,600.

What was he to do? What would any of us have done? There can be little argument as to what he *ought* to have done, which was write to Pinkus Fisch in Leipzig, tell him what he had found and ask for instructions. That is what a truly honest man would have done and what Anna, with her high standards of morality, would have insisted he do. But truly honest men are rare in this world, and Richard Hauptmann was not one of them. For months past he had been searching unsuccessfully for Fisch's assets in order to repay himself the $5500 plus $2000 traveling expenses that Fisch owed him: now here it was for the asking. If he disclosed what he had found to Pinkus, he would be in danger of losing it, for (apart from a note in his ledger) he had no documentary proof to back his claim. What about helping to reimburse Mrs Kirsten and Mrs Hile and Max Falek and all the other friends whom Fisch had swindled? He could hardly do that without telling them what he had found and making them accessories. And what about the balance of around $7000 after he had appropriated the $7500 he was owed? Well, he may have said, I'll cross that bridge when I come to it.[1]

But where to put it? Had the money been in regular greenbacks, he could have (and surely would have) put it on deposit account at his bank or credited his stock account at Steiner, Rouse. It being in gold certificates which it was now illegal to hold in bulk, he could do neither. So if he was going to keep it, he had to hide it. If he hid it in the apartment there was always the risk that Anna might find it and tell him he had no business to keep it. But it should be safe in the garage: no one went there except himself. So he hid the money in various parts of the garage, in a shellac tin stuffed with rags, in holes drilled for bits beside his pistol, on a boarded-in shelf wrapped in June and September copies of the *New York Daily News* and *Daily Mirror*.

He drew out a dozen or so notes for himself, however, and late in August and at the beginning of September he began to spend them in the stores; at Boccanfuso's fruit and vegetable store, at the Exquisite Shoe Corporation, and then on Saturday September 15 at the Warner-Quinlan gas station on Lexington and 127th.

[1] Later Uhlig wrote to his parents in Leipzig: 'According to my opinion, he said to himself: "He is dead, no one knows anything about it"; and so he just kept it. Anyhow, he had loaned him $7500.00.' (October 11 1934)

What was it he had said to the attendant there? 'I have only about a hundred of them left.'

Quite an understatement; but not the remark of a man who knows he is passing much-publicized ransom money.

*   *   *

Lieutenant James J. Finn was in a state of high excitement. He was, he believed, about to arrest the Lindbergh kidnapper. From the Bureau of Motor Vehicles he had obtained not only his name and address but two facts about him which seemed to clinch the matter: first that he was a German – it was now generally agreed that a German had written the ransom notes; second that he was a carpenter, which provided a powerful link to the ladder. That there were thousands of other Germans living in the Bronx who could equally well have penned the ransom notes, and that no professional carpenter would have fashioned the ramshackle affair that had been used to kidnap little Charlie were not thoughts that occurred to him. A German carpenter in possession of ransom money was enough.

Finn's first instincts were to collect a posse of men and go straight to Hauptmann's house to apprehend him. He rejected the idea because he wanted the arrest to be as unobtrusive as possible, and if, as seemed likely, Hauptmann had turned his apartment into a sort of mini-fortress, there might have to be a shoot-out; also, if taken in his house, Hauptmann might not have any ransom notes on him. If they were to follow him when he left the house, he might lead the way to confederates or to the cache where the ransom money was hidden.

So Finn called up Sisk and Keaton, and arrangements were made for three plain police cars to wait discreetly near Hauptmann's house; one containing himself, Corporal Horn of the New Jersey Police and Agent Seery of the FBI, one with Keaton and Sisk, and the third with Detectives William Wallace of the New York Police, and John Wallace and Trooper Dore of the New Jersey police. As his car traveled down 222nd Street Finn observed the houses – 'wood and stucco with shingled roofs and with neat bits of lawn and beds of flowers – homes apparently of simple, hard-working, God-fearing people'. But when he came to No. 1279, which was no different from the rest, his reflections were rather different. Here, he said, 'lived a creature who had not hesitated to go into the house of another man . . . and had so destroyed the happiness of that home that its owner and his young wife had been forced to abandon the house of their dreams and flee to scenes that had not been blighted by this filthy creature's foot'. One can assume that those with him felt the same.

The cars assembled near No. 1279 in the late afternoon of September 18. In the early evening the officers held a conference in a nearby German tavern (whose owner was later to find himself doing brisk business) where it was agreed that Finn should make the arrest, that a gunfight was to be avoided unless Hauptmann tried to shoot his way out, and that he should be allowed to travel some distance from the house before being halted. They saw the Hauptmanns leave the house in the car at 8 p.m. and return at about 2 a.m. on the 19th (they had been to the *Europa* to see a cousin of Anna, Hans Schmid, who was sailing for Europe). Then the lights were turned off in the apartment and they took it in turns to keep watch and doze during the night.

At 8.55 a.m. the front door of No. 1279 opened and Hauptmann came out. He was dressed in a double-breasted blue suit with brown shoes and a soft hat. Finn recalled the details of his motor vehicle application form – thirty-four, 180 pounds, 5 feet 10 inches, blue eyes, blond hair. This was the man all right. He watched Hauptmann walk briskly across the lane to his garage, unlock the doors and back out the Dodge. The numberplate read: 4U13.41.

Hauptmann closed and relocked the garage doors, climbed into the Dodge, and set off south. For him the day was little different from any other. After breakfast he had kissed goodbye to Anna and Manfred and was now on his way to Steiner, Rouse with possibly a stop-over for coffee at the Henkels.

From Fordham Road he turned down Washington Avenue to 189th Street, then west to Park Avenue. He drove fast and well, said Finn, so that the three police cars had difficulty in keeping pace with him. When they had traveled some five miles and were approaching Tremont Avenue, Finn realized that if Hauptmann got through on the last of the green, they might lose him. So he gave the signal to close in. The first car overtook the Dodge and edged it into the curb, the second drew alongside it, the third pulled up behind.

With guns at the ready, the detectives surrounded the car. Finn opened the driving door and looked into Hauptmann's bewildered face. 'What is happening? What is this?' Hauptmann asked. His first reaction was that he had been stopped for speeding. But why so many men to apprehend him, why the hostility and the guns?

'Get out,' said Finn.

He got out. Detective Wallace slipped the handcuffs on him. Then he was frisked. He had no weapon, but Keaton found a wallet in his back trouser pocket. In it was a $20 gold certificate bill. They checked it against the list of ransom money serial numbers and found it matched. But Finn didn't yet want Hauptmann to know what he knew.

'Where did you get this counterfeit money?' he asked.

Counterfeit money, thought Hauptmann. So this is what Fisch had landed him with. He wasn't altogether suprised.

'I have been collecting gold certificate money against inflation,' he said. 'At one time I had three hundred dollars' worth.'

'Don't you know the President has said that all gold money has to be turned in to the Federal Reserve Bank?'

'Yes.'

'How much more gold money do you have at home?'

He thought of the $14,600 hidden in the garage, and knew that if a charge of hoarding (let alone stealing) was not to be preferred against him, he had to lie. Remembering the gold coins he kept in a tin, he said, 'About a hundred and twenty dollars' worth.'

'We'll check on that,' said Finn; then, weighing up Hauptmann, he allowed his fantasies to run away with him. 'He was the bird we were looking for all right . . . I could defy any man who was a man to like him . . . I felt that he would kill a baby in a crib and never turn a hair.'

He went off to telephone Inspector Lyons about the arrest and to arrange for one of the officers to drive the Dodge back to 222nd Street. While waiting for Lyons to join them, Finn ordered Detective Wallace to sit with Hauptmann on the back seat of his car.

Wallace looked at the stupefied Hauptmann with the same sort of distaste as Finn had shown, seeing only what he wanted to see.

'So you're the Lindbergh kidnapper?' he said.

The what? The *what*? Hauptmann felt himself tossed about in a whirlwind of increasingly nightmarish dimensions, a world where normal expectations and reactions were in abeyance. First it was speeding, then passing counterfeit money, now this. It must be all a joke, a farce, some horrible mistake. When would it end?

Another detective smiled, with venom. 'You're going to burn, baby,' he said.

Book II

EFFECT

PART FIVE

THE INVESTIGATORS

'I have made a friend. There is nothing I would not do for Colonel Lindbergh. There is no oath I would not break if it would materially help his wellbeing. There is not a single man in my outfit who would not lay down his life for Colonel Lindbergh.'

HENCE ALL THE BULLSHIT

(Colonel Norman Schwarzkopf, *New York Journal*, February 15, 1935)

12

The convoy arrived back at 222nd Street, and Hauptmann was led upstairs to his own apartment. He was asked where the remainder of the gold certificate bills were, and he showed them the tin box containing $120 worth of gold coins. 'You were asked about gold *certificates*,' he was told. He didn't reply.

Still handcuffed to Wallace, he was made to sit on his bed while the officers searched the room. He realized now the deadly peril he was in. Where had Fisch got the Lindbergh money, and was he aware it was Lindbergh money when he gave it to him? With Fisch dead he would never know. *With Fisch dead, who would confirm his finding the money in the shoe-box?* Why did Fisch have to die? Why couldn't he have lived long enough to return to New York and claim his shoe-box? If there had been good reasons for lying about the existence of the money when he was arrested, there were even more now. Well, it was carefully hidden and with any luck the policemen would not find it. Now and again he rose a little to glance out of the window at the garage. 'What are you looking at?' asked Sisk, and Hauptmann said, 'Nothing.'

Anna came in. After Richard had left the house, she and Louisa Schussler and Manfred had gone for a walk, and then she had put Manfred in the backyard to sleep in the sunshine. There a detective had found her and brought her upstairs. Shocked to see the men turning her neat apartment upside down and her husband in handcuffs, she said, 'Richard, what is this?' One of the detectives said, 'You'll find out soon enough.' She went over and put her hands on her husband's shoulders and said, 'Did you do something wrong?' Richard said 'No,' and one of the detectives said, 'Take that woman outside.'

At around one o'clock Hauptmann was put back in the car, and they set off for the 2nd Precinct Police Station in Greenwich Street. This was an old police station near the Hudson Terminal on the lower west side, and had been chosen to avoid attracting the press: it was also where Finn had his office. On the way they stopped off at the Central Savings Bank at 73rd Street and Broadway to see if there were any ransom bills in Hauptmann's safety deposit box. They found it contained papers but no money.

Hauptmann was taken upstairs to the trial room for minor traffic cases, and looked into a sea of grim faces: Schwarzkopf with Lamb, Keaton, Bornmann and John Wallace from New Jersey; Sisk, Leslie and Turrou from the FBI; Lyons, Finn and William Wallace from the New York City Police. They looked at him with wonder and a certain awe. The man – or one of them – who had filled their waking thoughts for two and a half years, the human fiend who had kidnapped and murdered the Lindbergh baby, was now among them in the flesh. Strange, some thought, that he didn't look more the part.

Inspector John Lyons, as the senior New York Police officer present, conducted the questioning. For the first hour or so Hauptmann was asked about his childhood and early life, how he had come to America, what he had been doing since. He answered slowly but readily in a markedly guttural, high-pitched voice. Finn was impressed by his apparent frankness, and one of the FBI agents wrote that 'he gave the impression that he had blundered into our arms without a prepared alibi . . . There was nothing in his face to tell us he wasn't innocent. It was distressed and tired but clean of guilt.'

Without being reminded of the date of the Lindbergh kidnapping he was asked what he was doing in the early part of 1932, and said truthfully that he was working as a carpenter at the Majestic Apartments. He obtained the job from an agency on 60th Street, he said, and he was paid by the superintendent whom he described as Jewish (he had evidently forgotten the names of the Reliant

Employment Agency and of E. V. Pescia and Joseph Furcht). Asked how long he had worked there, he said a couple of months between February and April. What time did he quit work there? 'I guess five o'clock or six o'clock.' The police realized that if he was working at the Majestic Apartments until five or six on Tuesday March 1, it was unlikely that he was putting a ladder up against the nursery window at Hopewell three or four hours later; so Special Agent Seykora with one man each from the New Jersey and New York Police were detailed to visit the Majestic Apartments in the morning and try to trace the 1932 work records.

Then the questioning shifted to the gold certificate bills he admitted passing. Where had they come from? He repeated what he had told the detectives who had arrested him: from a stock of $300 worth which he had been saving when he could against inflation. They asked about the bill he had passed at the fruit and vegetable store.

'Where did you get that bill?'

'That is from the three hundred dollars.'

'Where did you save this money from?'

'I was going to the bank and getting bills.'

'Does it not strike you that it is a Lindbergh bill?'

'Yes, it does.'

'What explanation can you make?'

'None.'

They asked where he kept the gold certificates.

'I kept [them] right in the box, where the gold was.'

'And that is the only place where you kept [them], and you cannot make any explanation for having this Lindbergh ransom money?'

'No.'

'You do not expect us to believe that, do you?'

He didn't really, it sounded phoney even to him; but so long as they didn't find the money hidden in the garage, he should be all right. Asked about the $20 bill found on him that morning, he naturally said it was the last of the $300. Mercifully they didn't ask whether he expected them to believe that too.

Then Inspector Lyons said he was going to read out some dictation and Hauptmann should copy it down. This was a short composite statement consisting of various words used in the ransom notes and put together by a handwriting expert, Albert D. Osborn, son of another handwriting expert, Albert S. Osborn.

During the past two years various suspects had been required to copy the statement to see if their writing matched that of the writing in the ransom notes. None had. Now Hauptmann was asked if he would undergo the test.

'I'll be glad to,' he said, 'because it'll help get me out of this thing.'

Little did he realize that in the long run it was going to push him even deeper into it.

This was the composite statement that Hauptmann took down, not once but twice.

> Cross the street and walk to the next corner and follow Whittemore Avenue to the Sound. Take the money with you. Come alone and walk. I will meet you. The boy is on the boat. It is a small boat 28 feet long. Two persons are on the boat. They are innocent. You will find the boat between Horseneck Beach and Gay Head, near Elizabeth Island.

They gave him a break then while they wheeled in Hans Kloppenburg whom they had taken into custody that afternoon, thinking that as a friend of Hauptmann's, he might have joined him in the kidnapping. Had he ever made a box for Hauptmann? (Condon had handed the ransom bills over in a box.) Had Hauptmann ever given him money? Remembering the look-out at St Raymond's whom Lindbergh had seen waving a white handkerchief, they asked where he bought his handkerchiefs and must have been startled by his reply. 'I never bought any. I got a whole lot from Germany and some second-hand ones from a Chinaman.' Then, just in case he had written the ransom notes himself, they made him sit down and take dictation of a longer composite statement.

> We were not near Smith Hall where the robbery took place between six and twelve by our time. During all the time I was out of the house, but later came home. Did you not write letters to New York sending back anything that was stolen from Mr Conway? Police keep those letters and papers. They will be good for something later maybe. One of the letters stated, 'Dear Sir, Thank you for the bills and for your money. We will send back the bills later perhaps. Where shall we send them? The address we lost. Be at home every night so you will hear from us, you cannot tell when it will be.'

Hauptmann was also asked to write down this statement and again did so willingly, at least seven times.

Then Hauptmann and Kloppenburg were taken out, and Joseph Anthony Perrone, taxi-driver, was brought in.

*   *   *

People everywhere and at all times are notoriously gullible. Provided a thing is said with sufficient conviction and authority, there is almost nothing that men and women cannot be persuaded to believe and act upon. In mediaeval times religious people felt themselves so threatened by those whose dogma differed from their own as to justify breaking them on the wheel or putting them to the sword. In Germany in our own times thousands of otherwise rational people were led to think that Jews were such a menace to their society as to necessitate their extermination. In America before the war Orson Welles created panic with his famous radio drama about Martians landing on Earth.

So it is also in matters criminal, the perpetrators of horrendous crimes being seen as a threat to us all. Law enforcement agencies seize on a piece of evidence that leads them to believe that a certain suspect is the guilty party. When contradictory evidence appears, they ignore it, unwilling to admit that their original belief was false; and the longer the original belief is held, the more difficult it becomes to shift. When no corroborative evidence appears to reinforce the belief, it has to be manufactured – not with the object of framing an innocent man but, as the police believe, of bringing a guilty one to justice.

There are various ways in which evidence is manufactured, crudely by planting things in the suspect's pocket or forging incriminating documents, more subtly by persuading potential witnesses to give testimony against the suspect. To achieve this, the police employ highly effective methods. Several together (for there is always strength in numbers) tell the witness they have got the right man at last, there is not the slightest shadow of doubt about it, and all we want you to do is say you saw him when and where we thought you did. The witness is flattered to think that his opinion is of such importance; he is aware the police know far more about the case than he does; and as a law-abiding citizen he has no wish to obstruct the course of justice. So he agrees, if not at the first time of asking, usually (for the police are tenacious) at the second or third; then, having committed himself to an untruth, he – and everyone else – comes to believe in it. If he doesn't agree, the police, chameleon-like, can become hostile, threatening, and adopt an attitude that says, if you don't want to co-operate with us, man, we can make things tough for you, very tough indeed. In Hauptmann's case, as we shall see, almost all these methods of producing false testimony were used.[1]

In this case there was also another factor. Most crimes committed are unknown to the general public, except superficially. This one was not only known in detail but had shocked and outraged almost everyone in the country, filled them with a deep personal loathing of the perpetrators and a desire, almost an obsession, to see them caught and destroyed. Two and a half years later the feeling was no less strong; so that when this illegal German immigrant was found with ransom money on him, he became a ready-made focus for long-felt and previously unfocussed emotions of rage and disgust. No one was of a mind to doubt, to spare the time or effort to ask what other explanation there might be. As Agent Turrou said, 'From the start he was foredoomed. He *had* to be guilty.'

In this climate witnesses required little persuasion to say what the police wanted. They wanted to say it themselves. They felt proud and privileged to be in a position whereby they could play a small part in bringing this monster to justice. Millions of their fellow-countrymen envied them.

So Perrone was called, Perrone the taxi-driver who had had a fleeting glimpse in the dark two and a half years earlier of the man who had given him a note to deliver to Condon, and whom he had said unequivocally that he wouldn't be able to recognize again; Perrone who since then had identified a man called Chetel and various others who were nowhere near the Bronx; Perrone whom Schwartzkopf had labelled as a totally unreliable witness.

First Inspector Lyons gave Perrone a little pep talk and said, according to this verbatim report by Sisk: 'Now, Joe, we've got the right man at last. There isn't a man in this room who isn't convinced he is the man who kidnapped the Lindbergh baby. He answers the description of the man that gave you the note perfectly and there is no doubt about him being the man. Now we're depending on you, Joe. Take a good look at him when we bring him in, but don't say anything until I ask you if he is the man.' The same Schwartzkopf who had called Perrone a totally unreliable

---

[1] 'The real job [of a policeman] is to make a judge and jury, and especially a jury, agree with us that our prisoner is guilty. In the case of Hauptmann this was especially true . . .' Lieutenant James J. Finn: *Liberty Magazine*. It would be difficult to think of a more misguided view of a detective's role.

witness was present when this was said, and presumably approved. 'Inspector Lyons,' concluded Sisk, 'practically coerced Perrone into identifying Hauptmann.'

For the purposes of identification the law recommended a line-up containing others beside the suspect, so Lyons placed the bewildered Hauptmann between two beefy, 6-foot New York policemen, Patrolman Macnamara and Detective Croake. The three of them marched in like something from an early two-reeler. At a signal Perrone went up to Hauptmann and touched him on the shoulder. 'This is the man,' he said. Then, so there should be no doubt, Lyons asked Hauptmann to repeat the words that Perrone said were said to him about delivering the note. Hauptmann, always willing to oblige, said them, and Perrone lying in his teeth, said: 'I recognize the voice and manner of his speech. It was exactly as he spoke to me that night.'

And so, from this deeply corrupt source, the first of many nails was knocked into Hauptmann's coffin. And the police officers sat back relieved, happy to have their own beliefs confirmed. First they had brainwashed Perrone and then he had brainwashed them. Everyone was happy. It would have been awkward if he had failed to deliver.

Later they asked Hauptmann to comment on Perrone's identification. He had never seen him in his life, he said, and since owning a car he had had nothing to do with taxis. One of the officers said, 'You are not helping yourself by sitting there lying.' He paused and studied Hauptmann's face carefully. 'You don't look like a man who is concerned in a kidnapping,' he said; and then, misinterpreting Hauptmann's attitude: 'Our belief is that you are trying to help somebody out, but you are not going to get anywhere doing that. Now is your time to help us out.' How could Hauptmann explain that the only person he was trying to help out was himself?

He had a break then while they interviewed other friends, Lempke the chicken-farmer and Nostersky, thinking they might be involved, and then at 9.15 p.m., puzzled as to why they had not yet had a confession, they began interrogating him again. They were intrigued by the Hudson sealskins Fisch had left in the flat, and they asked him about his business arrangements with Fisch. He told them how Fisch had cheated him in the matter of furs ('he was a liar to me') and how he had searched for the furs Fisch said he had bought and couldn't find them, and how Fisch owed him

$5500 for furs. He was asked if he read the *Bronx Home News*
and he said No, he didn't like it, and whether he knew Betty Gow
and Violet Sharpe and he said No, and twice whether he had ever
been arrested in Germany and he said No, twice, which he was
soon to regret. He was asked about his dealings in stocks and what
he had lived on, and then they returned to the gold certificates and
where he had obtained them, and he gave them the same old dusty
answer.

It was now getting on for midnight, and Schwarzkopf was
keen for one of the Osborns to give an opinion on Hauptmann's
handwriting. So he telephoned the father, Albert S., aged seventy,
at his home in Montclair, New Jersey; he said he was in bed and
not feeling too good but if the matter was urgent, why not get in
touch with his son? The son, Albert D., agreed to go to his office
in the Woolworth Building, where presently Sergeant Ritchie and
Agent Turrou delivered to him the copies of the two statements
that Hauptmann had written as well as other samples of his writing
found by police in his apartment. There were nine sheets of dictated
writing in all; two of the first statement and seven of the second.
Sisk, who glanced at them before they went, said it was obvious
that Hauptmann had tried to disguise his writing. In fact the police
officers supervising the writing had asked Hauptmann to write the
seven versions with three different pens, some with an upright
hand and some slanting; so there were even greater discrepancies
between the various copies of the dictated writings than there were
between the dictated writings and the ransom notes.[1]

Schwarzkopf and the others had little doubt that Osborn would
declare that Hauptmann was the writer of the ransom notes. But
for Osborn, apart from the lateness of the hour, this was a routine
assignment (the news of Hauptmann's arrest had not broken in
the papers) and he wanted to take his time. After Ritchie and
Turrou had handed over the samples, he asked them to wait. They
waited fifteen minutes. Unconvinced that Hauptmann had written
the ransom notes, Osborn asked if he could be given some printed
specimens by him, particularly the name and address of Dr Condon
as it had appeared on the envelopes of the ransom notes. Turrou
and Ritchie hastened back to Greenwich Street with this information, Hauptmann was set to work writing out Condon's name
and address, and Turrou, this time with Zapolsky, retraced his

[1] Evidence of handwriting expert John F. Tyrrell. Trial 1168.

steps to Osborn. Asked if he had yet formed an opinion, all Osborn would say was that the samples were 'interesting', and that he would telephone Schwarzkopf with an opinion when he had one.

Convinced that Hauptmann was guilty, yet frustrated by Osborn's reluctance to confirm it, the police now resorted to their own methods of obtaining proof. We want you to write some more, they said. Hauptmann, by now exhausted, said he couldn't, he hadn't slept for twenty-four hours, and Kloppenburg who was also writing for them heard them say, 'You'd better write, it's bad for you if you don't,' and they hit Hauptmann in the ribs once or twice to keep him awake. 'You write,' they said to him, 'you write.'

This time Hauptmann was told to spell certain words as they had been spelled in the ransom notes. 'I was told to write exactly as it was dictated to me,' he said, 'and this included writing words spelled as I was told to spell them.' Kloppenburg said the same. 'I had to copy it the way it was spelt.' Many of the words mis-spelt in the ransom notes seem to have been done so haphazardly, without any recognizable pattern and, some think, deliberately. Among those Hauptmann was instructed to copy were 'bee' ('be'), 'The' ('They'), 'note' ('not'), 'mony' ('money'), and 'hte' ('the'), which last appeared only once in the ransom notes but *three times* in Hauptmann's dictated writings. Hauptmann was a good speller, and one has only to look at the reproduction of his letter to Mrs Begg (page 133) to see that he knew perfectly well how to spell 'money' (which he was dealing in every day at Steiner, Rouse) and 'not' and 'the'. 'Be' also is one of the first English words a foreigner learns, and when the notes were written Hauptmann had been in the States for ten years. Other words he was told to mis-spell were 'singnature' ('signature'), 'were' ('where'), 'ouer' ('our'), 'haus' ('house'), 'gut' ('good'), 'latter' ('later') and 'Sond' ('Sound') all of which had been mis-spelt in the ransom notes.

In addition to mis-spelt words in the dictation of the composite statements, Hauptmann was also told *to copy* both the two composite statements *and* the photostats of the actual ransom notes. There are a number of sources for this, the main ones being the *New York Times* of September 22 which reported, 'The New York Police disclosed that they had caused Hauptmann to copy the notes', that of Osborn Senior when he wrote of Hauptmann 'copying the prepared matter and other matter',[1] and of Agent

---

[1] Albert S. Osborn. *Questioned Document Problems.*

Turrou who spoke of Hauptmann 'having to work constantly at adding curlicues to "y"s or crossing "t"s in different ways'. He was also told to write a passage without dotting his 'i's (he almost always dotted his 'i's) because 'i's were not dotted in the ransom notes; to write many capital 'N's as 'и's (as on the ransom notes); and to write with the left hand (it was thought that the first five lines of the nursery note had been written

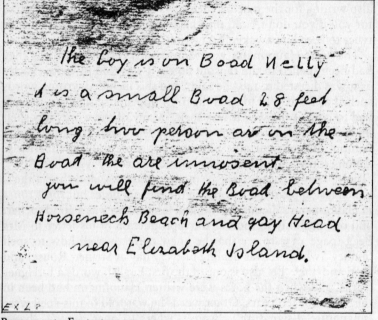

Ransom note. For text see page 109.

with the left hand). 'If I had known at the time,' Hauptmann wrote later, 'to what use the writing was to be put, I would never have undertaken the dictation.'

At around 4 a.m. the telephone rang. Schwarzkopf took it and when he heard it was Osborn, raised his hand for silence. According to Sisk, who was there, Schwarzkopf

listened to what Mr Osborn had to say for several minutes and then inquired as to whether further specimens would help out any, after which he remarked, 'We'll send them over.' He then hung up the receiver and advised those present, 'It doesn't look so good. He says that when he first looked at the specimens he thought they were the

Part of the composite statement prepared by Albert D. Osborn (see page 174) and dictated to Hauptmann on the night after his arrest. In (1) Hauptmann, whose spelling was good, takes down the statement correctly but in (2) he mis-spells certain words as they were mis-spelled in the ransom notes. The prosecution handwriting experts, not shown the first version and unaware that the mis-spellings in the second version were done on police instructions, naturally concluded that Hauptmann was the author of the ransom notes. Note too how the writing changes with the use of different pens.

same, and that there were some striking similarities, but after examining them for a while he found a lot of dissimilarities . . . and he is convinced he did not write the ransom notes.

'His father is coming to examine them in the morning first thing. I told him we would give them more specimens to work with, but he doesn't think that would change his opinion.'

Other police officers than those present might have paused to consider whether they might be barking up the wrong tree, and that anyway at this late hour enough was enough. But Osborn's verdict seems to have goaded Schwarzkopf and the others into even greater activity. More 'specimens' were demanded of Hauptmann, not just the two statements again but, said Turrou, other matter such as the *Wall Street Journal* and the *Congressional Record* into which Turrou admitted 'interjecting a word or two from the ransom notes now and then'. Bornmann, who must have been getting almost as sleepy as Hauptmann, said, 'Why don't you tell the truth, Richard, and get it over with? Why don't you get it off your mind?'

For what remained of that night, he was allowed to doze in his chair; but the questioning went on.

*   *   *

It was as obvious to the police as it must have been to Hauptmann that his story of accumulating Lindbergh ransom bills haphazardly from banks was too incredible to sustain, and at 10 a.m. the next day a posse of men from the three law enforcement agencies returned to 222nd Street to make a more thorough search. They turned over mattresses and chairs, went through drawers and closets, scattered on the floor the Hauptmanns' belongings and the baby's toys, but found nothing. At around 11.30 a.m. they moved to the garage, asking Mrs Hauptmann to accompany them; and there, before her astonished eyes, they unearthed the bulk of what Hauptmann had hidden: $11,930 beneath the rags in the shellac can and $1830 wrapped in the two newspapers, making a total of $13,760. At this juncture they did not find the $840 concealed with the pistol in the specially bored holes.

This news was speedily conveyed to Greenwich Street where two things happened. First, Lieutenant Finn telephoned the Woolworth Building where the Osborns, father and son, had been studying Hauptmann's request and acknowledged writings for the past two hours without finding anything to alter the son's previously declared opinion. Now Finn told them that the suspect whose writing they had been examining was under arrest, and that nearly $14,000 of the ransom money had been found hidden in his garage. Would they be good enough to reconsider their verdict?

This news put the Osborns in something of a fix. It was true that certain characteristics in both the ransom notes and Hauptmann's various writings – uncrossed 't's, 'x's formed like back to back 'e's, 'g's shaped like 'y's – indicated the writers of both as having German as their first language. It was also true that there were many mis-spellings common to both the ransom notes and the request writings. But when they compared the writings found in Hauptmann's house (a surer guide, they knew, than anything coming out of a police station) with the ransom notes, and saw how different were the formation of words and letters, the angle at which they were written, the shading, the spacing between words and lines, they knew that the writer of the one was certainly not the writer of the other.

And yet, supposing they were wrong! They had both been wrong before, and had seen plaintiffs or defendants for whom they had testified lose their cases in court. (In thirty-seven years' time the son was to make the biggest mistake of his career in testifying, along with another four 'experts', that writing said to be that of Howard Hughes but forged by Clifford Irving was genuine.) If the police were as certain as they seemed to be that the man they had arrested had written the ransom notes, who were they to contradict them? Less than an hour after Finn's call, Osborn Senior rang Schwartzkopf to say that the author of the specimens was also the author of the ransom notes. When this news was passed on to the other police officers in Greenwich Street, they burst out laughing. 'Those handwriting experts!' they said. 'Oh, boy!'

Earlier, after he had had a wash and shave and some coffee, they had begun to re-question Hauptmann. Quite friendly they had been to begin with, calling him Richard and asking if he couldn't think of anything else that might clear things up which, needless to say, he couldn't. Now, having been joined by J. Edgar Hoover and General O'Ryan, Commissioner of the New York Police, they brought him the news he had been dreading, the discovery of the ransom money in the garage. What had he to say about that? At first nothing: he was too stunned, knowing what they must think. Then, but too late, he told them about Fisch and the shoe-box and the water in the kitchen closet, but it must have sounded lame even to him. And now all their friendliness had gone and their arrows were deadly. All right, they said, let's assume for the moment your story is true.

'You knew the money didn't belong to you?'

'Yes.'

'You were stealing it.'

'Not exactly stealing it. This man owed me money.'

'Listen, you heard yesterday that was Lindbergh money, didn't you?'

'Yes.'

'When you heard it was Lindbergh money, why didn't you say that money was given to me by so and so under these circumstances? Why didn't you?'

'I lose on this fellow seven thousand dollars.'[1]

'Why didn't you tell us that story this morning and yesterday?'

'I was afraid to tell you about it yesterday. I figured, how can I explain how I got fourteen thousand dollars?'

'If you were an innocent or an honest man, as soon as you heard it was Lindbergh money you would come out and tell the truth. Instead of that, for twenty-four hours you sat there and lied.'

There was no answer.

Then they said, You were corresponding with Fisch's brother in Germany; when you found the money, why didn't you write to him? Wouldn't it have been the action of an honest man?

In a way, agreed Hauptmann, but he was thinking of the money Fisch owed him, the money Fisch had cheated from him.

All right, they said, but there was $14,000 there, and you were owed only $7000, which left a balance in favour of the brother. Wouldn't an honest man have written and told him so?

And he had no answer to that either.

And then out of the blue came another piece of bad news.

'Richard, do you remember telling me last night that on March 1, 1932 you were employed in the Majestic Apartments?'

'Yes, I was.' He had clearly remembered that on March 2, while at 225th Street Station on his way to the Majestic on the train, he had bought a paper and read of the kidnapping.

'You were lying when you told me that?'

'I was telling the truth.'

'We just sent a man to check up on that story and he says you

---

[1] Actually $7,500

didn't come to work until March 21st ... and you resigned on April 2nd, the night the money was passed ... You said you were sure you were working in the Majestic on March 1st?'

'Yes.'

'You still stick to that?'

'Yes. If the records say I wasn't, the records are wrong.'

Agent Seykora's report said that he and two officers visited the Majestic Apartments that morning and were referred to the owners, the Reliance Property Management Company, where they saw a Mr Birmingham. Seykora went on: 'Hauptmann first appears on the payroll time record for the half-month ending March 31st, 1932, in which he is credited with 11 days' work, his wages for this period being $36.67. On the following payroll for the period ending April 15th 1932, he is credited with two days' work, wages being $6.67. Mr Birmingham stated that this indicates that Hauptmann's employment terminated on April 2nd, 1932.'

That Hauptmann did not start work at the Majestic Apartments until March 21, 1932 was to be a linchpin of the prosecution's case. But if it were true, it also had to be true that not only did he not work on any of the preceding days *but that he did not come on to the company's books until that date.*

There are two documents against which this claim can be examined; the company's (a) timesheets and (b) payroll records for the periods March 1 to 15 and March 16 to 31. Seykora says that the Reliance Property Management told him that they did not have any payroll records for the period March 1 to 15, but this was untrue as will later be shown. Payroll records *and* timesheets for March 1 to 15 *were* in existence and, as we shall see, showed that Hauptmann was working at the Majestic Apartments throughout that period.

Turning to the second period, March 16 to 31, we have to ask what evidence there is that Hauptmann was not on the company's books on March 16 and therefore not working between March 16 and 21. If we look at the timesheets for the period March 16 to 31 (see page 186) we see that there are marks against Hauptmann's name for each day. This shows that he was on the company's books for the entire period: had he not been, there would have been no marks of any kind.

It is when we look at these marks a little closer that we are forced to a disturbing conclusion – that on the 16th, 17th, 18th, 19th and 20th round ink blobs have been deliberately superimposed to blot out the ticks indicating that Hauptmann was working. No other name has similar blobs or has been tampered with in any way. And if we look at the timesheets for the next period, April 1 to 15 (page 187), we can see that a similar large blob has obliterated the tick showing that Hauptmann was working on April 2, the day the ransom money was handed over (and on which day Mr

Majestic Apartments timesheet March 16–31, 1932.

Birmingham told Seykora that Hauptmann had definitely been working). Also there is the notation 'Out 4/4' in the Remarks column, showing Hauptmann quit on the fourth month on the fourth day[1]; the second '4' bears no resemblance to the first and has clearly been tampered with – almost certainly to obliterate a '2' showing that he quit work on the 2nd. It has been suggested that Hauptmann might have been away sick between March 16 and March 21 and that the blobs showed an error being corrected;

[1] In the writing of months and days in numerals, Europeans put the day before the month, the Americans the month before the day.

even so, it in no way invalidates the fact that he was on the company's books for the whole of the second half of March, and not just from March 21 as the prosecution were to claim.

When we look at the payroll records for the second half of March we find supporting evidence for the belief that documents were being tampered with (see page 188). Under the sub-heading

Majestic Apartments timesheet April 1–15, 1932.

'Days' in the 'TIME' column, an apparent attempt has been made to overprint the inverted comma (") indicating F.T. (full-time) with the figures '11'; while in the 'OVERTIME' column an attempt to delete the figure '2' in the 'Days' column and another '2' in the 'Hours' column has resulted in the erasure of part of the vertical lines enclosing them; and the base of the '2' in the 'Hours' column can still be seen.

And yet we are left with a dilemma, for the $36.67 in the 'Amount' column does not appear (unless very skilfully done) to be a forgery; and furthermore on September 20, 1934, the day after Hauptmann's arrest and long before any tampering was

PAYROLL TIME RECORD

BUILDING Majestic Apartments   WEEK ENDING   March 31st, 1932

Construction

OCCUPATION	TIME RATE	TIME HOURS	OVERTIME RATE	OVERTIME HOURS	RATE	NAME	AMOUNT	REMARKS
Supt.	F.T.				25	J. M. Furcht	12 50	✓
Carpenter	"	&	2	2	115	James Davis	66 00	See note.
"	"	&	2	2	100	Robert Lochhead	57 41	" "
"	"	&	2	2	100	Allen Wilkinson	57 41	" "
"	"	&	2	2	100	Gustav Kassens	57 41	" "
"	"	&	2	2	100	Joseph Burnsides	57 41	" "
"	11 days				100	Richard Kruptman	36 67	✓
Handy Man	F.T.				80	James Crosby	40 00	✓
"	"	&	2	3	80	James Cullen	46 22	See Note
"	"	&	1	5	85	David Davis	46 91	" "
"	"	&	1	5	90	John Covit	45 67	" "
"	"	&	1½	12	115	P. Harrigan	63 25	" "

Majestic Apartments payroll record for March 16–31, 1932.

possible, Mr Birmingham had told Seykora that this was the sum Hauptmann had been paid for eleven days' work.

What the answer is, is impossible to say. It could be that Seykora filed a false report, but in the time available I think it unlikely. It could be that Hauptmann was away sick for five days and so worked only eleven; but this does not dispel the suspicion that payroll records and timesheet were criminally tampered with.

Whatever the explanation, none of it matters. Whether Hauptmann was working at the Majestic Apartments or not during the second half of March has little bearing on his guilt or innocence. What does matter is what he was doing during the first part of the month and in particular March 1. And for that period, as we shall see, there is incontrovertible evidence that he was working full-time at the Majestic Apartments.

*   *   *

During the day the news that a suspect in the Lindbergh case had been taken into custody had somehow leaked out, and soon the Second Precinct Police Station in Greenwich Street was under siege from reporters and photographers. A press conference was hurriedly called, with New York's Police Commissioner, General O'Ryan, in the chair, flanked by Hoover and Schwarzkopf. There was nothing tentative in what they had to say: they were there to praise their own detective work and meet the public's expectations. With Perrone's and the Osborns' testimony under his belt, O'Ryan felt confident enough to assert (and he repeated it on the radio that night) that Hauptmann was the receiver of the Lindbergh ransom money. He went even further when asked if the prisoner was connected with the kidnapping itself. 'Yes,' he said, without the flicker of an eyelid or a shred of evidence to back him. On what grounds? No comment. Would his arrest solve both the kidnapping and the receipt of the ransom money? O'Ryan leaned over to whisper with Hoover and Schwarzkopf. 'All three of us,' he said, 'believe it will.'

Then it was the turn of the photographers, and Hauptmann was led in, like a prize heifer. According to the *New York Times*:

He was seated in a chair on a raised platform in front of the bench, and sat there, a stolid man, sullen and defiant, with a hang-dog look, while innumerable pictures were taken.

His hands were handcuffed in front of him, and he held them in his lap. He kept his eyes down most of the time. Once in a while a photographer would call for him to look up. Usually he would not respond. Once in a while, he would lift his eyes for a second, but then lower them quickly. Now and then a policeman would put the prisoner's hat on or take it off, as the photographers dictated. Once when the policeman was not looking and the photographers became insistent, the prisoner raised his handcuffed hands to take his hat off for them.

On the way out, Hauptmann passed Anna in the corridor. With the finding of the ransom money in the garage, she had been regarded as a suspect herself and brought down to the police station a short while before. She tried to embrace him but a police officer brushed her aside. Then she was taken away to be grilled by detectives using one of the oldest tricks in the business – the pretense that her husband had confessed, and that they knew everything.

'You tell the truth now,' she says they shouted at her. 'Your husband has already said you know all about the money.'

'That is a lie,' she answered with spirit. 'My husband would never say such a thing. He knows that I know nothing about the money.'

While they continued questioning her, her husband was taken up to the office of the Second Deputy Police Commissioner to attend another identification parade. Dr John F. Condon was on his way there and, everyone confidently believed, would pick Hauptmann out as the man he had met in the Woodlawn and St Raymond's cemeteries.

The line-up for the parade was even more bizarre than the one arranged for Perrone – eight detectives and five patrolmen. Hauptmann took his place among them. Agent Turrou, who was present, said, 'It wasn't much of a deception. The detectives were shaved, bright-eyed six-footers. Hauptmann looked like a midget who had wandered through a Turkish bath for two sleepless days and nights.'

Condon, however, was happy to play along with this farce. He walked up and down the line three times; then, to give the appearance of genuine doubt, asked for all but Hauptmann and three others standing by him to be eliminated. The four stepped forward, and now Condon was ready to go into his act. He knew that the eyes of three police forces, if not yet of America and the world, were on him, and he wanted every piece of kudos and limelight that was going. Addressing the little group but looking at

Hauptmann, he said: 'When I saw you, I gave you my promise that I would do all I possibly could for you if you gave me the baby. The only way in the world I think you can save yourself at all is to tell the truth. I gave you a promise that day. Follow that promise.'

He then asked the four men to hold their hands up, palms towards him, to see if any of them had the fleshy lump at the base of the left thumb he had observed on Cemetery John. None had.

Next in this highly injudicial interrogation (in which Hauptmann should have had no part and, if he had had the assistance of a lawyer, *would* have had no part) Condon asked the four to give their names and say whether they had ever seen him before. Three replied with the voices of New Yorkers, the fourth in a notably German accent.

Now Condon handed Hauptmann a slip of paper on which he had written a fragment of John's conversation, and said, 'Read it out loud.'

Hauptmann read, 'I stayed already too long. The leader would schmack me out. Your work is perfect.'

Unable to hear, or in love with his own handiwork, Condon asked Hauptmann to repeat it, which he did.

'Did you see me before?' asked Condon.

'Never.'

'You never saw me before?'

'Never.'

'What is your name?'

'Richard Hauptmann.'

'What is it again?'

'Richard Hauptmann.'

'Say "John".'

'John.'

'And you didn't see me before?'

'No.'

'Let me see your hands.'

Hauptmann showed his hands again and the four men were asked their names again, and then Condon said to Hauptmann:

'I gave the money and promised to help out if the baby was restored to me. Do you remember that?'

'No.'

'And I said I would help out.'

'No. I never talked to you.'

'I never broke my word in my life. What is your name?'

'Richard Hauptmann.'

'You don't remember speaking to me?'

'I can't say that I can.'

Condon tried a few words in very bad German which Hauptmann didn't understand.

'You never saw me before?'

'No.'

'Didn't speak to me?'

'No.'

'You have nothing to say to me at all?'

'No.'

'Why?'

'I don't know what to say.'

'Put your hat on, please.'

Hauptmann put his hat on.

'Pull it down at one side.'

Hauptmann did so.

'You didn't speak to me about the baby at all?'

'No.'

'Never said a word?'

'Never said a word.'

'Never had a conversation with me?'

'No.'

'You are positive of that?'

'Positive.'

Condon had been told by the police that Hauptmann was Cemetery John, there was no doubt about it, and he had been fully expecting him, as indeed they all were, to confess to it. Hauptmann's refusal to conform had entirely thrown Condon off balance. Inspector Lyons tried to retrieve the situation.

'Would you say,' he asked Condon, 'that he was the man?'

The pressure on Condon was even greater than that on Perrone, for while Perrone was an important bit-player, Condon was at center stage. He knew what he was expected to say and he knew from his encounters with Inspector Walsh and others how brutal the police could be if you crossed them. But – at this stage at least – the truth and his own integrity were still precious to him. He had given so many contradictory accounts of his meetings with John that even if the real John had been in front of him, it is unlikely he would have recognized him. But he was as certain as he could be that whoever this man was, he was not John. John was of lighter build, had almond eyes, a fleshy lump at the base of his left thumb, and a husky voice as opposed to this man's high-pitched one.

'I would not say he was the man,' he said.

Lyons, trying to salvage something from the wreckage, said, 'But you cannot identify him?'

Condon, happy to go along with this, said, 'No, I have to be careful.'

There was a sense of anti-climax in the room now and, anxious to end it, Condon wrote something on a slip of paper and asked Hauptmann to read it out loudly. It was another fragment of his conversation with John.

'What would your mother say?' read Hauptmann. 'She would not like it. She would cry.'

'Louder,' said Condon, 'I am not able to hear.'

'What would your mother say? She would not like it.'

'Still a little louder.'

'What would your mother say?' shouted Hauptmann. 'What would your mother say? She would not like it. She would cry.'

'Who were you afraid of up there?' asked Condon.

'Please?' said Hauptmann, baffled.

'Who were you afraid of there besides your mother? Do you remember Number Two, that you could not wait any longer because they would smack you out, the leader?'

Hauptmann said, 'I don't know what you mean.'

After more questions in the same vein, Inspector Lyons said: 'You cannot identify him?'

And Condon said, and one cannot help but admire him:

'No. I have to be very careful. The man's life is in jeopardy. I understand he has a wife and baby. If I identify him, it will mean the electric chair. I want to be sure.'

Agent Sisk observed that Condon appeared to be 'visibly nervous and shaken by the ordeal and in fact in a sort of daze'. Before leaving he said to Sisk: 'Everyone will mistrust me now. They will think that everything that's being said about me is true. I wish I could be sure, but I won't have it on my conscience, no matter what they think.'

13

On several occasions on September 19 and 20, wrote Agent Sisk, he had talked with Hauptmann alone in order to obtain a confession and learn whether others were involved with him; 'but he insisted he had nothing to do with the crime and that the gold certificates found in his possession had been left with him by Isidor Fisch'. Sisk spoke sympathetically to Hauptmann about his wife and baby and his mother in Germany 'but although he became emotionally disturbed and shed tears, he would not make even the slightest admission that he was in any way involved in the case'. Other officers, he said, 'also talked to Hauptmann alone in an effort to persuade him to tell the truth, but he remained adamant in his denials of complicity'. Agent Turrou concurred. 'We wanted a confession. We questioned him until our heads reeled, but we never got it.'

It is unlikely that the FBI men had any part in what followed, but by now some officers of the New Jersey and New York police forces were so frustrated and angry at what they regarded as Hauptmann's wilful obstinacy, that they resolved to try other methods; and Lieutenant Finn put through a call to Police Surgeon John H. Garlock to report to the station at 9.30 p.m. Garlock's brief was to examine the prisoner 'in order to determine the presence or absence of marks of injury'.

First, though, it was necessary to give the prisoner food, and he was taken across the street to a restaurant for dinner. There was now a big crowd in the street, and as Hauptmann emerged from the station there was a cry of 'Kill him, crucify him!' In the restaurant Hauptmann was too exhausted to eat anything more than a bowl of soup.

Back at the police station Dr Garlock and a colleague, Dr Loughlin, were waiting to examine him. It would be, he was told, just a routine examination, and as with the handwriting he took them at their word. After the examination Dr Garlock wrote:

Complete physical examination failed to reveal any evidence to suggest recent injury of any sort. Aside from the fact that this man was pale and suffered from loss of sleep, nothing was found. The heart was negative. All the joints of his body were normal. The head was normal, and there was no break in the skin. The patient's gait was normal. An entry to this effect was made in the police blotter.

With this lodged on the record the police went to work on Hauptmann. There is no official record of what happened that night at the Greenwich Street Police Station because when police beat a man up, they are careful not to leave any written trace. But later Hauptmann gave his own graphic account of it:

I was handcuffed in the chair and the police give me such a terrible licking that I falled downwards to the floor. They showed me a hammer and then they put out the lights and started to beat me on the shoulders, the back of the head and the arms. Then too they kicked my legs with their feet and kept yelling, 'Where is the money? Where is the baby? We'll knock your brains out . . .'

But Hauptmann could say nothing except plead ignorance and beg them to stop.

At 11.30 that night, with his body on fire and weeping uncontrollably, he was taken to the Bronx County Courthouse. Anna was already in the building, being grilled through the night before being taken to the Women's Prison. Five days later, by which time Hauptmann had a lawyer, an independent doctor, Dr Thurston H. Dexter, was able to examine him. He found, in addition to a scab and abrasions below the left eye,

. . . on right shoulder a tender lump an inch and a half, and a lump on the spine of the left scapula and above it . . . all of lower shoulder blade shows a swollen welt with discoloration and abrasions . . . in the lower abdomen close to the groin an area of three by five inches of faint greenish-yellow discoloration . . . in the upper chest a large irregular region discolored yellow and faint blue, superficially abraded . . . right thigh much swollen, very tender and markedly discolored.

'I conclude from this examination,' said Dr Dexter, 'that he had been subjected recently to a severe beating, all or mostly with blunt instruments.'

Hauptmann himself said that as a result of this beating he lost thirty pounds in weight, and that it took him two months to recover.

*   *   *

Nor was the ordeal of that Thursday night yet over. In the belief that an overwhelming desire for sleep and a release from seemingly endless probing would break down his resistance and lead to a confession, he was kept awake for further questioning until six the next morning. Such treatment by police often leads suspects to give false confessions, and it says much for Hauptmann's resistance that he did not succumb. He was asked if he had any more ransom money at home and, concerned about the pistol he had secreted with the remaining $840, stupidly replied that he hadn't. He was allowed a short rest and a clean-up before being taken to Barkley Avenue Police Station in the Bronx for the morning line-up and another interrogation, this time by Assistant Chief Inspector Sullivan. 'Worn and harried from more than forty-eight hours of questioning,' said one reporter, 'Hauptmann still retained his stolid, uncommunicative manner.'

He had in fact nothing more to say, to Inspector Sullivan or anyone else. He told Sullivan that he had had nothing to do with the kidnapping of the Lindbergh baby, that he had never been to Hopewell in his life, and didn't even know where it was. The money in his garage had been given to him by his friend Fisch.

On this negative evidence Sullivan told the reporters that there was no doubt in his mind that Hauptmann was the right man. There was a perfect case against him for extortion 'and if he was not actually at the scene of the kidnapping, he certainly had a hand in the machinery'.

Hauptmann was then taken to West Farms Court in the old Bronx Supreme Court Building at 161st Street and 3rd Avenue for arraignment. Reporters and photographers were there by the score and detectives 'pushed Hauptmann into the glare of the spotlights' so that the cameramen could get a better picture. At the request of the Assistant District Attorney and with the agreement of Hauptmann, the Magistrate adjourned the hearing until the following Monday.

Next day it was the turn of the Bronx District Attorney, Samuel J. Foley. He spent the afternoon and evening interrogating Hauptmann with as little success as everyone else; being the District Attorney, he was even more enraged than they by his failure. Not for one single moment did it occur to him, or to any of them, that Hauptmann's refusal to confess might not be due to obstinacy and wilfulness, as they believed, but to innocence; that despite earlier lies, he might not have had anything to do with the crime and, if so, would have had nothing to say to them. Had such a thought ever crossed Foley's mind, he could never have addressed Hauptmann in the brutal way he did, of which Sisk has left this account:

Mr Foley then advised Hauptmann there was no question in his mind or in the minds of any of the officers or prosecutors but that he was guilty and that he was the actual kidnapper or a participant with others in the crime; that his alibi about having obtained the ransom money from a dead friend was ridiculous and no one would believe it. Mr Foley asked Hauptmann if he expected any jury of intelligent men to believe his alibi, to which Hauptmann replied, 'I am innocent, I tell you I am innocent.'

Mr Foley pointed out that a Bronx County Jury would convict him on the evidence now at hand [for extortion] without even leaving the jury box; that he would then be taken down to New Jersey to stand trial on the kidnapping and murder and God only knew what would happen to him down there.

Mr Foley stated that Hauptmann's only chance was to come clean and tell the truth. He said, 'I want to get this case cleared up once and for all. It's been a headache for over two years. If you're protecting someone, tell the truth about it, and maybe I'll be able to help you . . . But if you don't open up and talk now, you'll never get another chance. The minute the door of this room closes on you, you're gone, you're sunk, and I will never talk to you again. The only time you will see me after today is in front of a jury.

'Now I want you to get this clear and straight. If you don't tell the truth, I am going to see you get everything in the book. I am going to ask the judge to give you the absolute limit, and that's forty years.'

Hauptmann, said Sisk, had nothing to say but was shedding tears with his head bowed down over his chest. Mr Foley then spoke at considerable length about Hauptmann's wife and child, among other things stating,

You have killed one baby and now you're going to ruin the life of another baby, your own child. I can see the first baby you killed might have met his death through an accident. You might not have intended to kill it. Maybe there is some excuse for that. Now you are deliberately, in cold blood, fully aware of what you are doing, wrecking and ruining the life of your own child.

Growing increasingly hysterical, Foley wound up with a truly shocking outburst:

Your wife is being held in the Women's Jail[1] [sic] with a lot of prostitutes. She is separated from the baby. It has no one who loves it, to take care of it. It may die of undernourishment. Your wife is hysterical. She will probably become an imbecile over the shock of this. If you have any

---

[1] This was not true.

speck of manhood left in you, you will come clean on this and do one manly thing in your life.

But I can see you're just an animal. You don't care what happens to your wife and baby. You don't care about anything. You're the lowest human being I ever had before me, and I've had a lot of bad ones. Why, the other night down at the police department, a mob were trying to get at your wife to hang her. That poor woman has put up so much from you. You were taking this blood money from this kidnapping and having a good time with a lot of fast women while your wife was visiting her people in Germany. Now you have a chance to redeem yourself, to do one decent thing in your life, and you won't do it.

While Foley was making these remarks, said Sisk, Hauptmann was shedding tears and appearing to be greatly shaken, constantly crying out, 'Stop, stop, I didn't do it! I told you everything. I don't know any more.'

That afternoon Anna was released from police interrogation and, with her own apartment a shambles and policemen all over it, went to stay with her niece Maria, who was already caring for Manfred. There a newspaperman found her, wearing a gray woollen dress, a brown hat and brown and white sports shoes; in contrast to her husband's broken spirit, she was in fighting mood.

The entire world [she told him] seems to have gone crazy. Some newspaper headlines have called my husband a kidnapper and a murderer. There have been comparisons between his handwriting and the handwriting of the Lindbergh baby kidnap notes. Even a blind person could see there is no similarity. Gradually the world is taking for granted the guilt of my husband in this horrible affair without having been given the opportunity to hear a coherent statement from either him or myself.

That night in the Bronx County Jail Hauptmann slept only fitfully, though he did not give way to further weeping as on the previous night. The next morning, September 23, was a Sunday, and for the first time since his arrest he was spared any further questioning. 'He spent the day brooding in self-imposed solitary confinement,' said the *New York Times*. 'Except at meal-times he remained sprawled out on his cot ... He did not summon the prison barber, he did not ask for newspapers or a magazine, which would have been allowed him. He did not try to speak with those set as guardians over him, nor did he try to communicate with other prisoners.'

It would have been surprising if he had done any of these things. After the nightmare experiences of the past few days and the turmoil exercising his mind, all he wanted was rest and silence, the chance to piece together his fragmented thoughts. There must have been many times when he dwelt on the bizarre and peculiar set of circumstances that had brought him there, on the twist of fate which but for his appropriating Fisch's money (and which had turned out not to be Fisch's money but Lindbergh's), he could so easily have avoided.

Was Fisch part of the kidnap gang? In spite of all his crookedness, Hauptmann thought it improbable; more likely that he had acquired the money in the course of some shady deal. This was Uhlig's view. 'I believe,' he wrote to his parents,[1] 'that he [Isidor] bought this Lindbergh money from some vagabond (as he knew many) with the money he had borrowed from his friends. And now perhaps the poor fellow [Hauptmann] must suffer for the dirty conduct of Isidor.' But why had Fisch not put the money in his safety deposit box at the bank? Perhaps because knowing it was 'hot' money, he would have been nervous about entering a bank with it. But why Hauptmann? 'My idea,' said Uhlig, who knew Fisch as well as anybody, 'is that there was nobody else he trusted. The rest of us would have opened up the package after a while and said, "What the heck has he left with us here?" He felt it was safe with Hauptmann.'

About the only encouraging thing in Hauptmann's life at this time was the appointment of a lawyer to assist him, James Fawcett, a friend of a relative of Anna. Hauptmann had met him briefly on the Saturday; on Monday, when the Bronx Grand Jury had assembled to hear Foley's case against him for extortion, he talked with him in his cell for more than four hours. By the end of the day, and despite the known evidence of Perrone and the Osborns, Fawcett was wholly convinced of Hauptmann's innocence; but then, unlike the police officers, he had approached him with an open mind. 'I do not believe he is the real culprit,' he said after his first visit. Two days later: 'I am becoming more and more convinced that Hauptmann is telling the truth when he says that he got the ransom money from Fisch.' And three days after that: 'I do not believe he is guilty of extortion. He trusted his friend Isidor Fisch. I have not found anything he has said to be untrue.' It may be said

[1] October 11, 1934

that as Hauptmann's lawyer, Fawcett would have been bound to take this view. But good lawyers develop a knack of knowing when a client is lying, and Fawcett had no need to be so publicly confident if he was unsure.

Those who knew Hauptmann well took the same view, and found his arrest incredible. They knew that whatever his short-comings, he simply was not the sort of man who, between carpentry jobs and visits to Steiner, Rouse, would have built himself a ramshackle ladder, found his way in the dark to Hopewell, known precisely where and when to place the ladder, snatched the baby unaided, killed and buried it, then come home late to Anna. Nor was he the sort of man who, between making wine with Victor Schussler and canoe trips with Louise Wollenberg and musical evenings with Hans Kloppenburg, would have written a dozen ransom notes with a special symbol, and made furtive nightly visits to cemeteries to collect $50,000 – all without Anna knowing or even suspecting a thing.

Kloppenburg was emphatic about his innocence. 'I was his best friend, you know. He never did it. How could he?' Uhlig was as positive. 'They got the wrong man. When the detectives came to see me, I told them, you found this money on him, so you're going to use him as a goat for the whole thing.' Hauptmann's sister Emma, her husband Charles and daughter Mildred, who had got to know the Hauptmanns and Kloppenburg well during their two-week visit in Los Angeles in 1931, were unanimous in their belief that he could not be involved. 'He was extremely fond of children.' Jaroslav Nostersky, with whom Hauptmann stayed when helping his friend Henry Lempke build a chicken-house, told the New Jersey Police: 'He was a fine fellow. I never would think he would do anything like that. At Hunter's Island he played the mandolin and had a boat. He was happy. There was always a policeman walking around there and it never seemed to bother him.' Lempke agreed, so did August Beeker, a fellow carpenter. 'He was a likeable, clean-cut chap . . . a hard worker and excellent carpenter. I can't understand how he would do such a thing.'

But against the wind that was to carry Hauptmann away, these were the voices of sparrows chirping in the wilderness. Sworn to secrecy (for the proceedings were *in camera*) the witnesses came and went before the Bronx Grand Jury: the filling-station attendant to whom Hauptmann had passed the ransom bill that had ensnared him, the policemen who had found nearly $14,000 hidden in his garage, Inspector Lyons to whom he had lied about the money in the garage, Perrone who testified that he had seen him when he hadn't, the Osborns *père et fils*. Old Osborn proved almost as big a windbag as Condon ('I have written two books on this subject,' he told Foley; 'I might be inclined to give one to you') and said that on first seeing Hauptmann's writings on Thursday morning, 'it was like meeting an old friend'. (He didn't add that telling the police about meeting this old friend hadn't occurred to him until an hour after hearing of the discovery of the ransom money.) He got round the marked dissimilarity between Hauptmann's writing and the ransom note writings by saying that Hauptmann had been trying to *disguise* his writing – a pointless exercise if, as Osborn maintained, much of the ransom note writing was 'disguised' writing in the first place. He was supported by a government handwriting man, Charles Appel Jr, who told the press that the chances against anyone but Hauptmann having written the ransom notes were one in a hundred million million!

And then massively, inexorably, supporting evidence from a variety of sources, much of it irrelevant and most of it false, began to pile up around the head of the hapless Hauptmann. First came news from Germany of his criminal record of fifteen years before. Never mind that the crimes committed had all taken place during one week. Never mind that nothing had been recorded against him since. What he had done was proof of the kind of man he was. So he'd used a ladder for one of his burglaries! And he'd held up two women pushing a baby carriage! A *ladder* and a *baby*! Just what you'd expect. True to form. History repeating itself.

Then along came Cecile Barr, cashier of a Loew's cinema in Greenwich Village. Nearly a year earlier, on the night of November 26, 1933, a customer had tossed a folded $5 bill at her which afterwards was found to be Lindbergh ransom money. She gave Lieutenant Finn a description of the man which, with one exception, was not dissimilar to that of Hauptmann. The exception (it is always the exceptions that get lost) was her claim that he was American, when you only had to hear Hauptmann utter two words to know that he was European. Also the date she gave happened to be Hauptmann's birthday when, with little Manfred just three weeks old, he and Anna were entertaining Maria Müller, Paul Vetterle and Isidor Fisch in 222nd Street, fifteen miles away. But, like Perrone before her, Cecile Barr had police encouragement and out of more than a thousand customers to whom she had issued

tickets that night, identified Hauptmann as the man who had given
her the ransom bill.

Next came a government financial expert, Mr Joseph A. Genau,
who had been examining Hauptmann's banking and brokerage
accounts and by an extraordinary sleight of mind had figured out
that the deposits Hauptmann had made since April 2, 1932 plus
the ransom money already found equalled (more or less) the total
ransom money paid of $50,000. This, needless to say, took no
account of monies Hauptmann had received from Fisch as profits
from furs and for stock investment, the cash that Hauptmann had
kept in his tin trunk, monies from carpentry work, and above all
the hundreds and perhaps thousands of dollars of ransom money
that had passed through the federal banks without trace and had
since gone for pulping. Nor was the only thing that mattered made
plain, that of the thousands of dollars Hauptmann had passed
through Steiner, Rouse & Co. and his banks during these years,
not one single ransom bill had been found. Even J. Edgar Hoover
had to admit, 'Identification of these funds is impossible.'

Another 'witness' keen to get in on the act was the wood expert
from Wisconsin, Arthur Koehler, whom we last met writing letters
to 1598 lumber mills to try and discover which one had the planer
with the defective knives whose markings he had noticed on
the 1- by 4-inch yellow pine Rails 12 and 13. After months of
correspondence and travelling, Koehler's persistence paid off; the
mill in question turned out to be the M. G. and J. J. Dorn Lumber
Company at McCormick, South Carolina, and inquiries there
revealed that in the relevant period (September 1929 to March
1932) it had shipped north forty-seven car loads of 1- by 4-inch
yellow pine planed in this manner. So on November 10, 1933
Koehler, accompanied by Detective Bornmann, set out to visit the
thirty East Coast lumber yards that had received them. Sometimes
sharing the same room, Bornmann was surprised to find that
Koehler (who was almost bald) wore a nightcap in bed.

From the beginning it was a pointless exercise. First, the turn-
around in lumber is very quick, and it was extremely unlikely that
any of the lumber yards would have any of that particular shipment
left; second, yellow pine 1 by 4 is so common and its sales so
extensive that it was even less likely that records of its buyers
existed; and third, even if the names of some of them could be
found, there was no guarantee that whoever had constructed the
kidnap ladder was among them – indeed to avoid attention he

would have been more likely to pick up the two planks he needed from some builder's yard or construction site.

The intrepid pair however set off. They visited eight yards in New York State, seven in New Jersey, six in Connecticut, four in the Bronx, three in Brooklyn and two in New York City. As expected, the vast majority had sold all their allocation of that particular shipment and had no records of who had bought them. One wonders why Bornmann and Koehler bothered to go on. However, they did, and on November 29 they revisited (it is not stated why) the National Lumber and Millwork Company at 3541 White Plains Road in the Bronx, and there found several lengths of 1 by 4 yellow pine which had been used to construct a wood bin, and which had exactly the same planer marks as in Rail 13.

At the time (November 1933) this information was totally valueless. In the report of his trip to Lamb and Keaton, Bornmann did not think it worth emphasizing, and Lamb and Keaton did not think it worth mentioning to the FBI. Indeed, whenever the FBI asked the New Jersey Police what progress was being made in investigating the origins of the ladder, they were told none. But when Hauptmann was arrested ten months later and it was discovered that the National Lumber and Millwork Company was where he bought his lumber and that Koehler had discovered planks similar to Rail 13 there, everyone said, Well there you are, that's further proof he did it.

In fact the discovery proved nothing. All it showed was that of the hundreds of thousands of feet of 1 by 4 yellow pine similar to Rails 12 and 13 which had been shipped north, the few planks to have survived happened to be in the yard where Hauptmann bought his lumber. It did not even prove that the maker of the ladder lived in the Bronx (though this was thought likely on other grounds). Any one of the National Lumber and Millworks' five hundred customers could have bought the yellow pine that made the kidnap ladder, or sold a couple of planks of it to the man who did. Yet not even this was certain, for the planks could also have been acquired from one of the other twenty-nine yards that had handled this particular lumber, in the Bronx, Brooklyn, New York and New Jersey. But few people were in a mind to appreciate this.

Then in quick succession came two more blows for Hauptmann. The first was the closet.

*   *   *

During the days following Hauptmann's arrest, his apartment on 222nd Street was the center of activity, not only for the police but for the press. In those days competition between newspapers was ruthless, and press and police were far more in each other's pockets than they are today. It was not unusual for newspapers to keep certain police officers on their payrolls in return for inside information for their chief reporters. One journalist so privileged was the *Daily News* reporter Tom Cassidy.

To steal a march on their competitors and produce a fresh lead for a long-running story, the press resorted to all sorts of dubious practices. One was to 'plant' bogus evidence at or near the scene of the crime, and then get a cameraman to take a picture of it. This had already happened twice, when Charlie's body was found near Hopewell. Sisk to Hoover: 'According to the newspapers some diapers were found near the body, but the State Police had conclusive proof that these were planted by a newspaper reporter. Also an old broken shovel was found there, but the State Police had a confession from a man who planted it and he admitted having received $5 from a New York reporter for making the plant.'

Tom Cassidy was one of the journalists given access to Hauptmann's apartment, and it was he who planted the 'evidence' there that began as a joke but was to have far-reaching effects. Either late on September 24 or on the morning of the 25th, while in the middle room of the Hauptmann apartment (Manfred's nursery), he opened the door of the closet near the window and high up at the back of it wrote in pencil Dr Condon's old address and telephone number ('2974 Decatur' and 'Sedgwick 3.7154') and on the jamb of the door '$500' and '1928', and the serial numbers of two dollar bills. He then smudged the writing as though an attempt had been made to wipe it out.

Three people who knew Cassidy confirmed that he had done this. Frank Fitzpatrick, a retired newspaperman, told the writer Anthony Scaduto in 1976, 'Tom Cassidy told me himself he wrote that in there. Hell, he bragged about it all over town. He even showed us how he wrote it.' Another old-time newspaperman, Russell Hopstatter, said to Scaduto, 'Sure, Cassidy wrote that phone number . . . he admitted that to me and Ellis Parker, he told everybody about it. He was sure Hauptmann was guilty so it didn't matter very much, that's how he felt about it.' And a report in the *Sunday Bulletin* of October 2, 1977 by Joe Sharkey quotes a former *Camden Courier-Post* reporter named Russell M. Stoddard as saying, 'He told a bunch of us he did it to get a new lead for the story the next day.'

Cassidy must have thought it unlikely that his jape would be taken seriously, for he knew that for the past five days every nook and cranny of the apartment had been examined exhaustively, and had the writing been there originally, it would have been discovered. Also, as Hauptmann had no telephone in his apartment, there would have been no point in his writing down Condon's telephone number, which was publicly listed, on the back of a closet door; while a check on the serial numbers would soon reveal they were not those of any of the ransom notes. He had however underestimated the prevailing climate of hysteria – the compulsion, even among those who should have known better, to latch on to any piece of evidence, however far-out and untested, that tended to incriminate Hauptmann.

Cassidy got word to the Bronx Police, and next morning they sent along their Inspector Bruckman, described by the FBI as 'evidently German, large, loud-spoken, easily excited and very brusque'. While accounts of searches of the apartment by officers like Bornmann, Wallace, Finn and Sisk were concise and direct ('Searched front room this a.m. Found two ledger books and photograph album, etc.'), Bruckman, in view of the tip-off, found it necessary to preface his report with a windy, half-apologetic preamble. 'As a result of a conference with Chief Inspector Sullivan . . . we felt there might be some possibilities in connection with a further search of the premises . . . the Assistant Chief Inspector authorized me to bring three police carpenters . . . to do such work in connection with the search as was deemed advisable.'

Why ask to bring police carpenters unless you know what you are bringing them for? Bruckman knew exactly why he was bringing them and what he was seeking, as this recorded telephone conversation between Agents Sisk and Wright shows.

SISK: 'Well, Mr Wright, do you remember telling me that Bruckman walked straight to that number as though he knew right where it was?'
WRIGHT: 'Well, he found it pretty quickly.'
SISK: 'He walked right up to it, I mean, as though he knew it was there and then made it known that he had found something . . .'
WRIGHT: '. . . he seemed to walk right into the room and hit directly for the closet where the number was found.'

Bruckman turned to those around him and said piously that this was a good example of the thoroughness of search; but he enjoined everyone to the strictest secrecy. In fact, said Wright, 'he even went so far as to tell me that if it became known he would hold me responsible.' What the explanation of this is, is hard to say; but it would seem likely that Cassidy had promised Bruckman a scoop for the Bronx Police in return for Bruckman giving Cassidy a scoop for his paper. Bruckman had the carpenters dismantle the door and jamb, then took them along to the District Attorney's Office where Foley announced that he would interrupt the Grand Jury proceedings to hear this fresh evidence.

Bruckman related what had happened, and stated categorically that the numbers on the jamb were serial numbers of the ransom bills. (Had Cassidy told him they were? Why hadn't he bothered to check?) Then it was Hauptmann's turn. It was unfortunate that his lawyer, Mr Fawcett, was not present, as he would have counselled silence. But having, he thought, nothing to fear, he saw no reason to refuse to answer questions that might clear him. As with the handwriting tests, he had no idea what he was up against.

Having been shown the jamb and the board with the writing, he was asked if the writing was his. If Hauptmann had been the kidnapper of the Lindbergh baby, if he had written the ransom notes and received the $50,000 from Dr Condon in St Raymond's Cemetery, he would either strenuously have denied that the writing was his or else kept silent. But who else but himself, he asked, would be scribbling things in pencil on the back of one of his bedroom closet doors? (The idea of a plant was as far beyond his own imagination as those of most other people.) Peering closely at the writing and saying he was unable to make it out (a great piece of acting, thought Foley), he was asked if it wasn't Condon's address and telephone number. 'I don't know,' he said. 'Why did you write it on the board?' Foley asked, and Hauptmann, knocking another nail into his coffin, replied, 'I must have read it in the paper about the story. I was a little bit interest, and keep a little record of it, and maybe I was just in the closet and was reading the paper and put down the address.' As he admitted later, it sounded a silly explanation even to him, but what other could there possibly be? Foley asked if he remembered what day he had written on the board, and he said No. 'You remember that you *did write it*?' asked Foley, and Hauptmann, giving himself the *coup de grace*, said: 'I must write it, the figures, that's my writing.'

For Foley, for the Grand Jury, for the three law enforcement agencies, indeed for the American people, here were the first glimmerings of the confession they had been waiting for during the past week, evidence that Hauptmann was the receiver of the ransom money and was at last admitting to it. Foley told the Grand Jury that this was 'conclusive evidence' that Hauptmann knew Condon at the time of the ransom negotiations (Condon changed his telephone number soon after), and that the extortion case against him was now complete.

When Fawcett heard what had happened, he told the press, 'I have told the defendant not to talk any further to anybody. He talked enough before I got into this case. He disobeyed that advice this morning before I got a chance to talk to him. When I saw him late this afternoon, I advised him again not to talk to the District Attorney.'

Bruckman returned to the Hauptmann apartment where, said Agent Wright, 'he invited every reporter and two news photographers into the house, spelled his name out for them, and explained the occurrences in detail.' History does not record whether Cassidy and his photographer were there, but the story duly appeared in the next edition of the paper.

And then came the second blow for Hauptmann: the discovery of the pistol and the remaining ransom money.

*   *   *

It was Detective Lewis Bornmann and his men who discovered the $840 and pistol in the holes bored for bits in the garage. He took them straight to the District Attorney's Office, where Foley had them put on a table and covered with newspaper. Then Hauptmann was called in.

'Richard,' said Foley, 'is there anything concealed in or about your apartment that you haven't told us about?'

'No,' said Hauptmann.

'Perhaps you didn't understand me,' said Foley. 'I will ask you again. Are there any things concealed in or about the premises connected with this case that you haven't told us about?'

'No.'

Foley pulled the newspaper off the wood containing the money and the gun. 'Well,' he said, 'how do you account for this?'

Later, looking back, Hauptmann said, 'I never felt so ashamed as I did at that moment.' He added, 'I know I did not speak the truth . . . but this was in order to avoid any charges about the pistol . . . this was the only reason for which I considered myself punishable.' When Foley announced this discovery to the press, he said that Hauptmann had declared that that was all that was left. 'But,' Foley added, 'he told us the same story after we found the first money last Thursday.'

At the end of that day, exactly one week after Hauptmann was arrested, the Bronx Grand Jury brought in a true bill against him for extortion, and Foley announced that, subject to any request from New Jersey for the extradition of Hauptmann on charges of murder and kidnapping, he would proceed to trial in two weeks' time.

If after Hauptmann's arrest there had been any doubts about his guilt (and there weren't), there were none now. The testimony of Perrone and the Osborns, the 'discovery' of the writing in the closet and now of the pistol and the rest of the ransom money, were for all Americans (except Mr Fawcett) conclusive and overwhelming proof of his guilt. Indeed, so concentrated was the national rage on Hauptmann and Hauptmann alone that few were any longer interested in who the rest of the gang might be. Hoover and Foley and Schwarzkopf hinted darkly that more arrests could be expected, but they knew that with Hauptmann silent and no evidence pointing elsewhere, this was no more than a pious hope.

The press, which had never been exactly reticent, now went overboard completely, not hesitating to print all sorts of allegations and rumors as fact. The worst offender was the Hearst Press who had it in for Hauptmann from the beginning and was to pursue him mercilessly until the bitter end. One Hearst paper, the *New York Journal*, claimed falsely that maps found in the Hauptmann apartment included those of the roads round Hopewell, that the chisel found on the lawn at Hopewell was the only one missing from a similar set in Hauptmann's tool-chest, that a 'canoeing' shoe of Hauptmann buried in his garage matched the footprint found beneath the nursery window at Hopewell, that the caliber of Hauptmann's pistol fitted a hole in the baby's head. But the *New York Times* was not far behind, with equally false stories that writing paper found in the Hauptmann apartment was the same as that used in the ransom notes, that ladder rungs found there were the same as those in the kidnap ladder, that the newspaper in which some of the ransom money had been wrapped was dated 1932, that Hauptmann had written to a man in a prison in Ohio saying he intended to kidnap the Lindbergh baby, that several people living near Hopewell had seen him there before.

No wonder that when the *Journal* picked out twelve men from the rush-hour crowd in Jersey City 'to act as Hauptmann's peers', they should have unanimously found him guilty both of extortion and kidnapping.

And when the US Attorney General, Homer S. Cummings, was asked as he passed through New York if he was satisfied that Hauptmann was the right man, he didn't say that that was for a jury to decide, but 'I didn't know that anyone doubted it.'

*   *   *

A last witness at the Bronx Grand Jury hearing was Colonel Lindbergh, who had arrived at Englewood the evening before after flying in with Anne from California. He had no evidence to give against Hauptmann as such; he had been called because of who he was, and to describe the evening when he had driven Condon to St Raymond's to hand over the ransom money. After he had recounted how he heard in the distance a man's voice calling out to Condon, 'Hey, Doc!', a juror asked Foley to ask him whether he thought he would recognize the man's voice if he heard it again. Lindbergh said he couldn't say positively. 'It would be very difficult for me to sit here and say that I could pick a man by that voice.' Asked if the man had a foreign voice, Lindbergh replied that he had 'a very distinct foreign accent' (though with only two syllables to guide him, it cannot have been all that distinct).

That Lindbergh hadn't completely dismissed the possibility of recognizing the voice obviously impressed Foley. Was it possible, he asked himself, that if Lindbergh was actually to hear Hauptmann shouting 'Hey, Doc!', he might recognize it as the voice in the cemetery? It was, he realized, one hell of a long shot, because he would be trying to recall two words said in the dark at a distance of 80 yards more than two years earlier – most would say a total impossibility. But at least it was worth a try, and what a coup if it came off! It would cook Hauptmann's goose more surely than anything.

He invited Lindbergh to come to his office next morning in disguise, and shortly after 9.30 the Colonel arrived, wearing a cap and dark glasses. He was taken to Foley's room and seated inconspicuously among a group of investigators. Then Hauptmann was brought in and the lives of the airman and the carpenter came together for the first time. Hauptmann was asked to walk up and down so that Lindbergh could try and figure out whether he resembled the man who had dropped the white handkerchief. Then he was asked to shout 'Hey, Doc!' in a variety of tones and strengths, and with no Fawcett there to tell him not to and once more believing it would help prove his innocence, he 'did not hesitate' (in Foley's words) to do so. Lindbergh did not say anything while Hauptmann was in the room, and Hauptmann did not know he was there. Later Foley issued a brief statement to say that at Lindbergh's request he had been confronted with the prisoner, but that the purpose of the visit and its outcome would not be disclosed by anyone present.

The outcome was not immediate. But a seed had been sown and, when it had ripened, its effect on Hauptmann would be devastating.

14

At this time too another seed was sown which, though longer in maturing, was to have an equally dramatic effect. It might be called the Bornmann-in-Wonderland story. It will be recalled (p. 145) that when Bornmann and Koehler were first studying the ladder in the spring of 1933, Koehler had given his opinion that Rail 16, of yellow pine, had probably come from an attic, barn, shop or warehouse. Since then Bornmann had kept this thought in the forefront of his mind, believing that when at last they found the guilty parties, there or thereabouts they would also find the wood from which Rail 16 had been taken. It was of course a fantasy idea, because although Rail 16 might well have been part of an attic, barn, shop or warehouse *originally*, it had almost certainly been fitted onto the ladder as a piece of discarded lumber.

Bornmann however could not get the fantasy out of his head. He and Koehler had been sweating up and down the lumber yards of the East Coast for eighteen months, and he knew as well as anyone how hollow were Koehler's claims that Rails 12 and 13 had come from the yard where Hauptmann bought his lumber. Were they not going to have anything to show for all their labours? He knew as a New Jersey policeman that whatever evidence New York might have against Hauptmann for extortion, New Jersey had absolutely none. If wood could be found on the Hauptmann premises from which it could be shown that Rail 16 had been taken, that would be a direct link between Hauptmann and Hopewell, evidence that he was not only the extortionist but the kidnapper and murderer as well.

So Bornmann, like some eager bloodhound, went sniffing around the Hauptmann premises. He had noticed that Hauptmann had built his garage of yellow pine, and a length of timber he was seen to have taken away on September 25 may well have been a plank from that. If so, it could not have matched Rail 16, for it is not referred to again. Where else to look? There was no shop, barn or warehouse here, but what about the attic?

The attic had already undergone a number of extensive searches in the six days since Hauptmann's arrest. It was a difficult place to get to, there being no stairway or ladder. The trap door into it was located in the roof of the passageway, opposite a linen-closet, and to reach it, the police officers had to remove the shelves from the linen-closet, climb up the closet on the cleats, push the trap door open and hoist themselves up by their arms. On September 19 it had been visited by Trooper Horn and half a dozen New York City detectives and FBI men. On the 20th two similar groups went through it, one in the morning, the other under Police Corporal Samuel Leon in the afternoon. On the 21st a fourth group visited it and on the 22nd Sergeant Zapolsky made a further inspection with three New Jersey State policemen and four New York City detectives. Between September 19 and September 25 a total of thirty-seven policemen and detectives made nine visits to the attic, and not one of them found anything remotely connected with the case.

On September 26 Bornmann decided to visit the attic himself, and at 9 a.m., according to his own report, he climbed up there with Detective Tobin, Superintendent Wilson and two carpenters. The flooring in the attic consisted of thirteen 20-foot lengths of yellow pine, the wood that Bornmann was looking for. But strangely his report makes no mention of it. 'Immediately proceeded to make a thorough search of the attic. Nothing of value was found,' is all he has to say. Yet visiting the attic for a second time that day he noticed what he failed to notice on the first visit – a similarity between the flooring and Rail 16. ' "Goodness, it looks familiar," I said to myself' (he told the author). 'When you've been looking for something for a year and then suddenly come across it, you get excited.' Why hadn't he been excited on the morning visit? It is when Bornmann states that on this second visit he noticed that an 8-foot section of one of the yellow pine planks was missing – which if true meant that it had gone unnoticed not only by himself in the morning but by thirty-seven other policemen in the week before that – that one begins to suspect that Bornmann is spinning a yarn. The missing plank, he theorized, had been used by Hauptmann to make Rail 16, and he says he ordered the carpenters to cut away a further section to see if it and Rail 16 matched. Or was the missing plank there when Bornmann paid his second visit, and did he at some later date have the carpenters take it up in order to fit Rail 16 into the vacant space?

  In his state of contrived euphoria it is unlikely that Bornmann considered the full absurdity of his thinking: that Hauptmann, in need of wood to make Rail 16, decided for some reason known only to himself not to obtain it from the lengths of wood he kept in the garage, not to obtain it from the yard where he obtained all his wood (and where according to Koehler he had already obtained the wood for Rails 12 and 13), but instead *had chosen to remove a plank from his landlord's flooring in the attic.* This meant an awkward and unnecessary journey heaving saws, chisels, nail-pullers, etc. up the cleats of the linen closet and through the trap door and then a tremendous effort to prise free the firmly nailed-down flooring. In addition the flooring was not 1- by 4-inch strips, as in Rails 12 and 13, but 1- by 6-inch tongue and groove, which meant he would then have had a further long sweat planing off the superfluous 2 inches. Why on earth would he want to do that?

  Aware perhaps on reflection that his theory was not quite as sound as it seemed, Bornmann was given authority and funds from New Jersey to take over personally the rent of the apartment. Trooper Englesteder was detailed to keep out any busybodies by day and a room was reserved for him (at $15 a week) at the Hotel Taft. Now Bornmann had the attic to himself.

                    *   *   *

In all of criminal history there can be few other cases where so much seemingly incriminating circumstantial evidence continued to pile up day after day; yet in which the more the police forces amassed, the more they felt they had to amass, subconsciously aware of the basic flimsiness of their case. There was a kind of desperation about some of the investigations they made. In Kamenz, Germany, Detective Johnson called on Hauptmann's old mother at No. 64 Bautzenerstrasse and, being told she was away visiting her other surviving son, Fritz, in Dresden, had the nerve to break in with the help of a locksmith and search the house from top to bottom in the quest of more ransom money. He also sought out Fritz Petzold, Hauptmann's former companion in delinquency, but Petzold, now a respectable citizen, got wind of his coming and fled.

In America J. Edgar Hoover suggested that Hauptmann might break down and confess if made to sit in his cell and copy out the ransom letters: no one thought to tell him that that was just what Hauptmann had been doing during the night of his arrest. Two police officers spent a frustrating day in the Hauptmann apartment searching for the instrument that had made the symbol on the ransom letters, while others had a merry time dismantling and blowing through bathroom pipes in search of more ransom money (which couldn't have been there if Hoover's and Genau's financial calculations had been correct). In the Bronx Jail Hauptmann had his ankles X-rayed for signs of a fracture caused by his falling off the kidnap ladder! And best of all, four 'alienists' (as psychiatrists were then called) spent a morning giving him the once-over to see if he were sane – a situation which, despite his predicament, he must have found quite entertaining. (Remarkably, they concluded he *was* sane which, in view of everything he had gone through, says much for his resilience.)

The fact was that the kind of hard evidence which the police, and particularly the New Jersey Police, were seeking and indeed expecting, had not materialized. A confession would have solved all their problems but, as the *New York Times* reported on September 29, 'he has resisted all the efforts of scores of questioners over the past week and a half to break him down, and it is now apparent that the authorities have virtually given up all hope of obtaining a confession'. Despite exhaustive fingerprinting (including joints and the palm of the hand) not one of his prints matched any latent prints that had been found on the ladder or at Hopewell (Captain Lamb asked wistfully if there was any way of counterfeiting fingerprints and seemed disappointed when told there wasn't[1]).

---

[1] Later Dr Hudson said that Trooper Kelly asked the same of him. (Scaduto, p. 383)
In 1981 it was revealed that in 1934 the FBI had found strong latent fingerprints on four

Hauptmann's shoes, size 9–9½, did not fit the footprint below the nursery window, nor the one in St Raymond's Cemetery. And other evidence was now emerging in his favor. A plumber called Miller came forward to confirm what Hauptmann had said about water having leaked into his kitchen closet and how he had been called in to deal with it; while chemical analysis of the ransom notes found in the garage combined with their musty odor showed they had recently been immersed in water, further confirmation of Hauptmann's story of the waterlogged shoe-box.

All this put the New Jersey authorities in something of a dilemma. As soon as the Bronx Grand Jury had returned their bill of indictment, it was expected that Governor Moore of New Jersey would apply at once for Hauptmann's extradition on charges of murder and kidnapping. But whereas the phoney evidence before the Bronx Grand Jury had related only to extortion in the Bronx, there was no evidence, phoney or otherwise, to connect Hauptmann with kidnapping in New Jersey. 'The New Jersey authorities,' Sisk telexed to Hoover, 'do not have one single reliable witness who can place Hauptmann in the vicinity of Hopewell prior to or on the date of the crime.' It does not seem to have even remotely occurred to the New Jersey authorities that one explanation for this might be that he had never been there; that while they had invented some reasons to show that he was the extortionist, there was no reason at all to think he was one of the kidnappers. But such thoughts were heresy. He *had* to be the sole kidnapper just as he *had* to be the sole extortionist.

Clinging to this belief like a baby to its nurse, Schwarzkopf issued a stream of statements to keep up his own and the public's expectations. On September 23: 'We now have sufficient evidence on kidnapping and murder to justify extradition.' They had none. On the 24th: 'We intend to charge him with kidnapping and murder' – yet asked by the press on what evidence, he refused to answer. On the 26th he scoffed at stories now frequently appearing in the papers that there were no eye-witnesses to place Hauptmann at Hopewell, and added that in any case the Osborns' testimony that he was the author of the first (nursery) ransom note was

---

of the ransom notes, and not only were these not Hauptmann's but they did not match those of any known criminal in the FBI's fingerprint files. It was this that led Agent Sisk to report on August 18, 1934 of the 'strong indications' that Cemetery John had no criminal record and had never been photographed. (*Hunterdon County Democrat*, Feb 5 and 19, 1981.)

enough. On October 5 he repeated this, adding for good measure the return of the baby's sleeping-suit, also allegedly sent in Hauptmann's hand. But he was whistling in the dark and knew it; and Governor Moore announced that he would not sign extradition request papers until the case against Hauptmann was 'iron-clad'.

But how to make it iron-clad? How to find a witness who would say he had seen Hauptmann near Hopewell? Well, if they couldn't find one, they would create one. And who more tailor-made for the role than Millard Whited?

*   *   *

Millard Whited was a 37-year-old hillbilly of the kind made familiar by the drawings of George Price, a long, lean, hollow-cheeked, cadaverous-looking man on whom one could say with assurance that fortune had never smiled. He had left school at eleven and could neither read nor write. He used old-time rustic phrases like 'I misspoke myself', 'I don't remember of saying', 'I memorized it down to heart' and 'I am not ashamed to tell my mind.' At the time of the Lindbergh kidnapping he lived on a small farm about a mile and a half from the Hopewell estate and worked as a woodcutter and wood trucker. With him lived his father, his brothers Howard and Ollie, his wife and four children. They were all extremely poor.

In the early hours of Wednesday March 2, 1932, Whited was woken by the barking of his dogs, and on opening the door found himself confronted by Colonel Lindbergh, Lieutenant Keaton, Trooper Wolfe and two other New Jersey policemen, desperately searching for Charlie and his kidnappers. Other troopers had been at the farm earlier the previous day inquiring about the whereabouts of a man in connection with a recent robbery, so Whited thought this nocturnal visit meant their suspicions had now fallen on him. But his fears were groundless. 'One of these men,' he said subsequently, 'questioned me as to how many children I had and if I saw any suspicious cars or persons around the last day or two. *I told them that I did not see anyone.* They asked me a few more questions about my neighbors and then they said goodnight and left.'

On April 26, some seven weeks later, Whited made a formal statement to Detectives Coar and Leon at Hopewell. It included (as well as the above) this extract:

Q   'Have you noticed any persons walking through the woods in the vicinity of the Lindbergh home before March 1st 1932 that acted in a suspicious manner?'
A   'No, I have not.'
Q   'Have you ever heard any one holding a conversation about the Lindbergh family or their baby?'
A   'No, I never did.'
Q   'Do you know where the Lindbergh baby is or who it's kidnappers are?'
A   'No.'
Q   'Is there any information you can give us that would assist us in this investigation, or help the police to recover the Lindbergh child?'

His answer was as unequivocal as Perrone's.

A   'No.'

In the light of this, it was difficult to see of what possible help Millard Whited could be. But Whited possessed, as it were, a secret weapon, one which only his neighbors and through them the New Jersey State Police knew about. It was this: he was very poor, thoroughly dishonest and a congenital liar. He owed money all over the neighborhood and he told lies as readily as most of us tell the truth. People in the Hopewell area who knew him, like William Diehl and George Lenz and William Whitehead, said his reputation in this field was legendary.

Since 1932 Whited had moved from the farm to a miserable little house in the main street of Lambertville, New Jersey, where he lived as a logger with his father, wife and now five children; and it was here that the police caught up with him early in October 1934. Schwartzkopf was taking a big risk in enlisting Whited, but he knew that unless he made the attempt, unless some person or other could be persuaded to place Hauptmann near Hopewell, the case against him would collapse. There is naturally no record of what was put to Whited and by whom, but it later became known that in return for identifying Hauptmann he was promised $150, $35 a day expenses and a share of the reward money.

On October 6, after being shown a photograph of Hauptmann, Whited was taken by Captain Lamb in a New Jersey Police car to the Bronx County Jail where a line-up had been arranged; and here Whited 'positively identified Hauptmann as the man he had seen twice in the vicinity of the Lindbergh estate'. The Bronx District Attorney's Office described Whited, presumably on the word of Captain Lamb, as 'a thoroughly honest man and reliable witness' which must have raised a horse-laugh back in Hopewell, and Schwarzkopf said that his identification would 'greatly strengthen' the case against Hauptmann, knowing that without it he had no case at all.

In two further statements Schwarzkopf showed a capacity for fibbing which even Whited might have envied. On the night of the kidnapping, he said, Whited had told the police that he had recently twice seen a man coming out of the bushes near the Lindbergh estate and had given a description of him that matched that of Hauptmann! Then, excelling himself in falsehood, he said, 'He is a poor man who is absolutely upright and honest. He is one of the witnesses we have kept "on ice" without anyone knowing about them.' It was astonishing the good Lord did not strike him dead. HAL

Naturally newspapermen wanted to interview this unexpected star witness but, anticipating that once Whited opened his mouth he would blow the gaff, the New Jersey Police told them that in return for coming to the Bronx to identify Hauptmann, Whited had been given an assurance that he would not have to answer reporters' questions. So the *New York Times* settled for the next best thing, which was to send a man down to Lambertville to interview his family. Here he found Whited's father, wife and five children ranging from fourteen years to two months 'living in very poor circumstances in a small and barely furnished house'. The family were at table when the reporter arrived and he observed that all they had to eat was soup containing pieces of broken bread. But father and wife were keen to talk, and in doing so showed that lies ran in the family.

'My husband is a truthful man,' said Mrs Whited, quite unprompted.

'That's right,' the father chimed in, 'he's never been known to tell a lie.'

Normally the press, trained professionally to disbelieve, would have been the first to voice doubts about such a heaven-sent witness, suddenly appearing when most needed and then heavily protected by the police from questioning. Yet most seem to have accepted the situation as presented to them, either in the belief that it would be unpatriotic to do otherwise or because they were as hallucinated as everyone else. One reporter however did ask Schwarzkopf if it were true that Whited had previously denied that he had ever seen anyone suspicious near the Lindbergh home.

It was fortunate that the Colonel was not wired up to a lie detector machine. 'There are no contradictions in his stories to us,' he said.

An embargo on reporters didn't stop cameramen and stills photographers descending on Lambertville, where the next day (Sunday) they found state troopers maintaining a 24-hour watch on Whited's house[1] and a stream of cars crawling past it, 'their occupants staring at the humble dwelling'. At first, said the *Times* man, Whited refused to have anything to do with the cameramen, 'then under the stress of financial considerations he changed his mind', and posed with his family in the backyard. One way and another Whited's betrayal of Hauptmann was proving quite lucrative.

Knowing that they could not keep Whited under wraps indefinitely, and that every day that passed increased the risk of the press rumbling him, the New Jersey authorities moved fast. Next day the Attorney General of the state, a young, ambitious lawyer by the name of David Wilentz, moved for a bill of indictment against Hauptmann on a charge of murder, and on the Monday following Whited's Saturday identification the Hunterdon County Grand Jury was convened in Flemington, New Jersey, to hear it. The charge of kidnapping had been dropped because, explained the Assistant Attorney General, Joseph Lanigan, it was not at that time a crime punishable by death. However, a killing committed in the course of a felony was so punishable, and the felony in this case was, in the words of Justice Trenchard to the jury, 'stealing the infant son in its clothing'.

The principal witnesses were of course Whited with his specially coached story of seeing Hauptmann in the bushes, the two Osborns, Cecile Barr the cinema cashier, a Princeton student called Lupica who claimed to have seen a man driving a 1928 Dodge containing a ladder near the Lindbergh estate on the day of the crime, but whose testimony both Schwarzkopf and the FBI had long regarded as worthless, Frank Wilson of the US Treasury to fantasize about Hauptmann's accounts, Koehler with his story about Rails 12 and 13 coming from the White Plains Road lumber yard (and which the FBI privately called 'fabricated evidence') and various police officers and FBI men.

There was also Lindbergh. At first it had been denied that

---

[1] To prevent reporters reaching him, state troopers also guarded him at work in the woods. (Harold Hoffmann: *Liberty Magazine*)

Lindbergh would testify, but at the last moment Schwarzkopf announced that he would. Ever since the Colonel's visit to the Bronx, Schwarzkopf and his men had been working on Lindbergh. They had told him, as they had told Perrone and the Osborns and Cecile Barr and Millard Whited, that Hauptmann was the right man, there was not the slightest, smallest conceivable doubt about it. Schwarzkopf knew that if Lindbergh could be persuaded to testify that the voice he heard shouting 'Hey, Doc!' in St Raymond's Cemetery was that of Hauptmann, it would have a more powerful effect on the jury than any other single witness. We can only speculate on the reasons that persuaded Lindbergh to change his testimony from that in the Bronx: partly Schwarzkopf's blandishments, partly no doubt his recent experience in hearing and watching Hauptmann shouting 'Hey, Doc!' in Foley's office, which must have set up painful echoes of that other voice he had heard so long ago. Whatever the reasons, he took the stand and gave evidence that the voice he had heard in St Raymond's was that of Richard Hauptmann.[1] From that moment Hauptmann was doomed.

It was a shameful thing to do, and did not pass unnoticed. Assistant Attorney General Lanigan smiled when he heard it, Agent Turrou thought it 'remarkable' that it had not been accompanied by any expression of doubt and Hoover in an internal memo was highly skeptical of it.[2] For, as Lindbergh himself had suggested in the Bronx, how could he say with any conviction that a voice he might hear now was the same as the one he had heard in the dark at 80 yards' distance two and a half years before? Even if the day after the incident at St Raymond's he had heard Hauptmann and half a dozen other Bronx Germans shouting 'Hey, Doc!' in succession, it is highly unlikely he could have distinguished one from the other. What was it he had written at the time of his trans-Atlantic flight in defence of the dismissive way in which he treated the popular press? 'Accuracy means something to me. It's vital to my sense of values. I've learned not to trust people who are inaccurate. Every aviator knows that if mechanics are inaccurate, aircraft crash. If pilots are inaccurate, they get lost – sometimes killed. In my profession life itself depends on accuracy.'[3]

Was accuracy less vital because the life at stake now was not his

[1] Lindbergh, said Foley, 'based his decision on a lot of other evidence besides the prisoner's voice,' which, it being hearsay, he had no business to do.

[2] Hoover to Tamm, October 9 1934.

[3] See page 24.

own but that of the man in the dock? Was his sense of values to be discarded when applied to someone else? For millions of lesser mortals Lindbergh stood as the epitome of manly virtues, courage certainly but also truth, and when the world came to hear his evidence about the voice, they believed it to be the truth. Yet it was an untruth – not a deliberate lie like those that Schwartzkopf told, but an untruth. The man who was supposed to be – and in some ways had set himself – above the common herd, had shown himself no better than the common herd. He of all people might have been expected to stand apart from the current stampede. Instead he had made himself part of it.

At 4 p.m. that day, after sitting for four and a half hours, the Hunterdon Grand Jury returned a bill of indictment against Hauptmann for murder.

The following day, if we are to believe Bornmann, Koehler showed up at 222nd Street with Rail 16 and, having obtained admittance from Watchdog Englesteder guarding the front door and negotiated the perils of the linen-closet and the trap door, joined Bornmann in the attic.

They took Rail 16 to where some of the flooring had been removed and laid it across the joists; by some deft pulling and pushing and by ignoring some rather awkward gaps that separated Rail 16 from the rest of the flooring, they claimed to have proved two things: that the nail holes in Rail 16 matched (if you forgot about the gaps) the nail holes in the joists, and that part of a knot in Rail 16 was a continuation (or would have been but for another gap!) of a knot in the flooring; and therefore, hey presto, this was where Rail 16 had originally been!

In reaching this preposterous theory they had conveniently over-looked several things: that when Koehler had first examined Rail 16 in 1933 (see page 145) he had declared that the spacing between the nail holes gave no indication of where it had been (had it ever been part of a flooring, Koehler would have recognized it instantly, for the spaces between the joists are 16 inch standard); that he had also declared that if Rail 16 had been prised from a floor, there would have been marks on it from the nailheads as it came loose, which there weren't; and that although he had stated in his 1933 report that the face of Rail 16 had been machine-planed, *it was still thicker* than the attic flooring by one sixteenth of an inch, which was impossible.

If their theory had had any substance to it, it would of course have been conclusive proof – as good as a set of fingerprints – that Hauptmann had been actively involved in the kidnapping of Charlie; and had these two jokers had any faith in themselves, they would have been eager to proclaim it to the world. But they knew it for what it was, and reckoned that for the time being, and so long as the faithful Englesteder was there to shoo others away (particularly the skeptical FBI) they had better keep it to themselves. Maybe it would come in handy later.

* * *

That same day, in Trenton, New Jersey, Governor Moore signed the extradition warrant against Hauptmann, and at seven that evening David Wilentz, accompanied by Foley, Lanigan, Captain Lamb and others, delivered it personally to Governor Herbert Lehman of New York in Manhattan. Next day in Albany, Lehman signed an order authorizing Hauptmann's removal to New Jersey, whereupon his defense lawyer James Fawcett issued a writ of *habeas corpus*. Asked if, should the writ fail and Hauptmann be sent to New Jersey to answer a murder charge, he would dismiss the case for extortion, Foley replied in his breezy way, 'Sure I'll dismiss it after New Jersey has electrocuted him.'

The hearing of the writ took place in the Bronx Supreme Court the following Monday, October 15, with the Honorable Justice Ernest Hammer presiding, and David Wilentz about to embark on his first murder case as Attorney General for New Jersey. The onus was on Hauptmann, as the applicant or 'relator', to prove that he was not in New Jersey but elsewhere on the night of March 1 1932. Knowing what harm his client did himself under questioning Fawcett had not planned to put him on the stand, but Hauptmann, eager as ever to clear himself, insisted.

In preparing his case Fawcett had one setback in that his plea to Judge Henry Stackell to be shown the minutes of the Bronx Grand Jury that had indicted Hauptmann for extortion had been rejected (Grand Jury indictment proceedings, it will be recalled, are held *in camera*). This was a gross denial of justice, for it meant that Fawcett had to go into court with one hand tied behind his back. However he had one trump card, at which he had hinted to the press on the day of the hearing at Flemington. 'We shall bring witnesses to prove that Hauptmann was not in New Jersey on March 1st,' he had said. Asked to elaborate, he refused, so as not to forewarn the prosecution.

The trump card was that he had obtained evidence from the Reliance Property Management Company that Hauptmann had worked at the Majestic Apartments on March 1, and he had subpoenaed their timekeeper, Edward F. Morton, to appear with his timesheets to affirm it. Morton was to be the first witness; but when the court had assembled and the court attendant called his name there was no response. Fawcett proceeded with another witness, then again called for Morton, but again there was no response. Fawcett couldn't understand it. The man had been subpoenaed and was therefore obliged, under contempt of court, to appear.

What seems to have happened was this. Soon after Fawcett had discovered that Hauptmann's name was on the timesheets and payroll records for the first half of March 1932, the District Attorney's office had discovered the same thing. Both these records, so highly damaging to the prosecution's case, together with the payroll records for *the last half of February 1932 – which must also have included Hauptmann's name –*.were then hastily removed. The payroll records were put under lock and key in the Office of the Assistant District Attorney, Mr Breslin, where they remained until October 29 when Breslin handed them to Detective Cashman of the New York City Police; Cashman's receipt for the payroll records will be found on page 223. The timesheets, according to David Wilentz, came into the possession of the police even earlier. It is inconceivable that Mr Wilentz, who was working in close co-operation with Foley and his staff, did not know the contents of both the timesheets and the payroll records, and know that if ever they saw the light of day, they would virtually clear Hauptmann.

Mr Morton therefore did not appear because the timesheets on which he was relying for his evidence had been removed; and in his place the Reliance Property Management Company sent along their assistant treasurer, Howard Knapp, not with the records for the *first* half of March which was what mattered, but with the altered and quite irrelevant payroll records for the *second* half (see page 188). He claimed that these showed that Hauptmann had not started work at the Majestic until March 21, and in support of this Wilentz produced a check for $36.67 dated March 31 1932, paid to Hauptmann by the Reliance Property Management for eleven days' work between March 21 and March 31, and with Hauptmann's signature of endorsement on the back. It would seem therefore that unless the checks were faked as the timesheets were,

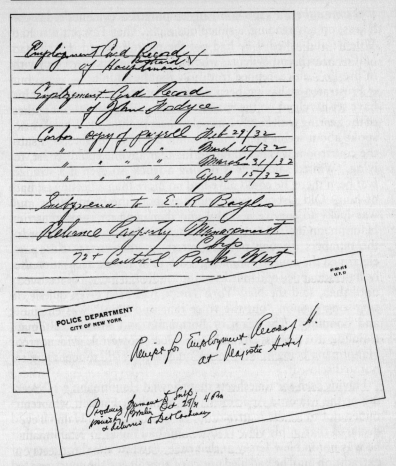

Detective Cashman's 'Receipt for the Employment Records of H [Hauptmann] at Majestic Hotel' listing 'Carbon copy of payroll Feb 29/32, March 15/32, March 31/32 and April 15/32'.

Hauptmann *was* away sick between March 16 and 21 and *had* only been paid for eleven days' work.

That the Reliance Company and Mr Knapp had gone along with the prosecuting authorities is clear from other evidence of Mr Knapp. Asked by Mr Fawcett where the records were for the first half of March, he gave a reply that put him in the same league as Whited and Schwarzkopf. 'Our records,' he said, 'do not indicate that any such records exist at this time,' then added lamely, '*or at that time either.*' As this company employed over a hundred people it was, on any reading, a ridiculous reply. Then Fawcett turned to Wilentz and asked if *he* had got the payroll records for the first half of March and Wilentz, who must also have known they were in Breslin's office, replied truthfully that he hadn't.

Frustrated at having been deprived of the evidence that might have set his client on the road to freedom, Fawcett sat out the rest of the hearing with barely concealed disappointment. When Whited spoke about seeing Hauptmann come out of the bushes, a voice in the courtroom was heard muttering that anyone could see he was lying. (Whited said he was driving a truck, so even if a stranger *had* been there, he could have had no more than a fleeting glimpse of him.) Old Osborn gave evidence about the handwriting, and was lucky to survive a skilful and damaging cross-examination. Hauptmann did his case no good by again claiming authorship of the numbers (though not the letters) in the nursery closet, yet electrified the court by shouting 'No!' to Wilentz's accusation that he had kidnapped and murdered the Lindbergh baby. His testimony until then, said the *New York Times*, had been given quietly, in sing-song fashion, 'but the voice that said "No!" was emphatic and booming'. The team of Bornmann and Koehler, although claiming to possess by far the most powerful evidence for Hauptmann being in New Jersey on March 1, still thought it wiser not to disclose it.

Having seen the timesheets that showed Hauptmann was working at the Majestic Apartments on March 1, Fawcett was determined not to let the matter drop. As soon as Justice Hammer had declared that in his view Hauptmann had failed to establish that he was not in New Jersey at that time, Fawcett asked for a stay of extradition until he had filed notice of appeal; and the court granted him forty-eight hours.

In the event it was not he who found the vital evidence he needed, but Tom Cassidy of the *Daily News*, the same Tom Cassidy who had been responsible for the writing in the nursery closet. It will be recalled that the superintendent who had taken Hauptmann on at the Majestic on February 27, 1932 was called Joseph Furcht, but that when questioned at Greenwich Street after his arrest, Hauptmann could not remember his name, nor that of E. V. C. Pescia of the Reliant Employment Agency who had sent him there. However Mr Knapp in his testimony had mentioned Furcht as the official responsible for the payroll records during the first half of

1932, and Cassidy, sniffing another good lead, immediately set about locating him.

Furcht worked for the Department of Public Welfare on Eighth Avenue and two days later, having just finished his lunch in the cafeteria, he saw Tom Cassidy bearing down on him.

Cassidy asked me if I was the Superintendent of the Majestic Apartments around March 1st 1932, and I said 'Yes'. He then asked me if I had any records and I said 'No'. . . Cassidy then told me that there were no records showing the employment agency which sent Hauptmann. I told him what the agency was and suggested that we go to the agency and get their records. We left the office about 2 p.m. and went to the E. V. C. Pescia Employment Agency, 779 Sixth Avenue, and there interviewed Mr Pescia. Pescia then presented the records to us . . . which clearly brought out the fact that Bruno Richard Hauptmann worked for me on March 1st 1932 . . .

At eight o'clock on the morning of that day Bruno Richard Hauptmann and Gus Kassens reported for work . . . and worked throughout that entire day until 5 p.m.; subsequent thereto they worked there the 2nd, 3rd, and 4th days of March 1932 from eight o'clock in the morning until 5 p.m. in the afternoon.[1]

With this information Cassidy took Furcht to the offices of the *Daily News* where he was interviewed by someone on the staff, and a photographer was despatched to Pescia's office to take a picture of the records. Next day Furcht informed Fawcett of his findings and also signed an affidavit before a notary public. At the end of the affidavit he wrote – and this is significant: '*Annexed hereto, and made a part of this affidavit, is a photostatic copy of the record of E. V. C. Pescia.*' [Author's italics]

Another photostat copy found its way to the Bronx District Attorney's Office where Foley and Wilentz, now deeply worried, saw the whole case against Hauptmann beginning to slide from under them. In a statement Foley said he had never heard of Furcht and Pescia before, showing how poorly his staff had done their homework. He was forced to admit that Hauptmann had worked at the Majestic Apartments on March 1 but added – in order to create time for Hauptmann to have reached Hopewell without rushing it – that he believed he quit work at 1 p.m. He gave no evidence to support this, and it was Hauptmann's first full day at work.

[1] Affidavit of Joseph Furcht.

Wilentz, equally disturbed, issued a statement saying he wasn't disturbed and, to lift his morale, brazenly declared that even if the statements of Furcht and Pescia had been before Justice Hammer, they would not have affected the outcome of the proceedings (he could have been right – in the prevailing climate of hysteria anything was possible). Indeed, so rattled was he that on returning to Trenton he issued a further statement in which he too admitted that Hauptmann had been employed at the Majestic Apartments on March 1 'but did not put in a full day's work'. He added, 'The police know that because they have the timecard record of the Majestic Apartments.' They certainly had, and no defense lawyer or nosey journalist who might upset the apple-cart was going to be allowed a peep at them. He went rambling on about records being a lot more definite that statements based on memory. Yet Pescia's statement was not based on memory but records, and the timesheet records in the hands of the police would have confirmed it. Later still, when reports that the police had been tampering with the payroll records were appearing in the press, Wilentz issued another statement that he was convinced this was untrue. 'The police at no time had possession of the payroll,' he claimed, but page 223 shows the police receipt for the payroll.

Next day, October 19, was the deadline for Fawcett's appeal, and in the Bronx Appeal Court he sought leave to bring Furcht and Pescia with Pescia's records before Justice Hammer for a presentation of fresh evidence. He added that he had subpoenaed the Reliant Company for their records before March 15 1932, 'but had been informed they had disappeared' (which must have given Wilentz and Foley a quiet laugh). The five judges of the Appeal Court turned down the proposal. The new evidence was in conflict with evidence already heard, they said, and issues of fact should await the trial of the action: the writ of *habeas corpus* would be dismissed.

Often in criminal proceedings when it is discovered that new evidence is likely to challenge the prosecution's case, certain things are found to happen: embarrassing documents disappear; new witnesses are discovered to counter the defense witnesses; and existing witnesses for the defense are persuaded (by various methods) to go back on their earlier statements.

In this case all three of these things happened. All copies of Pescia's records (and maybe the originals as well) mysteriously 'disappeared'; they have not been seen from that day to this. Gus

Kassens, the carpenter whom Furcht had engaged at the same time as Hauptmann, was run to earth and persuaded to sign an affidavit that Hauptmann 'had not started work until several weeks after March 1st' – though why any credence should have been placed on the memory of a man who had only met Hauptmann briefly two and a half years before, is hard to tell. (When Wilentz read it, did he remember what he had said about records being more reliable than memories?)

And then there was Joseph Furcht who, until now, had seemed so confident about the hours that Hauptmann had worked, who had told Fawcett (who had told Hauptmann) that he would take the stand for him at Flemington – he too was broken. What caused him to change his mind – threats or bribes or a call to duty – we shall never know, but on October 23, in the Office of the District Attorney, he went back on almost everything he had said.

> I wish to state that I do not know whether or not Bruno Richard Hauptmann worked on March 1st, 1932 at the Majestic Apartments . . . I have heard an affidavit given by Gustav Kassens[1] that Hauptmann did not work on March 1st but at a later date . . . I believe Mr Kassens as I know that he was always honest when he worked for me . . . If I knew at the time that I made the statement to the *Daily News* people what I know now, I never would have made that statement, but I would have stated that he did not work on March 1st at the Majestic Apartments.

It was a pathetic climb-down and when he read it through Furcht must have thought so himself, for right at the end he wrote,

> If the payroll from March 1st to March 15th 1932 does not contain the name of Bruno Richard Hauptmann for that period, and if the payroll is signed by me, then Hauptmann did not work on March 1st 1932.

He knew well enough that Hauptmann's name did appear in the payroll record for March 1 to 15, and that he had signed it himself. By lobbing the ball back into the prosecution's court, by challenging them to go and check the record for themselves, he had salvaged a little of his self-respect.

On conclusion of the *habeas corpus* proceedings on the evening of October 19, Hauptmann was put into a New Jersey Police car between Captain Lamb and Lieutenant Keaton, and with an escort

---

[1] His name was August Kassens.

of New York and New Jersey Police cars and a posse of motor-cycle outriders with sirens screaming, set out for Flemington. At the George Washington Bridge over the Hudson, which divides the two states, the New York Police cars turned back. As they crossed the river not far from Hoboken, did Hauptmann think back to the time he had stepped ashore there ten years before, his heart so full of hope, thanking God he had finally arrived? The convoy continued south by way of Jersey City, North Branch and Whitehouse. At Flemington meanwhile (said the *New York Times*),

> A crowd of about 1000 persons gathered round the jail after the news of Hauptmann's departure from New York became known and waited until he arrived. Twenty New Jersey state troopers helped Flemington's lone policeman keep the crowd in order, but there was no demonstration. The crowd watched silently in the glare of white flares which they held aloft or fixed on posts.
>
> Sheriff John H. Curtiss and Warden Harry O. Macrea received the prisoner and took over his papers from Attorney General Wilentz and Captain Lamb. He was searched and nothing was found in his possession. Hauptmann asked for cigarettes and Captain Lamb gave him a package. Then he was led away to Cell 1, up one flight, in the left wing of the jail.
>
> The warden ordered three guards on duty at all times, one at the cell door, one at the foot of the stairway and another at the warden's door near the stairway. Twelve state troopers were put on duty outside the jail for the night.

A few days later Special Agent Sisk came down to Trenton and reported to Schwarzkopf who (according to Sisk's report to Hoover) said to him: 'I wish you would convey to Mr Hoover my thanks for sending someone [i.e. Sisk] down here so quickly. We don't want to leave a stone unturned to convict this fellow now we've got him down here. I think your department ought to know that Colonel Lindbergh and the Morrow family are tickled to death about the arrest of Hauptmann. They are positive he is the right man, and they think that your department, the New York Police and all of us did a swell job.' Schwarzkopf then took Sisk across the street to meet Wilentz who 'said it was his intention to leave no stone unturned in his efforts to send Hauptmann to the electric chair. He said it would be a terrible thing if he were acquitted.'

In New York meanwhile Anna Hauptmann issued a statement saying she intended to fight on, as she knew her husband was innocent, and that she would soon come to live in Flemington with her baby. Later she made arrangements for them to stay in the house of a Mr and Mrs Eugene Latourette on Main Street, half a mile from the courtroom and jail: she would look after the baby and wash all their clothes, but meals would be provided.

On October 24 Hauptmann was led for the first time into the little courtroom he was later to know so well. He was wearing a freshly pressed gray suit and dark tie and was clean-shaven. Justice Trenchard took his seat on the bench.

'How do you plead?' Hauptmann was asked.

'Not guilty,' he replied in a firm voice.

The trial was set for January 2, 1935.

PART SIX

THE PROSECUTORS

'O judgment! thou art fled to brutish beasts,
And men have lost their reason.'

(Shakespeare. *Julius Caesar*.)

15

No one who visits Cell No. 1 in Flemington Jail and contemplates the thought of living in it for months at a time, can do so without a sense of shock and even disbelief; and it is good news that the block in which it is housed is soon to go out of use. Cell 1 is the first in a series of five adjoining cells, *each of which measures only 6½ by 5 feet* – the average dimensions of a railway couchette. Into this can be crammed a washbasin and lavatory set into the wall at the far end, a bed, a folding table and chair. Outside the vertical bars that front the five cells, and protected by a further parallel line of vertical bars, runs a narrow corridor or bull-pen, measuring about 25 by 5 feet, in which prisoners are sometimes allowed to mingle and take exercise. During Hauptmann's four months in Flemington the other four cells were empty, so he had the run of the bull-pen to himself.

But if he thought he was going to have some respite from his ordeal until the date set for the trial, he was in for an unpleasant surprise; for the New Jersey authorities were still determined to prise from him the 'confession' he had so far failed to give. They could not understand how a man so patently guilty – who had been caught with the ransom money hidden on his premises and had then tried to lie his way out of it – could withold a confession for so long. They found it puzzling, frustrating and a cause of some unease.

So, on top of the oppressiveness of the cell, they instituted for Hauptmann a regimen even more oppressive. Night and day they kept a bright light burning in the cell. Night and day he was watched by a detail of three guards under the command of Lieutenant A. L. Smith. When he slept he was obliged to keep his face and arms outside the blankets; when in his sleep he covered them, he was woken and told to take them out. To harass him further he and his tiny cell were searched *up to thirty times a day*. The three guards on duty were all forbidden to speak with him. To forestall suicide, they took away his tie, belt and shoe-laces (so that, as Oscar Wilde wrote, 'he might not rob the prison of its prey'). He was allowed no mail of any kind, and for the first few days no books – not even the Bible given him by the Little House Mission in the Bronx. From the time he rose in the morning through the fourteen or fifteen hours until he went to bed, there was nothing for him to do but sit on his bed and stare at the wall, or pace up and down the bull-pen like the caged animal he was. 'That whole time,' he said later, 'was a struggle against insanity.'

The treatment was deliberate, for police and military authorities the world over know that to isolate a man from his fellows is one of the most effective ways of getting him to talk, so desperate is the desire for human communication. A guilty Hauptmann would surely have talked long ago. As it was, his only response was to indulge in bouts of weeping. This also should have been a pointer, if those in charge of him had had eyes to see. For prolonged weeping is less a sign of guilt or even remorse than of grief arising from personal loss; the death of a near one, having to leave a much loved house, in Hauptmann's case the unexpected and now prolonged deprivation of liberty; desperation too at being unable to convince his jailers of the truth.

In Trenton meanwhile, thirty miles away, Attorney General David Wilentz and his staff were preparing the case for the prosecution. Wilentz was then thirty-nine, of Russian Jewish parentage, looking a little like George Raft, a little like Ben Gazzara. His appointment as Attorney General the year before had been a reward from Governor Harry Moore for persuading the electors of traditionally Republican Middlesex County to vote Democrat. Wilentz was a flashy dresser, sported an off-white felt hat, a velvet collared Chesterfield coat and a white silk scarf – more in keeping with Broadway, said one commentator, than with the Burlington Arcade. After war service in France, Wilentz had graduated from New York University Law School.

Looking at the evidence now before him Wilentz appreciated

there were still many obstacles to be overcome for, as the celebrated criminal lawyer Clarence Darrow said in an interview in Atlantic City, New Jersey's case against Hauptmann was anything but strong. 'I haven't seen anything there to indicate murder, have you?' he asked. 'Just the fact that Hauptmann had the ransom money on him doesn't prove that he had anything to do with the murder.' Darrow, being who he was, had the authority and standing to voice what others were thinking but lacked the courage to say.

Wilentz's major obstacle had been the evidence from Pescia's employment records that Hauptmann had worked at the Majestic Apartments on the day of the kidnapping. But with the documents to prove this either destroyed or locked away in police headquarters in New York, and with Furcht's recent recantation, they could now rely on the pay checks and altered timesheets showing that Hauptmann had first started work on March 21 (a strange action for a man who had just kidnapped and murdered a baby and expected shortly to collect $50,000 ransom money). The assistant prosecutor Anthony M. Hauck lied publicly when he claimed that he had more than fifty witnesses to prove that Hauptmann was not working at the Majestic on March 1.

Next in unreliability came Millard Whited, already, thanks to Hopewell old-timers, a somewhat discredited figure, and now made more so by a statement from his brother. Edward Whited said that he and Millard had been constantly together during the month before the kidnapping, and that not only had neither of them seen any strangers but that Millard had never said that he had; when taken to police headquarters for further questioning, he resolutely stuck to his story. It was obvious that the state would have to find other witnesses to place Hauptmann in New Jersey at the time of the kidnapping and that if the worse came to the worst and they failed, they might have to fall back on Bornmann's and Koehler's fantasies about Rail 16 of the ladder coming from Hauptmann's attic. Rumours about this so-called discovery had been gathering week by week, but the state realized that if they admitted to it prematurely, there was a likelihood of it being investigated and dismissed for the nonsense it was. With luck they might never have to use it, so why admit its existence? On December 8, in a joint statement, Wilentz and Koehler 'emphatically denied' that any wood from the ladder had been traced to Hauptmann's home. 'There is absolutely no truth in the matter at all,' said Koehler which, in view of his claim to have fitted Rail 16 to the attic floor with Bornmann just two months earlier, made him as much of a liar as Whited, Hauck and Schwarzkopf. Hauptmann, when told the story by Anna, was equally dismissive, indeed burst out laughing. 'It's nonsense,' Lieutenant Smith reported him as saying to Anna. 'Impossible!'

However, as the *New York Times* pointed out, the state's most crucial witness was Condon. Perrone and Whited claimed only fleeting glimpses of whoever they saw, but Condon had met one of the kidnap gang twice and on the first occasion had talked with him for an hour. If Condon failed to identify Hauptmann a second time, then the case against him must collapse.

Because of this, the police kept up an intense pressure on Condon. Agent Turrou informed Sisk that there had been constant police harassment and insinuations about his character ever since his failure at Greenwich Street to identify Hauptmann as Cemetery John. The psychiatrist Dr Dudley Shoenfeld, who was working closely with the New York Police, went further and wrote of intimidations to which Condon had been subjected, threats that if he failed to identify Hauptmann a second time he would be arrested and indicted for receiving part of the ransom money.[1] The police had the old man over a barrel, and he knew it.

There was also pressure on Condon from a different source. Lindbergh had already declared that the voice he heard shouting 'Hey, Doc!' in St Raymond's Cemetery was that of Hauptmann; yet he had not even seen the man. What would people say, *what would Lindbergh say*, if he, Condon, continued to drag his feet, refused to support his hero's unequivocal statement that Hauptmann was Cemetery John?

In the end he cracked. His wife, fearful that the police might take him away at any time, was heading for a nervous breakdown, and despite his unctuous moralizing he was not of the stuff of which heroes are made. Although he had no more reason now to think that Hauptmann was Cemetery John than when he had declared as much in Greenwich Street, he nevertheless made an appointment to see Wilentz at his home at Perth Amboy on the evening of October 23, the day of Hauptmann's arraignment. There, to Wilentz's surprise and delight, he told him that he would testify at the trial that Hauptmann was the man to whom he had handed

---

[1] *The Crime and the Criminal*, p. 391

the ransom money. It was as deplorable a commitment as Lindbergh's, and no less excusable. To ease his conscience he made two requests. The first was that until he gave evidence Wilentz would keep secret his sudden change of mind (no doubt he reckoned he could live with his intended perjury as long as only he knew of it, but it would be harder once it became the property of the world). The second was that he be permitted to have another meeting with Hauptmann. Because he had failed to identify Hauptmann as Cemetery John did not mean that Hauptmann was not Cemetery John. There was still an outside chance that Hauptmann might admit to meeting him in the two cemeteries. Furthermore, if Hauptmann did admit to receiving the ransom money, it would confirm that he, Condon, had not received a cent of it. Both requests Wilentz was only too ready to grant.

The meeting took place in the jail the following afternoon with Wilentz, Hauck and Schwarzkopf as witnesses in case Condon should somehow attempt to double-cross them. There are three accounts of what was said, all suspect: the memoirs of Condon and Hauptmann naturally favor their authors, while the report of Trooper Stockburger, a guard detailed to monitor the conversation, does not include anything he thought might offend his superiors. All three agreed that Condon made references to police harassment. In the Stockburger report Condon says the police called him 'whacky and screwy' and he spoke of his wife crying every day. In his own memoirs Condon says he told Hauptmann that he had been 'hounded, treated like a criminal, accused'; while Hauptmann's account says: 'He told me he was suspected by the police of having something to do with the crime. He told me that he had been very roughly treated by the police . . . he asked me if I would do what I could to help him out of the mess he was in. I said "I know absolutely nothing about the Lindbergh case; so I can see no way I can help you" . . . I told him I certainly felt sorry for him if he got the same bad treatment from the police that I got.'

For the rest of the conversation, we must rely on Stockburger and Hauptmann, for Condon's account is the usual nauseating blend of self-glorification, self-delusion and sentimentality. At one moment he claims to have said, 'Think of your mother! She sits waiting at your home in Kamenz, waiting for her boy to speak, to tell her the truth . . .' At another, after he had asked Hauptmann whether he wanted Manfred to grow up to despise him as a coward, 'I took a handkerchief from my pocket, reached forward and brushed from his face a tear that clung there.'[1] Later, according to Stockburger, he said, 'I am not one of the ordinary crowd, I am an educated man and was a professor in college . . . I went to Canada when there was twenty inches of snow, to the swamps of Mexico and Los Angeles. I have spent my money.' No wonder Hauptmann described his conversation as rambling.

There are several points at which Stockburger's and Hauptmann's accounts converge; what follows is taken from the two, with Condon opening the conversation:

'Have you ever seen me before?'

'I saw you once before. In the New York police station. This is the second time.'

'What is your name? What does your mother call you?'

'Richard.'

'May I call you John? It is a favorite name of mine.'

'You can call me anything you like.'

'The night I met you on the bench in the park I told you I was under oath . . . I told you I was the go-between. You told me that you had to do it, because they had something on you. I asked if you were German and you said Scandinavian.'

'The first time I met you was in the line-up. I had nothing to do with the Lindbergh case.'

At this point Condon seems to have shown Hauptmann drawings which Hauptmann didn't understand, and then according to Hauptmann Condon jumped up and shouted to Wilentz, 'I will not testify against this man!'

> Wilentz quietened him [said Hauptmann], but after this his conversation did not seem to be making sense. His mind seemed to be wandering, and he seemed to find it difficult to stay with one subject many minutes at a time. He said that he spoke to a man called John about the case while they were sitting on a bench . . . and the bench he had drawn on the paper was supposed to represent the bench they were sitting on. He then looked at me and said, 'Are you the man I talked to on the bench?' I said, 'No. You certainly know I am not the man you talked to. I know nothing of the Lindbergh case . . . if I did, I would have said so long ago.'

According to Stockburger this was how the conversation ended.

'No lawyer in this world will help you – no one but yourself, by telling the truth.'

---

[1] Condon was a great one for bringing on tears. See page 98, and footnote on p. 407.

'I can't tell any more. I can't make up a story.'

'No, don't tell stories, tell the truth . . . But how did you get the money?'

'I have told that already.'

'You are all alone, and you are the only one to help yourself from going to the chair.'

'. . . I haven't done anything.'

'You want to think of your baby, your mother and your wife . . . Were you glad to see me?'

'Yes, it feels good to talk to somebody.'

'I will come again with the permission of the man in charge.'

'I had nothing to do with it. If I knew just a little about the case, I would tell about it.'

But Condon never came again; and Hauptmann saw no reason in anything that had been said to think that Condon would now say that he was Cemetery John.

*   *   *

When it became obvious, after a few days of keeping Hauptmann in solitary confinement, blinded by lights and deprived of anything to read, that no confession was likely to be forthcoming, the conditions were slightly relaxed. He was allowed a daily newspaper from which all reference to himself or the case had been excised ('a good thing they have been,' Anna told him; 'you can't imagine the lies they are printing'), and books from the county library. He chose the biographies of heroic men: Abraham Lincoln; Manfred von Richthofen, the German war ace; Julius Lauterbach of the cruiser *Emden* who, after her destruction at the Cocos Islands in 1914, succeeded in returning to Germany alone;[1] and books on history and nature. The last he cherished as much as in the jail in Bautzen fifteen years earlier, as they enabled him to escape for a few hours from the awareness of his plight and the oppressiveness of his cell. The other restrictions continued. Mail continued to be withheld from him, including hundreds of letters from friends and well-wishers as well as from his mother from whom he longed to hear. Despite his many pleas, his cell light was kept burning day and night. When Anna visited him, she had to stand behind a kind of metal screen pushed up against the bars of his cell; when she asked if she might kiss him, she was refused.

---

[1] *Lauterbach of the China Seas* by Lowell Thomas.

Life for Hauptmann developed into a regular routine. He rarely went to sleep until after midnight, sometimes as late as 2 or 3 a.m. He was woken at 10.30 a.m. for the daily medical check-up (which he greatly resented and which was later discontinued as an unnecessary drain on public funds), then often slept again until lunchtime. In the afternoon and early evening he would receive visits from Anna (three times a week, later restricted to two) and/ or his counsel. In the early evening and after supper he would read and smoke. He ate two meals a day (the contents of which Lieutenant Smith dutifully recorded in his daily log) and seemed to have a good appetite. On Thanksgiving Day he was treated to turkey with all the trimmings, but to prevent him from killing himself its bones had been removed.

Having noted the very close relationship that existed between Hauptmann and his wife, the authorities felt certain that sooner or later he would say something to her in German (in which they always spoke) which would disclose some aspect of his participation in the crime. They therefore arranged for Deputy John Marut and Trooper Stockburger, who both spoke German, to monitor their every conversation. In the event they must have been dreadfully disappointed. During the ten weeks before Hauptmann's arrival in Flemington in mid October and the start of his trial on January 2, not a word was exchanged between them that was the least indicative of guilt. Indeed, the opposite. On several occasions both Anna and Richard referred to his arrest and imprisonment as a comedy, a joke. When she repeated what Hans Kloppenburg had told her about the police taking away an old pair of sailing pants they had found by Richard's canoe on City Island, they burst out laughing. Another time she was heard to say, 'The police are trying to pin something on you because they'll look fools if they don't.' And when one of the defense lawyers told Anna that her husband wasn't taking the charges against him seriously, she said, 'Why should he? He hasn't done anything.'

They talked much of Fisch. 'If he hadn't died in Germany,' Richard told her, 'I wouldn't be here behind bars and you wouldn't be standing out there ... I should never have started in business with him.' Anna said, 'Hans always used to say he was no good, but who would have thought he would have got you into this mess?' They were puzzled about Whited. 'How *could* he have seen me?' Richard asked her one day. 'You know I never went to Jersey alone; you or Hans were always with me. And I never went anywhere near the place where it happened.' In these first weeks the Hauptmanns had no idea their conversations were being monitored. Had the New Jersey law authorities been less blinkered in their thinking, less prisoners of a runaway juggernaut that they now had no means of halting, they might have stopped and asked themselves whether a man who thought his imprisonment a comedy and the evidence against him an enigma really was the kidnapper and murderer they believed.

Apart from this their conversation centered on the baby and the practicalities of Richard's defense. Manfred first visited his father on October 26, a week after his arrival. After Mrs Macrea, the warden's wife, had searched his clothing for concealed weapons, she handed him to Hauptmann in the bull-pen while Anna waited downstairs. Hauptmann spent the time hugging and kissing him, but seeing the boy in such circumstances made him extremely upset. 'After the departure of his wife and child,' reported Lieutenant Smith, 'the prisoner laid on his bed and cried for about half an hour, and seemed very downhearted and depressed.' Two days later Anna brought the baby again. At first, because it had been stipulated that Manfred should have only one ten-minute visit a week, Sheriff Curtiss wouldn't let him in, but Anna was so distressed that he relented. ('Blood is thicker than water.') This visit was no more successful than the first. 'Hauptmann was crying, his wife was crying and pretty soon the baby was crying,' the Sheriff said. After only five minutes Hauptmann handed Manfred back to Mrs Macrea, and it was agreed that he should visit only occasionally in future.

A more serious and pressing worry for the Hauptmanns was the question of defense counsel and defense costs. Richard had been pleased enough with Mr Fawcett who, although not a regular criminal lawyer, had believed in his innocence and worked hard on his behalf. Now Jack Clements of the anti-Hauptmann Hearst Press in New York had got hold of Anna and persuaded her to change to a well-known Brooklyn criminal attorney by the name of Edward Reilly who, he said, would provide a more professional defense. The Hearst Press would take care of most of Mr Reilly's fees as well as the cost of Anna's board and lodging for herself and Manfred in Flemington in return for which she (and, whenever possible, Richard) would give exclusive interviews to the *New York Evening Journal* and its syndicated associates. Clements and a woman reporter, Jeannette Smits, were assigned to cover Anna

Hauptmann; Smits would be with her most of every day. 'The other newspapers,' reported Lieutenant Smith, 'are angered at these conditions, and are trying to find some way to overcome them.' Once, when Anna did talk to a reporter from another paper, Clements rounded on her. 'Who do you think is paying for your room?' he said.

When Mr Fawcett was informed of the switch to Reilly, he was not pleased. He reckoned he had done as well for Hauptmann as anyone could, and was looking forward to appearing for him at Flemington. He therefore sent in his account for $4000 and informed Reilly that he would not be forwarding the papers on the case until it was paid. His expenses, Anna told Richard, 'included hotel bills in New York, and he lives in New York'. To raise some of the money Hauptmann told Anna to sell one of their mortgages, though it meant they would only get 75 cents in every dollar (Fawcett tried, unsuccessfully, to impound both of them) and to trade in a block of shares he still held. Wilentz managed to put a stop to the selling of the shares, presumably because he considered them to have been bought with Lindbergh money. This left Anna almost penniless. 'I tried to draw some money from the bank today,' she told Richard on November 1, 'but they refused to allow me any.' A week later she was unable to meet a police bill of $14 for Richard's cigarettes and cigars. Selling the four hundred Hudson sealskin furs that Fisch had left behind brought some funds, but not what they had expected. 'Isidor told us they were worth $6 a piece,' Richard said, and urged her to seek Henry Uhlig's advice. In the end they fetched only $1.75 a piece. 'You could see what a liar Fisch was,' said Anna.

Although not entirely happy about the switch to Reilly, she justified it by saying that Fawcett was too friendly with Wilentz, and Richard agreed. She reported that Wilentz was angry about the change, which was hardly surprising as Reilly was an experienced attorney with years of criminal practise. Had Wilentz known the kind of defense Reilly was going to provide, he would have been the first to welcome him. Even a non-criminal lawyer like Fawcett could have done better; while if Clarence Darrow or Sam Leibowitz had been handling Hauptmann's defense, the outcome might have been entirely different.

In contrast, the 52-year-old Reilly could hardly have been a worse choice. Large, florid, flamboyant and bespectacled, he was known either as the Bull of Brooklyn or Death House Reilly

because of the many hopeless homicide cases he took on. Married
to a French wife, he was an alcoholic who could only function on
several orange blossoms a day, and within two years, as a result
of tertiary syphilis, was to enter an asylum for the insane. He was
an exhibitionist who habitually wore striped pants, a cutaway coat,
fawn spats, and a flower in his buttonhole, none of which was
likely to endear him to a Flemington jury. Later one of the jurors
would complain of his 'pompous and strutting manner and his near
contempt for ordinary people in the courtroom'.[1] On accepting the
appointment he had special trial notepaper printed with a ladder
embossed in red at the head of it. Lindbergh was one of his heroes.
As a reservist, he had been proud to take part in the 'New York
Salutes Lindbergh' parade, and ever since had kept a photograph
of him on his desk. Worse, he had been so contaminated by what
he had read in the papers that he had already prejudged the issue.
'He told me,' Sisk said to Special Agent Tamm in the course of the
trial, 'that he knew Hauptmann was guilty, didn't like him, and
was anxious to see him get the chair.'[2]

Perhaps Reilly might have come to like the man he was defending
if he had managed to see him more. For days Hauptmann had
been looking forward to telling him about his situation and helping
him to plan his defense. But from the time of his appointment at
the end of October to the start of the trial early in the New Year,
Reilly visited his client on only four occasions *for a total of
thirty-eight minutes*. From November 14 to December 13, and
again from December 14 to January 18, he never came near him
at all. Perhaps he feared that if he visited for longer, he too might
come to believe in his client's innocence. The effect on poor
Hauptmann was shattering. 'Why doesn't he come to see me?' he
said to Anna in despair. 'Tell Mr Fisher I think he really ought to
see me.' On the few occasions when Reilly did come, he was the
worse for drink, and after he had gone Lieutenant Smith reported
Hauptmann as lying weeping on his bed.

Mr Fisher was C. Lloyd Fisher, the second of Hauptmann's
defense team, a much-respected member of a Flemington law firm.
Aged thirty-eight and described as a solid-looking man, he had
served on the Western Front and been invalided home. He liked

---

[1] 'From the start Reilly did all he could to show his contempt for us.' (Charles Walton,
foreman of the jury, quoted by Harold Hoffman in *Liberty Magazine*)

[2] Tamm to Hoover, January 22, 1936

cycling, wrestling and boxing, was an amateur tennis champion, and in 1932 had defended John Hughes Curtis (see pages 115–16) in the same courtroom where Hauptmann was to be tried. He made a point of seeing Hauptmann several times a week and was soon as convinced as Fawcett of his client's innocence – a belief he held until his dying day. On two occasions he brought Hauptmann little delicacies: the first time chicken sandwiches and mixed cake, which the officious Lieutenant Smith refused to sanction until over-ruled by Sheriff Curtiss; and on Christmas Day when Anna was busy with a broadcast, he twice left his own family hearth to visit the lonely, miserable man and bring him a message of comfort and cheer and half a dozen bars of candy. After he had gone, said Smith, 'the prisoner cried for a long time'.

The defense team was completed by the addition of two more local men, Egbert Rosecrans, President of the neighboring Warner County Bar Association and described as 'beaky and stooping, like a long bird'; and Frederick Pope, a former prosecutor and participant in many New Jersey murder trials and (which would stand the defense in good stead later) a highly skilled amateur carpenter. Dedicated to the case as they all were, they faced formidable difficulties. The lack of funds was the most pressing, and soon hardly a visit by one or more of them went by without a request for realizing more of Hauptmann's fast-diminishing assets. By contrast the State of New Jersey was pouring money into the case – by the time it was over, hundreds of thousands of dollars. Nowhere was the disparity more evident than in the engaging of the handwriting experts. The state booked no less than eight, all of whom would testify that Hauptmann wrote the ransom notes; the defense could have summoned as many to prove the opposite, but could only afford one. The fees and expenses of the eight, moreover, would equal the total costs of the defense for the entire trial.

Other unnecessary injustices inflicted on the defense were the obstacles that Wilentz and his staff put in their way. Naturally the defense wished to visit Hauptmann's apartment to inspec̶t̶ nursery closet where the writing had been found and ̶t̶ closet where the shoe-box had lain; to examin̶e̶ ̶t̶ it was alleged he had used to kidnap the bab̶y̶ ransom notes which it was claimed were in rejected the first two requests out of hand (whe̶n̶ Pope showed up at 1279 East 222nd Street on D̶ were refused entry) and said the last would be considered. And although Wilentz had permitted Condon to visit Hauptmann for more than an hour to suit his own purposes, and later authorized potential state's witnesses to gape at Hauptmann through the bars, Fisher's request to allow Hauptmann to meet potential defense witnesses was turned down flat by prosecutor Hauck.

Nor, according to Anna, were the New Jersey authorities above deliberately fabricating evidence (though in view of everything that had happened so far, she can hardly have been surprised). In mid November she had regained entry to her apartment where she found everything 'topsy-turvy', Manfred's teddy bear slit open as though for an operation, a miniature alarm clock, Richard's cuff links and the pen Fisch had given him on his thirty-third birthday missing. She went into the kitchen and opened the door of the closet where, she told Richard, 'it appeared to me as if something had been changed'. On closer inspection she realized it was the shelves. 'I think the top shelf used to be higher, and now it is about so high' (she pointed to a height at the level of her head). Hauptmann agreed, said the top shelf was level with a point some 6 inches above his own head, or a foot above hers. 'Why don't you take Hans up with you – he knows how high it was.' He urged her to tell Fisher about it, adding, 'They *would* do that,' by which he meant that if the state could show that the top shelf was level with Anna's head instead of out of sight above it, she would have been bound to have seen the shoe-box had it been there. Her not having seen it would prove it had never been there, and that her husband was a liar.[1]

She told Fisher about it, who told Reilly, who said to her, 'When you go on the witness stand I'm going to ask you about the box, and you say you saw it.' The upright Anna was shocked. 'I looked at him and I said, Mr Reilly, you want me to lie? I said, when I go on the witness stand I'm going to tell the truth, because the jury,

---

[1] Anna Hauptmann was right. When Lieutenant Robert Hicks took over the Hauptmann apartment early in 1936 on behalf of Governor Hoffmann he was able to confirm her suspicions:

> Examining the closet, Lieutenant Hicks decided that the walls had been painted within about a year. He applied chemicals to the paint, and what did he find under the outer paint but marks where a shelf had once been – many inches *above* where the shelf was when the State Police got through with the apartment. When Lieutenant Hicks placed a shelf at the point where the markings were, and then placed a shoe-box on the shelf, it was not possible for anyone to see the box unless standing on something.

> (*Liberty Magazine*, September 1938)

the judge and everybody would see I'm lying. I said, if I can't help Richard by telling the truth, I know I can't help him by telling a lie.' She added, 'I don't think Mr Reilly had much use for me after this. I very seldom saw him.'

Altering the closet shelves was not the only dubious activity in the matter of the shoe-box which, it was known, was a vital part of Hauptmann's defense. A key witness in the matter was Hans Kloppenburg, who had seen Fisch arrive at Hauptmann's apartment with the shoe-box, hand it to Hauptmann, and the two of them go into the kitchen with it. Before testifying to this in the Bronx, said Kloppenburg, 'the detectives or the DA's men took me into a private room and started talking about what electricity does to the body, all the terrible things that happen when a man is electrocuted. They were trying to scare me with the electric chair so that I wouldn't testify. And they threatened to put me in prison. But I testified anyway.'

Now prosecutor Lanigan, not wanting Kloppenburg to repeat this story at the trial and genuinely uncertain whether, as Hauptmann's best friend, he had been a member of the kidnap gang (no other candidates had showed up), ordered Schwarzkopf to bring Kloppenburg to Trenton for what he called 'a thorough grilling, even if it takes two or three days'.

Despite the unethical means the state was resorting to, the stark fact remained, as the *New York Times* pointed out, that the weakest link in the chain remained lack of proof that Hauptmann had ever been at Hopewell. Whited's testimony in the Bronx had been enough to ensure Hauptmann's removal to Flemington, but no one realized more than Wilentz the perils (quite apart from the morals) of putting him on the stand. Wilentz, Sisk reported, had told him that 'several neighbors of the Whiteds, as well as the brother of this witness, had given affidavits to the effect that he was a confirmed liar and totally unreliable'. Where else could they find a witness prepared to say he had seen Hauptmann in the vicinity of Hopewell two and a half years before?

On the face of it, it seemed an impossible task. Along the two-mile lane that separated the Lindbergh estate from the main road were only a handful of houses; at the time of the kidnapping all their occupants had been rigorously interviewed, and all declared they had seen nothing. These included a Mr Plum, a retired New York policeman who lived with his wife in the last house in the lane, the one standing at the junction with the main road into Hopewell. Visiting them from time to time was Mrs Plum's 87-year-old father, Amandus Hochmuth, and it was from him that the New Jersey Police now gained an unexpected windfall. Hochmuth had recently been boasting (in the way people do) to a neighbor, Frank Story, that on the morning of the kidnapping he had seen a car containing a man with a ladder turn from the main road into the lane. It is not even certain that Hochmuth was staying with the Plums at the time, but even if he was he had said nothing of it to the police. Frank Story told his friend Trooper Sawyer what Hochmuth had said, and Trooper Sawyer hurried along to the Plums.

Amandus Hochmuth was a little man with a goatee beard who looked like a retired European banker. He had fought for the Prussians in the Franco-Prussian war of 1870, and in America had been caretaker and porter at various institutions including the state mental hospital at Poughkeepsie, New York. Trooper Sawyer and his colleagues must have been disappointed to find that Hochmuth had cataracts in both eyes and was partially blind, indeed had been partially blind at the time of the kidnapping. Against this they discovered that while visiting the Plums he had given the New York Public Welfare Department a false address in the Bronx to draw public funds to which he was not entitled. This was the stick that made Hochmuth suggestible: the carrot was promise of a share in the $25,000 reward money. Shown a photograph of Hauptmann, Hochmuth peered at it and said, 'That looks like the man.' Then he was taken to Flemington Jail to look at Hauptmann and, in his own words, 'saw a figure but couldn't see him'; and by the time they were finished with him, he was prepared to say that at noon on the day of the kidnapping he had observed a car containing Hauptmann and a three-piece ladder turn from the main road into the lane to the Lindbergh estate. When Mr and Mrs Plum heard this, they expressed great surprise; he had never mentioned anything of the kind to them. The effrontery of the police in putting forward such evidence and of Wilentz and his staff in accepting it, is astonishing; but in this case disbelief was in abeyance and people would swallow almost anything.

Another matter exercising both prosecution and press was the failure of the prosecution to produce any others of the kidnap gang; with time going by and the trial approaching, prosecutor Hauck announced that the state would be proceeding on a one-man theory *and that Schwartzkopf had believed this from the beginning*.

Aside from the fact that Schwarzkopf had never believed anything of the kind (see page 121 for his belief that Violet Sharpe was involved), Hauck's statement was contrary to all accumulated evidence. It ignored the reports of the New Jersey Police and the FBI that taking the baby from his crib and down the ladder must have been at least a two-man job. It ignored the report of two sets of footprints on the Lindbergh lawn. It ignored the constant use of the words 'we' and 'us' by the author of the ransom letters. It ignored Cemetery John telling Condon that there were six in the gang, four men and two women. It ignored the look-out that Al Reich had seen at the Woodlawn Cemetery and the look-out that Lindbergh had seen at St Raymond's. It ignored the person whom Condon had heard his anonymous telephone caller address in Italian ('*Statti zitto*'). And it ignored the deposit of $2980 made in 1933 by the elusive 'J. J. Faulkner' (whose signature, all the experts agreed, was not that of Hauptmann). The whole story was shot through with evidence of the involvement of others. Yet in lieu of finding them, Wilentz and Hauck had no choice but to adopt their absurd one-man theory. Hauptmann's failure to name his colleagues they ascribed to Teutonic obstinacy; the alternative explanation, that he was innocent and therefore had no colleagues, was not one that ever occurred to them.

* * *

As the year drew to a close, both sides made their dispositions. Wilentz announced that for the duration of the trial his headquarters would be at the Hotel Hildebrecht in Trenton: a whole floor was taken over and a block of rooms permanently reserved for state's witnesses. The defense team would operate from Lloyd Fisher's law offices in Flemington by day and in the evenings at the home of Mr and Mrs Bartle Hawke, where Reilly would be staying. The full list of those appearing for the state would be: David Wilentz, Attorney General; Judge George K. Large, former prosecutor and judge and co-opted as Special Assistant Attorney General; four regular Assistant Attorneys General, Joseph Lanigan, Robert Peacock, Richard Stockton and Harry Walsh; and Hunterdon County Prosecutor Anthony M. Hauck. The defense team would consist of Reilly, Lloyd Fisher, Pope and Rosecrans. After Rosecrans had visited Hauptmann for the first time, he told reporters, 'He doesn't seem to know why he's there.'

As the New Year approached, Hauptmann's spirits seemed to

lift a little, although with a murder charge to face, he told Anna,
he could no longer regard his situation as a joke. But soon the
waiting would be over, and he would have the chance to tell the
world that his arrest and imprisonment were a ghastly mistake.
His weight went up from 150 to 155 pounds as a result of an
increase in appetite. Before retiring on December 18 he asked for
an apple, and on the 19th for a sandwich: both were refused, as
was his request on Christmas Eve for a second helping of hash.
('Prisoners in the jail,' commented Lieutenant Smith in the manner
of Mr Bumble, 'are not allowed second helpings.') He was asked
if he wanted an interpreter at the trial and said no. Whether this
was the right decision is a moot point. Having every word of
testimony translated for him could have affected the jury in one of
two ways: stressing how alien and therefore suspect he was; or
making them ask whether such a man would have had enough
grasp of the American scene in general, and of the lives of the
Lindberghs in particular to plot and carry out such a crime on his
own. On the other hand, he still thought in German, which meant
that, if he mounted the witness stand without an interpreter, he
would have to double translate before replying; and there was
always the danger (it had happened in New York) that he would
not understand everything said.

Good
point

Aware (though they may not have voiced it) of the extreme
flimsiness of the evidence so far amassed against Hauptmann,
the law officers of New Jersey must have been understandably
apprehensive about how it would be viewed by the Hunterdon
County Jury. How humiliating if, at the close of a long, expensive
and much publicized trial, Hauptmann were acquitted! They could
not of course pick the jury themselves, but when in early November
the list was published of the 150 talesmen from whom the twelve
jurors would eventually be chosen, orders went out for them to
be thoroughly (but secretly) investigated, and reports made for
necessary action to be taken. This was not only contrary to natural
justice, but showed the measures to which the State of New Jersey
had been reduced in order to secure a conviction.

The task of organizing this undercover operation was headed by
Special Assistant Attorney General Judge Large from his office in
Flemington, with Detective Sergeant John Wallace of the New
Jersey State Police directing troopers in the field. Two of the
troopers have left accounts of the clandestine way in which they
operated. On November 19 Trooper Sawyer was sent to Wearts-

ville to investigate one of the talesmen, Jonathan Voorhees. 'On the pretext of trying to locate a man formerly of Weartsville, Mr Voorhees was engaged in conversation . . . he is very friendly with Lloyd Fisher.' (Attitudes to Fisher, a prominent man in the district, were to become a key question in the investigation.) Two days later Trooper Genz was in the back room of Cutter's Drug Store when Voorhees came into the front shop. 'I told Mr Cutter to engage him in conversation and lead up to his view about the state convicting Hauptmann. I could hear them talking from where I was standing and Mr Voorhees stated that he had not made anything definite in his mind as yet.' At Neshanic Station Genz made informers of a Mrs Yandell and the local doctor, by the name of Anderson. 'Mrs Yandell will obtain any information she can for us and turn same over.' Dr Anderson, asked to comment on Mrs Verna Snyder, was equally obliging. 'Anderson thinks she would make an honest juror, but is not too sure if her husband would turn her against the State Police because he has been arrested a few times for disorderly conduct . . . Anderson said he would be on the look-out for further information on Verna Snyder.'

When all the reports were in, they were collated into 150 separate entries of around half a dozen lines each, the main specifications being place of residence, age, married or single, political persuasion, ethnic origin, property-owner or not, nature of employment. As prospective jurors they were rated as Good, Fair or Poor. Some of the entries listed as Poor make interesting reading:

Archie Diehl, Republican, aged 45 . . . Advised he is a German Communist. *Poor type of juror for state.* Don't let this person serve on jury.

Leslie Mile, Hungarian, farmer . . . not related to Fisher but friendly to Fisher. *Would make a poor juror.*

Edward S. Payne, garage owner, second wife German. Mrs Hauptmann supposed to have visited the Payne home about the week of Nov 19th 1934. *Poor type juror for the state.*

Wesley M. Schuyler . . . Learned that this juror has been doing a lot of talking lately stating that the state has a weak case against Hauptmann. *Poor type juror.*

Albert Mathews . . . very timid type of person, may easily be swayed to life imprisonment instead of the chair. *Poor type juror.*

Frances Opdyke, nurse . . . very friendly with Fisher and his staff, Mrs

Hauptmann residing at the Opdyke home.[1] *Very poor juror for the state.*

The good type jurors, those recommended for final selection, usually had one of the following qualifications: American origin, believers in capital punishment, previous jury duty which had resulted in a guilty verdict, unacquainted with or (better still) unfriendly to Fisher, having a relative in the State Police. Of the 150 entries, half were rated Good, a quarter Fair and a quarter Poor. None of those rated Poor was included, two thirds being rated Good and one third Fair. For these unsavory activities Judge Large was paid $8043, the informers $100 each.

On Christmas Day the *New York Journal* columnist Jeannette Smits was along early to the room that Anna Hauptmann and Manfred shared in the Opdykes' house. 'In one corner of the room,' she wrote, 'stands a little Christmas tree, jaunty with tinsel and bright ornaments. Baby Manfred reaches chubby hands towards the glittering baubles, and smiles as he plays with fascinating new toys.' This was the kind of thing *Journal* readers wanted to hear; Condon would have enjoyed it too. In the old days, Anna told Jeannette, Richard had always dressed the tree. 'I worked almost every Christmas Eve in that bakery until late at night. I would go home so tired – and there would be the tree he had fixed up for me.'

Later Anna was interviewed on radio and film in the Union Hotel. Carried throughout the East Coast, the broadcast seems to have been a personal triumph. 'Shaky in the language, unfamiliar with the microphone,' said Jack Lait, her interviewer, 'she delivered a more workmanlike broadcast than many of the hundreds of professionals who have been my guests in the past. This uncultured, distraught woman became transformed.' Those who witnessed Anna Hauptmann's appearance on the NBC *Today* show fifty years later can well believe it. In 1982, as in 1934, the passionate certainty of belief in her husband's innocence was self-evident.

It was at this point announced that Lindbergh would attend each day of the trial and that Mrs Lindbergh would be called as a witness for the state. Lloyd Fisher said she had no relevant testimony to give and that the sole purpose of calling her was to influence the jury through sympathy. When Jeannette Smits told

---

[1] Mrs Hauptmann and Manfred had earlier moved from the Latourettes to the house of Mr and Mrs William Opdyke, only a block away from the courthouse and jail.

Anna Hauptmann the news, she expected her, as the wife of the man who had murdered Mrs Lindbergh's baby, to show some fear or concern. To her surprise, 'Mrs Hauptmann did not wince. Her honest face did not change expression. The only emotion in her deep-set hazel eyes was one of lively interest. "That does not worry me," she said. "What can Mrs Lindbergh say that would harm my husband? He did not kill that baby." She went further. "We are both mothers. She loved that baby the way I love my darling Manfred. I believe I can understand just what terrible grief she experienced when she discovered he had been stolen." '

16

Since their dramatic flight east at the end of September for Lindbergh to testify before the Bronx Grand Jury, Charles and Anne had been living at Next Day Hill while awaiting further developments. Although their privacy and Jon's safety were guaranteed by State Police at the entrance gate and the ever comforting presence of the dog Thor, this was one of the least happy periods of Anne's life.

First, although she and Charles had their own quarters in a wing of the huge house, she felt a sense of oppression which she was not able to analyze until years later: 'When a married daughter goes back to live at home, a curious unconscious regression seems to occur. Despite the best intentions on both sides, the old patterns for mother and daughter tend to take over. Willy-nilly, one falls into the trap and begins acting the out-worn role.'

In addition, the arrest of Hauptmann and consequent legal proceedings meant more of the publicity from which they had been comparatively free.

> The morbid and intense pressures that had surrounded us at the time of the kidnapping returned with added force. The newspapers were full of details of the crime and case as it unfolded day by day . . . the familiar crowd of reporters gathered at the entrance to our driveway . . . threatening letters increased in our mail . . . an armed guard roamed the grounds. My husband, following every detail of evidence and testimony to be given, plunged again into long conferences with police, lawyers and advisers . . .'[1]

[1] One wonders what these long conferences were about, and the role that Lindbergh played in them. He was, after all, no more than a minor (though important) witness.

She felt trapped, without as well as within, for where else but Next Day Hill could afford the protection and seclusion they needed or would be more convenient for commuting to Flemington? Furthermore, Anne realized how much her mother needed her support and companionship, and that because of her absences on flying trips her mother and Jon had formed a close relationship which it would be cruel to break. Today she would have seen an analyst but, as she wrote, 'at that time . . . one saw a doctor for physical illness, and I was well, even if sleepless. Psychiatry was for those who had nervous breakdowns, and I did not break down.'

Yet there were compensations, not least of them Jon, who now filled her life as much as Charlie had done three years previously. Jon could be difficult in wolfing bacon but refusing everything else, squeezing his cereal into pulp and throwing his toys in the swimming-pool, but at other times he was angelic. 'Jon,' his mother wrote to his aunt Elisabeth, 'is so terribly precious. Do you think I should not call him "Darling" and try to be restrained?' The loss of Charlie, she admitted, tended to make her over-loving. Only once did the drill touch unexpectedly on that particular nerve: 'I take a bath and get ready and come down to supper. C is not there. The evening paper headlines: a little girl kidnapped, body found, skull crushed, shallow grave. I don't mind the columns about us and the case, it is dead sorrow, but that was living anguish. I felt I could not bear it. I went up to Mother's room but could not get over crying – could not stop.'

Forty miles away across the state in his cell in Flemington, Hauptmann was crying too: it was a day when Reilly and Fisher were badgering him for money, saying they had none and their investigators needed to be paid. Smith said Hauptmann cried for an hour after they left; he, no less than Anne, was a long-term victim of the anguish and havoc Charlie's murderers had left behind.

The event that brought Anne the greatest joy that fall was the coming to Englewood of the English writer Harold Nicolson, who had accepted an invitation to write her father's life. Nicolson had already visited North Haven, which he found 'wild and rugged as one would wish', but like other American homes in the wilderness, 'tamed and trimmed to look suburban'. On the way south he stayed with Anne's friend Mina Curtiss, who told him uncharitably and arguably that but for his flight to Paris, Lindbergh would have been in charge of a gasoline station on the outskirts of St

Louis. She also divulged that Dwight Morrow Junior was backward and heard voices and that Mrs Morrow was none too nice to him. In Vermont Judge Learned Hand told him that Morrow Senior had been physically revolting and lacked charm. Such tit-bits of gossip Nicolson cherished. Later he was to write that Morrow had had 'the mind of a super-criminal and the character of a saint'.

Nicolson reached Next Day Hill in the evening where Banks the butler told him that Mrs Morrow was dining with the Lamonts but that Colonel and Mrs Lindbergh were at home:

He led the way through the hall to the boudoir [Nicolson wrote next day to his wife, Vita Sackville-West]. There were Anne and Charles. Anne like a geisha – shy, Japanese, clever, gentle, obviously an adorable little person. Charles Lindbergh – slim (though a touch of chubbiness about the cheek), schoolboyish, yet with those delicate prehensile hands which disconcert one's view of him as an inspired mechanic. They were smiling shyly. Lindbergh's hand was resting upon the collar of a dog. I had heard about that dog. He has figured prominently in the American newspapers. He is a police dog of enormous proportions. His name is Thor. I smiled at him a little uncertainly: not for a moment did Lindbergh relax his hold upon the collar. It is this monster which guards Jon Lindbergh.

'What a nice dog!' I said.

'You will have to be a little careful at first, Mr Nicolson,' he answered.

'Is he very fierce?'

'He's all that. But he will get used to you in time . . .'

I stretched a hand towards him. 'Thor!' I said, throwing into the word an appeal for friendship that was profoundly sincere. He then made a noise in his throat such as only tigers make when waiting for their food. It was not a growl. It was not a bark. It was a deep, pectoral regurgitation – predatory, savage, hungry. Lindbergh smiled a little uneasily. 'It will take him a week or so,' he said, 'to get used to you.' He then released his hold upon the collar. I retreated rapidly to the fireplace as if to flick my ash from my cigarette. Thor stalked towards me. I thought of you and my two sons and Gwen and Rebecca, and my past life and England's honour. 'Thor!' I exclaimed, 'Good old man!' The tremor in my voice was very tremulous. Lindbergh watched the scene with alert but aloof interest. 'If he wags his tail, Mr Nicolson, you need have no fear.' Thor wagged his tail and lay down.

The more that Nicolson saw of the family, the more he liked them. 'It is all nonsense people saying that Lindbergh is disagreeable. He is as nice as can be.' He was astonished at the breakfast table to find that although the case was front-page news Lindbergh did not so much as glance at the morning papers. 'It is not a pose,' commented Nicolson. 'It is merely a determined habit of ignoring the press.' He concluded: 'I like the man. I daresay he has his faults but I have not yet found them. She is a little angel.' He went for walks in the grounds with Anne, Jon and Thor. 'Jon is bad at going down steps and has to turn round and do them on his tummy. He is a dear little boy with the silkiest fair curls. I think of his brother.' For Mrs Morrow, too, he had nothing but affection and respect, particularly after she heard that her eldest daughter, the ailing Elisabeth, had developed pneumonia after an appendix operation, and was going to fly out to California to be with her.

> I feel quite bruised with pity for her. She seems so lonely in her misery, poor little thing. I do admire that woman. She never breaks down under these blows. For the first time tonight she mentioned the baby and in such a pathetic way. I said something about her control and courage. 'Courage?' she said. 'Do you know that I cry about that baby of ours every night even now. That is not courage!'

It was blowing a gale that evening and Lindbergh's company, Trans World Airlines, did not think it safe to fly. But another company agreed to provide a plane, and at 8 p.m. she left for Newark Airport. 'I shall always think of her,' wrote Nicolson, 'in the doorway with her little hat and bag. A gale outside and the rain lashing down. There she was, about to fly three thousand miles in the night. And she loathes flying in any conditions. So small and pathetic she looked. But what guts that woman has got!'

Nicolson however was also a snob, *par excellence*, and in another letter to Vita he assessed the Morrows in the light of his own, obsessive preoccupation with English class divisions. The entire family (and no doubt others he met) were 'bedint' – the Nicolson family name for 'common', not out of the top drawer, not like us. Despite his liking for Mrs Morrow, 'one feels that even with her, there is the housemaid's room atmosphere. She is like the very best type of retired upper servant. (How Gwen will squirm at this snobbishness.) Anne is like Emily Booth [the wife of the Knole butler], Charles Lindbergh like a bright, young chauffeur.'

He added that he felt rather ashamed at putting these feelings on paper, 'even to you', since nothing could equal the kindness he had received. Nicolson, as those who knew him will recall, had a reserved, patrician manner ('hard to tell whether he is shy or bored,' wrote Anne; 'perhaps a little of both') and it would seem that he instilled in the intuitive Anne what was felt by other well-to-do Americans, 'a terrible inferiority complex about English people on the whole'. The English, she added, 'are older and more assured – real assurance, I mean. We can't help comparing ourselves and feeling country-bumpkin in the comparison ... It seems impossible ever to catch up.'

What pleased Anne most was his genuine appreciation of her writing. He had asked her to let him see an article she had written in the *National Geographic Magazine* about the Pan Am proving flight to Europe, and expressed himself delighted. 'You ought to do more of that,' he told her. 'I'm not just being polite – I really mean it.' Encouraged, she gave him notes about her father which excited him even more. Ninety-seven per cent of humanity, he told Vita, was unobservant, but Anne belonged to the 3 per cent minority. 'She noticed every detail about her father and remembered it. She sat there graceful and shy upon the large chintz sofa reading her notes slowly and with precision. "He would rub his right forefinger over the back of his left hand as if feeling a lump." "He would tear off little bits of paper while talking, roll them into spills and then work the spills into his ears. These spills would lie about the floor." ' (Morrow in some ways does sound repulsive.) After so many Morrow friends had given him nothing but gush, this was like a jet of clear water. She had written a description of family breakfast, he told Vita, which was so good that he would include it in the book *in toto*. And did.

All this temporarily lifted Anne's spirits. 'I was so extremely happy that it is hard to analyze ... it was being treated *seriously*, a kind of recognition or respect.' Often she had felt, 'I can't write. Someone should kill this thing in me,' but now an established writer had told her that she could. She had been given a spur to finish *North to the Orient* and, on Nicolson's advice, to expand the *National Geographic* article into a book.[1] 'For twenty-four hours I felt young and powerful. I felt life was not long enough for all I wanted to do, and I lay awake all night, my mind racing and my heart pounding.'

Yet this sense of release was only temporary, a shaft of sunlight in the gathering gloom. With her damaged heart valves poor Elisabeth was in no condition to weather her pneumonia, and at the end of November she died. For Anne, as for her mother, it was a terrible blow – in three years she had lost a father, a son, a sister.

[1] Later published as *Listen, the Wind* and widely acclaimed.

neral service at Next Day Hill on December 11.
ed lovely – chrysanthemums and sunlight . . . The
iful – Daddy's service which Elisabeth had picked
he room was quiet and natural. No one wanted
ing the hymns gratefully. We did not face anyone,
but went out, and waited upstairs for everyone to go.'

For the last entry in her diary for 1934 she made some New
Year resolutions. 'You can't count on anything, but there is next
week and next month; not to disappoint C at the Trial, to finish
the book for him, to give him a home and a sense of freedom and
power and fulfilment.'

*   *   *

Nothing that had happened in its history so far had prepared the
little town of Flemington and its three thousand inhabitants for
the tornado that hit it on January 2, 1935. Originally the territory
of the Lenni-Lenape Indians, then settled by the Dutch, the 105
acres that comprise the town were part of a land parcel of some
nine thousand acres acquired in 1712 by Daniel Coxe and William
Penn, the founder of Pennsylvania. In 1756, Samuel Fleming
bought some of the 105 acres and on Bonnell Street built an inn
which still stands today. Hence 'Fleming's town'.

Surrounded by fertile land, Flemington became the marketplace
for the crops and later the chickens and dairy produce of the local
farmers. In 1785 it was chosen in preference to Lambertsville on
the Delaware as the seat of Hunterdon County, and a county
courthouse was built. In the early 1800s English and German
settlers (who named the Sourland Mountains after their own
Saarland) set up industries dependent on farming such as spinning,
weaving and milling, and in 1854 the coming of the railroad
opened up new markets. Later still pottery and cut glass factories
were established, but the essential character of Flemington as a
quiet market town never changed.

The center of the town was, and still is, Main Street, and the
center of Main Street was, and still is, where the county courthouse
and the Union Hotel face each other. There had been two other
hotels but Prohibition had put an end to them. The Union Hotel
is a square, rather austere, four-storey, red-brick edifice which then
had fifty rooms and an outside balcony running the length of the
building and supported by eleven slim, white pillars. The old
county courthouse was burnt down in a fire and replaced by the

present one in 1828. It is an elegant neo-classical, colonial-type building whose main features are a portico with four big, white Doric pillars and a roof whose apex is a cupola containing a bell and supporting a golden ball and weather vane. The bell is rung in serious cases when juries have reached a verdict.

The main courtroom where Hauptmann was to be tried is approached by a pair of winding stairs, flanked by attractively carved wooden banisters and balustrades. It is a squarish room (30 by 45 feet), about the same size as a tennis court, with white walls and four long, graceful windows on either side. At the far end is the judge's dais, supporting a crescent-shaped oak bench which is curved inwards towards the judge's chair. Above this are rust-red curtains and, high up beneath a Grecian pediment, the Hunterdon County Seal with its stook of golden corn. Facing the judge's dais, a door behind it on the left leads to the judge's chambers and to the cells, and it was through this each morning and evening that Hauptmann would be led. Below the dais is the well of the court, separated from the body of the courtroom by a low, chestnut balustrade, and containing tables for prosecuting and defense counsel. To their right is the jury-box, and between the jury-box and the judge the plain wooden chair (Ford Madox Ford called it 'a common kitchen chair') used by the witnesses. In the body of the court, between the balustrade and the entrance doors, are six benches like church pews for spectators, and which still look much as they must have done in 1828. Above is a small curved gallery, resting on four white pillars, for more spectators.

For Hauptmann's trial the spectators came in an avalanche, from all corners of the United States and beyond for, as H. L. Mencken said, it was the greatest story since the Resurrection, with something in it (said the editor of the *Chicago Daily News*) for young and old alike. As a result there was hardly a paper in America that didn't send a correspondent; some sent several, and the Hearst Press sent fifty. There were representatives from the European press, such as *Paris Soir* and the London *Daily Telegraph, Daily Mail, Daily Express*. Estimates of the number of newsmen varied from 300 to 350, and of cameramen from 100 to 130. In empty rooms above the courtroom, telegraph and telephone facilities had been set up for correspondents to file directly, and a cat's cradle of wires carried forty-five direct lines to such places as Paris, Berlin, London, Buenos Aires, Sydney, and Halifax, Nova Scotia. A makeshift airfield was organized on the edge of town for half a dozen planes a day to take film to New York for developing in time for the next day's editions, and the Black Diamond Express of the Lehigh Valley Railroad was halted nightly at Flemington Junction. (Cartoonists like Harry Haenigsen didn't finish their work in time for either, and had to drive to and from New York, often in snow, every day of the trial.)

Many papers sent celebrity writers to provide additional comment: they included Alexander Woollcott, drama critic of the *New Yorker*; Damon Runyon, sports and short story writer (and said to be the best-dressed journalist at the trial); Dorothy Kilgallen, Ford Madox Ford (experiencing hard times because of poor sales of his novels during the Depression); Adela Rogers St John, daughter of a famous lawyer; Earl Rogers, described by Clarence Darrow as 'the best of all'; Heywood Broun, Edna Ferber, Walter Winchell and others. Winchell, who from an early date had proclaimed Hauptmann's guilt, had a privileged position near the balustrade and was sometimes observed passing notes to the prosecution. He habitually wore dark glasses, uncommon at the time said one reporter, and unknown in winter, which made him easily recognized, if that was their purpose. He began his broadcasts against a chatter of telegraph keys and with the words, 'Good evening, America, and all ships at sea.' Other radio correspondents included Gabriel Heatter on WOR, Boake Carter with his English accent and catch-word of 'Cheerio!' when signing off on WABC and the lawyer Sam Leibowitz, who broadcast an evening summation of each day's proceedings on WHN. On another channel actors acted out the day's proceedings from hastily prepared texts. The newsreel companies managed to bring a camera into the courtroom and conceal a microphone at the far end of the jury-box, either without the court's knowledge (hard to believe) or with its tacit approval. At any rate no formal objection was made by the judge until just before the end of the trial when sequences were shown in theaters all over the country.

This saturation coverage did not pass unchallenged, even among the press. Indeed, so sickened was the White Plains *Daily Reporter* by what it called 'the droves of sporting writers, society scribblers, magazine authors, short-story specialists, scenario specialists, sob-sisters, sobbing brothers, actors, chorus girls, lawyers, doctors and psychiatrists, Broadway columnists and managing editors' that it refused to carry any news reports from Flemington, only syndicated photographs. 'These people, experts all,' the paper said, 'are trying

Hauptmann more completely and perhaps more convincingly than will be done during the trial.'

The demand for copy was staggering – the coverage given to the trial exceeded that of any other comparable event in American history, including the Armistice and the Olympic Games. It was estimated that an average of half a million words spewed out of Flemington daily: the trial transcript alone took sixty thousand. David Davidson had to deliver five thousand words a day for the *New York Evening Post*, which meant that as soon as he had finished one page in the courtroom, a messenger boy whipped it upstairs for telegraphing to Manhattan, then ran down to wait for the next. Joe Alsop had to write *ten thousand* words a day for the *Herald Tribune*. To fill their quotas, many reporters found themselves scraping the bottom of the barrel. One was driven to compose a patronizing piece on local farmers, 'coming into town, booted and bewhiskered for their simple shopping'. Another claimed that the owner of the Flemington Stoneworks, Standish Hartman, had offered Hauptmann a free tombstone and choice of epitaph if he were electrocuted (a story which Hartman hotly denied).

The *Hunterdon County Democrat* lost count of the number of times that out-of-town correspondents had called the town sleepy, the townspeople backward and its tradesmen out to make a fast buck. And when all else failed there was always the comings and goings of the visiting firemen to fall back on, celebrities like Ginger Rogers, Lynn Fontanne, Jack Dempsey, Moss Hart, Robert 'Believe-it-or-Not' Ripley, Jack Benny, Elsa Maxwell, Lowell Thomas, Clifton Webb, Margaret Bourke White *et al*, many of whom, along with conservative *chic* like Mrs Ogden Livingston Mills who came down from New York in their Rolls-Royces with liveried chauffeurs and Pekes, had wangled their way into the courtroom (stretched to hold five hundred instead of two hundred) by getting one side or the other to issue them with subpoenas. Some failed and went off in a huff. Of those who succeeded many were disappointed to find that much of the testimony, as at most trials, was repetitious and boring, and so paid little attention to the proceedings. 'A few read magazines, some did crossword puzzles and several women knitted.' Even their most famous chronicler, the gossip columnist Cholly Knickerbocker, could not condone their behavior. 'What a sorry spectacle New York society has made of itself these last few weeks.' And Edna Ferber wrote:

'We sit and stare like vultures on a tree. We are like the knitting women watching the heads fall at the foot of the guillotine. We have got into the room through cajolery, bribery, trickery, lies.'

Working under pressure all day, the newsmen sought somewhere to relax after telephoning their copy each evening. They found it in the former pool emporium behind the Union Hotel, now converted into a huge bar and christened – after a black and white mongrel bitch which had attached herself to the newsmen – Nellie's Tap. Here, on bourbon, Scotch and local applejack, many caroused the night away, and here too was born the trial drinking song. It will be recalled that Hauptmann in his request writing was alleged to have written 'singnature' as in one of the ransom notes; the prosecution also claimed to have found the word 'boad' in his notebook similar to 'the boad Nelly' in the last ransom note:

> Is das nicht ein ransom box?
> Ja, das ist ein ransom box.
> Ist das Fisch ein clever fox?
> Ja, Fisch ist ein clever fox.
>> Ransom Box?
>> Clever fox!
> Ist das nicht ein singnature?
> Ja, das ist ein singnature!
> Ist das nicht peculiar!
> Ja, ist damn peculiar!
>> Singnature?
>> Peculiar!
> Ist das nicht ein ransom note?
> Ja, das ist ein ransom note!
> Is das nicht ein Nelly boad?
> Ja, das ist ein Nelly Boad!
>> Ransom note?
>> Nelly boad!
>> Singnature?
>> Peculiar!
>> Ransom box?
>> Clever fox!

The influx of so many people put a great strain on the resources of Flemington, whose population almost doubled overnight. But with the Depression not yet over, the boost to trade was welcome.

Anyone with a spare room found willing takers at inflated prices. The Union Hotel engaged an additional thirty-four hands and served meals from 7 a.m. to midnight (regular dishes included Lamb Chops Jafsie, Baked Beans Wilentz, and Lindbergh Sundaes). The *Hunterdon County Democrat* reported takings in The Candy Kitchen up 80 per cent, in the Blue Bowl Tearoom up 65 per cent, in the Puritan Restaurant up only 20 per cent (with a name like that, hardly surprising). And to cope with extra demand the Women's Council of the Methodist Episcopal Church laid on simple lunches in the church each day, patronized by lawyers and journalists alike. The menswear shops reported a sharp increase in the sale of socks – it was well known, said the *Democrat,* that reporters were traditionally hard on socks.

As well as the journalists and celebrities who had come to observe the trial, there was a further invasion by those who had come to observe the journalists and celebrities. For many the chance of seeing at close quarters Charles Lindbergh, Walter Winchell, Damon Runyon – even the jury as they were escorted twice a day to and from their quarters at the Union Hotel – was too good to miss; and as they jostled down Main Street, street vendors did a brisk trade selling toy replicas of the kidnap ladder, book-ends in the shape of the courthouse, photographs of Lindbergh with forged signature. One enterprising copyboy sold 'certified locks of Baby Lindbergh's hair' at $5 a packet; as the trial progressed, his own grew noticeably sparser. On Sundays people came in their thousands from as far away as Washington and Chicago. On the first Sunday it was estimated that sixty thousand people in twenty thousand cars descended on Flemington, choking the streets and reducing traffic to a crawl. They parked where they could, then headed for the courthouse where all day long sightseers were taken round in batches of two hundred. They posed for pictures in the judge's chair, in the witness chair (nailed to the floor lest it be seized as a souvenir), in the jury-box: some had to be restrained from carving their initials on the woodwork. All this led more than one observer to dub the trial and what it spawned as a circus. 'For two months,' wrote Norman Levy in the *American Mercury*, 'the world went mad and the center of the universe shifted to the sleepy town of Flemington. All sense of proportion and much of decency was lost.' And Edna Ferber wrote, 'It made you want to resign as a member of the human race.'

*   *   *

This, then, was the background to what was called then and for a long time afterwards the Trial of the Century.

It had snowed in Flemington over the Christmas holiday, and on the morning of January 2 a light layer of it still lay on the town's roofs. At 8 a.m. after a restless night in which he had been observed 'tossing around', Hauptmann rose and washed, and for the first time in two and a half months dressed not in the prison garb of open shirt, shapeless khaki trousers and laceless shoes, but in his own blue shirt and tie, newly pressed double-breasted gray suit and tan shoes. He breakfasted on cereals, bread and butter and coffee, and at 10 a.m., with Corporal O'Donnell holding his right arm and Deputy Sheriff Hovey Low behind holding his left, he was led from his cell to the courtroom and took his seat just behind the table of defense counsel.

Observers noted his thinness and the extreme pallor of his skin – 'My poor Richard,' said Anna aloud, 'what have they done to you?' – but as he hadn't seen sunlight or breathed fresh air since October 19 this was understandable. Otherwise impressions were favorable. 'He doesn't quite meet our melodramatic visions,' wrote Adela Rogers St John, 'of the Lindbergh kidnapper' – indeed, with his smart suit and confident demeanour he looked more like a successful young businessman than a kidnapper and murderer. As the days went by many commentators found it difficult to square the image of the man sitting among them with the stereotype they had formed in their minds. His air of smiling confidence, even of a kind of relaxed superiority, both puzzled and annoyed them, for this was not how a guilty man should look; and Adela Rogers St John, like others equally *bouleversés*, confessed to a feeling of 'intense perturbation'. Yet Hauptmann could not help looking superior – in one way he was superior. For he knew what no one else knew, that the State of New Jersey and all its officials were making supreme asses of themselves, that the important witnesses that had been arraigned against him were liars, that the complex ritual about to unfold before him was a gigantic charade which should never have been allowed to happen. Yet despite everything, and because he was by nature an optimist, he had sufficient residual faith in the workings of justice to believe that truth would prevail.

This was the court of Oyer and Terminer, and court crier Hann rose to cry, 'Oyez, oyez, oyez! All manner of persons having business with this court . . . on this second day of January in the year of Our Lord One Thousand Nine Hundred and Thirty-five,

let them draw nigh, give their attention, and they shall be heard.'
Judge Trenchard entered and took his seat on the bench. At
seventy-one he was the longest-serving judge on the New Jersey
Supreme Court with twenty-eight years of continuous service.
He had presided over ninety-one murder trials, passed the death
sentence in eleven, and had never once been reversed.[1] Gray-haired
and moustached, dignified and scholarly, with a reputation in court
for clarity of thinking and in private for being kindly and polite,
he would, as many correspondents were to note, be the only
element of sanity and order – though later there would be moments
when even he found it hard to disguise a bias in favor of the
prosecution.

The first day's proceedings were given over to the selection of
twelve jurors from the sixty-two talesmen shortlisted. As each man
or woman took the stand he or she was asked: Had they formed
any firm view about the guilt or innocence of the defendant, had
they been unduly influenced by anything they had read in the
papers, especially the *Daily Mirror* column of Walter Winchell,
did they have any religious or conscientious scruples about capital
punishment, would they be ready to deliver a fair verdict in
accordance with the evidence? One by one, on this day and the
next, they were whittled down to the regulation twelve: eight
men and four women. The men were Charles Walton, fifty-five,
machinist (and foreman); Charles Snyder, forty, farmer; Elmer
Smith, forty-two, insurance salesman; Robert Cravatt, twenty-
eight, educational adviser; Philip Hockenbury, fifty-eight, railroad-
man; George Voorhees, fifty-four, farmer; Howard Biggs, fifty-five,
book-keeper and described by the *New York Journal* as 'a thin-
beaked, hatchet-faced man with a bobbing Adam's apple'; and
Liscom Case, sixty, retired carpenter. Case had a dicky heart and
the prosecution were so worried that he might not stay the course
(and thus bring about a mis-trial) that the judge allowed him to
have lunch in the jury-room instead of traipsing back and forth to
the hotel. Hauptmann watched the choosing of the jurors intently
and Wilentz, watching him, was puzzled by his apparent cheerful-
ness. 'He chatted with his counselors,' wrote George Waller, 'as if
he and they were a group of spectators who had dropped in to
watch the trial, rather than a man accused of kidnapping and
murder sitting with the men who hoped to save him from the chair.'

[1] *New York Times*, October 10, 1935.

Three of the four women were very large. Mrs Verna Snyder
(she whose blacksmith husband had on occasions fallen foul of the
State Police) weighed 261 pounds and was observed to yawn a lot.
'She had difficulty in understanding the questions put to her,' one
paper reported, 'and appears deeply uninterested in the whole
proceedings. The defense are surprised that the state did not
challenge her immediately.' Mrs Rosie Pill, fifty-five, was described
as 'stout, very well dressed, of mixed German and American
descent' and Mrs May Brelsford, thirty-eight, active in local civic
affairs, as 'a housewife of ample proportions'. On the other hand
Mrs Ethel Stockton, thirty-two, was 'a vivacious brunette who
smiles easily and frequently' and as frequently caught the eye of
many a spectator and correspondent. She was the only one to have
any kind of legal experience, having been a stenographer in a
Flemington law office.

The jury (paid $3 a day) were double-booked in six rooms on
the top floor of the Union Hotel, where in the evenings they could
hear the broadcasts from a makeshift radio station along the
corridor and the clatter of typewriters on the floor below. They
were escorted by constables to and from the courthouse, and when
the snow began falling again Judge Trenchard ordered rubbers to
be provided for one jurywoman who had none (their health, for
fear of a mis-trial, was paramount). They were strictly segregated.
They were not allowed to read papers or listen to the radio and
when they ate their meals in the main dining-room they were
separated from other diners by a large screen; but they still heard
much of what was being said. On Sunday they were forbidden to
go to church, but allowed walks, morning and afternoon, and later
in the trial bus-rides organized by Oden Baggstrom, one of the
constables, around Hunterdon County. Most evenings they played
cards, particularly '500', a favorite Hunterdon County game, and
sometimes the gramophone. One evening, we are told, Verna
Snyder, having eaten fifteen bread rolls, danced to a recording of
Casey Jones. It must have been a memorable sight.

Next day, January 3, after the last juror had been chosen and
the jury sworn in, was the start of the trial proper; and it was
announced by the prosecution that two of the state's first witnesses
would be Anne and Charles Lindbergh. They were in court for
Attorney General David Wilentz's opening speech, and when Jeannette Smits of the *Journal* pointed Anne Lindbergh out to Anna
Hauptmann, she expected as before some reaction, recognition

that here in this courtroom and a few feet away from her was the mother of the baby her husband had murdered. But, said Jeannette, 'Mrs Hauptmann was not interested, save in a detached, impersonal way, like any other spectator. "She's tiny, isn't she?" Anna said. "I've always felt so sorry for her. It was a terrible thing to kidnap her baby in that way." ' Jeannette looked for some indication that Anna realized the drama of the situation but could find none; nor, equally, of any sign that she was acting. The *Journal* also set up an exclusive interview with Hauptmann conducted by Jack Clements through Reilly. Hauptmann repeated what he had said a hundred times before, that he had nothing to do with the stealing or murder of the baby, that on the day of the kidnap he was working at the Majestic Apartments, that the shoe-box story was true and that he had since found out many things about Fisch that he had not known before. He admitted to being worried about his predicament, 'but I believe it will come out all right because I am innocent. I know it, and I want the whole world to know it.'

But it was Hauptmann's guilt, not innocence, that was the dominant theme of the Attorney General's opening speech, as impassioned in delivery as it was speculative in content. The Lindbergh's child, he said, was 'a happy, normal, jovial, delightful little tot . . . blue-eyed, curly-headed, blond-haired . . .'

> . . . the state will prove to you jurors that the man who killed and murdered that child sits in this very courtroom – the gentleman in the custody of the Sheriff's guards right in the rear of the distinguished members of the bar who make up the defense counsel.
>
> The crime had been planned for some time. The defendant Hauptmann had conceived this plan and had undertaken it, had plotted it, prepared it and we will show you that by the fact that he was in and about the vicinity of the Lindbergh home on many occasions before as well as at the time of the crime.
>
> He came there with his ladder, placed it against the house. He broke into and entered at night the Lindbergh home with the intent to commit a battery upon that child and with the intent to steal that child and its clothing. And he did . . .
>
> Then as he went out that window and down that ladder of his, the ladder broke . . . And down he went with this child. In the commission of that burglary that child was instantaneously killed when it received that first blow . . .

For the last part of this imaginary reconstruction of events, Wilentz's flights of fancy knew no bounds:

Getting down there, he took the ladder and about seventy feet away the load was too heavy. In the one hand he had the ladder and in the other he had this bundle, this dead package to him. The ladder was of no particular use to him. He abandoned that. Then he proceeded on his way until he had gotten about a half mile, the child dead. Knowing it was dead, he wasn't a bit concerned about it, and there, three thousand feet away and still on the Lindbergh estate, he yanked and ripped the sleeping garment of that child off its body . . .

Then of course at the very first convenient spot, some miles away, he scooped up a hastily improvised and shallow grave and put this child in face downwards . . .

Hauptmann, sitting a few feet away, gave no indication of what he must have been thinking. But there was more to come. After listing all the other things Hauptmann was supposed to have done, writing the ransom notes, sending Perrone to deliver one, returning the baby's sleeping-suit, collecting the $50,000 from Condon in the cemetery, Wilentz said this:

When Hauptmann was arrested, what do you suppose we find? We find he worked at the Bronx lumber yards, he bought lumber there, not only that, he has got this ladder right around his neck . . . one side of that ladder comes right from his attic, put on there with his tools, and we will prove it to you, no matter how difficult it may sound – we will prove it to you so there will be no doubt about it.

So, in the end, and after emphatic denials, the state had decided they would use Bornmann's and Koehler's preposterous story. And one can see why. The evidence of Condon and Lindbergh that they had been in contact with Hauptmann in Woodlawn and St Raymond's was, as evidence, strong enough. But it related only to the Bronx; and for Hauptmann's presence in New Jersey, they had only Whited and Hochmuth to rely on. The former had already been half discredited, the latter might be too if defense lawyers ever learnt of his blindness – and they would want to know why he had not come forward to say what he had seen two and a half years before. Further, there was nothing in Whited's evidence about a ladder, and even if the jury accepted that Hochmuth had seen a man with a ladder, they might not be convinced that it was Hauptmann. What the state needed was evidence that would connect Hauptmann personally to the ladder as closely and indissolubly as links in a chain; and the Bornmann–Koehler story would give it to them.

There was a risk of course that such an outlandish tale might also be discredited, that the jury would be curious (and skilful counsel would pose the question for them) as to why Hauptmann, with his own lumber yard a couple of blocks away, would want to go to the sweat of chopping up bits of Mr Rauch's attic. But, Wilentz must have decided, it was a risk he had to take; for without such testimony there was a real danger of Hauptmann being acquitted.

Finally, said Wilentz, what was the motive of the crime? 'It was money, money, money. The very day Hauptmann collected the $50,000 he quit his job ... so that he could live a life of luxury and ease ... so he could go to Florida, so he could have a boat on Hunter's Island and other places [what other places?], so he could have a radio, so that he could gamble and speculate with thousands and thousands of dollars. Why, he used Lindy's money to buy sweepstake tickets with! What do you think of that?'

This state, he concluded, will not compromise with murder or murderers. 'We demand the penalty of murder in the first degree.'

Reilly, relaxed, world-weary, lumbered to his feet and said what was in the minds of many:

'If your Honor please, I move now for a mistrial on the impassioned appeal of the Attorney General not being a proper opening, but merely a summation and a desire to inflame the minds of the jury against this defendant before the trial starts.'

But the caravanserai had only just got rolling, and at this stage not even Trenchard was prepared to consider halting it.

'The motion is denied,' he said.

17

The first witness was a surveyor by the name of Walter Roberts whose evidence about the lay-out of the estate at Hopewell was important but boring; by mid afternoon those spectators booked for the duration of the trial had some idea of what they were up against. Five hundred people were pressed as closely to each other as books in a shelf. They were jammed together in the pew-like benches, they sat huddled on radiators and tables, they squeezed against each other as they squatted in the entrance ways and aisles and window recesses. 'If one itched and scratched,' said one writer, 'his neighbors felt it.' When dull witnesses like Mr Roberts were giving evidence, there were so many coughs and sneezes that much of it was missed. And when the body heat of the five hundred was added to the heat from the radiators, the windowpanes became so wet with damp you couldn't see across the street. The fug and the wish to escape from it gave birth to another verse of the trial drinking song:

> Ist das nicht der noon recess?
> Ja, das ist der noon recess!
> Schmells der Court like Bronx Express?
> Ja, like rush-hour Bronx Express!

After Mr Roberts came Anne Lindbergh, wearing a jacket and skirt of black silk with a pink belt and black satin beret. She was tiny, as Anna Hauptmann had said, with the figure of a young girl, and the hearts of those looking at her pale but dignified face could not fail to reach out to her. This was what Lloyd Fisher had predicted and David Wilentz had intended: that her presence would somehow color the trial, and that when the time came for the jury to pass judgment on Hauptmann, they would remember that sad, frail figure and the terrible wrong done to her, and weigh it in the balance. In fact she could have been spared the ordeal of being put on the stand, for she had little to say that could not have been (and was) said by others: an account of that nightmare evening at Hopewell when the world seemed to come to an end. Yet now, nearly three years on, it had become history. Wilentz spoke of 'the baby' and so did she: Charlie, with his small vocabulary and winning ways, was now less a person than an object. Reilly, sensing the mood of the court, had the grace not to cross-examine.

Then it was her husband's turn, and as his long gangling figure moved over to the witness chair, cartoonist Harry Haenigsen was struck by the similarity between him and Hauptmann: both young men in their early thirties; both slim, clean-cut; both with a habit of crossing their legs and leaning forward in their chairs to concentrate on whatever was being said. Others noticed that when Lindbergh's jacket was left open, they could see the bulge of a revolver. (It had gone when he returned to continue his evidence next day.) He too gave his account of the night of the kidnapping, the receiving of the ransom notes, the acceptance of Condon as intermediary. Then the Attorney General took him to the night he had gone to St Raymond's Cemetery for Condon to hand over the ransom money (but pointedly asked no questions about the look-out with the white handkerchief, for that would have destroyed the state's case that Hauptmann had acted alone). While sitting in his car, Lindbergh claimed, he observed Condon crossing Whittemore Street next to the cemetery, some seventy to one hundred yards away.

'When he arrived at about the center of Whittemore, I heard very clearly a voice coming from the cemetery, to the best of my belief calling Dr Condon.'

'What were the words?'

'In a foreign accent, "Hey, Doctor!" '

This (though most people, including Reilly, failed to notice it) was a departure, an embellishment of what he had said before. Before the Bronx Grand Jury on September 25, 1934 he had stated that what he had heard was 'Hey, Doc!' (as had Condon). Since then he must have realized that it would be hard, if not impossible, to distinguish between a foreigner shouting 'Hey, Doc!' and an American shouting 'Hey, Doc!' But 'Hey, Doctor!' or maybe even 'Hey, Dok-*tor*!' with the emphasis on the last syllable made it more plausible.

Then Wilentz said:

'Since that time, have you heard the same voice?'

'Yes, I have.'

Now there was complete silence; not a cough or a snuffle anywhere.

'Whose voice was it, Colonel, that you heard in the vicinity of St Raymond's Cemetery that night saying "Hey, Doctor!"?'

'That was Hauptmann's voice.'

'You heard it again the second time where?'

'At District Attorney Foley's office in New York, in the Bronx.'

Of all the evidence massed against the hapless Hauptmann, this, coming from the mouth of the father of the murdered child, perhaps the most revered man in America, was by far the most damaging; moreover, it called for the most stringent cross-examination from Reilly. Something like this: 'Colonel, are you seriously asking the jury to believe that you can identify a man's voice from two words he said in the dark 80 to 100 yards away in 1932? Without *any* doubts? Is it not true that until the arrest of Hauptmann you never mentioned to anyone that the voice you heard had a foreign accent? Would you agree that to an American the voice of one German immigrant speaking English is much the same as that of another?'

It was a point which others were quick to latch on to. In addition to the doubts already expressed by Lanigan and Hoover, Frederick Pope, interviewed by the *New York Times* that evening, said: 'It is impossible to believe that Colonel Lindbergh would remember a voice for more than two years. Even a superman like him could not do that.' It was unfortunate that Pope rather than Reilly was not cross-examining. Yet if Pope was *parti pris*, the *New York Law Journal* was not. 'Without corroboration we doubt [the identification's] legal sufficiency . . . several members of any jury would be inclined to discredit an identification hanging upon so slender a thread.'

Reilly however was not a man disposed to throw his cap in the ring, publicly to make dents in the image of his and America's Number One hero, whose photograph for eight years past he had been proud to rest on his desk. He did not ask – and it was a terrible omission – one single question to test the validity of Lindbergh's claim to have identified Hauptmann's voice. Instead he pursued his own theory of the crime being an inside job ('of the baby being carried down the stairs and let out the front door') and quizzed Lindbergh on the loyalty of Betty Gow, Violet Sharpe and others of the Morrow and Lindbergh households – allegations which the Colonel had little difficulty in refuting. Reilly's homework, too, was sadly deficient. He had only a dim understanding of the lay-out of the house and he persisted in calling Condon's friend Al Reich 'Mr Ricci'. Then, towards the end of his cross-examination, he fell into a trap by pressing Lindbergh to say whether at the time of the kidnapping he had stated that he had believed it was the work of a gang. Wilentz was on his feet to say he had no objection to the Colonel answering this question provided that he was also allowed to say what were his beliefs now; and the court upheld him.

So after Lindbergh had agreed that yes, he had at one time thought a gang was involved, Reilly said: 'Colonel, I will ask you, as suggested by the court, and I assume your answer will be that the defendant, you believe now, is guilty of the kidnapping. Is that correct?'

'I do.'

It was a question which no English court of law would have allowed, for the answer was entirely prejudicial. Had it been put by the Attorney General, it should have brought Reilly to his feet objecting that it was incompetent, irrelevant and immaterial. For

Lindbergh's *views* as to Hauptmann's guilt were in no sense evidence at all, and in the scales worth no more or less than anyone else's. But the effect on the jury, coming after his identification of Hauptmann's voice at St Raymond's, and bearing in mind who he was, must have been considerable.[1]

In a letter to her mother-in-law next day, Anne Lindbergh wrote of her husband, 'He was a wonderful witness . . . sure of the trust of his statements which withstood any test of cross-examination.' In fact he made such an impression of integrity in the courthouse that one reporter remarked, 'I think *Reilly* withstood the cross-examination very well.' [Author's italics]

The effect on Hauptmann was rather different. 'There has been considerable change in the demeanour of the prisoner since the court adjourned,' wrote Lieutenant Smith. 'The prisoner paces his cell continuously, and although he asks for reading matter, he reads only for a period of five or ten minutes . . . He ate only a small portion of his supper, then tore the paper dish into pieces, apparently in a fit of temper.'

It could be said that he had something to be in a temper about.

* * *

At the beginning of the second week of the trial a succession of witnesses gave evidence of the night of the kidnap: Elsie Whately (whose dead husband Reilly unsuccessfully attempted to show was an acquaintance of Condon); Betty Gow, who had since left Mrs Lindbergh's service but had been brought from Scotland at New Jersey's expense and was now staying with the Lindberghs at Next Day Hill (and whose friend Red Johnsen, the Norwegian deckhand, Reilly suggested was involved with her in the kidnap); and Troopers Wolf, Bornmann, Kelly and de Gaetano of the New Jersey State Police. Wolf and de Gaetano, it would be recalled (pages 82–3) had reported finding *two* sets of footprints leading away from the ladder on the night of the kidnapping, but so as not to disturb the state's theory that the kidnapping was a one-man job, this evidence was naturally suppressed. 'How many footprints did you see?' asked Reilly, and Wolf replied, 'One.'

[1] Under the headline LINDBERGH WANTS TRIAL TO BE SCRUPULOUSLY FAIR in the *New York Times* of January 7, Lindbergh was reported as refusing to answer press enquiries as to what his feelings were being in such close proximity to Hauptmann at the trial. His reason: 'So as not to affect the judgment of the jury'! After the trial Adela Rogers St John canvassed the jury who told her that Lindbergh's evidence had been a determining factor in reaching their verdict.

During Bornmann's evidence the famous ladder was brought into court and, as the first of many officers and others to handle it, Bornmann admitted that it had been dismantled by his colleagues in the police, nails, rungs and dowel pins having been removed and put back again. This led Pope to object to its introduction as evidence.

In the first place, its custody has not been traced, down to the present time. We don't know who has had an opportunity to play with this ladder, toy with the ladder or to change it or alter it. And in the second place, it definitely appears from the testimony of this witness that in several respects the ladder is not now in the same condition that it was at the time it was found, namely that some of the rungs have been removed from the ladder, that it has been taken apart, that nails have been drawn out of it . . .

The court however would go no further than say that the ladder was to be marked for identification, but that counsel should produce evidence relating to its custody and treatment. Hauptmann was observed to smile several times while listening to evidence about the ladder, and when asked by a *New York Times* reporter as he left court what he thought of it, said, still smiling, 'If I made that ladder, I would be a second-rate carpenter.' Hans Kloppenburg, another carpenter, described it as 'a shoemaker's ladder'.

Then came the first of the visual identification witnesses, the 87-year-old half-blind Prussian war veteran, Amandus Hochmuth, who, as an entirely fresh witness, had been promoted in the batting order above the heads of the already much-publicized Perrone, Whited and Condon. This was not his first visit to the court. Because of his defective eyesight, a trooper had taken him there the day before, so he could make a mental note of where the man he would be required to identify was sitting. Now, while waiting in the witness chair for the first question (said the *New York Times*), 'his body trembled, his head moved back and forth and his hands shook as he folded them together in his lap'.

At about noon on the morning of March 1, 1932, Hochmuth said, he had just come onto the porch of his daughter's house where the main highway joined the road leading up to Lindbergh's estate. A dirty green car[1] had turned into the Lindbergh road at a pretty fast speed and momentarily come to a halt. In it was a

---

[1] Hauptmann's car was blue.

ladder; and the driver, who had a red face,[1] stared at him as though he were a ghost. Asked if the driver was now in court, he said he was, and pointed a trembling finger in Hauptmann's direction. Then he was asked to come down from the chair and put his hand on Hauptmann's shoulder. In the event he touched Hauptmann's knee. As he did so, Hauptmann was observed to shake his head, lean across to Anna and say, '*Der Alte is verrücke!*' ('The old man is crazy!')

Reilly had observed that Hochmuth was wearing glasses, but didn't know that without them he could hardly see a thing. So when he asked him if he was near- or far-sighted and Hochmuth replied untruthfully, 'My eyes are all right,' he was in no position to press the matter.

In testing the worth of Hochmuth's testimony, however, he was marginally more successful than with Lindbergh.

'When did you first tell this story to anybody?'

'Never spoke to anybody about it.'

'Before you took the witness stand, you never told a soul about what you were going to testify to today, is that correct?'

'That is correct . . .'

'Not even your son-in-law?'

'No.'

'Your daughter?'

'No.'

Here was the perfect opportunity for Reilly to press Hochmuth hard. ('The day after you saw this car, you heard the news of the kidnapping. And the police came and questioned you, asked you if you had seen anything suspicious. Why didn't you tell them about the man with the ladder then?') But Reilly left the questions unasked, and went on to other things. *What a waste!*

Then, right at the end of his cross-examination and almost by accident, he was given a second bite at the cherry. It was the court's impression that the first time since March 1, 1932 that Hochmuth had had an opportunity of seeing what Hauptmann looked like was when he viewed him in his cell. Now he admitted to Reilly that at the time of Hauptmann's arrest he had seen pictures of him (and some took up the entire front page) 'in every newspaper'. Again Reilly might have said, 'Why did not you tell the police or your daughter or son-in-law then that this was the man, or looked

---

[1] Hauptmann's features were always markedly pale.

very like the man, you had seen driving the car with the ladder?'
But all Reilly said was 'That is all,' and sat down.

   After Hochmuth came Arthur Koehler, at this stage to comply
with the court's directive that more evidence should be heard as
to who had handled the ladder and what had happened to it since
March 1, 1932. Koehler, like Bornmann, had to admit that he too
had dismantled it, had removed all the rungs and nails, had made
a sawcut in one of the rungs, had noted when he received it a
second time that one of the rails had been sawn in two and joined
together, and had no idea when the nails were put back whether
they were the same nails or different ones. This led Pope to make
a second impassioned plea that the ladder should not be permitted
in evidence. Not only had it been here and there, been dismantled
and reassembled at least twice and tampered with on both occasions so that it was nowhere near in the same condition as when
it was first discovered, but there was another reason why it should
not be admitted:

> a very great reason and a very strong reason – there is absolutely no
> connection, either by circumstance or by direct evidence between this
> ladder and the accused, and until this ladder has been placed in the
> possession of the accused, or until there is some evidence in this case
> which would be sufficient to go to the jury, to have them consider
> whether or not the ladder was ever in the possession of the accused,
> this ladder is not evidential against the accused.

Impressed by these arguments, Judge Trenchard ruled that he
would defer the admissibility of the ladder as evidence until there
was more information regarding its history. Wilentz wasn't worried; he had made contingency plans. He (and Bornmann and
Koehler) had a story to tell about the ladder and Mr Rauch's attic,
and when the time was ripe, they would tell it.

   In the afternoon came the taxi-driver Joseph Perrone, short and
stocky with black hair and glasses, and told of the night when a
man had given him an envelope to take to the house of Dr Condon.

   'Who is the man,' asked Wilentz, 'who gave you that envelope?'

   Perrone, who had spent the night as guest of the State Police at
their barracks in Trenton, and had been accompanied to court by
a trooper, had been well coached.

   'Bruno Richard Hauptmann,' he said in a firm voice.

   Asked to come down from the stand and point him out, Perrone
walked across to where Hauptmann was sitting between his two

guards and said, touching his shoulder, 'That is the man.' And Hauptmann looked up at him and said, loudly enough for several people to hear, 'You're a liar.'

In a useful piece of cross-examination Reilly established that Perrone's first interrogation by the police did not take place until six weeks after delivery of the note (and so he had little reason to remember the events of that day – indeed, when asked by Reilly, couldn't recall a single other thing that had happened); also that ever since his police interrogation he had illegally been accepting unemployment charity relief work while continuing to drive his cab – and although Reilly's questions hinted that the police might have set this up, or at least turned a blind eye to it, he failed once again to press the line of questioning home.

One by one, as a result of his having lied about the hidden ransom money back in September, Hauptmann's pigeons were coming home to roost; after he had put on his prison garb that evening, Lieutenant Smith noted in his daily report: 'The prisoner did not eat his breakfast and only part of his dinner and supper. His sleep was broken and not sound. Upon returning from court at 4.30 p.m. the prisoner was apparently very nervous and paced up and down the bull-pen as fast as he could walk.'

With his troubles fast multiplying, he had much to be nervous about. Next day Condon was going to take the stand.

* * *

Earlier, the defense team had issued a statement saying there was no truth in the rumors that there was dissension among them, and that they all believed in Hauptmann's innocence; they stated that in their view New Jersey's case would stand or fall on the evidence of Dr Condon. They made this assertion with confidence and on the basis of Condon's outburst to Wilentz while interrogating Hauptmann in his cell – 'I will not testify against this man.' What they could not know was the degree to which, since then, Condon had sold out to the devil.

Condon's evidence was now not just the same old mixture of exhibitionism, false sentiment and pedantry, but of calculated and repeated perjury – all in all one of the most contemptible performances by a man of his standing inflicted on any court. Three times in his examination by the Attorney General he was asked who Cemetery John was, and three times, in measured, ringing tones he declared, pointing at the defendant, 'Bruno –

Richard — Hauptmann.'[1] He expressed no doubts of any kind. Asked to describe John, he gave a good description of Hauptmann: 5 foot 9–10, well-built, athletic, muddy blond hair, 158–165 pounds[2]; and swore falsely that this was what he had told the New York and New Jersey Police at the time (not a word of his statement to Lieutenant Finn that John had almond eyes, a husky voice and a fleshy lump at the base of his thumb). He retold his story of chasing John from the gates of Woodlawn Cemetery into van Cortlandt Park ('Hey, come here, don't be cowardly, you are my guest!') and of handing over the money at St Raymond's ('He was crouched under the hedge, and I said "Come on, stand up like a man."') And he offered a new piece of evidence about the conversation in Woodlawn that no one had ever heard before. To find out whether John really was one of the kidnappers, he told Wilentz, he had asked him, 'How am I to know that I am talking to the right man?'

'And what did he say?' questioned Wilentz.

'That the baby was held in the crib by safety pins.'

'Who said that? John?'

'John.'

'And . . . did you have the pins with you?'

'I had the pins with me, because I took them out of the baby's crib on the night that I slept there.'[3]

This was the first time that Condon had mentioned the safety pins — he had said nothing about them in his statement to Finn nearly three years ago or to anyone since; of all the lies that he told against Hauptmann, this was by far the wickedest. For if the jury believed that Hauptmann was Cemetery John, they would also believe that Hauptmann was the kidnapper, for who else would have known that there were safety pins attached to the baby's crib?

Then it was Reilly's turn and he tried to puncture Condon's pretensions by reference to amateur dramatics and asking Condon is he was enjoying his day in the sun. But Condon, stung, proved more than a match for him, correcting Reilly's grammar and use

[1] These were the only occasions in his lengthy examination that he said Hauptmann's name. Elsewhere he insisted on calling him 'John', as though deeply reluctant to continue repeating what he knew to be a lie. (See Scaduto, page 138.)

[2] This was Hauptmann's current weight, information with which Condon had been fed. In 1932, according to his vehicle licence, it was 175 pounds.

[3] See page 99.

of English, mimicking Cemetery John's voice and the way he turned his collar up, telling Reilly not to raise his voice ('Don't shout. I can hear you. I can hear every syllable that you utter if you use your lips.') until finally both Wilentz and Trenchard had to bring him to order. Reilly, as usual, had little grasp of his material, referring to the *Bronx Home News* as the *Little Bronx News* and Judge Hammer of the Bronx as Judge Hadding. He did make some attempt to press Condon about his failure to identify Hauptmann as Cemetery John at Greenwich Street, but Condon was ready with a smoke-screen of verbiage about the distinction between identification and declaration that left the court quite limp.

'You didn't identify him, did you?'

'No, sir. Beg pardon, there is the word identification again. I take exception to your language . . . when you begin to divide the identification and declaration and denial, you would make it appear as though I was dishonest, and I am not.'

Turning to Trenchard, Condon said, 'Is that too severe, Judge?'

And the judge, who might have told him to address himself to counsel, said politely, 'No.'

'Come on,' said Reilly, 'I can take it.'

'That is good,' said Condon. 'I want you to know, Counselor, that the identification is purely a mental process after the senses have known . . . and unless that is taken that way to answer quickly, fast, I don't know but what it might be a kind of trap you were setting me. The declaration is where I tell it to others. Identification is what I know myself.'

Poleaxed by this nonsense, Reilly didn't have the strength to ask Condon what had prevented him from making a declaration of identification at Greenwich Street that yet allowed him to make one (or rather three) now.

Wilentz was delighted with Condon's evidence; it was all he had been hoping for. Lindbergh too was pleased, for it amply confirmed his own false testimony. After he had returned to Englewood that evening and given Anne a run-down of the day's proceedings, she wrote in her diary: 'Dr Condon on the stand. Evidently he made a wonderful witness.'

But for Hauptmann it was a different story. Having to sit captive and mute and listen to the lies as they came tumbling out hour after hour, he longed to stand up and shout in protest. 'Many times,' he wrote, 'I could only keep myself back with a great effort.' He did so because of his counsel's repeated warnings that any public demonstration would do his case no good. Nothing that Condon had said to him in his cell, he reflected, had prepared him for this. 'I was happy when I saw him take the stand,' he wrote, 'because I supposed, following his conversation with me, that he would say the same thing he had said in my cell. But the whole world knows how he completely changed his story . . . apparently the power of the Lindbergh name, the power of the governments of the State of New York and of New Jersey were too strong for him to withstand, and he took the weakest way out.'

Hauptmann's troubles that afternoon were not yet over. For now Corporal Horn, Sergeant Ritchie and later Colonel Schwarzkopf (all of the New Jersey Police), Lieutenant Finn of the New York Police and Thomas Sisk of the FBI all took the stand in turn and told of the night in Greenwich Street when after ten hours of questioning Hauptmann first took dictation from Osborn's composite test statements. All were agreed that Hauptmann had undertaken this voluntarily and because, as he had told them, it would help to clear his name. (Did they never ask themselves why, if he *had* written the ransom notes, he had not shown some reluctance in Greenwich Street to write *anything*?) They did not add that they had made him *copy the ransom notes* (had they forgotten admitting this to the *New York Times*?) or that they had asked him to spell words in different ways, which he had also agreed to, thinking this too would clear his name.

Indeed, they said the opposite. The spelling was his own, lied Schwarzkopf, and Sergeant Ritchie said he had pronounced words one way and Hauptmann had written them another. Now, for the first time, Hauptmann realized the full extent of the trap he had fallen into; that when he had agreed to write 'not' as 'note' and 'the' as 'hte' and 'be' as 'bee' because he believed it would prove his innocence, they were intending it to confirm his guilt.

Listening to these further lies, he could hardly contain himself. 'He gave signs,' said Smith, who was watching him closely, 'of being under a great mental strain, his hands clenched tightly in his lap . . . his face turned the color of putty.' And after he had returned to his cell that evening and they had taken away his tie so he wouldn't hang himself and he had picked at his supper of meat sandwiches, potatoes, cookies and tea, he paced up and down the bull-pen showing more signs of nervousness than ever before.

Next came Frank J. Wilson, Special Agent in the Internal Revenue Service, who had arranged with Lindbergh and others the make-up of the ransom money back in March 1932. He said one thing favorable to Hauptmann, one unfavorable. The favorable thing was that some of the ransom money could have found its way to the US Treasury without being detected, so great were the number of deposits after Roosevelt had called in gold certificates. The unfavorable thing was his denial that any more ransom money bills had shown up since Hauptmann's arrest. In fact one had shown up as recently as December 19, but because this had been handed in by someone other than Hauptmann, news of it had naturally been kept quiet.

During the next four days came the state's handwriting experts. There were eight altogether, led by the septuagenarian Albert S. Osborn; their names were Elbridge W. Stein, John F. Tyrrell, Herbert J. Walter, Harry M. Cassidy, William T. Souder, Albert D. Osborn and Clark Sellers. They were unanimous that it was Hauptmann's hand that had written all the ransom notes, 'as surely,' said one, 'as though he had signed his name to every one of them'. Looking like senior members of an old folks' bowling club, they posed together for a newsreel company; and reading from a prepared statement Albert S. Osborn said their conclusions were 'irresistible, unanswerable and overwhelming'.

We can see with hindsight that they were nothing of the kind, that all eight were as much victims of the current epidemic of hallucination as everyone else. As their combined testimonies run to some five hundred pages of the trial transcript and are much concerned with technicalities – the shape of a 't' or the curl of a 'y' – and as their conclusions were later challenged by the defense's lone expert using the same material (see also Appendix 3), it is not proposed to go into these in any detail. We must however ask how it is that eight handwriting experts, all acknowledged professionals in their field, should arrive at a verdict so contrary to the truth.

The first thing to say – and it is a general point – is that the study of handwriting is not a profession in the sense that medicine, the law and accountancy are professions, with firm ground rules to be studied and learnt. There are no examinations to be passed or degrees to be taken; it is an empirical, subjective activity with few yardsticks against which judgments can be measured. As a result handwriting 'experts' often find themselves on opposite sides in American courts, reaching contrary conclusions from the same material, and the profession as a whole has been particularly prone to error. Reilly confronted Osborn Senior (though not as effectively as he should) with a whole stack of cases where, he claimed, Osborn's testimony had been proved wrong. Elbridge Stein and Osborn Junior admitted they had been proved wrong in the Mowell case, John Tyrrell agreed that a man had been wrongly convicted and sent to prison as the result of his evidence in the Morgan case, and Lloyd Fisher reminded Osborn Junior of a case in which they had appeared on the same side and the verdict had gone against them. (In addition, as already stated, in 1971 Osborn Junior made the biggest mistake of his career when he declared unequivocally that writing purporting to be that of Howard Hughes was genuine when it was a Clifford Irving fake.)

To understand the background to the conclusions that the eight reached, we must follow the chronology of events from the time that Hauptmann wrote the request writings in Greenwich Street Police Station on the night of September 19. After comparing these with the ransom notes, it will be recalled, Osborn Junior informed the police that in his view the writer of the one was not the writer of the other, but that when his father came into the office in the morning he would ask for a second opinion, and if there was any different conclusion, he would call back. In the morning, Osborn Senior compared the two sets of writings and came to the same conclusion as his son. But when, later that day, the Osborns were informed that some $14,000 of ransom money had been found on the premises of the man who had written the request writings, they called back within an hour to say that they had reconsidered the matter and the writer of the ransom notes and the request writings was the same.

At that time Osborn Senior was regarded as the foremost hand-writing expert in the United States. His conclusion (by inference) that Hauptmann was guilty was followed in the days ahead by other evidence – the closet writing, the identification by Perrone, etc. – which seemed massively to confirm it. The Attorney General of the United States, when asked his opinion, said he didn't think that anyone doubted it. And he was right. Soon there was not a man, woman or child in America or elsewhere who didn't think Hauptmann was as guilty as if he'd been caught climbing the ladder at Hopewell.

It was not therefore in a spirit of impartial inquiry that the six other experts approached their task, but in a climate where Hauptmann's guilt was universally assumed, and where anyone who doubted it was considered something of an oddball. From the

The Hunt for Evidence

33. Crowds outside Hauptmann's home in the Bronx after his arrest. The large window on the upper floor is that of his sitting room, those on the side *(from left to right)* the sitting room, Manfred's room, and the Hauptmanns' bedroom. The small window above is that of the attic. The garage is on the extreme right.

34. Police carpenters demolishing Hauptmann's garage in search of ransom money.

35

Trial of the Century

35. Colonel Norman Schwarzkopf escorting Mrs Morrow and her daughter from the Flemington courthouse after Mrs Morrow had given evidence. 'I thought with a pang in the middle of it, How incredible that my baby had any connection with this,' wrote Anne.

36. Ollie Whateley and Betty Gow in court.

37. The Flemington jury. *Front row, left to right:* Elmer Smith, Ethel Stockton, Charles Snyder, Mrs Verna Snyder, Mrs Rosie Pill, Charles Walton, foreman. *Back row, left to right:* Robert Cravatt, Philip Hockenbury, George Voorhees, Mrs May Brelsford, Liscom Case, Howard Biggs.

37

38. Hauptmann confers with his wife across his two guards, Deputy Sheriff Hovey Low and Lieutenant A. L. Smith.

39. The crowded courtroom, stretched to hold five hundred instead of two hundred. (*a*) George Large, (*b*) David Wilentz, (*c*) Walter Winchell, (*d*) Hauptmann, (*e*) Mrs Hauptmann, (*f*) Edward J. Reilly, (*g*) Lindbergh, (*h*) Egbert Rosecrans, (*j*) Samuel Foley, (*k*) Norman Schwarzkopf.

The 'Experts'

40. Detective Bornmann with the three sections of the kidnap ladder, the numbers corresponding to the vertical side rails. Note the exceptionally large space between the rungs.

41. Arthur Koehler, the wood expert, examining one of the side rails.

42. The Hunterdon County Prosecutor, Anthony M. Hauck (left) and Special Assistant Attorney General Judge George K. Large with enlarged charts of specimens of ransom letter and of Hauptmann's handwriting to show they were one and the same. 'From the start the experts were not looking for dissimilarities (which they all admitted were numerous) but for what they could find that matched.'

43. Handwriting expert Albert D. Osborn with his father Albert S. Osborn.

42

43

44

45

The Prosecution

44. *Left to right:* Bronx District Attorney Samuel Foley, New Jersey's Attorney General David Wilentz, Dr John Condon, Assistant Attorney General Richard Stockton, and Captain John Lamb of the New Jersey State Police.

45. Amandus Hochmuth, aged eighty-seven, who claimed two and a half years after the event to have seen Hauptmann near Hopewell. 'Cataracts in both eyes…when asked to identify a vase with flowers ten feet away, declared it was a woman's hat.'

46. Millard Whited and his family posing for the press outside his shack in Lambertville, New Jersey. 'In exchange for identifying Hauptmann he was promised $150, $35 a day expenses and a share of the reward money.'

47. Whited in the witness chair.

Yale
somewhere
Bob ♡

STRAIGHT UP WHITE TRAILER TRASH

46

47

48

49

The Defense

48. *Left to right:* Edward J. Reilly, C. Lloyd Fisher, Frederick A. Pope, Hauptmann, Egbert Rosecrans.

49. Hauptmann's chief counsel, Edward J. Reilly, and Mrs Hauptmann entering the Flemington courthouse. 'I said to him, "Mr Reilly, do you want me to tell a lie? … If I can't help Richard by telling the truth, I can't help him by telling a lie".'

50. Three defense witnesses: handwriting experts J. M. Trendley and Hilda Braunlich with Hans Kloppenburg *(right)*. Mrs Braunlich, who told Reilly that strokes in the ransom letters had been forged, was never called.

51. George Steinweg, the steamship agent who sold Fisch his ticket to Germany. 'Surprised to see so much money come out of the pocket of a fur-cutter…'

52. Joseph M. Furcht, Superintendent of the Majestic Apartments. 'The records … clearly brought out the fact that Hauptmann worked for me on March 1st 1932 … until 5 p.m.'

[Handwritten annotations:] YES YOU CAN THE PROSE CUTIO WHOLE CASE IS BUILT ON LIES, HALF TRU AND TOTAL FABRICAT

50

51

52

IT'S TIME FOR THE D-UP TO START LYING,

Conviction

53. Mrs Hauptmann with Manfred after visiting her husband in Flemington Jail.

54. Hauptmann poses for photographers near the entrance to the bull-pen, the day after being sentenced to death. The entrance to his own cell is at bottom left.

55

56

Stay of Execution

55. Announcement by Governor Hoffman on January 16, 1936 that he had granted Hauptmann a thirty-day stay of execution, and by Attorney General Wilentz that he would not set a new execution date until the reprieve had expired.

56. Handwriting expert Samuel Small showing marked dissimilarities between Hauptmann's writing and that of the ransom notes.

57. Part of the letter of thanks from Hauptmann to Governor Hoffman before his execution.

58. Governor Hoffman reading the above letter.

BEAUTIFUL

PRICELESS

57

58

60

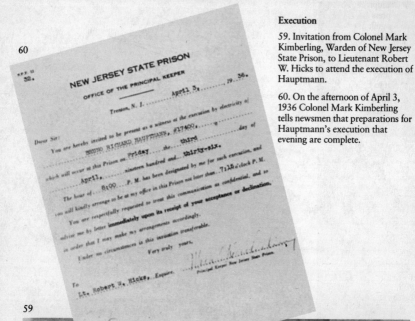

N.P.F. 32.

NEW JERSEY STATE PRISON

OFFICE OF THE PRINCIPAL KEEPER

Trenton, N. J. .... April 3, ... 19. 36.

Dear Sir:

You are hereby invited to be present as a witness at the execution by electricity of

BRUNO RICHARD HAUPTMANN, #17400, ... "g" ....

which will occur at this Prison on .... Friday, ... the ..... third ..... day of

.... April, ... nineteen hundred and ..... thirty-six.

The hour of ..... 8:00 ..... P. M. has been designated by me for such execution, and

you will kindly arrange to be at my office in this Prison not later than ..7:15 o'clock P. M.

You are respectfully requested to treat this communication as confidential, and to

advise me by letter **immediately upon its receipt of your acceptance or declination,**

in order that I may make my arrangements accordingly.

Under no circumstances is this invitation transferable.

Very truly yours,

Mark .... Kimberling

Principal Keeper New Jersey State Prison.

To Lt. Robert W. Hicks, Esquire.

Execution

59. Invitation from Colonel Mark Kimberling, Warden of New Jersey State Prison, to Lieutenant Robert W. Hicks to attend the execution of Hauptmann.

60. On the afternoon of April 3, 1936 Colonel Mark Kimberling tells newsmen that preparations for Hauptmann's execution that evening are complete.

59

61. Hauptmann executed.
The press maintain belief
in his guilt until
the end.

62. Reporters outside the door of
Mrs Hauptmann's hotel room, as
the news of her husband's death is
about to break.

63. Mrs Hauptmann is told of
her husband's execution.

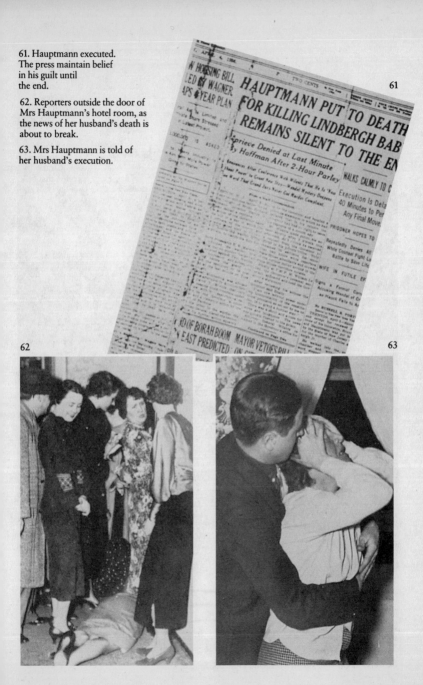

61

62

63

64. Mrs Hauptmann after her husband's funeral, April 6, 1936.

start therefore they were not looking for dissimilarities (which they all admitted were numerous) but for what they could find that matched. ('You hunted all through the ransom notes to find a 'p' like that one?' Pope said to Souder, and Souder had to agree.)

The first similarity that hit them was one that Hauptmann could hardly have foreseen. The writer of the ransom notes, it was generally agreed, was a man with German as his first language who had since learnt English. Hauptmann was also such a man, and Germans who have come to learn English (as the experts admitted) tend to write it in a broadly similar way. Thus, in both ransom and request writings, were 'o's not joined at the top, 't's shaped like triangles which could be mistaken for 'b's, 'g's looking like 'y's, 'N's with the diagonal inverted. But how to distinguish between a national characteristic and an individual one was not an exercise the experts (or for that matter the jury) were invited to undertake.

It was the second similarity that clinched things for the experts: the extraordinary fact that certain simple words in the ransom notes which had been spelt wrongly were spelt in exactly the same way in the request writings. 'I can't believe,' declared Osborn Junior, 'that this is just a coincidence,' and Fisher, who had a different explanation to Osborn, said, 'Neither can I.' Introducing his composite statement, Osborn explained that he had included in it many words which had been mis-spelt in the ransom notes:

... I put the word 'where' in to see how a suspected writer [i.e. Hauptmann] would spell it. In the first line, 'We were not near Smith Hall where the robbery', this writer wrote it as in the ransom notes, 'w-e-r-e'. In the second line I put the word 'our' in to see how the suspected writer would write 'our'. It is written in the ransom notes 'o-u-e-r', and when the suspected writer wrote it, he also wrote 'o-u-e-r'. The next line I put the word 'later' in because in the ransom notes it is spelled 'l-a-t-t-e-r' ... And when this suspected writer was asked to write that word, he wrote 'l-a-t-t-e-r', and it is the same throughout this specimen.

Listening to this evidence, and not knowing the background to it, how could anybody doubt that the suspected writer, Hauptmann, was also the writer of the ransom notes? Elbridge Stein admitted that his entire testimony was based on these mis-spellings, while Harry Cassidy declared that the possibility of two people mis-spelling the same words in exactly the same way was so small as to be negligible. Fisher put it to Stein that it would be improper to ask a suspect to copy the disputed (i.e. ransom) writing, and Stein, unaware that the New York Police had already admitted to it, said he thought it would be highly improper. Fisher asked Cassidy and Osborn Junior point-blank to consider the possibility of Hauptmann having mis-spelt the words because the police told him to. But middle-class people in those days, and especially those who relied for their work on friendly relations with the police, did not believe in such things. 'I am going on faith,' said Cassidy. 'I have got a certain amount of faith in humanity and I just can't think those officers would do a trick like that.' Osborn Junior echoed him. 'I cannot believe that the people getting those specimens would do anything like that.' The jury didn't believe it either. And yet that is what had happened.

There were other points that Fisher and Pope (who had done their homework far better than Reilly) made to good effect. Why hadn't Stein included numerals in his comparison of ransom and request writing? Because, Stein admitted, there were no similarities between Hauptmann's numerals and the numerals in the ransom writing. Wasn't it highly significant, Fisher suggested to Tyrrell, that the writer of the ransom note could manage quite difficult words like 'hazardous' and 'circumstance' and 'accordingly' and yet manage to mis-spell 'not' – 'perhaps one of the first words he ever learned to spell?' Tyrrell agreed it was significant (Osborn Junior's explanation was that he used a dictionary for the difficult words, but thought he knew the simple ones!) Tyrrell was also struck by there being more differences between the various request writings than between the ransom notes and the request writings – further evidence of the police having told Hauptmann to write with different pens in different ways (Osborn Junior's explanation was that Hauptmann was attempting disguise).[1] Fisher and Pope did their best to draw the witnesses' attention to things Hauptmann had written long before his arrest, like the letter to Mrs Begg, in which he had spelt 'the' and 'not' and 'money' perfectly correctly, but their difficulty was that the prosecution, knowing that the more documents they introduced of Hauptmann's writings before his arrest, the more obvious the dissimilarity between them and the ransom notes would be, kept these to a minimum – a few vehicle licence applications, lists of shares, the letter to Mrs Begg,

[1] It is clear that the request writings of Hauptmann that the state offered as evidence were only a fraction of those he had written at Greenwich Street Police Station, and that their choice had been highly selective.

a short deed of agreement. And because the police had cleared Hauptmann's apartment of all his other writings, the defense were unable to offer any themselves. So the rebuttal that Hauptmann's counsel might have made of the evidence of the experts, all so immensely assured, largely went by default.

* * *

An interesting event occurred on the morning of Thursday January 17, when Dr Charles Mitchell, who had performed the autopsy on Charlie's body, was due to give evidence. That day Mr Pope had invited his brother-in-law to attend the trial and, concerned that he might not be re-admitted to the courtroom after the noon recess, Mr Pope advised him to wait in the judge's chambers. While he was there, the brother-in-law heard one of the prosecuting team coaching Dr Mitchell to say that Charlie's death was instantaneous: this was essential if the murder charge under the burglary indictment was to be proved as having taken place in Hunterdon County. A death that was not instantaneous could be assumed to have taken place in Mercer County, where the body was found, and thus Judge Trenchard would have been compelled to declare a mistrial. In the event Dr Mitchell did his stuff: 'The fracture was so great, covered such an area in my estimation that proved conclusively it was instantaneous or almost so'.

That afternoon the court heard two outbursts. Earlier, other witnesses besides Dr Mitchell – the truck-driver William Allen, Sergeant Zapolsky, Inspector Walsh, and the Trenton coroner Walter Swayze had given evidence of the finding and identification of Charlie's body. But as the body was badly decomposed and as Charlie's paediatrician, Dr Van Ingen, had said at one stage that even if offered a million dollars he still wouldn't be able to identify it, the thrust of Lloyd Fisher's cross-examination of these witnesses was to cast doubts on whether the body found really was Charlie's. Wasn't there a Catholic orphanage across the road from where the body was found, he seemed to suggest, and inferred that the body might have been that of one of the children there.

To counter this (somewhat far-fetched) suggestion, Wilentz called the custodian of the orphanage, Mrs Elmira Dormer, to say that at the time in question none of her charges was missing. Whereupon Reilly rose to declare: 'I will say now that there has never been any claim but that this was Colonel Lindbergh's child that was found there.' Fisher, aghast at finding his line of question-

ing reduced to tatters and from a source where he had least
reason to expect it, shouted angrily at Reilly, 'You are conceding
Hauptmann to the electric chair,' and strode briskly from the
room; and Hauptmann was heard to mutter, 'You are killing me.'

Reilly has been much criticized for saying what he did, for
having, as one writer put it, 'destroyed the slimmest chance to save
Hauptmann's life'. In fact it was no chance at all. In addition to
Sergeant Zapolsky and Dr Mitchell, others – Betty Gow, Dr Hawks
and Lindbergh – had all identified the body as Charlie's, while
Betty, Elsie Whately and Anne Lindbergh had testified that the
little scalloped shirt with the blue Silko thread found on his body
was the one they had put on him the night he had disappeared.
While Reilly might have found a more tactful, less public way of
disagreeing with his colleague's tactics, he had for once saved time
rather than wasted it.

After Mrs Dormer came the dark-haired, boyish-looking FBI
agent, Thomas Sisk, the first of several police officers to testify to
the arrest of Hauptmann and the finding of the ransom money in
his garage; it was during his evidence that the second outburst
occurred. Sisk described how he had found beneath the garage
floorboards a jug with a lid on it containing 2 or 3 inches of water.
'We questioned Hauptmann as to that jug. He denied knowing
anything about it but the next day when we questioned him, he
admitted that he had that money in there three weeks before he
was arrested.'

Now this was an unexpected development, and one that the
defense was hearing for the first time. Its purpose was to explain
why the money was damp and also to discredit Hauptmann's story
(which he had related to many police officers and never once
departed from) that it had become damp because of the water
leaking into the shoe-box. To those unaware of the complexities of
the case, it must have seemed a small point. But to Hauptmann it
was the linchpin of his defense, for it was the water dripping into the
shoe-box that had revealed its contents to him for the first time.
Now he could contain himself no longer. 'Mister, Mister,' he
shouted, raising himself from his chair, 'you are lying!' And, as his
guards pulled him back, 'You are telling a story!'

There was a third outburst the next morning, this time from
Anna Hauptmann. A woman called Mrs Ella Achenbach took the
stand, a middle-aged German immigrant. She said that she had
employed Anna as a waitress in 1928 and that a day or two after

the kidnapping in March 1932, the Hauptmanns had called on her. Although this in itself was in no way damaging to Hauptmann, Mrs Hauptmann knew there wasn't a word of truth in it – she hadn't seen Mrs Achenbach in months – so she shouted out, 'Mrs Achenbach, you are lying.' After Judge Trenchard had asked her not to intervene again and she had said, 'Well, I will try . . . but sometimes I just can't help it,' Mrs Achenbach said that during the Hauptmanns' visit she had noticed that Richard was limping (this was designed to tie in with the kidnapper having fallen off the broken ladder). In cross-examination it emerged that there was bad feeling between the two women, for Mrs Hauptmann had taken Mrs Achenbach's daughter with her to Germany and back in 1928, and claimed that Mrs Achenbach had consistently refused to repay her the child's return fare. To the jury it must have seemed yet another link in the growing chain of evidence against Hauptmann.

In the afternoon Inspector Bruckman described how he had found the writing in the closet, and Foley's stenographer read the verbatim account of Hauptmann admitting to Foley that the writing must be his. Observing Hauptmann during this testimony, Lieutenant Smith wrote: 'While damaging evidence was being produced on the stand, prisoner appeared to be laboring under great strain. Although he sat fairly quiet, his hands were clenched tightly. He quivered at times.'

Then, as it was a Friday, the court adjourned for the weekend. Back in his cell in prison garb, Hauptmann had several visitors: Anna for ten minutes, Fisher for nearly an hour, Reilly (the first time for a month) with Fisher for another twenty minutes. As usual Reilly was the worse for drink and spent much of his time shouting. 'You could have heard him,' said Fisher, 'all over the prison.' 'After being interviewed by his wife,' Smith wrote, 'the prisoner cried for some time. After being interviewed by his attorneys, he paced the bull-pen rapidly and also cried.' He spent the rest of the weekend looking through his bank and brokerage accounts in preparation for the evidence of William Frank of the US Treasury on Monday. At last he had something relevant to occupy his time. 'Slept and ate well,' noted Smith, 'no nervousness.'

18

William E. Frank, a small, bright-eyed man, had been eight years in the Intelligence Unit of the United States Treasury, and during the past three months he had been analyzing Hauptmann's financial transactions from the time of the handing over of the ransom money on April 2, 1932 to the time of his arrest on September 19, 1934. If Frank had approached his task with an open mind, his conclusions might have turned out rather differently. But like the Osborns and Koehler and Bornmann and everybody else, Frank believed Hauptmann guilty; if he was guilty, his accounts had to reflect the fact, and if they didn't he, Frank, would be failing in his job. So the conclusions he did arrive at after several hours of mind-numbing testimony were, even more than those of Genau in the Bronx, breathtakingly precise: between April 1932 and September 1934 Hauptmann had unaccounted-for assets of $49,950.44 – just $49.56 short of the $50,000 ransom money.

Like Genau, Frank had omitted those things that didn't suit his case and grossly exaggerated others. He had ignored Frank Wilson's evidence that much of the ransom money could have passed through the banks undetected, he had ignored the various monies that Hauptmann had received from Fisch, the cash he had at one time kept in the front room at home, the monies he had received in cash for freelance carpentry. He had, as Reilly pointed out, treated as 'real' money the 'paper' money credited to Hauptmann's brokerage account as a result of his trading on margin. And because Hauptmann was constantly passing the same monies from his bank to his brokerage account and back again, there were occasions when Frank double-counted. 'His arithmetic,' wrote Hauptmann, 'would make Professor Einstein appear as a novice! He figured . . . that if I put $2000 in the bank and took out $1000 and invested it somewhere in order to make a profit and after some time I put back $1400, then . . . I must now have $3400 saved!' While researching for his book *Scapegoat* during the 1970s, the writer Anthony Scaduto discovered a 65-page FBI document analyzing Hauptmann's finances. This makes it clear, he says, that far from depositing the large sums of money the prosecution claimed, the amount of equity in Hauptmann's accounts never exceeded $12,000 and that Frank in his evidence was 'bending the truth'.

The next witness was a man who, if he had spoken the truth and brought with him untainted records, could have blown the case against Hauptmann wide open. He was Edward F. Morton, timekeeper for the Reliance Property Management Company at the Majestic Apartments, the man whom James Fawcett had expected to appear at the Bronx *habeas corpus* proceedings and who had failed to show up. The reason he didn't, it will be recalled, was that the timesheets which showed that Hauptmann was working at the Majestic on March 1, together with the payroll records for the same period, had been discreetly removed from the Reliance to the Office of the Assistant District Attorney, Mr Breslin, before being handed over to Detective Cashman of the New York City Police. In Morton's place had appeared the Assistant Treasurer of the Reliance Property Company, a Mr Knapp, who had been persuaded to say that Hauptmann had not started working at the Majestic until March 21 and that he couldn't produce any payroll records for the first half of March *because none had ever existed*.

Aware of this (for he was in the Bronx court at the time) Wilentz was yet able to ask Morton:

'I show you a book and ask you if this is your original book of entry with reference to the employment record of the employees of that company?'

This, it turned out, was nothing less than the company's timesheets, presumably now retrieved from Detective Cashman of the New York City Police; the ones that Mr Knapp had said had never existed.

'Yes, sir, it is.'

'Particularly with reference to March and April 1932?'

'Yes, sir.'

'. . . *does your book include the time from March 1st to March 15th?*'

'It does.'

'Will you tell us whether or not Bruno Richard Hauptmann worked on any day from March 1st to March 21st for your company?'

Knowing that Hauptmann *had* worked during that time, Morton couldn't bring himself unequivocally to deny it.

'Bruno Richard Hauptmann,' he said, '*started* work on March 21st.'

Wilentz's effrontery in this line of questioning, indeed in calling

Morton and his timesheets at all, was staggering. Was he hoping that people had forgotten that a bare three months earlier – on October 18 – he and Foley had both admitted that Hauptmann had worked at the Majestic Apartments on March 1? Did he not know that Hauptmann's timesheets for the periods March 16–31 and for April 1–15 had been doctored? No doubt he was bargaining that Reilly, ignorant of so much about the case, and with his superficial line of questioning, would not ask to see Morton's book. But what if he did?

Knowing how dangerous this area was for him, Wilentz asked no more questions about March 1 or March 21, but concentrated instead on Hauptmann's movements on the day the state alleged he had taken the money from Condon, Saturday April 2; and Morton lied that Hauptmann's last day of work before resigning was Monday April 4, and not Saturday April 2. It was important for the prosecution to establish this untruth, for a scenario in which Hauptmann had spent the Saturday earning $3.33 before collecting $50,000 from Condon the same evening was hardly one which any self-respecting jury would find credible. (Come to that, their case that Hauptmann had started work on March 21 while halfway through the ransom negotiations and had then gone back to earn another $3.33 two days *after* collecting the $50,000 was hardly more credible.) In fact, as will be recalled, Hauptmann did work that Saturday and in the evening had his usual musical soirée with Hans Kloppenburg.

Then it was Reilly's turn, and right at the outset he came within an ace of upsetting the prosecution's applecart. Instead of accepting Morton's evidence at face value, he asked if he could have a look at Morton's book. For Wilentz it must have been an uncomfortable moment, but he said 'Surely' with grace and handed it over.

'Will you find the Hauptmann entry for me, please?' Reilly asked Morton.

'Of what period, please?'

'When he first started . . .'

Morton turned the page.

'Right here, sir.'

'What day do you say he came to work for you?'

'On the 21st March.'

Had Reilly believed in his client's innocence as Fisher did, had he been aware (as he should have been) of Pescia's employment records showing Hauptmann had worked on March 1, of Furcht's affidavit that Hauptmann had worked on March 1,[1] of Foley's and Wilentz's admissions that Hauptmann had worked on March 1, of Knapp's statement that no records for March 1 existed, the first thing he would have asked Morton to show him would have been the entries in his book for March 1–15 – and the second thing the entries for March 16–31. We know (from page 186) what he would have found from the March 16–31 entries: Hauptmann's record tampered with. Would he have found similar tamperings with Hauptmann's record in the March 1–15 entries? Or would Morton have said that, after all, he had forgotten to bring them? We shall never know, for Reilly let the opportunity pass. As most of Wilentz's examination had been to do with the entries for April 1–15 (see page 187), he moved to that, but this time carefully studied Morton's book.

'You have Joe Burnside?'

'Yes, sir.'

'And you have Gustav Kassens?'

'Yes, sir.'

'Then you have Richard Hauptmann crossed out?'

'Yes, sir.'

'But you have a check[2] there for April 1st before it was crossed out, haven't you?'

'I drew that line through the name after he had resigned, sir.'

Morton was side-stepping: Reilly hadn't asked about a name. And anyway, why put a line through Hauptmann's name only and not those of others who resigned?

'I am asking you,' said Reilly, 'whether or not you have a check there for April the 1st?'

'Yes, sir, I have.'

'And you have a naught for April the 2nd, right?'

'Yes, sir.'

'Underneath the naught – which I suppose indicates he didn't work – there is a check mark, isn't there?'

Cornered, Morton pretended not to see.

'Underneath the naught?' he queried.

'In other words,' said Reilly, *'there was a check mark there and you put a naught over it.'*

---

[1] On January 16, five days earlier, the *New York Times* was reporting that Hauptmann's lawyer in the Bronx was still refusing to hand over his papers on the case to Reilly until he had been paid.

[2] What in Britain is called a tick, i.e. ✓

What could Morton say now? He had been caught fudging the books.

After a bit, he said, 'I didn't notice that,' although it was as plain as could be.

'You didn't notice it,' said Reilly, witheringly. 'Then you drew the line and wrote on the side something, didn't you?'

'Yes, sir.'

Now Reilly was ready for the *coup*.

'You didn't draw the line through for Lieutenant Finn, did you?'

'No, sir,' lied Morton, 'I did not.'

And that, amazingly, was all. Reilly had Morton on the ropes but left him there. A few well-placed questions – 'Why did you draw that line through Hauptmann's work record and no one else's?'; 'Wasn't it because you had recorded that Hauptmann *had* worked that Saturday and the knowledge of that would have greatly damaged the prosecution's case?'; 'Can I now see your entries for March 1st and March 21st?' – and Morton (and Wilentz) would have been out for the count.

But Reilly didn't say that or anything like it. He asked a question or two about check marks on Sundays and requested Mr Morton to write his name and address on a piece of paper, and then he sat down. Fisher might *then* have said with justification: 'You are conceding Hauptmann to the electric chair.'

*   *   *

Edward Morton was followed by Cecile Barr, the cashier of Loew's Sheridan movie-house at 12th Street and 7th Avenue, who had claimed that on the evening of Sunday November 26, 1933 a man whom she had identified as Hauptmann in September 1934 had bought a ticket with a $5 ransom bill. Not only would it have been quite out of character for Richard to have left Anna on a Sunday night to travel on his own to a movie-house fifteen miles away, but the date was his birthday and we know he was at home that evening celebrating with Katie Fredericksen, Paul Vetterle and Isidor Fisch.

One of the strangest things (at least to one familiar with British law) about the procedure followed at Hauptmann's trial was the prosecution's reluctance to offer documentary or other corroborative proof of oral evidence, and the defense's reluctance to insist upon it. Edward Morton's unverified and unproved claim that Hauptmann had first started work at the Majestic on 21 March,

1932 was one example. Similarly with Mrs Barr. She should have been asked to tell her full story; how Lieutenant Finn had showed her the $5 ransom bill the bank had given him and asked her if she could describe the man who had handed it to her; how she *was* able to remember him because of the curious way the bill had been folded 'three times in eight parts'; and how ten months later, after Hauptmann had been arrested and she had been shown his photograph, she declared that this was the man. What she told the police should have been offered in evidence. One reason it wasn't was because she had said that the man was American; and nobody could mistake Hauptmann for that.

In place of proof Wilentz gave the court this:

'Do you know the defendant, Bruno Richard Hauptmann?'

'Yes, sir, I have seen him.'

'When was the first time you saw him?'

'When he purchased a ticket at the window, November 26th 1933.'

Such a breathtakingly unsupported statement called for a response: called for Reilly to demand to see Mrs Barr's statement to Lieutenant Finn; called for him to examine in great detail the circumstances in which she had declared Hauptmann was the man, nearly a year after what could have only been a fleeting glimpse of him. But he failed to make such a response. He had another opportunity to find out what Mrs Barr had said when Lieutenant Finn took the stand to identify the ransom bill. But after Wilentz had given him the witness, all he could say was, 'I don't think there is anything we want.' It pretty well summed up his attitude to the whole case.

It will be recalled that the state had so far made two attempts to have the ladder introduced in evidence, and both times the judge had refused, saying the court needed to know more about it. So now Bornmann returned to the stand to trace its chequered history. For the defense Pope again argued skilfully and passionately against admitting it: 'There is no connection between this ladder and the defendant here on trial. No one has even suggested that this ladder was ever in the possession of the defendant. No one has even suggested that he had anything to do with building it; and it is therefore immaterial and irrelevant . . .' But crafty Wilentz had insured himself against this contingency by dredging up Amandus Hochmuth. Was there any doubt, the judge asked Pope, that Hochmuth had seen the defendant in possession of this ladder?

Not *this* ladder, said Pope, Hochmuth did not say it was *this* ladder. And that was true enough. But however the judge regarded Pope's plea – whether as an important point of law or as a splitting of hairs – he knew that if he refused to admit the ladder a third time, that could be the end of the state's case. 'I feel constrained to admit the ladder in evidence,' he said, 'and it will be admitted.'

Then came two more identification witnesses: Whited and a newcomer to the case, Charles Rossiter. Whited told the same lies as he had told in the Bronx, and admitted that on the previous Sunday and because he couldn't read, some man on Wilentz's staff had read over to him his Bronx testimony so that he wouldn't contradict himself. (He still managed to, nevertheless.) Then Fisher did what Reilly never did: he took the witness back to what he had said *at the time*. If Whited's claim to have seen Hauptmann was as strong as the prosecution claimed, thought Fisher, then the police must have taken a statement from him soon after the kidnapping. So he put the question of a statement to Whited, and Whited, not expecting it, nearly gave the game away.

'Have you signed any statement yet about this man that you say you saw along the—'

'Yes.'

'When did you sign that?'

'. . . I think it was the latter part of March or perhaps the middle of April [1932].'

'You signed a statement about *seeing* this man?'

Whited paused. He knew that in this statement of April 26 (see page 216) he had categorically denied seeing *anyone*.

'I signed a statement of all I knew,' he said.

Fisher tried again.

'Well, did you include in the statement the fact that you saw this man along the road on two occasions?'

Whited hedged.

'I won't say whether I did or not.'

Fisher pressed him.

'At the time you said nothing about this man you saw on the road?'

Whited hedged again.

'I wasn't asked no questions and I didn't answer nothing.'

And then a little later, after Whited had rambled on about seeing some strangers among Ten Eyck's loggers in the mountains, Fisher's persistence paid off.

'Nothing was said about seeing this man in that statement?'
And Whited, fed up with prevaricating, said 'No.'

If Wilentz had been more anxious to see that justice was done to Hauptmann and less anxious to win at all costs, he would have seen to it that Whited's statement of April 26 saw the light of day instead of being suppressed. But that, as he well knew, would have destroyed Whited's testimony entirely, and left only Hochmuth as the thin thread connecting Hauptmann with Hopewell. For Hauptmann it was also unfortunate that Fisher did not challenge Whited on his brother Edward's statement to the press and police that he and Millard were continually together and had seen no one. And why did the defense not subpoena Edward as a witness?

Then it was Wilentz's turn to re-examine, and in an unashamedly leading question (to which Fisher objected) he invited Whited to repeat his monstrous lie:

'On the very morning after this kidnapping and crime, you did give a statement verbally, that is, you spoke to the police officers and told them the story you are telling now?'

What else could Whited say but 'Yes, sir.'

* * *

It has already been suggested that this was a case in which the groundswell of opinion for a conviction was so great that people were prepared to suspend their critical faculties and believe whatever evidence was offered them, however outrageous. The story that was now unfolded was another of these. Soon after Hauptmann's arrest and the appearance of his picture in the papers, hundreds of people telephoned or wrote to the New Jersey Police to say they were sure they had seen him somewhere. Among these was a young man named Charles B. Rossiter (who was later discovered to be a thief) and his story, told to the New Jersey Police on September 22, was that he remembered seeing Hauptmann for a few minutes in the dark standing by his car on a road near Princeton on the Saturday before the kidnapping two and a half years before – a feat of memory almost unparalleled. He was then taken to the Bronx Jail to view Hauptmann, and declared that he was the man.

The New Jersey Police had been flooded with stories of this sort, and Rossiter's being scarcely more credible than anyone else's, they had allowed his statement to lie on the file. Now, however, with aspersions being increasingly cast on the only two witnesses to

place Hauptmann in New Jersey, Hochmuth and Whited, the
prosecution decided to dust him over and put him on parade. His
story was that while motoring to Philadelphia to stay with his
wife's parents, he had seen a car stopped, with the driver standing
beside it, on the road near Princeton Airport. It was 8 p.m. and
dark. He himself had stopped to see if the driver needed assistance,
but the driver said he didn't. Wilentz asked if Rossiter had then
proceeded on his way, and he said, 'No, I stood there and looked
the man over pretty well' (a statement designed to give his story
more credence). WHAT BULLSHIT

  Reilly was rather more successful with Rossiter than with others,
making Rossiter admit that he had mistaken people's identities
two or three times before, and that he was well in with the New
Jersey State Police. ('At a conservative estimate I know about ten.')
Then, in one single question and answer, Reilly came halfway to
nullifying Rossiter's evidence entirely.
  'Describe the car.'
  '. . . I didn't distinguish the make of the car . . . the car that I
saw had on the rear of it a three-pronged tire holder . . .'
  Now Hauptmann's car was distinctive in that it had no tire
holder on the rear, three-pronged or otherwise, but a large canvas-
covered wooden box which, it will be recalled, Hauptmann and
Kloppenburg had made for their 1931 trip to California. It had
never been removed. That Rossiter was unaware of this showed
how badly he had been briefed. But, incredibly, Reilly didn't seem
to know of it either – if he had known, he would have been bound
to ask Rossiter whether he was aware of the existence of the box.
And so another great opportunity to damage the prosecution's case
was lost, and Rossiter was allowed to stand down. Alone, his
testimony – like that of Mrs Achenbach and Millard Whited and
Edward Morton and Cecile Barr – was not all that impressive; but
collectively and cumulatively their weasel words were like water
dripping on a stone.

                    *   *   *

Now the prosecution were almost at the end of their case against
Hauptmann, and to wrap it all neatly up, to prove beyond doubt
that Hauptmann was Charlie's kidnapper and murderer, they were
ready to present their final, conclusive chapter: how the wily
Bornmann and Koehler proved that part of the kidnap ladder came
from Hauptmann's attic.

Hauptmann, it will be recalled, was arrested on September 19, and there began several lengthy and systematic searches of his small apartment, all of which included the attic: in the week following it was visited on nine occasions by no less than thirty-seven detectives and policemen. 'We were unable to find anything connected with the Lindbergh case,' reported Corporal Samuel Leon on September 20, and that went for the other searches too. Then on September 26 Bornmann went up there, accompanied by Detective Tobin, Superintendent Wilson and two carpenters. 'We immediately proceeded to make a thorough search of the attic,' he reported to Lamb. 'Nothing of value was found with the exception of several small pieces of wood and shavings and several cut nails . . .'

The court that was trying Hauptmann knew nothing of these things and so Bornmann, when he took the stand again, was able to tell a completely different story. On searching the attic on September 26, he said, he found that an 8-foot length of flooring 'had been removed'. How was it, he was asked, that this wasn't noticed before? His answer was breathtaking in its mendacity. Because, he said (knowing that nobody would contradict him) *he was the first policeman* to venture into the attic. Of all the lies told at Hauptmann's trial, this was one of the worst.

He then told his story of thinking that Rail 16 might have come from this missing 8-foot plank and, as a result, of ordering the carpenter to remove another 7 feet from the same section in order to compare it. He didn't realize that this entirely contradicted the evidence of Hauptmann's landlord Max Rauch, given only the day before, that when he visited the attic a week later, only 8 feet were missing; all of which suggested that whatever Bornmann had done or said he had done did not take place on September 26. He then described how he and Koehler had returned to the attic on October 9 with Rail 16, laid it in the space where the missing plank had been and, with a bit of pushing and shoving, found that the nail holes in Rail 16 were flush with the other nail holes in the joists beneath. QED, Rail 16 was part of the missing plank.

Before Bornmann stepped down, Pope complained that his taking over the Hauptmann apartment meant that the defense had been persistently refused permission to enter it, to see this famous attic for themselves. Could they do so now, Pope asked? And Bornmann replied, 'You have my permission, sir.' In fact, until the trial was over, all access for the defense to Hauptmann's apartment continued to be denied. To those acting for a man on trial for his life, it would be difficult to think of a greater injustice.

Then Arthur Koehler, the wood expert, was called and for most of one day and the morning of the next he blinded the court with wood expertise, supporting everything Bornmann had said and adding esoteric touches of his own. For instance the grain in Rail 16 and the grain in the plank that Bornmann had removed were similar (as grains in yellow pine often are); a knot in Rail 16 was clearly part of the same knot in the board (or rather, would have been but for an unfortunate 1¼-inch gap); and if the color of Rail 16 was different to that of the board, why that was because Rail 16 had been stained by chemicals used in searching it for fingerprints. In addition certain plane marks on Rail 16 were the same as marks made by a plane found in Hauptmann's garage (which if true would have meant that Hauptmann had not sharpened the blade in two and a half years) and saw cuts made by a saw found in Hauptmann's tool-box were similar to saw cuts found on Rail 16 (both 35 to 37 thousandths of an inch).

Then, as though all this were not enough, the ¾-inch Buck's chisel found beneath the nursery window at Hopewell was brought in and identified, and Koehler said a chisel of the same size had been used to fashion recesses for the cleats in the ladder. He was obviously reckoning that no one would remember that in his report of March 4 1933 (see page 145) he had stated unequivocally that it was impossible to say what width of chisel had been used; or that the defense would be aware that when Dr Souder examined the ladder and chisel for the FBI in May 1932, he had categorically stated that 'no conclusion that the chisel was used in building the ladder is warranted'. Finally, to clinch matters, one of Hauptmann's tool-boxes was brought in – naturally not the one containing his modern set of Stanley chisels, but a collection of old cheap Buck's chisels which was all that he could afford when he first came to America. This enabled the following dialogue to take place between Wilentz and Koehler:

'Do you know what sizes of chisels make up a carpenter's chest of chisels?'

'As a rule a good carpenter's tool-chest should contain a quarter-inch chisel, half-inch chisel, three-quarter-inch chisel, one-inch, one-and-a-half- and possibly two-inch.'

'Take a look at these chisels found in the Hauptmann place and tell me whether there is a three-quarter-inch chisel there or whether there is one missing . . . Take your time.'

Koehler poked around and came up with the answer Wilentz wanted.

'There is a quarter-inch chisel, a half-inch chisel, and an inch-and-a-half chisel.'

'Is there any three-quarter-inch chisel?'

'No.'

The inference of course was that Hauptmann had taken the missing chisel with him to Hopewell and left it on the lawn as he fled; and no doubt this is what the jury believed. The truth was simpler, and even less attractive: the chisel had been quietly removed and taken to New Jersey State Police headquarters in Trenton, where in a basement room some forty years later the writer Anthony Scaduto discovered it. Looking through Hauptmann's tool-chest Scaduto found that the ¾-inch Buck's chisel was still missing. He mentioned this to the trooper helping him, and the trooper (who obviously knew nothing of the background to the case) 'pulled from a tall metal locker filled with boxes a rolled-up manila envelope. "This could be it," he said. There was some writing on the outside of the envelope. It said: 'Two old chisels found in Hauptmann's garage'. . . Both were ¾-inch chisels. One of them was a Buck's Brothers brand similar to the one found under the nursery window . . . the other a Stanley.'

Pope's cross-examination of Koehler was not what it might have been, for while his own knowledge of carpentry told him that Koehler was talking nonsense, he lacked the hard evidence on which to nail him. Had he been able to lay his hands on Koehler's 1933 report, it would have been a different story. He would have read what Koehler had said about being unable to determine the width of chisel used to make the cleats; what he had said about the lack of marks on the nail holes in Rail 16 which indicated they had been removed by pushing from below (impossible if Rail 16 had been part of a flooring); and what he had said about the spacing between the nail holes giving no indication as to what Rail 16 had been used for (had Rail 16 ever been part of a flooring he would have recognized the standard 16-inch space between joists). As it was, Pope, although tenacious and sometimes passionate, was largely fumbling in the dark.

What was the real story behind the phoney evidence that Bornmann and Koehler had cooked up? Anthony Scaduto probably came nearest to the truth in *Scapegoat*:

What I believe most probably occurred in the attic is that either Lamb or Bornmann, remembering the comment of the wood expert, Arthur Koehler, that Rail 16 had once lain indoors and that a search of any suspect's home should be made for a place where the rail had previously been used, decided to fake the evidence once it was clear all prior searches were fruitless.

Bornmann then went into the attic. He laid Rail 16 down across one of the floorboards so that the nail holes in the rail would lie above one of the joists. Measuring only roughly, he cut off a length of lumber that would approximately correspond to the length of the ladder rail, but he cut it at least eight inches too long, forced to do so perhaps because of the 16-inch spacing between joists. He threw that length of lumber away. He then placed Rail 16 over the joist nearest the remaining piece of floorboard, took four of the square-cut nails which he had found in Hauptmann's attic, and slid them into the nail holes in the ladder rail. He then hammered them home, so that they would create holes in the joists precisely corresponding to the angle and spacing of the holes in the rail. When he removed the nails, he had his evidence to directly link Hauptmann to the ladder . . .

There is other circumstantial evidence which tends to further support the conclusion that Bornmann created the attic scenario. For one thing, through all the days in which Hauptmann was questioned by police and the Bronx District Attorney's staff – questioning that continued after the date Bornmann claims to have found the attic proof of the prisoner's guilt – no investigator ever questioned Hauptmann about it. He was repeatedly interrogated about the ransom money, about the board with Condon's telephone number which had been found in his closet, about his tools and his purchases of lumber, and dozens of other questions connected with the ladder. But not once was he asked to explain the missing board in the attic . . .

After making another point put forward here – that if the attic evidence was true, Foley and Wilentz would certainly have used it at Hauptmann's extradition hearing in October, it being by far the strongest evidence to put Hauptmann at the scene of the crime – Scaduto continues:

Bornmann, who lived in the Hauptmann apartment from the day after the arrest until the trial, must have manufactured the attic evidence long after September 26th and then back-dated his reports so that it would appear he had simply decided to make another search of the attic on that date. He could not pretend to have found the evidence before September 26th because his report and the reports of other investigators said that up to that date nothing of interest had been found. And he could not have filed a report a week or a month after that date, because the delay would have been more suspect. So he filed his fake report with a date and time immediately following his last authentic report of the fruitless search of the attic.

The evidence discovered by Bornmann is probably the most demonstrably false of all the evidence against Hauptmann. And it is Bornmann's evidence upon which the credibility of Koehler's testimony hinges. Without that ladder rail, none of Koehler's testimony can be considered even circumstantial evidence connecting Hauptmann with the kidnap ladder; without that ladder rail, in fact, Koehler's testimony is absolutely valueless.

And later, long after the trial had ended, would come FBI support for the belief that Bornmann and Koehler had faked the attic evidence. In a memorandum from Special Agent Rosen to Mr Tamm, dated May 26, 1936, it was stated:

The identification of the wood in the ladder, resulting in the opinion that the wood in the attic of Hauptmann's residence was identical with that of the ladder, was developed subsequent to the withdrawal of this Bureau from an active part in the investigation, and occurred after the New Jersey State Police had rented the Hauptmann residence.

You will also recall that at one stage of the trial of Hauptmann it was indicated that efforts would be made by the defense counsel to subpoena records of this department relative to Arthur Koehler, with the thought in mind that the defense could establish and check that Arthur Koehler's story concerning the wood identification could be proved as having been fabricated by the joint efforts of the New Jersey State Police and the New Jersey Prosecutor's Office in co-operation with Arthur Koehler. However this request was not received by the Bureau from the defense attorneys.

Naturally the jury had no inkling of this. The last of them to survive, Ethel Stockton, said to me in 1982: 'It was the expert witnesses, like the handwriting people and the wood man, Mr Koehler, who impressed me most. You can coach ordinary witnesses to say what you want them to say. But you can't coach experts.' (Unless, she might have added, the experts coach themselves.) It was not a view shared by Anna Hauptmann. Also in 1982 she said to me: 'All those lies they told in the witness chair. I could understand it if they had been making mistakes, but these were lies and they knew it.'

On the afternoon of Thursday January 24, the Attorney General rose and said to the court:

'The state rests.'

*   *   *

In order not to interrupt the narrative flow of the presentation of the prosecution case, no mention has been made of the interruptions to the testimony by counsel on both sides. They were frequent, often lengthy and at times acrimonious. Seldom more than a few minutes of uninterrupted evidence were heard before counsel of one side or the other were on their feet to complain of a breach of procedure, a question wrongly put, an answer wrongly given. Wilentz was the worst offender, Reilly was not far behind; and in the great majority of instances Judge Trenchard upheld the arguments of the state and rejected those of the defense.

In addition it was said that both Wilentz and Reilly contravened Canon 20 of the American Lawyers' Canons of Professional Ethics by making frequent public statements in the press and/or on the radio about their current view of the case. Early on Reilly had boasted he would name four people who were the real kidnappers but, when pressed, refused to do so. Later he issued a statement that the defense's case would be that Fisch was the kidnapper, aided by Violet Sharpe! And he tried to keep up his spirits and those of his client by continually stating that he believed Hauptmann would be acquitted, that no jury in the world could possibly convict him. Wilentz was not much better. 'We are going to wrap that kidnap ladder around Hauptmann's neck,' he declared to the press on one occasion, exhibiting a vengefulness that characterized his entire approach to the case. 'What a horrible thing if this man got away with it. Wait till you see what follows. I can't wait myself.' Writing in the *American Mercury*, Newman Levy said Judge Trenchard had ample powers to discipline any lawyer who broadcast and talked to the press, but had failed to exercise them, and that he had equally failed to discipline the press under the powers given him. It was fear, said Levy, that traditionally inhibited judges from these tasks; being elected, not appointed to office, they were dependent on the press for the furtherance of their careers.

The other unattractive features bordering the trial continued. Flemington remained a carnival town, the dark mornings and evenings punctuated with exploding flashbulbs to freeze the arrival and departure of celebrities. The boom in the sale of toy ladders was maintained and there was continuing nightly revelry in Nellie's Tap. Reilly (who by now had abandoned his striped pants for a business suit) did nothing to enhance his dignity when a small fire broke out in the offices of Fisher's law firm, and afloat on orange blossom he leapt onto the fire truck to pose for photographers. On another occasion Ethel Stockton saw him dancing round the courthouse flagpole. Inside the court the judge had frequently to rebuke gigglers and chatterers who, bored with the evidence, gossiped among themselves. On the first Sunday in February a stream of sightseers – nearly 3000 in all – traipsed round the courtroom, while members of the American Legion stood by to prevent them taking souvenirs or scratching their initials on the woodwork. The same day Mrs Hattie Trimmer, a Methodist minister, conducted her usual Sunday morning service in the jail for twelve short-term prisoners; she'd been doing it for twenty-seven years. 'We sang "What a friend we have in Jesus" and "There is a fountain filled with blood",' she said, 'and I'm sure Hauptmann heard every word.' If he did, there is no record of it; but in the afternoon Anna and Manfred came to visit him, their entry to the prison watched by a score of photographers and the twelve jurymen exercising on their balcony in the Union Hotel across the street. Inside the prison Manfred's blue woollen suit and white knitted outer garment were again thoroughly searched, 'to make sure,' said the *New York Times,* 'that the clothing did not conceal an article which would enable Hauptmann to escape or commit suicide'. After the visit Hauptmann wept. His current reading, said the paper, was *Gentlemen of Courage* by James Oliver Curwood, and stories of expeditions to the North and South Poles.

The press continued to berate the conduct of the case, if not their own role in it. Ford Madox Ford missed the solemnity and reverence of a British court of law. Edna Ferber said that 'the jammed aisles, the crowded corridors, the noise, the buzz, the idiot laughter, the revolting faces of those who are watching are an affront to civilization.' A letter in the *Brooklyn Daily Eagle* called the trial 'the most disgraceful thing that ever happened; we must be the laughing-stock of the world.' And the criminologist Arthur Reeve declared:

> There is an urgent need to revise our crime detection methods, our criminal law and practise. In a case like Hauptmann's, the best attorney available should have been appointed by the court and have been granted the time and funds necessary to meet the points raised by the state in order that the defendant's guilt or innocence should be established beyond any reasonable doubt.

PART SEVEN

THE DEFENDERS

'I had no more idea it was Lindbergh ransom money than the man in the moon.'

(Hauptmann: 'Why did you kill me?'
Liberty Magazine)

19

Before the defense formally opened, Egbert Rosecrans applied to the court for a motion of acquittal on two grounds: that the prosecution had produced no evidence to show that the baby had been murdered in Hunterdon County rather than Mercer County where its body was found (and in which the court had no jurisdiction); and that there was no evidence to place Hauptmann at the scene of the crime. Both propositions were true, and in his counter-arguments Wilentz said nothing to invalidate them. However, he reminded the court of what he alleged the prosecution had proved: that Hauptmann had written the ransom notes, returned the sleeping-suit, collected the ransom money, built the ladder and been seen in the neighborhood; and it would have required a steelier character than Judge Trenchard to fly in the face of such seemingly powerful circumstantial evidence. 'The motion for direction of acquittal,' he said, 'will be denied.'

Lloyd Fisher opened for the defense and said they would produce an alibi for Hauptmann on March 1, the day of the kidnapping; on April 2, the day of the handing over of the ransom money; and on November 26, 1933, the day of his birthday. They would show that in analyzing Hauptmann's accounts the prosecution had grossly over-estimated the monies that had been in Hauptmann's possession. They would bring witnesses to prove that Hochmuth suffered from hallucinations and that Whited was a congenital liar. They would show the worthlessness of the evidence about the ladder, and they would produce a handwriting expert who would declare that the writing in the ransom notes was not the hand-writing of Hauptmann – they could not produce more than one expert because they could not afford to. 'We will show you that the funds of this man Hauptmann are completely and totally exhausted. He is before you here in the court without one dollar that he can call his own, without a penny in the world. And his defense has been almost entirely financed through the members of his counsel.'

Fisher sat down and Reilly rose.

'Bruno Richard Hauptmann,' he said, 'take the stand.'

Although Hauptmann had gone to bed before midnight, he had lain awake until 2 a.m. before falling into what Lieutenant Smith called 'a troubled sleep' which lasted until 8.30 a.m. But he had breakfasted well on hot cereal, bread and butter and coffee, and after Smith had shaved him and he had put on his double-breasted gray suit, light blue shirt, new dark blue spotted tie (specially bought by Anna at Nevius Brothers, Flemington) with a white handkerchief sticking out of his breast pocket, he could almost have passed for any up and coming young business executive. As he moved briskly across to the witness chair, impressing the spectators with his composure and self-confidence, Lieutenant Smith's guards took up their new positions: Deputy Low behind the witness chair, Trooper Stockburger beside the jury-box, Trooper Green at the end of the judge's bench, Smith beside Mrs Haupt-mann, and Troopers Piana and Zickwolf in the lanes beneath the courtroom windows (to catch Hauptmann if he decided on a headlong leap to freedom?).

Now there was silence in court; this was the moment for which everyone had been waiting. For seventeen days the spectators had seen the prisoner enter the court in the morning and leave it in the evening, and in between times had seen the back of his head. Now, as he settled down in the raised witness chair he faced them all. Soon he would speak. How would he sound? What sort of account would he give of himself? Might he at long last confess?

The examination started off in a low-key fashion. Reilly, who called Hauptmann 'Bruno' throughout (a name he disliked and never used), asked him about his early life in Kamenz, schooling, war service, arrival in America, marriage and jobs. Hauptmann answered, according to one newspaper report, 'slowly, quietly, without vehemence ... there was even a hint of drabness in the color of his clothing, unrelieved by a face which seemed from a front view, one flat plane . . . His legs assumed many postures . . . he would cross and uncross them, then spread his knees so that the soles of his shoes faced each other; again, one would be drawn under the chair, the other extended.' Others noticed how high-pitched and guttural was his voice, at times how unsure his use of English. He related his business dealings with Fisch, the money Fisch owed him when he died, his discovery of the gold certificate bills in the shoe-box. He spoke of the beating-up he had received in the Greenwich Street Police Station (which evidence Wilentz unsuccessfully tried to have suppressed) and the threats made by the police in making him write far into the night.

'How long a period was it before they finished with you as far as the writings were concerned?'

'From the hour of my arrest to, I'd say, around two o'clock in the morning the next day.'

'And how many times did they request you to write?'

'I don't recall how many times.'

'Many times?'

'Many times. I fell asleep on a chair when they poked me in the ribs and said, "You write!" '

'Were you hit during the writing, during the different periods you wrote?'

'I got a couple of knocks in the ribs when I refused to write.'

'Now, in writing, did you spell the words of your own free will or did they tell you how to spell the words?'

'Some of them words they spell it to me.'

'How do you spell "not"?'

'N-o-t.'

'Did they ask you to spell it "n-o-t-e"?'

'I remember very well they put an "e" on it.'

Reilly asked about 'signature'.

'Did they tell you to spell it "s-i-n-g"?'

'They did.'

'So when they were dictating the spelling, that was not your own free will in spelling, was it?'

'It was not.'

Although Wilentz complained, rightly, that these were leading questions, they were only repetitions of what Hauptmann had maintained all along. But to satisfy the court, Reilly put the question comprehensively:

'As far as the spelling of those words I have indicated, *and other words that are mis-spelt in these request writings of yours*, was that your voluntary spelling or your voluntary act, or was it the act and spelling dictated to you by policemen and officials who wanted you to write it that way?'

Hauptmann's answer was unequivocal:

'It was because of the dictation.'

He was unequivocal too about other things. He had not known the Lindberghs had a baby, he had never seen it alive or dead, and he had no knowledge of the location of Hopewell, Woodlawn Cemetery or Dr Condon's house. But his most effective moment came with the bringing into court of the three sections of the ladder. They were placed against the wall to the right of the jury-box.

'Now how many years, Bruno,' asked Reilly, 'have you been a carpenter?'

'About ten years.'

'You have seen this ladder here in court, haven't you?'

'Yes.'

'Did you build that ladder?'

Hauptmann smiled.

'I am a carpenter,' he said. It was a telling reply and raised laughter in court.

'Did you build this ladder?'

'Certainly not.'

'Well, come down and look at it, please.'

Hauptmann did so and, heartened by the response to his first comment, said, 'Looks like a music instrument.'

Baffled, Wilentz asked for a repeat.

'He says in his opinion,' said Reilly, 'it looks like a music instrument.' Turning to Hauptmann, 'In your opinion does it look like a well-made ladder?'

'To me,' said Hauptmann, 'it [hardly][1] looks like a ladder at all.' He observed the 18-inch gap between the rungs. 'I don't know how a man can step up.'

Were these the answers, some asked, of a kidnapper and murderer who was also a consummate actor; or of an innocent man?

Now it was Wilentz's turn, and from the start he went in fighting, getting Hauptmann to admit that he had not always told the truth,

---

[1] This word or one similar is missing from the trial record.

listing his convictions in Germany (and for good measure adding two mythical ones) so that the jury could see the kind of man he was; saying how 'unfortunate' it was that Fisch had died and so could not corroborate the shoe-box story; trying to dirty his relationship with Gerta Henkel, even with Anna ('Do you know what you are talking about?' Hauptmann shot back angrily. 'You are talking about my wife and me'); producing a child's drawing of a ladder and a window found in Hauptmann's apartment and endeavoring to make something of it; showing the similarities between letters in his hand and those in the ransom notes ('o's with open tops, 'x's as back-to-back 'e's, 'light' as 'lihgt' etc.) to which Hauptmann retorted, 'Many German people got about the same handwriting.' Wilentz produced a notebook of Hauptmann's and declared that the word 'boat' in his writing had been spelled 'boad' as in 'the boad Nelly' in the last ransom note. In fact he had spelt it 'boat', his 't's in the shape of triangles bearing some slight resemblance to other people's 'd's; and in any case, as Hauptmann pointed out, 'boat' in German is not 'boad' but '*Boot*'.

Then Wilentz produced one of the ransom notes and asked Hauptmann to read it aloud. Only a counsel who believed as passionately as Wilentz did in the prosecution's case would have made such a request, reckoning that having a guilty man read out in court the letters he had written demanding money would produce some signs of guilt. But the firework Wilentz had hoped for proved a damp squib. 'It's hard for you to read, isn't it?' he said, thinking Hauptmann was hesitating, and Hauptmann, battling with the ill-formed mis-spellings, said, 'You bet it is.' He peered closer. 'I can't make out the next word' – 'I don't know what the next word means' – 'Can't make out the next two words' – 'When you tell me, I can make it out.' Once again those in court had to decide whether these were the responses of a genuinely puzzled man or of a brilliant performer.

Everyone present was agreed that during the first hour or so of his cross-examination Hauptmann was extremely nervous, but that when he settled down he gave as good as he got. 'He simply leaned forward in the witness chair,' said the reporter from the *New York Times*, 'fixed his cold, hard stare upon the prosecutor and shot back his answers with the same force as Mr Wilentz fired his questions. As in a few other clashes earlier in the day, he raised his voice in a loud and angry tone and spoke rapidly, in contrast to the low, deliberate and cautious manner in which he testified most of the time.'

His most telling moments came when he was able to smile; when, as one reporter put it, 'he assumed the air of a man who considered himself master of the situation'. This first occurred after he had agreed with Wilentz that at the end of 1928 his accounts showed a credit balance of $5780.

'Did you ever have that much money when you were in Europe?'

Hauptmann, remembering Germany's post-war inflation, smiled and said, 'I got billions.'

Puzzled, ignorant about inflation, aware that Hauptmann had somehow got the better of him, Wilentz said,

'Billions in Europe?'

'Yes,' said Hauptmann, and to help out, 'Inflation it was.'

'Inflation time?' said Wilentz, as he might have said 'Party time?'

'Yes.'

'You had billions?'

Still smiling, Hauptmann said 'Yes', and in the vacuum left by the Attorney General's silence, the court laughed; when the laughter had died away, all that a discomfited Wilentz could think of to say was, 'This is a sort of hallucination with you, isn't it, this billions business?' It was this kind of stumbling that led Kathleen Norris to say, 'One feels that Attorney General Wilentz isn't entirely satisfied with the way things are going, but an older hand than he would have trouble with this elusive witness . . . Hauptmann has the air of being pleased with himself.'

Another occasion occurred after Wilentz had been questioning Hauptmann about Tom Cassidy's writing on the inside trim of the nursery closet. Because Hauptmann's admission to Foley of the authorship of part of the writing was the nearest that Hauptmann ever came to a confession, Wilentz would not leave it. He went on and on about it, trying to force Hauptmann to admit once again what he had admitted in the Bronx. If he *had* written what was there, said Hauptmann, he had no idea it was Condon's address and telephone number. So you admit you did write it, said Wilentz. No, said Hauptmann, I thought I must have done when asked in the Bronx because I didn't realize then exactly where the board had come from. But now I know, I say it's impossible to write or read in the closet, it's too dark. You chose a dark place, suggested Wilentz, because you didn't want anyone to find it. Not true, said Hauptmann, I only wrote things down and left them where I could see them. To and fro the battle raged. Only once did Hauptmann request a truce. 'I am thinking in German and I have to translate in American language, and it needs quite a bit of time, so excuse me.' Then they were at it again. 'Wilentz,' said one reporter, 'tries by tireless attacking to break down the prisoner's resistance, but Hauptmann doggedly, stubbornly, eludes pursuit.'

In the end Wilentz gave up, exasperated that he hadn't obtained the confession he was expecting; and Hauptmann, with his attacker's guns temporarily silent, could afford to smile again, not in triumph but because, alone of all those in court, he knew the absurdity of the proposition Wilentz was making. Goaded, Wilentz said:

'This is funny to you, isn't it? You're having a lot of . . .'

'No,' said Hauptmann, 'absolutely not.'

'Well, you are doing very well, you are smiling at me every five minutes.'

'No.'

'You think you are a big shot, don't you?'

'No,' said Hauptmann, then taking the initiative, 'Should I cry?'

Rattled, Wilentz answered the question instead of ignoring it. 'No, certainly you shouldn't.' Then, recovering his balance, 'You think you are bigger than everybody, don't you?'

'No,' said Hauptmann, 'but I know I am innocent.' And he repeated it with assurance a moment later. 'I feel innocent and I am innocent and that keeps me the power to stand up.'

This wasn't in Wilentz's scenario at all.

'Lying when you swear to God you will tell the truth,' he shouted. 'Telling lies doesn't mean anything?'

'Stop that!' Hauptmann shouted back.

'Didn't you swear to untruths in the Bronx courthouse?'

'Stop that!' shouted Hauptmann again.

But nothing would stop Wilentz now: he had become a very angry man.

'Didn't you swear to untruths in the courthouse? Didn't you lie under oath time and time again? Didn't you?'

'I did not.'

'You did not?'

'No.'

'All right, sir. When you were arrested with this Lindbergh ransom money and you had a twenty dollar bill, Lindbergh ransom money, did they ask you where you got it? Did they ask you?'

'They did.'

'Did you lie to them or did you tell them the truth?'

'I said not the truth.'

'You lied, didn't you?'

'I did, yes.'

'Yes. Lies, lies, lies about the Lindbergh ransom money, isn't that right?'

'Well, you lied to me too.'

'Yes, where and when?'

'Right in this courtroom here.' MOTHERFUCKIN' RIGHT BRUNO.

Exhausted, Wilentz dropped to a lower key; but in his mind things still rankled.

'You see, you are not smiling any more, are you?'

'Smiling?'

'It has gotten a little more serious, hasn't it?'

Hauptmann agreed.

Wilentz paused, looked at the jury, round the courtroom, then at Hauptmann.

' "*I am a carpenter!*" he said.' The brazenness of the utterance, the fact that everyone in the case remembered it, still incensed him.

'I am,' said Hauptmann.

'That was funny, wasn't it?'

'No, sir, there is nothing funny about that.'

'There is nothing funny about it? You had a good laugh, didn't you? Did you plan that in the jail there, did somebody tell you to give that answer when I asked you about the ladder,[1] to stand in front of the jury and say, "I am a carpenter"?'

'No, sir.'

'You thought that out yourself?'

He had, but he said, 'No, sir, I didn't think a thing about it.'

'Let me ask you something,' said Wilentz. 'You have got a peculiar notion about willpower, haven't you?'

Wilentz was losing his grip: Hauptmann had said nothing about willpower, and it brought Pope to his feet.

'Well,' said Pope, 'I think this has gone just about far enough . . . this patent abuse of the witness. It seems to me it is about time we protested about it. It has been going on for quite a while.'

Had the judge been a stronger character he would have stopped the abuse himself. Instead he granted a recess; and after it, when things were cooler, Wilentz went on to other things.

[1] In fact Reilly had asked him.

In Reilly's re-direct examination Hauptmann was able to list several of his possessions which he claimed the police had seized from his apartment and then suppressed as evidence: the ledger which contained all his accounts, and six or eight letters sent to him from Fisch in Germany proving their business partnership. Shown his tool-box he found that his two iron planes were missing, also his half-, three-quarter- and one-inch Stanley chisels which he had last used only two days before his arrest. Confronted with the plane which Koehler had said had been used to make Rail 16, he smiled and said it was a cheap, wooden one which he had bought on arrival in America and had last used in 1928.

Thanks mainly to Anna, who continually urged him not to get angry or over-excited, Hauptmann maintained his composure until the end. During the noon recess on the third day of his testimony, when back in his cell for lunch, Lieutenant Smith noted: 'He seemed in good spirits due to the fact that he believes he is more than holding his own during the cross-examination by the Attorney General.' As he resumed his seat he felt confident enough to smile at the jury, and several were observed to smile back. And when he finally stepped down after seventeen hours of giving evidence, eleven of them to the Attorney General, the *New York Times* observed that 'he seemed stronger and more composed at the end of the experience than when he started last Thursday afternoon'. Reilly expressed satisfaction at his performance and even Wilentz could not forbear a word of praise, though naturally the prosecuting team were disappointed not to have heard, as they had expected, a 'confession'. The prosecution's Judge Large attributed it to Hauptmann having 'a lot of nerve and gall', and Wilentz explained it away by saying, 'A man who is strong enough to commit this crime is strong enough to withhold a confession.'

To most spectators Hauptmann was as much an enigma at the end of his testimony as he was at the beginning. The evidence pointed so clearly to his guilt, and in many of his responses he had been less than convincing. Wilentz had him contradicting himself several times about his accounts (though Hauptmann, being unable to refer to his ledger, was under a considerable handicap); his replies as to why he had put the shoe-box in the kitchen closet rather than somewhere else were unsatisfactory; his having lied in the Bronx about the ransom money was particularly damning; while his telling Wilentz that he intended to give the money in his garage to Pinkus Fisch *even if he hadn't been arrested* was plainly ridiculous.

There were also many like Wilentz who mistook his self-confidence and composure for arrogance, who saw in him a typical member of the master race now asserting itself across the Atlantic.

Yet if he was guilty, how could he afford to be so dismissive about so much of the evidence, to apparently take things so lightly, to break into the occasional smile which, one observer said, was his most telling offensive weapon? And how to square the image of the meticulous keeper of accounts with that of the semi-literate writer of the ransom notes; the professional carpenter with the maker of the ramshackle ladder; the father of a much-loved child with the kidnapper and murderer of a baby? Instead of clearing the air, as many had expected, Hauptmann's seventeen hours in the witness chair had made him more mysterious than ever.

It was a mystery which might have been dispelled had Reilly had the intelligence and drive to explore deep into that area of evidence which held the key to his client's innocence – his employment at the Majestic Apartments in March and April 1932. By now one would have expected the defense to have learnt from *somewhere* – from Fawcett or Furcht or Pescia, from Wilentz's or Foley's admissions – that Hauptmann was speaking the truth when he declared in Greenwich Street that he was working at the Majestic on March 1. Incredibly, and tragically, the very opposite happened. When Reilly questioned him on this early in his examination, he said he had registered for the job at the agency on Saturday February 27, left his tools at the Majestic on Monday February 29, reported for work at 8 a.m. on Tuesday March 1 *and been told by the Superintendent there was no work and to come back on March 15, which he did.* It is impossible to say what powerful evidence made him change his mind so drastically. Had Wilentz assured Reilly privately that there was no evidence of his working there between March 1 and 15, and had Reilly taken him at his word and believed him? And had he then passed this on to Hauptmann as though it were gospel truth? Later Reilly asked Hauptmann if there had not been some doubt in his mind in his testimony in the Bronx as to whether he had worked on March 1, and he replied truthfully enough, 'If it wouldn't be so long ago, I would probably have ten to twenty witnesses that I worked.'

So in cross- and recross-examination, Wilentz, clever as a monkey, produced the check for $36.67 which Hauptmann admitted had his signature on the back and which (unless it was a forgery) confirmed that he had worked for only eleven days (at $3.33 a day) between March 16 and 31. As further confirmation Wilentz produced the doctored payroll sheet for the second half of March (see page 188) but was careful not to bring into evidence the more blatantly doctored timesheets (pages 186–7) for the same period. And when Reilly called on him to produce Morton's records, Wilentz was quick to say 'Ending March 1st and April 15th?' before they were handed over. So Reilly never saw the doctored timesheets for March 15–31, nor the vital timesheets or payroll record for March 1–15. Why did he not ask, why did he not insist on seeing them? Had he learned that they contained information that would clear his client? And had he then shied away from them, knowing that it was not for this that the anti-Hauptmann Hearst Press had employed him? One trusts not, but in this most extraordinary of trials anything was possible.

20

It was now the turn of Anna Hauptmann – described by Kathleen Norris in the *New York Times* as 'a thin, fuzzy-headed woman, plain, long-nosed, pale', who had won the admiration of all by her stoicism and unwavering belief, conveyed to Jeannette Smits and printed in the *New York Evening Journal* almost daily, in her husband's innocence. Kathleen Norris misinterpreted what she read and saw. 'How long should a woman stick by a man anyway?' she wrote. 'How far should wifely loyalty carry her against her self-respect, her sense of honesty, her true belief? Does anything like love still linger for him, or is it only pity?' She would have been startled to know that fifty years later Anna would be loving him as truly as ever, and that her self-respect, honesty and beliefs were all intact.

She mounted the stand. She was wearing a blue crêpe dress with a high neckline, a rhinestone pendant, a black felt hat and a fashionable short veil. 'She spoke in a thin voice with a German accent, slurring her words and using a low tone which made her voice barely audible. Although she appeared frightened, she was calm, and from time to time a crooked smile appeared at the corner of her mouth.'

Reilly took her through her early years in America, her life with Richard, relationships with the Henkels, Hans Kloppenburg, Isidor Fisch, the birthday party on November 26, 1933, the farewell party for Fisch a week later. Then Reilly asked about the shoe-box. Having failed to persuade her to say she had seen it when she hadn't, he now listened to her saying she hadn't seen it because she never used the top shelf; it meant getting on her toes to do so. In cross-examination, however, Wilentz managed to draw from her a small list of domestic things – a tin box for soap coupons, some old cleaning rags, shelf trimming and curtain rods – which she kept up there and was too honest to deny. Having made his point by inference (that if the shoe-box had been among these other articles on the top shelf, she must have seen it – and if she hadn't, it was never there) Wilentz was content not to press it.

'I want to direct your attention to the closet again and make sure that I haven't done you an injustice. Now when you were nursing your child, you had difficulty about reaching the closet, didn't you?'

'The doctor told me I shouldn't stretch, I shouldn't reach high.'

'So you didn't reach for that closet many times on account of that condition, I suppose?'

'I didn't.'

With many of the rest of his long list of witnesses Reilly was less fortunate, partly through his own incompetence, partly due to circumstances beyond his control such as lack of funds and harassment by the opposition. It will be recalled for instance (see page 79) that on the morning of Monday February 29, 1932 Hauptmann left his tools in the cellars at the Majestic Apartments, then spent the afternoon on Hunter's Island with two friends, Emil Müller and Ludwig Kübisch; and in the course of conversation told them he was starting on a new job the following morning, Tuesday March 1. From a report by Detective Joseph Meade of the New Jersey Police it seems that Ludwig Kübisch mentioned this to Gerta Henkel who, realizing its importance, urged him to tell Müller to see Reilly. Accordingly, on the last day of 1934 Müller went to Reilly's office. Meade's report goes on:

Mr Reilly took Müller's name and address and made a few pencil notes. The entire interview did not last five minutes. Müller said that Reilly did not appear to be very much interested in his story. Müller at this time appeared to be very discouraged due to the fact that Reilly was disinterested in his story and he is very much in fear of being called to Flemington as a witness. He said that Kübisch knows just as much about the events of those weekends in question, but that he [Kübisch] was smarter than he as he kept quiet about it.

Needless to say Müller was never called – the second occasion on which Reilly rejected information that tended to show that his client was working on the day of the kidnapping.

Similarly with a German woman, Mrs Hilda Braunlich, whose name doesn't appear in any contemporary account of events, but who surfaced, aged seventy-nine, in Clearwater, Florida in 1977. She told the press then that she was a European handwriting expert who, with several others called by the defense, had on January 12, 1935 been permitted briefly to study the ransom notes and Hauptmann's request writings with a trooper on either side of each person. She had come to the conclusion then not only that Hauptmann had not written the ransom notes but that the notes themselves, when observed under a strong magnifying glass, clearly showed forged strokes. 'Rounded structures in the ransom notes showed a thickening like a point which was typical of Hauptmann's writing, and a different blend of ink had been written over.'

'What I saw shocked me,' she said, and she proposed to Reilly that the original notes be brought into court and projected on a large screen that would reveal the forged strokes. 'I told Reilly I could prove Hauptmann innocent in five minutes,' she said. The suggestion seems to have horrified Reilly who, she said, became very angry and ordered her to leave Flemington immediately. 'Reilly,' she said, 'didn't want the truth to come out.' She was so frightened that she hid that night in the house of a farmer and left in disguise the next day. It is clear from the newspaper reports that Reilly's rejection of what she (rightly or wrongly) regarded as crucial evidence had rankled with her for more than forty years.

In Uhlig too ('the plum-faced Uhlig' one paper called him) Reilly wasted a splendid opportunity. Uhlig had been brought to Trenton by the prosecution in mid January because, as Fisch's closest friend, it was thought he might say that Fisch was a pauper who could never have been in possession of $14,000, let alone put it in a shoe-box. But Uhlig knew that for the Knickerbocker Pie Company and other bogus ventures Fisch had conned from his friends more than $13,000; and Pinkus had told him in Leipzig (as he later told the *New York Times*) that he believed Isidor had considerable funds in New York. Knowing Fisch as he did, Uhlig told the press, 'it seems entirely plausible to me that he left the money with Hauptmann and did not tell Hauptmann what it was'.

All this was anathema to Wilentz but manna from Heaven for

Reilly, who at once put Uhlig on his list of witnesses. But when Uhlig took the stand, Reilly made no use of it at all, contenting himself with routine questions about his friendship with Fisch and their trip to Germany. Worse, almost at the end of his brief examination, he declared Uhlig to be a hostile witness. This was because he was basing his defense on the shaky proposition that Fisch, not Hauptmann, was the kidnapper of the baby; and Uhlig, he knew, believed Fisch to be as innocent as Hauptmann; believed that Fisch had bought the $14,000 of ransom bills as 'hot' money from a man in a downtown pool-room, then handed it concealed in the shoe-box to Hauptmann for safekeeping. And so another witness who, in other hands, might have been of great help to Hauptmann was allowed to fade away.

Other witnesses failed to materialize for a variety of reasons. Some, declared Reilly, because having written or telephoned to say they had information on the case, 'they ask for transportation and their day's pay and the Hauptmanns have no money'. Others because of Schwartzkopf's dirty tricks department. 'The State Police,' said Reilly, 'have interfered enough with defense witnesses. Some of my witnesses have been told to go home, they would not be needed, and when I wanted to call them, they were gone. The public should not forget that Schwarzkopf is up for reappointment with a new Governor in the chair.' As a result, the chairs set aside for defense witnesses were often barely occupied, and Judge Trenchard warned Reilly that if at any time he was without witnesses, 'something unpleasant is likely to occur'.

The worst example of harassment of a defense witness was the treatment accorded to Hans Kloppenburg. Kloppenburg, it will be remembered, was a key witness for the defense in that he was the only person to have seen Fisch hand the shoe-box to Hauptmann when he arrived for the party on December 2, 1933. In November the prosecution had ordered him brought to Trenton for 'a thorough grilling' (see page 243). At the grilling Kloppenburg had stuck to his story. Now, on the eve of giving evidence for his best friend, he was summoned to see Wilentz in his suite at the Hotel Hildebrecht: 'When I came in he was very friendly, you know. "You want something to eat and drink?" The waiter was there to take an order. But I'd just had something to eat and I wasn't hungry.'

Wilentz, said Kloppenburg, told him how far on he was with the case, that he'd pretty well won it already. Then:

... after telling me he wouldn't let me into the jail to see Richard, he said to me, 'If you say on the witness chair that you seen Fisch come in with the shoe-box, you'll be arrested right away.'

I was very surprised that he said that. I told him, 'But I seen it. I seen him come in the house with the shoe-box. It's the truth.' And he said if I talk about the shoe-box, I'm going to be in a lot of trouble. Then a day or so later, I think it was the day before I testified, there was a story in the newspapers that police were about to arrest a second man in the kidnapping. *That was me they were talking about.* They were trying to scare me so I would shut up. And I was scared. So when I testified, I never called it a shoe-box. I described the size, I gave the measurements – six by eight by fourteen or something – but I never used the word.

Some of the most damaging witnesses to the defense were those who volunteered helpful information to Reilly but whose backgrounds and character he had not bothered, or had not the staff or funds, to check on. As soon as each witness took the stand, the whole of the resources of the New Jersey and New York police forces were harnessed to discovering whatever discreditable information they could; and sometimes Wilentz spun out his cross-examination all afternoon to give the police overnight opportunities to make enquiries.

A Mr Elvert Carlstrom was called to the stand. He remembered seeing Hauptmann in Fredericksen's Bakery on March 1, 1932 because that was his birthday; in rebuttal Wilentz called a witness named Larsen who testified that he and Carlstrom had been in a place called Dunnellen that day and had never left it. A Mr Benjamin Heier testified that he saw Fisch near St Raymond's Cemetery on the night of April 2, 1932, but he admitted to a criminal record, and another testified that at 10 p.m. that night he and Mr Heier had been involved in a motor accident miles away. A Mr Sam Streppone said that in May 1933 Fisch had left in his shop a package like a shoe-box; then he told Wilentz that he had been five times in a mental institution and once judged insane. Mr Lou Harding, who had seen a car containing two men and a ladder near Princeton on March 1, 1932 and had reported it to the police at the time, had a conviction for assaulting a woman;[1] Mr Peter

---

[1] 'Although negative, Harding's testimony fits in with the defense attempt to convince the jury that someone other than Hauptmann committed the crime, that the authorities, especially the State Police, neglected opportunities to follow up clues such as Harding's, and that they are now trying to cover up their failure to investigate the case properly by "railroading" the accused man.' (*New York Times*, February 3, 1934.)

Sommer, one of several who claimed to have seen Violet Sharpe with a baby at a Hudson ferry terminal [1] on the evening of the same day was a professional witness. Mr Theron Main who saw Fisch in August 1933 holding a gold certificate note 'with a yellow back to it' had to be told by Wilentz that gold certificates had no yellow backs. A Mr Philip Moses did an impersonation of Will Rogers.

The cumulative effect of these witnesses on the court was one of farce and incredulity, and some wondered whether they had been 'planted' on the defense by Schwartzkopf's dirty tricks brigade. Even Reilly was heard to quip when presenting a new witness that he had the disadvantage of not having a criminal record or having been judged insane. Most agreed with Arthur Reeve in the *New York Post* when he wrote that 'a damning indictment is replied to by as frivolous a defense as has ever been offered in a major trial'. And the effect on poor Hauptmann was catastrophic: day after day Lieutenant Smith recorded his concern, both in and out of court. On February 1, 'the prisoner seemed disgusted with the way things were going'. On February 4, 'by his attitude in court he showed that he did not like the witnesses that were put on the stand by the defense'. On February 7, 'he had a very disgusted expression during some of the testimony . . . endeavored to talk to his attorneys on several occasions'. Back in his cell Hauptmann said to Fisher, 'Where are they getting these witnesses from? They're really hurting me.' And speaking of his growing gloom, the *New York Times* said that, formerly confident he would never be convicted, 'now for the first time he has begun to brood over the possibility he might be sent to the electric chair'.

Yet among the dross there was some gold. It was said earlier that the kidnapping of the Lindbergh baby (like the assassination of President Kennedy) was an event so traumatic that long afterwards people could remember where they were when they heard of it. Two of these were Mr August van Henke and Mr Louis Kiss, and their accounts of having seen Hauptmann with Mr Fredericksen's dog (which, it will be remembered, he often used to exercise) on the evening of March 1, tended quite independently to support each other.

In the middle of February 1932 Mr van Henke, a German-born restaurant owner, lost his German Shepherd dog Rex. He said that

---

[1] Some said Weehawken, others Yonkers.

on the evening of March 1, while returning to New York from New Rochelle, he stopped at a gas station not far from Fredericksen's Bakery and there saw a man with a dog that looked very like his. He accosted the man, recognized him as a fellow countryman and said in German that if, as he believed, the dog was his, he would have him arrested. The man, who gave his name as Hauptmann, replied that the dog belonged to the baker down the road and offered to take Mr van Henke there to prove it. However, the dog didn't answer to van Henke's call, and on closer inspection he saw that on its neck were black spots which Rex didn't have.

Mr Louis Kiss, a silk painter, was having cake and coffee in the bakery when Hauptmann returned with the dog. In evidence he said he heard Hauptmann say to the waitress (Anna) in German, 'Somebody wanted to take the dog!' Kiss also remembered the date, not only because it was the same night as the kidnapping but because it was 'exactly a week earlier' that his son had been rushed to Bellevue Hospital with a kidney complaint. Unlike some others, Mr Kiss was an impressive witness. 'If I had happened to be on the jury,' wrote Adela Rogers St John in the *New York Evening Journal*, 'I would have listened very carefully to Mr Kiss because I had a conviction he was telling the truth.'

Naturally Wilentz did all he could to discredit both Kiss and van Henke, though in van Henke's admitting that he had once run a speakeasy and used more than one name, and in Kiss's that he brewed and sold rum, the damage was minimal. Ferret-like, Wilentz checked on the records of the Bellevue Hospital and found that the Kiss boy had been admitted at 1.20 a.m. on February 22, 1932. 'And exactly a week after that,' he said triumphantly, 'was February 29th and not March 1st' – so Mr Kiss was wrong in his recollections. Here was the perfect opportunity for Reilly to say that as Hauptmann only ever came to fetch Anna from the bakery on Tuesdays and Fridays when she worked late, it could not have been February 29 (a Monday) when he saw Hauptmann there with the dog and must have been March 1 (a Tuesday); this also tied in with the recollections of Mr van Henke. But, as usual, Reilly let the opportunity pass.

There were other helpful minor witnesses. Paul Vetterle and Anna's neice Maria Müller testified that Hauptmann had been at home on his birthday, November 26, 1933 (and so wasn't passing a ransom bill to Cecile Barr in a cinema fifteen miles away); Victor Schussler who lived downstairs disclosed that many of his tools, including a chisel, were missing (supporting Hauptmann's claim that the police had taken away all of his); George Steinweg, the steamship agent who had booked Fisch's ticket in the *Manhattan*, had noticed the considerable amount of money Fisch was carrying in his wallet;[1] Gustave Miller, plumber, confirmed that in August 1934 Mrs Rauch had called him to fix a bad leak in Hauptmann's kitchen closet (supporting Hauptmann's account of the water-logged shoe-box). Mr Miller added that he went up to the attic to trace the source of the leak, and that at that time 'all the boards appeared to be in the right place'. Had 8 feet of one been missing, he could hardly have failed to notice it.

Another impressive witness was Dr Erastus Mead Hudson who within days of the kidnapping had traveled to Hopewell to show the New Jersey Police his new method of silver nitrate fingerprint-ing. He had spent an entire three or four days with police officers Kelly and Kubler examining the ladder for prints and was able to produce 'more than five hundred of value'. When Pope pointed out that none of the five hundred belonged to Hauptmann, Hudson said that if Hauptmann had made the ladder, there would have been bound to be some. But the most startling piece of Hudson's evidence was his absolute insistence that when he examined the ladder minutely in 1932 *there was only one nail hole in Rail 16*. He stuck to this view like a limpet, even after Wilentz had shown him a picture of Rail 16 showing four nail holes, which he claimed had been taken in 1932. Even if the picture had appeared in a US Government report, said Hudson, he still wouldn't be convinced. He remembered Rail 16 vividly because of a particular knot in it which had caused a split in the wood and had had two or three nails driven either side of it for strengthening; he knew for certain that there was only one nail hole in the face. Angry and frustrated, Wilentz did everything he could to belittle Dr Hudson and his evidence, and showed his feelings when his irritable cross-exami-nation ended. Told he could step down, Hudson said politely, 'Thank you.'

'Did you say, "Thank you"?' replied Wilentz. 'You are welcome.'

The defense's lone handwriting expert also had helpful things to say. He was 67-year-old John M. Trendley and had volunteered his services because in his view Hauptmann's writing and the

---

[1] But he did not say that he had been paid in Lindbergh ransom money, which one would have expected if he had been. It would have been of prime importance to Hauptmann's defense, as good as confirming his shoe-box story.

writing in the ransom notes were not by the same hand: he had been examining questioned documents for forty years, had testified in court more than 387 times and, like his colleagues for the prosecution, admitted that on occasions he had made mistakes. But he was quite sure this time. He pointed out that in the whole of the first ransom note Osborn Senior had claimed only one word, 'is', which bore any resemblance to Hauptmann's writing and that when you looked at them both closely, there was no resemblance. Nor had Osborn compared the word 'singnature' in Hauptmann's request writing with the 'singnature' in the first ransom note. If he had done (and Trendley did it letter by letter) he would have seen there was no resemblance at all. In addition there was a marked difference between ransom 'a's and request 'a's, while twenty-nine ransom note 'k's turned to the left and twenty-seven of Hauptmann's didn't. The way that Hauptmann wrote his 'x's and 'y's and put a hyphen in 'New-York' was typical of Germans who had learnt English. In short, the ransom writing was wide with unnatural shading and many rough lines, while Hauptmann's writing was characterized by a light upstroke and graduated shading in the downstroke, a modification of the Palmer method.

Nor was Trendley the least shaken by Lanigan's cross-examination. After describing (as Mrs Braunlich had done) how the state had done their best to keep the handwriting documents from him (two hours under police supervision was all he had been allowed to study the original ransom notes), he gave a view of the mis-spellings common to request and ransom writings that differed sharply from those of witnesses for the prosecution. Having been told that the request writing had taken place in a police station, he saw no significance at all in finding 'the' spelt 'hte' in both ransom and request writings. 'I wouldn't take anything written in a police station,' he said. 'You would spell what they told you to spell.' And he added (*pace* Mrs Braunlich) that the word 'expenses', when examined under the microscope, appeared to have been 'written over . . . worked over'.

The best of all the defense witnesses came right at the end, and spoke about wood. First came a wood pattern maker named Stanley Seal, an expert on the use of planes, and his answer to Koehler's claim that Hauptmann's wooden plane made similar marks to those found in the ladder was that it entirely depended on what angle you held the plane. Demonstrating to the court with Hauptmann's plane and a piece of wood, he showed that by holding the plane at a variety of angles, there was a difference in the marks it left of between five-eighths and three-quarters of an inch.

If this evidence made a dent in Koehler's credibility, the next (and last) two witnesses set about demolishing it altogether. One was Charles de Bisschop, a general contractor from Massachusetts who had read Koehler's earlier testimony in the press, considered it nonsense and volunteered to come to Flemington to testify at his own expense. The other, Edward Mielk, was a millworker and carpenter. They were both practical, forthright witnesses and neither had the slightest doubts that Rail 16 had no connection at all with the attic board from which Bornmann and Koehler had claimed it had come. At the start Wilentz tried to discredit de Bisschop as a qualified witness by asking if he had ever tried matching grains in two different pieces of lumber to see if they were the same. 'I've been doing that for the last thirty years,' replied de Bisschop. 'Hardly a day goes by but what somebody wants a piece of wood to match something they broke.'

As for the grains in Rail 16 and the attic board looking alike, he went on, why, grains in North Carolina yellow pine boards of the same age did look alike. He produced two pieces of yellow pine attic boards in which the grains looked identical, then said that one had lain in one building for forty-seven years, the other in a different building for five or six years, but that the age of the boards (in terms of growth) was the same. He gave several powerful reasons why Rail 16 and the attic board were not related: the knots were different ('the lower rail has three knots and the top one seven which is contrary to anything there ever was'); the 'V's were different; the saw cuts were different; the nail holes in Rail 16 were smaller than those in the board; and while the end grains appeared to match, they didn't when laid end to end. The reason for the gap between Rail 16 and the attic board, he suggested, was because the grains *didn't* match and also so that the holes in Rail 16 could fit over the joists. Holding up Koehler's drawing of Rail 16 and the attic board with the gap between he said, 'whoever has drawed these lines has drawn them to correspond and make it look as though they were meeting . . . look at the width there . . . they are tightening together . . . *they had to do it to make them look the same*'. He even challenged the prosecution's claim that their so-called attic board had come from the attic. 'There are no marks on its under side to show it has lain on joists for the last few years, and no marks to show that it has been removed by hammer and chisel.' In his view it had never been part of the attic flooring.

Then came Edward Mielk who gave additional reasons: the rings in the attic board were darker and had more life, there was a marked difference in the size and spacing of the knots, and the board was thinner than Rail 16. As Wilentz saw his evidence being demolished brick by brick, and no doubt cursing the day he ever decided to introduce it, he became increasingly jumpy, popping up and down like a jack-in-the-box to object to almost every question put or answer given – an exercise in which the judge mostly sustained him. But Mielk stuck to his guns: Rail 16 and the so-called attic board were not and never had been part of the same flooring.

Although Mielk was the last witness to give direct evidence, Wilentz was now entitled to call additional or former witnesses to rebut witnesses for the defense. The areas he considered most dangerous to the state were: Hudson's insistence that there was only one nail hole in Rail 16 when he examined it; the testimony of de Bisschop and Mielk about Rail 16; the defense's contention that far from being destitute, Fisch had accumulated large sums of money; and a variety of dubious witnesses who had stated that they had seen Violet Sharpe with a baby at a Hudson ferry terminal on the night of the kidnapping.

To counter Hudson's claim Wilentz first called George G. Wilton, described as a photographer in the New Jersey State Police, to testify to two photographs showing Rail 16 with four nail holes and which were alleged to have been taken on March 8, 1932. From the way Wilentz worded his questions it was clear he was intending to give the court the impression that Wilton had actually taken the photographs, but when Reilly took over it emerged that all he had done was enlarge them, and as they bore no date or signature, and looked remarkably fresh and clean, the enlargement could have been made at any time.

Brought back to rebut de Bisschop and Mielk, Koehler was not impressive, blinding the court with technicalities concerning curvatures and butt ends, in which the amateur carpenter Pope proved a reasonable, if equally boring, match. Koehler was forced to agree that the two boards were of different thicknesses and that the saw cuts in each were different, but insisted that despite the gap between they were a 'perfect match'. He also said that in November 1935 he had made a diagram indicating the distance between the nail holes in Rail 16 and that 'these matched with the holes in the joists in the attic when I came to fit them'. Incredibly, he did not proffer his diagram as an exhibit, and even more incredibly (except that this was routine now) Reilly did not insist on his producing it.

To prove Fisch's poverty Wilentz called his landlady, Selma Kohl, at 149 East 27th Street who said he had the smallest room in the house for which he paid $3.50 a week, and very few clothes. 'He had a working suit and a Sunday suit with two pants and a cheap-looking raincoat, and he had a winter suit and a blue dark winter overcoat.' She was supported by Hanna Fisch, Isidor's sister whom, with her brother Pinkus, the state had brought over at vast expense from Leipzig. She was still dressed in semi-mourning and was described as 'a slim woman, dark-featured, with a thin face, prematurely lined'. All she had to say was that Isidor had brought with him 'nothing of real value' from America, and would not be drawn when Reilly suggested that the family had consulted a German lawyer to discuss Pinkus coming over to New York to assess Isidor's estate; yet she must have known what Pinkus had said about Isidor having raised $17,000 from friends for investment, and about Isidor being a business partner of Hauptmann and leaving behind scores of unpaid bills. As a result, Hauptmann's claims of having a close business relationship with Fisch, and the extent of Fisch's swindling, were never brought out at the trial.

Finally, to scotch Reilly's suggestion, supported by a number of dubious witnesses, that Violet Sharpe and a baby had been seen at a Hudson ferry terminal on the evening of March 1, Wilentz called several witnesses to show that Violet Sharpe was elsewhere – either at Next Day Hill or at The Peanut Grill roadhouse with friends. Among them was Mrs Dwight Morrow.

* * *

Although Lindbergh had not so far missed a single day's attendance at the trial, being greeted like royalty, lunching with Schwarzkopf or Judge Large, dominating the courtroom with his presence, a constant reminder to the jury of why they were there, Anne and her mother had purposely kept away. Like most women, they were not interested in a blow-by-blow unraveling of events (in her diary for the first six weeks of 1935 Anne barely mentions the trial); if anything unusual happened, the Colonel would tell them at the end of the day.

Spurred on by Harold Nicolson, Anne's main interest at this

time was completing *North to the Orient*. Charles – 'very kind and helpful' – read each chapter as it was completed, and when the Breckinridges came to lunch, gave Henry the chapter about flying in fog. Henry 'says very little but I'm sure he does not like it. He objects only to my saying "God" so often, but in reality I think he objects to . . . the whole thing. I think he feels it not courageous – that we all feel fear, but should not admit it . . .' When the first five chapters of her father's biography by Harold Nicolson arrived, she read them at a stretch. 'I cried and cried . . . They are terribly good – much better than I dreamed they would be.' Nicolson, expected back at Next Day Hill soon, promised to have five more chapters ready by the time he arrived, and to have completed the book by May. She thought of her own sluggish progress: 'Oh God, why try if I'm so far behind the standards?'

Her general mood seems to have been calmer, but the black dogs returned with a nightmare about Elisabeth, and again when Charles vetoed a trip to Boston to see *The Yeomen of the Guard* which she was planning with Constance – 'the appearance of going off to a theater while the trial is on would look disrespectful and light'. She agreed the decision was right, but felt terribly frustrated and discouraged.

But there were happier days; playing with Jon in the snow, trips to New York to lunch with her friends Margot Loines and Lincoln Kirstein (Mina Curtiss's brother), a visit from her childhood friend Corliss Lamont, reading Elisabeth's journal (with nostalgic entries about their time together in Paris) and the unashamed joy of physical pleasures. 'Hot baths and eau de cologne on one's body, and the heat pad at one's feet at night. And things to eat, too, toast and sherry . . .'

On February 9 came her mother's summons to Flemington. With Charles they passed the airport where Mrs Morrow had embarked that stormy night to fly to the dying Elisabeth ('She had left with hope. It must have been awful to see it'), then reached Flemington with its 'gingerbread houses, the streets crowded with people, snow, cars'. They went through the cameras the back way to the courtroom, and were shown to where Anne had sat six weeks before. Some in court thought how alike mother and daughter were.

I felt as if I'd been sitting there for ever. The crowded rows, the slat chairs, the fat bored-looking woman opposite me in the jury,[1]

[1] Verna Snyder.

the high windows behind; outside the red bricks of an old building, lit by the sun.

Koehler was testifying about Rail 16 and the attic flooring when they arrived, so they had a long wait.

That sad-eyed sob sister looking at me every time I looked up. People breathing behind me. That pale profile of Hauptmann startling one through a gap in the heads. The pathetically bedraggled thin face – tired, bewildered – of Mrs Hauptmann. The smart stenographer, taking down the record, stooping as she walked back and forth in front of the Judge's box. The Judge exactly the same, dignified, unruffled.

It was a far worse day emotionally than when I testified. That long, long morning of wood testimony; tiny minute points, technical haggling, vernier scales, how marked, etc. I thought with a pang in the middle of it, How incredible that my baby had any connection with this.

She would have found it even more incredible to be told that he had no connection at all.

The noon recess was called and after lunch Wilentz called the people who had been with Violet Sharpe the night that Reilly's witnesses had said she was elsewhere. Anne was angry at Reilly's snobbery in calling Violet 'just an ordinary servant girl', when Wilentz always referred to her as 'Miss Sharpe'.

Mrs Morrow told Wilentz that Violet had been at Next Day Hill serving dinner the early part of the evening and she had seen her again after eleven, and then it was Reilly's turn; and the *New York Times* noted another aspect of his snobbery in that he questioned Mrs Morrow 'in a low, deferential voice, in striking contrast to the loud voice with which he had hammered at previous rebuttal witnesses . . .'

Reilly's trap questions: 'Who served you the night before?' 'The night before? I don't know because I was on the train.' He jumped quickly to 'Who served you the night after?' 'You mean March 2nd?' 'Yes.' 'I don't know – of course, I was in Hopewell!'

He dropped her quickly and we went out and escaped quietly and drove home. Mother *so* relieved.

Now all that remained was what in English law are called closing speeches and in American law 'summations', and the judge's charge to the jury; and there can have been few people in court, especially the jury, for six weeks almost as much prisoners of the law as Hauptmann, punch-drunk after trying to absorb a million and a half words of testimony and 380 exhibits, who did not feel a lifting of the spirits as they spotted daylight at the end of the tunnel. Even Hauptmann shared it, relieved that his long ordeal would soon be over, hoping that within a few days he would be walking from the court a free man. 'I believe,' wrote Lieutenant Smith in his report of February 9, 'that he anticipates an acquittal.'

First to rise was the Hunterdon County Prosecutor, Anthony M. Hauck, who gave a brief run-down of the state's evidence. It was mostly a rehash of false claims and assertions already made. 'We have proved to you that the baby was killed by the fall from that ladder . . . and secondly that death ensued immediately.' They had proved nothing of the kind. He repeated the lies about Whited having first described Hauptmann to the police on the morning after the kidnapping; the lies about Rail 16 and Hauptmann's plane and chisel ('Mr Koehler,' he said, 'gave the most wonderful testimony I have ever heard'); Hochmuth's lies, Perrone's lies, Condon's lies; and the mistaken conclusions of Lindbergh, Frank, the Osborns and others. 'Remember,' he finished, 'we are not required to have a picture of this man coming down the ladder with the Lindbergh baby; but we have shown you conclusively, overwhelmingly, beyond a reasonable doubt, that Bruno Richard Hauptmann is guilty of the murder of Charles A. Lindbergh Junior.'

There had been some talk as to whether Reilly or Fisher would make the defense's summation. Hauptmann wanted Fisher, who believed in his innocence, had already proved himself more competent than Reilly, and as a local person would be more sympathetic to a jury of local people. Fisher himself wanted to do it. But Reilly was adamant. 'I'm running the show here,' he told Fisher, 'and I'm doing the talking.' The decision cannot have given much comfort to Hauptmann or to the rest of the defense team, but in the event Reilly largely redeemed himself. Perhaps he had been awoken by a sense of professional pride, perhaps at this late stage even he was beginning to nurture doubts about his client's guilt; apart from his usual shakiness over names ('Johnnie' instead of Joseph Perrone, 'Hans' instead of Otto Wollenberg, 'Arthur' instead of Henry Johnson) he laid bare the essential weakness of the prosecution case.

Within minutes of rising he went to the heart of the matter. 'How in God's name,' he asked the jury, 'did Hauptmann in the Bronx know anything about the Lindbergh home?'

> The evidence is that the first time in the history of Colonel Lindbergh's life that he ever stayed a Tuesday night in that house was this Tuesday night. Every other weekend was over Sunday night or early Monday morning. Who knew the baby had a cold and had to stay in Hopewell on Monday? Not Hauptmann ... Then comes Tuesday, and Mrs Lindbergh, believing that the child's cold is sufficiently important, sends for Betty Gow ...

If nobody but the family and their close staff knew about the intention to stay over Tuesday as well, how did Hauptmann get to know it? Furthermore:

> Hauptmann would have to know what room that child was in, and he would have to know whether the Colonel was home or not home; he would have to know whether Mrs Lindbergh was home or not home; he would have to know when the baby was put to bed, and he would have to know when there was no person in that house at that present minute in the nursery. *Is there any evidence he knew anything like that?*
>
> A man can't come up to a strange house with a ladder and stick it against the wall and run up the ladder, push open a shutter and walk into a room that he has never been in before. That is what they would have you believe.

He turned to the time and place of the baby's death:

> You must find that the child came to its death between the hours of the kidnapping and midnight March 1st on the estate of Colonel Lindbergh. You must find that from the evidence. Now, nobody saw it; nobody comes here and says, 'Hauptmann, you hit the child.' You haven't a particle of evidence in this case when that child died. All you have, and the law is very strict ... there must be no doubt, no circumstantial evidence or inference or guess-work on this part of the case, the child's death must be established by direct evidence ... Now where is there any evidence at all?

It was the same with the disposal of the baby's body:

No proof in the world that Hauptmann ever dug that grave, nobody ever saw him over there or anything, notwithstanding the speech of Mr Hauck this morning that he ran there that night and was afraid and dug the grave and put the baby in there. That's all guess-work on the part of the prosecuting officers. But there is no evidence.

After showing the impossibility of Hauptmann (or any other man) climbing the ladder in the dark, opening the shutters and window, hoisting himself into the room, seizing the baby, regaining the top rung of the ladder (2½ feet below the windowsill), closing the window and shutters while holding the baby and with it negotiating the 18-inch spaces between the rungs to the ground, *all completely unaided,* he declared that the kidnapping must have been the work of a gang, 'and by a gang I mean a collection of people bent on an evil undertaking'.

He elaborated. The ladder hadn't been used at all. The ladder was a plant, to divert attention. The kidnapping was an inside job: the baby had been taken down the back stairs and handed to someone waiting outside. It had to be an inside job because none but the Lindbergh staff knew that the family intended to stay over. Wasn't it suspicious that Betty Gow hadn't been near the baby between 8 and 10 p.m.? What was her telephone conversation with Red Johnsen about except for her to say the coast was clear? Why had the dog Wahgoosh not barked – unless Ollie Whately was muzzling it? Why had Violet Sharpe committed suicide – unless she too was involved in the affair and was fearful of a further session of questioning by Inspector Walsh? And wasn't Condon, who had always acted alone and whose stories of meeting one of the kidnappers in Woodlawn and St Raymond's were entirely uncorroborated, wasn't he yet another member of the gang? 'General Wilentz describes him as a patriotic gentleman of the old school . . . Well, General, I don't share that opinion with you.'

This was a far-fetched theory, but if Reilly was going to offer some alternative to Hauptmann as the kidnapper, it was about the only alternative open to him. If he could do no more than sow some doubts in the minds of the jury, shake their belief in Hauptmann's guilt just a little, such doubts might be reflected at the end of the day, if not in outright acquittal then a lesser verdict than first-degree murder.

He went through the testimony piece by piece, and for the first time (but knowing nothing of Hauptmann having shouted 'Hey,

Doc!' for Lindbergh's benefit in Foley's office) challenged the reliability of his hero's identification of Hauptmann's voice:

> Colonel, I say to you it is impossible that you, having lived for years in airplanes, with the hum of the motor in your ears . . . and the change of climatic conditions that you have lived under since you made your wonderful flight, to say with any degree of stability that you can ever remember the voice of a man two and a half or three years afterwards, a voice you never heard before and never heard since.

He suggested that a man torn by grief such as the Colonel had been, who had seen before him a man charged with the crime, could unconsciously make a mistake of judgment – 'and that, Colonel Lindbergh, I think you have done in this case.' It must have required an effort for Reilly to voice this allegation with Lindbergh only a few feet away, and he rather spoiled it after the court had risen by apologizing to Lindbergh for having doubted him – an apology which Wilentz overheard and had no compunction in using to his own advantage next day.

Then, with vigor, commitment and at times passion, Reilly dealt with the major items of evidence against his client:

The handwriting of the first ransom note:

> Now of course it is very important for the prosecution in this case to try and pin the nursery note on Hauptmann. This is part of what I call their scenario.
>
> But I ask you this, please, before finding that this is Hauptmann's handwriting . . . keep in mind the fact that *there is no evidence except this* . . . which puts Hauptmann in the nursery March 1st; and this places him there through the opinion or guesswork, we will call it, of Mr Osborn and those who followed him.
>
> I think you will agree with me that to take one word, 'is', out of all those lines and compare that 'is' to one 'is' of Hauptmann's and say then that because that 'is' looks something like an 'is' that he wrote, that is pretty slim evidence . . . to put a man in a nursery of a house he knew nothing about . . .
>
> Every expert that took the stand said that this was disguised writing. Now what benefit is a disguise?
>
> If a person puts on a disguise and hides his own face and figure . . . then he ceases to be what he was and assumes the character of the person he is attempting to disguise.
>
> If this is disguised handwriting, where is there any standard by which it can be examined with that certainty with which you will send a man to his death or with that certainty with which you could send a man away for life imprisonment? One 'is', one 'is'?

Hauptmann's accounts:

They write the scenario and they say, 'Well, look at what Hauptmann did. He went into Wall Street. He spent money in Wall Street.' They add up a set of figures and they show you that from April 2nd 1932 down to the time of his arrest, he spent $50,000 or $35,000, just enough to make, with the $15,000 found in the garage, the $50,000 of the Lindbergh money.

And when we took the accounts with Hauptmann, and their Inspector for the United States Government was sitting here – I think his name was Ward [in fact, Frank] or something like that . . . we ask,
'Did you buy this?'
'Yes.'
'Did you sell it the next day?'
'Yes.'
The sales offset the buying. He showed it clearly. Nobody went back on the stand and contradicted him. He lost $5000. They would have you think that he was spending Lindbergh money down to the day of his arrest, and yet when you look at the accounts, you will see that . . . from July 2nd, 1933 . . . this defendant didn't put a dollar into his Wall Street account excepting one or two small dividend checks . . .

Now why try to fool you? . . . It isn't right and it isn't decent. Not a dollar of that ransom money ever went through Wall Street or a bank [of Hauptmann's]. One bank might slip up. But there was a bank in Mount Vernon. There was a Central Savings Bank. There was the bank the brokers did business with. Then there was another brokerage account. I think there were three brokerage accounts. There were three or more banks. And not a brokerage account, not a bank account from anybody in this world found a dollar of this money.

Spending the ransom money:

. . . let's say he has got this money and he knows it is Lindbergh money, and he goes around the Bronx, leaving it in stores where he deals all the time; he goes to a gas station where they can write down his number . . . and when the man said to him, 'Have you any more home?' – instead of saying to the fellow, 'Now don't bother me, I just got that from a cigar man down the street', evasive or crooked, he said, 'Sure, I have got ten or twelve or a hundred more home' – and the man writes down his automobile licence.

Now if he had the guilty knowledge that this was Lindbergh's money . . . wouldn't he go home and pack a bag and go in the garage and take the rest of the money and leave the Bronx, so . . . when they came looking for him, after the bill had gone through the bank, they wouldn't find him?

Doesn't it strike you that he was acting as an innocent man would act?

SO TRUE!

The request writing at Greenwich Street:

They take care of him down in Greenwich Street. And they try to get him to confess or make a statement, and he says, 'I don't know anything about this at all.' And then they say, 'Will you write?' He says, 'Sure, I will write. I am anxious to write. I want to be cleared of this thing.' Now, is that the natural reaction of an innocent man, 'I want to write, I want to be cleared of this thing'? And they say, 'Write this and write that.' And Hauptmann says, 'I wrote as I was told to write. They spelled words for me and I spelled those words as they told me to.' And not one soul went back on that witness stand in all the rebuttal to contradict Hauptmann on that score.

The writing in the closet:

They'd have you believe, the New York City Police – past masters in fixing evidence on people – that a man who never had a telephone in his life . . . would crawl into a closet . . . a dark closet, mind you . . . and over in a corner on a board he would write Dr Condon's telephone number as it was three or four years ago before they made the change . . . this board on the inside of a closet is the worst example of police crookedness that I have seen in a great many years.

Why, if Hauptmann, as dumb as they want you to believe one minute or as smart as they want you to believe the next minute, ever wrote to Dr Condon, you can bet he would never write down anything on wood in a closet that you have got to back into to find it.

The taking over of Hauptmann's apartment by the New Jersey State Police:

Well, they hadn't a very good case in the Bronx against Hauptmann up to now . . . there had got to be something else.

Go out and get something else on this fellow now. We will rent the apartment to the New Jersey State Police at sixty or seventy-five dollars a month, and we won't let anybody in to look at it.

And when *we* are getting ready for trial, when *we* ask permission to go into the attic and into the Hauptmann apartment, it is denied. What are they hiding? What are they hiding from us that they won't want us to see where this board was ripped out, if it ever was ripped out? What is the State of New Jersey, if it is on the level in this case, hiding from the defense?

Hauptmann's employment at the Majestic Apartments:

There was another little plant, as we call it in these cases, in the Majestic Apartments . . . Hauptmann did not work April 2nd is what they say, and with a big hullabaloo they brought a man down here with a timebook.

This man testified . . . 'Yes, I kept that book.' There was a check
mark April 1st, April 2nd was a circle. When you go into the jury room
and get that timebook, please put the magnifying glass on it and
underneath the circle you will find a check mark. They didn't know
that I had in my possession a photostatic copy of the payroll, but I
knew it and I let the fellow go, I cross-examined him and let him go.
But he would be willing to send a man to the electric chair by changing
the record of the man's employment.

It was a nice little plant to show that on April 2nd he was only
concerned in the ransom money, therefore he didn't work.

The attic board:

Now, do you suppose that this board was ever taken out of any attic
floor? Examine it carefully. There isn't a mark on this board from any
hammer.

Now you have got a board that is supposed to be nailed down,
covering a catwalk in an attic, and the distance between the bottom of
this board and the top of the ceiling of the room below is about eight
inches.

'Oh,' the detective said, 'all I had to do was to reach in with my
hand or something and pull it up. The nails came right out.'

You might think that board was putty or something. Now you know
they would have to take a pinch bar and pry it in and lift it up, and
those nails that had been in there for all the time the house was built,
seven years, would be in there so solidly that they would be part of the
house.

Not a mark of a hammer, not a mark of a pinch bar, not a mark of
anything!

The number of holes in Rail 16:

Let me have those photographs, please, the big photographs with the
four holes.

Dr Hudson I don't believe would commit perjury for President
Roosevelt. I don't think he would commit perjury for anybody, much
less for Hauptmann. Dr Hudson stakes his professional integrity and
honor on that witness stand. He says there was one hole.

Oh (says the state) we will get around that: we will bring in the
photograph taken when Koehler saw it in 1932; and they bring in a
great big photograph that was so fresh, so nice and so clean you
could almost see it had been printed within forty-eight hours. His
photographs that were taken last September or October – see the way
they have been handled and torn.

'When were they taken, officer?'

'Oh, they were taken in 1932, May 13th.'

'Where?'

'Down at Hopewell.'

'When you examined the ladder?'
'Yes.'
'Where is the plate?'
'I don't know where the plate is; this is an enlargement.'
'Where is the date on the back of the plate?'
'I don't know.'
'Was there ever a date?'
'I don't know.'
'Who was there when you took it?'
'I don't know.'
'Have you got any proof?'
'I don't know.'
I will ask you, looking at those photographs, those enlargements, nice and clean and lovely as they are, whether you believe they were made in 1932, showing the holes in this board here and the side of the ladder and all this stuff?

Now why plant things in this case? Why are they so desperate?

Rail 16 and the attic board:

We brought down here a man from Massachusetts and I will stake his common, good old variety type of horse sense against any Koehler . . . You men on the jury have handled boards. Here we have down in North Carolina, South Carolina, billions and billions of board feet a year; and then Koehler has the nerve to come and tell us there never were two boards in all the billion feet alike; and he says, 'This board here was once a part of this board here.'

De Bisschop says, 'Nothing of the kind. The grain isn't alike; the knots are not alike. The general appearance and the general characteristics of this board are nothing like this board.'

We started this case with practically nothing, but we sent an appeal out through the radio and through the news and in the theaters: 'If there is any soul on God's earth that knows anything about this case, please come forward and tell us.'

And this man up in Massachusetts, who doesn't know a soul in this courtroom, reading the Koehler testimony, says, 'That fellow is wrong and I am going down there and I am going to show he is wrong.'

Now would he come down here and commit perjury, come down here and make a fool of himself, go to all this trouble? And his stuff rings true. He points it out to you that it is true, and he says *that* board and *that* board were never the same. We can't get into the attic and see where the board came from.

I don't know who cooked up this idea of trying to make this ladder and this board agree, but I don't think this jury is going to stand for that kind of evidence.

Koehler was wrong many times. He was wrong on his measurements . . . Mr Pope took them over with a measuring instrument and found,

I think [it] was one sixteenth or one twelfth of an inch out of the way, planed differently, different saw marks.

No, I am afraid this board was prepared; I am afraid this board was prepared for this trial. I am pretty certain these pictures were prepared.

Reilly's last sentence before sitting down was anti-climactical; an obeisance to Lindbergh, a piece of unashamed schmaltz to make up for having doubted his word earlier — 'and I am quite sure that all of you agree with me that his lovely son is now within the gates of heaven'.

But what he hoped the jury would remember were things he had said earlier:

I don't know what was behind the kidnapping, whether it was for greed or for gain, for spite or hate or vengeance. I don't know. It was a horrible, a horrible thing. And, my God, it couldn't have been planned by any one person . . . It had to be planned by a group.

But the state stands here and says, 'Kill Hauptmann. Close the pages. Let everybody sink into oblivion and obscurity. Kill the German carpenter!'

The mob wants the German carpenter killed, as mobs for the past two thousand years have cried for the death of a person . . . then afterwards it was discovered that the person that was killed by the mob's vengeance wasn't guilty at all . . .

No, if you want to convict Hauptmann because the mob wants you to — and by the mob I mean the people of the world — and thinks it should be done, then all my prayers and pleadings won't do him any good. But I don't think that is the way you value your oaths.

Hang this man and cover up our sins. Hang him and ten years from now, after he is dead, have somebody on their deathbed just about to meet their Maker, turn over and say, 'I want to make a confession, I was part of the Lindbergh gang', and then where is our conscience, where are our feelings when we have sent an innocent man to his death, and we think about the real culprit — he must be somewhere in the world. There must be two or three of them still alive, because no one man could do this.

I believe this man is absolutely innocent of murder.

* * *

Nothing human is alien to me, said Dostoevsky, and reading Wilentz's summation one has to remember it. It has never been the task of a public prosecutor to involve himself emotionally in the justness of his cause or the horrendousness of the crime, but to present his evidence as factually and coolly as possible. Yet as one reads Wilentz's summation today, watches and listens to his courtroom performance on old newsreel film, one feels as though he had chosen to take on his shoulders alone the collective sense of outrage and desire for retribution of the entire American people. He may also have seen himself (others certainly did) as the standard-bearer for persecuted German Jewry, with Hauptmann (the former machine-gunner) personifying Nazi brutality and arrogance.

Whatever the cause, Wilentz's summation must rank as one of the most distasteful on record. It was not composed to prove guilt; from the beginning it assumed it. Its only redeeming aspect was that despite all the contrary evidence that had come his way, nobody could accuse Wilentz of knowingly framing an innocent man. Every day and night since October 1934, he told the jury, 'the more convinced I was that I was pursuing a righteous and proper cause'.

He began quietly enough:

> My delightful adversary says that you are not to be governed by the clamor of the mob that wants the life of this man. Let me say to you if there is such a clamor . . . it is not because of anything that you have done or I have done. It must be because of the evidence that has come from the lips of credible witnesses sitting here under oath.
>
> 'Judge not, lest ye be judged,' my adversary says, but forgets the other biblical admonition, 'And he that killeth any man shall surely be put to death.'
>
> For all those months since October 1934, not during one moment has there been anything that has come to the surface or light that has indicated anything but the guilt of this defendant, Bruno Richard Hauptmann, and no one else.

He assured the jury that he had not sought to become prosecutor in the case; he had only done so because the prosecutor for Hunterdon County had asked him to. ('Why, the very thought of prosecuting a man for a crime goes against the very soul and the very grain of my system.') Now he welcomed the approaching end of the trial. 'I want to get away from it all. I am naturally a home-loving person. I want to get back evenings to my children.' The disclaimer over, he gradually warmed to his task:

> There may be some questions you can't answer, but there sits the man that can answer them. He will be thawed out, he is cold; yes, he will be thawed out when he hears that switch; that's the time he will talk.
>
> Who would be the type of person that would take a child like that and murder it? Who could there be?

Why, men and women, if that little baby, if that little, curly-haired youngster were out in the grass in the jungle, breathing – just so long as it was breathing – any tiger, any lion, the most venomous snake would have passed that child without hurting a hair of its head.

Now what type of man would kill the child of Colonel Lindbergh and Anne Morrow?

He wouldn't be an American. No American gangster and no American racketeer ever sank to the level of killing babies. Ah, no! . . . It had to be a fellow that had ice water in his veins, not blood . . . it had to be a fellow that was an egomaniac, who thought he was omnipotent. It had to be a secretive fellow. It had to be a fellow that wouldn't tell anybody anything . . .

It would have to be the type of man who wouldn't think anything of forsaking his own country and disgracing his own nation . . . the type of man that would forsake his own mother, sixty-five years of age, and run away. Yes, it would have to be the type of man that would hold up women at the point of a gun, women wheeling baby carriages.

And let me tell you, men and women, the State of New Jersey and the State of New York and the federal authorities have found that animal, an animal lower than the lowest form in the animal kingdom, Public Enemy Number One of this world, Bruno Richard Hauptmann; we have found him and he is here for your judgment.

He referred to Hauptmann as an animal several times in his summation; and then,

I never even walked [into his cell] to ask him a word. I never went in to annoy him for a second. I wouldn't get close enough to him. If I had my choice, I wouldn't get in the same room, I wouldn't become contaminated, I wouldn't breathe the same air.

I think too much of my friends and my wife and my kids to be around him at all – I feel itchy, I feel oozy, I just couldn't stand being anywhere near him. I never walked into that jail even to get a confession from him.[1]

He complained of Reilly's character assassination of the state's witnesses, and asked several of them to stand up in court. 'Jury, look at Colonel Schwarzkopf. Take a look at his eye. Does he look like a crook? Jurors, take a look at Inspector Bruckman, who became an inspector after twenty-seven years, risking his life many days and nights, with an invalid wife at home. Does he deserve

---

[1] Sam Leibowitz, listening to all this, was appalled. 'No matter how much a prosecutor feels he must obtain a conviction, he must be fair in his analysis of the evidence. No prosecutor has the right to say to a jury, "I know that this defendant is guilty." No prosecutor has the right to use inflammatory, incendiary arguments calculated to arouse the passions of the jury instead of cold arguments based on reason and logic.'

that sort of treatment for this burglar, this murderer and convict?'
Then he began to ridicule what was common knowledge, the lack
of adequate funds for the defense:

> They talk about the defense not having any money. There is not . . .
> the slightest bit of proof that they haven't any money.
>   I think they have got lots of money . . . money coming from cranks
> and idiots and fools, un-Americans all over the country, pouring in
> enough money to hire what they consider the four best lawyers avail-
> able, to get the best criminal lawyer in the East . . .
>   No money? Who said no money?
>   Just an effort to prejudice this jury.
>   Why, I think they have probably spent more money than the state.

And this from a man who knew the state had spent hundreds of
thousands of dollars.

He demolished Reilly's suggestions of Betty Gow, Violet Sharpe,
Ollie Whately being involved in a conspiracy; then, after the lunch
recess, returned to the attack:

> Let me tell you, men and women, that this murder even of the Lindbergh
> child would shrink into absolute insignificance in comparison to the
> crime that would be committed if this man were freed. *That* would be
> the crime of the century.
>   To let him roam the streets of this country and make every woman
> in her home shudder again; that would be a real tragedy, an American
> tragedy!
>   That is why I told you, men and women, that is why I told you I am
> so consumed, every inch of me, every ounce of me cries out to you,
> 'Please do your duty!'

Now his emotionalism knew no bounds, so that even truth
became a casualty. In his opening speech, he had declared that the
baby had met its death falling off the ladder, a supposition repeated
by Hauck.

> But let me tell you this: this fellow took no chance on the child
> awakening. He crushed that child right in that room into insensibility.
> He smothered and choked that child right in that room. That child
> never cried, never gave an outcry. The little voice was stilled right in
> that room.
>   He wasn't interested in the child. Life meant nothing to him. That's
> the type of man I told you about that we are dealing with.
>   Public Enemy Number One of the World! . . . Take a look at him
> as he sits there. Look at him as he walks out into this room, panther-like,
> gloating, feeling good.

Did he use the chisel to crush the skull . . . ? Is that a fair inference? What else was the chisel there for?

There were times in his summation when Wilentz appeared hardly sane; as when he picked up a ransom note and pointed to the colored symbol at the foot:

There it is. You couldn't reproduce it. There it is: the blue circle, the red center and the holes. 'B' in blue for Bruno; 'R' in red for Richard; Holes, 'H' for Hauptmann. Our *sing*nature. Nobody could reproduce that except Bruno Richard Hauptmann . . .

And in relation to the word 'singnature', he said, Hauptmann had committed 'downright and absolute perjury', declaring that that was the way he had been asked to spell 'signature' in the request writings. But, said Wilentz, 'you go through every one of those mis-spelled writings and there isn't the word 'signature' on one of them to show that we ever asked him to spell it, right or wrong.' Wilentz was wrong. Hauptmann *had* written '*sing*nature' in the request writing, and the defense handwriting expert Trendley *had* compared it with the 'singnature' of the ransom note and found no similarity. But Wilentz was not in court at the time (Lanigan cross-examined Trendley) and so was ignorant of it.

This was how he justified denying the defense access to the attic:

Oh, they say, we wouldn't let them get up into the attic. The poor boys, we wouldn't let them – terrible thing . . .

Why do they have to get up into the attic? What is there about the attic that [Hauptmann] doesn't know? He has lived there. What is there about the attic that Mrs Hauptmann doesn't know? . . .

What would they see up there? Counsel wanted to go up there on a Sunday morning while the Attorney General was at home sick in bed and couldn't make arrangements that Sunday morning, and I told him any other morning, but no, it had to be Sunday morning. Any morning during the week they could have gone up with their wood expert.

So the charge is made here in open court that has absolutely no basis for it, that they would not be permitted up in the attic.

What have we got to hide up in the attic or anywhere? What do I care about hiding anything?

Elsewhere he was full of inaccuracies, declaring that no other ransom bills had been found since Hauptmann's arrest, that Perrone had given a true description of Hauptmann in 1932, that Lindbergh was so near to the man who had called to Condon in St Raymond's Cemetery that he could almost touch him. He libelled

Dr Hudson, who had been such a thorn in his flesh earlier ('he entered this case in order to attract the attention of the world to what he considers a good solution for fingerprinting . . . and if he gets away with his testimony he would make millions of dollars') and he described Mr de Bisschop, who had cast such doubts on Koehler's evidence, as 'a little poppy-cock'. He continued to insist that Hauptmann had not worked on Saturday April 2, but wisely avoided mentioning March 1, knowing (and having previously admitted) that Hauptmann had worked at the Majestic Apartments on that day.

He concluded:

> Now, men and women, as I told you before, there are some cases . . . in which a recommendation of mercy might do. But not this one, not this one. Either this man is the filthiest and vilest snake that ever crept through the grass, or he is entitled to an acquittal. And if you believe as we do, you have got to convict him . . .
>
> We have proven it overwhelmingly, conclusively, positively. Now jurors, there is no excuse, you would never forgive yourselves if you didn't do it, you wouldn't be happy, you wouldn't feel right, honestly you wouldn't.
>
> You convict this man of murder in the first degree . . .

* * *

A few minutes after 10 a.m. on February 13, 1935, the last day of the trial, Judge Trenchard in his brown suit and black robes and carrying a sheaf of papers and a yellow pencil entered the court, took his seat on the bench, and faced the jury. He began, as judges the world over do, by saying that he would instruct them on the law, but they were the judges of the facts; then he set out the heads of evidence and invited them to draw their own conclusions.

Ford Madox Ford spoke for many when he wrote that the judge's charge to the jury seemed absolutely fair to him; and reading it today, it would be hard to disagree. But as those with experience of criminal trials know, there is all the difference between how words spoken in court sound at the time and how they read afterwards. Stress and emphasis are missing from the written record, and it is by use of stress and emphasis that judges, if they have a mind to, can indicate subtly where their own preferences lie.

It was Lindbergh, oddly, who was one of the first to observe that Trenchard's charge read more impartially than it sounded.

'For instance,' he later told Harold Nicolson, 'he kept on saying to the jury, in going over some of Hauptmann's evidence, "Do you believe that?" Now that sounds all right in print. But what he actually said was, "Do *you* believe *that*?" ' A good example of this was when Trenchard said: 'The defendant says that these ransom bills, moneys, were left with him by one Fisch, now dead. Do *you* believe *that*?' Other examples of bias were his asking the jury whether they had any doubts about the truth of Hochmuth's testimony, without adding that it had first been given two and a half years after the event; and again in asking them if they had any reason to doubt that part of the ladder had come from Hauptmann's attic. ('Mr Koehler declares that Rail 16 did come from the attic,' he might have added, 'and Mr de Bisschop and Mr Mielk declare it didn't. Now which of those gentlemen's testimony are you going to believe?')

Elsewhere Judge Trenchard was pretty fair. The evidence was mostly circumstantial but it was not enough for the circumstances to render Hauptmann's guilt probable. 'They must exclude to a moral certainty every other hypothesis but the single one of guilt, and if they do not do this, the jury should find the defendant not guilty.' If the state had not satisfied the jury beyond reasonable doubt that the death of the child was caused by the act of the defendant, he must be acquitted.

He explained the law. If murder was committed in the course of a burglary, which was what the state maintained, it was murder in the first degree, whether intentional or not. It was open to the jury to include in the verdict, if they wished, a recommendation that the penalty should be imprisonment at hard labor for life.

Mr Pope and the rest of the defense team made their objections to the charge, standing at the side-bar close to the judge's bench; while they did so Anna Hauptmann (wearing a beret, said one report, with a brave red feather) was seen to lean across the knees of Trooper Stockburger to talk to her husband – 'very much like a lady and gentleman in the orchestra stalls,' wrote Ford Madox Ford, 'politely talking across the faces of members of their party, as if discussing a new play'.

The most important of the defense's objections was the judge's telling the jury that they could conclude from the evidence that the child had met his death on the Lindbergh estate. 'The dead child's body was found in Mercer County,' Pope said, 'which raises the presumption that that was the place where death occurred, and there is no evidence to justify the conclusion that death occurred elsewhere . . .'

Sam Leibowitz, who believed Hauptmann guilty but was a stickler for the law, agreed. Kidnapping, he wrote, was a continuous crime and so long as the baby was in the possession of the kidnapper he was guilty all the time. However, the charge was not kidnapping, which in 1932 in New Jersey didn't carry the death penalty, but murder in the course of burglary, which did. Yet burglary was not a continuous crime and to make the death penalty stick, the death of the child had to take place while the burglary was being committed. Where was the evidence, he asked, that the child was killed during the perpetration of the burglary? 'What is there . . . which does not show it is just as likely that the baby was killed a hundred yards from the Lindbergh home, a mile or three miles away, hours after the burglary, or minutes or days?'

The judge granted the defense their exceptions which would be heard before the New Jersey Court of Errors and Appeals, and at 11.14 a.m. the three men and three women constables were sworn 'to safely keep the jury until they have agreed upon their verdicts'; their leader was Oden Baggstrom, in whose bus the jury had been taken for rides during Sundays in the trial. After the jury room had been inspected for hidden microphones, they escorted the jury out of court. The eight men and four women passed directly in front of Hauptmann, but none of them glanced at him.

The judge rose and disappeared into his chambers. Hauptmann rose, manacled to Trooper Stockburger and Deputy Sheriff Low, to be led back to his cell. Fisher gave him a few words of encouragement and Pope patted his shoulder, but Reilly 'walked off in another direction and did not look at him'. Lindbergh, with a streaming cold, rose for the thirty-third and last time and went out the back way to drive home to Englewood. The rest of the court slowly emptied, leaving only newsmen, troopers and officials.

On the way to his cell Hauptmann asked the short, be-spectacled Hovey Low, who, as one of his regular courthouse guards, had come to know and like him, what he thought the verdict would be.

Low said, 'Richard, that's in the lap of the gods.'

Hauptmann said, 'I'm innocent.'

Low smiled and said, 'Don't worry.' It didn't seem adequate, but it was all he could think of at the time.

22

The most trying time in any trial is waiting for the verdict. For all those involved, whether participants or observers, it is a kind of no-man's land, a vacuum. The routine of days or weeks has suddenly ceased, the conveyor belt of evidence and argument has ground to a halt. People find themselves deprived of their usefulness, their roles. Nor can a new role be found, for no one can tell when the jury will return, whether it will be minutes or hours before they reach a verdict. So it is a time of restlessness, hanging around, lighting and extinguishing cigarettes, exchanging small-talk, reflecting.

The Hauptmann trial was no exception. It being afternoon when the court recessed, the thoughts of many turned to lunch. In the courtroom, newsmen and counsel, reluctant to leave in case something unexpected happened, sent over to the hotel for coffee and sandwiches. In his cell Hauptmann, now so near to knowing whether he was to be condemned to live or die, lunched alone as he had done these past four months. In their room the jury ate hamburgers, green peas and French fries prepared by Margaret Macrea, the wife of the warden.

As the afternoon wore on, correspondents in the courtroom began filing for the morning papers. Russell B. Porter described what he saw around him for the *New York Times*. 'In the same place where laughter and noise brought a threat to clear the court, the air is hazy with tobacco smoke, men sit reading newspapers with their hats on and women perch on tables and chairs to gossip about the case. There is an incessant hum of conversation where formerly the barking of the bailiff's "Quiet, please" stopped even a whisper.'

Damon Runyon did the same for the *New York American*, reporting a checker game in progress at one end of the press table, the litter of milk cartons and paper bags on the floor, paper arrows being sailed around the room; he observed the principal participants too, like Schwarzkopf, now relaxed and smoking a cigarette. 'When he is not with Lindbergh,' he wrote, 'the Colonel is inclined to unbend.' Wilentz came in, wearing his famous white hat. 'His best friends and severest critics should inform the dapper gentleman from Perth Amboy that the white kady is all right for

Tom Mix, but not for one of Jersey's well-dressed gents.' He described Reilly as sitting glumly at the back of the court with his *chic* French wife. Asked if he had ever lost a case involving the death penalty, Reilly said, 'Lots of them. I get the most desperate cases. When it looks as if a man hasn't a chance, the courts assign Reilly. But I never take a case just because I think I can beat it.'

With interest now on the jury, James Cannon wrote up his notes on them. The attractive Ethel Stockton, often dressed in bright red: 'Smiled with a mischievous frequency at Hauptmann on the stand. Bats her eyes at Wilentz.' Verna Snyder: 'Gained thirty pounds since the case began.' Robert Cravatt: 'Ages every day. Seems depressed by trial. Slumps in seat. Moves slowly. An industrious reader.' Philip Hockenbury: 'Clasps hands impatiently all day. Sour. Looks straight ahead.' Mrs May Brelsford: 'Nibbles on knuckles during testimony.' Charles Snyder: 'Neatly dressed in conservative fashion. Looks like Hauptmann. Looks at prisoner as if he were peering in a mirror. Never smiles.'

In purplish prose Adela Rogers St John assessed the performance of the principals: Trenchard: 'true as steel, wise as Solomon, undismayed by uproar and undisturbed by excitement'; Wilentz: 'beating himself to pieces with his own desperate conviction of Hauptmann's guilt'; Reilly: 'big and bland, able and quiet, persuasive as only an Irishman can be.' She concluded: 'These weeks have been horrible, haunting, desperate, even when for a few brief hours they touched laughter, laughter which was a little hysterical with sheer relief . . . a trial none of us will ever forget.'

And Ford Madox Ford, sitting alone in the balcony above the entrance door, asked himself what verdict he would reach if he were the jury. 'I have no hesitation about the matter. I should vote for acquittal and I would stand for acquittal till the skies fell . . . I cannot think the fox was given enough grace. The prosecution was too keen. It is in my blood to think that prosecutions should have some of the impartiality of Justice herself . . . There must remain, over the vast expanses that the record of this affair will reach, some reasonable doubt.'

Afternoon gave way to early evening. The jury sent out for a magnifying glass to examine the closet writing. Reilly, now more cheerful, joined two messenger boys in a rendering of 'Let me Call you Sweetheart'. Hauptmann, who had been moving restlessly between cell and bull-pen all afternoon, sent word that he would like Fisher to visit him, but was informed that regulations did not

permit it while the jury were out. The judge sent word to Baggstrom
that the jury would not be allowed to leave the jury room until
they had reached a verdict, even if it meant remaining there all
night and all the following day.

At 7 p.m. a church bell started tolling for the regular
Wednesday evening prayer meeting, and people swarmed towards
the courthouse, thinking it was the courthouse bell announcing
the jury's return. They stayed, most of them, knowing that the
verdict could not be much longer delayed, and in the hope of
influencing it they began chanting, 'Kill Hauptmann! Kill the
German! Kill Hauptmann!' What the jury made of it is not on
record; but Hauptmann, pacing the bull-pen, was struck with
fresh terror, for it was the voice of the angel of death.

The shouting died away. Time dragged on. More coffee and
snacks were sent over from the hotel. People ate and sat and
smoked in silence, for doing nothing all day had exhausted them,
and anyway they had nothing more to say. At 9.24 the courtroom
lights went out: there were cheers and sighs and a few laughs, and
Wilentz told Schwarzkopf to send in some troopers to prevent
disorder. In the silence that followed someone began singing 'Oh,
Lord, please take away the darkness'. Presently He did.

Soon after, things began moving to a conclusion. Reilly and
Judge Large, who had been over at the hotel, came into court and
joined the other counsel, and then tubby little Sheriff Curtiss came
in. 'His face is gray and his bald spot reflects a sickly gleam and
he looks tired to death,' said one report, 'but he wanders round
the railed audience as though he were a theatrical manager looking
over his house.' In contrast, Reilly was overheard talking light-
heartedly about the verdict to Wilentz who, true to form and
according to the *New York Times*, 'loudly made a joke about
betting on a horse race – "first-degree or nothing, right on the
nose" '. There Anna Hauptmann took her seat: she had spent the
afternoon washing her own and the baby's clothes, confident of
returning home with Richard that night.

At around 10.20 p.m. several things happened. The courthouse
bell was heard tolling, announcing a verdict; and with it the crowd
again began baying for Hauptmann's blood – 'Kill Hauptmann!
Kill Hauptmann!' In the courtroom one of the bailiffs stood up
and ordered everyone else to sit down. Wilentz gave instructions
for the windows to be closed and the drapes drawn, and a trooper
to be posted at each one – 'so that no wise guy can leave by the

window'. Schwarzkopf told other troopers to lock the doors.

There was a hush in court as Hauptmann was led in, so that the yelling of the crowd penetrated the closed windows. This time he was manacled to his guards, for though innocent now he might, after the verdict, be a convicted felon. His head was bowed as he walked to his seat, and people noticed how deathly white he looked and how prominent were his cheekbones. Anna, pale and exhausted, moved nearer to him, and they exchanged a few words, across one of the guards. Fisher leaned over and said, 'Don't show a sign, because if you do, it will count against you. And remember, whatever the verdict, this is only the beginning.' Then he put his arm round Mrs Hauptmann's shoulder.

Sheriff Curtiss announced: 'The jury has reached its verdict and is ready to report.' He went out to bring them in, and a dozen troopers in blue and yellow formed an aisle between the door and the jury-box, like a guard of honor at a wedding. Curtiss was followed by Baggstrom, Baggstrom by Charles Walton the foreman, Walton by the eleven others. As they processed between the troopers and took their seats in the box, Hauptmann and Anna anxiously scanned their faces. Not one of the jury looked their way; their faces were grave and Verna Snyder was almost in tears. Still Hauptmann searched, desperate for a glance, a half-smile, some sign that he could still hope. Then he knew they had no hope to give him, and in despair turned his head away.

Now the court waited only for the judge. But for some reason he didn't come. The minutes ticked by in silence, and the tension became almost unbearable. Eventually Wilentz rose to confer with the Sheriff, and Reilly and Fisher joined them; nearly ten minutes after the jury had returned to the box, the Sheriff went to the judge's chambers to fetch him.

The judge was preceded by the white-haired court crier Hann with his cry of 'Oyez, oyez' and everyone rose and stood until the judge had taken his seat. He tapped lightly with his gavel and said, 'All those who wish to leave the courtroom before the verdict may do so at once.' No one did. 'Poll the jury,' said the judge, and in turn each of them answered to his name.

When the twelfth had answered, Hann reported, 'The jury is in the box.' The judge motioned with his hand, and the court clerk said, 'The jury will rise.'

They rose. The judge said, 'Let the defendant rise,' and Hauptmann and his two guards rose too.

'Members of the jury,' asked the court clerk, 'have you agreed upon your verdict?'

Quietly, raggedly, they answered, 'We have.'

'Who shall speak for you?'

'The foreman.'

'Mr Foreman,' said the court clerk, addressing Walton, 'do you find the defendant, Bruno Richard Hauptmann, guilty or not guilty?'

With trembling hands Walton unfolded a piece of rustling paper. 'Guilty,' he said. 'We find the defendant Bruno Richard Hauptmann guilty of murder in the first degree.'

There was a murmur in court and a kind of drawn-out sigh, which for different people meant different things: satisfaction, surprise, wonder, awe. All eyes turned to Hauptmann, but he had his back to the court and apart from a slight swaying, gave no reaction that could be seen. Some pressmen dashed to the doors, but were not allowed to leave: there had to be further proof of the unanimity of the verdict.

'Members of the jury,' said the court clerk, 'you have heard the verdict, that you find the defendant, Bruno Richard Hauptmann, guilty of murder in the first degree, and so say you all?'

Barely audibly, as though half ashamed of what they were being asked to say, they murmured, 'We do.'

But even this was not enough, for now Reilly demanded, as was his right, that the jury be polled individually; and each had to stand and say 'Guilty of murder in the first degree.' Verna Snyder could hardly force the words out. It was she and Rosie Pill, according to Ethel Stockton, who had stood out on the first and second ballots for life imprisonment, and only on the third ballot had been persuaded to change their minds.

Wilentz moved for immediate sentence, and after calling for the indictment, the judge announced he would impose it.

'The defendant may stand,' he said.

Once again Hauptmann and his guards rose.

'Bruno Richard Hauptmann, you have been convicted of murder in the first degree.' He looked down at his papers, then back to the convicted man. 'The sentence of the court is that you, the said Bruno Richard Hauptmann, suffer death at the time and place and in the manner provided by law.' He said it quietly and with authority for he had said it many times before. 'And the court will hand to the Sheriff a warrant appointing the week beginning

Monday the 18th of March 1935 as the week within which such sentence must be executed in the manner provided by law.'

This meant death in the electric chair in the State Prison in Trenton in five weeks' time; but everyone knew it would be long after that before all the processes of law would be exhausted.

'You are now remanded to the custody of the Sheriff.'

With Stockburger and Low on either side, Hauptmann was led from the room. He did not look at Anna as he walked away, though she with red-rimmed eyes looked despairingly at him. When he reached his cell he collapsed on the bed and was heard to mutter, 'Little men, little pieces of wood, little scraps of paper.' Later still a police officer came to his cell and said that it might help him to avoid the chair if he revealed what he had done with the other $30,000 of ransom money. Hauptmann replied that Wilentz had just proved that he had spent it.

The judge rose and returned to his chambers; now the doors were opened, and the pressmen ran out in search of telephones to file their stories. In more orderly fashion the jury filed out too and were escorted across the street by the constables for a last night at the Union Hotel.

* * *

Harold Nicolson heard the news on the radio at Next Day Hill where he had arrived the day before, his book on Dwight Morrow almost completed. Dinner, he wrote to Vita Sackville-West, had been a strained affair, for they were all keyed up waiting for the verdict.

> They knew that the first news would come over the wireless, so that there were two wirelesses turned on – one in the pantry next to the dining room and one in the drawing room. Thus there were jazz and jokes while we had dinner, and one ear was straining the whole time for the announcer from the courthouse. Lindbergh had a terrible cold which made it worse.
>
> Then after dinner we went into the library, and the wireless was on in the drawing room next door. They were all rather jumpy. Mrs Morrow, with her unfailing tact, brought out a lot of photographs and we had a family council as to what illustrations to choose for the book. This was just interesting enough to divert, but not to rivet, attention.

Another guest came over to talk to Nicolson, while the others went into the drawing room.

> We discussed Dwight for some twenty minutes. Suddenly Betty put her

head round the huge Coromandel screen. She looked very white. 'Hauptmann,' she said, 'has been condemned to death without mercy.'

We went into the drawing room. The wireless had been turned on to the scene outside the courthouse. One could hear the almost diabolic yelling of the crowd. They were all sitting round – Miss Morgan with embroidery, Anne looking very white and still. 'You have now heard,' broke in the voice of the announcer, 'the verdict in the most famous trial in all history. Bruno Hauptmann now stands guilty of the foulest . . .' 'Turn that off, Charles, turn that off.'

Then we went into the pantry and had ginger beer. Charles sat there on the kitchen dresser looking very pink about the nose. 'I don't know,' he said to me, 'whether you have followed this case very carefully. There is no doubt at all that Hauptmann did the thing. My one dread all these years has been that they would get hold of someone as a victim about whom I wasn't sure. I am about this – *quite* sure. It is this way . . .'

And then, as if to bolster his beliefs, Lindbergh went through the case point by point though not entirely accurately, and just as the New York and New Jersey police forces had earlier succeeded in convincing him that Hauptmann was guilty, so now he succeeded in convincing Nicolson. 'It was very well done,' wrote Nicolson. 'It made one feel that here was no personal desire for vengeance or justification; here was the solemn process of law inexorably and impersonally punishing a culprit.'

He rounded off his letter with a paragraph which could well have found a place in any Hearst newspaper editorial:

If Hauptmann had been acquitted, it would have had a bad effect on the crime situation in this country. Never has circumstantial evidence been so convincing. If on such evidence a conviction had not been secured, then all the gangsters would have felt a sense of immunity. The prestige of the police has been enormously enhanced by this case.

Lindbergh, he ended, told him that Hauptmann was a magnificent-looking man, splendidly built. 'But that his little eyes were like the eyes of a wild boar. Mean, shifty, small and cruel.' Lindbergh, no less than others, saw what he wanted to see.

*   *   *

In the courtroom Anna Hauptmann had not moved since hearing her husband sentenced. 'Up to now,' wrote Craig Thomson, 'she had been staring at the floor, the only sign of life on her face the blinking of her heavy-lidded eyes.' But now the woman whose dignity and stoicism had won the admiration of all had reached breaking-point. 'Suddenly her shoulders shook, the tears came silently, without sound or warning, and she was crying. From her pocket-book she took a small blue handkerchief and began dabbing at her eyes.' Seeing her situation, John Walters, Flemington's Chief of Police, stepped forward and chivalrously offered to take her home; soon after she left for her room at the Opdykes'.[1]

Counsel on both sides gathered up their papers and made their way out of the building, some to go home, others to join the pressmen for a last get-together in Nellie's Tap. Reilly was not among them. He paid a brief visit to Hauptmann's cell, expecting that with nothing left to lose Hauptmann would now confess. Surprised and disappointed (for he had hoped his conscience might be eased) by Hauptmann saying he had nothing to confess, he left for the station and the last train to New York.

Now, apart from paper bags and candy wrappings and milk and coffee cartons, the main courtroom at Flemington was empty. The night watchman on his rounds turned off the lights. The Trial of the Century was over.

*   *   *

Reactions to the verdict could hardly have been more varied. Adela Rogers St John, who earlier had been racked by doubts and had written, 'We feel we will forgive him much if he will give us a complete explanation', now tried to dispel her doubts with the jury's certainties. 'Bruno Hauptmann murdered the Lindbergh baby,' she declared. 'Hold to that, cling to that, never forget that.' New Jersey's officials were blander. Wilentz congratulated the jury on its courage, Judge Large and District Attorney Foley said the verdict was fully justified by the evidence, Schwarzkopf that the ends of justice had been served, Peacock that the result was an answer to the prayers of the nation's mothers. The *New York Daily News* said it would put a crimp in the snatch-racket that would be felt for a long time.

Others however took a different view. Fisher said, 'This is a cry for blood. It is the clamor of the crowd for no matter whom.' Rosecrans said he had expected an acquittal and was sure that on

[1] This was in marked contrast to the behavior of Jack Clements of the Hearst Press who next day, said Anna, having driven her and Manfred to Manhattan, handed her a $5 bill for them to find their own way home.

appeal the verdict would be reversed. The *New York Times* called the case an unsolved mystery and Eleanor Roosevelt expressed the concern of many when she said, 'The entire trial has left me with a question in my mind.' Clarence Darrow, as forthright as usual, said that no man should be executed on such flimsy evidence; while the man at the center of it said: 'I was sentenced to death for murdering a little child I never saw in my life.'

And this was the paradox at the heart of it all; that those who had testified against him had lied and lied and been believed; and that he who had told the truth had been disbelieved and condemned to die.

PART EIGHT

THE GOVERNOR

'But only agony, and that has ending;
And the worst friend and enemy is but Death.'

(Rupert Brooke)

23

With verdict and sentence now established, the American people believed it would be only a matter of time before Hauptmann gave the world a full confession; Lloyd Fisher therefore made immediate arrangements with Sheriff Curtis for representatives of the media to visit Hauptmann in prison and hear a declaration of innocence from his own lips. The day after sentence a newsreel company was permitted to set up its equipment outside the bull-pen, and Hauptmann, standing behind the bars (and allowed for the occasion to wear shirt and tie) to make a statement direct to the camera.

'I want to tell the people of America,' he said, 'that I am absolute innocent of the crime of the murder. My conviction was a great surprise. I never saw the Lindenbergh (*sic*) baby and I never received any money. I want to appeal to all people everywhere to aid me at this time. A defense must be raised to carry my appeal to a higher court. Before God, I am absolute innocent. I have told all I know about the crime.'

Perhaps Lloyd Fisher had told him not to show his feelings. If so, it was a pity. Nervous of the occasion and still not at ease with the language, he read the statement in a high-pitched, awkward monotone that carried little conviction.

Then came two reporters, representing the American news agencies and press; for them Hauptmann was told to change back into prison garb of undershirt, old gray trousers and laceless shoes. The reporters noted that the harsh electric lights which had glared down on Hauptmann night and day during his confinement were still shining brightly, that there were two guards with Hauptmann in his cell, another in the bull-pen and three others within call. After telling them that he was going to try and raise money from the public to finance an appeal because he was now penniless, he was asked if it was true that he had been offered a large sum of money to confess everything. 'If I had anything to confess,' he told them, 'I would have done so months ago, so as to spare my wife and mother all they have gone through.' He added, 'If they came to the door and opened it and said, you can go free if you tell the whole truth, I couldn't tell them anything because I have already told the whole truth.' Not once during the months of life that were left to him was Hauptmann to depart from this view.

Asked about the trial, he said he was disappointed in some of his witnesses who were clearly out for publicity, in the judge's charge to the jury which he thought favored the state too much, and in the daily presence of Lindbergh which he felt must have influenced the verdict. The only time he chuckled during the interview, the reporters said, was when they brought up the evidence about Rail 16 coming from a board in the attic. 'That was the most ridiculous thing,' he said, smiling. 'I got so many boards in my garage, why should I want to go to the attic?'

Asked if he felt afraid of the electric chair, he said, 'You can imagine how I feel when I think of my wife and child. It is them that I fear for. For myself I fear nothing, because I am innocent.' Discussing reports in the newspapers that he was not religious, he replied, 'I am probably more religious than most people who go to church. I am a friend of nature. I have always been a Lutheran. I pray in my heart and not only since I was here.' He concluded, 'If there is anybody in the United States to whom I did any wrong and from whom I took a penny in any dishonest way, I'd like that man or woman to step forward and say so . . . I make an appeal to the whole American public to help me . . . so I will not have to die in the electric chair.'

The same day, half a world away in Kamenz, Saxony, Hauptmann's mother heard news of the verdict and sentence while out shopping, and burst into tears. Later a *New York Times* reporter came to No. 64 Bautzenerstrasse and sat with her on the bench beside the stove where so long ago Richard had confided in her his innermost thoughts and feelings. ('There was nothing in my life, good or bad, that I did not tell her; the twilight hours passed on wings.') 'I know my son is not guilty,' she said, 'but

Lindbergh wanted it, and so everything went that way.' She sat down at the table and in Gothic script wrote a letter to President Roosevelt for clemency. '. . . the World War has already taken from me my husband and two of my sons. I am seventy years old. It would mean my death if you, Mr President, don't pardon my son, because then I shall be all alone . . . Bruno isn't a bad man. Therefore I beg you to be merciful to him.' While she was writing, a telegram arrived from Anna. 'DON'T WORRY. DECISION ONLY TEMPORARY.'

Next day Hauptmann signed an oath that he was now a pauper, so that his attorneys might apply for a copy of the trial record (some five thousand pages) for the purpose of preparing an appeal, and he issued a statement through Lloyd Fisher for funds to subsidize his appeal, estimated to cost some $20,000. 'I being the father of a baby boy now almost the age of the Colonel's child at the time of its death, feel very sorry for the Colonel and Mrs Lindbergh . . . and it seems inconceivable to me that a man devoted to his wife and child as I am, could possibly commit such a violent crime.' After pointing out that he had had no record for violence in Germany, and that since coming to America in 1924 his record had been spotless, he asked, 'Is it possible then that people can believe that I could commit this most violent of all crimes?'

That evening Anna and Manfred left the Opdykes to stay with Anna's niece Maria Müller in the Bronx, while Wilentz, Judge Large and Condon went south in search of sunshine to (respectively) Florida, Bermuda and Panama. Next morning while it was still dark a convoy of three sedans containing Hauptmann and an escort of fourteen state troopers (they were taking no chances!), with lights flashing and sirens wailing, accompanied by a score of cars containing pressmen and photographers, set out on the forty-minute journey to Trenton. For more than five months Hauptmann's eyes had seen no further than the stone walls and steel bars of his cell; now, as day dawned and despite his situation, the sight of clouds and the open countryside, the woods and fields of New Jersey, must have delighted him. But soon the journey was over and they drew up at the main gate of the fortress-like State Prison, adorned like the Tombs in New York with effigies of serpents, rams, eagles, and kneeling human figures. Manacled to his two guards he stepped from the car wearing his hat and double-breasted suit and, remarkably, still smiling. He posed briefly for the photographers, and a man in the crowd shouted out (and you can hear parts of it on the newsreel film today), 'We all know you're innocent, kid.' Then he was led into the prison and the door clanged behind him.

At reception Hauptmann was given his prison number, 17400, was issued with prison uniform of blue shirt, blue trousers and heavy shoes, was medically examined, photographed, finger-printed, and had his hair cut off. The prison's six hundred inmates were gathering in the mess hall for their midday meal, and as Hauptmann was led past the hall on his way to Death Row at the other side of the prison, they broke out with cat-calls and hisses: rapists and robbers, muggers and buggers, contract killers and con men the world over have always held in low esteem those who maltreat children, especially a golden one like this.

Today the death house in Trenton is no longer in use; but along the length of its empty, echoing cells, in the dust that accumulates daily on the unswept floors, in the abandoned electrocution chamber where the outline of the chair, like some obscene fingerprint, disfigures the wall, there is still the smell of death. There are two tiers of nine cells each, one above the other. They were built in 1907, the year when executions in New Jersey changed from hanging to electrocution. Each cell measures 10 by 9 feet and contained a folding bed, a desk and chair and a combined wash-basin and lavatory. There were times in the old days when every one of the eighteen cells was occupied by condemned men and an overspill of perhaps half a dozen others were held in the main body of the prison. Some had to wait five, six, seven years for death or reprieve: one man was electrocuted thirteen years after committing his crime.

There were six other prisoners in Death Row when Hauptmann arrived, but to avoid incidents the warden had placed them all on the top tier, with Hauptmann alone on the bottom tier in Cell 9, next to the execution chamber. In some ways Hauptmann's regime here would be better than Flemington, in others worse. His 10 by 9 cell gave him more room to move about; the light kept burning there was not as harsh, he would not be required to sleep with his arms on the coverlet, he could exchange conversation with his guards and write up to six letters a month (including one, for the first time, to his mother). As a condemned man he would be given the same food as the prison officers which included butter, eggs and fresh vegetables from the prison farm. Against this there was no bull-pen where he could pace up and down, and he was not entitled (unless the warden decreed otherwise) to more than one visit a month, one hour's exercise a day and one bath a week. On arrival the first thing he asked for was a Bible.

Next day the bad relationships that had been simmering throughout the trial between Reilly and the rest of the defense team, especially Fisher, finally surfaced. Asked about lodging a writ of error with the Court of Errors and Appeals – the first stage of any appeal and one which would automatically postpone the execution, now only four weeks away – Reilly said that as a matter of courtesy he proposed to wait until David Wilentz had returned from his vacation in Florida. Fisher exploded. 'Mr Reilly has not conferred with any of us, and I think it is an outrage,' he declared. 'When our man is scheduled to die the week of March 18th, we should not be wasting time waiting for Mr Wilentz to return from Florida. It will be a job to get that record printed in time now, and if we were to follow Reilly's suggestion, he would be dead and buried before we can get it.' That suggestion, he went on, was in keeping with Reilly's entire conduct of the case, and he launched into a bitter denunciation of some of the witnesses Reilly had chosen to call.

Reilly came back with a blustering reply ('I am sick and tired of all this fooling around, and Fisher's double-crossing') but, ignoring him, Fisher went ahead with petitioning Judge Trenchard for the record to be printed, and when that was successful, lodged a writ of error with the Court of Errors and Appeals. This meant an indefinite postponement of the execution, but the question now arose as to whether Reilly or Fisher was Hauptmann's chief counsel. The matter was partly resolved at a three-hour meeting at the prison between the four attorneys and the Hauptmanns, at which the lawyers seemed to have made up their differences for the sake of their client. Asked outright who was leader of the team, Pope told reporters: 'Cut out your damned chiefs and seniors. We are four musketeers, all for one and one for all.'

A week later the first of several public meetings to raise money for Hauptmann's defense fund took place in the Yorkville Casino, center of a predominantly German-speaking area of the Bronx. The hall was filled with 2500 people and a further 3000 overspill waited outside. Anna spoke with passion of her husband's innocence ('I know he is not capable of a crime like that') and to show solidarity Reilly joined her on the platform. He declared to the audience, as he had done recently on several occasions, that he too believed Hauptmann innocent – by which it seems that he did not think him guilty of what he called 'the actual murder', though continuing to believe, as many did, that he must have been involved in some way. 'The man who did this crime,' he said, 'deserves to be drawn and quartered, but that man was not Bruno Richard Hauptmann.' With him on the platform was Hauptmann's spiritual adviser in prison, the Reverend D. G. Werner of the First Adventist Church, who, after only a few visits to the condemned man, had also come to believe in his innocence. The meeting raised some $600 in admission fees and a similar amount by way of collection. On the same day two further ransom bills were located at East Boston Airport.

Hauptmann meanwhile had settled down into the boring routine of life in Death Row, reading avidly (his latest book was *The Travels of Marco Polo*), signing his autograph to raise money for his appeal, making notes from the trial record for his attorneys, writing to his mother not to despair because he was sure (and he believed it) that the appeal would be successful. On March 15 three of the men on the top tier, Connie Scarpone, Michael Mule and George de Stefano went to the chair for having murdered a friend of de Stefano for $500. They were led down to the execution chamber at seven-minute intervals and on the way shook hands with Hauptmann who told them to pray to God. All three were despatched in the course of the next twenty minutes. Twelve days later a 22-year-old murderer, Kurt Barth, trod the same path, and Hauptmann urged him too to put his trust in God. Now there were only two men left with Hauptmann in Death Row.

The sweetness and light which Reilly had recently been bestowing ended abruptly at the beginning of April when, having cast his beady eye on the mounting defense fund and ignoring the fact that the Hearst Press had already paid his $7500 retainer, he whacked in to Hauptmann an account for professional services of $25,000. Anna (who had paid him $5000 from the defense fund the week before) was outraged and, after consultation with Richard, wrote to Reilly dismissing him. Unabashed, Reilly told the Brooklyn Masonic Luncheon Club, 'Lawyers must be paid. Whether Anna likes it or not, she is going to pay, and pay through the nose.' But, he said, he would continue to believe in Hauptmann's innocence, and would not be surprised if someone, some day, were to make a deathbed confession. Pope, asked what the defense team would do now, said they would continue without Reilly and without charging a fee. 'There is no use presenting a bill to a man who is pauperized,' said Fisher, and Pope added, 'We're in it for the love of the cause.'

On May 2 (a week after Millard Whited had been clapped into jail for stealing a road grader and selling it for $50) the Court of Error and Appeals met in their room in the State House annexe at Trenton. The Court consisted of Chancellor Luther A. Campbell, New Jersey's highest judicial officer, Chief Justice Thomas J. Brogan, seven of the remaining eight Supreme Court Justices (Judge Trenchard had naturally disbarred himself) and four lay members. They were to hear a petition from Hauptmann's attorneys, additional to the main appeal which would be presented later, that the jury at his trial were not properly sequestered, that there was a circus atmosphere in the courtroom, and that press and radio reports were grossly prejudicial. The court rejected these arguments, but did give leave to the defense to include in the record the summation of David Wilentz which, the defense had claimed, 'was inflammatory, far beyond the evidence and unduly influenced the jury against the defendant'.

Six weeks later in the same room came the hearing of the main appeal. It was an impressive occasion with the judges sitting in two rows of high-backed, leather-cushioned chairs. 'The heavy mahogany furniture, the thick purple carpeting, the great windows overlooking the Delaware River and the general air of spaciousness,' said the *New York Times*, 'was in striking contrast to the overcrowded and unventilated courtroom at Flemington.' Security was strict. The general public were barred, Hauptmann was not allowed to be present by law, and even Anna and the Reverend Werner were turned away. Reporters were at first barred but later allowed in, though instructed not to leave or enter while the court was sitting. Photographers were kept at some distance from the building.

The defense's case was presented by Egbert Rosecrans. In the three hours allotted to him he began by arguing that the verdict had breached the Fourteenth Amendment (deprivation of life and liberty without due process) and the Sixth Amendment (trial not held in district where crime was committed). He went on to submit that the charge against Hauptmann of the commission of a felony in the crime of burglary had no legal precedent. Burglary, he said, was not a statutory crime in New Jersey; and even if a burglary had been committed, which he was not admitting, a garment [the sleeping-suit] that had not been proved to be of value could not be offered as proof of theft. In any case the theft was petty larceny, and so the child's death was not murder in the first degree. It was these submissions that interested the court most, with one judge querying the failure of the state to prove grand larceny and a felony, and another asking whether proof that the house had been broken into and entered was not enough.

Rosecrans turned to Wilentz's inflammatory summation, and several judges wanted to know why this had not been objected to at the time. Pointing out that Reilly was chief defense counsel at the time, Rosecrans said, 'We may have been neglectful and we may have been ignorant, but that doesn't make any difference. The trial judge should not have allowed these things to go on. Because counsel did not object is no excuse.'

Other points he brought up were the contradictory theories Wilentz had advanced in his opening and closing speeches as to the cause of the baby's death (the latter specifying 'a wilful, deliberate and premeditated killing in all its aspects'), the bias in Judge Trenchard's charge to the jury, his wrongful admission of the ladder as evidence, and the unreliability of the evidence of Hochmuth, Osborn Senior, Arthur Koehler and Cecile Barr. After lunch, he dwelt on the circus atmosphere of the trial, from which the jury could not have distanced themselves, and the daily presence of Lindbergh, 'constantly presenting to the jurors the living picture of a bereaved father, for whose sorrow the world demanded a sacrifice'. (He might have contrasted Lindbergh's daily attendance at Flemington with the refusal of the present judges to allow Hauptmann, or even his wife, to attend the appeal proceedings.) Hauptmann's trial, he concluded, had been unfairly prejudiced: the weight of evidence was against the verdict, and he submitted it should be reversed.

Wilentz, in rebuttal, was in no mood for compromise. He said angrily he saw no need to retract anything in his closing speech. He had dubbed Hauptmann Public Enemy Number One and an animal because that was what he was; the jury had found him guilty as charged and he deserved the punishment that was coming to him. He went through all the evidence that had been amassed against Hauptmann at his trial, and defended Lindbergh's presence in court and the conduct of the press and public; he left it to his chief assistant Mr Lanigan to deal with the matter of felony. Under the old common law, said Lanigan, both petty and grand larcenies were felonies; under the statutory law a burglary could be said to have been committed if there was proof of felonious intent. 'We are within both the common law and the statutory provisions in saying that a felony was committed which resulted in first-degree murder,' he concluded. 'We submit there was no error.'

At 4 p.m. the court rose and the judges took away with them the briefs of both sides, to which counsel had spoken. They would study them at leisure during the summer recess, and hand down their judgment in the autumn. Meanwhile the date of Hauptmann's execution would remain in abeyance.

*   *   *

'The trial is over,' Anne wrote in her diary the day after the verdict. 'We must start our life again, try to build it securely – C and Jon and I.' They continued living at Next Day Hill, though with her mother away in Cuernavaca with Harold Nicolson, the pressures of that relationship were lifted. She was putting the finishing touches to *North to the Orient*, while Charles commuted to New York each day to work with Dr Alexis Carrel on their heart-pump machine at the Rockefeller Institute. 'We look at each other with surprise and joy and feel young and on a honeymoon. Jon is mine again and runs to my arms.'

Elsie Whately wanted to return to England. 'She is very tired,' Anne wrote her mother, 'and hasn't been home since Whately died.' Anne hated losing her. 'She seems part of our marriage, which is a funny thing to say, but at least part of the *feeling* of being married, for she was with us when we first started housekeeping in the little farmhouse.' It was there, near Princeton, arriving back from New York, that Anne would look up at Charlie's window to see if his light was on and he still awake. Elsie had been with them at Hopewell too and, since Betty Gow's departure, was the last link with Charlie.

But the highpoint of Anne's life that spring was taking up Harold Nicolson's introduction to his New York publishers; and any author reading Anne's diary for the end of April and beginning of May 1935 will hear the echo of his own footsteps. 'I went down to Harcourt, Brace with *North to the Orient*. I was pretty trembly about it and before I went, I did a stupid thing. I counted the number of words. It was 42,000 something. I was in a panic. It was much too short and I was already committed to talk to them.'

This didn't worry nice Mr Harcourt ('How long is a piece of string?' he asked) or his colleague, nice Mr Sloan. Nor were they concerned that the events in the book were three years old, or at having to meet criticism that they were publishing it (if they did) because it was written by Lindbergh's wife. She didn't leave the manuscript, because it needed corrections. How long would these take? A week, said Anne, and went out 'still trembly, but happy.'

Later she had misgivings ('two or three good chapters, several poor ones, the rest mediocre') but with Charles's help beavered away at corrections. Mr Sloan came down when they were finished, listened unimpressed to Anne's disclaimers about the book's merits and took it away. Then the agony of waiting to hear. On Friday, 'They're not excited about it or they'd call up. I don't think it's good . . .' (Harold Nicolson was then expressing similar doubts to Vita about his Morrow book: 'I am terribly discouraged. It is as heavy as lead.')

'Six o'clock and no word. It would be till Monday then. I did not feel exactly disappointed – just tired. It was what I expected.'

At a quarter to seven she was in the garden when Banks the butler announced Mr Harcourt on the telephone. 'Mrs Lindbergh? Mr Sloan brought in your manuscript this morning and I've just finished it. I couldn't put it down. It's splendid. I would take it if it were written by Jane Smith. It's a good story, it's moving, it's well constructed and parts of it border on poetry . . . You've written a book, my dear.'

She stood looking out of the window, overcome with happiness. 'It's true. I have it, then. It's here.' In the garden she remembered other landmarks in her life, other moments of personal joy or triumph.

The Jordan Prize announcement in chapel, my first proposal and my first kiss, and then C asking me to marry him, and my first child and my second. And soloing a plane and that moment off Africa when I got WSL.[1] And H.N.[2] after reading the *Geographic* article, telling me I should write.

C came home and said I looked as if I had swallowed the canary. When I told him, he *beamed* with pride. He was terribly, childishly proud.

In mid June she returned to Smith College to be given an honorary degree and then, on the day that Rosecrans was putting Hauptmann's case to the Court of Errors and Appeals, and the

---

[1] The radio station in Massachusetts.

[2] Harold Nicolson.

Rockefeller Institute for Medical Research was announcing the successful development of the Lindbergh/Carrel heart machine, she took Jon to North Haven for the summer.

With Charles they were there until early fall. It was a happy, soothing time, the days active with golf and tennis, swimming and sailing: on a day trip to remote Matinicus Island they had daydreams of building a house there, shut away from the world. Proofs of *North to the Orient* arrived: it was to be published on August 15 (books which take a year to be published today took four months then).

Jon, like Charlie before him, had to suffer their father's policy of early toughening up. 'C,' said Anne, 'has been taking Jon every day to the pool and throwing him in' – and although he had a life preserver, he was still only two! Anne confessed she couldn't watch, but that Jon seemed to thrive on it. And she was right: before his third birthday he was swimming on his own.

Guests came and went, including Harold Nicolson and his eighteen-year-old son Ben, later to win fame as an artist ('Ben wants to be a painter,' wrote Anne, 'but he really doesn't think he can, or can afford to waste a year finding out . . . I know exactly how he feels.') The Nicolsons stayed in a cottage on the estate to allow Harold to correct *his* proofs from Harcourt, Brace. He adored North Haven and wrote ecstatic letters to Vita about 'the air scented with fresh seaweed and pines' reminding him of the west of Scotland. They played tennis and aquaplaned, and Lindbergh took Ben flying in his scarlet plane. Harold longed to go too, but ever since a near miss in 1923 had promised Vita he would never fly again. 'I did so envy him, damn you,' he wrote to her. 'That perfect summer's day, that lovely island-studded sea, those distant mountains and that vault of blue above the scent of pines.'

Lindbergh has the reputation of being an extremely silent man, yet with us he chatters the whole time. Yesterday he made a huge bonfire, cutting down whole pine-trees to improve his landing-ground. I puffed and puffed. Ben very languidly stooped, picked up a pine cone and with infinite forethought flung it on the bonfire. I was goaded by his example to wield an axe. He stood there, watching. The smoke was all resinous and drifted in a huge yellow turban out to sea. The sea-gulls yelled. Little Jon from a safe distance watched us entranced. Lindbergh hewed and hacked . . . It was an odd occupation to render one so happy; but it did.

After Anne had taken Nicolson to the boat, she wrote, 'I mind that we will not see him again. I wish people did not mean so much to me.'

At the end of July they took to the air again, bound for Charles's boyhood home at Little Falls, Minnesota. They landed at Fort Ripley, then drove into town past a water tower with a sign, 'Charles A. Lindbergh's home town welcomes you.' At the West Side Hardware Store, they called on old family friends, Mr and Mrs Engstrom, who drove them to the homestead, now a museum. A good-sized house,' Anne called it, 'clapboard, of no particular form or style.' In the attic they found family trunks, discarded bits of furniture and an incubator Charles had once made; in the basement the old Saxon Six in which he had driven his mother to California. They visited the duckpond Charles had built, the creek where he swam but which now was dried up, the field where he lay and looked up at the sailing clouds, thinking how wonderful it would be to fly. 'C plunges ahead with Engstrom,' wrote Anne, 'zeal on his face', so that she and Mrs Engstrom, in wet shoes and fighting off mosquitoes, had difficulty keeping up.

They were back at North Haven for Jon's third birthday party, but he was not a very good host, telling his guests when they arrived, 'I'm going upstairs now,' which he did, clutching a balloon, and when everyone sang 'Happy Birthday' he searched for a ball under the bench. Soon they were airborne again, this time to Falaise to stay with the Guggenheims and then to Detroit and points west. Anne found the trip to Long Island terrifying, with rain, fog and thunderstorms, and believed as she often did that they were going to be killed: the fact that their dear friend Will Rogers and the record-breaking pilot Wiley Post had been killed in Alaska the week before added to her terror. But at Long Island Lindbergh, rock-like as always, came out of low cloud to make a routine landing in driving rain.

They went on to visit more Lindbergh relations and were back at North Haven again at the end of August. *North to the Orient* had been published and reviewed while they were away, and they found many letters of congratulation. Mina Curtiss had written, and Harold Nicolson included a tribute from Vita Sackville-West. 'This is thrilling,' Anne wrote, 'faith pouring back into me.' Charles took Jon on his first flight ('Jon is not at all frightened . . . I on the other hand am paralyzed with fear') and in mid September Charles took off on his own to pick up Harry Guggenheim for rocket-firing experiments in the desert in New Mexico. Leaving, he dipped his wings, then roared past into the sun. 'I feel incredibly empty and realize suddenly that without C, I would lose life and the whole purpose of life.' Four days later he sent his first letter since they were married. 'Comforting, and *so* much him, wrapped up in a sock with a watch.'

Her mother and Con left, then Elisabeth's husband Aubrey and, shutting up the big house for the winter, she and Jon moved into the guest cottage. On September 30 the scarlet plane again roared overhead, but was unable to land because of the wind. She chased it in the car, lost it, returned to find it already landed, 'and C in the little house going upstairs with Jon in his arms'.

Her last North Haven entry before returning to Englewood is for Tuesday October 8. Next day, Hauptmann's tenth wedding anniversary, the Court of Errors and Appeal met again in Trenton to give judgment on his appeal.

24

For Hauptmann it had been a rather different summer, especially during July and August when the sticky East Coast heat was at its most uncomfortable and he was confined day and night to a windowless, airless, 10 by 9 cell. But he had not been unoccupied. To read (in addition to books from the library) he had the five thousand pages of the trial record, which he would pore over for hours. On Fisher's advice and to raise additional funds, he had been writing the story of his life from childhood at Kamenz to the present day: it came to 218 manuscript pages, and Fisher hoped to sell it to a New York paper. In July Hauptmann was heartened by a report from a committee of the American Bar Association that castigated both prosecuting and defense attorneys at his trial for having given prejudicial interviews to press and radio. 'To treat a simple trial as a public show, as was done in the sensational case of Bruno Hauptmann, is to cheapen life itself,' they said; and they recommended that a committee of distinguished lawyers and pressmen be appointed to set guidelines for the future. Hauptmann remained optimistic about his own future, believing that all that had happened so far was a kind of ritual which for form's sake had had to be exercised, and that the judgment of the Court of Errors and Appeals would finally free him. On July 20 (when Anne

Lindbergh was playing golf at North Haven – 'swinging at daisies, the wind blowing through me and feeling perfectly happy') he expressed his optimism in this touching letter to Anna – written in English because of prison regulations:

My dear Anny,

It is nearly two weeks since I saw you last time, so therefore I will write to you; if it would permit it to write in my mother tongue, you certainly would get one letter after another. But you know, dear Anny, I can not express myself as I would like to and as I feel in my heart.

The last time you was visiting me you said you would like to bring our baby to me. O dear Anny, you know how I would like to see my baby, all my thoughts are by him and you. But I can not allow you to bring our child, our sunshine, behind these walls. Even when he don't know where he is when he see me, this would not give me any justification. As long as I can prevent it, our child shall never come behind those walls. So, therefore, I have to wait till I come home again.

Furthermore, dear Anny, can you imagine how I would feel when I see you and the baby, my heaven on earth, going from me and I have to stay in this terrible place. It would be a struggle against madness. I have stand a great deal of suffering already, but that would be the end. You said, people said I was never asking to see my baby. Of course they will say I must be a madman. Did people ever understand me or was trying to understand me? They probably will better when they have read my life story.

Dear Anny, I know positive that I will be home again and then our happy family life will continue. Just now, I have to be satisfied to have only the picture from you and the baby in here. Every night between seven and eight, I kiss the baby and you, like before as we did together. Brahms's beautiful lullaby, I know it is the time to put the baby to bed. To be in thought of my family is one thing nobody can take away from me; it is all what remains left and there is no possibility for stealing it.

My love for you and the baby and my belief in God, no one can lay his hand on it. These are two supremes that cannot be stolen through circumstantial evidence.

Dear Anny, when I say I am positive sure, that I have to come home free, is based on my belief in God. I know he will never permit that some persons commit a murder on me. Just now, I am like a ball in a child's hands and they like to play with it. But the dishonor will not rest on my shoulder, but it will rest on the shoulder of the State. Because the State must be responsible on the group of men who was working only in their own interest and not in the course of justice, this was only a matter of secondary consideration, but to win this case and so to climb higher on the political ladder was more important as justice. Therefore this false sentence never will stand, not before God and not before the American nation.

Dear Anny, you are wondering always when you come visiting me that I am so happy. It is not only the happiness in seeing you, it is also a quiet happiness that I have in my heart that I know the time will come when the truth comes out and then the people will say that I am innocent. For this time, my dear Anny, let us pray together and fold the hands up of our child to pray to God; God is with us, then we will soon be together in happiness and love.

Your Richard

Kiss the baby from me and when possible bring some pictures to me.

Meeting again at the State House annex at Trenton, the court gave no warning that it was about to hand down judgment, so no attorneys and no press other than the resident court reporters were present. It was only when Case 99 was called, and each Justice in turn affirmed the verdict of the court at Flemington, that it was realized what they were discussing. The judgment itself, which ran to twelve thousand words covering forty-five pages, was left on the file. Justice Charles W. Parker delivered a précis of it.

It has seldom been the task of Courts of Appeal, especially in countries which practise the adversary system of justice, to re-try cases referred to them; to usurp the function of the jury who heard the witnesses in court and evaluated the evidence offered. Rather do they see their role as ensuring that the trial was conducted according to the dictates of the law, and that the weight of evidence did not lead the jury to a perverse verdict. The Court of Errors and Appeals was no exception. Having accepted at face value the mass of false evidence that was offered against Hauptmann, their conclusion was inevitable: 'The evidence pointed to guilt from so many directions that no reasonable doubt was left and no verdict other than the one found by the Flemington jury would have been justified ... the verdict was not only not contrary to the weight of evidence but one to which the evidence inescapably led.' As regards defense evidence that rebutted that of the state, they did not so much argue it through as largely ignore it. They rejected outright the submissions of Rosecrans that there was no evidence as to where the death of the child took place, that the stealing of the sleeping-suit was not a felony, that the remarks of Wilentz and Trenchard were prejudicial. And, although Hauptmann had not been tried at Flemington for extortion of the ransom money (which was a Bronx offense) they felt confident enough to speak of 'the moral certainty, beyond a reasonable doubt, that he collected the ransom money and was therefore the kidnapper ...'

About the discovery of the ransom money in the shoe-box, they said this: 'The explanation of the source of this money offered by defendant was incredible, and we find not the slightest evidence to corroborate it. The defendant's handling of the money makes clear his guilty connection with the enterprise ... It is inconceivable that Fisch, if he had this money, would have left it in defendant's custody in the manner claimed.'

Despite the restrictions under which they were obliged to operate, it is curious that, in view of all the doubts that had been raised about the case, the strongly worded report of the committee of the American Bar Association, the general unease and puzzlement expressed both in the press and by Mrs Roosevelt, the writer H. L. Mencken, Clarence Darrow, General Hugh Johnson and others, the judges were prepared to accept the Flemington testimony so uncritically. But then, wise and upright though they all were, they too had become as hallucinated as everyone else.

Most people of course, especially those who had come to wonder if they *were* hallucinated, were relieved to have the common view sustained. The *New York Times* editorial spoke for many when it said that the judges had patiently and carefully examined the whole case: 'By this unanimous decision of the Court of Errors and Appeals the case has been brought to a fitting end. Judge Trenchard who presided at the trial and now the judges of the highest Jersey court have so borne themselves in a very difficult case as to heighten the reputation of their state in the administration of justice.'

Six of the jurors, when canvassed, expressed satisfaction at the judgment, and Mrs Ethel Stockton said: 'It would have been a terrible disappointment if the higher court had reversed our verdict.'

So everyone could relax! But for Hauptmann the decision was shattering. Lloyd Fisher was leaving the prison after seeing him at around 1 p.m. when his secretary Laura Apgar brought him the news; he at once retraced his steps. Hauptmann took it well, he said, his only comment being, 'What a terrible wedding anniversary present for my Anny.' Anna said she would do all she could to carry on, adding, 'I hope and pray the true facts will come out before they can do anything to my poor man.'

All that afternoon, his guards noticed, Hauptmann sat motionless on his bed, staring at the floor. Now he knew that everything that had gone before was not the empty formality, the shadow-boxing he had imagined. They really did mean to kill him.

Was there nothing or nobody that could help him now? He had been told that the new warden of the prison, Colonel Mark O. Kimberling, owed his appointment to his friendship with the Governor of New Jersey, Harold Hoffman; and that the Governor was not only the chief executive of the state whose servants were mainly responsible for his present plight, but also the *ex-officio* chairman of the Court of Pardons, the only body that had the power to commute his sentence to life imprisonment. Several times recently Hauptmann had mentioned to Colonel Kimberling that he would like the Governor to come and see him. Now, more urgently, he repeated the request.

*   *   *

At this stage of his career Harold Hoffman had two claims to fame: at thirty-nine he was the youngest Governor in the country, and in 1934, when he was elected, he was one of the few Republican Governors to take office. Of Dutch and Scottish extraction (his great-grandfather, James Thom of Ayrshire, was a sculptor in sandstone), he was born in South Amboy, New Jersey, not far from the home in Perth Amboy of David Wilentz whom he had known from boyhood. On leaving school he joined the *Perth Amboy Evening News* and at the age of twenty became its sports editor. On America's entry into the Great War he enlisted as a private in the infantry and rose to the rank of captain. After demobilization he went into politics and was Republican Party Chairman of Middlesex County when David Wilentz was Democratic Party Chairman. Thereafter his advance was rapid: City Treasurer and then Mayor of South Amboy, a member of the New Jersey Legislature, a member of Congress for two terms, and for five years before being elected Governor, New Jersey's highly successful Commissioner for Motor Vehicles, in which office he established himself as an expert on highway safety.

Hoffman at this time was a stocky, chubby-faced man, married with three daughters, a Methodist and member of numerous charitable organizations such as the Shriners, the Elks, the Masons and the Rotarians. His secretary Andrew Dutch said he had an enormous capacity for work, an astonishing memory and an independent mind. Told by a friend that some action he proposed to take would lose him political support, he answered vigorously, 'I know what I'm doing is right. The votes can take care of themselves.'

Although he had not taken office until Hauptmann's trial was under way, he was as Governor and Chairman of the Court of Pardons more interested in it than most. One of his first acts as Governor was to re-appoint Justice Trenchard, whose term of office would otherwise have expired in mid-trial; and he had approved the extra monies which Wilentz claimed were needed for prosecuting the case. He had been perturbed by what he saw as the rail-roading of the defendant. 'I have never in my life,' he told Andrew Dutch, 'seen more hatred shown to a man than at that trial.' His interest grew when an old friend and brilliant investigator, Ellis Parker, chief of Burlington County detectives and asked by Hoffman's predecessor Governor Moore to look into the case, had assured him that Hauptmann was not guilty. Then came a call from a friend of Capitol Hill days, Charles Curtis, a former Vice President of the United States. 'Governor,' he said, 'there are a lot of funny things about that case. I've read some of the testimony, and it doesn't seem to me that Hauptmann was adequately represented or had a fair deal. I think you ought to look into it.' And now here was Colonel Kimberling in his suite at the Hildebrecht with Hauptmann's request to come and see him.

But what did Hauptmann want to see him *about*? Was he now ready to confess, to 'thaw', as Wilentz had crudely promised he would when faced with the certainty of the electric chair. If so, then as the state's chief executive, he would be lacking in duty not to comply. In any case the temptation to talk with the man who for months past had gripped the attention of the world must have been well nigh irresistible. So on the night of October 16, five days after the judgment of the Court of Errors and Appeals, and when an evening appointment was suddenly cancelled, he decided to visit Hauptmann on the spur of the moment. 'As to the propriety of my going, one of the highest judicial officers in the state had assured me that such a visit would not conflict with any existing statute. Not only that: governors before me had visited the Death House.' Nevertheless he was anxious to avoid publicity; a visit in darkness and under the personal supervision of the warden would ensure that it went unreported.

Concerned that he might not understand everything that Hauptmann said, Hoffman telephoned Ellis Parker's secretary Anna Bading, a fluent German speaker and professional stenographer, to ask her to accompany him. She lived at Mount Holly, fifteen miles away, and was at a function being given the accolade of Worthy Matron of the Chapter by the *Eastern Star*. She had no time to change before answering the Governor's call, and joined him at Kimberling's residence in full evening dress. Kimberling lent her a big overcoat and they drove round to the 3rd Street entrance which gave access to Death Row. There they were let in by the deputy warden, Colonel Selby, who had served with Hoffman in the infantry. They walked through the darkened death house, a flashlight picking out the electric chair, 'covered in white muslin', said Hoffman, 'like a seated ghost'. Hoffman asked Mrs Bading to sit on a bench near the chair and said he would call her if needed. Then he was taken through the iron door on the other side of which lay Hauptmann's cell.

Hoffman's account of his visit to Hauptmann is taken from a series of articles he wrote in *Liberty Magazine* (and in which he spelt Hauptmann's words phonetically so that readers might catch the flavor of his voice). Noticing that Hauptmann was dressed in a blue-gray open shirt and dark blue trousers, that there was a Bible and the paper-bound volumes of the trial record on the table and photographs of Anna and Manfred on the wall, Hoffman sat down on Hauptmann's bed, bracing himself to hear a plea for mercy to be conveyed to the Court of Pardons. Instead he found himself facing an angry and frustrated man. 'Vy does your state do to me all this, Governor?' Hoffman records as Hauptmann's opening remark. 'Vy do they want my life for something sombody else have done?' Hoffman interjected to say he had been found guilty. 'Lies, lies, lies!' Hauptmann almost shouted back. 'All lies. Vould I kill a baby? I am a man. Vould I build that ladder? I am a carpenter?'

Ironically Hauptmann found that Hoffman was prepared to give more time listening to him than had his own counsel, Edward Reilly; Reilly had talked with Hauptmann for a total of thirty-eight minutes in four months; Hoffman now gave him an hour. This was the first opportunity Hauptmann had had of putting his case to a New Jersey official, uninterrupted; and all the manifold weaknesses in the prosecution's case which Reilly had failed to stress or even state came tumbling out in a flood.

Why (he asked) hadn't it been emphasized at the trial that the police, despite taking numerous sets of his fingerprints, hadn't found a single one on the ladder or in the nursery, and that the two footprints found on the Hopewell lawn and in St Raymond's Cemetery didn't match his own? Why did they infer that the chisel found on the lawn was his chisel, when the chisel he used and which they had taken away was a quite different type? Why had they suppressed all the letters Fisch had written him from Germany? Would he as a carpenter build a ladder that would not bear his own weight? If guilty, would he have been so foolish as to write Condon's telephone number in a closet and not rub it out? – and, even more foolish, say to the police that it looked like his writing? Why would he go up to the attic to tear up a floorboard to make the ladder when he had plenty of boards in the garage? How could the nicks in the ladder have been made by his plane unless he had not sharpened it once in two and a half years? Would he have told the gas station attendant who took his car number that he had a hundred more gold certificate bills at home if he knew they were Lindbergh bills?

All this and much more; and he finished bitterly: 'The poor child haf been kidnapped and murdered, so somebody must die for it. For is the parent not the great flyer? And if somebody does not die for the death of the child, then always the police will be monkeys. So I am the one who is picked out to die.'

As Hoffman rose to go, Hauptmann asked to be given the lie-detector test. 'Vy won't they use on me that?' he asked. 'And on Dr Condon also use it?' He added, 'If he vill tell the truth, I vill be a free man.'

The Governor collected Anna Bading from her gruesome vigil beside the chair, left her at Kimberling's residence, then returned to his suite at the Hildebrecht and wrote all he could remember far into the night. He had been deeply disturbed by what had occurred because it was so different from what he had expected. 'Here was no cringing criminal pitifully begging for mercy but a man making a vehement claim of innocence, bitter in his denunciation of the police and the prosecution and their methods . . . and bitter too in his excoriation of his former chief counsel, Reilly.'

If Hauptmann had not asked for mercy, he had asked for further investigations, and in the interests of justice the Governor determined he should have them. 'His story and his unanswered questions put new doubts in my mind and aided in fashioning a firm resolution to search out, within the limits of my resources and my ability, the truth and the whole truth in this mysterious and challenging case . . . My duty,' he concluded, 'seemed clear.'

And next day he motored over to Flemington to buy the eleven volumes of the trial transcript.

*   *   *

Fisher meanwhile had not been inactive, although defense funds had again become exhausted and apart from the sale of Hauptmann's memoirs to the *New York Daily Mirror* for what he called 'a low figure', there were few prospects for attracting more. However, he went ahead with a petition to the United States Supreme Court to review the judgment of the Court of Errors and Appeals and it was lodged in mid November; until that was determined, the date of Hauptmann's execution would be postponed. From now on Hauptmann seems to have developed a calmer and more stoical attitude, putting his trust increasingly in God, almost indifferent to whatever fate had in store for him. When John Favorito who had killed a garage proprietor for $4 went to the chair at 8 p.m. one evening, Hauptmann, having gone to sleep an hour earlier, knew nothing of it.

Dr Condon however, to ease his conscience, was not above continuing to tell lies, and when in Boston declared that Hauptmann had sent for him three times in order to make a confession. In a dignified statement from his cell Hauptmann categorically denied it ('I have never put such a request to anyone') and suggested that Condon was the one to make a confession. ('He himself is holding the key to my cell.') At this time the Reverend John Matthiesen of the Trinity Lutheran Church, Trenton, took over from the Reverend Werner as Hauptmann's spiritual adviser; like Werner, within a few days he declared his belief in Hauptmann's innocence.

On the evening of December 4 Governor Hoffman was at New York's Madison Square Garden as a spectator at the six-day bicycle race. Asked by reporters if Ellis Parker was investigating the case, he replied that Parker had been working on it since a few days after the kidnapping. Next morning, under the headline 'Lindbergh Case Reopened', the reporter incorrectly quoted Hoffman as saying that *he* had engaged Parker to investigate. At a New York Advertising Club lunch that day Hoffman was quizzed about the story by other reporters. Pat McGrady of Associated Press asked:

'Governor, have you ever seen Hauptmann?'

'Yes,' replied Hoffman, 'once.'

'Where?'

'In the State Prison at Trenton.'

In answer to further questions Hoffman said that he had recommended to his fellow members of the Court of Pardons that they too should visit Hauptmann in his cell. 'He insisted to me he was innocent,' said Hoffman, 'and we were together for more than an hour.'

There was an immediate scramble for telephones and by next morning the case was back on the front page, with Hoffman portrayed as the New Jersey Governor who was doubting Jersey justice. In many papers he was bitterly attacked as an interfering busybody, the fiercest attacks coming from those who thirsted most for Hauptmann's blood. The re-opening of the case, declared New Jersey Assemblyman Crawford Jamieson, 'represents nothing but the exploitation of this celebrated crime for the purpose of providing our Governor with national publicity'. He charged Hoffman with having impugned the integrity and fairness of New Jersey's courts, and demanded a full inquiry. Yet the Governor did have allies. The *Newark Sunday Call* approved of his visit to Hauptmann, saying the responsibility for determining life or death was a heavy one, and that he was entirely justified in seeking out all the information he could. He himself issued a statement that he had no opinion as to Hauptmann's guilt or innocence, but in view of the many rumors that had been circulating since the trial, he intended to ensure there had been no possibility of error. As the weeks went by and the controversy grew, he revealed that despite a largely hostile press, he had received some 800,000 letters and telegrams, 'the vast majority of which approved of what I was trying to do'.

On December 9, in a one-line statement, the United States Supreme Court declined to consider Hauptmann's petition, and Justice Trenchard set the new date for Hauptmann's execution in the week beginning January 13, 1936. On December 16 Hauptmann wrote to Hoffman, 'With clear conscience I have fought my case. In my heart I cannot believe this state will break the life of an innocent man,' and he called again for Condon and himself to be given the truth serum or any other lie-detector test. This news was conveyed to Condon in Lynn, Massachusetts, where the old creep was making money from his perjury by appearing in a vaudeville show several times a day and by posing in a furniture shop window. Told of Hauptmann's request while having a haircut, he laughed. 'Let him take the truth test if he wants to,' he said. 'I know I told the truth and that's all there is to it.'

By the year's end Hauptmann's date of execution was only two

Col. Kimberling.

Dear Sir!

In translation of this letter
I realy would be very thankful.
What I have written is only
the truth.

The same, I would be glad
if the Governor would read
this letter over.

I know dear Sir it is quite
some trouble for you, but I realy
don't know to whom I shall
go in my present affair

Thanks for your kindness

Very respectfully
R. Hauptmann.

Dear Sir!

In translation of this letter
I realy would be very thankful.
What I have written is only
the truth.

The same, I would be glad
if the Governor would read
this letter over.

I know dear Sir it is quite
some trouble for you, but I realy
don't know to whom I shall
go in my present affair

Thanks for your kindness

Very respectfully
R. Hauptmann.

The covering note to Colonel Kimberling that accompanied Hauptmann's letter to his mother.

weeks away, and not knowing how much false information about him had been reaching his mother in faraway Kamenz, he wanted her, before he died, to hear the truth from his own lips. So on December 27 he wrote her a long letter in reply to one he had received from her on Christmas Day. A translation of it will be found in Appendix IV. It is a moving letter because it comes from Hauptmann's heart. Unfortunately his mother never received it. When Colonel Kimberling read it, he decided it might 'result in unfavorable reaction if released in Germany and place us in an embarrassing position'. So he put it among his personal papers where it was discovered in 1977, forty-two years later.

On the day that Hauptmann wrote it, Charles, Anne and Jon Lindbergh were halfway across the Atlantic, in a ship called the *American Importer*, bound for England.

* * *

The same volume of correspondence critical of the death sentence on Hauptmann that had been reaching Hoffman had – in cruder and harsher terms – been reaching Lindbergh too. Threats of death, threats to kidnap Jon and demands for money had been arriving in their hundreds by almost every post; even allowing for the fantasies of cranks and others, the menace was continual. Again the Lindberghs found themselves living under siege, photographers permanently at the gate. Twice there had been ugly scenes when Jon was being taken to school; once when the curtains of a van parked outside the school entrance were drawn aside to reveal a telephoto lens, again when the car in which he was travelling was forced into the kerb and cameramen jumped out to take close-ups of the little boy and his teacher clinging to each other in terror. With the rejection of Hauptmann's appeal by the Court of Errors and Appeals and by the Supreme Court, coupled with Hoffman's reopening of a case they had regarded as closed, the threats increased, so that any kind of a normal life in which Anne could write undistracted and Charles continue his work on the heart-pump machine with Dr Carrel, became almost impossible. On December 7 he told Anne he was thinking of taking the family to Sweden or England for the winter, maybe longer. 'Be ready to go,' he told her, 'at twenty-four hours' notice.'

Anne was not best pleased – she had just taken a room in New York to write undisturbed – but remained philosophical. ('All my life seems to be trying to "get settled" and C shaking me out of it. But you like it? Yes.') Charles opted for England rather than Sweden: he had been there twice and enjoyed it. His brother-in-law Aubrey Morgan had offered them the run of his estate in Wales until they found something more permanent, or there was the possibility of finding something near the Nicolsons in Kent. He spoke to Basil Harris, vice president of the United States Lines, who said that to avoid publicity he would book them on a freighter with passenger accommodation, sailing from Manhattan on December 21.

They went on board that evening after dark, unobserved. When the ship was far out at sea Lindbergh's newspaper friend Lauren D. Lyman broke the news in the *New York Times*. Most editorials sympathized with the decision, suggesting it made its own commentary on the American social scene. Speaking of British virtues – restraint and respect for individual rights and privacies – the *New York Herald Tribune* said, 'Now that Americans have driven one of their leading men to flee in secrecy from a life which they made intolerable for him, they would do well to meditate upon the value of those virtues.' Others took a contrary view: Mayor Kelly of Chicago thought the trip un-American and the *New York Daily News* declared that Lindbergh had always attracted publicity by shunning it, after the manner of Greta Garbo. 'We do think he would have been pestered less if he had acted more as a popular hero is supposed to act, and been less embarrassed in the public gaze.' Condon took the event as an opportunity for more self-publicity. In a letter to the *New York Times* he declared that Hauptmann in America was a poor exchange for Lindbergh in Europe, referred to the kidnapping as the most disastrous case since the Crucifixion, claimed falsely that he had seen $49,680 of the ransom money returned to Hoover's G-men, and climaxed in an orgasm of muddled, chocolate-box prose: '. . . the ashes of the darling baby, victim of a fiend urged by greed of gain and seeking pleasure, are mute witnesses of the crime, while within every American's breast there is a beating of the heart, tolling the death-knell of every gangster, while the Stars and Stripes fly from every staff and masthead . . .'

The trip across was rough but uneventful. Charles and Anne ate in their private cabin, waited on by a white-haired English steward who had fought in the Boer War and First World War and was now waiting the next 'to settle the question'. Jon found a kitten to play with; on Christmas Day he had a tree and presents. 'I am with him every minute and adapt my schedule to his,' Anne wrote. 'It is *so* absorbing.'

They docked in Liverpool on the last day of the year. It was misty and damp as Charles carried his son down the gangplank and through the gauntlet of waiting cameras. Then came the drive through the streets: 'trams, buses, chimney-pots, red-cheeked children, women with shawls, nursemaids wheeling prams, brick houses, raincoats, drably-dressed women . . .' She found it all 'terribly English', and while the newsboys shouted 'Lindbergh in Liverpool' as they entered the Adelphi Hotel, she wondered how long before she saw things American again.

So ended 1935, a year which had brought the world a little closer to the conflagration that was soon to engulf it (and, on the far side of it, to technological advancements as yet beyond men's dreams). It was a year in which Italy had invaded Abyssinia and in which Germany had repudiated the Versailles Treaty, made the swastika the national flag and banned jazz as decadent. It was a year in which the Chaco war between Bolivia and Paraguay ended, Persia changed its name to Iran, the French liner *Normandie* crossed the Atlantic in under five days, Malcolm Campbell broke the world land speed record at Daytona Beach, Florida, at 278 m.p.h., T. S. Eliot published *Murder in the Cathedral*. On Broadway it was the year of *Porgy and Bess, Tobacco Road* and *You Can't Take It With You*; in films *Mutiny on the Bounty* with Charles Laughton and Clark Gable, *Top Hat* with Ginger Rogers and Fred Astaire, and *A Night at the Opera* with the Marx Brothers; while from Tin Pan Alley came two Cole Porter classics, 'Begin the Beguine' and 'Just One of Those Things', Noël Coward's 'Mad About the Boy' and Irving Berlin's 'Cheek to Cheek'. One way or another it was quite a year.

25

On New Year's Day 1936 Hauptmann concluded his memoirs in the *New York Daily Mirror* with a reflective epilogue about his past life 'from the happy years of childhood to the place where I now find myself. I have called up again my sunny days . . . I have not thrown a cloak over the sad and rainy days.' Declaring that much had been written about him which was untrue, he could yet not bring himself to hate anyone, not even (remembering Wilentz) 'the man who used the lowest type of language against me . . . I feel sorry for him as the language only reflects a picture of his soul.' It was not quite what the *Mirror* or its readers were expecting; the editor described it as 'an extraordinary document to come from one who is probably the most cold-blooded and crafty criminal on record'.

Now there were only thirteen days to the beginning of the week set for the crafty criminal's execution. On January 6 it was announced that the Court of Pardons would meet on Saturday January 11 to consider clemency, and that if the vote went against Hauptmann, his execution would take place on Friday January 17; having engaged the services of the executioner Robert Elliott for $150 and his assistant John Bloom for $50, Colonel Kimberling sent out the first eighteen of some fifty invitations to the press and others to witness the event at eight p.m. Two days later he briefed the press, who seemed obsessed about a possible last-minute 'confession'. Asked whether he would postpone the execution if a confession was 'in the air', and whether if one was made it could be recorded on sound equipment, Kimberling said he would be guided by his conscience.

The Court of Pardons consisted of the Governor and the Chancellor, Luther Campbell, and the six lay members of the Court of Errors and Appeals. Four of these, who were lawyers, had with Luther Campbell already declined to reverse the Flemington verdict; the other two, a publisher and a retired butcher, were coming to the case fresh. None of them had taken up the Governor's suggestion that they visit Hauptmann in his cell, but Hauptmann hoped that they would look favorably on his request – unprecedented if granted – to appear before them. 'I could show them I am not the man who committed the crime,' he said. 'My life is at stake and only a little of their time will be lost whatever they do. It seems to me to be the fair thing to do.'

At this time the *New York Daily Mirror* was serializing Anna Hauptmann's memoirs, and on January 9 they arranged for her and three friends to visit the Hopewell area and the scene of the crime. 'We passed the house of Amandus Hochmuth,' she wrote in the paper next day, 'and *could not even see* the porch where Hochmuth said he was standing when he saw Richard come around the corner.' They drove to the entrance to the Lindbergh estate and stood in the snow, not daring to go further but trying to imagine the exact location of the house. They measured various distances, then drew up on the Hopewell–Princeton road close to where Charlie's body had been found. ('I looked into the woods from the car window. They ask me to believe that my Richard carried the body of the poor little child in there and left it there . . . It is impossible.') Next day she told Richard about Hochmuth's porch and everything else she had seen in the hope of providing some crumb of information that might sway the Court of Pardons. But on the eve of its meeting, the Court of Pardons turned down Hauptmann's application to appear before them.

The court met at 11 a.m. Wilentz appeared for the state, Fisher for the defense; Colonel Schwarzkopf and Colonel Kimberling were also present. No press were admitted and the proceedings were confidential, but two small items of information did leak out: Colonel Schwarzkopf insisted that Rail 16 was part of the ladder found at Hopewell, and Colonel Kimberling declared that in all his utterances to him and others Hauptmann had maintained his innocence.

Two further affirmations of belief in Hauptmann's innocence were laid before the court. The first was a letter from Paulina Hauptmann in Kamenz, valueless as evidence but touching in its plea for clemency:

> As the mother of the condemned man, who bore and raised him in a God-fearing family, I may be forgiven if, nevertheless, I cannot believe in Bruno's guilt. Although certain outward appearances may be irrefutably against him, I feel distinctly that Bruno, who was always a model son to me, and is himself the loving father of a little boy, could not be and is not the real perpetrator of this dastardly crime.
>
> Up to the last of the many letters which Bruno has written me from his prison cell, he has again and again firmly stated his innocence. Moreover thousands of people, personally unknown to me, who followed all the details of the trial, have spontaneously written me that the prosecution merely insisted on having him pay the penalty of death because, otherwise, the blame for not having cleared up the mystery of the murder would permanently rest upon them.
>
> Almighty God in his infinite wisdom has invested Your Excellency with the supreme prerogative of pardon and clemency. I beseech you to exercise them for the benefit of Bruno Hauptmann, my beloved son, whose ignominious death on the electric chair would break my heart. I implore you, Mr Governor, to use the dignity of your high office in not permitting that a man undergo the one penalty that is irreparable on merely circumstantial evidence.

Hardly less moving although more impressive, because its author had no axe to grind, was the submission by the Reverend James Matthiesen, Pastor of Trinity Lutheran Church and one of Hauptmann's two spiritual advisers:

> I have had fifteen very intimate and soul-searching interviews with Bruno Richard Hauptmann, and am convinced that he tells the truth. If Hauptmann had had a reliable defense lawyer at the outstart, and if he had asked for an interpreter during the trial, the very evidence used against him would have spoken in his favor. Hauptmann felt no need for them until it was too late. After careful study of that case I have come to that conclusion.
>
> First, know Hauptmann as he really is, and his wife Anna, and then study the evidence; and you will arrive at the same conclusion. Hauptmann does not fit into the frame of circumstantial evidence. I bring these findings to your honorable members of the Court of Pardons not because of sympathy for Hauptmann, although I claim to know

him better than anyone with the exception of his wife, but I want to see justice prevail.

I would ask for the supreme penalty if Hauptmann were guilty. My creed has no objections to that. There is nothing else in my mind than this: that I may serve the State of New Jersey with my findings. I feel it is a sacred duty I have to discharge.

For having the courage to discharge this sacred duty the Reverend Matthiesen was rebuked by his parish council, so angry were they at his having questioned the received wisdom.

Nor did his plea have any effect on the Court of Pardons who, like his parishioners, did not want to have their conclusions disturbed. When the vote was taken at the end of the day, Hoffman declared in favor of commutation to life imprisonment, the others against. Fisher went to the prison and with Kimberling broke the news to Hauptmann. Fisher told Hauptmann that no other channel of clemency now remained, and that if he had anything to say he had not said before, he should reveal it. Like a music box which repeats its tune *ad infinitum*, Hauptmann said once again he was innocent; he had never changed his story and never could. Outside the prison Kimberling and Fisher met reporters. 'As we were leaving,' said Kimberling, 'Hauptmann asked Mr Fisher to see his wife and tell her he was all right. His eyes were filled with tears as he said that.' And Fisher told them, 'You might add that I believe that Hauptmann is innocent and nothing has happened in any shape, form or manner to change that. He is as guiltless as any of you.' Later Anna arrived at the prison to see her husband, but was told that visiting hours were over and she should return on Monday.

Now there were only five clear days before Friday January 17, when Hauptmann was to die. When Anna visited him on the Monday, she found him calm but despondent. Hadn't eleven months' prison been enough suffering for something he hadn't done? he asked her. Did they really have to kill him as well? And why didn't the real perpetrators of the crime come forward? One day the truth would come out, but they couldn't bring him back then. Anna was distraught. 'I cannot sit here and watch this terrible thing happen to Richard,' she wrote in the *Mirror*, 'but I do not know what to do. I know he is not guilty and yet I can do nothing to save him.' On Tuesday she moved into the Stacy-Trent Hotel in Trenton so as to be near him up to the end, and on Wednesday morning was allowed a special visit. During it, on the other side of the wall, John Bloom tested the electric chair.

Meanwhile the defense team of Fisher, Rosecrans and Pope, temporarily strengthened by two young Washington lawyers, Nugent Dodds and Neil Burkinshaw, were pulling out all the stops they could. On the Monday they petitioned the US Circuit Court of Appeals for a writ of *habeas corpus* on the grounds of a mis-trial, but this was rejected by Judge Warren Davis. Then in a last desperate attempt to stave off the inevitable, they again petitioned the US Supreme Court, also for *habeas corpus*, and this was denied just thirty-six hours before Hauptmann was due to mount the chair.

But there was still the Governor. On the evening of Wednesday January 15 (before the Supreme Court had reached its latest decision) Hoffman was traveling to New York to stay the night. He was a deeply worried man, for more and more information had been arriving on his desk to cast doubts on Hauptmann's guilt. His investigators had begun to unearth the facts about the blindness of Amandus Hochmuth – and Dr Condon (whose money-making activities as a vaudeville artist had been stopped by the protests of twenty-five Massachusetts clergymen) was on the brink of publishing a series of lucrative articles about meeting Hauptmann in the two cemeteries. Hoffman had read these in proof and found they contradicted much of what Condon had said to the police and at the trial. He had hoped to question Condon on them, but the old fox, seeing things hotting up, had slipped away as quietly as Lindbergh had, on a cruise to Panama. Finally Hoffman had learnt that Hauptmann had turned down an offer from Sid Boehm of the *New York Evening Journal* to pay Anna Hauptmann $75,000 (later increased to $90,000) if he would give them a full, confidential confession to the crime, only to be published after his execution. Hoffman knew how devoted Hauptmann was to his wife and son, and how concerned he was about their future. How could he possibly refuse such an offer unless he really did have nothing further to say?

At the New Yorker Hotel, Hoffman learnt that David Wilentz was dining with friends in the Terrace Room. This was too good an opportunity to miss and after dinner Wilentz came to Hoffman's suite for what Hoffman called 'a long, earnest and important talk'. Having known Wilentz since schooldays, said Hoffman, he didn't have to pull his punches. 'We have disagreed in politics; we certainly disagreed, without any personal feeling, on the Hauptmann case.' Hoffman told Wilentz his doubts about the state's identification witnesses, particularly Hochmuth and Whited. Well, said Wilentz, even if they had been untruthful, there was still the evidence of Condon, and Hauptmann's admission to the closet writing, and the entry in his diary of the word 'boad'. True, said Hoffman, but that only concerned the extortion charge, not the murder. 'Then,' said Wilentz, not fully understanding, 'why the hell doesn't he tell the truth?' (i.e. that he was guilty of extortion but not of murder.)

In the end they agreed it was more important to get the complete story – 'just how a man could conceive and execute such a ghastly plan single-handed' – than it was to take his life. And they made a solemn pact: that in the morning the Governor would see Mrs Hauptmann and ask her to tell her husband that if he made a full statement of his involvement – however great or small – he and Wilentz would jointly recommend to the Court of Pardons that the death sentence be commuted to life imprisonment. By another strange chance the Director of the FBI, J. Edgar Hoover, was also at the New Yorker that night, and after Wilentz had gone Hoffman stayed talking with him into the small hours, again expressing his doubts. He told Hoover that he had it in mind, so that further investigations could be made, to grant Hauptmann a temporary reprieve.

After three hours' sleep, Hoffman left on the 7 a.m. train for Trenton. He knew that Mrs Hauptmann was staying at the Stacy-Trent Hotel, and made arrangements to see her in the manager's suite. As the hotel lobby was swarming with pressmen and photographers, Hoffman arrived by the back entrance and reached the suite by way of the freight elevator. Fatigued and red-eyed by worry and lack of sleep, Anna Hauptmann was waiting for him.

'Mrs Hauptmann,' he said, 'tomorrow, as you know, your husband is to die. I wanted to help him, but he has not been telling me, or anyone else, the truth.'

Anna became galvanized into life.

'*No, no, no!*' she shouted. 'That isn't so. Richard *did* tell the truth. He *is* telling the truth.'[1]

He waited for her to calm down, then told her of the pact he had made with the Attorney General.

'You must go to the prison this morning and see your husband.

---

[1] In his *Liberty* articles Governor Hoffman wrote what Anna Hauptmann said to him phonetically (as with Hauptmann) but this has been rendered in plain English for easier reading.

You must tell him that he can save his life. You must tell him that you want him to tell the truth.'

Anna exploded. '*No, no, no!*' Hoffman reported her as saying. 'My husband has only a few hours to live. Could I do that to him – make him think that I, too, believe that he would kill a baby? Would I make Richard think I too have believed those lying witnesses who, for money, would send a good man to die? No, no! Never would I do that. Not even to save my Richard's life would I do that.'

Hoffman made one last attempt, but realized it was useless. 'The truth he *has* told,' said Anna. 'What more can he say? Yes, maybe he could make up lies to say he did it and save his life. But soon it would be found they were not the truth. No! Always I – and some day Bubi[1] – would be sorry that he would say he had done such a thing even to save his life.'

Hoffman, seeing Anna for the first time, had expected a run-of-the-mill housewife, not this outraged woman of courage and principle. Listening to her, he asked himself whether she was telling truths that burned deeply in her heart or staging a scene that would rival those of the great actresses of America. 'It was hard to think of Anna Hauptmann as an actress.'

Well, he said, if she wouldn't do what he had asked, would she ask her husband if he would talk further to Hoffman and someone from the Attorney General's office, and answer any questions? Yes, she said, she would gladly do that, she would do anything except tell her husband that she doubted he was telling the truth.

Hoffman gave her his telephone number at the Hildebrecht, and an hour later she rang from the prison. 'Richard says he will be glad to see you and Mr Wilentz. He will be glad to see anybody. But, Governor, his story is just the same. He has told everything he knows – nothing more he can tell.'

Hoffman rang Wilentz and told him what had happened.

'The hell with it, Harold,' was Wilentz's reply. 'If that's still his attitude, I'm damned if I'm going to do anything to help him.'

But the Governor was now ready to act on his own: there were still too many unanswered questions which, if Hauptmann were to die the following night, might never be answered. He did not have the power, as some Governors did, of commuting the death sentence to life imprisonment; but he was entitled to grant a

[1] The Hauptmanns' nickname for Manfred.

reprieve of up to ninety days. It was true that any reprieve was supposed to be granted not more than six months after sentence, but there had been at least fourteen cases in the past when they had been granted after this time. Hoffman decided on a thirty-day reprieve, but before announcing it he informed Wilentz; and to allow Hoffman enough time for further investigations (about whose outcome he had no fears), Wilentz said he would not ask Trenchard to set a new execution date until the thirty days had expired. As an execution had to take place not less than four and not more than eight weeks from the date it was determined, this meant that Hauptmann could expect at least another two months of life. Announcing his decision, the Governor said there would be only this one reprieve – unless some event occurred which led him and the Attorney General to consider a further stay.

That same day in Chicago the Executive Committee of the American Bar Association put forward new guidelines for the conduct of press and radio in criminal trials in order to prevent what it called 'the prejudicial publicity' that had accompanied Hauptmann's trial. 'The Bar Association,' said the *New York Times* in an editorial, 'is to be applauded.'

*   *   *

Hauptmann took the news of his reprieve calmly, Anna said 'God be thanked,' and in Kamenz old Paulina Hauptmann, woken from sleep, said, 'This is the happiest day of my life. Now everything will be all right.' But the effect on others was extraordinary. Although, as Hoffman said, Governors' reprieves were customary and justification for granting one had never before been demanded, this time there was a burst of popular indignation: solid citizens for whom the death of Hauptmann would be catharsis and expiation feared the experience was to be denied them. Death threats began arriving at Hoffman's home at South Amboy (also at the homes of Wilentz and Hauck) and guards were posted. The newspapers too condemned him. An hysterical editorial in the *Trenton Times* declared that the Governor had 'flaunted [*sic*] the highest courts of state and nation . . . dishonored himself, disgraced the state and converted New Jersey into an international laughing-stock . . . sacrificed all legal and moral right to serve as Chief Executive of New Jersey', and called for the House of Assembly to institute immediate proceedings for impeachment. Even the staid *New York Times* called his action 'a desperate gamble' and 'indefensible'.

But, said Hoffman, the letters he was receiving applauding his action far outnumbered those criticizing it, and in answer to his critics he issued a long and reasoned statement: if impeachment was the price he had to pay for following his own conscience, he was ready to pay it. He had never expressed a view as to Hauptmann's guilt or innocence and did not do so now:

> I do however share with hundreds and thousands of our people the doubt as to the value of the evidence that placed him in the Lindbergh nursery on the night of the crime. I do wonder what part passion and prejudice played in the conviction of a man who was previously tried and convicted in the columns of many of our newspapers. I do, on the basis of evidence which is in my hands, question the truthfulness and mental competency of some of the chief witnesses for the state. I do doubt that this crime could have been committed by any one man, and I am worried about the eagerness of some of our law-enforcement agencies to bring about the death of this one man so that the books may be closed in the thought that another great crime mystery has been successfully solved . . .

He made no apology for the reprieve. It would provide time for investigating some of the most baffling aspects of the case and, in particular, Hauptmann's continued refusal to admit to any part of the crime, even though he knew that an admission to the Court of Pardons would spare his life and an admission to the *New York Evening Journal* would guarantee his family financial security after his execution. Nor, said Hoffman, as the father of three children himself, was he motivated by maudlin sentiment. What he was interested in was 'that thing we have rather proudly called "Jersey Justice" ', and he concluded, 'I hope that real and full justice will finally be done in this case.'

*   *   *

One of Hoffman's first actions after the reprieve was to appoint a Washington detective, Lieutenant Robert Hicks, and a small team of investigators to look into every aspect of the case including the files of the New Jersey State Police; as well as Ellis Parker he was helped by a man he refers to as 'a retired state trooper', who had worked on the case and had grave doubts about Hauptmann's guilt. One of Hicks's first actions was to take a lease on the Hauptmann apartment from Mr Rauch (Bornmann's lease had ended after the trial) in order to make an examination of the floorboards in the attic.

Hoffman's initial investigations uncovered all the evidence, unknown to the jury at the trial, that showed that if Hauptmann *was* guilty, he certainly had accomplices: this included Condon hearing one of the kidnappers on the telephone say to a third party '*Statti zitto!*' ('Shut up!'); Cemetery John telling him there were four men and two women in the gang; John going off to talk to another of the kidnappers before accepting the money; Al Reich's statement that he had seen an Italianate look-out at Woodlawn and Lindbergh's that he had seen a look-out with a white handkerchief at St Raymond's; J. J. Faulkner handing in nearly $3000 of ransom money, Schwarzkopf's and Walsh's statements declaring the kidnapping to be the work of a gang.

In the light of this Hoffman wrote to Schwarzkopf on January 26 with what he called 'abundant evidence' of other participants. (He wrote to the Director of the FBI and to the Commissioner of the New York City Police in the same vein.) To let any of them escape trial and punishment, he said, would be as grave an offence against justice as the punishment of any person not guilty, and there was even the possibility ('which you may consider as being very remote') that Hauptmann was not guilty. 'As Governor of the State of New Jersey,' he concluded, 'I direct you, with every resource at your command, to continue a thorough and impartial search for the detection and apprehension of every person connected with this crime . . . you will report to me in writing at least once weekly.'

Schwarzkopf's rage and resentment at receiving this letter can be imagined. Ever since Hauptmann's conviction he had received congratulations from all over America on the successful conclusion to the case and the leading part he had played in it. Now here was his own Governor not only questioning the conviction but, in calling for the police files, doubting his word as well. For the next four weeks his reports in writing were brief, perfunctory and non-committal. By the fifth week, exasperated and knowing he was beaten, Hoffman ordered the reports to be discontinued.

Elsewhere the investigations wholly justified the Governor's uncertainties. In the police files Hoffman found Whited's statement of April 26, 1932 that he had seen no one suspicious in the neighborhood, and a statement by Trooper Wolf holding out to Whited a share of the $25,000 reward money; Schwarzkopf's references to Perrone as a totally unreliable witness and Perrone having previously identified a whole variety of different people including a man called Steiner (who, Hoffman told the press, no more resembled Hauptmann than Condon's 6 foot 4 inch bodyguard Al Reich resembled one of Singer's midgets); four statements by Lindbergh to the police that the voice he had heard in St Raymond's Cemetery had shouted 'Hey, Doc!' and not, as he later said, 'Hey, Doctor!'; and a record of Condon being told by the police that if he failed to identify Hauptmann a second time, he would be indicted as an accessory.

The bogusness of Hochmuth's evidence was revealed, too. In the files of the Division of Old Age Security in New York City's Department of Public Welfare Hoffman found two reports on Hochmuth's health. The first, dated June 29, 1932 (less than four months after the kidnapping), described Hochmuth as 'partly blind' and the second, a month later, referred to 'failing eyesight due to cataracts'. Also unearthed was a statement by Hochmuth to a state employee in 1932 that he had not seen anyone in the vicinity that day (which the prosecution had naturally suppressed) and a memo doubting if he had been in New Jersey at all. Hoffman wanted to interview Hochmuth, but the old man refused to come, saying to inquirers as he shoveled snow from the porch, 'I said what I had to say at the trial.'

Knowing that Hauptmann's movements on March 1 1932 were really the linchpin of his case, Hoffman made contact with E. V. C. Pescia, manager of the Reliant Employment Agency, who had engaged Hauptmann to work at the Majestic Apartments. Pescia, consulting his records, told him that on February 26, 1932 Furcht had given him an order for eight men: a carpenter/cabinet-maker, a weather-stripping carpenter, four porters and two painters. He went on:

> At about 8.20 on the morning of February 27th, Hauptmann . . . came in. He impressed me as being a very fine, clean-cut type of German mechanic, gentlemanly, neat, with a very snappy appearance. He was soft-spoken; in fact, to get a closer grasp to answers to my questions, I had to move my chair nearer to him – there was less than three feet between us. I decided to send him to Mr Furcht as weather-stripping carpenter.
>
> I got in touch with Mr Furcht and he told me that Hauptmann would start work March 1st and to bring his tools with him.

Pescia, stated the Governor, said that Hauptmann had paid an engagement fee of $10 *and that if he had not appeared for work on March 1, he would have been so advised by Mr Furcht. He was not so advised*. Confirmation that he had worked on March 1, said Mr Pescia, would be found in the Majestic Apartment timesheets for *the latter half of February and first half of March*. When Hoffman asked for these, he was told they were missing. He had no means of knowing they had been handed over by Bronx Assistant District Attorney Breslin to Detective Cashman on October 29 1934 (see page 223), and were now under lock and key in the offices of the New York City Police.

On February 16 Hauptmann's thirty-day reprieve expired at midnight. On February 20 it was announced that the new date for his execution would be during the week beginning March 30. That same day the great Samuel Leibowitz announced the failure of his mission to persuade Hauptmann to confess.

*   *   *

Known as 'the Great Defender' and 'the greatest actor-lawyer of his time', Samuel Leibowitz at forty-three was the most successful criminal counsel in New York. Son of a Lower East Side Rumanian immigrant, he had won all but one of seventy-eight cases of murder in the first degree, including a triple murder charge against Al Capone; and for three years he had been unpaid chief counsel for the Scottosboro' Boys, nine blacks who had been wrongly indicted for raping two white girls in a freight train in Alabama, a case which had caused much controversy at the time.

The Hauptmann trial had defeated him. Although he believed Hauptmann guilty, and had said so repeatedly in his radio broadcasts and in the *New York Evening Journal*, he was another who could not understand why Hauptmann had not yet named his accomplices. So when he was approached as someone who might succeed in wresting the truth out of Hauptmann, he readily agreed. It was explained to Mrs Hauptmann that Mr Leibowitz wanted to ask her husband some questions, and in view of Leibowitz's reputation, Hauptmann agreed to answer them. Fisher was sceptical: 'If Mr Leibowitz thinks Hauptmann is going to change his story one iota he is mistaken . . . He is as innocent as I am.'

To gain entry to the prison Leibowitz temporarily joined the defense team as additional counsel. On his first visit he was accompanied by Anna Hauptmann. Hauptmann was looking forward to meeting the man who had saved so many from the chair and might do the same for him. Leibowitz opened the conversation by saying that now that the reprieve had expired, his death in a few weeks' time was certain. There was only one way he could save himself: tell the truth and name his accomplices.

Hauptmann stared at him, appalled. He had endured this line of questioning from Finn and Foley and Wilentz and a dozen others, but to hear it from this man, at this time and place, was beyond credence. He burst into tears. Anna did her best to comfort him. Leibowitz rose and, unabashed, promised to return in a day or two. Outside the prison he told reporters, 'I had a very gratifying interview with Bruno. He broke down and cried like a child. I am coming to see him again on Sunday.' Tears of despair for Hauptmann had for Leibowitz become tears of guilt.

Realizing her mistake, Anna had no wish to see Leibowitz return, but Fisher told her that a refusal by her husband to see him might be interpreted as an unwillingness to answer awkward questions. And Hauptmann, believing as always that the truth could only help him, was ready to answer any questions anyone wished to put. So the two men (Leibowitz now accompanied by the Reverend Matthiesen) met again, the one believing he could persuade the other to 'confess', the other believing he could convince the first of his innocence. Many of the questions were less awkward than hypothetical, Leibowitz thinking that an oblique approach might be more effective. How did Hauptmann think the baby had been taken from the nursery? What would he have done on finding it had met with an accident? If he had been Isidor Fisch, would he have put the money in a shoe-box and left it with a friend? Instead of telling Leibowitz that these questions were irrelevant, he did his best to answer them. Naturally he was somewhat hesitant, for he could no more read the minds of the kidnappers than Leibowitz. This enabled Leibowitz to tell the press that Hauptmann's answers had been as evasive and untruthful as he had expected, but that he felt that sufficient progress had been made to justify a third meeting (i.e. he was damned if he was going to be defeated).

Anna, now desperate at the harm Leibowitz was doing, insisted that Fisher be with Leibowitz at the third meeting. Leibowitz met Fisher beforehand and told him that Hauptmann would have confessed long ago had not Fisher kept bolstering him up by declarations of his innocence. If at the interview Fisher would hold in abeyance that belief, would give the impression of agreeing with whatever Leibowitz said, then he believed Hauptmann would break.

Here is Fisher's account of the interview, as told to Governor Hoffman:

> We were there for four hours and twenty minutes – from two o'clock to six-twenty. Leibowitz, in the most brutal language possible, pointed out to Hauptmann that the chair was inevitable; that there wasn't a chance in the world to escape. He drew mental pictures of the chair; talked about the smell of burning flesh. He pointed to the death chamber just a few feet away.
>
> He went into lengthy theories, asking Hauptmann . . . how the crime had been committed. He started playing with figures in connection with the handwriting and finally had it worked out to a point where it was 670 to one that Hauptmann didn't write the ransom notes. As Leibowitz would make what he considered a telling point, he would look at me and ask, 'Isn't that so, Lloyd?' and in line with the arrangement, whether or not the statement was true, I would agree with him.
>
> After four hours Leibowitz reached a point where he could stand little more. He was perspiring and bedraggled and he had broken a small vein in his eye. Every single argument he had advanced had been met, freely and frankly, by Hauptmann. Finally Leibowitz announed he was ready to leave.

As they took their departure, said Fisher, Hauptmann called out through the bars, 'Come back if you have any more questions to ask, Mr Leibowitz. You know I have plenty of time!'

That night a defeated Leibowitz issued a petulant statement washing his hands of the whole affair. 'I cannot see how I can serve the interests of justice any further by my continued participation in the case . . . Therefore I want no further part in any of it.' As Fisher said, having declared his belief in Hauptmann's guilt so frequently, he could hardly now be seen to change his mind. 'You don't want the world to know,' Fisher told him bluntly, 'that the great Leibowitz could make a mistake.'

26

These events – the Leibowitz visits and Hoffman's continuing exposure of the lies and contradictions in the prosecution's case – were being aired almost daily in the press, with markedly divisive effect. Some New Jersey politicians said that Hoffman was seeking to divert attention from his disastrous economic policies. The press was almost solidly against him, 'ascribing to me deeds I had never thought of, words I had never spoken'. One group of Jersey citizens was so enraged at what they considered an unlawful reprieve that they proposed serving a writ of *mandamus* on Colonel Kimberling to carry out the execution without further delay. And a judge in Texas wrote that it was better that Hauptmann, whether guilty or innocent ('he is after all an alien') should die, rather than reflections be cast on American courts. Against this he was supported by the state's Young Republican Executive Committee and several individual members of the state legislature. Prominent figures such as Clarence Darrow continued to voice support, and the majority of letters in his postbag, he said, continued running in his favor.

It will be recalled that before Dr Condon had left for Panama, Hoffman had wanted to interview him about the discrepancies and contradictions between his statements to the police, his testimony at the trial and his recently published articles in *Liberty Magazine*. In mid March, with Hauptmann's new execution date less than two weeks away, the old man returned. A courteous telegram from the Governor requested an interview in New York at a mutually convenient place and time. Anticipating this, Wilentz and a senior Jersey police officer had already visited Condon to tell him to stand firm. Thus bolstered, Condon found courage for an arrogant reply, telling the Governor he had no authority for his investigations and doubting his sincerity and good faith. He would however 'permit' the Governor to come to his home for an interivew; but Wilentz must be present, and questions and answers would be in writing.

Such conditions were unacceptable to Hoffman, as Condon knew they would be. 'I will not submit any questions in writing. Anyone might answer the questions if put in that form. I do not intend to spend an evening with Dr Condon merely to chat with him. I had only a sincere desire to obtain a complete solution to this crime . . .' Thus was lost a last, slim chance of discrediting one of the state's key witnesses and perhaps saving Hauptmann's life.

For Hauptmann now the sands were running out fast. On March 21 Colonel Kimberling set the new execution date as Tuesday March 31. Invitations to press and officials were again sent out, and the executioner and his assistant re-engaged. Fisher broke the news to Hauptmann, who took it calmly.

During the next ten days there was a burst of activity by Hoffman's investigators in last-minute efforts to prove

Hauptmann's innocence. A wood technician in the Public Works Administration by the name of Arch Loney had publicly disagreed with Koehler's findings regarding Rail 16 and the attic, and after Lieutenant Hicks had taken over the Hauptmann apartment, Loney was invited to inspect the attic for himself. He came to the conclusion that Rail 16 had not formed part of the attic flooring, and on March 26 Hoffman invited Wilentz and Hauck to come along to the apartment to see the evidence for himself. Wilentz insisted that the two men who had furnished the attic evidence, Koehler and Bornmann, should come too.

They managed to climb up the cleats of the linen-cupboard and hoist themselves into the attic (Bornmann said that the trapdoor was only 15 square inches so that Hoffman's portly frame had to be pushed through) where Loney confronted Koehler and Bornmann with his evidence. The board from which it was alleged that Rail 16 was taken, he said, was the odd man out. There were thirteen boards on either side of a plumb-line from the centre of the roof, but this board made an unsymmetrical fourteenth; and while all the other boards had seven nails fastening them to the joists, this one had twenty-five. Simple, said Koehler, carpenters often laid flooring unsymmetrically and the reason it had so many nails was that it was the first board laid and needed to be securely fastened. ('Carpenters have advised me', Hoffman wrote later, 'that it would not take anywhere near twenty-five nails to anchor the first board, and they have also pointed out that approximately the same number of nails required to anchor the first board would have been required to anchor the last board.') Loney then pointed out that Rail 16 was a sixteenth of an inch thicker than the other boards, but Koehler didn't have an answer to that one.

Then came the great experiment, which was to place Rail 16 over the joists where the state had contended that it had lain, and drive the nails through the holes in both. When this was done, it was found that not one of the nails could be made to sink in to its full length: each one protruded above Rail 16 by about a quarter of an inch.

Convinced by this that the attic evidence had been fixed, Hoffman took Wilentz and Bornmann to a room below, flatly accused Bornmann of perjury and told him that unless he wanted to be broken, he should come clean. Bornmann replied with confidence that he had been speaking the truth and Hauck backed him. Sections of the joist were then cut out and taken to a physics laboratory at Columbia University, where fibrous fragments were found at the base of each hole. Hauck claimed that these had been planted, and threatened to have Hoffman impeached. But Hoffman was told that fibrous fragments were just what you would expect in nail holes that were comparatively fresh.

> The wood fibers in the nail holes have not died [he said]. There are no signs of rust from the nails, and it is apparent to anyone with an open mind that eightpenny cut nails had never remained in those holes for the nine or ten years that the flooring had been laid. Other nail holes in the joists . . . are lined with rust and there are no projecting fibers. It seems to me that . . . the disputed nail holes were made by nails driven in the joists and pulled out almost immediately.

Supporting evidence came later, too late to be of any service to Hauptmann. 'I have in my possession,' wrote Hoffman the following year, 'a photograph of the ladder made the day after the commission of the crime. It is a clear photograph, in which the knots and grains are distinctly shown, and Rail 16 can be easily identified; *but neither in the original nor in a copy magnified ten times can the alleged nail holes be found.*' (Author's italics.)

Submissions that cast fresh doubts on the handwriting evidence were also received in those last days. An expert by the name of Samuel Small came to see Hoffman at the Hildebrecht, bringing with him the blown-up exhibits of the ransom notes and Hauptmann's admitted writings, and declared that Osborn had testified against his own beliefs. 'In a lifetime of effort,' said Small, 'a man cannot change the way he was taught to write. Look at these. The shadings are different – the downstrokes and upstrokes. Every letter has different characteristics . . . the smartest criminal in the world couldn't do that.'

Another attempt to have Hauptmann's sentence reduced to life imprisonment was made by the psychiatrist Dr Dudley Shoenfeld, who was as capable of fantasies as wild as those of any of his patients. He believed that Hauptmann was a victim of schizophrenia (or *dementia praecox* as it was known then) and had killed the Lindbergh baby because as a great air ace Lindbergh had supplanted his own hero, Manfred von Richthofen, after whom he had named his own son. Like others, Shoenfeld believed that Hauptmann must have had accomplices; and he succeeded in raising enough money for a year-long psychiatric examination of Hauptmann in order to reach the full facts. Wilentz, whom he had come to know during the trial, agreed that it would be better for society to know the full facts than for Hauptmann to die, and said that if Hauptmann could be persuaded to confess, he would go to the Court of Pardons along with Shoenfeld and the Governor and ask for commutation of sentence.

Shoenfeld made an appointment with Hoffman, told him what Wilentz had said, and urged him to do what he could do to bring about a confession: it might be difficult to obtain, he said, because Hauptmann had been buoyed up by so many people's publicly expressed doubts about his guilt. Any appeal to Hauptmann, he went on, would have to be on the basis of asking him *not* to die, *pleading* with him to live, 'for if it were presented to him on the basis that he himself was asking for life, the confession would never be obtained'. This was the same path Leibowitz had traveled, and Hoffman knew it was doomed, for Hauptmann never would confess. But as to *why* he wouldn't, none of them – neither Wilentz or Reilly or Leibowitz or Shoenfeld or anyone else – could recognize the simple truth staring them in the face: that he had nothing *to* confess, that he had had no part in the affair at all. That was too fanciful and heretical and dangerous an idea even to consider.

By now the Governor had formed the view that the execution of Hauptmann would be a gross miscarriage of justice, and in a long statement released on the Saturday before the Tuesday of the execution, he declared that the case reeked with passion, prejudice and unfairness. He demolished the credibility of the only three witnesses who had placed Hauptmann in New Jersey – Whited who was a liar, Rossiter who was a liar and a thief, Hochmuth who was blind – and all three because they had been promised reward money. He revealed that he had been to see Justice Trenchard to inquire whether the new information would permit him to set aside the conviction and order a new trial and that Trenchard had said he could only entertain such a motion within six months of conviction. It seemed to the Governor that there was no loophole left, for he had said he would grant only one reprieve, and the Constitution did not allow him another. 'I would willingly grant another reprieve,' he said, 'if Prosecutor Hauck and Attorney General Wilentz can find a way to advise me that I have a legal right to do so.'

The day before there had been a new and extraordinary development in this most extraordinary of cases in that all members of the Court of Pardons had received a twenty-five-page confession to the Lindbergh baby kidnapping and murder by a fifty-year-old disbarred Trenton attorney and convicted perjuror (who was also wanted for fraud) by the name of Paul Wendel. This was not as crazy a confession as at first thought, since it had been made to none other than Ellis Parker, Hoffman's friend and the chief of Burlington County detectives. Ellis was instructed to deliver Wendel to Mercer County detectives who took him before a Justice of the Peace to be arraigned for murder before being lodged in the Mercer County Jail. Once there he immediately repudiated the confession, claiming he had been kidnapped by Ellis Parker and his son Ellis Junior, taken to a mental hospital for a number of days, tortured there and forced to sign the confession under duress. It seemed to many that this, if true, was a last desperate effort by Parker, convinced that Hauptmann was innocent, to save him from the chair.

In the light of this development, however, and at Fisher's request, the Court of Pardons was convened for a second time on the Monday morning, just thirty-six hours before the time set for the execution. The night before, an agitated Samuel Small, the handwriting expert, had come to Hoffman's suite at the Hildebrecht to ask if he could testify before it. Hoffman replied it was impossible, the rules didn't permit. 'But,' said Small, breaking down and crying, 'do you mean to say that your state will send to the chair a man who *couldn't possibly* have written those notes?' He paused, momentarily too distressed to continue. 'Listen,' he said, 'it isn't a question of *if* Hauptmann wrote those letters. It is a question of whether he *could* write them. I tell you, Governor, that if you went to the prison and said to Hauptmann, "I will let you free if you can write a single sentence the way it is written in the ransom letters", Hauptmann would have to stay in prison the rest of his life. A person cannot change his handwriting from one known system to another.'

At 11 a.m. the court met in the State House annex. Fisher argued for clemency on two grounds: it was now established that Rail 16 could not have come from Hauptmann's attic, and if Wendel's confession was true and his repudiation of it false, then Hauptmann *ipso facto* could not be guilty. Wilentz and Hauck argued that nothing new had been found in the attic and that no one was taking Wendel's confession seriously. Wilentz also claimed that the first ransom note (which on the strength of the one word 'is' Osborn had declared was in Hauptmann's hand) placed

Hauptmann firmly in the nursery on the night of the crime. How Hoffman must have wished that Samuel Small could have been granted his request to testify. He himself said little, knowing that colleagues who had rejected Hauptmann once in the Court of Errors and Appeals and a second time at the first meeting of the Court of Pardons were hardly likely to have a change of heart now.

The court was still in session when Anna Hauptmann went to see Richard for the last time. The prison band was practising and the sound of the music reduced her to tears. But, said the *New York Times*, she controlled herself quickly, 'and with the aid of a little face powder, put on her best appearance before meeting her husband'. It was what she had always done, whatever her feelings, whatever the state of her purse. They talked of little Manfred whom his father had not seen for more than a year because, as he had said then, 'I do not belong here', and the idea of Manfred in later life remembering such a visit was abhorrent to him. 'You must have faith,' Anna told him; 'something may still happen.' But she could see from his face that there was little faith left. They were allowed to hold hands through the bars, and they cried together, aghast and incredulous that nine years of married happiness had to end like this. Then she left.

By mid afternoon a huge crowd had gathered outside the State House annexe to hear the decision of the Court of Pardons. Wilentz, Lanigan, Stockton, Schwarzkopf, Lamb and Keaton had gathered in the Attorney General's office; Fisher, Pope and Mrs Hauptmann were in the Stacy-Trent Hotel. At 5 p.m. the clerk of the court, Albert Hermann, fought his way through the mob to the State House and there, holding aloft a piece of typewritten paper, announced that the appeal had been denied. Fisher told the press that with Wendel arraigned on the same charge for which Hauptmann had been convicted, the judgment was incomprehensible. 'We are very bitterly disappointed,' he said.

He took the news to the prison. Despite Wendel, Hauptmann had been half expecting it. After Fisher had gone, Hauptmann called to one of the guards for pencil and paper. Now that all hope had gone and his death was a certainty, he wanted to write a farewell letter.

It was addressed (in German) to Governor Hoffman and was a kind of last testament. 'My writing,' he began, 'is not for fear of losing my life, this is in the hands of God. It is His will. I will go gladly, it means the end of my tremendous suffering. Only in thinking of my dear wife and little boy, that is breaking my heart. I know until this terrible crime is solved, they will have to suffer under the weight of my unfair conviction.'

Once again he emphasized his innocence and lack of knowledge about the case ('I passed the money without knowing it was Lindbergh money . . . up to the present day I have no idea where the Lindbergh house in Hopewell is located'); railed against Dr Condon ('Why did Dr Condon say in my cell he cannot testify against me? My God, Dr Condon, did you ever realize what you did?'); attacked Reilly ('Why did my chief lawyer send important witnesses home without even bringing them on the stand? My God, my God, I can't hardly believe all what happened at my trial'); but kept his bitterest comments for the state's prosecutor:

> Mr Wilentz, with my dying breath, I swear by God that you convicted an innocent man. Once you will stand before the same judge to whom I go in a few hours. You know you have done wrong on me, you will not only take my life but also all the happiness of my family. God will be judge between me and you.
>
> I beg you, Attorney General, believe at least a dying man. Please investigate, because this case is not solved, it only adds another dead to the Lindbergh case.

He concluded with a message for the Governor. 'I see this as my duty, before this state takes my life, to thank you for what you have done for me. I write this with tears in my eyes. If ever prayers will reach you, they will come from me, from my dear wife and my little boy.'

When his supper came that night, he didn't touch it. After it had been taken away, unable to reconcile God's will with the workings of so malevolent a fate, he wept.

Next morning he didn't eat his breakfast or his lunch either. After the lunch hour, as was customary with condemned men, he was moved from his own cell to Cell 8 on the other side of the death chamber: this was in case he had hidden some weapon in his own cell by which he could cheat the executioner, and also to be made ready for death. Apart from a chair and a table the cell was empty of furniture. Hauptmann was allowed to bring his Bible there, but nothing else, not even the photographs of Manfred and Anna. Fisher, visiting him, found him deeply distressed. 'I have been a good prisoner,' he said, 'I have never made anybody any trouble. Why should they do this to me? Why should I be pushed around when this is my last day to live?' Later the prison barber arrived to shave the crown of his head: this was where the executioner would fix one of the electrodes. Then a fresh suit of clothes was brought in, a blue shirt and dark-striped khaki trousers. Hauptmann noticed a long slit in one of the trouser legs and was told this was for placing the second electrode.

Alone again in the bare cell, Hauptmann broke into another fit of weeping, less perhaps at the thought of his extinction or the wrongfulness of it, but because of the pitiful, degraded figure they had now reduced him to. He was still weeping when the warden came to see him, and asked for time to recover his composure. Kimberling said he'd heard Hauptmann had had nothing to eat for nearly twenty-four hours and encouraged him to eat now (though with death only hours away it is difficult to see why); the warden said he could order a special meal of anything he liked. Hauptmann suggested he send it to Condon, then made one last impassioned assertion of innocence. Could not the warden arrange for him to make a radio broadcast to the American people, beg anyone who knew the truth about the kidnapping and murder to come forward before it was too late? Colonel Kimberling shook his head.

After Kimberling came the defense attorneys, Fisher and Rosecrans and Pope, who did their best not to show their distress at seeing this man whom they had grown to admire and like appear before them like some grotesque clown, ashen-faced, hair shaved like a monk's tonsure, one trouser leg obscenely different from the other. He shook hands with them and thanked them for what they had done, and then the two pastors, Werner and Matthiesen, who had already visited him once or twice that day, came again to comfort him. The Reverend Werner asked if there was anything he wanted to say about the case, and for about the millionth time he said no, he had nothing to add to the truth. They asked if he would like to pray, and when he said his mind was too full to concentrate, they reminded him of the solace St Francis of Assisi had derived from murmuring to himself the single word 'God'. Then, together, they read the Bible.

From around 6 p.m. crowds began gathering outside the main gate of the prison: they saw, beneath the floodlit walls, two fire trucks and ninety fully armed policemen and state troopers, for Kimberling was taking no chances. An hour later the first of the forty-five guests arrived and walked down an aisle formed by some of the troopers, beneath the frieze of rams and serpents above the entrance gate, and into the prison. Thirty of the forty-five were press, the others New Jersey officials: these included two members of the state legislature; Dr Charles Mitchell, the Mercer County coroner who had performed the autopsy on Charlie; the two prison doctors; Albert Hermann, clerk of the Court of Pardons; Captain Lamb and Lieutenant Keaton, Inspector Harry Walsh and Lieutenant Robert Hicks. At the top of the entrance steps the guests were frisked for cameras and weapons, and the state police officers had their pistols removed. A more detailed search was made in a small office and carried to almost ludicrous lengths. 'The guards,' said the *New York Times*, 'examined everyone's hatband, coat and trouser linings and cuffs, buttons, pencils, fountain pens, matchboxes, watches, wallets, keyholders, envelopes, notebooks, papers, and the soles and heels of shoes.' They were then taken to another office and asked to wait.

They had been told they would be taken to the death chamber soon after 7.30, but the hour came and went and the clock moved on towards 7.45. There had been some muted chatter to begin with and the lighting of cigarettes, but now, thinking they would be summoned almost any moment, they fell silent, extinguished cigarettes. Meanwhile, in Cell 8 at the other end of the prison, Hauptmann was waiting too, using up the last minutes of his life in prayer with the Reverends Werner and Matthiesen. 'The Lord is my shepherd . . . he shall feed me in green pastures . . . yea, though I walk through the valley of the shadow of death, I will fear no evil; for thou art with me; thy rod and thy staff comfort me.' Soon he would be in Paradise, his sufferings over.

As the voices droned on, Hauptmann heard the sound of footsteps on the stone floor. They were not what he expected, the slow, heavy footsteps of the guards come to summon him next door, but quicker, lighter steps. The ministers stopped praying. Hauptmann looked up. Fisher was standing outside the bars. He was smiling. 'They've postponed it for at least two days,' he said.

Anna heard of the decision in her room at the Stacy-Trent. She had seen her husband for the last time the day before, and today she could do nothing but think of him, wondering how he was coping with the hours of waiting, knowing that he too was thinking of her. She had been out once, to buy herself a black dress, hat and veil, in recognition that the state was about to make her a widow. Now she lay on the bed wearing the dress, still thick with cold, drowsy from the sedative the doctor had given her. The telephone rang; it was Fisher with the news. Anna leapt from the bed, crying, 'I knew it! I told you so!' and went to change into a blue print dress with red and white flowers in readiness for the waiting photographers. She was overjoyed, interpreting the decision more as a cancellation than postponement. There must be some overwhelmingly strong reason for it taking place at the eleventh hour, she decided; and the state, having taken them all to the brink once, surely could not do so again.

The forty-five witnesses were led back to the main gate, half relieved, half disappointed. They mingled with the crowd, now nearly ten thousand strong, and disappeared into the night. The crowd itself refused to believe repeated announcements of the postponement, thinking the troopers wanted to get rid of them, and stayed around until after ten when the newsboys came round with the extras' banner headlines, HAUPTMANN REPRIEVED.

And the reason for the postponement? The Mercer County Grand Jury had taken it upon themselves to consider a possible bill of indictment against Paul Wendel for the murder of Charles Lindbergh Junior. They had sat all day and, not having reached a conclusion by evening, instructed their foreman, Alleyne Freeman, to telephone the warden to ask that the execution be postponed. Kimberling, having discretionary powers to carry it out on any day within the same week, now ordered it to take place on the evening of Friday April 3.

*   *   *

Public reaction to the news of the postponement was as divided as had been the response to Hoffman's thirty-day reprieve. Many read into it a further sly attempt by the Governor to pervert the course of justice. Hauck expressed himself outraged, a front-page editorial in the *Trenton Times* made a fresh call for Hoffman's impeachment, and a Professor of Astronomy and thirty-four other members of Princeton University faculty staff petitioned the state legislature to inquire whether grounds existed for removing Hoffman from office. Also, in a fit of pique, the Church of Seventh Day Adventists, Christians to a man, were so incensed by the Reverend Werner having publicly voiced his belief in Hauptmann's innocence that, despite his having been a pastor for thirty years and not now in the best of health, they declared him unfrocked and deprived of his pension.

Against this the Governor received many letters and telegrams applauding the postponement, including one from Clarence Darrow who had himself received numerous letters 'from all classes of persons including countless mothers of children'. Many of these letters condemned Condon, 'heretofore so eager to occupy the limelight, but now prevented by Wilentz from shedding further light on the situation'. To Darrow the immediate death of Hauptmann seemed unprofessional. 'In the face of such widespread public disapproval, he should be granted a new trial.'

But it was a foreigner, not an American, whose comments on the postponement caused the greatest stir. Writing in *Le Figaro*, the distinguished French man of letters André Maurois expressed the views of many Europeans who deplored the cruelty which condemned men were often obliged to suffer in the long-drawn-out American judicial process. Three times, he said, Hauptmann had awaited death on a date known to him:

> He has counted days, hours and minutes. Three times during these fearful days his mind has turned, supposedly for the final time, to the dreadful scene in that room, to the signal, the final shock and convulsions to follow. The last time his imagination was further stirred by the gruesome preparations in the death chamber, and by the shaving of his head for contact with the electrode.
>
> This is not all. This man has a mother and a wife. For them as well these three frightful rehearsals have taken place. Three times the wife said her last farewell, and on Monday, while leaving the prison, she saw the workmen hastily installing telegraph equipment for newspaper reporters. Nobody can picture such things without feeling pity.
>
> Whether Hauptmann is guilty or not is no longer the question. The death of a guilty man may be necessary for the good of society. But all civilized people ought to admit that a man who has had the order of his execution countermanded at the last moment, should not then be forced to die.

The condemned man however had managed to recover some of his composure and appetite. On being taken back to the familiar surroundings of Cell 9 after the postponement, he had changed back into regular prison clothes, eaten a good dinner and then fallen into a sound sleep from which he didn't wake until ten the next morning. Anna Hauptmann was allowed a two-hour visit and reported him cheerful and hopeful of another reprieve.

Next day, after confessing to Anna transient doubts about God, he wrote, 'He has put it into my heart that I should live and that I should see you and Manfred again. God forgive me and help me in my lack of faith. From now on I shall leave everything in His hands . . . He will stay with me whatever will become.'

The Mercer County Grand Jury sat all Tuesday and Wednesday and then decided to discontinue their deliberations without a finding. If they had returned a true bill or a no-bill, Kimberling would have known what to do. But without either and yet with Wendel's arraignment for murder still on the file, he was in a dilemma. Should he make a further postponement to the end of the week or go ahead as planned? He asked Wilentz for a ruling and Wilentz was quite definite. The execution must be carried out as ordered unless (a) there was another reprieve from the Governor, (b) a direction from the Hunterdon County Court or some other competent court, or (c) commutation by the Court of Pardons. So Kimberling had all the witnesses telephoned to confirm that the execution would take place on the night of Friday April 3.

Fisher meanwhile was doing all he could to bring about a further postponement, persuading Anna to go to Flemington to lay a charge against Wendel for Hauck and the Hunterdon County Grand Jury to consider, petitioning the Governor for a second reprieve. And right up until the last moment the Governor himself was looking for any loophole that might enable him to put off the inevitable. When Stephen Spitz in a Chicago prison announced that he had bought $5000 Lindbergh ransom money at discount, Hoffman made great efforts (in the end unsuccessful) to bring him to Trenton. He was unaware that on that very same day another ransom bill had been passed in the Bronx, or that Colonel Schwarz-kopf, fearful that the finding of more of them in any quantity would demolish the state's evidence that Hauptmann had received the lot, advised J. Edgar Hoover and others that if more bills were found, they should be taken out of circulation and destroyed.

So now there was no going back; the demand for a burnt offering was irresistible, the public thirst for expiation could only be assuaged by Hauptmann's death. On April 3 he was moved back to Cell 8 where in the course of the day Fisher had a long talk with him, found him more composed. 'You don't know, Lloyd,' he said, 'what I went through three days ago. Even now I don't know what I do. If I cry like often I want to do when I think of Anni and Bubi, everybody will say I am guilty. If I fight with my heart and soul they will say I am cold-blooded fellow like one who would commit such a crime.' He asked Fisher to let Anna know he was all right, and not to mention about being moved to another cell.

Once again, this time at a little before seven that evening, the first of the fifty-odd witnesses made their way towards the main gate of the prison. It was a cold, gray, blustery evening, unlike the picnic weather of three days before, and although the fire trucks and police and troopers were again in position, it looked as though there would be no need for them; for tonight the crowd, half expecting another reprieve, numbered no more than five hundred. As before, the witnesses were first thoroughly searched by prison guards, then taken to Kimberling's office where they signed affidavits that they were not carrying cameras, weapons, drugs or other contraband. Then the deputy warden, Colonel Selby, took them to the prison centre, a circular space from which corridors radiated to the various cell blocks. He told them he would return presently and they could smoke. A clock on the wall showed close to 7.30.

Hauptmann meanwhile, back again in execution clothes – gray shirt, trousers with one leg split, slippers – and with a re-shaved scalp, was praying with Matthiesen and the loyal Werner. Earlier, in an article which would be published after his death, Hauptmann had written of his feelings sitting within ten feet of the chair and preparing to walk 'that last mile'. He imagined that the witnesses would include some who had helped prepare the case for the prosecution. 'It is my belief that their suffering, their agony, will be greater than mine. Mine will be over in a moment. Theirs will last as long as life itself.' (True, if they could ever have brought themselves to admit they had made a mistake, which they naturally never did.)

Fisher, still half hopeful of another last-minute reprieve, came to say goodbye. Matthiesen handed him a piece of paper on which Hauptmann had written a statement in German; it would, said the minister, be his final statement. He translated:

I am glad that my life in a world which has not understood me has ended. Soon I will be at home with my Lord. And as I love my Lord, so I am dying an innocent man.
Should however my death serve for the purpose of abolishing capital punishment . . . I feel that my death has not been in vain.
I am at peace with God. I repeat, I protest my innocence of the crime for which I was convicted. However, I die with no malice or hatred in my heart. The love of Christ has filled my soul, and I am happy in him.

Hauptmann stood up, shook Fisher by hand and thanked him again for all he had done ('You have been very kind to me, Lloyd'). Fisher looked at the shaven crown, the putty-like face on which for eighteen months the sun had never shone, reluctant to admit that everything he had done for him (and it was considerable) had been in vain. He had given Hauptmann a part of his life; until his own death things would never be the same again.

Fisher went along to the warden's office, where Kimberling told him the Governor had sent word there would be no further reprieve and Hauck had said he would not present Anna Hauptmann's charge against Wendel to the Hunterdon County Grand Jury until their next session. Fisher reminded Kimberling that his discretion in ordering the time of the execution lasted until midnight on Sunday. Would he defer it until then? The warden shook his head. But in case there was a last minute change of heart somewhere, he would postpone it by forty minutes.

And so the witnesses left standing in the draughty prison centre smoked more cigarettes and grumbled among themselves and asked what the delay was; it wasn't until just before 8 p.m. that Colonel Selby arrived to form them into two rows and not until 8.15 that Kimberling arrived to address them. They would watch the execution in silence; anyone who cried out or spoke would be removed by the guards; if Hauptmann spoke, if he indicated he wanted to confess, the warden and no one else would give whatever response he deemed necessary. Finally, because there had been persistent rumours that there would be an attempt to photograph the execution, there would be another search, beginning with himself, before they entered the chamber.

They set off two abreast in a file a hundred feet long, through the middle cell block, the dimly lit mess hall and kitchen corridors and out into the prison yard. The clouds had cleared, the stars were out, there was a pale moon. Ahead of them lay the squat shape of the death house, two guards with rifles and fixed bayonets patrolling its floodlit roof. A sound as of the murmur of the sea same to them: the voices of the crowd on the other side of the walls, now some two thousand strong.

They went through folding doors to the death house courtyard and after being searched were allowed one by one into the execution chamber. It was a bare, square, brightly lit room with poorly whitewashed walls and a skylight in the roof. Resting against the centre of the far wall was the chair, like some tawdry throne awaiting the crowning of a new occupant. Between it and the ten rows of plain, wooden chairs had been draped a three-foot-high white canvas strip, to separate, as it were, the spectators from the performers.

Behind the chair was a cabinet enclosing an instrument panel and a large wheel, and standing beside it Robert Elliott, the executioner, and his assistant John Bloom. Elliott, in a gray suit, was gray-haired and had a deeply lined face, not unconnected with the nature of his job. 'I dreaded this assignment more than any other,' he wrote later. He had read the trial testimony, spoken to friends who had attended it, and was much concerned about the rightness of the sentence. 'I wondered whether justice would best be served by the snuffing out of the life of this man.' His not to reason why: killing people was his job.

The witnesses took their seats. The warden, still wearing hat and topcoat, moved in front of the chair and asked everybody to button their coats and keep their hands out of their pockets. Reporters who wanted to make notes could do so as long as pads and pencils could be clearly seen. He motioned to a guard who held up a large clock: this was to fix the exact time of the execution. It read 8.36 p.m. He said to another guard, 'Before we call Hauptmann, I think it would be wise to telephone the central office and see if there is any message.'

The guard nodded and left. Elliott placed a wooden bar with light bulbs on the electric chair, then turned a switch on the instrument panel: the bulbs lit up. He removed the bar, and now everyone waited. They were waiting outside the prison walls too; in New York's Times Square a huge, silent crowd was waiting to see the announcement go up on the big illuminated ticker-tape; all over America and the world families and individuals waited by their radios to hear the words that would at last write *Finis* to this terrible story. So long overdue was the news that many thought there had been yet another postponement. Only those in the death house knew the event was imminent.

The guard who had gone away returned. There were no messages. Kimberling looked at Elliott who signified all was ready. Kimberling still hesitated, as though reluctant to assume reponsibility of the final, irrevocable act. Then he turned and told the guards to bring in Hauptmann. Lieutenant Robert Hicks looked at Kimberling's face. 'I could read there,' he said, 'an immense distaste for his task.'

The guards went through the steel door and closed it behind them. Now there was dead silence, for they were about to see a pornographic live show and live shows, whether of copulation or killing, instil a certain awe: both are about the mystery of life, its renewal and its ending; both are acts normally performed in private. A minute later the doors opened again. First came the guards and behind them Werner and Matthiesen, chanting a prayer in German; after them the semi-bald Hauptmann, pale and expressionless, one trouser leg flapping, shuffling to his doom in brown carpet slippers. He walked past the chair and would have collided with one of the attendant doctors had not a guard guided him back. He sat down heavily, laying his arms on the armrests as in the famous Abraham Lincoln statue. For a fleeting moment he glanced at the witnesses, and there were those who thought they caught the flicker of a smile. Some of the press still had pencils poised for a confession. 'Here was Hauptmann's chance to talk,' said Edward Folliard of the *Washington Post*, and seemed surprised he didn't.

The guards strapped Hauptmann's arms, chest and legs firmly to the chair. Elliott took one of the two cup-shaped electrodes dipped in brine, placed it on his head like a sort of coronet and secured it with a strap under the lower lip, as with the busby of a Coldstream guardsman. It took but a moment to fix the second electrode through the slit in the right leg. Then a mask was placed over his face, so that the spectators might be spared the horrific contortions that two thousand volts do to a man's features, forcing his eyes almost out of his head.

Elliott walked to the control panel, looked at Kimberling. The guard held up the clock: it said 8.44. Kimberling nodded. Elliott turned the wheel, there was a drawn-out mournful whine from the dynamos, like the wind in the Hopewell treetops, the bulbs in the control panel lit up as if on a Christmas tree, and the full charge drove into Hauptmann's body. He went rigid, strained against the straps, dropped back as the whine of the dynamos fell. One rookie spectator, unable to contain himself, cried out, 'Christ, it's terrible!' The process was repeated a second and third time. Against it could be heard the chanting of the defrocked Reverend Werner, continuing to give comfort to one already far beyond it, at 8.44 a sentient being, at 8.45 a corpse. ' "I am the Resurrection and the Life," saith the Lord. "Whosoever liveth and believeth in me shall never die." ' The spectators noticed a wisp of smoke above Hauptmann's head.

404 Crime of the Century

Elliott switched off the current, the three attendant doctors put their stethoscopes against Hauptmann's chest. Dr Wiesler, the prison doctor, spoke for all three. 'This man is dead,' he said, and again, 'This man is dead.'

The guards unstrapped the body and carried it into the autopsy room next door. The spectators, stunned and silent, rose from their chairs. Kimberling went outside to give the news to the press. Under the arc lights movie cameras and microphones had been positioned; some reporters had set up typewriters on little make-shift tables, others stood poised with pads and pencils at the ready; nearly all wore hats and many were smoking cigarettes.

There was only one question they wanted to ask. 'Did he make a statement before he went? Did he confess?'

'No,' said Kimberling, 'he made no statement after he left the cell.'

Why not? Expecting it, they felt puzzled, cheated, let down. But then the whole case had been a puzzle from the beginning, and as yet no one had been able to figure out why.

Presently, in New York, a sub-editor of the *Times* roughed out a Page One headline for the next day's paper: 'HAUPTMANN SILENT TO THE END'.

Silent? It was a travesty of the truth, as great a lie as the headline that had told the world of his arrest back in September 1934 – 'LINDBERGH KIDNAPER JAILED'. Far from remaining silent he had from the outset, and with every breath in his body, unceasingly asserted his innocence to anyone who would listen. But to this the American press and people remained deaf: it was not, and never had been, what they wanted to hear.

So ended the brief life of Bruno Richard Hauptmann, guilty beyond a doubt of appropriating monies not his (yet part of which he believed was due to him); but of kidnapping, extortion and murder as ignorant, and innocent, as you or I.

Epilogue

Anna Hauptmann with a woman companion from the Hearst Press was waiting in her room at the Stacy-Trent. During these past few agonizing weeks there had been a parallel in Anna's life with that of Anne Lindbergh after the disappearance of Charlie. Both women had lived in hope; hope against the coming of the angel of death, hope which those who loved them had encouraged them to sustain. For Anna now that hope was about to be extinguished, just as Anne's had been when her mother had told her, 'The baby is with Daddy.'

Outside her locked door stood half a dozen women reporters and cameramen with instructions from the editors to record in words and pictures her reactions to the news of her husband's death. They stood around like so many vultures, knowing the promised feast could not be long delayed. Some got down on hands and knees to peer through the crack beneath the door to see if they could wrest a story from feet or furniture.

It was Fisher's secretary, Laura Apgar, who brought the news. Pushing her way through the press, she knocked at the door and was let in. Anna had only to look at her face to know the worst. 'I'm sorry,' said Laura lamely, 'it's all over.' Bursting into tears, Anna rushed into the bathroom and locked the door. She was still there, sobbing hysterically, when Fisher and Werner arrived. Werner, in German, entreated her to come out. She did so at last, and at once a photographer, who with two reporters had forced his way in after Fisher unnoticed, began taking photographs. One reporter said, 'Our editors . . .' Enraged, Fisher turned on them. 'Get out!' he shouted. 'Let this poor woman alone.' Anna threw herself on the bed, hardly knowing what she was about. Fisher took out a handkerchief to dab his own eyes and then, realizing he could be of little help, left.

Late that night and guarded by six policemen, Anna was taken downstairs in the freight elevator and to the popping of flash-bulbs and, in front of a large crowd who had waited hours to see how this newly widowed woman would comport herself, was put in a car to return to the Bronx. She was back in Trenton in a day or two to collect from the prison a bundle marked 'The property of Inmate No. 17400' – a toothbrush, a few books and letters, the pictures of herself and Manfred – and with a Bronx undertaker her husband's body. To the undertaker Colonel Kimberling handed a letter which said, "Under Chapter 79, Laws of 1906, no religious or other service shall be held over the remains after such execution . . .' Disregarding this (for they had nothing further to lose), Werner and Matthiesen officiated at the service at the Fresh Pond Crematory in Queens on April 6; after it, Hauptmann's body was cremated.

Hauptmann's mother Paulina had also been living in hope, as a reporter found when he visited her at Kamenz in the early hours of the morning after the execution. 'She was almost smiling despite her anxiety,' he wrote, 'clearly expecting news of another reprieve.' When the reporter told her the news, she did not seem to understand. 'That can't be,' she said, 'it's impossible, quite impossible.' She asked the reporter into her living room where she began to tremble and her eyes filled with tears. 'She said nothing for a while. Then she said, "My son was my only hope. What have they done to my boy? Oh, God, how could it happen?" Then, with obvious effort, she asked: "Did he send me any greeting?" The reporter said yes. For a few minutes Mrs Hauptmann ceased weeping; then she said, "Please go. I want to be alone," and broke down completely.'

Lloyd Fisher's comment was, 'This is the greatest tragedy in the history of New Jersey. Time will never wash it out.' Hoffman's predecessor, the former Governor Harry Moore, said it was a triumph for justice. The two witnesses most responsible for Hauptmann's conviction, Condon and Lindbergh, maintained a discreet silence. The European press (less Germany) gave the execution massive coverage, most agreeing with André Maurois's strictures and the editorial in the Viennese *Die Stunde*: 'The way in which they played with the life of this man was a world scandal.' In Britain the interest was such that in many papers the execution drove the European situation, Amy Johnson's record-breaking flight to South Africa and the Oxford and Cambridge boat race off the front page. If the American public were as divided after the execution as they had been before it, most newspapers approved. The fairness of Hauptmann's conviction, said the *New York Times*, was weighed again and again. 'Recourse was had to every safeguard provided by the American system of jurisprudence against a miscarriage of justice and the punishment of an innocent man.' Two days later the paper made a slashing attack on Governor Hoffman for setting himself above the law, and hoped that the petition of the Princeton University professors to the New Jersey state legislature for a full inquiry into what it called 'the unwarranted and illegal meddling with the processes of criminal justice' would succeed.

But Hoffman, knowing he was on solid ground, welcomed an inquiry, indeed wanted it broadened to cover every aspect of the case. 'If an earnest desire to see truth and justice prevail is an offense against my oath of office,' he said, 'I am guilty and should be impeached.' And far from apologizing for anything he had said or done, he pursued his own investigations with renewed vigor, continuing to peel away layer upon layer of the numerous malpractices that had led to Hauptmann's conviction. He had Whited brought to his office, Whited who at the trial had denied receiving anything for testifying in the Bronx except his dinner money, and now admitted to receiving $150 fee, $35 a day expenses and a promise of reward money. He had Hochmuth brought to his office, Hochmuth who had said at the trial that his eyesight was all right and who now, when asked to identify a vase with flowers ten feet away declared it was a woman's hat. He compared Trooper Wolf's statement made on the night of the kidnapping that he had seen *two* sets of footprints leading away from the house with his evidence at the trial – 'How many footprints did you see?' – 'I saw one.' He found the contradictions in Condon's various statements to the police and subsequent testimony in New York and at Flemington so marked and so numerous as to make it impossible to believe a word he said.[1]

Then there was the matter of the $25,000 reward money. Although Hoffman had asked Schwarzkopf on the day after Hauptmann's execution to submit recommendations for its distribution, he wanted to complete his own investigations first. So it wasn't until two years later that he called a press conference to announce what had been decided. The biggest recipient, at $7500, was Walter Lyle, the gas station manager who had noted down the number of Hauptmann's car, next at $5000 was William Allen, the truck driver who had found Charlie's body. The two bank

---

[1] In Condon's evidence to the Bronx Grand Jury about his meeting with Cemetery John, Hoffman found this: 'I said, "What is your name?" He said, "Call me John." "Well, John, did you ever think of your own mother?" "Yes – *and a tear came into his eye*." ' What vision the venerable doctor had on that dark night, commented Hoffman, when he spied that tell-tale tear!

tellers who had spotted the gas station bill and the one passed to
Cecile Barr at Loew's movie house were awarded $2000 each.
Hochmuth, Whited, Barr, and Perrone received $1000 each, as did
John Lyons, the gas station attendant. Charles B. Rossiter received
$500 and the remaining $3000 was divided in small denominations
between bank tellers who had turned in ransom bills. Condon had
not had the nerve to put in a claim, but Koehler had: it was rejected on the grounds that, like the detectives in the case, he had
been an employee of the state.

Hoffman's subsequent career was one of decline. After he had
appointed Kimberling to succeed Schwarzkopf in 1936 because of
Schwarzkopf's handling of the Lindbergh case, he himself (and
partly because of *his* handling of it) failed to win re-election as
Governor in 1938. He later served in various state administrative
positions, but in 1954 had to resign as the head of the Division of
Public Security as a result of investigations headed by – an ironic
touch – the same Norman Schwarzkopf into financial irregulari-
ties. Six weeks later he died of a heart attack in a New York hotel,
leaving a letter for his daughter in which he admitted having em-
bezzled $300,000. It was a tarnished end to what had once been a
promising career, yet in no way diminishes the courageous stand
he took in championing the cause of Hauptmann's innocence in
the face of preponderantly hostile public opinion.

Schwarzkopf, after his dismissal, became president of a New
Jersey bus line and also gained fame as moderator of a weekly
radio programme, 'Gang Busters', a dramatization of the activities
of the FBI. In 1942 he went to Iran as commander of the US Military Mission there, served five years, and on return was awarded
the Distinguished Service Medal. After the war he served in army
posts in Italy and Germany, rising to the rank of Major General,
and later headed various official inquiries for the New Jersey state
government. He died in 1958. His son, also named Norman, also
entered the US Army and became famous as Commander-in-Chief,
Army General in the 1990–91 Gulf War.

Of the other main participants Wilentz continued as Attorney
General until 1944 when he entered private law practise. He remained active in Democratic politics and became state party leader
in 1949. In 1953 he quit the post because of illness, but continued
to practise law until well into his eighties. One of his sons became
Chief Justice of the New Jersey Supreme Court.

Edward Reilly entered a mental hospital the year after the

end of the Hauptmann trial, suffering from paresis, an untreated syphilitic condition. On application by his lawyer, Sam Leibowitz, he was released after fourteen months but was barely able to resume his law practise and died of a stroke in 1940, aged sixty-four. Two years later Judge Trenchard, who had retired in 1941 after thirty-five years in the Supreme Court, died of a cerebral haemorrhage. Lloyd Fisher was appointed by Governor Hoffmann to succeed Anthony Hauck in 1937 as Prosecutor of Hunterdon County. He practised in Flemington for the rest of his life, becoming secretary and president of the Hunterdon County Bar Association, and died of cancer in 1960, aged sixty-three.

In 1936, while renting a house belonging to Harold Nicolson in England, Lindbergh received an invitation from General Goering, head of the Luftwaffe, to inspect the German air forces. On this and two further visits he showed himself to be as gullible in accepting inflated information about German air strength fed to him by his hosts as he had been in accepting Schwarzkopf's certainties that Hauptmann was the kidnapper and murderer of his baby. Back in England he wrote alarmist reports to the Chief of the American Air Staff that the Luftwaffe was invincible and the best that the English could do now was to bow to the inevitable.[1] In this he had the full support of the American Ambassador in Britain, Joseph P. Kennedy, father of the future President.

By the time war broke out and the Lindberghs were back in America, Charles had become an advocate for Nazi Germany, and began a succession of speeches and radio broadcasts urging America to keep out. In April 1941 he became chairman of the isolationist 'America First' Committee which his many pro-British friends such as Harry Guggenheim (who after the fall of France saw Britain as America's front line) found puzzling and distressing and which was a source of some embarrassment in the family circle, particularly to Mrs Morrow and to his brother-in-law Aubrey Morgan, now head of British Information Services in New York.[2]

---

[1] His 1938 report estimated that Germany possessed around 10,000 war planes of all sorts and was building between 500 and 800 a month. But German official figures show that *two years later*, total German air strength was still less than half Lindbergh's figure and no more than 125 fighters and 300 bombers were being produced each month. (Leonard Mosley: *Lindbergh*, 225)

[2] After Elisabeth's death Aubrey Morgan had remained in the family by marrying her sister Constance in June 1937.

President Roosevelt was not pleased either and when America entered the war after Pearl Harbor, Lindbergh's application to rejoin the Army Air Corps was refused. His courage however had never been in doubt. After testing the P.47 Thunderbolt fighter at high altitudes for the Mayo Clinic in Minnesota (and nearly losing his life when the oxygen failed at 42,000 feet) he joined a fighter wing in the Pacific as a civilian consultant, made recommendations for increasing the range of the P.38, and flew on several unauthorized combat missions, shooting down one enemy plane. He knew that if he had been captured by the Japanese, he would have been shot.

After the war Lindbergh gradually eased back into the mainstream of American life. He was allowed to rejoin the Army Air Corps, interested himself in rocket development, took up his former technical consultancy with Pan Am, wrote his best-selling account of the flight to Paris, *The Spirit of St Louis* (made into a movie with James Stewart) and in later years devoted himself to ecology and conservation. He and Anne lived in two houses, one at Darien, Connecticut, the other on the Hawaiian island of Maui. Lindbergh died at Maui in 1974, aged seventy-two.

Anne continued to bear children – after Charlie and Jon, two more boys and two girls – and to write books; after *North to the Orient* and *Listen, the Wind*, poetry and the five volumes of diaries and letters stretching from 1924 to 1944, and more recently the philosophical best seller *Gift from the Sea*. With the passage of time, the references to Charlie in the diaries inevitably become fewer, though in the last volume, *War Within and Without*, she found that news of the disappearance of well-loved aviators – Amelia Earheart, Phil Love (Lindbergh's fellow pilot on the early St Louis to Chicago mail run), the French airman and writer Antoine de St Exupéry – produced similar emotions to those of hers at the kidnapping. Reports that St Exupéry (whom she had met only once briefly but admired greatly as airman and writer) was missing she found particularly distressing. 'I know the pattern well – the first shock, then the false hopes, and time passing, passing . . . The heart will not take it all at once; it rejects it, it has to be told – a fresh telling, a fresh shock, a fresh thrust over and over again . . .'

After her husband's execution Anna Hauptmann faded quickly from the public gaze. For most Americans, whatever their views, the case had been a traumatic experience which they all now wanted to forget. Helped by a friend, Anna moved to Philadelphia. For many years she had a desperately hard time, sharing a bed with Manfred, working in a bakery by day, office cleaning at night, in order to bring in enough for the two of them to live.

In all those years she never ceased to revere Richard's name and to assert his innocence to anyone who would listen. But few were interested and most were disbelieving. She never thought of marrying again or of changing her name, either of which might have made life easier. In all those years, she said, she felt strongly that her husband was with her.

For the last years of her life, 'this truly upright Christian woman', as Richard once called her, lived in a trim house in a Philadelphia suburb close to that of Manfred and his own family. Well into her nineties she remained extraordinarily active and mentally alert. From time to time newsmen asked her to describe again the events of half a century ago. Many asked how she had managed to live so long, and to all of them she gave the same answer: "I am waiting for the truth to come out. When it does, I die next day. And I die in peace."

In the film she says to Richard when he knows he has to die, 'The truth shall make us free'. And because she herself knew the truth and knew that a growing number of others had also come to know it, she was enabled, in my view, to die in peace. At least I like to think so.

Yeadon, January 29-1984

Dear Mr. Kennedy:

I want to thank you + Mrs. Kennedy very much for the beautiful Christmas card, I have never seen one like it.

Most likely you are very busy finishing the Book + I hope + believe that people after reading it, see a different Richard Hauptmann.

My Husband did not Kidnap the Lindbergh Baby, he was with me + together we drove home that evening

We did not know a Baby was stolen until we read it the next morning in the Newspaper

The State of New Jersey murdered an innocent man, they Killed my Husband God knows he was innocent I have told the truth.

Most sincerely,
Anna Hauptmann

Appendix I

Extract from FBI Report 62-3057 on the method of kidnapping

The Police found two rectangular ruts in the soft ground under the window and observed that the ladder fitted exactly into these ruts, and upon re-enacting the crime noted that the kidnapper upon climbing up the ladder would have had a very difficult time entering the window, because of the fact that the ladder was two feet short of reaching the window, the fact that it had been placed to the right of the window, and it was necessary to reach up with his left hand, pull the shutters apart, and then to climb in the window and over the suitcase to gain entrance into the nursery. It is extremely doubtful that a large man could have accomplished this feat without making a lot of noise and disturbance. The New Jersey State Police have a ladder made of identically the same wood and materials as the kidnap ladder and conducted tests with same, determining that it would not hold a weight of over 155 lbs. Regardless of the significance placed upon this test the kidnap ladder was a flimsy affair and anything but strong. After the kidnapper gained entrance into the nursery, he had the problem of getting the child down on the ground. It is agent's opinion, from observing the size of the window and considering the circumstances that it would have been almost impossible for one man to have climbed out of the window with the child in his arms and Lt Keaton stated that he has the same opinion as to the matter. He stated that the State Police feel reasonably certain that at least two persons perpetrated the kidnapping; that one of them entered the nursery and took the child out of its crib, while the accomplice climbed the ladder and received the child through the window from the hands of the kidnapper who actually entered the room.

Appendix II

Note on the identification of Charles Lindbergh Junior's body

Over the years doubts have been expressed as to whether the body found was that of the Lindbergh baby. This has led two men (Kenneth Kerwin and Harold Olson) each to advance the ludicrous claim that he himself is the Lindberghs' son, and at least one author, Theon Wright, to publish a book (*In Search of the Lindbergh Baby*)[1] advancing Olson's claim.

There are three main reasons for these doubts.

(1) The post-mortem showed the baby to be 33½ inches long, but a Missing Person poster issued after his disappearance, and given wide distribution, declared him to be only 29 inches; and, it has been argued, he could not have grown 4½ inches between the time of his disappearance and the discovery of his body.

(2) A New York specialist, Dr van Ingen, who had examined Charlie for rickets two weeks before he was taken, said when asked to identify the remains: 'If someone were to come in here and offer me ten million dollars, I simply wouldn't be able to identify those remains.'

(3) Dr Mitchell's post-mortem showed that the two big toes of the right foot were overlapping which, if the body was Charlie's, wasn't true.

As regards (1) and (2) the figure of 29 inches instead of 2 foot 9 inches (i.e. 33 inches) was given out erroneously by Colonel Breckinridge's office. The corrected figure was given out immediately and appeared, among other of the baby's statistics, in a feature in the *New York American* and other papers on March 7 1933. An FBI report of April 28 1933 stated that Dr van Ingen conferred with Dr Mitchell at Trenton, 'and it was found that the measurements and other characteristics noted by Dr van Ingen at [his] examination . . . tallied almost exactly with Dr Mitchell's measurements of the body . . . except that Dr Mitchell's overall measurement of the body showed one half inch longer than did the overall measurement made by Dr van Ingen . . . and that this additional half inch difference . . . could be accounted for by muscular relaxation in death.'

Despite his remark about not being able to identify the remains, Dr van Ingen nevertheless 'expressed the opinion that it was the body of the Lindbergh baby'.

As regards (3), this would seem to be a genuine mistake, either in dictation, transposition or typing (in major cases contradictions of this

---

[1] Tower Publications, New York, 1981

kind invariably occur). Had the two big toes been overlapping as well as the two little ones, Lindbergh and Betty Gow could hardly have failed to spot such a gross double abnormality.

Confirmatory evidence for Betty Gow's identification (which she is as certain about today as she was then) comes from three sources. Inspector Walsh, on being shown the piece of flannel with the scalloped, embroidered edge from which the flannel shirt with the blue thread had been cut, declared that the two were identical. Dr Mitchell, on comparing the face of the baby (in much better shape than the rest) with a photograph of him, said he was 'very much impressed it was the same child'. And finally, on leaving the morgue at Trenton, Condon had asked Dr Edward Hawks, the doctor who had attended Charlie's birth:

'There's no possible question concerning the identity of the child, is there, Doctor?'

And Hawks had replied: 'None whatsoever. The unusual overlapping of two of the child's toes would be, in itself, sufficient identification. It is Colonel Lindbergh's baby.'

Supporters of the Kerwin/Olson theory have never faced up to the consequences of their own logic, which necessitate a belief not in one kidnapping but two. If Charlie was spirited away secretly to grow up as Kerwin or Olson or anybody else, then it follows that the kidnappers miraculously found another male child 33–33½ inches long, with curly golden hair, eye-teeth just showing through the gums and overlapping little toes, kidnapped him, knocked him on the head, dressed him up in Charlie's flannel shirt and sleeveless overshirt marked 'B. Altman Co., New York', and dumped him in the woods near Hopewell. Does anyone think such a bizarre scenario likely?

Appendix III

Extracts from the report of Gunter P. Haas, British handwriting expert

After the showing of the BBC film on the case, Mr Gunter P. Haas, a leading British handwriting expert, expressed an interest in it and subsequently examined in great detail the state's handwriting exhibits, i.e. the ransom notes, Hauptmann's request writings, and Hauptmann's acknowledged writings.

At the end of a twenty-page report which listed thirty separate examples of how the ransom note writing differed from the writing of Hauptmann, Mr Haas concluded:

The differences between the ransom writing and Hauptmann's writings which have been pointed out in this report are very prominent and, I submit, far outweigh occasional similarities to which the reader's attention has been drawn.

If one studies two kinds of writing extensively, one would expect to find similarities, which would not necessarily persuade one that such writings stem from the same person. Yet Osborn says, quite rightly, in his book *Questioned Document Problems*, 'One permanent and distinctive difference of course *more than outweighs* several similarities.'

Here we are confronted with two sets of documents, both written by foreigners, both of German descent. This is clear from the frequent use of German words, spelling errors due to the mispronunciation of German words, and the angled writing.

The general appearance of Hauptmann's writing is reasonable. It shows some control, some tidiness, some discipline. The ransom note writer is a very poor writer. His writing on the whole is slow, clumsy, smudged, slovenly, you could say 'creepy-crawly': there is very little difference between pressure in upstrokes and downstrokes. This produces a different line quality which is virtually impossible to copy or disguise. In my view it would have been impossible for Hauptmann to write as the writer of the ransom notes did, or vice-versa.

In *Questioned Document Problems* Osborn claims that Hauptmann disguised his writing and that 'some of the repeated [i.e. request] writing was disguised *exactly like the ransom letters*'. The words 'exactly like' suggest that the similarity of the writings is obvious, yet I cannot find any ransom note writing so similar to Hauptmann's writing as to make one think Hauptmann had written it. Some superficial similarities are due, in my view, to the circumstances in which the dictated and/or copied documents were written and the various pens used. Yet all the Hauptmann request writings retain many if not all of Hauptmann's normal writing characteristics. So if he was trying to disguise his writing, he didn't make a very good job of it.

In any case, why would he want to disguise his writing, which would only create a greater discrepancy between his normal writing and the writing of the ransom notes which, Osborn claims, was also his?

Some of the differences I have found in comparing Hauptmann's writings with the ransom note writings have been quite startling. Hauptmann's use of the letter 'd' for instance is quite unlike anything in the ransom notes; for not only does he frequently end the letter with a downstroke well below the line, but the line becomes thinner instead of showing pressure which is more normal. Differences in the figure 'o', the capitals 'B' and 'S' and the small 'k' are equally startling.

I conclude this summary by re-affirming my opinion that the ransom letters were not written by Hauptmann.

Gunter P. Haas.
March 23rd 1983

As this book was going to press, another handwriting report was received from Mrs Hauptmann's lawyer, Robert Bryan. It had been prepared by an established American hadwriting expert, Mr Gus R. Lesnevich, formerly a documents examiner in the US army and US Secret Service. Mr Lesnevich was asked by Mr Bryan to make an independent, unbiased (and unpaid) evaluation of all the relevant writings, which he did with great thoroughness. I am grateful to Mr Bryan and to Mr Lesnevich for allowing me to publish his conclusions.

'An examination, comparison and analysis of the questioned ransom notes and known writings not used by the police, along with the additional known writings, has resulted in the conclusion that Mr Richard Hauptmann did not write the questioned ransom notes.'

Appendix IV

Letter from Richard Hauptmann to his mother, December 27 1935

Dear Mother,

Yesterday, on Christmas Day, I received your dear letter of December. Your kind words made me very happy and I thank you, dear mother.

Dear Mother, this letter will be somewhat long, for I want to go into some points regarding my trial. I will and must always, suitable to my situation, go according to the records. Also, a lie cannot help me, but would rather hurt me.

In every arrest it is customary to take fingerprints of the person arrested the first thing. So they did with me. A few days after this occurrence, two members of the N.J. State police came to me in the Bronx prison and requested further prints. I told them that the N.J. State Police had already taken my fingerprints a few days previously. I did not make this statement, perhaps, because I wanted to refuse, but it seemed somewhat unusual to me. The men replied that the prints which they had were not clear enough, so they wanted to take them again. That evening they took my prints, very firmly – altogether about six sets. My astonishment was great when one or two days later they came again with the same statement that several spots were not yet plain enough. So! they worked anew on my prints. This time they made still more sets than before and also some of the sides of the hand, which they did not take before, especially the joints of the fingers and the hollow part of the hand. Since they made these impressions ever firmer than before, I began to be worried for I had a feeling that something queer was happening.

Well, what came out at the trial when my counsel asked about finger-prints: Believe it or not, the prosecutor's staff said simply 'O, well, there were no fingerprints in existence, not on the ladder or in any part of the room where the child was, nor on the window or windowsill.' But as though to fill the measure completely, the prosecutor's staff came out with the fairy tale that they also did not find any prints of the father or mother of the unfortunate child, nor of the child's nurse or of other house servants. So! they invented another story. They said, simply, that I had worked with gloves. O, what a worthless statement: for accordingly then, all the servants and the child's nurse must also have worked only with gloves. Good heavens! is it possible when the father or mother go into the child's room in order to take joy in their child, they also put on gloves?! In that case I would truly like to know why they twice came extra to New York for my fingerprints, when none were at hand with which to compare them. Why isn't the prosecutor's staff honest and why doesn't it say openly that the fingerprints, as well as the foot prints did not match with mine. That a distinguished fingerprint expert from N.Y. found hundreds of fingerprints on the ladder alone was laughingly not recognized. They could not honor the truth for nowhere was there an impression of mine. But instead they built up indirect evidence, which cries to heaven.

The peak of the indirect evidence which was built up was the ladder story. The prosecutor said at the trial that a part of the wood of which the ladder was made came from the house where we lived – and that was not enough – I was supposed to have torn up a board from the floor of the attic (only half of which was boarded up) and to have used half of it for the ladder. This false assertion borders on the shameless. When I moved into the house, I went up into the attic and came up there (hardly to be wondered at?) only two or three times in that year. Still up to this hour, I can not say whether or not a piece of board was missing. But the most ridiculous thing about the whole ladder is, it is altogether no ladder. It is only a wooden rack and I do not believe that this rack was ever used as a ladder. Its construction shows too plainly that it never came from the hand of a carpenter, not even from a poor one. The prosecutor said, to wit, that I am not a good carpenter. I say, herewith, only that I have often worked for myself as a foreman. Every master could depend on me. Indeed, I often had to figure out the whole requirement of wood for a new construction and order the material and was also responsible for the whole job. If I wanted to make anything at home I almost always had enough wood lying in my garage, and if not, there is lumber yard only a block away from my house . . .

Mother, I could write on, but it makes me sick when I think of it. For so it went through the whole trial. State's witnesses could never swear away the blue of the heaven – it was all believed. Also they were protected by the state and this even when they contradicted themselves 200 per cent. All that played no part. The circus was on. What may the symbol of justice have thought when it had to behold all that. For the band was removed from her eyes, so that her person could see all. Well, I was a German carpenter.

How my chief counsel at the trial acted or how he could act so, I can not comprehend. According to my opinion, I believe that I was 100 per cent certain when I say that he worked with the prosecutor. I had an opportunity to explain my case to him only five minutes. He simply did not come to me, or if he came for three to five minutes, he was often drunk. How could I talk with him then.

Thus the prosecutor in his final speech changed the whole view [opinion] of the death of the poor child. But why he did it is easily explainable, for he himself could not believe the story of the ladder, for it had become in itself too threadbare, he simply changed the whole discussion of the culmination. For it was the assumption of the state that the ladder broke when the ostensible man climbed down with the child, and for six weeks it was discussed thus that the ladder broke in this manner. But all that meant nothing to the prosecutor. So when the hearing of everyone was over and my counsel had also spoken, so that there was no more opportunity to refute it, the prosecutor changed the whole view. I hardly believe that such a thing has ever been in history before. So much sand was thrown in the eyes of the jury and their minds so inflamed through the speech of the prosecutor that they hardly knew longer what was in or out.

The packet with the money I found again in the middle of August, 1934, and since I did not know what money it was, I spent it the same as any other money. I never tried to hide my identity in so doing. I also told the police immediately that I had spent 12 to 15 bills. That is all, and this was after the 15th of August, 1934. The police tried everything possible to prove that I passed a $5 bill on November 26, 1933 in a movie. It was fortunate that this day happens to be my birthday, so I knew where I was, for on that day and at this same hour, I celebrated my birthday with friends at our house. This my witnesses swore to also.

Dear mother, you can hardly conceive how I feel when I think about the whole 'built-up' affair. I must be here in this place and suffer for something of which I know nothing and people who laugh outside and hold festivals amuse themselves at my expense. I cannot see my child, in whom my whole heart is placed, in this world. My God, my God! Where is justice in this world.

Where I was arrested, they almost crippled me by beating in order to apprehend something which is not in me. There are, indeed, societies for prevention of cruelty to animals, but, unfortunately, not for men. Where is the humanity steering, which is in this world in Christ's name.

Dear mother, I have written you only a small part. If I wanted to write down everything, it would comprise volumes. If there is any shame in this case then it lies on the shoulders of the prosecutor, for I have carried on in this case with a clear conscience.

In the hope that justice will conquer, I greet you most affectionately,
Your dear son,
Richard

Chronology

Lindbergh		Hauptmann
	1899	Born in Kamenz, Germany.
Born in Little Falls, Minnesota.	1902	
	1914–18	Apprenticeship in carpentry and
Leaves school to farm homestead.	1918	mechanical engineering.
	1919	Returns to Kamenz. Convicted of
Learns to fly and joins flying circus.	1920	charges of robbery and larceny and sentenced to five years' imprisonment.
	1923	Released from prison.
Joins army air corps.	1924	After two unsuccessful attempts reaches America as a stowaway.
	1925	Marries Anna Schoeffler.
Chief pilot, airmail service St Louis to Chicago.	1926	
First man to fly Atlantic alone. Journey from New York to Paris in single-engine Spirit of St Louis takes thirty-three hours. Overnight becomes America's Number One hero. Flies to Mexico City as special guest of US Ambassador Dwight Morrow, and falls in love with his second daughter Anne.	1927	
Charles and Anne married at Englewood, New Jersey.	1929	
Birth of Charles Augustus, Junior.	1930	
	1925–31	Earning good money as carpenter and waitress, Richard and Anna save more than $10,000.
Charles and Anne fly to China via northern Canada, Siberia and Japan.	1931	
	Summer	The Hauptmanns go on automobile trip to California with Hans Kloppenburg.
	October	They move into upper apartment at 1279 222nd Street. Hauptmann builds garage on adjoining plot.
Their house near Hopewell, New Jersey, is ready for occupation.	1932	
Charles Junior kidnapped. Demands for ransom money.	March 1	Hauptmann begins work at Majestic Apartments on Manhattan's West Side.
Lindbergh accepts Dr John F. Condon as intermediary with the kidnap gang.	March 10	
Condon meets one of the gang in the Bronx's Woodlawn Cemetery.	March 12	
Condon hands over $50,000 ransom money to one of the gang in the Bronx's St Raymond's Cemetery. Sitting in car, Lindbergh hears voice in cemetery shout to Condon, 'Hey, Doc!'	April 2	Hands in notice at Majestic Apartments. Musical evening with Hans Kloppenburg.

First ransom bill found by a bank teller. In the months to come, others follow.	April 4	
Body of Charles Junior found murdered in woods near Hopewell.	May 12	
Violet Sharpe, English maid in the Morrow household, commits suicide.	June 10	
	June–September	Anna in Germany.
	October	Hauptmann begins ill-fated business partnership with Isidor Fisch, a furrier.
	1933	
	January	Trip to Florida. Anna conceives.
	Summer	Continuous business dealings with Fisch who, unknown to
Charles and Anne on proving flight to Europe via Greenland, Iceland and Shetland and back via Spain, West Africa and Brazil.	July–December	Hauptmann, is conning money from mutual friends for defunct Knickerbocker Pie Company, and also buying 'hot' money at discount.
	November 3	Manfred Hauptmann born.
	November 26	Richard's birthday party. Fisch gives him a pen.
	December 2	Richard and Anna give farewell party for Fisch who is going on a visit to Germany. Fisch leaves with Hauptmanns a batch of skins, two suitcases and a shoe-box wrapped in paper.
	December 6	Fisch sails for Europe with Henry Uhlig, owing Hauptmann $5500 on their fur account and $2000 for Fisch's steamship ticket.
	1934	
	March 29	Fisch dies of consumption in Leipzig.
	May–June	Hauptmann and Uhlig make exhaustive searches for Fisch's assets in New York, but find nothing.
	August	Hauptmann discovers more than $14,000 in gold certificate bills in Fisch's shoe-box, and begins to spend them.
	September 16	Gold certificate bill presented by Hauptmann to a Bronx filling station is recognized as part of Lindbergh ransom money.
Lindbergh testifies before Bronx Grand Jury. Later, in disguise in the office of the Bronx District Attorney, he listens to Hauptmann shouting 'Hey, Doc!'	September 19	Hauptmann arrested. Ransom money found in his garage.
	September 25	Hauptmann indicted by Bronx Grand Jury for extortion.
	October 19	Hauptmann loses plea to Bronx Appeal Court against extradition to New Jersey on charges of murder and kidnapping, and is taken to Flemington, N.J., to await trial.

	1935	
	January 2–	
At trial of Hauptmann Lindbergh testifies that voice he heard at St Raymond's Cemetery on April 2, 1932, was that of Hauptmann.	February 13 January 3	'The Trial of the Century', which makes national and international headlines. Hauptmann found guilty of first degree murder, sentenced to death and taken to Death Row at the State Prison at Trenton, N.J.
Lindbergh attends trial daily.	January 4– February 13	
	May 2	Hauptmann's appeal lodged with Court of Errors and Appeals
Lindberghs at North Haven, and on flying visits to his relations in Minnesota.	Summer	
	October 9	Appeal rejected.
	October 16	Governor Harold Hoffman visits Hauptmann and has doubts about his guilt.
Harassed by press and public, and with Hauptmann's execution scheduled for the New Year, the Lindberghs sail for England on an indefinite stay.	December 21	
	1936	
	January 11	New Jersey's Court of Pardons confirms death sentence, set for January 17.
	Janaury 16	Hoffmann grants Hauptmann thirty-day reprieve.
	March 30	Court of Pardons refuses further appeal.
	March 31	Execution postponed by Warden of State Prison.
	April 3	Hauptmann electrocuted, maintaining innocence to the end.

Sources

GENERAL BOOKS

CONDON, John F. *Jafsie Tells All*, Jonathan Lee Publishing Corporation, New York, 1936

DAVIS, Kenneth S. *The Hero*, Longmans, London, 1960

DUTCH, Andrew K. *Hysteria*, Dorrance, Philadelphia, 1975

ELLIOTT, Robert G. with Albert R. Beatty. *Agent of Death*, E.P. Dutton and Co, New York, 1940

HARING, J. Vreeland. *The Hand of Hauptmann*, Hamer Publishing Co, Plainfield, New Jersey, 1937

LEES-MILNE, James. *Harold Nicolson, A Biography*, Vol II 1930–1968, Chatto and Windus, London/Archon Books, New York 1981

LINDBERGH, Anne Morrow. *North to the Orient*, Harcourt Brace, New York, 1935

LINDBERGH, Anne Morrow. *Listen, the Wind*, Harcourt Brace, New York, 1938

LINDBERGH, Anne Morrow. *Hour of Gold, Hour of Lead. Diaries and Letters 1929–1932*, Harcourt Brace Jovanovich, New York, 1973

LINDBERGH, Anne Morrow. *Locked Rooms and Open Doors. Diaries and Letters 1933–1935*, Harcourt Brace Jovanovich, New York, 1974

LINDBERGH, Anne Morrow. *The Flower and the Nettle. Diaries and Letters 1936–1939*, Harcourt Brace Jovanovich, New York, 1976

LINDBERGH, Anne Morrow. *War Within and War Without. Diaries and Letters 1939–1944*, Harcourt Brace Jovanovich, New York, 1980

LINDBERGH, Charles. *The Spirit of St Louis*, John Murray, London/Charles Scribner's Sons, New York, 1953

LINDBERGH, Charles. *Boyhood on the Upper Mississippi*, Minnesota Historical Society, 1972

MOSLEY, Leonard. *Lindbergh*, Hodder and Stoughton, London/Doubleday, New York, 1976

NICOLSON, Nigel (ed). *Harold Nicolson, Diaries and Letters 1930–1939*, Collins, London/Atheneum, New York, 1966

OSBORN, Albert D. *Questioned Document Problems*, Boyd Printing Co., Albany, New York, 1944

ROSS, Walter S. *The Last Hero*, Harper and Row, New York, 1976

SCADUTO, Anthony. *Scapegoat*, Secker and Warburg, London/Putnams, New York, 1976

SHOENFELD, Dudley D. *The Crime and the Criminal. A Psychiatric Study of the Lindbergh Case*. Covici-Friede, New York, 1936

SULLIVAN, Edward Dean. *The Snatch Racket,* The Vanguard Press, New York, 1932

TURROU, Leon G. *Where my Shadow Falls*, Doubleday and Co, New York, 1949

WALLER, George. *Kidnap*, Hamish Hamilton, London/Dial Books, New York, 1961

WHIPPLE, Sidney B. *The Lindbergh Crime*, Blue Ribbon Books, New York, 1935

WRIGHT, Theon. *In Search of the Lindbergh Baby*, Tower Publications, New York, 1981

WILSON, Frank J. and DAY, Beth. *Special Agent*, Holt, Rinehart and Winston, New York, 1965

REFERENCE BOOKS

The Bronx. New York City Guide, Random House, New York, 1939
Plan for New York, Vol II. The Bronx, New York City Planning Commission, 1969
World Encyclopaedia and Book of Facts, 1932–34

MAGAZINE ARTICLES AND PERIODICALS

ANON. 'The trial of the century' in *Exploring Hunterdon's Heritage*, Vol 1, No 1, Winter 1981

BENT, Silas. 'Lindbergh and the press' in *Outlook*, April 1932

CONDON, John F. 'Jafsie tells all' in *Liberty Magazine*, January 18, 25; February 1, 8, 15, 22, 29; March 7, 14, 21, 1936

CURTIN, D. Thomas, and FINN, Lieutenant James J. 'How I captured Hauptmann' in *Liberty Magazine*, October 12, 19, 26; November 2, 9, 16, 23, 1935

DAVIDSON, David. 'The story of the century' in *Worldwide Magazine*

FISHER, Lloyd C. 'The Case New Jersey would like to forget' in *Liberty Magazine*, August 1, 8, 15, 22, 29; September 5, 12, 1936

HAUPTMANN, Bruno Richard. 'Why did you kill me?' in *Liberty Magazine*, May 2, 1936

HOFFMAN, Harold G. 'Things I forgot to tell' in *Liberty Magazine*, July 2, 1938

HOFFMAN, Harold G. 'More things I forgot to tell' in *Liberty Magazine*, July 9, 1938

HOFFMAN, Harold G. 'What was wrong with the Lindbergh case' in *Liberty Magazine*, January 29; February 5, 12, 19, 26; March 5, 12, 19, 26; April 2, 9, 16, 23, 30, 1938

HYND, Alan. 'Everybody wanted to get in on the act' in *True*, March 1949

KOEHLER, Arthur. 'Technique used in tracking the Lindbergh kidnapping ladder.' *Journal of Criminal Law and Criminology*, Vol 27, No 5, 1936–37

LEVY, Norman. 'Justice goes tabloid' in *American Mercury*, April 1935

PROSSER, William L. Review of George Waller's *Kidnap* in *Minnesota Law Review*, Vol 46, 1962

ROBBINS, Albert D. 'The Hauptmann trial in the light of English procedure in.' *The American Bar Association Journal*.

SEIDMAN, Louis M. 'The trial and execution of Bruno Richard Hauptmann' in *The Georgetown Law Journal*, Vol 66, October 1977

THACHER, Thomas D. 'Trial by newspaper' in *The American Bar Association Journal*, September 15 1936

WEBSTER, Goodwin B. 'The Press invades Hopewell' in *Christian Century*, April 27 1932

WEDEMAR, Lou. '50 unanswered questions in the Hauptmann case' in *Liberty Magazine*, January 4 1936

WILSON, P.W. 'The Lindbergh case' in *North American Review*, January 1934

YAGODA, Ben. 'Legacy of a kidnapping' in *New Jersey Monthly*, Vol 5, August 1981

ZEITZ, Carl. 'Hauptmann letter discovered' in *Trenton Times*, March 28 1977

ZITO, Tom. 'Did the evidence fit the crime?' in *Life Magazine*, March 1982

NEWSPAPERS

Atlantic City Sunday Press, Baltimore American, Baltimore News Post, Bronx Home News, Camden Courier Post, Chicago Daily Tribune, Detroit News, Hunterdon County Courier News, Hunterdon County Democrat, Jersey Journal, New Jersey Record, New York American, New York Daily Mirror, New York Daily News, New York Evening Journal, New York Herald Tribune, New York Times, New York World Telegram, Philadelphia Evening Ledger, Philadelphia Record, Salt Lake Telegram, Sunday Bulletin, and many others.

OFFICIAL DOCUMENTS

Reports by and/or statements to:
Bronx District Attorney
Jersey City Police
Metropolitan Police, District of Columbia
New Jersey State Police
New York City Police

US Department of Justice, Division of Investigation
US Treasury Department, Internal Revenue Service

Report by Lieutenant A. L. Smith, Flemington Guards' Details, October 20 1934 – February 12 1935

Trial of Bruno Richard Hauptmann. The trial record (pp. 1–4791) and state exhibits.

Appeal of Bruno Richard Hauptmann to the New Jersey Court of Errors and Appeals, June 20 1935, and Reply Brief for the State of New Jersey.

Judgment of the Court of Errors and Appeals, October 9 1935

Petition of Bruno Richard Hauptmann to the United States Supreme Court, October Term, 1935, No 582

Suit of Anna Hauptmann against the State of New Jersey and others, October 14 1981 and second, third and fourth amended complaints.

Opinion of US District Court Judge Frederick B. Lacey, dismissing the above, August 11 1983

MISCELLANEOUS

Hawke, George. Trial by Fury. A thesis presented to the Department of Politics, Princeton University, April 27, 1951

Television interview between Eric Severeid and Anne Morrow Lindbergh, 1977. (Museum of Broadcasting, New York City)

Speech of Charles A. Lindbergh to the Washington Press Club, June 11, 1927 (Museum of Broadcasting, New York City)

Correspondence and/or interviews with:

Mr and Mrs Albert Axelrod, Lewis J. Bornmann, Robert R. Bryan, Betty Gow, Gunter Haas, Anna Hauptmann, Hans Kloppenburg, Anne Morrow Lindbergh, Trudi Morris, Cornel Plebani, Ethel Stockton, Henry Uhlig.

Index

Nothing
Happened

Nothing Happened

molly booth

HYPERION

Los Angeles ✶ New York

First Edition, May 2018
10 9 8 7 6 5 4 3 2 1
FAC-020093-18089
Printed in the United States of America

This book is set in Avenir LT Std, Bembo MT Pro, Wingdings/Monotype; Bambusa Pro, Brandon Grotesque, Hey Comrade, Janda Elegant Handwriting, Larissa Handwriting, Marcello Handwriting, Museo, TT Berlinerins, Wanderlust/Fontspring
Designed by Whitney Manger

Library of Congress Cataloging-in-Publication Data

Names: Booth, Molly, author.
Title: Nothing happened / Molly Booth.
Description: First edition. • Los Angeles ; New York : Hyperion, 2018. •
  Summary: "Modern-day retelling of Shakespeare's Much Ado About Nothing
  taking place at an idyllic summer camp where the counselors have to cope
  with simmering drama"— Provided by publisher.
Identifiers: LCCN 2017034518 (print) • LCCN 2017045796 (ebook) • ISBN
  9781484758533 (ebook) • ISBN 9781484753026 (hardcover : alk. paper)
Subjects: • CYAC: Camps—Fiction. • Interpersonal relations—Fiction. •
  Love—Fiction. • Family life—Maine—Fiction. • Maine—Fiction.
Classification: LCC PZ7.1.B668 (ebook) • LCC PZ7.1.B668 Not 2018 (print) •
  DDC [Fic]—dc23
LC record available at https://lccn.loc.gov/2017034518

Reinforced binding

Visit www.hyperionteens.com

For Bonnie
whose insight and support flicker between
every word in this book

CHAPTER 1

Bee

I FOUGHT THE URGE to crumple the paper, shove it in my mouth, and eat it.

Flip-flops for the shower

Bucket for toiletries

Notebooks, pens, etc. will be available at the store

Why did my college's packing suggestions look so much like a list for summer camp?

Ugh. I wasn't supposed to have to deal with this for months. Packing. Moving. Boston.

"What's that?" My sister, Hana, peeked over my shoulder.

"Nothing!" I stuffed the list back in the envelope.

"If it's not about camp, you can look at it later," my mom said. We were all in the living room on our faded yellow floral sofa, huddled over the coffee table stacked high with mail. Our annual Leonato family spring camp paperworkfest! Every year, my parents picked a weekend in April—shortly after the application deadline—for us to organize our camp's employment for the coming summer. Counselor and activity leader applications; CITs.

I felt Hana's eyes watching me and my envelope with concern.

I knew my family was really going to miss me when I left—especially after this year, with everything Hana had gone through.

They didn't need to know how my stomach sank every time I thought about college.

Hana opened her mouth to say something, but I quickly cut her off—

"Good idea, I'll look at it later!" I resealed the envelope and hurled the entire packet behind me. It landed with a *smack!* somewhere in the dining room. Hana smiled. Sadness avoided, for now.

"Bee . . ." Mom's severe brow furrowed in my direction.

"What?" I said. "You told me to!"

"You could've broken something."

My dad carried in another gigantic armful of envelopes and dropped them in a pile on the floor. "That's it: next year, Camp Dogberry is going digital." Mom shot him a look. He gestured emphatically at the mountain of mail. "Nik, come *on*! Look at this! We're the opposite of eco-friendly. We're eco-mean."

Mom sighed. She abhorred technology. "I know you're right. As much as I hate to admit it. But, no"—she pointed a finger at my sister—"that does not mean you can use your phone at camp, Hana."

Hana turned red. We'd both gotten smartphones a few years ago, and ever since she'd been glued to hers.

"The no–cell phones rule is important," I said. "Don't forget the legend of *The Idiot CIT and the Bear.*"

"I don't think I remember that one." Dad grinned. "Bee, would you—"

"Maine is known for blueberries and bears," I began, in my narrator voice, standing up and taking my place in the living room archway. No sense in not being completely dramatic about this. "Camp Dogberry, in Messina, Maine, was practically bursting with blueberries. As for bears, rumors floated around camp. Largely because of one dangerous incident: *The Idiot CIT and . . . the Bear.*"

"Dun-dun-duuuuuun," Dad added in.

"One summer, loooong ago, a young, dewy-eyed counselor-in-training was going for his early morning run, with headphones in." I mimed a slow jog, bobbing my head back and forth. "The headphones were plugged into his cell phone, on which he played *loud music.* This was his fatal mistake."

"Not quite fatal," Mom said, undermining my narrative.

"He set off around the coastline, blasting music into his ears instead of enjoying the harmonious sounds of nature. So loud were his tunes that he didn't hear rustling in the bushes. Thus, it came as quite a shock when a real live bear cub tumbled onto the path in front of him. Awww! he thought. A baby bear! How cute! I am clearly not in any danger!"

"Have we confirmed with the original source that this was his exact thought process?" Dad asked.

"The CIT stood transfixed by the adorableness of the bear cub. With the music still blasting into his ears, he was unaware of the approaching danger. Suddenly, he felt hot breath on the back of his neck. He froze." I froze. "He turned." I turned. "And directly behind him was an enormous black bear. A mama bear's job is to protect her kids, and she was afraid this clueless human was somehow going to hurt her baby bear. She didn't know the CIT was harmless. What would the CIT do now? What would you do? Because I guarantee, it's not this:

"The CIT grabbed two pine branches and waved them back and forth as he backed away, screaming, 'OLD MACDONALD HAD A FARM. EEEEYI EEEYI OOOOOH!!!'

"At this noise, Mama Bear stopped in her tracks, dumbfounded, and quite frankly, artistically offended. She realized that this creature was not dangerous, but totally ridiculous. She let the CIT turn around and run back to camp, where he did about five hundred jumping jacks to release his adrenaline, and then passed out on Monarch field.

"And that, kids," I finished, "is why we don't use cell phones at camp."

My family dutifully gave me a round of applause, to which I bowed deeply.

"Excellent performance as always, Bee," Dad said. "But I don't remember this cautionary tale making fun of the CIT quite so mercilessly. For instance, I don't think *idiot* is in the title."

"Okay, so I made some changes." I rolled my eyes and stepped over the table to drop down next to him again. "Stories evolve." I ignored the itchy guilt that crept up the backs of my arms. This story was funnier when the idiot CIT and I were still friends.

"Dad's right." Mom moved a handful of forms down the line. "We don't use the word *idiot* at camp. You know that."

"Obviously, I won't tell it like that *at camp*," I assured them.

"You can tell it however you want when you run the place." Dad smiled. "You can fill it with swears."

"I *am* running the place!"

"You're the assistant improv leader," Mom corrected. New title this year—it sounded so official. I loved it. Plus it meant I got to spend most of the camp day with our longtime improv leader, and one of my best camp friends, Raphael.

"Preeetty sure that means I'm a boss."

"Okay, boss, have a look at this application and let me know what you think." Mom passed me an envelope.

I bent back the metal fastener and slid out the packet of papers. The heading *Camp Dogberry Counselor Application* in our official green camp font, with little pine and dogwood trees on either side, greeted me. When my eyes landed on the applicant name, I had to fight another urge to crumple up the papers and shove them in my mouth. The staple would pose a problem, but I could spit it out like a cherry pit—

"What the hell?" I finally managed. I looked up right into Mom's eyes. Same eyes as Hana—big, light brown in the middle, dark brown on the edges. Like tree rings. Mom's usually reflected that firm, parental love, but now they were straight-up laughing at me.

"Seems promising, right?" She tried to keep from smirking. But not that hard. "Ben Rosenthal. He's applying for sports leader."

"Ben?!" Hana gasped.

"Do you think he's right for the job?" Mom asked.

Was this a joke? "Sure, unless we care about the sports program," I replied, still dazed.

"Wait, seriously, it's really him?" Hana hopped up and looked over my shoulder. I wanted to block her view, but my arms and hands didn't move when I told them to. "Ben? Ben's coming back?!" She squealed in my ear.

"I guess?" I handed her the application.

"Huzzah!" Dad clapped his big bear hands.

"But I thought last year was his *last year*?" Hana said, examining the application critically. I'd done the same thing, but it was definitely his handwriting—it looked like a chicken on a seesaw had filled it out.

"He certainly announced that many times," I growled. "What a dingus. I should've seen this coming."

Mom had moved on and was waving the next envelope. "Well, he's not the only one going back on his vow. Here's *Donald King* too."

"Both of them?" I demanded. "Unreal. They kept calling dibs on stuff last summer because it was their *last summer*. They got more breaks and chocolate and beer—" I stopped, quickly. Neither parent reacted, thank goodness.

Hana hopped over to Mom and grabbed the packet. "This is awesome!"

Truthfully, yes, I was excited that Donald was returning to camp. He always brought a special something to Camp Dogberry that no one else did. He was really cool—too cool—so he made everything at camp seem cool for the campers. And for the counselors, too.

"You're right, it's awesome," I said. "But what is *Ben* doing back at camp? Isn't he a doctor or something?"

"He's only been in college for a year!" Dad laughed.

"Well, it's pathetic." I shook my head. "He made this huge deal about 'moving on,' and now he's just, like, applied? Without saying anything?"

"What else would he say?" Mom asked.

That was a loaded question—one I was not prepared to answer.

"I don't know!" I sputtered. "He didn't call either of you, did he?"

Mom and Dad exchanged a glance. "Colleen might've mentioned something," Dad admitted. Colleen. Ben's mom.

Mom tapped his application. "And Ben might've called me a few weeks ago—"

"Seriously?!" I yelled.

"—to ask if applying for sports leader would be appropriate."

"He's a nice kid." Dad nodded.

"He is." Mom smiled back.

"I'm going to kill you both!" I threw up my hands. What were parents good for? I turned on Hana: "Did you know about this?"

"No!" she said quickly. "I haven't heard from him since he texted me on my birthday. . . ."

Ouch. I hadn't heard from Ben on *my* birthday. I looked down and scowled into my hands. Imagined his face on a grape. Squished the grape in my palm.

"But, Bee?" Hana's soft voice interrupted. "Isn't it better to have Ben back? Camp wouldn't be the same without him."

I looked up. She blinked at me. Hana acts all naive, but she's sneaky, that one. I shot her a death glare, extra death. Then I threw another application toward her.

"What about *you*, Hana? Would camp be the same without *Claudia*?"

She saw the name on the envelope and immediately dropped it like a hot marshmallow.

"Of course!" she said, voice screeching up an octave. "It's great they're *all* coming back!"

My parents looked at us both dubiously. Then Hana attempted her own version of a death glare. Her round eyes twitched. I laughed—it was like a stink eye from a baby seal. My sister was the cutest person alive, and glares didn't even work on her face.

"Ben, Donald, Claudia, and here's Margo!" Dad raised up another application. That broke up some tension: we all cheered for Margo. I already knew she was coming back, because we had one of those summer friendships that kept going the rest of the year.

"Excellent!" Dad smiled. "The Dogberry dream team. We're barely going to have to hire anyone new."

"I wouldn't be that heartbroken if, say, *Bobby* or *John* didn't come back," I muttered.

"That's not a very *teamwork* attitude," Mom chided.

Dad held up John's application. Crap. Well, he came with Donald.

"Okay." I nodded. "But more importantly, if *Ben* had miraculously got a life, would it really be that much of a loss?"

"All right." Mom sighed, running a hand along her right temple. "Bee, you have a couple months before camp starts, so work on losing that attitude. I can't take another summer like last year. You and Ben are friends."

"Not till it snows in July," I retorted. Friends. Friendly, friendly friends. "He's the biggest pain-in-the-butt friend I've ever had," I added. "And a seriously lazy employee." I cringed even as I said it. She was right, though—I needed to shut up. The bigger deal I made out of this, the worse the whole situation would be. And besides, it had been almost a year. When was I going to stop associating Ben with that one awkward night? I'd known him for six years before that. It made no sense, and it made me want to slap myself.

"You know Ben's got his strengths," Mom said. "Not everyone's good at getting up early."

"He *is* champion of Capture the Flag." Dad grinned at Mom. "Man. I really can't wait for camp to start."

"I'm starting to dread it." I stood up. "I need a break. I'll go into town and get us lunch."

"Pizza, please!" Dad brightened. "And can you stop at Reny's and grab us a pack of highlighters?"

"And clothespins," Mom added. We'd just hung up our laundry line.

"You got it!" I hurried toward the front door.

"I'll come with you!" Hana jumped up.

Argh. I wanted to be alone, but I didn't want to tell her no. She'd been a little clingy since my college acceptance letters. Look at me, I mentally muttered. Calling my sister clingy. This was Ben's fault. Before last summer, I never needed time alone to think. I did my best thinking *with* Hana. Now I had secrets.

"Parents—" I turned back to them as I pulled on my boots. "Let's not be hasty. I'm sure there are other qualified sports candidates."

"Bee, your promotion to assistant improv leader does not, I'm afraid, give you hiring and firing power." Mom waved me away. Insulting.

"Sorry, kiddo." Dad nodded. "Capture the Flag is my favorite part of camp, and Ben *is* Capture the Flag."

"I repeat: ugh."

I let the screen door slam on our way out. I usually looked forward to this time of the year. I felt the climbing anticipation—every form we filled out, every permit stamped and hire made, was another step toward starting day. Sun and sweat and laughter.

But this Ben thing pulled me up short; threw me.

Out the door, Hana had a mission. "Want to go look at the waves real quick?"

My sister loved all bodies of water, but particularly our waterfront, the pebbly edges of Messina Harbor. This coming summer would be her first as a full-fledged lifeguard and swim instructor, which meant she got to spend all day teaching campers to swim. And when she wasn't doing that, she'd be swimming just for herself. I'd known Hana since she was three and I was five, when my parents adopted me and brought me to the US from Ethiopia. They'd originally planned on adopting a baby, but when they got to the adoption center, I'd jumped into their laps and demanded a story, and that was the end of that. Luckily, it was a love-at-first-sight kind of deal for Hana and me. Being sisters was clearly our destiny.

I remember watching her in the pool, though, at our YMCA, and feeling slightly five-year-old suspicious. When I showed up, she could already dive and swim across the deep end.

These suspicions had not waned. I'd never been able to confirm Hana wasn't actually a mermaid.

"Sure, let's go."

We set off down the trail. I tried to shake off Ben, but my thoughts kept drifting back to him. Well, things around/adjacent to him. Sparklers and snowflakes. Grass blades and eyelashes.

"Are you okay?" Hana poked my side.

I smiled instantly. "I'm fine!"

"It *is* a little weird Donald and Ben are coming back," she ventured. "When they swore so many times they wouldn't."

"Yeah." I nodded. *Don't take the bait, Bee.* We walked the trail in silence for a few moments, while I fought my dangerously impulsive mouth. Hana checked her phone five times in a minute. She caught me looking at her and blushed.

"Maybe you're right," she admitted. "Maybe I am looking forward to seeing Claudia."

"Oh really?" I teased, relieved by the change of subject.

"Really," she admitted. "But I don't know if I'm over Christopher."

I bit my tongue. Come *on*! At least Claudia was someone new for Hana to obsess over. Not that jerkwad Christopher, who'd yanked her around all year, then dumped her, reducing my beautiful Hana to a phantom who could barely get out of bed.

"Okay," I said. "But what if this summer, we just did our own thing?"

"What?" I could already hear the defensiveness in her voice.

"I just mean . . ." I fought for the right words. "What if we just swim, and play improv games, do crafts, and hang out with Margo—"

I cut myself off with a sharp breath in. We had reached the part of the path where it divided into three separate trails: One led to the center of camp and our giant log cabin mess hall—Beaver Dam—and the sandy clearing out front with the flagpole. The second led to our swimming waterfront. Docks, buddy board, all that camp swim stuff.

And then there was the third option: a steep, scraggly path, hidden in the summer by ferns that were just starting to revive now. This little trail led up to Eagle's Nest, a clearing at the top of a hill hidden by trees, with a perfect view of the stars. AKA Nest, one of our counselor party spots.

Last Fourth of July, after our annual sparkler party, two of the counselors had stayed behind to clean up and had returned to their respective cabins just before morning meeting, causing wild intrigue and rumors to fly throughout camp.

That night.

"Bee," Hana's soft voice ventured.

"What?"

"Last summer . . . with you and Ben—"

"Oh my God." I groaned and stalked toward the water. "I've told you a hundred times: *nothing* happened."

CHAPTER 2

Hana

BEE WAS TERRIBLE at keeping secrets. She always cracked and spilled her guts. When we were little, if we did anything wrong, like take extra cookies or break a glass, I knew Bee would confess the second Mom walked in the room.

"Mom, I am *so* sorry, but we *betrayed* you *again*!" she would announce, bursting into tears. Eventually I figured out that if I wanted extra cookies, I had to keep my big sister in the dark.

So how had she kept this secret all year? I wished for the millionth time that she would confide in me. But I'd learned to let the question go, and for the millionth time, I did.

The sea felt gorgeous—wind danced across the water, flicking spray onto my face. Thick fog had rolled in, concealing the little island off our shore. I scooped some of the freezing ocean into my water bottle.

Bee stood on the swim dock, arms crossed, staring ahead into the haze. Her tall, dark silhouette almost disappeared into the mist. I wondered what song from *Les Mis* was playing in her head.

"Bee!" I called cheerfully. "Let's go get pizza!"

ﻭﮭ

After dinner, Bee announced she was done for the day, and she'd be in the den studying. My parents both looked at me pointedly— Bee's love of paperwork was legendary, and I knew they wanted me to follow, ask her what was wrong. But I just shrugged back at them; I knew she wanted to be left alone.

Instead I went up to my bedroom and poured this afternoon's saltwater into one of the glass vases on my windowsill. The bits of sand and plant swirled. This vase was halfway full now—it was my seventh. A long line of little vases, holding bouquets of waves.

My therapist, Louisa, and I had developed these "coping skills" to help with my depression. "Exercise" (swimming), "sleep schedule" (I'm not great at this), "school" (I kind of didn't do homework last fall), and "self care" (semi-insane craft projects).

My bedroom reflected the last one. A line of water vases, a stack of "adult & teen!" coloring books, and a shoe box full of tiny lucky origami stars, which I folded obsessively. I'd cleared out the camp art building, Painted Turtle, of all the rainbow origami paper. Still have to tell Mom about that.

When summer started, Donald and Ellen, our art leader, would give me new crafts to do. Tie-dye T-shirts, friendship bracelets, lumpy handmade candles . . . I could spend all day between the ocean and Painted Turtle. Just swimming and crafting.

And absolutely no Christopher.

I paused my social studies reading to check my phone.

No Christopher, even if I wanted him.

My ex . . . whatever. I guess I couldn't really call him an ex-boyfriend. We'd never been official. But he was still my ex-*something*.

I just needed to get through the next month and a half of school. Three more swim meets, three more papers, one guy I still couldn't shake. I mean, he mostly ignored me at school anyway, which was good. My therapist and I agreed it was good.

Except that I spent most of the school day waiting for him to accidentally make eye contact with me. I didn't tell Louisa that.

Suddenly, my phone lit up. Three texts in a row, all from Claudia.

> No way. I had no idea they were coming back. Texting them now

> Those idiots. What happened to "this is our LAST SUMMER"?!

> TBH I'm excited though. That just made this summer even better

I smiled and quickly typed back.

> Same!! I really can't wait

Claudia. Once we got going, we'd be up till two or three talking. It didn't matter what we talked about. I just liked this routine: I liked that someone else was awake that late, too; I liked that the later it got, the flirtier we'd get; I liked that every part of me would grow warmer, just for a few hours.

> Seriously. School needs to be over

> ☹ I know those feels. But we're so close!

> Yes. And then we'll be together

Together. That was such an incredible word. I melted reading it. Being apart made that word different. *Together* meant in the same place, her body in front of mine, and hearing her voice, soft and smoldering, like charcoal pencil strokes.

Claudia lived in Connecticut, hours away. We never saw each other, except for summers. All of this texting started a few months ago, during a weekend when Christopher had blown me off again. But it got more intense in the last couple months, when Chris and I had split. Well, he'd split from me. And I'd just wanted someone to talk to—and suddenly, she was there, in my messages, whenever I needed her.

And I'd felt that glow begin.

Sometimes I looked at pictures of her online and just stared, dumbfounded. Black hair streaked with gray and white strands, wiry arms, serious lips that grudgingly loosened into smiles. Could this beautiful person really be on the other end of these conversations? It didn't feel real.

Somewhere around eleven, Bee appeared in my doorway, catching me by surprise. She looked at the phone in my hands, said a tight "Good night, I love you," and then I heard a knob click.

I knew she was just worried about me, but it still hurt.

> Sometimes I wish my sister wasn't so judge-y

> Ha! It's not like she doesn't have secrets too. *Cough cough* Ben *cough cough*

We stayed up till three thirty, the longest we've ever talked. Claudia complained about her old, crappy group of friends. I told her about drama on our swim team. We whined about school and would it ever end? I think we both knew, even if we couldn't say it, what the end of the year meant:

The beginning of us. Maybe?

In between texts, I folded star after star, pinching my summer hopes into the paper points.

CHAPTER 3

Ben

FOR THE LAST EIGHT YEARS, the end of June meant one thing—the beginning of Camp Dogberry. But Camp Dogberry meant a lot of things: wheezing in dusty cabins, no sleep, mosquito bites on sunburns, complete responsibility for a million children, the same food for two months straight, and boats. I hate boats.

Also, camp meant this one person, whose wicked laughter and glares I brought home at the end of summer. And like every June, I felt, like, so excited to see her. But I tried to squash those habitual feelings, told them to cool it. We hadn't so much as texted this entire year. Did she hate me? I had no idea where we stood anymore.

And *also* also, whatever, more importantly, Camp Dogberry meant my best friends and the best place in the entire world. Especially after spending a year trapped in the city of Boston, summer camp in Maine seemed like a rural paradise.

But this June wasn't supposed to be about camp. I'd made a solemn vow last year that it was my *last year.* I'd declared this, publicly, many times. I knew finding summer internships during college would be important, and any part of me that still clung to the idea of coming back was blown to smithereens that one night. After that

I'd just plain sworn off Camp Dogberry forever. Which was terrible, because I loved it.

Life was so complicated.

And there I was, year nine, waking up at fudge o'clock, rolling off the couch, grabbing a sleeping bag, kind of brushing my teeth, kissing my sisters' sleeping heads . . . then getting Layla a cup of water because she'd woken up when I'd kissed her sleeping head.

Finally, I wrote a note to my mom and left it on our new kitchen island.

"Ben! Look! Our own private island!" Mom had said, beaming, when we'd moved in the week before. I still wasn't used to her real smiles, but they automatically made me grin back.

I stumbled down the apartment building stairs, outside, and into Claudia's car.

The great thing about Claudia was that she understood I was not a human before ten a.m. I got in the car, we grunted at each other, she turned on the radio, and next thing, I woke up to the sound of tires crushing gravel as we pulled into the familiar Dogberry parking lot. Counselors' families and cars swarming, the smudged white check-in tent waiting to the left. I felt at home, but also like I might throw up.

"Ben, are we gonna get out or what?"

I startled, realizing that I'd been spacing out into the bushes in front of the car. When I looked at Claudia, I startled again at her new hair. For as long as I'd known her, Claudia'd had this long black sheet of hair. Now it was clipped short, shorter than mine. You could really see all her little white hairs peeking up throughout the black. She was the only seventeen-year-old I knew who actually had salt-and-pepper hair.

"Yeah, sorry, let's go."

Camp smelled like pine needles, saltwater, and good old dirt. It was a sunny morning, still chilly for June, but that was Maine for you, especially a little farther north. We grabbed our gear out of the trunk. A couple other cars were already there—I saw Donald's ridiculous green Mercedes and couldn't help smiling. It would be awesome to have everyone back together again, even if it felt like cheating adulthood.

"Oh hey." Claudia pointed ahead. "There's Hana."

Leonato Jr. held the check-in clipboard under the welcome tent. Her whole face lit up, and she waved us over. Claudia hesitated for just a second and fell behind me as we walked up. Jesus. Put Claudia in the path of a pretty girl, and she became a ball of idiot.

"Ben! Claudia! It's so good to see you!" Hana reached out for a hug. She must've had a growth spurt or something—she was nearly as tall as me now. Maybe a little taller?

"Hey, Hana!" I squeezed her back. "Did you grow or did I shrink?" She laughed in my ear.

"Hey," Claudia mumbled behind us.

Hana pulled back and reached out tentatively to hug Claudia, who went in for an intense grip for one second, then let go immediately. Weirdo.

"I'm so glad you both came back this year!" Hana smiled, unflustered by Claudia's bizarro hug. "I thought you weren't going to?" That last part was directed at me. It only stung a little.

"Well, here I am!" I said cheerfully.

"Yeah—wasn't last summer your *last summer*, Ben?"

A voice stopped me cold. I tried to compose myself, but when I turned around, I still wasn't prepared for Bee Leonato. Fierce, beautiful, perfectly witty and weird. Always an inch or so taller than me, now even more so—her black hair was braided in intricate spirals that pulled into a faux-hawk on top of her head. Gold hoops hung from her ears, trembling in the force that buzzed around her.

Had I ever stood a chance?

Our gazes met. My eyelids fluttered rapidly, like I was looking into the sun. I forgot about replying and just focused on looking at my feet without falling over. My heart pounded into the dirt.

Bee didn't miss a beat. "Claudia!" She turned and gave her a quick smile and a non-awkward hug. "Great to see you."

"You too."

"So, Ben, what's up?" Bee tried again. "Are you here to drop off the girls? That's next week."

"What?" I fumbled. Another three seconds to prepare had not helped. Especially since her eyes were now fixed on me in their familiar glare. "No, I'm sports leader."

"Right . . ." Her glare slid over me. My stomach gulped. "You're sports leader this year. Even though you said you were done with this place, a *million* times."

"I . . . um . . ."

I glanced at Hana, for support, but she just blinked at me apologetically and pulled Claudia off to the side. Great.

So much for my hope that everything might be magically forgotten.

Bee was still staring at me, arms crossed. How was it she looked the same but everything was completely different? We should be catching up on the past year. I wanted to know where she was going to college. Plus I was full of news too—about the move, my sisters, Boston. I was bursting to tell her everything . . . but she kind of looked like she wanted to murder me.

"So yeah—" I tried—

"Why did you come back, Ben?" She had cut me off, her dark eyes clouding over, unsearchable.

"Family stuff." I lowered my voice. "We moved out. My mom and my sisters and me. It's complicated." Where did that come from? I'd sworn I wasn't going to tell anyone.

"Oh." Her glare softened the tiniest bit, and I instinctively leaned in closer. We could fix this. If I could just figure out the right thing to say—

"Bee, can we—"

"Beeeeeeee!" We both turned as Margo threw herself into Bee. I stepped back to shield myself from the hug explosion. Margo's hair sprang every which way, which was normal, but usually, it was a bright, fiery orange. Now it was a deep, shiny purple. Did Dogberry send out a memo that we all needed new hair this summer? After a full minute of squealing and jumping around, Margo finally noticed me.

"Ben! You're back!" She grinned, like this was just a little amusing.

"Hey, Margo."

We hugged, and then they went back to yelling in one another's faces. Bee and I were clearly done for now. Hana, while being squeezed by Margo, told Claudia and me that we could wait in Dam, where we'd all be meeting soon.

I hiked my orange duffel bag higher over my shoulder and led the way down the wide, shady dirt path, vaguely aware of Claudia trailing somewhere behind me.

My reunion with Bee was over, just like that. I'd been daydreaming about it for months, but in my dreams, I was a lot cooler, and Bee was a lot happier to see me.

We approached the biggest building at camp, an enormous pseudo–log cabin with a large porch and a flagpole area out front. Claudia tripped up the stairs. I wasn't the only one in a daze.

We pushed open the double screen doors; they shut with a comforting slam behind us. Rows of colorful tables and chairs, white twinkle lights wrapped around the rafters, the big welcoming window to the kitchen, the wafting smell of blueberry pancakes. Home.

"Hey! Nerds!" Donald called out as he sauntered across the hall and pulled each of us in for bro hugs.

"Hey man, how ya been?" I clapped his back.

Sunglasses, Afro, always the tie-dye shirts with designer jeans. Did he even own shorts? "Killin' it," he assured me. "It's good to see you."

He pushed his sunglasses back on his head. "Claudia, your hair's gone!"

"Really? I hadn't noticed," Claudia said sarcastically. Well, almost sarcastically—it had that awkwardness that kind of ruined the effect of sarcasm. I made a mental note: the hair thing was sensitive.

"Huh." Donald stared at her head for a moment before turning to me. "So, freshman year! How'd you do?"

"Oh, fine." I shrugged. "Good grades."

"Who cares? Do you have a girlfriend?" Donald pointed an eyebrow at me.

"I'm premed," I reminded him.

"So nobody wanted to fuck you?"

"I don't have time."

He snickered. "Please—virgins have tons of time on their hands."

I shoved him.

"Claudia?" He turned to her. Her entire upper half had disappeared into her duffel bag, rooting around for something.

"No, I don't have cash for a beer run," she answered from inside. I laughed.

"That too. But I was asking if you got a girlfriend this year."

Claudia pulled her head out, blushing. "Shut up. No." I laughed again. I really had missed Claudia. She reminded me of myself when I was twelve. Not that I would ever tell her that, since she was seventeen and a lot more muscular than twelve-year-old me. Or nineteen-year-old me.

"That makes three of us, then." Donald sighed and shook his head. "Single and back at summer camp. Pathetic."

"So nobody wanted to fuck you?" I asked innocently.

Claudia fist-bumped me. Donald laughed but then got serious and pushed both of us toward the corner of Dam with the drink machine—pretty much the only place at camp you were guaranteed privacy—glancing back over his shoulder. I looked in that direction: John, his half brother, with Connie and Bobby. They had formed a trio last summer.

"Actually, yeah, someone *did* want to fuck me," Donald whispered, under the buzz of the machine.

"Can I submit that to the camp newsletter?" I whispered back. Claudia smirked.

"But that guy"—Donald jerked a thumb in John's direction—"screwed it up for me."

"Screwed up the fucking," I summarized. Claudia laughed.

"Seriously!" Donald groaned quietly. "*Why* did my dad have to get that ingrate into Yale?"

Donald and John's dad was Josiah King, a New York senator. Their family was . . . complicated. Senator King had had an affair with John's mom and kept it quiet, but the whole thing blew up when the guys were in middle school, for reasons I never totally grasped. Nobody could really believe when Senator King had called the Leonatos last summer about John working here. John was an okay guy and okay at his job—but he and Donald did *not* get along.

Senator King had pulled strings to get *Donald* into Yale, too, but it probably wasn't a good idea to bring that up right now.

"Wait," Claudia whispered. "How could *John* get in the way of you having sex? That doesn't even make sense." I didn't voice aloud the image that question brought to mind.

"Well, because Yale sucks," Donald explained, like he was reviewing a pair of headphones online. "John and I were in the same dorm, on the same floor, so we knew a lot of the same people, went to the same parties."

"Right." Donald's college life sounded wildly different from mine. A month later, I was still recovering from finals and the one end-of-year party I had attempted to go to.

"So in the first few weeks, I was hanging out with this girl, Joanna, and man, she was *hot* and *cool*," Donald continued. "And we were so close, man. Like, so close. I got to third multiple times."

"Again, newsletter-worthy," I interjected. I was trying to keep it light—Claudia was a little younger than us, and as far as I knew, she'd never hooked up with anyone before.

"So we're supposed to go to this party together, right?" Donald's whisper became more of a hiss. "But she bails on me. And then the next night, she bails on me again. And then one of her friends tells one of *my* friends that Joanna told *her* that John told *everyone* that I'm a *virgin!*"

Claudia and I took a beat to react.

"Damn, Donald," I observed.

"But . . . aren't you?" Claudia asked him, at the exact same time.

"Yeah, but you don't *tell people* that at college!" Donald smacked his forehead. "At college you get to start over. People ask you how many girls you've been with, and you say, 'I don't know, I lost count.'"

"Smart." Claudia nodded.

I had to admit, I kind of wished I'd thought of that.

"So he told her that I'm a virgin, and she didn't want to be my first, so she ghosted me. Except that we kept bumping into each other in the bathroom and avoiding eye contact."

"What a jerk."

"Yeah, John's the worst," Donald said, glancing darkly over his shoulder.

"I meant Joanna," I said, lightly hitting his shoulder. "She didn't have to ghost you just because you'd never had sex."

"Uh, what's ghosting?" Claudia asked. "I'm getting some weird mental pictures right now."

"My only solace is that John's clearly not getting laid either," Donald said, completely ignoring both of us.

"Clearly." I yawned. "I'm going to get pancakes."

Just as I turned to go, Dam's doors banged open, and in walked Bee and Hana with Margo between them.

"Hey!" Bee called out. "Time to circle up!"

All the counselors gathered in the middle of the room, dutifully forming a large, misshapen circle. I glanced longingly at the breakfast bar one more time before falling in line.

Nik and Andy Leonato appeared at the head of the circle. Nik was our camp director. Technically Andy was the co-director, but Nik really ran the thing. She was short, tan, and intimidating, with an angular face and an impressive forehead. I used to be scared of her, and I still was a little bit, 'cause she was my boss. But I'd seen her soft side now too.

Where Nik was little and pointy, Andy was towering and doughy. He had a ton of curly hair and an impressive brown beard. I think I'd seen him frown maybe once in my life. Put it all together with his love of Jell-O, and it was totally obvious why a lot of campers called him Santa. Andy was a school nurse during the year, and he ran the Dogberry first-aid building, Black Bear.

"All right, kiddos!" Nik shouted. The hubbub died off immediately. "Welcome back to Dogberry, and welcome to our newest counselors—Dave, Doug, and Jen. As for you old-timers, it's good to see *all of you* back this summer."

Donald nudged me. I winced.

"We're in for another year of hard work, and our session numbers, miraculously, look good. Your cabin and age assignments are on the green lists going around, and the orange paper is the training schedule for the week. CITs and activity leaders will be here this weekend, and the first session starts Monday. Everyone needs to get certified, or recertified, in first aid and CPR. And if you need lifeguard or swim certs . . ."

Nik read off the list, and then Andy announced the activity leaders and assistants. Donald assisting in art, Margo in nature, and Bee in improv. We were the oldest counselors now. Totally weird.

Even weirder that I'd somehow landed sports leader, with Claudia as my assistant. I mean, Nik had told me to apply, but still. Even back when I thought I'd work at Camp Dogberry forever, I never thought I'd get promoted to leader before anyone else.

" . . . so now you have a few minutes to settle in," Nik finished. "We'll see you all in an hour at Monarch."

The games field. My office for the summer—so much better than my admin work-study job. I couldn't wait. The circle broke up with a happy racket, and Nik and Andy sauntered over to us.

"The mighty hath returned from war!" Andy clapped Donald and me on the back. "Glad you're back from college in one piece. How's Yale, Donald?"

"Failing everything."

"That's what we like to hear," Nik said, then looked at me. "How's BU, Ben?"

She knew. She'd talked to my mom last week. But I appreciated her not mentioning that. "It's good," I said. "Not Yale, so I'm doing well."

"Excellent." Nik nodded. "And it's still a great school. Bee applied there."

"Really? Where did she—"

"Claudia?" Andy leaned down and smiled at her.

She startled. "Uhh, I'm not in college yet?"

Andy smiled. "Great. Glad everyone's on top of their educations."

"Nik, the first-year counselors look so young," Donald whispered. "Are you sure they're not campers?"

"That's a sign you're getting old, Donald," Nik chided, "when you see the fifteen-year-olds as babies."

Andy chuckled.

Donald looked over his shoulder. "They *are* babies."

"Hana was a baby a second ago, and she's taller than me now!" I offered. "And since when is her hair all curly, like Andy's?"

Nik laughed. "Well, she is his daughter. Or that's what I told him, anyway."

Donald and Claudia cracked up. Nik grinned and kissed Andy's cheek. He raised his eyebrows at me, and they both retreated into the kitchen.

"I just meant," I mumbled, "I haven't seen her in a while, and it looks curlier now—"

"Why're you still talking, Ben?" Bee strolled over with Margo and Hana. "Nobody's listening."

"I . . . uh . . ."

"You know, Bee"—Donald leaned an elbow on her shoulder—"in some circles, Ben is actually smooth."

Everyone laughed. Thanks a lot, Donald.

"He's a city guy now," he continued. Please shut up. "He's got city game."

"Oh, is that so?" Bee turned back to me. "So . . . what? Did you get a *city* girlfriend?"

"Well, no," I sputtered. "I'm too busy studying."

"Oh, thank God." Bee smiled. "I'm so relieved for all the girls in Boston." Donald and Margo both laughed.

"So you've got a boyfriend?" I asked, before I could stop myself.

"No," she snorted. "I'd rather eat a handful of glass."

"Good!" Donald slung an arm around both of us. "So we're *all* pathetic and single. Maybe we can change that this summer."

"Some more pathetic than others," Bee singsonged, shooting a pointed look at me. "Some of us are actually single by *choice*."

"Whatever," I sighed. "Can you cut it out, Bee? I'm already so over this."

The group went awkwardly silent. Everyone glanced at Bee, waiting for her witty reply.

Bee's face fell, but her expression quickly morphed into a scowl. "Whatever, Ben. If you're over it, you shouldn't have come back."

The silence was less awkward this time. More hushed. Was this actually happening? Yes, that night—well, really the next day—had been the worst, but did that really mean we were done? Forever? I kept waiting for her to laugh, to take it back. But she didn't.

"Well, too late now." I grabbed my bag and headed over to the table to get my cabin assignment before anyone could notice how red my face was.

I was living in Snowshoe this year. Cool. There was an electrical outlet under the counselor bunk in that one. That was good. Forget Bee. Things were looking up. I headed out the door, and Donald and Claudia caught up with me. Neither one said a word about the train wreck they just witnessed, which was merciful of them. We went down toward the waterfront, where the path split for the cabins. Donald snatched my cabin assignment right out of my hands.

"Snowshoe. Nice. I'm in Coyote."

"Red Fox," Claudia sighed. "I wish I was over with you guys."

I was grateful they weren't bringing up what had just happened.

"Margo's in Moose," Donald continued, examining the list. "And Hana and Bee have the usual."

Bee and Hana shared a cabin every year—Little Bat. It was the nicest cabin, with two secret outlets, and built-in bunk beds. Plus it was closest to the big house, the Leonatos' year-round home, Big Bat. *And* the waterfront, Dam, and the nicest bathrooms.

"Seriously?" I just felt angry at everything right now. "They get that every year. It's total nepotism."

"Yeah." Donald started to head out. "At least you're not John. He's in Otter again. Serves him right."

"Whatever, he's a newer counselor," I replied. We'd all done our time in the crappy cabins farther out.

We parted ways at the split. Donald walked ahead while I paused at the waterfront and took it all in. The dock. The paddleboats and kayaks. Our little island.

That was the thing about summer camp. The job made sense: Wake up, set up the field, play sports all day, keep kids from killing each other. Try to eat and sleep in between. Sing songs, roast marshmallows, dress up in costumes, dominate Capture the Flag, sit on trial at Kangaroo Court.

It was pretty idyllic in every way. Or it had been, until last year.

As I set up my bunk, I came to a decision. If Bee wanted to be enemies, fine. But that didn't mean I had to fight back. I made a solemn vow, one I'd actually keep this time: no matter how I felt, I would not be involved in any camp drama this year. With my stepdad, Tim, and my mom's divorce, I'd had enough real drama to last a lifetime. This summer, no secrets, no fighting, and absolutely no *feelings*.

CHAPTER 4

Bee

"BEE, THAT WAS A little harsh," Margo said, once Ben had ducked out. "Can't you two bury whatever this fight is already? Have you even tried?"

"We're not in a fight," I retorted. "And I have to help with some food stuff. I'll see you in an hour?"

"Sure, darlin'." She shook her head, kissed my cheek, and grabbed Hana.

I ducked into the kitchen, found my way to the paper goods closet, and huddled on the floor. Shane, the cook, didn't see me. Or pretended not to see me. Thanks, Shane.

Ben hadn't even looked back. He'd just left Dam and disappeared forever. Well, probably disappeared into his cabin. And I'd have to see him in an hour anyway. I stood up, grabbed a stack of napkins, and started doling them into our little green table baskets.

Truthfully, I didn't know if I could handle this. His maddening, twinkly eyes and dusky-brown hair that flopped every which way. Something inside me still expected him to treat me like . . . like there was something between us. When there wasn't. Clearly. Margo was right—I needed to cool it, or they'd all start talking again. And plus, I didn't want Ben to think I actually cared.

Maybe that could've occurred to you a little earlier, Bee?

I kept forgetting what I was supposed to be doing, how I was supposed to feel. Like I was in a play, trying to play ten characters at once, with ten different sets of motivations. Where was Raphael when you needed an acting coach?

I made several trips back and forth from the kitchen, setting out the baskets on our blue-and-yellow picnic-style tables, imagining my character as an efficient lady with more important things to do than miss a boy.

The thing was, I did miss him—I missed my *friend*. Ben and I used to tell each other everything each summer. And sometimes we'd text each other funny links during the year. Not like Hana and Claudia, who couldn't go a day without texting each other. But Ben and I had a similar silly sense of humor. There were certain things I'd find online that I knew he would get and no one else would, so I'd send them, and the stuff he sent me *always* made me laugh. His texts were bright spots during the long weeks of studying and rehearsals. It made me feel . . . special, like he was always thinking of me, even when we weren't at camp.

This past year had been weird—looking at schools without talking to him. Picking a school without talking to him. Picking a school *in Boston* without talking to him.

He still didn't know.

As if he'd care. I was kidding myself if I thought *he'd* ever felt special because of *me*. To him, all we had ever been was that barely-a-friendship friendship. And what had happened last summer had killed even that pretty effectively.

WHAT HAPPENED: PART 1

Bee

EVERY FOURTH OF JULY, the whole camp goes to the nearby lighthouse to watch Messina's fireworks together. Then the counselors ditch the campers, put the CITs on watch, and meet at Nest. We call it the sparkler party.

This particular sparkler party progressed like usual: At first everyone was cripplingly awkward. Sometimes when you work with kids 24/7, you forget how to socialize without them. But then we remembered that alcohol helps with the awkward thing. I had a few beers, Ben had a few beers, and Donald had a few beers and proceeded to set three sparklers off at once in one hand and start screaming. Claudia calmly shook up a can and doused him. Margo videoed the whole thing.

Eventually, Donald insisted on Truth or Dare, which meant we all got to see Bobby streak across the clearing in the moonlight. While everyone was hooting at him, Ben and I stood next to each other, nearly silent in shock.

"Jesus Christ." He shook his head. "Why didn't we close our eyes?"

"I know," I whispered back. "I can't unsee that." He snickered, close to my ear. His breath made my skin prickle like saltwater. I tried to ignore it.

At the end of the night, the senior counselors packed up their blankets and headed back down the path. Like robots, everyone started to follow them. But I was still awake, and I realized the torch was being passed to us. Or, the sparkler bucket with blackened sticks. And blankets, and a warm cooler of floating beer cans, and cards everywhere. In grand tradition, we were being stuck with the cleanup.

"Hey, all—we need to get this cleared before we go." I crossed my arms.

"Aww, Bee," Donald groaned. "We're exhausted. We were up at six thirty."

"So was I!"

"Sweetums . . ." Margo drawled into a yawn. "We can take care of it tomorrow."

They didn't get it. My parents didn't mind counselor parties, but there was an unspoken agreement that we left no trace of them. We couldn't leave Nest like this overnight. What if they came up here early?

"Never mind." I shook my head. "I'll do it myself." Hana opened her mouth to protest, but I waved at her. "Get some sleep, babe."

"Are you sure?" Margo asked half-heartedly, already drifting backward, toward the edge of the trail. They thanked me again and filed down the path. I turned away and sighed to myself. *Whatever. You're always the one who gets it done.* Then I heard shuffling feet, and realized someone was still there, to my right, carefully collecting the scattered cards. My cheeks flushed, like they knew something I didn't.

"Ben, you don't have to help."

He shrugged, smiled. "Eh, I'm not that tired."

I grinned. "Me neither."

CHAPTER 5

John

FIFTEEN MINUTES AT CAMP, and I was already pissed.

The cabins were lined up along Camp Dogberry's shoreline, and for the second year in a row, I'd been tossed into the farthest one out, Otter. Cramped, ancient, devoid of electrical outlets, with no place to install your mosquito netting poles, which meant I had to duct tape them, and duct tape all the kids' poles too.

It was only my second year at camp, but I was *eighteen years old*. I'd just finished a year of *college*. Even one of the *first-year* counselors had a better cabin than me.

I collapsed onto the smelly mattress and sighed.

"Camp's not so bad, right, Johnny?" my mom had asked, anxiously, watching me pack last night.

"I like it there," I had assured her.

Camp Dogberry was one of King's stupid plans.

Last summer's press:

John Hernandez will be working at Camp Dogberry in Messina, Maine, with his brother, Donald King. "We're getting these city boys some fresh air!" Senator King said, to a friend at the ACLU benefit dinner.

I'd hated that my mom was letting him tell me how to spend

my summer, but then it had actually turned out okay. I had friends, there was a girl I liked, I made some money. Not a bad way to spend a couple months, but I did have to get past the whole it-was-a-sham-my-asshole-politician-father-put-together-for-his-own-image thing.

I hadn't planned on coming back this year, but then Donald had chickened out of his swanky internship, and my mom and I had gotten the call. Not like I had my own plans, like chilling for the summer at home with my mom in NYC. No, of course not. My entire state of being was waiting for instructions from King, obviously.

But at least I got to see Claudia again.

"This cabin's still the worst." Bobby swung the creaky door open, with Connie hovering just behind him. I got to see my weird Dogberry friends too, I guess.

"I know." I sighed and got up to unpack my stuff into the drawers under the counselor bed. "I don't get it. There's a new guy in Whitetail, and in Snowshoe with Ben, so why am I out here?"

"Did you ask Nik?" Connie, all legs and elbows, sat on one of the beds.

"Why bother? They're not gonna change it now."

"At least there's some privacy out here," she said. Privacy at camp? Not a thing. "So, guess what? I'm headed to Wash U in the fall."

Bobby, Connie, and I were all around the same age, but I graduated a year early, got into Yale a year early.

"Yeah? Congrats."

"Thanks." She smiled. "I'm pumped to go out west. Bobby's going to USM." She jerked a thumb at him. Bobby pretended to chug an imaginary beer. "So now you have to tell us," she continued. "What's college really like?"

"It's tough," I said. "I worked my ass off and still got a couple Bs."

"Not bad," Connie said.

"I don't care about your grades," Bobby clarified. "What's the party scene like?"

"Boring," I said firmly. "New Haven's nothing like the city."

"Aww, man," Bobby sympathized, even though he's from Maine, so he has no idea what I'm talking about.

"Yeah," I said. "And the *worst* part was that Donald lived on my floor." He was no doubt telling all his friends what a pain that had been, so I might as well tell mine.

"Seriously?!" Bobby laughed.

"Yeah, can you believe that?" I replied. "King's idea, I'm sure. They wanted to put us in the same room, but I got out of it." Actually, Donald had thrown a fit, but they didn't need to know that.

"That's such bullshit," Bobby groaned. "Can't your dad be cool for, like, five seconds of his life?"

"He's supporting the better health care bill—" Connie offered. Bobby threw my pillow at her.

"Yeah, so anyway," I said, swinging my legs around over the edge of the bed. "Donald shows up to campus with a truckload of stuff—"

"And another U-Haul for his ego?" Bobby asked.

"Nice." I reached over to slap his hand. "Yeah, and we're at the same boring parties, where he's bragging about all the girls he's slept with. And we have two classes together, and he doesn't even acknowledge me. Looks right through me. I couldn't take it anymore."

"What did you do?" Connie leaned forward.

"There was this girl he was hooking up with, and I told one of her friends that Donald was a virgin."

"What?!" Bobby shouted, cracking up. *"Dude!"*

"Oh my God!" Connie squealed in laughter.

"I know, and she *dumped* his ass."

"Dude!!" They both lost it. I grinned at the ceiling.

"So, then, you two are kind of even now, right?" Connie said, sounding hopeful. "So maybe you can just relax this summer?"

I wanted to point out that King and his family had pulled so much shit that nothing I did could even come close to leveling the playing field. But being a drama queen was Donald's thing, not mine.

"Sure," I said instead. "Relax and hook up with Claudia. She got even hotter this year."

"You mean balder?" Connie snickered.

"Jealous?" Bobby raised his eyebrows at her.

"As if."

"Short hair is a thing," I explained patiently. "Tons of girls have that cut in New York."

Connie looked doubtful. These Mainers, man.

"It looks pretty good," Bobby offered. "Her neck is, like, really elegant." He winked at me. I laughed. This effing kid.

"Dear lord," Connie groaned.

"The point is, I'm totally asking her out this summer."

"Hell yeah!" Bobby high-fived me. "I'm totally hooking up with Margo again this year."

"Oh excellent." Connie rolled her eyes. "So she's going to act like it's not happening, and you can spend another summer whining about it?"

"She's got you there." I smiled. I had to admit, Margo was definitely the dude of that hookup situation.

Bobby sighed. "I mean, I'd rather not keep it a secret and sneak around all the time," he acknowledged. "But at least I'm getting some." He pointed at Connie. "Who are *you* going to hook up with?"

Connie turned red. "Like you care."

"You're right," Bobby said happily. "I don't care."

She got up and smacked the back of his head. "Come on, guys. We're supposed to meet at Monarch."

As we left the cabin, I felt almost a fondness for the creak in the creaky door. It felt good to be back at camp but have friends this time. Even these two.

At CPR training, I made sure to get paired up with Claudia. I cracked a joke about how all the breathing dummies were white, and she laughed. Unlike the rest of Dogberry, I felt so chill with her. We'd been thrown together to teach the knot-tying elective last year, and she'd been so cool about it. Just handed me a rope and showed me knot after knot, almost silently. Even though she was friends with Donald, I never felt judged around her. That's why I liked her.

That, and her intense gaze—the way she looked at me, like I needed to be untangled. Her eyes were what most people would call honey-colored, but with Claudia, it was more like fierce bronze. Fierceness doesn't come from an easy life, and I knew, I felt, that we got each other. Knot after knot, I'd fallen for that bronze gaze. But I didn't have the balls last summer, and I didn't think I'd ever see her again.

Now I had another shot, and no way in hell I wasn't going to take it.

CHAPTER 6

Vanessa

COUNTDOWN TO CAMP: four days.

Which was good, because my sisters were driving me absolutely up the wall. Like I was clinging to the ceiling.

"It's *my* night to sleep on the top bunk!" Ava insisted.

"But you always take Smooshie up there with you!!" cried Layla, cat lover.

"Two bedrooms is what I can afford right now, but we'll find somewhere bigger when we can," my mom had explained apologetically, biting her lip, when we'd first seen the new place. I'd looked at the small white box-shaped room, with one window, too high at the back.

"Totally!" I'd agreed, smiling. "Not a problem, Mama." Immediately, my nose had started burning in that fuzzy, pre-cry way. When she'd turned around, I'd wiped the tears out of my eyes. Ben had seen and quickly given my shoulder a squeeze. Sigh. I knew better than to complain. Ben had to sleep on the couch. But still, it was pretty clear then that this rooming situation was going to cost me my sanity.

I wasn't wrong. Writing in my journal, I became aware of deadly silence. I looked up from my bed: Ava and Layla were rigging some kind of cat pulley–system. Smooshie watched, naively curious.

"Hide," I whispered to him.

Sharing a small room with seven-year-old twins made a cabin with patchy mosquito netting sound like a fancy hotel.

A knock came at the door—

"Vanessa, phone call!" My mom poked her head in, smiling. The way she said it, I already knew it wasn't my dad.

I jumped off the bed, grabbed the cordless from her, and ran out onto our teeny back porch.

"Hello?"

"Hey, Ness, how's it going?"

"Ben! Do you really want to know? The girls are bouncing off the walls, and Smooshie's about to die in a tragic elevator accident."

"Our place doesn't have an elevator."

"It does now."

"Oh good." He laughed.

"How's camp?"

"Orientation's fine," he said. "We did some team building stuff on the ropes course today. And I double checked for you—Sophia and Wallace are both on the CIT list, for the whole summer, just like you."

"Yes!! Thanks, bro." My best camp friends. They'd both said they were coming back, but you never knew.

"No problem. Yeah, so, we did CPR, which you'll do on Sunday, and first aid—"

"Cool, cool," I said. "But what's the camp *news*?" Not that I didn't care about CPR, but, like, c'mon. There had to be more important stuff happening at Camp Dogberry. There always was.

"Let me think." I could hear him running his hand down his face. "All right. Claudia got a real short haircut."

"She *did*?"

"Yeah, it looks pretty cool."

"Oh. Well, that's good. Anything else? Who's my counselor?"

"I don't want to spoil everything—you'll be here in a few days, and you can do all the gossiping you want."

That was a lot of gossiping. "Reaaaaally, Ben?" I whined. "You can't even tell me, like, one more thing?"

"Fine."

"Yay!"

"Andy got a new car. It's a blue hatchback."

I groaned. "I hate you."

"And I love you." He laughed. "I have to go to lunch. Hang in there with the girls."

"I'll try."

"How's Mom?"

"She really likes it here." I smiled. "I think it makes her happy." I didn't think, I knew. She'd told Aunt Deb on the phone, like, five times.

"Good. See you in a few days. Call if you need anything, but unless it's an emergency I have to wait to—"

"Call at the end of the day. I know."

We said our good-byes, and he hung up. I secretly wished he could've stayed until I left for camp too. It had been awesome to have Ben with us for a whole month—I'd missed him so much during the year, when he was at college. The new apartment had felt better with him here.

I brushed my bangs back, tried to think positively. Maybe it was a little cramped, but at least we'd moved out of Aunt Deb's. And no matter what, it was still better than *home* home, living with Dad. I didn't miss him hovering around like a storm cloud in scuffed-up loafers.

I took a deep breath and went back inside, read my camp packing list for the four hundredth time, using it as my calming mantra.

Watershoes optional, watershoes optional, watershoes optional.

CHAPTER 7

BEN

I THREW A STACK of plastic mats out onto the one patch of pavement at Camp Dogberry: the foursquare court. Claudia turned the hose on them, spraying away the layers of dust and grime built up over a year in the sports shed. Training week had passed quickly, in a blur of CPR, child psych overviews, and so. Much. Cleaning. The CITs and other leaders were coming tomorrow, which meant the campers would be here in two days. That was kind of terrifying.

Except that meant I'd get to see my Vanessa tomorrow. It'd only been a week, but I missed all three of my sisters.

Claudia and I had also been prepping Monarch this week. Repainting the white soccer lines, setting up the volleyball/badminton net in its patch of sand, and writing lists of games that worked last year and games that didn't: notably, Dodgeball had been a disaster—the kids didn't like the confines of organized teams, because they wanted to whip the squishy balls at whoever they wanted to (their friends and secret crushes). Thus, Sproutball was born, which was every-kid-for-themselves, free-for-all chaos. It was a new addition, but I liked it almost as much as Mashed Potato War or Capture the Flag. And I got to plan all of it now. Aces.

When I thought about that, I seriously couldn't wait for camp to start.

But.

All week, as I sorted the balls (soccer, volley, beach, squishy, etc.), I felt more and more pathetic. Here I was, back at this camp where I'd been since fifth grade, planning to pit children against one another in Sproutball death matches. Part of me wished I could've gotten an internship, like all my other premed classmates. But then I wouldn't have been able to help Mom move—most internships don't start *you know, whenever you're done moving.*

"Done," Claudia said, winding up the hose. "We should spread these bases out to dry in the grass."

I followed her lead, and then we spread ourselves out to dry too. The grass was still pointy and hard from its first summer cutting. It poked through my shirt and athletic shorts like needles. It wasn't a particularly pleasant sensation, but I found it comforting. That's how the grass was at the start of camp. Soon the whole field would be torn up.

"Can I ask you something?"

I kept my eyes closed. "Yeah, sure."

"What do you think about Hana?"

Something in Claudia's voice made me nervous.

"Hana's the best," I said. "She's a good kid."

I heard Claudia roll over, felt her look at me, and ignored it. "She's pretty, right?"

"Not like Bee," I mused, then quickly realized what I'd said. "I mean, yeah, whatever. I can't think of the Leonato girls like that. I've known Hana since she was, like, eight or something." That should shut Claudia up.

"Well, I think I'm in love with her."

I sat up so I could stare down at her. "What?!"

Claudia turned red, all the way up to her sticky-out ears. "I said I think I'm—"

"No, don't say it again," I pleaded. "Unsay it. Right now."

"What?" she asked, confused. "No—I'm in love with her."

I'd forgotten that though Claudia didn't speak often, when she did, she didn't know how to do the shutting up part. It was one of her talents.

I scrambled to my feet. "You've just ruined the entire summer!"

Claudia looked baffled. "But—"

"Who's ruined the summer? I'll kill 'em!"

We both jumped: Donald had appeared on the field, sunglasses on, hands and forearms splattered with paint, sucking a purple freezer pop.

"Claudia! Kill Claudia!" I demanded, pointing at her. "She's 'in love'! Or something."

Claudia stood, defensively, and turned a shade of red I hadn't realized was humanly possible. I felt bad, for a split second, but then I envisioned all the drama and gossiping and PDA that would happen as a result of this. I hated when camp became high school. Like what had happened last summer—or hadn't happened (whatever Bee wanted)—*that* had been totally high school.

"She's in love?" Donald smiled, his teeth a violent shade of grape. "With Hana?"

Claudia narrowed her eyes. "How did you know?"

"Oh my God!" I stumbled a few yards away and threw myself back onto the field, facedown in the pointy grass this time. "This is a nightmare."

"C'mon, Ben." Donald gently kicked me. "This is adorable, man. What's better than two of our favorite people getting together?"

"No," I said into the dirt. "It's a disaster. Plus, who tosses the word *love* around like that? What happened to *like*?"

"I know what I feel," Claudia said indignantly. "We've been talking all year—"

"Just because *you've* sworn off dating women," Donald chided me, "doesn't mean Claudia has to."

I stood up. The prickly grass had won. "I just don't want to waste my time *dating*. I'm premed."

"We *know*." Claudia sprayed me with the hose. Donald cheered.

"You guys are such jerks." I took off my soaked shirt and started down the path toward Dam. They followed, not drenched.

"We're the jerks?" Donald laughed, with kind of a snap. "Claudia just told you something personal, and you had, like, the worst possible reaction."

I glanced behind me at Claudia, who was staring pointedly at the ground. Oh, crap.

"God, you're right." I stopped in the middle of the trail, wringing water out of my shirt. "I'm sorry, Claud."

"It's cool." She shrugged. But it clearly wasn't.

"It's just . . . romance, or whatever, creates drama." I slid a hand over my face. "I think we'd all be better off just staying friends."

"We *are* being friends!" Donald shoved me. "We're going to help Claudia, our *friend*, get the girl!"

"*See!*" I protested. "Games! Drama! You're doing it right now! You're like the drama activity leader!"

"I kind of like that!" Donald smiled. Then he started rubbing his palms together—never a good sign—and focused on Claudia. "So, first party tonight. What are you gonna do?"

I bit my cheek and pulled my wet shirt back on.

"Umm . . ." Claudia thought for a moment. "Go for a little while, feel awkward, drink, and leave?"

"No! Well, probably." Donald led the way up to the veranda outside the dining hall. He jumped up onto the banister. "But you're also going to make a move! Tell her how you feel!"

"Oh." Claudia shook her head. "Yeah, no. I don't think I can do that. I wouldn't know how to . . . what to say."

"That's true, she's pretty bad at that," I added, hoping to squash this idea.

"What if I told her for you?" Donald hopped down in front of Claudia.

"You?"

"Yes!" Donald clapped. "I'll pull Hana aside at the party, one-on-one, and tell her that—"

I glanced around: "Maybe we should shut up about this outside of the—"

"Hey, all." Nik, our *camp director* at our *place of work* (who also happened to be *Hana's mom*) had appeared at the top of the stairs. Exactly what I was afraid of. Donald was being so unprofessional it was ridiculous.

Claudia backed into the corner, like a terrified wild animal. A flickering feeling of déjà vu hit me. Didn't I feel extra terrified of Nik last summer? Guess I didn't anymore. . . .

"You all coming in for lunch?" Nik asked.

"Sure, yeah."

"Absolutely, in a minute." Donald smiled.

"Great." She opened the door and called into the dining hall, "Donald, Ben, and Claudia are coming in a minute! They have to talk about all of you first!" She tuned back and beamed at us.

Claudia looked like she was going to be sick.

"Um . . . thanks?" I said to Nik.

"Sure thing." She cackled, clearly delighted with herself, and held the door open. Donald threw an arm around Claudia and steered her into Dam. I let them go and took a somewhat private moment on the veranda to deeply regret my choice to return this summer.

WHAT HAPPENED: PART 2

Ben

OKAY, IF I'M BEING real, I did not stay behind just to help Bee clean up. I mean, yeah, that was the right thing to do. But also, I had this idea.

A year and a half before, Bee and I had kissed. In January, under a half moon, snow falling all around us like a terrible movie. And I'd wanted to kiss her again ever since. And it was my *last summer* at camp, so I had to go for it.

The going for it, however, proved harder than I'd anticipated. We'd cleaned up slowly, circling each other, picking up sparklers and trash in muggy silence. I thought about asking Bee to hang out on her own, just for a sec, so I could do a quick run down to the cabins and wake up Donald for advice.

After a few more silent minutes, I couldn't take it anymore. The awkward, burning sensation that I was thoroughly screwing this up. So I did exactly what I felt like doing—I collapsed facedown in the middle of the clearing, on a forgotten, scratchy picnic blanket.

My own breath bounced back and hit me in the face repeatedly. As long as she didn't notice, I could stay there, slightly suffocating, forever.

Good move, I told myself. *Until you figure out what to do, don't do* anything.

Then I heard a laugh—her laugh. Cackling, like Nik's, but sweet, like a really nice witch. Suddenly, I felt a weight drop onto the blanket next to me. I turned my head and opened my eyes. She'd sat down. Aces.

"I thought you weren't tired?"

I couldn't see her face—just her legs. That felt creepy, so I quickly sat up too. She passed me a warm beer.

"Definitely not tired," I replied. "It's just so hot out."

"Yeah, it's really gross." She opened her beer, the noise thunderous, and took a long sip. I waited for *Come on, dingus, we need to get back to work.* Nothing. Weird.

I looked down at the beer in my hand, and a thought hit me in the gut like a kick ball: *She has the same idea. Of how this could go. Maybe?*

"So, do you think . . ." she began, and my breath caught. ". . . that Margo and Bobby are going to hook up again this year?"

"What?" I sputtered, spitting out a little bit of my beer. She laughed at me again.

"Margo and Bobby." She sipped from her can and stretched out her legs. I tried not to stare at them. But then, if I didn't look at them at all, would she think I didn't like her legs?

"Were they flirting tonight?" One part of my brain somehow kept on top of the conversation.

"Uhhh, duh!" She rolled her eyes. "Didn't you notice?" I used this question as an excuse to properly look at her: hair tied up in an elegant knot, the moonlight illuminating her skin, her eyes— widening, prompting me, indicating my incompetence.

I tried to clear my mind enough to answer. "Yeah, I mean, I really mostly noticed Bobby's ass?"

She laughed. That was three. "Right, yeah, that was pretty spectacular. I bet Donald'll do a beautiful impressionist collage of that sprint someday."

"Titled 'Truth or Dick'?"

We both cracked up.

"Anyway, that was Margo's dare," she continued. "Not a coincidence."

"And you don't like the whole Margo-Bobby thing?" I guessed. I knew she wasn't Bobby's biggest fan.

She sipped her beer, wrinkling her nose. "Bobby's immature. But they kept hooking up last year anyway, so . . . maybe they're meant to be or something."

Aha! I had something to say about that. "*Meant to be* is kind of a bullshit concept," I declared.

"Oh?" She turned to face me, brown eyes pinning mine. I almost lost my words again.

"Yeah." I looked at the blanket so I could talk. "Because we're not *meant to be* with just one person."

"Huh," she replied. I felt her go cold—then it dawned on me what I'd just said.

"I didn't mean it like that!" I said quickly. Back up, Ben. "I meant *fate* doesn't exist, we have free will, so how can anyone be *meant to be*?" I said the last part as more of a demand. Whoops.

Bee sipped her beer again. I'd said too much. Maybe I was ruining the mood. Eventually, she murmured: "I guess I didn't really think about it like that."

"Right?!" I turned to her excitedly. "I didn't either. But it's total bullshit. Because you can choose: you can be with someone, or you can leave them. It's not already written out for you. None of it is."

A bead of sweat trickled down her neck. I wanted to lick it. Ew no, no I didn't. What the hell was wrong with me?

I waited for another response, but again, didn't get one. I looked away.

Maybe, I thought, you're not supposed to tell a girl that you think fate is bullshit on the same night that you badly want to kiss her.

CHAPTER 8

Bee

"MUSHROOM FAIRY!" Margo said sternly. "Get in here, darlin'!"

The jet-black baby pygmy goat stared back at her with his bizarre rectangular pupils. Then he looked away and kept eating. Margo might sound no-nonsense, but she looked downright charming standing there with her purple pigtails and knee-high rubber boots.

"Bee, can you give him a nudge?" Margo held open the shed door, blocking the opening with her leg so the other four kids wouldn't escape.

"Probably have to do more than nudge." I eyed him.

Margo spent most of her time here, at Salamander, the dusky green nature building, complete with accompanying goat shed. It was her favorite place at camp. As soon as Margo arrived every summer, my parents relinquished animal care to her. We had turtles, lizards, a pair of rats, and a new crop of baby goats each year, in addition to whatever our grandma-like nature leader, Doc, would show up with tomorrow.

I grabbed Mushroom Fairy's collar and led him up to the door. "*How* did he grow an extra set of horns?"

Farmer Amy, who'd lent us the goats for the summer, had removed their little baby goat horns that spring, but Mushroom Fairy's had freakishly begun to grow in again.

"He's clearly the alpha," Margo said, shoving his bum into the shed. "And destined for greatness."

We grabbed pitchforks and started mucking out the goat pen, big shovelfuls of hay and poop. I was always thankful that when the CITs and campers arrived, we'd divide up the chores.

It had been a slow afternoon, for the first time all week. We'd been recertified, I'd gone over every inch of CIT paperwork, and we'd had the diversity and "camp-appropriate" talks with Dad. Now we were almost ready for campers. One more weekend of spending way too much time around Ben, and then the kids would get here, and it would be so hectic I would hardly notice him. Right now he was, well . . . noticeable. Twinkly and floppy. I hated the sight of his adorable bare chest at the waterfront.

"So, island party tonight?" Margo asked, casually flinging muck into the fertilizer bin.

Right, I also had to survive the *island party with Ben*.

I dug my fork into the muck with my boot. "Donald's collecting the booze money. I still don't know how he's going to get it."

"Yeah, he's kind of booze magical," Margo said. She passed me a heap of straw, and we started laying it down on the less poop-y dirt.

Margo tossed a handful behind her. "So, can we talk about my boobs?"

I laughed. "Sure, what's up with your boobs?"

We deposited our pitchforks in the bucket and made our way to the side of the building to wash our hands in the squeaky outdoor sink.

"Have you not noticed?" She gestured to her chest, soapy water drops flicking onto her shirt.

"I've noticed you have boobs," I admitted. "Is there something in particular you're referring to?"

"Is there something in particular?" Margo flung her hands down, exasperated. "Bee, they're *huge*! They just like, *popped* at the end of the school year. I bet Max is *really* regretting dumping me now."

Awww. Margo'd had her first boyfriend this year, but he'd broken up with her a couple months ago.

"If Max is regretting dumping you for that reason, he's a jackass."

"Well, he *is* a jackass." She laughed. It teetered off into what she'd call a big ol' sigh.

Poor babe. I struggled for the right words to say. I almost wanted to tell her I knew how she felt—but something stopped me. I couldn't . . . It was just easier if nobody knew. Instead, I slung an arm around her and pulled her into Salamander. Once inside, Margo grabbed a chunk of lettuce from the mini-fridge and started tenderly feeding the turtles. I sat at one of the old soft wooden tables, etched with claw marks.

"Okay," I said. "So what was it you were going to say about your boobage?"

"Well—"

The door flew open. Margo scowled and turned pink all at once—maybe she was expecting one of the guys, but it was just Connie.

"Hey!" Connie kind of shouted.

"Hey," Margo and I chorused.

"Have you guys seen Donald?" she asked. "I'm trying to find him to . . . get him cash. I've heard he's making a run after dinner."

"He's probably in Turtle," Margo replied. Her face was returning to normal, her freckles slowly reappearing.

"Or illegally napping," I added. "I'd check his cabin, too."

"Okay, thanks, guys," Connie said. "You excited for the party tonight?" She slid onto the bench next to me.

Margo and I exchanged glances. Connie DeAngelo had been at Camp Dogberry for years—she'd done her CIT training here and everything. She was so cute: tall, dark tan skin, shiny black hair. She was nice, kind of friendly, but *just so awkward* sometimes. A few summers back she and Bobby led a hiking trip and returned best friends, and then they glommed on to John last year.

"Not really." I made a face. "I heard Donald's getting tequila."

"Is he?" Margo's face lit up.

"Yuck." Connie stuck out her tongue and stood up. "Well, that'll be fun—adding tequila to the Donald mess. That won't backfire at all."

I'd kind of been phoning it in, but at that, I turned and blinked at her. "Donald mess? What?"

"Yeah, huh?" Margo looked at her, bewildered, then at me. I shrugged. Connie paused, leaning her right elbow up against the doorway, but, like, all wrong. It just kind of stuck into the wood. It looked super uncomfortable, and I wanted to tell her and her elbow to chill out.

"You know . . . that rumor going around camp?" she said, but her voice sounded less certain. "The one about how Donald likes Hana?"

"Hana?" I asked. "Ha!"

"No way." Margo's eyes went wide. "Who told you that?"

"Ellie," Connie said. "She heard Ben, Donald, and Claudia

talking outside Dam at lunch. Donald said he was going to make a move on Hana tonight. At the island party?"

Ellie, a second-year counselor. Not the best source, but . . . Mom had made this funny comment at lunch, about how those three were standing outside talking about us. I'd assumed she'd made it to embarrass them. What if they actually were talking about us?

Donald liked *Hana*?! Hana was a baby! What the hell?

But it's not like he'd tell you, a voice reasoned in my head. *And Hana doesn't look like a baby anymore.* . . . But really? Donald liking my little *sister*?

Suddenly, I realized Connie was nervously glancing between Margo and me. I tried to come up with something to say that didn't give away how disturbing this was. "Uhh, well . . ."

"*Bee*, we should muck out the goats before dinner," Margo said quickly, saving me. "See you later, Connie?"

"Sure." She nodded. "See you. Um, sorry?" She and her strange elbow stance disappeared from the doorway.

Margo immediately sprang across the room to me. "What is *going on*?"

"I don't know." I shook my head. "But I think we need to tell Hana."

CHAPTER 9

Hana

AT DINNER, EVERYONE BUZZED about the island party. The beer, the fire pit, the s'mores . . . all I could think about was the moonlight. Claudia in the moonlight, specifically. And her text this afternoon.

> I can't wait to be together tonight

> Same ☺

I had to believe we were speaking in code. There were times that I began to doubt and felt a little unsure—Christopher had spoken in code, too, but like a code nobody, like none of my friends, could crack. I'd known Claudia longer, so my gut told me to trust her. Although my gut had told me to trust Christopher, too. . . .

She sat toward the other end of the table at dinner, every so often glancing in my direction in a way she thought was sneaky. Her shorter hair brought out her cheekbones and made her look older.

And hotter. This entire week had been torture. I'd crushed on her last year, but I knew how to kiss now, and I wanted to kiss *her*.

"Hana!" Bee poked my shoulder. I looked up, dazed.

Margo poked my other shoulder. "Dinner's over. Let's go get ready."

"Definitely!" I smiled, stood up, scraped my leftover food, almost the whole plate, into the compost bucket.

"Girls!" On our way out, Mom and Dad called us over to their table in the corner. Margo recognized a family conference and went over to wait by the door.

"So, morning meeting is tomorrow at eight," Mom said in a lowered voice. They were both polishing off bowls of red Jell-O with whipped cream, a Camp Dogberry special.

"Might wanna make that nine," Bee suggested. "Or noon?"

I nudged her.

"Noon?" Dad looked alarmed, which was not normal for him. It looked weird on his face. "If you're *staying up* so late that you can't get up before noon, we have a problem."

"Relax!" Bee laughed and waved a hand at him. "I was joking. Ten is fine."

"Eight thirty," Mom pointed her spoon at Bee.

"Nine thirty."

"Nine."

"Done." They nodded solemnly—their version of a handshake.

"And be careful." Mom's brow wrinkled into her worry lines. "I don't want anyone getting *rowdy* and pushing someone into the water."

"Well, *we* don't get *rowdy*," Bee reminded them. "But I can make no promises about pushing people into the water."

"I'm not worried." Dad stood up and shoved his chair in. "If Ben drowns, we'd know immediately who to blame. I think you're smarter than that, Bee."

"Am I?"

Our parents started walking toward the dish pit, but Mom stopped and lowered her voice even further. "Call us if you need help." She held up her walkie-talkie. "We'll leave this on. I expect you"—this was mostly directed at Bee—"to keep the madness to a minimum. And be watchful for the first-year counselors, please."

"Of course." Bee was suddenly serious.

"I can help too."

We both jumped and turned around. Ben had been hovering nearby, hands behind his back, looking eager. Bee eyed him for a moment, then turned back to my mom.

"Yeah, don't worry, *I* got this."

"Thanks, Ben." Mom squeezed his shoulder as she walked past him. Bee wasn't going to like that. "And, Bee, if Ben's boat capsizes . . ."

Bee threw up her hands. "Ben's *really bad* at boats!"

"Not *that* bad," he protested, but Bee was already walking away. I shot Ben what I hoped was a supportive smile, then caught up to her.

After changing and grabbing our supplies, Bee, Margo, and I went to the bathroom for the girl cabins, Opossum. I'd changed into a white eyelet tank top and khaki shorts, nicer than anything I could wear during a normal camp day. Margo wore a blue halter top with leggings, and Bee hadn't changed anything: she still wore her ripped jean shorts and green camp T-shirt. Once in the bathroom, she slipped on a pair of large gold wind-chimey earrings. That's all it took for my sister to go from camp to party.

"Hair?" she asked.

I looked in the mirror. I had some zits and flyaways. Not all of us could look so flawless with zero effort.

"Half up, half down, with a braid!" Margo called, from her position at the sink. She was doing eyeliner calligraphy—little wing tips. It looked really dramatic with her pale complexion and loose, dark violet curls.

"Sounds good." I nodded.

Bee sat me down on a stool and carefully moved her fingers through my hair, which had started curling out of of nowhere this year. I still didn't really know how to wrangle it. I felt lucky to have Bee and Margo figuring it out.

Bee gave me a little scalp massage, and it felt so good, I closed my eyes, relaxed, and let myself think about the space between Claudia's ear and her neck.

"So, dearest, there's something we should tell you." Margo's voice floated in.

"Now?" Bee whispered.

"What is it?" I was still mostly thinking about ear-neck situations.

"Well . . . the thing is . . ." Margo's voice came closer. "Donald likes you."

"What?" My eyelids sprang open. Margo cringed in the mirror.

"Don't move!" Bee corrected my head forward again. My sister was somehow still concentrating on my hair! "Margo, maybe this wasn't the best time."

"Sorry, but when did you want to tell her? Five seconds before we got there?" Margo bit her lip and eyed me warily. "It's true, Hana darlin'. Donald likes you."

I watched the sunburn drain right out of my face. "No way. Did he say something?"

"No. Connie told us this afternoon," Bee said, still working on the back of my head. "She thought we already knew."

"Apparently, Ellie heard Ben, Donald, and Claudia talking about it outside Dam at lunch today," Margo confirmed. "I asked Ellie about it at dinner, and she said it was true."

Bee tied off the braid in my hair. "Done!"

The top half was pulled back so you could see my face, and the bottom curls fell down around my shoulders. It looked really cute, but I couldn't enjoy it, because Donald? *Donald?!* It didn't make sense. He was like an older brother.

"So . . . do you like him?"

I turned to Margo. "No, of course not."

"Didn't think so." She sounded a little relieved. "So what are you going to do?"

"What do you mean?" I said, not comprehending most of this.

"Oh, that's the other part." Bee grimaced. "The rumor is he's going to tell you he likes you tonight—"

"Tell me!" My stomach plummeted. What would I say to him? Donald, who I'd known forever? Maybe I could tell him I was gay. But that was a lie—I was bisexual or pansexual. I didn't know for sure, but I knew I didn't just like one gender. I could tell him I had a boyfriend—but that was a lie too. And if Claudia heard that . . .

"I don't think I should go." I felt tears well up in my eyes.

"No, you have to go!" Margo turned away from Bee's cheeks.

"Hana." Bee waved Margo's brush away and put her hands on my shoulders, looked straight into my eyes. I relaxed a little. "If Donald likes you, and you don't like him, it's okay to tell him that."

"But—"

"I know he's our friend, and he's great, but you can't control how you feel," Bee continued.

"Totally." Margo came over and slipped an arm around my waist. "And I'm pretty sure you feel things for a certain salt-and-pepper babe."

"And wasn't tonight kind of, like"—Bee smiled at me gently—"kind of a big night?"

I smiled, my ears burning a little. "Well, yeah . . . maybe. But what if Claudia knows that Donald likes me?"

"It doesn't matter how many people like you, it matters who *you like back*." Bee hugged me.

"Real." Margo nodded.

Bee pulled back. "So if Donald confesses his love, just tell him you like someone else! We can't let dramatic boys ruin the evening."

"Okay." I smiled and wiped the beginnings of tears off my lower lids. I checked my eyeliner. Waterproof—I was good.

"Besides . . ." Margo had slipped back in front of the mirror and was applying bright red-orange lipstick. "I could probably be persuaded to comfort Donald."

Bee rolled her eyes. "Could you really?"

We all laughed.

We finished up like everything was normal. I took some deep breaths while Margo fussed over Bee, finishing up dusting some shimmery powder on her cheeks.

As we walked down to the dock, I tried to calm down and push away thoughts of what might or might not happen. *You can't control or predict what comes next*, my therapist's voice reminded me. *Just take it moment to moment.*

CHAPTER 10

Ben

THAT NIGHT, AS THE sun disappeared into the tree line, we fitted on our headlamps and headed down to the docks. As we got closer to the waterfront, something buzzed in the air. Probably Claudia's nerves. She and Donald had been scheming all through dinner. I wished there was some kind of anti-drama product I could use—like bug spray, but for feelings.

With some help from the others, we pulled a handful of paddle-boats off the rusty racks. Kayaks were faster, but much harder to steer drunk, and Donald was counting on everyone being hammered for the trip back.

We sat on the dock, dangling our feet over the water, waiting for Bee and co. Everyone but Claudia, who paced up and down, her footsteps rattling and clanging against the metal slats. I checked my watch. *Who's late now, Bee?*

Claudia's pacing made me antsy. I got up and pulled aside Dave, Doug, and Jen, our new first-year counselors, to talk about the one beer per hour rule. I'd now been to enough unmonitored drinking parties (one) at college to understand why it was important.

"And drink water. We don't want any of you throwing up," I

explained. "Throwing up from drinking is not actually cool. It just makes you smell bad and feel like shit the next day."

They nodded at me, eyes wide. This was their first party, their first summer as real counselors. The CITs weren't here yet, but even if they had been, they wouldn't have been included. "Babies" were never invited out after sunset.

Finally, just as Claudia looked like she might explode, Bee, Hana, and Margo arrived, carrying backpacks I hoped held marshmallows and chocolate. I saw Claudia freeze. I guessed *not* out of excitement at the possibility of s'mores.

"What're you all standing around for?" Bee called out.

"We got the boats, Your Highness!" Donald called back.

They leaped out onto the dock. Margo and Hana were all dressed up, but Bee just looked . . . Beeish. I couldn't look anywhere else, so I attempted to look everywhere else. Water. Trees. Boats. Donald. Awkward eye contact with Doug. Whoops.

"You're late!" Donald announced. "Let's go! I wanna get drunk!" The younger counselors giggled nervously.

"Not *drunk*." Bee walked up and pointed her flashlight at him. "Just buzzed." Donald batted the light away.

"Listen, Bee," he said, climbing into a paddleboat and motioning for me and Claudia to follow. "You need to learn how to drink, for school. Don't worry—Ben and I can teach you."

Claudia hopped in the front next to Donald. I paused. Logically, I knew these paddleboats were sturdy. I'd ridden in them every year and supervised other kids riding in them every year, for seven years. Nobody'd ever drowned off a paddleboat. But God, in the dark, gently bobbing in the water, they just looked straight out of a nautical horror movie. The "trustworthy" boat would randomly spring a leak, and a shark would be waiting, right under the surface, in five feet of water—

"Thanks for the offer, Donald." I woke up to Bee's voice, sounding annoyed, standing right next to me. "But I think I know how to drink."

She'd crossed her arms. Donald grinned at her, which made me want to punch him.

"Not like us," he insisted, looking at me. "We're gonna get hammered, like a real party. Right, Ben?"

Bee raised her eyebrows at Donald, then me. I looked away quickly, before I turned to stone.

"Um, yeah," I agreed. "Long week. Let's get hammered."

Bee looked almost disgusted as she strode over to her own boat. Hana followed, but Margo stopped to whisper, "Hey, teach me to drink?" She winked.

"You got it!" Donald whooped. "Let's get fucked up!" She laughed and jumped in the back of Bee's boat. Almost everyone was seated now. I needed to get in before they noticed I wasn't and started in on me. With as little a hop as humanly possible, I lowered myself into the back seat. The boat wobbled slightly to the right, but hardly made a splash. My sneakers planted on the slimy plastic. Success.

Once settled, I glanced around—it seemed like nobody'd seen my awkward entrance. But then I felt someone staring: of course, directly across, Bee sat in the front seat of her boat, facing me, eyes laughing. She'd seen the whole thing.

Just as I saw her, something bumped our boat, and I almost screamed.

"Where's your yacht, bro?" John asked from the boat that had just grazed ours.

"Hey, bro." Donald whipped around. "Fuck off."

"Can we get that again for a sound bite, Senator?" Bobby quipped, as they moved along past us. They cracked up at their own hilariousness.

"Bastard," Donald muttered.

Bee's right, I thought. All we need now is this fun bunch to get drunk.

"Whatever, let's go," Donald decided, and we sped off into the moonlight. And by that I mean we slowly paddled away from the dock like a school of geriatric turtles.

I watched the silhouette of Bee's faux-hawk against the navy-blue sky, just starting to sparkle with stars.

Maybe we just needed more moonlight. Maybe that could fix everything.

CHAPTER 11

Claudia

IT TOOK TWENTY MINUTES to get the fire going, but in the meantime, we got a show: Ben and Bee attempting to start it together.

"Shouldn't we be building a pyramid?"

"Are you seriously using a lighter?"

"That kindling is green."

"Back up. Do you want to burn your eyebrows off?"

I thought about helping, but their arguing actually produced a well-constructed campfire.

The island is small, maybe less than half a mile across, and in the middle, there's a fire pit with log benches circled around. I sat across from Hana, too nervous to attempt sitting next to her. The fire popped, the stars came out, and Donald passed out beers like it was Halloween and we were trick-or-treaters. Bee let him, and then situated the beer cooler in the clumps of bayberry bushes behind us.

"Stop being paranoid!" Donald laughed. "The police are not going to show up on the tiniest island *ever* in northern *Maine* and card us."

That got a laugh from the group. But I kind of understood it. Bee was the camp directors' kid. She needed to set a good example. Of hiding the alcohol.

Once everyone was settled in around the fire, and the bug spray had been passed around, Bee opened a beer for herself and raised up the can.

"To Camp Dogberry, the most beautiful place in the world."

A murmur of agreement.

"To old friends returning, new CITs coming—"

"Our fresh crop of servants," Donald interjected, to a round of cheers.

"And our beloved campers, soon to be here, to make us want to give up and torch the place."

Another cheer.

"And to summer." She paused, to look up at the sky. Then she grinned at Hana. "*This* summer."

A toast of cans smacking into each other.

Bee was right. We only had one summer. Who knew what would happen after that?

Across the fire, I watched Margo whisper something to Hana. She smiled in reply. Hana didn't laugh a lot, not unless she was really comfortable. She mostly smiled. Tonight, her dark curly hair was pulled back from her face and hovered loosely on her shoulders. Her skin was already starting to tan from hours on the water this week. I wanted to run my fingers down her arms, then catch her hands at the bottom.

"Hey, Claudia, can you pass me a beer?"

I looked up. John. I grabbed him a beer from the cooler and another for myself. I opened mine and drank half in one go. I needed to calm down.

Hana, so pretty. So perfect. Calm down.

"Claudia?"

I looked up again. John was still there.

"Did you get your beer?" I asked, checking around me. "I gave it to you, right?" Who knows what I'd done with it.

"Yeah." He stared at me for a second and then walked away. Weird. Bee passed around a bag of marshmallows, and I found a stick and roasted one, on autopilot.

Hana sat across the fire, carefully rotating two at a time. I wanted to be sitting over there, talking to her. I felt like it was an attainable goal, but how to get from here to there?

Donald. Wasn't he supposed to be helping me? He was talking to Ben. I reached forward and tapped his shoulder. His shoulder was so much bigger than mine. I needed to work out more.

Donald turned away from his conversation with Ben to look at me.

"Yeah?" he asked.

I widened my eyes. Bat signal.

But he just raised his eyebrows back, like he somehow did not recognize the bat signal. Shit.

"No, umm . . can you umm . . . go talk to . . ."

Expressionless, he watched me fumble. Maybe he'd forgotten about the entire plan. God, it was so annoying to bring it up again. *Stop it, Claudia.* Then Donald suddenly cracked a smile and shoved my arm.

"I'm just kidding, Claud, I got this."

He hopped up and sauntered his way around the fire pit, like I never could. I am rarely, *rarely* attracted to dudes, but Donald was so good looking it hurt. Dark, smooth skin; Afro; and a loud, infectious smile. Teased you all the time. He was unstoppable. And it wasn't just me—he had that effect on the younger counselors, CITs, even the campers. They swooned over him.

John might be like that too, I thought, if Donald wasn't around. He was kind of good looking, too—smooth, tan skin, buzzed hair on the sides, black curls on top. But he had none of Donald's confidence.

As I watched Donald approach Hana, I felt my legs start to shake, knees almost knocking.

What if, on this moonlit walk, Donald charmed the hell out of Hana? He *did* say Hana was really cute, and he had offered to talk to her . . . and how could you not like a guy like Donald?

But I noticed Hana's smile faltered, just a little, when Donald offered her a hand. She glanced at Margo, who glanced at Bee, who nodded at Hana, encouragingly. What the hell? Were they all secretly shipping them, and nobody'd told me?

Wait, didn't I *want* Donald to talk to Hana?

Donald laughed, made some joke, and Hana looked a little less terrified. As they disappeared from the firelight onto the trail, he slung an arm around her, in a friendly kind of way, like he'd done to me or Ben or Bee a thousand times.

Okay. Calm down. It's Donald we're talking about. He's got your back.

I took a breath, switched gears. A walk-around couldn't take more than fifteen minutes. After a year of waiting to see her again, of hanging suspended between text messages, I could make it fifteen minutes. No problem.

The group had dispersed some. I noticed Connie and John wandering onto the trail. Maybe they were an item too. And a few younger counselors were missing. Ooo freakin' la la.

"Claudia, that's your third beer in, like, twenty minutes."

I looked up. Ben stood over me. I hadn't even realized I'd opened another one, but there it was, half-finished in my hands.

"Slow down, yeah?" He sat down next to me. "And if you don't stop staring longingly at the trail, I *will* vote you off the island."

"You don't have the power to do that," I countered. "And I'm taller than you now." I'd grown a couple inches, and now I totally looked down at shorty Ben.

He snorted. "Just wait till Capture the Flag. We'll kick your asses."

"Not this year," I vowed.

It must've come out really serious, because Ben cracked up, which admittedly made me smile and forget about Donald/Hana for half a second. But then it came back—I glanced at the trail entrance again, wondering where they were on it. Ben started talking about something, school maybe, but I couldn't really hear him. I jiggled my leg. Then the other leg.

"I'm gonna pee." I stood up. I needed to move, and conveniently, when Ben had pointed out I'd had three beers, I'd suddenly felt them in my bladder.

Ben sighed and went to go sit with Rachel and Doug. He was friendlier to the younger counselors than the rest of us were. Guess it was all those little sisters he carted around. I was pretty grateful to be an only kid, even if that made the gay thing more intense with my parents. Sometimes I found myself wishing I had a nuisance older brother, the kind that always got detention.

I wandered onto the trail, and then off it a ways. As I went to unzip my shorts, someone's voice scared the crap out of me.

"Whoa, whoa!"

I jumped—to my right, in a bayberry bush, Bobby.

"Dude!" I yelled.

"Sorry!" he yelled back. "I was looking for somewhere to take a leak."

"*I'm* leaking here," I protested. Whelp. I was definitely drunk.

Bobby laughed. "Right, sorry, man." He waved his hands in apology and started to walk toward the trail, still talking. "With all the hookups, it's hard to find a spare tree."

"Sure." Wait. I turned. "Who's hooking up?"

"Dave and Jen."

Oh. First years. Who cared about them?

"And Doug and Ellie . . . and Donald and Hana . . ."

I immediately didn't have to pee anymore. Or maybe I'd peed myself. I wasn't sure. Everything had gone numb.

"Donald and Hana?"

Bobby paused at the edge of the trail and yawned. "Yeah. I heard him asking her out. And then—you know where that big rock is on the other shore? I saw them over there."

He didn't say it, but we both knew that was the *kissing rock*. What the hell was happening? My face felt hot as a sunburn. Something boiled in my stomach, like I might puke.

"Cool," I heard myself say. And then I pushed past, our shoulders thunking into each other.

"Hey, are you—"

I ignored him. I rifled through my options: I had to get back to the campfire. Act normal, grab another drink if Ben would let me. I couldn't paddle back and disappear. People would notice.

Don't explode, Claudia, don't explode.

Donald and Hana, his fingers in her hair, his lips on her lips—

I stopped on the trail. I couldn't go back there. I was still too hot. My insides churned. I reached up to a smaller, low-lying branch on the nearest tree, and tore it off, stepped one leg up onto a stump, and split the branch over my knee. It hurt, but I felt a little better.

I wrapped my arms around my stomach, trying to hold myself in place.

The ocean roared to my left. Hana was the water, and I'd been pulled under. As I was sinking, she'd made me forget the rest of the world.

And now I'd never be hers.

Well, who wanted that, anyway? I could barely remember the Claudia who did.

"Claudia?"

It was just Ben, with his dopey, concerned face. He had a beer in his hand. I wanted another beer.

"Are you okay?" he asked, walking up.

When I didn't respond right away, he poked my foot with his.

"Did something happen? You look like crap."

"Thanks," I bit out. A shiver went through me. It was cold. I'd worn a ribbed tank top because I thought Hana would like how it looked.

Ben didn't say anything, but he shuffled off his sweatshirt and held it out. I took it, fought it on. He sipped his beer, waiting.

"Donald's kissing Hana," I whispered finally.

"Wait, that's what this is about?"

I hated the laughter in his voice.

"It's *true*." Hot tears blurred my vision. "They're down on the kissing rock."

Ben actually laughed at that. "Okay. And Bee's making out with Dave in a paddleboat?"

"Seriously," I said.

"Did you actually see them making out?"

"No. But everyone else has."

"Okay." Ben sighed, like I was a seven-year-old camper throwing a tantrum. "Do you really think Donald would do that to you?"

Drunk thoughts swam through my brain.

"All Donald wants is to get laid."

"True," Ben replied, too calmly. "But he's a good friend. Bros before . . . you know, whatever. I wouldn't believe this till I saw it."

"Fine." I said. "So I'll go see it."

CHAPTER 12

Bee

WHERE HAD EVERYONE GONE?

It had been twenty minutes at least, and Margo and I had watched all of our friends vanish, in varying degrees of drunk and huffy.

As I bit into a crinkly golden marshmallow, a scene flashed in my mind: Hana rejecting Donald, him bursting into tears, and Hana, unsure what to do, then awkwardly comforting him. Or maybe he was shouting and being a dick. Either way, I'd let this go on long enough.

"Don't you think melted chocolate kind of looks like poop?" Margo giggled at her s'more.

"I need to pee," I announced, and stood up.

The crowd around the fire startled and looked up at me. Was I that loud?

"I need to go with her," Margo also announced, with a hiccup.

"Ooookay," Ellie offered.

We grabbed our beers and stumbled over the logs toward the trail. It was a good thing we were senior and kind of in charge, because otherwise we'd have been real weirdos.

"So are we looking for Hana and Donald?" Margo whispered to

me, once we got on the trail. Luckily, the Maine sky had turned out tonight. The stars were breathtaking, if you weren't worried your sister was currently getting Nice Guyed somewhere underneath them.

"We're not *looking* for them," I whispered. "But we're not *not* looking for them."

"Goooootcha."

"I also do have to pee."

"Me too!!" Margo giggled.

I wobbled, just a little. Two beers in. I really wasn't good at holding my drinks. Both metaphorically and physically—I tripped and dumped a splash of beer into the dirt. Margo steadied me, and we found an adequate pee clearing in the shallow woods. As I peed, hugging a tree, I contemplated how, if it was daylight, definitely harbor boats could see us.

We hopped back on the trail, and I led the way in the opposite direction of the fire. Maybe now I was officially on the Hana hunt.

"Did you see Ben?" I whispered to Margo as we walked.

"Where?" She turned around. Had she been sneaking extra drinks? Maybe to impress Donald and his drunk boasting.

"No, not here." I rolled my eyes. "At the campfire earlier. He was talking to *Janine*." It came out darker than I intended.

"No!" Margo almost yelled. Margo and I both have loud voices normally. Give us a couple beers, and we're belting a duet. "But isn't Janine, like, *fifteen*?!"

I shushed and pulled her closer. "She *is*. But they were totally talking, for, like, half an hour." She'd shoved him playfully and everything. But if I'd told Margo all of that, she'd know I'd been watching them, and not exactly 100 percent listening to her rehash her break up with Mike.

"Whoa," Margo whispered. She reached an arm around my waist to steady herself. "But, like . . . maybe he was just talking to her. You know, Ben talks to a lot of people."

Super astute. This girl was hammered. "Or maybe," I whispered, "Ben's trying to date someone on his maturity level."

Margo giggled. "Noooo. I don't believe it. Maybe she's just got a crush on him, and he's being nice. Ben's really nice."

"Marf," I replied. Which wasn't a word, but it was how I felt.

We'd almost looped halfway around the island by then, with no sight of Hana or Donald. We even stopped to check the kissing rock, but nothing. As we made our way back to the main trail, Margo's arm over my shoulder, she asked me:

"Hey, Bee, have you asked them yet? Why they came back? Donald and Ben, I mean."

I hesitated. Somewhere in my brain a warning signal flashed: SECRET, SECRET, SECRET. Right. Ben's family moved. *You will not say that*, I briefed myself. *You will say something else.*

"I bet Donald's dad made him come back," I fake speculated. "So that he and John still look buddy-buddy."

"Oooh." Margo nodded. "That makes sense."

"Yeah, and then Ben just followed, like a lost puppy."

Margo liked this. "You think so?" She smiled. "Ben kind of does look like a puppy."

"Oh yeah." I steered us around a fallen tree in the path. "Ben wouldn't have had the guts to come back alone."

"Well, I probably wouldn't come back without you or Hana," Margo said. "Who'd want to be stuck here without our friends?" She swung her arm down and grabbed my hand, which made it easier to walk on the uneven path. We stopped to check another make-out spot, the kissing cove, and kind of walked in on Doug and Dave. Whoops.

"So sorry, guys!" I called back. Margo was just a giggle now. There was nothing else left of her.

Privately, I felt a teeny stab of jealousy. I remembered when I felt like Hana did, and clearly like Doug and Dave did. Like something exciting might happen at one of these parties, something that might change the next day.

Things were better this way, though. Friends were better. Just friends.

"How do you feel about it?" Margo asked.

"About what?" We were nearly to the other side again. Maybe Donald and Hana were already back at the campfire.

"About Ben coming back?"

It took everything in my physical power not to stop in my tracks. I mean, I knew Margo suspected . . . but did she actually know something? Had Ben talked to Donald and Claudia, and they'd talked to her?

"I wish he wasn't here," I said quickly. When I said it, I realized it was really true. If only he'd stayed away, like he was supposed to. Then maybe I could finally get rid of these feelings, these memories. "He's just—"

A snap in the bushes cut me off. I could see a shadow looming. Someone was there.

Margo and I looked at each other. The shadow from the bush had a suspiciously floppy-haired head. Was Ben eavesdropping on us? Margo's laughing face confirmed that she'd had the same thought. Her chin quivered from the effort of not giggling. I threw up my hands.

"Anyway," I said, much louder than before. "What a great summer it would've been *without Ben*."

"What?" Margo's eyes went wide. She hadn't picked up on the plan I'd just sent her telepathically: smoke Ben out.

"Yeah, I was *really* looking forward to it." I sighed. "I mean, the last thing we need around here are *childish* employees."

Margo still didn't get it. "But what have you really got against him?" she demanded. "He sleeps late sometimes—"

"And is so disorganized, never remembers anything—"

"Well, yeah, but he always figures out the lessons in the *moment*—"

"He makes my life harder," I said. "He's immature, he follows Donald around like a puppy, he's obnoxious and spineless, and never says what he's thinking."

"What?" Margo sounded confused, but I was barely paying attention.

The bush was practically shaking with anger. Any second now Ben would jump out and yell at me. I couldn't wait.

"Okay, okay," Margo's voice got soft. She laid a hand on my shoulder. "I get it. You guys don't . . . get along anymore. I mean, I still don't get *why*, but . . ."

Too close, too close! Suddenly, I really hoped that *wasn't* Ben in the bushes. I backpedaled so fast the boat nearly turned over.

"Let's just get back to the campfire." I looped my arm through hers. "I think we missed them."

"Okay." Margo looked over her shoulder. I pulled her forward but snuck a glance back myself. The bush looked like it knew my secrets. Fuck you, bush.

WHAT HAPPENED: PART 3

Bee

IT WAS FINALLY ALL happening: Ben and me. We were up far past our bedtimes, on purpose. And he'd stayed behind to help me, and now we were sitting on a blanket together, happily drinking warm beers. And we were laughing, and tipsy, and some kind of energy coiled in the space between us. Maybe just static from the scratchy blanket, but it felt like more.

But then he'd started ranting about how "fate is bullshit," and I started to get the idea this was maybe not as romantic as I had begun to let myself think.

"Ben, what are you *really* trying to say?" I asked. "Like, you don't believe in relationships, or what?" *Wow!* That sounded a lot bolder than I felt. Thanks, beer. He was dancing around something, and I wanted him to spit it out. No more dancing. Just spitting.

"Okay, fine." He let out a big rush of breath before continuing. "It's nothing like that. It's like . . . my mom."

"Your mom?" We were jumping all over the place.

"Yeah," he murmured. "My mom, and my stepdad, Tim. He's an

asshole. He screams at my mom. And me. Not at the girls, anymore. Not since last winter."

"Last winter?"

"When we showed up at your house."

I swallowed. We'd never talked about that night.

He sighed again. "But yeah, Tim's not my mom's soulmate. He's just a shitty guy. This wasn't *meant* to happen to my mom, it just did."

I waited for more, but he only scrunched up his face and rubbed his nose. The clearing went silent. That was the end of the confession. I'd known things weren't perfect in Ben's home, he'd alluded to it before, but he'd never laid it out for me like that, in plain terms.

I thought about him at home, with Nessie, Ava, and Layla. I thought about all of these years struggling to protect them. About how he'd never really dated anyone.

"I'm so, so sorry, Ben," I said, trying not to let my voice catch. This wasn't about me.

"Thanks," he said softly. "My mom's making a plan, so . . ."

"Can I do anything to help?"

"Well, I mean, your parents have helped a lot already. Nik took my mom to a group, and she's got a job now."

I nodded, slowly putting everything together. That made sense. Mom never told me why their family had shown up that night, but after, that spring, I sometimes heard her whispering to Dad about seeing Colleen, Ben's mom. And sometimes she'd gone over "to visit" two hours away.

"That sounds like them," I whispered.

"Yeah." He nodded. "They're good people. Camp Dogberry's always been the best place to escape."

I felt my eyes widen. Of course. Since fifth grade, Ben had come here, every summer, for the whole summer.

Suddenly, I turned to face him. He copied me, but before he could ask why, I reached forward, wrapping my arms around his shoulders. He felt so much bigger than I thought he would. Slowly, his arms circled my waist. My chin hovered awkwardly, but then I relaxed and rested it between his neck and shoulder. We were locked, chests pressing up against each other.

After a few moments, we both pulled back, but paused with our faces close.

His brown eyes twinkled, his nose an inch from mine, his lips—

"Do you think . . ." he began, his breath alighting on my skin. "Do you think at some point tonight we're going to kiss?"

CHAPTER 13

John

I HAD ONE MISSION for the island party: ask Claudia to hang out. Slow, yes, but I *liked* Claudia. I didn't want this to be a drunk hookup that got awkward in the morning.

Down at the waterfront, everyone waited for the rest of the ringers to show up. Claudia wore a black tank top, shorts, and high-top sneakers. She looked chic as fuck.

Once we got to the island, I had to admit, it felt good to be outside, partying around a fire, instead of cramped into a sorority house or dorm room or apartment. Some part of me filed it away—I could tell my New York friends about drinking under the stars, like it had been romantic, and then I'd tell them about the girl.

It was hard to get close to Claudia at one of these things. She and Ben were Donald's lackies. I didn't hold that against her though, because everyone thought Donald shat gold. I guess that's what happens when you're insanely rich your entire life.

Donald finally disappeared. This is it, I thought.

Drinking makes me nervous, but you have to drink at a party. I had a couple beers, and then jitters crept into my legs. I steadied myself and walked over to Claudia and asked for a beer. She seemed out of it though, annoyed, and I chickened out and sat back down.

"Where're your balls now?" Bobby snickered.

"Wanna go for a walk?" Connie asked.

I glanced at Claudia. Ben had swooped back in. So why not? We ditched Bobby and hopped on the trail. Connie peered around at the bushes and trees.

"Do you see Donald and Hana?" she asked.

"Who cares?" Gross. My older brother making a move on a vulnerable sixteen-year-old. Pathetic, but unsurprising. Like father, like son.

"I don't think she's going to go out with him," she continued. "If it makes you feel better. Bee and Margo got really weird when I told them about it earlier."

I nodded. That actually did make me feel better. Shot down by a high schooler was good ammo for the fall, if Donald pulled any crap at Yale. I wouldn't even have to make it up.

About halfway around the trail, we spotted Bobby.

"Guys!" He ran up in the dark.

"Not a guy," Connie grumbled.

"Claudia," Bobby said, breathless. Dude was not in shape. "I bumped into Claudia, and then I saw her head down to the rocks."

"She's alone?"

"Definitely. We almost peed on each other."

Connie and I looked at each other.

"Accidentally," Bobby clarified.

"Gotcha."

"Make your move, dude!" He punched my shoulder.

Fuck. He was right. This was my moment. Man up.

"Thanks." I clapped his shoulder and took off in Claudia's direction. My heart drummed in my chest, my ears. I rounded a corner, pushed through a couple bushes and out into moonlight, and then I saw her, down on the flat "kissing rock" (camp was so cringeworthy) overlooking the harbor. She sat with her knees pulled into her chest. She'd put on a camp sweatshirt.

"Hey! Claudia!" I jumped down the small, steep trail.

She turned her head. "Oh, John, hey."

She made no move to stand up, so I sat down next to her.

"What's up?"

She stared out at the water.

"Sucky night," she said, finally.

"That . . . sucks," I said. Not the smoothest.

"Yeah," she sighed. "I'm just trying to cool down."

I glanced at her. She wasn't lying. Her jaw clenched tightly. Something was really pissing her off. This was why I liked Claudia—she was real, like a real person. Not like other girls, who pretend like everything's fine, and then flip out at you.

"Sorry," I said, scooted a little closer. I reached into my pocket, pulled out a set of strings. "Knots?"

She looked at my outstretched hand and actually smiled. "Yeah, thanks." She grabbed the black strings and began folding them, pushing, pulling until she had a fish hook. Straightforward, perfectly done.

"This helps," she said. But not enough. Her jawline still looked like the Hulk. "So how's your night?"

I thought about it. "Fine," I said. "But I did want to ask you a question."

"Okay, shoot," she said. She started on a monkey's paw.

"Do you want to, like, hang out sometime?"

She paused. "Like, how?"

A fair, vague question. She was good. I tried: "Like, on the weekend? Not at camp?" I hoped she got the message. I couldn't go further than that without feeling like I was handing her a bat to bust my nuts.

"Do you mean like a date?" she asked, still staring at the string. I was super affronted. That sounded so old school. *Date.* It was pretty cute, though.

"Like, *hanging out*," I clarified.

She paused again, then nodded. Phew. Hard part over with. But then came something worse: silence. Not actual silence, because the small waves broke softly on the rocks in front of us. I counted waves instead of seconds: One . . . two . . . three . . .

"I'll think about it," she said finally.

"Really?" I said.

Someone else's voice jumped out. "Hey, friends, what's going on?"

Claudia freaked and shoved the rope back into my hands.

CHAPTER 14

Ben

I WATCHED BEE AND Margo go, then stepped out of the bush, prickled and dazed.

Bee. Talking to Margo. About me. Behind my back.

Well, technically, in front of a bush, but whatever.

Cool. Real cool. I loved parties.

I kicked a pebble. Camp Dogberry was really something else. You stop to pee and get to hear all your worst qualities listed systematically. Bee's words echoed all tinny in my head: *childish, disorganized, immature, obnoxious, spineless, puppy-like.*

I wish he wasn't here.

I shivered. So, the moment with the boats, the bantering over starting the fire . . . I was a moron. None of that meant anything. I breathed in and out.

It's fine. *You knew she didn't like you, Ben, you just let yourself get carried away for an hour.* That's nothing after getting carried away every summer for eight years.

I would walk back to the campfire, but from the other direction. I didn't want Bee to think I'd overheard their conversation.

Or did I?

I stood there in the dark, unable to decide.

Goddamn it. Immature? A terrible employee? I mean, I was late to morning meeting a lot. And yeah, I was never great at planning ahead. And sometimes I forgot things, like deodorant or my sleeping bag. And okay, one summer I forgot pants. Just all my pants.

Did she really think I'd just do whatever Donald did?

Well, you did feel like you could reapply once Donald told you he was coming back.

Fuck you, self, it was also because of the move.

Did you even really want an internship, or were you just afraid you wouldn't get one?

You totally are *spineless.*

Shuuuuuut uuuuuuup.

I'd changed. Didn't she know I'd done a whole year at college? I'd never missed a class, had aced my work, and spent every waking hour studying. Not that she'd heard about any of that, I guess. Because we weren't friends anymore.

It shouldn't have been that big of a surprise that she felt this way. I knew things were bad between us. I knew that I might've done something wrong that night. The problem was, I didn't know what it was.

Or maybe this was how she'd felt all along. I mean, from that conversation, it *sounded* like Margo didn't know anything about that night last summer, and Bee and Margo were close. So the only logical explanation was that Bee super regretted what had happened, and she was horrifically embarrassed, and she didn't want anyone to know.

I was so sick of guessing. Would I ever actually know the truth?

Whatever the case, clearly, she hated me, and she never wanted to kiss me again, maybe she never had. I shouldn't have come back here, with the harbor and the trails and the drama and the stars so gorgeous they almost reminded me of Bee.

When I got back to the campfire none of my friends were there. I grabbed another beer and sat down to discuss Capture the Flag strategies with Dave. I laid out a tentative plan for this year.

"Isn't that against the rules?" he whispered, concerned.

"Do you want to play by the rules, or do you want to win?" I whispered back darkly.

He looked confused. "Both?"

"Wrong. Answer."

"We're *baaaaack*, losers!" Donald had appeared on the other side of the fire. As my eyes adjusted, Margo and Hana materialized next to him. Where was Claudia? And—

"Where's Bee?" I called out. Shit. This second beer had gone straight to my mouth.

"She's coming!" Margo assured me, with a giddy smile.

I shook my head, stood up, and walked across the campfire area. Like I figured, Donald wasn't holding Hana's hand, so it looked to me like Claudia was just being her usual paranoid self. Not that she didn't have good reasons, but this was camp, not school, and nobody here was looking to make her miserable. That settled in my mind, I made a decision.

"I think I wanna go," I said.

"What?" Donald laughed. "Absolutely not."

"I'm tired," I explained, as if that had ever been a good enough reason for Donald. When I said it, Margo looked at me, then away quickly. Had she seen me on the way back? Did she know I'd heard their conversation?

"You're not tired." Donald shook his head. "It's, like, ten thirty. Why do you want to go?"

"Look, I just don't want to deal with Bee right—"

"The feeling's mutual."

I turned around, and there she was, illuminated by the fire, casting a ten-foot shadow, the flames' light shimmering across her cheekbones. *Goddamn it.*

Focus, Ben, she just trashed you.

CHAPTER 15

Bee

SO I *HAD* BRUISED Ben's ego. Serves him right, I thought, for snooping on our conversation. I couldn't help it—my gaze flickered over to him, and his eyes flashed hurt back at me.

Whatever.

"Donald"—I turned and addressed him—"you asked me to get Claudia." I stepped aside and revealed Claudia, who was scowling powerfully. "I found her sitting on the rocks, sulking." I left out *with John*. Something weird was going on there, but we'd left him and his buddies on the trail. No need to make any of this more complicated.

"Oh, come on!" Claudia cried, startling all of us. "I was not sulking!"

"You were hunched over on the rocks," I pointed out. "And you had a big pouty face on."

"Can everyone just leave me alone?" she asked loudly. "I just want to get off the island." Had everyone had too much to drink? Wasn't Ben supposed to be keeping track of this? Incompetent.

Hana bit her lip and glanced at me.

"Me too," Ben interjected. "I want to go to bed." He stood not quite upright, leaning to the left. So much for teaching me how to drink.

"All right, all right." Donald tried to put an arm around Claudia, but she shrugged him off. Tipsy was not a good look on her. I glanced at Hana, whose forehead pinched in worry. All the other counselors watched us like we were onstage. Which, I guess, we kind of were up here, front lit by the fire.

"Maybe bed isn't a bad idea," I said quickly. "Ben, can you take Claudia—"

"Got it." Ben nodded at me and strode toward her. I guess he wasn't so incompetent, under direct orders. I felt warmth spread in my cheeks, but it wasn't the beer or the fire. It was that feeling that I could count on Ben, even when we were at odds, in moments like these.

"No, no, no, no, no, no. No." We froze. Donald pushed Ben away from Claudia. "No sleep till *kissing*!"

Our audience erupted in laughter. Ben threw up his hands. Margo giggled so hard she sputtered her sip of beer. But one of us still wasn't having it.

"Who's kissing, Donald?" Claudia snapped.

"*You're* doing the kissing, dummy." Donald rolled his eyes and held out his free hand to her. Claudia didn't move.

"I don't think she wants to kiss you," Margo whispered loudly. More laughter, including Margo, cracking up at her own joke. I shushed her.

"I don't want to kiss her, either," Donald whispered loudly back. "She's going to kiss"—he pointed to my sister—"*Hana.*"

At Hana's name, Claudia's whole body changed. Her arms uncrossed, her jaw unclenched. She panicked, looking at Donald quickly, then Hana, who braved a small smile. Donald dropped his beer in the dirt, *thunk*. He grabbed Hana's hand first, then Claudia's, and brought them together.

"Hi," Hana whispered. I swooned at the cuteness, just a little.

"It's official: You two totally like each other! You both told me!!" Donald proclaimed giddily. "Now, kiss! Or something."

Hana stood there, hand clasped in Claudia's, her smile soft and hopeful. Claudia, meanwhile, looked like she'd been punched in the brain.

"Kiss! Kiss! Kiss!" Donald started a chant, Margo immediately caught it, and soon everyone was chanting and clapping. The strangest repeat-after-me song ever. Claudia looked up, suddenly realizing what was happening, and stared at the mass of chanting weirdos with absolute terror. Hana registered Claudia's alarm, and the bubble popped. She went from thrilled to seriously uncomfortable in a snap.

I grabbed them both and ushered them toward the trail, away from the fire, to an "Aaaaww!" from the disappointed chanters. The new couple both looked at me, dazed, waiting for instruction.

"The kissing rock"—I nodded down the trail—"has a really lovely view of the harbor."

"Ooooh." Hana smiled.

She glanced shyly at Claudia, who nodded in reply, still looking like a moose in headlights.

"Thanks, Bee," Hana said, and without another word or look, took Claudia's hand and led her down the trail.

"No problem!" I called after, and watched them float off into the darkness. A couple whistles and hoots came from the campfire behind me, but it didn't seem like they could hear it. I'd never seen Hana look at someone like she'd looked at Claudia. Well, I'd never seen her look at someone that way and have them looking back. Their connection sparked visibly in the dark air.

Without warning, tears welled in my eyes.

"You gonna keep creeping on your sister?" Donald shouted to me.

I pulled down my sweatshirt sleeve, wiped at my eyes, and walked back to the campfire.

"It's just nice to see something actually working out," I said, and sat down directly across from Ben.

CHAPTER 16

Hana

IT DIDN'T REALLY MATTER that the rock had a nice view. The only thing that mattered was the kissing part.

Kissing Claudia was like ascending a flight of stairs that seem to go on forever — every height you reach, you realize there's more. It kind of hurts, but you keep going because you know, you feel, that there's something magical at the top.

Claudia

Kissing Hana was everything I'd ever wanted.

Hana

Our lips touched, again, and again, and again. Sometimes for a few seconds, sometimes barely brushing. My head reeled, softly. I stroked her cheek, her neck, under her ears. One of her arms wrapped around my waist, and it fit perfectly.

Claudia

I glanced up toward the trail, the fire pit in the distance. I tried not to worry about if anyone could see us. Because this incredible, beautiful person was kissing me like her life depended on it, and I'd never kissed like this before.

I wondered if she had.

Hana

Lips, hands, lips, eyes, skin. Claudia, Claudia, Claudia.

Claudia

Eventually, I pulled back. When I did, she looked confused, and kind of dizzy. I tried not to smile at how cute she was.

"We should probably go back up," I whispered. My fingers tentatively reached out to touch her cheek. She brought her hand up, placed it on top of mine, and closed her eyes. I didn't know what to do.

Hana

I closed my eyes, took a breath, pulled myself together. I really wanted to keep falling apart, with her, in this new way.

"If we have to." I sighed and looked at her. She smiled. Her smile was so genuine. I felt like I knew everything behind that smile. I realized I trusted it.

I took her hand in mine as we stood up. We made our way back to the fire pit. Right before we got within earshot of the rest of them, I whispered, "To be continued?"

Claudia

Hana asking *me* that was a joke. But I nodded at her. "To be continued."

Would I really get to touch her again? Would I get to keep

touching her? Was this summer going to be the best summer of my entire life?

When we sat back down, I could've sworn the fire danced just a little higher.

CHAPTER 17

Bee

"ANOTHER HAPPY COUPLE, brought together by *me!*" Donald crowed.

"You're praaaactically cupid!" Margo singsonged.

I rolled my eyes but laughed, too. It was late—we were on our way down to the dock for departure. Claudia and Hana were walking slightly ahead of the group, so blissfully into each other that they couldn't hear the group of tipsy, tired counselors fumbling behind them.

"*Another* couple?" Ben asked Donald. "Pretty sure this is your first success. Unless you count Kangaroo Court."

Kangaroo Court was our mock trial performance game at Camp Dogberry. Raphael, our improv teacher and my favorite person ever, ran it. We let the campers put the counselors "on trial" for silly things, like not wearing enough sunscreen (Margo), or singing loudly and badly in the shower every morning (Donald).

Raphael also liked to perform fake weddings at Kangaroo Court. He married Mom and Dad last year, and Donald had convinced him to marry Francis and Sam, a couple of older counselors, a few years ago.

"Well, first of all, I *do* count Kangaroo Court," Donald said over his shoulder. "But I have a *real* couple success rate, too." He turned, and flashed his flashlight into Ben's eyes.

"Hey! Ow! What?"

"You and Bee, four years ago, second-year CITs?"

I snorted.

"That *really* doesn't count," Ben said. Why did that make me want to smack him?

"Oh, that magical summer," Donald sighed. "When you two couldn't get enough of each other."

"Ooooh! Right!" Margo wrapped an arm around me. Then something horrific dawned on her: "Hey, did you guys kiiiss? Were you *first kisses*??"

Ack. "No," I said firmly. "We didn't do anything. It was just one of Donald's stupid schemes."

"But . . ." Margo's face screwed up in tipsy thought. "You *were* his girlfriend, right?"

"She was," Ben interjected, glancing over his shoulder at us. "For three entire days." I glared at him. "And we slow danced," he continued. "At the dance party that year."

"Ooooh!" Margo giggled. "Scandalous!"

I couldn't believe Ben. I took a breath and reminded myself that I promised my parents I wasn't going to murder him.

Buuut you only said you wouldn't drown him, I realized. *You could still murder him in other ways.*

"If I remember correctly, I dumped you *during* that slow dance." I settled for death by humiliation.

"Right," he agreed, too easily. "For being *childish*, *obnoxious*, and *spineless*."

Crap. My own words from earlier echoed back at me. Ridiculous, eavesdropping Ben. My eyes rolled and my cheeks burned all at once.

Great, Bee, you brought this completely on yourself, vis-à-vis the most absurd boy in the world.

"But hey," he continued. "I don't think that actually counts, either—can you even dump someone if you weren't technically dating them?"

"You totally can." Donald sighed and shook his head. "She's got you there, bro."

"Hey, Ben." Margo reached out a hand. "You just found out you were dumped four years ago. Do you need anything? Ice cream? A hug?"

And now we were laughing again. I couldn't decide if I was fine with all of this, or if I wanted to set myself on fire. And because this was still an enormous joke, everyone quickly grabbed paddleboats and left me with two options: 1. Hop in the moping boat, John's vessel, or 2. Enjoy a paddle for two with Ben.

"Jerks!" Ben shouted at the other four, as they pulled away from the dock.

I stomped into the front seat. "Let's just get this over with."

He looked at my outstretched hand, sighed, and took it. Shaking violently, he stepped forward, then collapsed awkwardly next to me.

"Thanks," he muttered, righting himself.

"No problem."

As we chugged away from the dock, my right hand buzzed on the steering handle. I told it to stop. It kind of listened. I felt Ben to my right, maybe looking at me. A small silence passed over us, and I almost felt something reset in my chest. The boat, the water, the island, what if last summer had all been a dream—

But by the time we reached the Dogberry shore, we were arguing again.

"Capture the Flag is *always* at the end of the week," Ben complained.

"I know," I said as I steered us toward the hazy outline of the beach. "But it's always a nightmare to do that the same morning the session checks out."

"So what are you suggesting?"

"I'm not *suggesting* anything. It's a done deal," I said. "My parents asked me to set the events schedule for the summer, and I did. Capture the Flag is on a Wednesday." I hopped out of the boat into the knee-deep water and pulled the boat in closer.

"But I'm the sports leader!" he complained, still sitting in the passenger seat. "Shouldn't I get a say in this?"

"Capture the Flag isn't a sport," I snapped. "Can you get out of the boat, please?" He grumbled and climbed, very slowly, onto the dock. I was regretting any and all of this. Tonight, the last week, last summer, every summer leading up to that . . .

All the counselors had pulled in and were helping each other stow their boats back on the racks. Margo and Donald helped with ours. John and co. had already disappeared. The younger counselors wandered off toward their cabins, promising they'd hydrate. I looked for Hana and Claudia, and saw them lingering in the water. Was it possible to enjoy kissing with your feet that cold?

Slowly, I became aware that Ben was still muttering about Capture the Flag, sort of directed at me. I decided to ignore it on purpose now.

"You know." Donald came up behind me and swung an arm around my shoulders. "It kind of seems like you two aren't in love anymore."

That brought Ben up short. He shoved his hands in his pockets.

"Tragedy." I laughed. "I guess I'll give up. I'll never love again." Kind of pleased with how that sounded so over it. I was. I was so over it.

"Never?" Donald turned to me, his face close to mine. Alcohol breath. I inched back a little.

"Please," I sighed, in spite of myself. "The potential dudes at my school were the worst. Maybe I'll have better luck in college."

I thought I could feel Ben's eyes on the back of my neck. I turned to glare—

"Well, what about me?" Donald asked.

"Ha!" I snorted. But when I looked at Donald, he wasn't laughing. By the yellow light of the buddy board, I could see him watching my face intently. Wait, was he serious? I couldn't tell, and I'd already laughed. Shit. Shit. As Raphael would say, *commit*.

I laughed again and shoved him away. "No way, Donald. You're too fancy for me—I couldn't go to those big black-tie senator events every weekend. I'd end up stabbing someone in the eye with my salad fork."

There was an awkward pause, in which I freaked out that I'd erred to the point of no return. Who was listening to us? Ben? Crap.

But then Donald cracked his familiar smile. He clapped his hands, hooting. "I'd like to see that!"

"I didn't say I wouldn't be stabbing *you*," I pointed out.

"Damn, Bee!" He reeled, laughing. I couldn't tell if his reaction was genuine or overkill.

"Sorry, not sorry," I said, shooting him a smile.

"No apologies, please." Donald shook his head. "Happy to be roasted by your wit."

"That's why we love Bee!" Margo popped in between us and slipped her hand through mine and squeezed. "She's the wittiest, silliest Queen of the North. Plus, she's a Libra."

I squeezed back. "You and your *astronomy*."

"What, it's true!" Margo insisted. "The stars don't lie—your planet is Venus, hon, and you're beautiful, just, and super sarcastic."

"How scientific." I laughed. "Well, my birth mom *did* warn the adoption center that I was 'born under a dancing star.'"

Immediately, the group around me went silent, pity hanging in the air, and I cursed myself. Sometimes I forgot how people acted about my childhood and adoption, even my close friends.

Everyone panicked. Donald looked at Margo, who looked at me, then glanced at Ben, who took a step forward—and suddenly, bringing a great wave of relief, Hana was at my side.

"I've always thought that star must've had some serious dancing skills."

"You know it!" I laughed, too loudly. Hana held out a hand, I twirled into her, and she dipped me. Everyone laughed a slightly hysterical laugh, glad the awkward was over. For them, anyway.

"Now, unlike you jerks," I said, standing up, "I have to be awake to help Mom and Dad set up before morning meeting. So I'm going to bed."

They whined about me skipping the after-party, but I yeah-yeahed, kissed Margo's cheek good night, and started back to Little Bat. Halfway there, I heard small footsteps running to catch up behind me, and Hana's soft voice:

"Bee! Are you okay?"

My little baby seal. I pulled her in.

"I'm A-OK. Now tell me everything!!"

CHAPTER 18

Ben

THE BALLS OF MY feet tried to push me forward, to run after Hana and Bee. My ears rung, and my chest burned from wanting to so much. I was dying to go after them, to apologize, and make sure Bee was okay. Everyone had acted so weird. But considering everything that had happened tonight, and I guess the last year, I was pretty sure I wouldn't be welcome.

I turned and trudged after the other three instead, toward Donald's cabin for the "after-party."

"I'm such an idiot," I heard Donald say as I caught up. "And Bee's *such* a queen." Was he an idiot for a dumb joke? Or for actually trying to ask Bee out?

"Agreed to both." Margo patted his shoulder. "The queen bee among us workers."

"Yeah, but she's changing the day of Capture the Flag," I said with a scowl.

"Which makes sense," Claudia said over her shoulder. Seemed she'd recovered enough from kissing to speak. "We're always scrambling afterward to get everyone packed up."

"But ending a session on Capture the Flag always leaves the

kids super pumped about camp, and all the great times they had," I complained. "Even if they were homesick and miserable the whole week."

"Like Dale." Donald nodded.

"That's not a bad point," Margo offered.

"Besides, I'd already planned a kick ball tournament for that Wednesday."

"No offense," Claudia said. Yay. "But considering your disorganized track record, Bee probably didn't suspect you'd planned anything."

I groaned. "Well, she could've asked!"

We'd arrived at Donald's cabin. He flicked on the porch light, nearly blinding me. Donald looked hungover already—Claudia had all the kissing energy to eat up the alcohol.

"Well, dude, she's had it in for you since last summer," Donald pointed out. "But I can't imagine she changed the camp schedule just to spite you."

"Can't you?" I demanded. "She hates me now! She thinks I shouldn't even be at camp. Even though I *run the sports program*, I'm, like, a hopeless kid to her."

Margo shifted, arms hugging her stomach. "Umm, Ben . . ."

I looked around and realized everyone was staring at me. Probably waiting for the downer to leave so they could party.

"Sorry, guys." I sighed. "I'm going to bed." I was getting out of line, and I didn't want to make Bee's stinging opinion of me stick with the rest of my friends.

"Night," Claudia called after me. I waved in her direction. I couldn't *really* be mad at her for falling in love with Hana. But if tonight was any indicator, I'd been totally justified in my rant about

drama. Or was nobody else disturbed by Claudia's earlier flash trans-
formation into a possessive, paranoid snapping turtle?

Whatever. All's well and all that.

I walked back to the waterfront, just past my cabin. I grabbed a
few flat stones, skipped them on the top of the little waves. From
here, I could see Little Bat's windows glowing in the dark.

And I could almost see my younger self, staying up late with the
Leonato girls, playing Uno, drinking bug juice till our teeth were
stained red.

Why had I tried? How had I messed this up so badly?

Why had I come back?

WHAT HAPPENED: PART 4

Ben

SO I ASKED HER if we were going to kiss, and she laughed right in my face. Classic. And then I laughed too. What an asshat thing to say. *You barf your heart out about your family, and she was nice to you, so what, now you get to make out with her?*

"Ben!" she managed to say, through the giggling. "What in the world—"

"Sorry, sorry." I waved my hands. "That was uncalled for."

She bumped her shoulder against mine, still laughing.

"But I mean," I ventured, "it is my *last summer. . . .*"

She landed a thorough smack in the middle of my chest.

"Well deserved." I nodded. "Sorry, I'm buzzed."

"I'm buzzed too," she pointed out. "And *I'm* not proposing ideas completely devoid of any sense."

"That's fair." *Devoid of any sense.* Right. I collapsed again, falling back onto the blanket. This was *really* why I never dated anyone, I thought. Because I am the most awkward human being alive, and any attempts I made to be otherwise were pointless.

"But I am going to lie down too," Bee announced. I looked over, but suddenly, she was there already, her head resting on my arm.

"Can I use you as a pillow?" she asked all nonchalant. "I'm a little sleepy now."

"Sure." I could barely believe it, but then she snuggled up into my armpit. I stared into the sky, praying silently to the Maine stars that my deodorant had lasted. I scooped my hand up and around her shoulder. And then, like magic, I was lying on a blanket, with my arm wrapped around Bee Leonato, the greatest girl in the universe. Breathing in tandem, our bodies slowly syncing. I could've lain there with her forever. The leaves above us could've changed, the snow could've buried us, I wouldn't have cared—we'd just thaw out in the spring.

"I have one," Bee said.

"One what?" I murmured.

"A personal confession."

That woke me up. "Okay, go!"

"Well . . ." she began. I tried to look at her, but I couldn't without moving, which would probably ruin everything. "When I was five years old," she continued, "when my mom and dad brought me to the US, it was obviously a big adjustment. I didn't know English when I first came, just basic phrases, and they only knew some basic Amharic. So I liked everybody and all that, but it didn't feel like home."

"That makes sense." Maine was nothing like Ethiopia. Even I knew that.

"During that time, I thought a lot about running away . . ."

I knew the feeling.

". . . I think partly for the adventure of it. I'm not sure." She paused. "But anyway, the day I decided to actually do it, I told both my parents."

I laughed, thinking of little Bee, the honest rebel. I could sense her smiling next to me.

"I know, right?" She laughed, too. "And Mom said, 'Okay, I don't want you to go, but if you're going to, we should pack you a bag first.' So they packed my backpack with my clothes and my toothbrush. They put on my puffy coat and sent me into the woods behind Big Bat. And as I left, Mom said, 'Bee, before you get too far, check the front pocket of your backpack.' So a few steps in I did, because I was convinced it was candy."

I couldn't help laughing again, and then I gave her shoulder a small squeeze. I didn't plan it, it just happened naturally. Instinctually. Did I have good instincts? I think she liked it, because for a moment, she stayed closer, in the squeeze, her head farther up my shoulder.

"Anyway." She relaxed. "It wasn't candy. It was a note from my parents, which was at first a bit of a letdown. But then I read it. It said: 'Bee, we love you, please don't go.' Simple English," she explained.

"Right," I whispered.

"And every time I decided to run away, which was a lot in that first year, they'd pack my backpack and put a note in the front. And eventually I named it the Bee-Don't-Go Bag. And then I stopped wanting to run away."

"Bee-Don't-Go Bag," I repeated, dumbstruck.

"Mmmhmm."

I'd seen framed photos of little Bee at the Leonatos'. Braids, shining cheeks, that huge grin, one arm planted firmly around little Hana, always. I'd envied her perfect family, getting to live at Camp Dogberry all year long. Here, it was safe. I never really thought about how maybe it hadn't always felt like that to her. I pictured Nik and

Andy, dutifully packing a backpack for her, and then waiting for her to return. Hoping the next time that she wouldn't feel she had to go. . . .

. . .

"Ben?"

. . . . . .

"Ben, are you crying?"

"No. I mean, I can't help it."

She laughed and sat up. My shoulder felt cold. I sat up too, and rubbed at my nose, trying to wipe off all the gross happening on my face. I must be pretty wimpy and disgusting to her, I thought.

"But, uh." I wiped my hands on my shorts. "That was such a beautiful story." I finally looked at her again. Our eyes met. And I realized she really didn't think I was disgusting.

"Aww." She smiled. "Well, you're the only one outside my family who knows it. This probably goes without saying but—"

"Never. What happens at Nest stays at Nest."

"I promise too." She put her hand on top of mine.

We were looking at each other like that again. Like when I'd asked if we were going to kiss. I forced myself to hold steady—I wanted us to keep looking at each other like that, to stay in one of these moments, because inside them, there was this tiny possibility of something.

Like it might actually happen.

CHAPTER 19

Hana

AFTER FIFTEEN MINUTES OF sister talk, Bee yawned enormously and said she was going to sleep. I ducked out to go to Donald's, and as I walked away from Little Bat, I stopped in my tracks: Bee might've been faking the yawn.

I turned back to look at our cabin—a flashlight lit one of the windows. I wondered if I should go back and make sure she wasn't being upset on her own. I'd been so wrapped up in Claudia (literally) that I'd only caught the end of the adoption conversation. Once we were alone, she'd given me a quick rundown, at my urging, and mentioned something about Donald "making a joke" about asking her out, and then things getting weird. When I tried to ask more, she'd insisted we talk about the whole Claudia-and-I-kissing situation instead.

On my way to Donald's, I filled my water bottle up with the shallow water, just at the spot Claudia and I had lingered. It had been amazing to me we hadn't been electrocuted. I swear, I had felt sparks between our lips. I bottled up the memories with the water, and screwed the lid on tightly—later, I'd empty it all into one of the vases in my bedroom.

Coyote's screen door fell sharply on the frame behind me.

"Hana!" Donald looked up, delighted, as I stepped inside. Coyote was a cavernous cabin—twelve beds, *two* lights. Every Dogberry cabin had camper signatures all over the walls and bedposts, written in permanent ink, but only Coyote had signatures in every color. Donald always brought a pack of rainbow Sharpies.

Steady rap music played on Donald's laptop on the floor. Margo and Donald sat on his counselor's bed on the back wall, a bottle of something between them. Above his bed, Donald had pinned up the big collage he'd made last year: a coyote's face, with enormous yellow eyes, constructed out of tiny newspaper and magazine clippings.

Claudia hovered next to the door, wearing boxer shorts and a not-loose-enough-fitting gray T-shirt.

I needed to sit down.

"Hey." I smiled and slid onto the bed opposite Donald's. Claudia immediately sat down next to me. I felt my smile widen. "I couldn't sleep."

"Kind of glad." Claudia nudged me with her shoulder.

"Excellent!" Donald proclaimed. "Welcome to the exclusive after-party!"

"Where's Ben?" I asked.

Donald shook his head. "He went to bed."

Margo made an "eek" face. "I don't know how he's going to fall asleep over all that angry muttering coming out of his mouth."

"I think he'd been chewed up enough by Bee," Claudia offered. I winced.

"Well, they chewed up each other. . . ." I trailed off.

Donald smirked, and Margo giggled.

"Umm, never mind." Claudia blinked at me, her honey eyes laughing. She held up her left arm, and I scooted in under her shoulder. Her hand kind of flopped over the side of my arm. It was sort of awkward, but that didn't make it any less magical.

"No!" Donald shouted. "*Do* mind, because we have an idea."

"Mmm!" Margo agreed, smiling a little too wide. "And we need your advice." These two were going to be real gross in the morning.

"Oh?"

"Yeah," Claudia sighed. "Donald wants to do another setup."

"*You two* can hardly complain." Donald pointed a finger at her, at *us*.

I let out a giggle; Claudia shivered. I put a hand on her leg to steady her. More teeny shocks. How many body parts could we touch before lightning struck?

"Okay, who's getting set up?" I asked. "Margo and Bobby? Officially?"

"Ew, no!" Margo said quickly. *"Bee."*

I looked at Donald. "With who?"

You?

The last few years, I'd noticed Donald around Bee. Donald was always funny, always on top of it, but around Bee, there was this tiny falter, this small hitch in his game. He always pushed through like it hadn't happened, but I'd got the sense he felt something for her. I'd never mentioned it to Bee, because it was pretty clear to me she didn't feel that way about him.

Which was partly why that whole Donald-liked-me rumor had been super weird today. Thank goodness it had been nothing.

If Donald's feelings had been hinted at before, I was pretty sure they'd been confirmed tonight. Even if he'd played it off as a joke, and then put his foot in his mouth.

"We're setting her up with *Benjamin*!" Donald declared, raising his bottle. "Those two have been into each other since . . . seventh grade?"

"Years!" Margo yelled in agreement. "They're my OTP."

We laughed. I guessed they were my One True Pairing too. I'd always thought they were going to get together.

"Right," Donald nodded. "And we *know* something happened between them last summer."

All eyes turned to me. I held up both hands. "I don't know anything," I assured them. I felt guilty even confirming that piece of non-information.

"And she wouldn't tell us if she did." Margo toasted the bottle at me.

I smiled at her. "No, I wouldn't."

"But something *did* happen!" Margo continued. "It's so obvious. They've been acting weird ever since last year's sparkler party."

I watched Donald's face. Was that the tiniest flinch ever, or a blink?

"Well, they've always made fun of each other," Claudia said.

"Oh, come on," Margo said. "It wasn't like this before. Before it was friendly. Or *flirting*."

"That's true," I said. "They were friends." I turned to Claudia. "Good friends."

"And this could be Ben's last shot!" Donald hopped off the bed in excitement, held out his arms wide. A presentation was beginning. "Bee's gonna get scooped up by some hottie this fall."

"Totally." Margo nodded. "She's already joined, like, nine clubs."

I felt a pang. Had she?

Donald laughed and pointed at Margo. "Exactly. She's a hot nerd, and there's gonna be a line of guys banging down her door. So Ben's got one last shot, this summer."

I wasn't a fan of discussing Bee's love life behind her back, but Donald was probably right. Bee was going to have her pick of guys at college. My mom had sometimes said this to Bee, when she'd bemoaned her dating options at Messina High. Unlike me, she'd never even sort of dated anyone at MHS. But in Boston, that big, looming skyline in my head, she'd have so many options. Odds were she'd meet at least one guy she might actually want to spend time with.

Maybe this *was* Ben's last shot.

"Well," I managed. Claudia gave my shoulder a squeeze. She'd figured out what to do with her floppy hand. I loved this.

Donald clapped at me. "Hana's on board. Claudia?"

"I don't know what I'm agreeing to yet."

"Good point." He climbed back on the bed, put one arm around Margo, and leaned in. He motioned for Claudia and me to come over. We glanced at each other, quickly acknowledging neither one of us wanted to move, and then we did. We crowded around Donald on his squishy, orange sleeping bag.

"I have a plan," he whispered.

"Of course you do," Margo said, tipping over onto his shoulder.

I should've guessed. He was on a roll. He'd been so proud earlier, taking me for a walk, little by little revealing that Claudia liked me, while at the same time making sure I liked her back before he did. I'd been so terrified that *he* liked me, the entire thing had worked perfectly.

"What's the plan?" I asked him.

"We're going to *trick them* into admitting they like each other!"

Donald said triumphantly. "You and I," he said to Claudia, "will set up Ben so that he overhears us saying that Bee likes him but won't tell him. And then *you two*"—he gestured to me and Margo—"will do the same thing with Bee. Reversed."

Margo squealed and hit my arm excitedly.

"I actually like that idea." Claudia raised her eyebrows. "It's like Battleship."

I smiled, but I wasn't so sure. I wasn't going to bring it up again, for fear of more speculation, but we *didn't* know what had happened between them last summer. We didn't know what we would be getting in the middle of. What if it was serious?

But wouldn't Bee have told me if it was?

"I'm a genius." Donald twirled his pointer fingers.

"But, *genius*," Margo whispered, "what comes after that? After they hear they like each other?"

"Yeah, how do they get together?" Claudia asked.

"Aha! That's the best part!" Donald bounced on the bed. "They have to figure it out, and *we* get to watch!"

Claudia lit up. "Okay, that's good. But what if they don't figure it out?"

"Oh, they will." Margo nodded. "Eventually. Probably. Hana, what do you think?"

Three pairs of eyes on me.

I wanted Bee to be happy. And right now, when she and Ben weren't busy shouting at each other, they were ignoring each other. Something had happened, and she wouldn't even talk to me about it, but I could tell she was still upset by whatever it was. I wanted to fix that for her. Maybe this would.

"Let's do it," I said, finally.

"We have the sisterly blessing!" Donald whooped. "Let's start this week, so they're paired up for the sparkler party."

Margo shook her head. "Darlin', you're one part schemer, one part disgusting romantic."

"Darlin'," he twanged back, "I've never claimed otherwise. And now you all get to share in my glory!" Donald grinned. "Because we'll *all* be the camp cupids this summer. And this will be our ultimate victory, in the name of *love*!"

Claudia, Margo, and I looked at one another, wide-eyed. Donald had finally lost it. I grabbed his water bottle from the floor and tossed it to him.

"Bro"—Claudia moved toward the door with me—"go to sleep."

We slammed out into the night air, and Margo followed a few moments after.

"I tucked him in," she whispered.

On the trail back, Margo couldn't stop giggling about our plan, and her giggles combined with the night peepers made a soothing, happy soundtrack for our walk.

At Little Bat, she turned to us and said, "Well, I'll leave before this gets awkward," and bounced away.

"Good night!" I shouted after her.

"Thanks for not making it awkward!" Claudia called half-heartedly.

In the dark, I couldn't quite see Claudia's face. But I could feel her hands, and then her lips, her breath. I could feel her. I wanted her. My mind pulsed, begging this night to never end.

But eventually, the kisses got longer and sleepier. One more kiss on my cheek. A whisper:

"To be continued."

Forever, I thought.

I watched her leave, striding back to her own cabin, her shoulders slightly hunched. This adorable, awkward, perfect human was mine.

I stayed outside for just a few more moments, and then, as if just for me, the moon peeked out from behind the clouds, lighting up the world in a blue crush. I stood on Little Bat's porch, listening to the peepers and the waves, still feeling Claudia's lips on mine, aching for them for one more second. I wouldn't need to make any paper stars tonight. I was already filled up with my own.

A light caught the corner of my left eye. I turned to see Margo and her flashlight, popping up back down the other side of the trail, near the boys' cabins. The *exclusive* exclusive after-party. I wondered how any of them could even stay awake. I'd just been kissed within an inch of my life, and I'd never been so happy to snuggle down into my sleeping bag. It was easier to fall asleep when you were happy.

CHAPTER 20

Vanessa

COUNTDOWN TO CAMP: *zero* days, one hour.

I had been waiting *my entire life* for this. Well, umm, about five years. But that's still a long time. Fine. I had been waiting *more than a third of my life* for this.

My mom found Camp Dogberry when I was eight, and she'd sent us here every year since. My sisters came for the first time last year, but they'd been to camp to pick us up and drop us off so many times it was a tradition for them too. We all loved camp. The food was great, the cabins were cozy (especially Little Bat—and it has a skylight roof), and I wasn't one of those campers who got homesick. In the past, it had been this big escape, but I still got to be with Ben. So it was perfect.

Mom woke me up with a finger to her lips. She pointed to the girls—they were still asleep. She whispered she'd gotten a babysitter for the morning so we could drive up to camp alone together.

"And get breakfast?"

"Yes, we'll get breakfast."

I quickly showered and threw on the first-day outfit I'd prepared: well-worn red Camp Dogberry T-shirt, so I looked official, running shorts and Keen hiking sandals. I said good-bye to Smooshie. I felt bad I couldn't say good-bye to Ava and Layla, but they were sleeping like logs. Snoring logs. I hoped I didn't have eight-year-olds in my group.

We put my big bag out in the car. It was heavy, but I was positive I hadn't forgotten anything. *And* I'd brought an extra pair of Ben's pants, just in case.

Mom and I talked about everything at the diner, even though we'd talked about all of it for the last week straight. Which counselor and cabin I wanted, which campers I hoped were coming back, what they'd name the goats this year. I told Mom the story of Capture the Flag two years ago again—the one where Ben had defeated Claudia with a gorilla suit.

We finished breakfast and got back in the car. As we passed the town line, I felt an itty-bitty pang of sadness. We'd just moved here. Even after the month at Aunt Deb's, I still wasn't used to walking around a home freely, no longer waiting for a bomb to go off, a burst of ringing anger.

Dishes! Money! Your mother! Your brother! You people!

I winced. How long would it take to forget all of that?

Camp. Think camp.

Countdown: thirty minutes.

I'd wanted to be a camp counselor since that first summer. The counselors were so cool. They were all best friends, and they got to stay up late and decide which games we were going to play, which art projects we were going to do. I wanted so badly to be a part of that.

Ben always said it wasn't as glamorous a job as it looked, but I think he just told me that so I wouldn't be jealous. Now I didn't have to be jealous anymore, because this year I'd get to spend the entire summer at camp as a counselor-in-training. CIT. I loved saying the acronym out loud. It felt professional.

We roared up I-95, and the trees and bushes got wilder and wilder the farther north we went. Mom chatted on the way up about the girls, and how they'd be there in a week so I didn't have to miss them too much.

"Can't wait!" I said. I knew in my heart that was true, it's just my heart was kind of full of other things at the moment. Like my cabin assignment and being on staff with my favorite counselors.

Countdown to being a first-year counselor: 1 year, 364 days.

"Nessie, are you going to get out of the car?"

We were here!!

Warm, sunny Camp Dogberry, which always felt warmer than the rest of Maine. I opened the door and breathed in that camp air: boat grunge, saltwater, animal poop, and rising bread. I hopped out of the car, grabbed my backpack, and tried not to run to check in. The dirt parking lot felt like a red carpet under my sneakers. I was a *CIT* this year!!

"Vanessa!" Bee checked me in with a big hug. Her hair was up in this braided faux-hawk do. She looked so cute. No wonder my brother secretly loved her.

"Bee!!" I grinned. "Where's Ben?"

"In Dam, stuffing his face." She smiled.

"Sounds like Ben." Mom came up behind us, carrying my bigger bag. "Hey, Bee"—she kissed her cheek—"is your mom around?"

"In the office." Bee nodded. "She said to tell her when you got here."

"I'll go find her myself, thanks!" Mom said. She kissed my forehead. "I'll see you next week, okay?"

"Sure, sure!"

I hugged Mom, and she went off in search of Nik. Our good-byes at camp were never super sad or long, because she came to visit a lot. Or to drop off something Ben forgot. And she always wrote me letters and postcards, even though we were only a couple hours apart.

I was just about to ask Bee what my cabin was, when I got *slammed* by Sophia, right in the stomach.

"Your bangs are so cute I'm going to die!!"

"Sophia!" I laughed. "You're going to kill me!"

"With love!!" she screamed, squeezing tighter.

When she finally released me, I took a moment to check out my best camp friend: dark tan skin, brown curly hair, wicked grin, shorter than me this year!! Wearing an all-pink ensemble, complete with pink handkerchief and pink sunglasses. Sophia took her color coordination seriously.

"I missed you so much!" she squealed.

"I couldn't tell!!" I smiled.

Somewhere behind her, my other best camp friend, Wallace, waved at me. I smiled—the same black, cowlick-y hair, ridiculously pale skin, and a *new* NASCAR T-shirt. He was tall and gangly this year, which was weird. I waved back through Sophia's bubbling, and eventually made it over to say hi.

Before we could really catch up, though (I had to tell them both about the divorce and the big move), Bee ushered us into the dining hall with the rest of the CITs for our first meeting.

Walking into Dam was how I would imagine walking into the great hall in a castle. The big main room was made of beautiful, spiral-y wood. Slabs of enormous trees were loosely shaped into long tables. The walls were covered in fading charts and maps of Maine's animals and plants, and an abandoned wasp nest hung like a disco ball from rafters in the center of the room. The poles and cross-beams were wrapped in twinkle lights that were never turned off. At the back, there was a friendly window—the drive-thru window, we called it—where you could talk to the cook, Shane. And where you ordered eggs. Next to it, a narrow wooden door led back to the kitchen for dish duty.

Not even dish duty could make this place less magical.

"He-llo! Nessie?" Sophia's voice cut through my dreamy entry. "Come on!" Most people at camp called me by Ben's nicknames, which I always forgot at first. I jumped and went to go sit down with her and Wallace. At the table were the other CITs this year, Joe and Isabelle. This was their second year, which meant they got to be first-year counselors *next year.* I was so jealous.

"So," I said as I slid in next to Sophia and Wallace. "Did you guys know that Claudia chopped off *all her hair?*"

Wallace's eyes widened. Sophia's mouth dropped open. "*No. Way.* Why would she—"

"All right, kiddos! Welcome back!" We looked to the top of the room, near the fireplace, and there stood Nik and Andy, both in cargo shorts, green camp T-shirts, and baseball caps; both smiling; and both holding clipboards. If I'd taken a picture of them right now, that would be, like, the quintessential Nik and Andy shot.

First, they doled out cabin assignments. I got Moose with Margo!! I'd wanted Little Bat, but I guess it was covered, since it already had two counselors, and the Leonato sisters were the best counselors ever. But Moose was a cute cabin, with a cute purple bench out front. And I loved Margo, and now I'd get to hear her bedtime songs all summer.

Sophia got Connie in Puffin, and Wallace got Donald in Coyote. Wallace was really excited about it, and Sophia just shrugged. I knew she probably wanted Margo—she kind of worshipped her style. I felt a little bad.

"We're all so excited to have you here," Andy finished, after the last assignment. "And to get you guys trained so you can be the best Dogberry counselors ever someday."

"Much better than this year's," Nik added. "They're terrible."

"Hey!" called voices from the kitchen. Everyone laughed.

"We'll give you"—Bee looked at her watch—"fifteen minutes to stow your stuff, and then it's back here for the first hour of orientation. Now, we need three volunteers."

There were six of us total, and we all raised our hands.

"Excellent." Nik laughed. "You can *all* take out the compost buckets on the way to the cabins. Pairs are better anyway, since they're heavy. Let's get going!"

A couple other CITs, including Sophia, groaned loudly. I didn't say anything. Okay, so compost was gross—every piece of food scrap from the camp went in there—but *I* was determined to be the most hirable, helpful CIT there ever was. No way was I screwing up my chances of working here like Ben. Speaking of, guess who was waiting at the compost buckets?

"Hey, Nessie!"

I ran up and threw my arms around him. He gave me a squeeze, ruffled my hair, and turned and greeted the other CITs warmly.

"Now, who's ready to help the environment??"

The other CITs looked doubtful, but I raised my hand. After we lugged the gross glop to the garden, he grabbed my big bag and walked me to Moose.

"Everyone's really excited you're a CIT this year," he chatted happily. "All the girl counselors fought over you, gladiator-style."

"And Margo won?" I smiled.

"Naturally." Ben nodded. "She called on her vicious woodland creatures to help."

I laughed. I liked my brother even more at camp—he was more energetic and just . . . happier. He had that layer of magic camp dust on him now. Soon I'd have it too.

We paused outside my cabin. I wondered where Margo was. I wanted to make a new, profesh impression on her.

"So everything's good at home?" Ben asked. I knew what he wanted to know.

"Everything's good," I assured him. "He hasn't called more than he's supposed to. Layla and Ava are so excited to come next week once Jewish Community Center camp is over."

"Good old JCC."

"And Mom got an A on her first quiz in her summer courses," I offered.

He laughed and shook his head. "I don't even want to know how you found that out."

I smiled. "I have my ways."

Mom leaves her computer open sometimes. Or sometimes she leaves her phone out. Or not out, but easily accessible. I just like to make sure everything's okay.

"But yeah, everything's good," I finished, anxious to get into my new space. "Except Smooshie's definitely mad you left again. I feed him treats, but I don't have those magic Ben chin-scritching skills."

Our cat inexplicably loved Ben with every long, floofy gray tuft of fur on his body.

"I miss him," he said wistfully. "I hope he writes."

I laughed and gave him one more hug. "Okay, I need to go in."

"See you later, on Monarch!"

Oooooh right, evening games tonight, special for just CITs and counselors. I loved evening games. I guessed I would love them even more with Ben running them now.

The cabin was empty, but there was a colorful note from Margo on my bed—the one on the opposite side of the room from hers.

Nessie!

You're my CIT now. I promise to rule over you with fairness and as little gloating as possible. Here is a tiara I made Donald make for you. Also, I saved one of the baby goats for you to name.

Love love love,

Can't wait to see you,

Margo

I sighed happily, put on the daisy crown, and held the note to my heart for a brief second. And then I ran to orientation, because I realized I was already five minutes late!!

CHAPTER 21

Bee

THE ACTIVITY LEADERS WERE set to come that afternoon for a few hours to organize and set up their spaces, which meant Ben and I would be on opposite ends of camp, thank goodness, since I was Raph's improv assistant this year. Margo would be with Doc in nature, Donald with Nell in art, and Claudia, lucky her, with *Ben* in sports. Seriously, I couldn't believe he was leading an activity. Mom would neither confirm nor deny, but I suspected that he'd planned *nothing* this week. What a Ben-shaped train wreck.

"Raphael's here!" Mom called when I walked into Dam. She was sitting at the paperwork table. Dad was in the corner with the CITs, happily supervising their camp nametag creation.

I looked around wildly. No beautiful man. "Wait, *here* here?"

"Luna!"

"Thanks!" I grabbed a camp calendar and dashed back out the door, hearing the group chuckle on my way out.

Luna Moth was our all-purpose building, in between Painted Turtle (art) and the boat shed. It was newer than the other buildings and had bright green trim instead of red. The first floor of Luna's kind of a catchall for stuff we have at camp that doesn't have any other place. Part library, part counselor hangout, part trial room for Kangaroo Court. It was big and sunny, with enormous windows on all sides, and since there were squishy purple-and-pink rugs piled on the floor, it was the only building where you were allowed to take off your shoes. It was also where all improv classes took place, which made it the *best* building.

But it was only the *best* building when the *best activity leader ever* was inside it. And, actually, the only person in the world who knew my last-summer secrets.

I burst through the door and saw him at the back of the room, hanging up posters. "Raph!"

"Bee!"

I slid off my shoes and toppled into him. I was a lot bigger than he was. I barely had time to take in his slick new haircut—short on the sides and long, styled, and suave on top. I wondered if he partially did it to smooth out his receding hairline. Well, it totally worked. He wore his usual brightly colored shorts, salmon this time, and a striped tank top.

"It has been *forever*." He smiled. Raph had a perfect small mouth, with perfect small teeth.

"I can't believe you're finally here!!" I squeezed his hands. Now it really felt like summer had arrived.

"Neither can I, let me tell you." He sighed. "I had such a bad health year in New York. I got terrible asthma. Thank God for camp! I can actually breathe out here." He closed his eyes and took a big breath.

Raphael was in his late twenties, doing a masters program in directing in New York City.

"That's awful!" I shook my head. "I know you love it, but I get so claustrophobic when I'm in a city."

We'd done family trips to Portland and Boston, and one to New York City to see some shows. Amazing theatre, way too many people for me, and not enough trees or stars.

"So this means you're going to New Hampshire?" he asked.

"Oh." I'd forgotten that I'd told him about my acceptances but not my final choice. He'd written one of my recommendation letters. "No, I mean, I guess I'll get used to city life, because I'm going to EBU." East Boston University.

"Bee, I am so proud of you!" He pulled me in for another hug. How did he smell like a Macy's, even at camp? "You're going to love it!" He pulled back and handed me a poster to hang. *In the Heights.* "You're majoring in . . . ?"

"Education with a minor in theatre."

"That's my girl! Oh, I am just so thrilled for you."

When I said my major aloud to Raph, it sounded cool and confident. Like I knew what I was doing. Wouldn't it be nice if that were real?

We started moving around chairs and organizing Luna into our usual setup. We chatted about the shows we'd worked on this year—Raph had assistant directed *Sunday in the Park with George*, and my school had tried to do a production of *The King and I*, but I'd gathered a petition against it, seeing as we had *all white students.* Except me, and I'm not Thai. I'd won.

Raph shook his head. "I can't believe they even tried. That drama director is—"

"Out of touch as fuck?"

He laughed. "Putting it mildly, yes. What'd you do instead?"

"*Bye Bye Birdie.*"

"And you were Kim?"

"Naturally."

"Could've been worse."

"Could've been the most racist *The King and I* ever."

"Dear *God*."

I'd missed him so much. After thoroughly Broadway-ing the space, we spread out on the rugs to plan the games for the first session. Starting off with Statues, Machine, What Are You Doing?, Park Bench, and then more complicated games as the week went on. I was trying to figure out how to bring up Ben stuff with him, without sounding like I wanted to talk all about me. So far, no balanced phrasing had presented itself in my head.

"Well, I'm sure your new theatre department will be much more informed," Raph assured me, while he color-coded the lesson plan by age group. He'd given me the calendar to mark up for special events and theme days. His organization skills were on point.

"Oh yeah, I'm sure." My new theatre department. I didn't want to think about it.

"You'll get into the city, and it'll be such a relief, Bee," he continued.

"Right."

"That's totally how it was for me," he explained. "In New York, I could finally be myself. And then it was easier to be me here in Maine too."

"Great." I tried not to grit my teeth. Even if I was the only black girl in my class, Messina was still my home. Raph and I weren't coming from the same place on this. Maybe I'd made a mistake and I should stay here—

"Have you told Ben yet?"

I froze.

"Umm, told him . . . ?"

"That you're going to EBU?"

"Oh right, that. No. Nope. Definitely not." I'd managed to only answer college questions when Ben was conveniently out at Monarch. Or out on the trails. Or peeing.

"Iiiinteresting," he replied, drawing out his green highlighter with the word. "So, is there anything new to tell there? He's here, right? That wasn't the plan, if I remember correctly."

I bit my lip. Though I'd wanted to bring him up, now that the opportunity was there, I wanted to scream and duck into the pile of pillows, or make an emergency exit. Where was the closest fire alarm?

I took a breath. I was so used to hiding the Ben stuff from everyone, it felt weird to finally talk about it. But I really, really wanted to. I passed Raph the finished calendar.

"Yeah, he's here," I said, finally.

"And how's that going?"

I thought back over the week. "I'm, uh . . . not handling it well." By the end of the sentence, my eyes had filled with syrupy tears. I grabbed my lips to try and stop them from quivering.

"Aw, Bee." Raph put a hand on my shoulder. "I'm sure it's not as bad as you think."

I swallowed, forcing some crying down. "No, it totally is." I hated my choked voice. "And he's totally given up. I really think the whole thing is just dead now. Like, in the water. Like a dead seagull carcass floating in the water."

Raph nodded, his big blue eyes widening with sympathy. "I know, sweetie. It's the worst when you've thought about it for so long, and then it's over, like it never mattered."

I nodded back. I didn't want to speak again until I could sound like a grown-up human, not a homesick baby camper.

"I promise, it'll heal," he continued. "It'll always hurt, but it won't be everything, all-consuming, and you'll feel like yourself again."

I took a shuddery breath and sighed. Did I want to be myself without my feelings for Ben?

"Thanks. Sorry." I stood up. "I know you're right, I just wish he hadn't come back. It would be so much easier if I didn't have to *see* him."

"I hear you." Raph stood up too. "Here's some advice from the great beyond: *do not* hook up with your roommate just because he says he's moving out." He rolled his eyes at himself. "Because the housing hunt is brutal and he's probably actually not moving out."

I laughed. That's why Raph was awesome. He was older; he'd been through this stuff before. He made it all sound normal.

Of course, this was why love and sex and whatever was so unappealing to me. Because who the hell wanted this to be their normal?

We finished, and I walked Raph out to his car. Another hug, because tomorrow morning was a long way away, and he and his white SUV pulled out of the lot. I trudged back to Dam, his words sitting heavily on my shoulders: *it'll always hurt*. I pushed away the Ben stuff, but there was a lot left over.

The city, a new theatre department, a new life. The MHS theatre department was a nightmare, but I knew everything about it. It was mine. When there were problems, I felt like I could fix them. I didn't even know what the EBU theatre problems were yet.

I went to bed that night and woke up clammy from a dream that my new theatre was putting on an all-white production of *Hamilton*. With some water and the soundtrack, I coaxed myself back to sleep.

The next dream was one more familiar.

WHAT HAPPENED: PART 5

Bee

WE'D TOLD EACH OTHER secrets and promised to keep them. Our hands were touching, mine on top of his, skin-to-skin, and we were looking at each other like, like, like—it was too much. I broke it off.

"Wanna go for a walk?" I asked, standing up quickly

He paused for a beat, then jumped up too. "Sure."

We folded the blankets and stacked everything in a corner of the clearing. Donald and Margo and the rest could carry it down in the morning. Well, later in the morning. The stars had already begun to fade. I tried to ignore that.

Wordlessly, we wandered toward the opposite edge of Nest, toward the path that led down around the cabins. Getting down off Nest was steep and tricky, the path dirt was loose, and I had to carefully place each step. I felt Ben next to me, concentrating on his steps, too.

We're not drunk anymore, are we? But I pushed that thought backward. Because if we weren't drunk, what were we doing?

The trail leveled out. The water grew louder, waves hitting the shore nearby. We followed the sound down a small side trail that led by the off-season boat shed, Stickleback. We stored the kayaks and paddleboats there during the winter.

Past the barn, the trail came to a small point—rocks with a view of the water. We pulled up short at the edge. You couldn't swim here or anything, too many sharp edges below. But you got the nice view of Messina's cove, with the harbor, houses on the other side, and sailboats in the middle, rocking gently.

"The fog . . ." Ben trailed off.

The paling sky and still-bright moon illuminated levels of mist, a bridge over the water. It was pretty, but cooler down here. I pulled my hair out of the topknot and shook it all out so it would cover my ears.

I glanced over at Ben. His eyes squinted at the ocean. Neither of us said anything.

What now? I panicked. *I've ruined everything by taking us down here. We never should've left Nest.*

"We should probably go—" I turned around, but I must've been distracted, or tipsier than I thought, and misjudged the edge of the point.

As scary as it was, it only took about two seconds. I tripped, I started to fall to the side, saw my life flash before my eyes, my body splayed across the rocks below, and then I was scooped up into Ben's arms immediately. He held me close, and we breathed hard into each other.

"Hey, you okay?"

It wasn't even that far a fall; I probably wouldn't have died. I was fine. But automatic reactions took over: my heart pounded, my eyes watered, my cheeks grew hot.

"Ahhh! I'm sorry," I said, wiping my eyes. "I'm so tired, I must've—"

"I know," Ben said gently. "It's okay though, you're okay. You're fine."

I'd heard him use that soothing voice with campers, with his little sisters. It was kind of humiliating he was using it on me, even more that it worked. My breathing softened, *You're okay*, my heart slowed, *You're fine*. After a few deep breaths I looked up at him.

"Fudge," I whispered, laughing a little. "That was so. . . but thanks."

"What are friends for?" He smiled.

I smiled back.

And then we didn't kiss.

CHAPTER 22

Bee

MY DAD WOULD'VE SAID that the parking lot on the first day of camp was "abuzz," but that was too light a word for it. It was more ablaze, and it was our job to be constantly at the ready with a massive hose.

I stood under the tent with the group signs—the kids dropped their stuff off by age and cabin. Donald, Margo, Bobby, and Ellie were on lice check duty, supervised by Dad in the chairs set up outside the office. Hana was down at the waterfront, conducting swim tests with the Dogberry swim team. The CITs and John and Connie took care of lugging the gear, while Doug, Dave, and Jen were at the mini trading post we'd set up in Dam, selling mosquito netting and Dogberry T-shirts to the new campers and families. Ben, of course, was nowhere to be found, because that would've meant he'd been on time.

I tapped the top of my clipboard. This was my first year running check-in out here—usually we had another, older counselor. Somehow, now I was that older counselor, and as much as I hated to admit it, I was really nervous. What if I said someone's name wrong? Or put off an unprofessional air? What kind of air *was* I putting off? How did I change it? From where did that kind of air originate?

A yawn interrupted my worries—Ben, ten minutes late, the skin under his eyes still swollen from sleep. Like a troll. I'd somehow avoided him since the island party, but now there was no escape. Had he known Donald was going to ask me out? Was he just totally okay with that?

"Morning!" He gave me a tight smile. "We're under the big top, huh?"

"I am." I stiffened. "*You're* just getting here."

"I know, I'm sorry, I got stuck in my sleeping bag."

"Only Peter gets to use that as a valid excuse." Peter was our camper who got stuck in things. The bathroom, his sleeping bag, his luggage . . .

"Hey, look! It's Jay and Maddie!" Ben pointed to the entrance, where a big tan van had parked, and two kids were jumping out. Suddenly, all my nerves and Ben-related annoyance evaporated. Right, I reminded myself. This is about these awesome kids, not my checklist, and not my *coworker.*

Jay and Maddie tore toward us, their mom following at a normal human pace.

"Slow down!" I shouted. They almost tripped, taming their sprints into Olympic speed walking. When they were finally close enough, they flung themselves into our arms. Sometimes being a camp counselor was kind of like being a celebrity.

"Bee!" cried Maddie. "And *Bunny*!"

"*Bunny!*" Jay cackled, jumping up and down with evil glee in the middle of hugging Ben.

I watched Ben's expression flip from elated to a fake smile. "Okay, guys. LOL. But I'm not Bunny this year, just Ben."

"Oh, but you'll always be Bunny to us." I smiled.

"Not. This. Year. *Bee.*" Ben grabbed Maddie and Jay's bags, and huffed over to their group's drop-off zone.

Whoops.

Last summer, for the first session, before the Fourth of July, Ben and I had led a group hike together to Blueberry Mountain. The trip was a *disaster.* It started pouring on the way, but we had half a dozen strangely determined kids, so we'd handed out extra ponchos and hiked anyway.

About halfway up the mountain, when we were basically climbing through mud and the kids were miserable, I got stung by a wasp. I'm really allergic to wasps, so I had to take a bunch of Benadryl, and we had to turn the group around.

Benadryl makes me *really* loopy.

So there we were, in the pouring rain, Ben trying to get these kids back down a mudslide safely, and me yammering on, high as a kite.

"Come on, kids!" Ben had yelled, as encouragement. "This trip wasn't a mistake if nobody dies!"

That got a laugh out of them, but they were still exhausted, soaked, and hungry. So my loopy self was keeping them preoccupied by asking them icebreaker questions. Like their favorite movies and colors and animals.

At the time, the older campers had it in their heads that Ben and I were dating. So when I asked their favorite animals, they asked me the same question, and I said:

"I *love* bunnies."

They'd figured out by then that I was out of it, so they egged me on.

Sophia, a camper at the time, giggled and said, "As much as you love Ben?"

"More," I'd shouted. "I love bunnies more than Ben!"

"What if Ben *was* a bunny?" asked Rudy helpfully.

"Thanks, Rudy," Ben had grumbled.

"That would be *the best case scenario.*" I'd laughed. "Bunny Ben. Hey, let's call Ben *Bunny* from now on. Ben, your new name is Bunny!"

And it stuck. All summer. It caught like wildfire, and it super bugged him. Even Doc and Judy called him Bunny. And I swear, John, Connie, and Bobby told each new session of campers coming in. Probably Donald did too. Ben hated it.

And he blamed it all on me. Clearly. Fantastic. "Guys, if Ben doesn't want to be called Bunny, we shouldn't call him Bunny," I said to Maddie and Jay, diplomatically. "Respect, remember? It's an important thing at camp."

Ben shot me a grateful look. It was probably the most civil moment we'd had yet, and it almost made me blush. I shook him off with a smile and changed the subject with Maddie and Jay. "So, did you have a good school year?"

"Jay has a pet frog now," Maddie told me, pointing at him as if he was being accused of something terrible. "He named it *Maddie.*" Oh, he *was* being accused of something terrible.

Jay snickered, holding his hand up to his mouth to hide it.

"Frogs are cool," I explained to Maddie. "I'm sure it was a compliment."

"Was not."

"Hey, you two," Ben said, returning from stashing their duffel bags. "You need to go get a lice check and then change and do your swim test."

Maddie tugged on the hem of my T-shirt. "Are you doing polar bear swim tomorrow?"

Ben grinned as I stifled a groan. Polar bear swim was a hellish tradition at Camp Dogberry, and the only one I fantasized about axing once I took over the camp someday. The kids were given the opportunity to wake up at *six a.m.* and go dunk in the ocean. If you perform this satanic ritual four times during your session, you get a certificate when you go home. I did this once as a camper—it was freezing and terrible and my least favorite thing ever, but I was *determined* to earn my certificate.

After one bone-chilling round of this, I realized the certificate was a sheet of blue paper with a polar bear on it. I could totally print that myself. I haven't participated since.

"If *you* want to go, just tell your counselors," I said.

"We will." Jay nodded. "But *you're* going to come, right?"

"Never." I laughed. "Not in a million years."

"But, Bee, you always say that!"

"Correct!" I smiled. "Because I'm never going to do it again."

"But you always tell us to try new things!" Maddie pointed out. These kids must've joined debate club this year.

"And she's already *tried* polar bear swim," Ben chimed in, taking Jay gently by the shoulders and turning him toward the lice-check area. "Now go get checked for bugs."

"But—"

"Go!" Ben prodded them.

Wow. Was Ben actually taking my side? "Don't worry. You can berate me more at lunch, if you want," I told the kids.

"Fine," Maddie said. "We'll berate you then." As they walked off, I heard Jay whisper to her, "What's *berate* mean?"

Next I checked in Meredith, the tiniest, gangliest, freckliest eleven-year-old in the world. She was a longtime camper and was notorious for losing her toiletries every year. This year we'd given her counselors an extra set already, so they'd be prepared.

"Hey, Bunny." She grinned a toothy grin at Ben, handing over her bag. "Long time no see."

"I'm not even going to dignify that with an answer," Ben groaned, tossing me a look. But his eyes were twinkling, just a little, and I let myself smile back.

CHAPTER 23

Hana

"OKAY! ERIC, BACK UP the ladder. Toyah, how would you like it if a giant fish tried to catch you? Leave that little swimmer alone, please."

First day of camp as a swim instructor was different. The youngest swimmers were the hardest. They *really* tried, but most of them needed to stay in the shallow end, no question. After Judy, the head swim instructor, announced the verdicts, they all sighed and slid back into their flip-flops dejectedly.

I *loved* being in the water the entire morning. Bee always said I was a mermaid because I floated like a balloon and my skin never pruned. Maybe that was true, because being in the water felt like my other world, and I forgot about everything else. On swim team, I wasn't particularly good at keeping track of laps, though. It never mattered to me how many I'd done—once I started swimming, I never wanted to stop.

When we finished our last swim test before lunch, I pulled myself up onto the dock and wrapped a towel around my waist. Technically, I was supposed to change out of my suit for the dining hall, but if I didn't, then Claudia might see me in it. My rash guard top, lifeguard official, hugged my chest, and though I wasn't Margo-epic, I knew I looked good.

I slipped on my flip-flops and thanked George, our day lifeguard, on my way out. I found Margo outside of Dam, by the flagpole, lying out on a towel in the sun.

"Hey, darlin'," she said, sitting up. "Nessa and Rachel are getting my group changed for lunch. How cool is that?" Margo had the littles, our youngest group of campers.

I smiled. "Pretty cool. Don't let my mom catch you tanning, though."

"Not tanning." She sighed, standing up and shaking out her towel. "Just freckling more."

"Beautiful freckling," I said. "We should head in and help set up."

"Oh wait!" Margo caught my hand and pulled me away from the veranda steps. "I forgot: I have a *plan*."

"You're starting to sound like Donald," I pointed out.

She steered us around the side of Dam, through the gate and into the garden near the carrot tops, where she shot the fluffy greens a brief glare, like she was threatening them not to repeat anything.

"Okay, so this morning, I got Jay and Maddie for lice check," she whispered.

"Oh, I got them too for swim test!" I said, normal volume. "They both passed into the deep end this year."

"Cuties!" Margo whispered, face lighting up for a moment as she temporarily forgot her mission. "Right," she said, becoming serious once more. "So, they were talking about how Bee never goes to polar bear swim."

"Oh, never." I shook my head. "She hates waking up that early and hates cold water." Two of my favorite things.

"That's a lot of hate," Margo admitted. "*But* what if we got Raph to take her to Kangaroo Court tomorrow and sentence her to a morning of polar bear swim?"

It was kind of evil, but I did love getting everyone to go to polar bear swim, and a public Kangaroo Court sentencing would be such good press.

"I'm in," I agreed, and Margo clapped in excitement. "But what does polar bear swim have to do with Donald's plan?"

"That's the *brilliance* of it," Margo said. "*Bee* is groggy in the morning."

"Yes." Bee was really out of it early in the morning. Sometimes she left for school without her books or tried to get in the car wearing pj bottoms. She was never late, but she was never with it, either.

"So it's the perfect time to *stage our trick*."

"You mean—"

"We plan it so she's coming down to the bathroom to change, and we're already there waiting outside, hidden, right?" Margo's voice got faster as she talked. "So we wait until she goes in, and then *we* go in, and talk about how Ben is *in love with her*!"

"Oh." This just got real, real fast.

"And she's so out of it that she actually believes us. What do you think?" Margo bit her lip.

I considered Bee's grogginess. I considered our acting skills. "I think it's our best shot?"

"Yes!" Margo squealed. "I'll go catch Raph." With one more silencing frown at the carrot tops, she hopped around the corner. Then reappeared a second later, and made funny eyebrows at me, whispering, "By the way, you look real cute in your swim top." She winked, and disappeared again.

Okay. That was sort of random. But a second later, it made sense: Claudia tentatively peeked out from around the corner. I smiled, and she closed the distance between us.

Back here in the garden, we were shielded from the world for a moment, and I could see her eyes take me, and my swimsuit, in. I took her in too, in her athletic shirt and cargo shorts. I imagined we felt the same way about each other's clothes. Like we'd rather we weren't wearing them?

"Hey," she said, voice low, wrapping her arms around my waist. She didn't seem to mind I was soaked.

"Hi," I whispered. "How was your morning?"

"No lice," she said. "How about you?"

I smiled. "No one drowned."

"You'll never believe what Donald's planned for Ben." Her eyes sparkled with laughter.

"Oh, I can probably believe it." Before I realized what I was doing, I'd gently grabbed her shirt. One small movement, and we crashed together. Our lips pushed against each other urgently. Her fingers entwined through my damp hair. My hands found their way onto her back, grasping her closer.

Was kissing Claudia ever not going to make the world spin double time? If it kept going like this, we were going to disrupt the solar system.

All at once, we broke apart, breathing heavily. Whatever was happening, it was super not camp appropriate. Breathing like that, looking into each other's eyes, I realized this was moving fast.

"To be continued?" I whispered.

"Mmm," she hummed back.

CHAPTER 24

Vanessa

OH MY GOD. My first day of camp was *exhausting*. I fell asleep as soon as the kids finally did. And then I had to get up and go to breakfast and start all over again.

I didn't even *think* about the fact that being a counselor would be like babysitting twenty of my sisters at once. Margo and I had seven-year-olds, who were a year younger and cuter than the twins, but maybe even more of a handful. One of them peed themselves the first afternoon, and another one turned into a dinosaur, which Raph and Bee *did* work into improv class flawlessly. Still, it wasn't as useful for our nature hike, because he scared away most of the birds and chipmunks.

"*RRRRGH!*"

Margo salvaged the hike with icky-looking plants. "Look at these gross *mushrooms*, though!"

"Ooooooh!" "Nice. That's disgusting." "Can we eat them??"

We spent all day ordering our littles in and out of places: in and out of the water, in and out of the bathroom, on and off the field, in and out of Dam. And half of them couldn't sleep that first night because they were homesick. Luckily, Margo had a bunch of stories up her sleeve.

"The trick is," she whispered, once the last one had drifted off, "to *start* the story really exciting, and then make it more and more boring. And voilà!" She gestured to our snoring cabin. "I'm going to go get a snack!" How she had the energy to move after all of that, I had no idea. I fell asleep ten seconds later.

The next morning, we were up at eight, changing, bathroom, breakfast. I barely said a word except "No, Howard. No." I never wanted to admit it, but Ben and I were both bad before ten a.m.

Standing in the breakfast line, the comfy smell of pancakes started easing me back to sleep. I felt my lids start to flutter. Could I sleep standing up? And then Sophia leaped in next to me, in a blinding shade of lime green. What a scary alarm clock.

"Nessa, you'll never believe what I heard."

"How did you hear anything?" I yawned. "Over all the kids?"

"Mine are eleven." Sophia pointed to a group of older kids in line at the eggs counter. Tall kids. Almost-our-age kids. Kids who looked like they could express when they had to pee, before the fact. I felt a little pang of envy.

"They're kind of mopey." She tilted her head at them.

"Lucky," I sighed. But then I saw my dinosaur camper, sneaking around the muffin basket, hunched over like a velociraptor. At least my group kept things interesting.

She poked my side. "Yeah, but ask me what I heard."

Gossip, Vanessa. Wake up. Get in the zone. "Okay, what did you hear?!"

"I *heard* that Claudia and Hana are *dating*."

That woke me up. There was nothing better than counselor

relationship gossip. Although it was weird when, like last summer, your brother was in the middle of it.

"Seriously?" I whispered. "Who told you?"

"Isabelle, who heard it from Rachel and Doug."

"Whoa." This was big. Actual counselor information. I guess being pre-counselors now, we got more reliable gossip. We grabbed plates of pancakes and fresh-cut strawberries. I eyed Hana at one end of the dining hall, pouring herself coffee, smiling at her mom. Dark hair in a curly knot, already damp, wearing board shorts and a short-sleeved lifeguard swim top. So pretty, no matter what. I looked and found Claudia sitting with her group, the nine-year-olds, playing table hockey with a melon rind.

Hmmm. They weren't looking at each other longingly or anything. But they weren't supposed to either. We'd found that out at orientation. *NO PDA. Boundaries, boundaries, boundaries.* Boundaries sure made it hard to snoop.

"But can you believe it?" Sophia continued seamlessly, as we got our tea.

"Believe what?" Wallace asked.

"Hana and Claudia," I whispered. "There's a rumor—"

"Oh man, yeah." Wallace smacked his forehead. "So embarrassing. I accidentally saw them kissing yesterday before lunch."

Sophia let out a little shriek, and I spilled hot water all over the table. We quickly mopped it up.

"You *did*?"

Wallace scratched his head. "Yeah. I mean, I didn't *watch*, but I went to cut through the garden, and they were . . . you know . . . *in the garden.*"

I had so many questions: Was it like a peck? Or were they in a *romantic embrace*?? But Wallace looked embarrassed enough already.

"Amazing," Sophia breathed.

"Well, I think they'd look pretty cute together," I said, picturing it in my head. Automatically, my brain put them in front of a wedding altar with Hana in a flowy white dress and Claudia in a sharp black suit. "I can see it."

"Yeah . . . but they're both girls?" The way Sophia said the last part, I wasn't sure whether she thought one of them was a dude, or whether she wanted to know if I didn't like gay people.

"Weren't you at orientation?" I fired back, suddenly terrified my friend was homophobic. "We had a talk about diversity, you know."

"Oh, I know," Sophia whispered. "I've just never *known* any girls who date, you know, each other."

"Well, now you do," I said firmly. They were the first girl couple I knew, too, but Ben had told me about that stuff. And now that we didn't live with my dad anymore, I didn't have to hide that I supported everyone.

"Hey, you're right!" Sophia brightened. "This is going to totally *shock* my school friends."

"I don't think that's—"

"Let's go discuss with Isabelle."

She jumped up, Wallace followed, but then three of my campers asked if I would come sit at their table. Who could say no to those little faces? As we crossed the dining hall to their perfectly selected spot, I scouted the rest of the room.

Rachel and Doug? Rachel and Jen? Doug and Dave? Who else was dating?

I could not *wait* to find out.

CHAPTER 25

John

IF I'M BEING HONEST, Hana and Claudia making out at the island party, after I'd asked her out, wasn't my ideal. My ideal was me making out with Claudia. So yeah, a small setback in the plan, but hey, everyone's gotta do their thing, and I didn't hold it against Claudia for liking girls too. That just made her hotter, as Bobby pointed out. And I couldn't deny Hana was cute, even though she was super boring. All that girl did was swim and smile. But she was fine for a hookup buddy.

I barely saw Claudia over the first two days of camp. I had the ten-year-olds, and damn did they have energy. And concerns. So many concerns. I missed working with younger kids (they were usually just cute as all hell), but Margo and Rachel got them this time. I did get to see Claudia, briefly, during sports, and she smiled and joked with me like usual. I figured I was in a good position to ask her to hang out on the weekend. Maybe for Saturday. The sparkler party was Friday, but my real aim was to get Claudia alone.

I snuck glances at her in the dinner line. The piercings all along the back of her right ear. The gentle smirk she threw at campers. She seemed to operate in the world so easily, so herself.

If I asked her out tonight, after Counselor Hunt, was that too desperate? Maybe I should wait till tomorrow?

"John, Lis says she *doesn't like* our president," one of my boy campers complained, jerking his thumb at one of the girls. "Isn't that unpatriotic?"

Out of the corner of my eye, I saw Connie by the piano, motioning at me to come over.

"What's to like?" I replied, nodded at Lis, and ducked out of line. I heard the boy huff as I dodged into the bathrooms hallway. Connie poked her head out of one of the single occupancies, and I followed her in. She shut the door hard, behind her.

"Pretty sure we're not supposed to be in the bathroom together," I pointed out. Suddenly, I was paranoid: if Claudia saw us come in here, would she think I liked Connie?

There was a knock at the door, and Bobby slipped in too. Would Claudia think I was having threesomes with these knuckleheads?

"What's up?" Bobby asked.

"I have bad news," Connie announced.

For bad news, she didn't look real upset. "All right," I said. "Make it quick. I have kids out there, and some of them have *dietary restrictions*."

"You know how Claudia and Hana . . . ?"

"Only wish I'd seen it." Bobby sighed. I hit him in the gut.

"Yeah, so?" I prompted. I was pretty sure Connie was into me. She'd seemed overly excited that Claudia had made out with someone else.

"So they're a thing."

"A thing?"

"Like a dating thing."

My stomach dropped. They weren't supposed to be a thing, of any kind. A sexy thing, at the very most. "How do you know?"

"A bunch of people saw them in the garden yesterday, kissing."

"Where am I when all of this is happening?" Bobby demanded. I hit him in the gut again.

"Ow."

More kissing? In the fucking garden? That sounded sickeningly romantic. "So they're kissing." I tried to blow it off. "That doesn't mean anything."

"Well." Bobby held up a finger. "Combined with the fact that all the CITs know they're dating—"

"What?"

"Yeah, that was my second piece of bad news." Connie nodded. "Ellie told me, and apparently everyone else, that Hana and Claudia are a legit couple."

Fuck. Fuck, fuck, fuck. These girls always knew each other's business. And Ellie was friends with Hana, and she might've talked to her.

I kicked the door. Now I was back at this goddamn camp, because of my goddamn brother, and my goddamn pseudo-*father*, and my one chance . . .

No. That's not how this worked. People dated all the time. Hooked up all the time. They hooked up with people they liked, and people they didn't like. . . . All we had were rumors. And some kissing.

"This doesn't mean anything," I decided. "Until there's actual proof."

"But what more proof—" Connie started.

Bobby cut her off. "John's right," he said. "It's just two girls doing that experimenting thing. You know." Connie glared at him. But I'd seen plenty of girls go through that phase.

"But keep an ear out, yeah?" I said. "For actual proof. Like, online or something."

Connie rolled her eyes, clearly frustrated—she so wanted me—and shoved her way out of the bathroom.

"Dude, I'm totally hooking up with Margo later," Bobby whispered. "She gave me the nod."

"Good for you, man."

I slapped him on the back affectionately. Dude was in to get his heart mashed into papier-mâché pulp, third summer running, but who was I to stop him?

We split up. I went and found Marigold, who needed gluten-free pasta, and Caleb, who needed soy-free sauce. I had to stop myself from talking to them like my grandma: *When I was your age, if someone was allergic to peanuts, they ate a peanut, died, and got it over with.*

CHAPTER 26

Ben

DAY TWO OF SPORTS went smoothly; I didn't have to send any-body to Andy/Black Bear for any kind of medical attention, which might've been a first for the sports program. I dug being in charge of the games we played, the sportsmanship lectures. When I'd been Pete's assistant, I had helped out, but *my* assistant, Claudia, was so disgustingly in love, I got to do everything myself!

Lucky me!

But whatever, I still liked it a lot, in spite of space cadet Claudia. I'd made her the permanent catcher that morning during tee ball so that she didn't have to hold a bat. That seemed wisest.

The routine of camp had wrapped itself around me like my cozy sleeping bag. I loved having every inch of the day planned for me. I loved being busy. I didn't love when I had time to think—like this weekend, and Fourth of July. We had the rare Friday Fourth, which meant the kids would go home after lunch. Which meant maximum sparkler partying.

Fireworks.

Picnic blankets.

Warm beer.

Bee . . .

I tried to shake it out of my head, like an Etch A Sketch.

Donald, however, could not shut up about it. He whispered to me in hushed tones when I sat in on the afternoon art class. Hana had volunteered to help out with an origami unit on her break, so everyone who was free came to hang out. Luckily, Bee wasn't free. Some kind of ropes course disaster.

"I'm making a booze and fireworks run on Thursday," Donald murmured, creasing a blue paper creation. "You want to come?" He handed me the finished product.

I ignored him for three reasons. One, seriously, a bunny? Fuck off. Two, I didn't really want to think about this party and all the memories that went along with it. And three, folding tiny origami stars takes a lot of concentration.

"Donald, I can't make a crane," Reading whined. "Can you do it for me?"

"Did you *try*?"

"No . . ."

⌒

After dinner, en masse the kids poured onto Monarch for evening games. Tonight, a classic and a favorite, Counselor Hunt. The rules were simple: counselors hid, campers sought.

Each counselor was worth a different amount of points. The more points the counselor was worth, the harder they were to find. We used to ask the kids to assign the points, but now we did it randomly, because it became a terrible popularity contest, and Donald always won.

One setting sun, sixty or so campers, a dozen counselors, half a dozen CITs. *Mayhem.*

"All right!" I called out over the field. The murmuring and excitement began to die away, but Bee's voice cut it down like a machete:

"Listen *up*, Camp Dogberry!"

Sixty silent, attentive faces. You could hear the peepers.

Skills.

"Thank you." I nodded at her. She winked in response and my heart backflipped. It was almost like old times. "So tonight, we're playing Counselor Hunt!" Applause erupted from the field, but they quieted down quickly for the rules. I ran through the basics for the new kids and then looked behind me on the grass, where I'd set down the points cards—colorful poster board with lanyard ties. The counselors wore them around their necks, like nametags.

"Where—"

"Bee is worth *one thousand* points!"

I turned. Donald was already assigning Bee her points card, dramatically placing it over her head. The campers clapped, giddy. Great.

"Donald . . ." I tried. He dodged around me and continued.

"Hana is worth *an entire birthday cake!*" Everyone cracked up. "Which is equivalent to three hundred points." Hana dipped her head through the loop and gave a little wave. "Claudia is worth *five hundred* points, *and* half an ice cream cake."

All right, well, he'd taken my job, but the entire field was rolling in laughter. Except John and Bobby, who were, predictably, worth ten points each.

Finally, he got to the end of the line, awarded himself a thousand points plus the best sunglasses award. That was not a thing at all. Then he got to me—

"Finally," he said, holding up a points card. "Our young Benjamin is worth *three thousand points*."

We didn't even have that card. I looked at what he put over my head: he'd added two zeros to the thirty points card.

"You, my friend, are the Golden Snitch!" he announced proudly. That reference was lost on the majority of our campers, but they clapped anyway.

After the fancy part was over, Donald handed it back to me for the actual game work. We divided the kids into teams and assigned them each a CIT or first-year counselor. They had to give us ten minutes to start hiding, and then BLAM. The older counselors had a quick huddle before we set off.

"No hiding inside, under, or on buildings," I reminded them. "And nobody take the waterfront." I put my hand in the middle, we all did: one, two, three, *Camp Dogberry!* And we broke off.

"Better hide somewhere good, Rosenthal," Bee whispered, as we headed out. "Gotta live up to those points."

There wasn't even any sarcasm in her voice. I grabbed the olive branch and tried not to do a maypole dance around it.

"Back at you, Leonato." That sounded normal.

"Pshh," she scoffed. "I'm apparently only worth a third of you."

"It's hard being the best," I admitted. "But someone's gotta make the game interesting."

Pink sunrays hit her brilliant smirky smile; I tripped over a tree root. By the time I got up, her snickers were echoing down the trail. Donald, Claudia, Hana, and Margo had already disappeared.

Hide, Ben.

Right.

Three thousand points. We'd never assigned that many. I ran

through my options: goat shed, haystack, tire swing pine trees, under the outdoor clay sink? Could I burrow into the sand at the volleyball court? Impersonate a log at the sing-along fire pit?

Suddenly, a thought occurred to me. I didn't *like* the thought, but my feet started moving without my consent, as my stomach twisted.

Quickly, I jogged past the waterfront, behind Dam, up the trail, out into Nest, where I found the fuzziest dogberry bush of the bunch, crouched down, and inserted myself into the branches. The raw, sticky wood rubbed at my skin, but eventually I found a position I could tolerate. It *was* the perfect spot: Nest was an easily forgettable location. The campers didn't come up here often, maybe only for stargazing once in a while. And three thousand points was a lot of hiding responsibility.

Still, I thought. I had other options. Why had I returned to the scene of the crime?

A few minutes later, I heard distant hoots and hollers: the race was on!

Over the next hour, voices floated up from Dam and the garden. There were screams of victory, and cries of defeat carried up to me on the wind as counselors got away.

Finally, I heard footsteps coming up the trail. At this point, I was ready to be found. Usually I was a patient hider, but this spot I'd picked . . . I'd just been staring out into the middle of the clearing, watching the sun set, the stars come out, the scene in my head projected onto the space before me. There was Bee, there was me, there was my arm around her, there was the briefest hint of possibility. I couldn't decide whether I wanted our former selves to scrap the whole thing and go to bed, or whether I wanted them to try harder. To be more honest with each other. What if she had just told me that she only wanted to hook up—nothing more? Would I have said fine and done it and been hurt anyway?

So yeah, after an hour of that circle of hellish thinking, I was A-OK with being found.

But it wasn't campers.

"Is he here?" Donald's voice at the top of the trail.

"I don't see him, but where else could he be?" Claudia.

They must've been found already. Suddenly, I saw this for what it was: an excellent opportunity to scare the crap out of my friends. I could see their outlines in the dark—they turned and started seeking on the other end, making their way around Nest's edges. Soon they'd be close enough that I could reach out and grab their ankles.

Their voices were lower on the other end of the clearing, so I couldn't hear them. I was mostly focused on the space in front of me, holding my breath till I could see their shoes.

Footsteps and voices sounding closer, closer, closer. Shoes. Yes. I could grab one of each foot. I slowly, silently wove my hands through the bush's branches. I was just about to reach out—

"I told you: we definitely can't tell Ben," Claudia said.

Wait, what?

"Bee is *in love with him*, and we're not going to tell him?" Donald asked.

CHAPTER 27

Claudia

"NO WAY," I REPLIED. "We're not telling him. What good would that do?"

Donald eyed the bush, trying not to laugh. We'd both just heard Ben *squeak*.

"I don't know . . ." Donald managed, grinning like a madman. "I feel like he deserves to know."

He looked at me expectantly. Crap. I'd completely lost my lines. Everything we'd rehearsed had gone right out of my head. And I hated improv.

Donald mimed smacking his forehead but picked it up: "I know Hana told you *not to say anything*."

"Right!" I said. "She *did* say that! She told me not to tell anyone!" This didn't sound super realistic coming out of my mouth. What were words, what was saying things? Did I ever sound realistic?

"I get that, but how can she drop this news on you and not expect us to tell our friend?" Donald continued. *Okay, okay, Claudia. Focus.* What came next?

"Yeah." I snapped my fingers. "She said that Bee was *going crazy* with Ben being back this summer."

"Like how?" Donald prompted.

"She's so obsessed with him she can't think about anything else!" I said. That sounded good. And currently what I was experiencing with Hana. "And she can't sleep! Or . . . eat dairy!"

"Dairy?" Donald said, genuinely surprised. I was on a roll.

"Yeah, her stomach gets upset," I explained. "Bad poops. She's so stressed. She can't even shower!"

"Shower?" Donald repeated, raising his eyebrows.

"Yeah, she keeps forgetting to shower," I said. "Because she's so in love with him?" This was starting to sound fake. I quickly added: "That's what Hana said, anyway."

Donald held a hand over his mouth, literally holding in laughter. Jerk. After heaving a few deep breaths he finally spoke in a rush of air: "Well, you know, love is a powerful thing, man. So is stank, though. I hope she's swimming . . . and avoiding dairy."

"Me too," I said. Was this over yet?

"So anyway, I guess what you're saying is, we can't tell Ben because he would never, ever admit to liking her back."

"What do you mean?" I asked. *Stick to questions, Claudia, not statements.*

Donald glanced in the direction of the dogberry bush, then winked at me. "Well, you know Ben. He's got the emotional depth of a dinner plate."

"Maybe a canoe?" I offered.

Ben

Seriously? Fuck these guys!

Claudia

We heard another small, indignant noise from the branches, and out of the corner of my eye, I thought I saw the shadow of a middle finger.

"Did you hear a mouse?" Donald asked innocently. We both cracked up, silently, but I pulled out of it fast: I didn't know how much longer Ben could hold it together. "So yeah. I don't think he's, um"—there were a few stray tears of laughter running down Donald's face—"I don't think he can deal with . . . *feelings*."

"Tell me about it." I rolled my eyes. He'd been such a jerk when I'd told him about my feelings for Hana.

"And he's never even *had* a girlfriend."

"So true," I said, feeling the smug slip out. I mean, *I* had a girlfriend.

"Now that I'm thinking about it," Donald pondered. "Even if he liked Bee, he would totally shoot her down or fuck it up somehow." I couldn't tell if that was acting or not.

"You're right," I said. Because that seemed to be what Donald wanted.

"And Hana's right," he said firmly. "We wouldn't want Bee to have to deal with that. It's probably better this way. Her feelings'll fade eventually."

"Yeah. I wouldn't want that to happen to her. *Rejection* from *Ben*. Double ouch." We both laughed.

"Me neither." Donald sighed. "Bee's kind of the greatest."

"Well . . ."

"Yeah, yeah." Donald shoved me lightly. "Something about how 'her sister's cool, too.'"

"She *is*."

"Speaking of which, shouldn't we go? The game's almost over, and I feel like you're gonna want to gaze adoringly at Hana across the fire."

I frowned at him. But then I realized that's totally what I wanted to do.

"Yeah, let's go."

He put an arm around my shoulder and started steering me toward the trail again. As we left, I tried not to look back at Ben, who I'm sure was throwing the most dramatic fit of all time.

CHAPTER 28

Ben

THEY WALKED BACK TO the trail, trampling through my dreamscape of Bee and me on the picnic blanket. I waited for an extra thirty seconds, just to make sure they were really and truly gone, then I stepped out into the clearing and sat down. Hard.

Dam's generator whirred from down below. The moon and starlight hummed. A beetle landed on my forearm and stared up at me judgmentally.

Bee *liked* me?

The back of my neck burned. Was I sunburnt or blushing or both?

I closed my eyes, pictured Bee. Her high forehead and cheekbones, her round, dark eyes flanked by darker lashes. That smirk on her lips—*her lips*—that so easily broke into a grin. Crossing her arms. Bursting into laughter. Pointing one finger with such command that an entire room of children pretending to be jungle animals instantly became taxidermy.

The greatest. Donald was right. She was.

And she liked me—*loved* me?

My heart beat into my stomach, into the grass and ground beneath me.

I loved her.

If a nearby pine tree had fallen on top of me, that would've been a lighter blow than this.

"Ha-ha, *what*?" I said out loud. To no one. Maybe the judgmental beetle.

I launched off the ground, almost blacked out from dizziness, steadied myself, and started pacing around in circles.

I loved Beatrice Leonato. *Really, her full name?* a part of me protested.

My pacing picked up—I jogged in wider and wider circles. It helped me think, break this down.

Claudia had *said* that Bee was afraid that I'd reject her if she'd said anything. But I had told her last year that I liked her, and she'd rejected me: *just friends. She'd* rejected *me*! But maybe she regretted it now? And thought I wouldn't forgive her?

Or had something else happened that night? Something I hadn't understood?

Donald and Claudia clearly thought I would fuck things up if the opportunity presented itself. Maybe they weren't wrong.

Sidenote: Why had I spent so much time in bushes listening to people making fun of me this summer?

WHAT HAPPENED: PART 6

Ben

THE MUSIC SWELLED, THE stars danced, and fireworks went off—prematurely. Because we were standing on that rock, holding each other, our pulses racing, lips moving closer. And then we were distinctly doing none of those things.

Okay, so she didn't want to kiss me. Or . . . well, we'd both jumped back before it could happen. And then I'd tromped behind her on the trail, trying to wrack my brain for a memory made a moment ago. Did one of us jump back first? Which one?

The brown boat shed, Stickleback, came into view. If we took a hard right, it was a fifteen-minute walk back to camp. A rough fifteen minutes. I wasn't looking forward to it. I felt all of this, whatever it was, slipping away as the sky grew ever so slightly brighter.

"Do you think the Bandytails are in there?"

I almost bumped into Bee. We'd stopped. She walked up to one of the murky windows and was peering in.

"We could check?" I offered. My heartbeats grew more deliberate.

"Why not?" She opened the door. I followed her inside.

Stickleback was dark and dusty, but my eyes adjusted. The air smelled stale and musty, but my nose adjusted. Odd wooden chairs and heaps of sunfish sails, looming empty boat racks.

A pair of raccoons, called the Bandytails, often camped out in Stickleback. They left behind plenty of poop, footprints under the windowsills, and sometimes tufts of fur caught on the metal racks. Staff and campers had logged only a few actual sightings because they seemed to invade at night exclusively.

Bee and I checked the couple old paddleboats in the back—no cute faces staring up at us. We checked in the tackle cubbies. We checked the closet with rigging, too. Nothing. We gave up.

So much for those deliberate heartbeats. This was so over.

Except on our way out, I tripped on a rope. I swear I didn't mean to. I don't think.

I grabbed Bee on my way down, and laughing tiredly, we both fell onto a pile of tarps. We landed with Bee on top of me, face-to-face, chests pressed against each other. She stayed there.

"This is actually pretty comfortable," she whispered. I nodded. "Is there any poop?"

"I don't think so."

With those magical words, her lips were on mine.

CHAPTER 29

Ben

MAYBE SOMETHING HAD TANGLED that night. A misunderstanding. This whole time, I'd thought that I was the one confused and Bee had known what had happened. But it sounded like we were both in the dark. So maybe this wasn't over.

Holy crap, this isn't over.

A shadowy figure appeared at the top of the trail.

"Ahhhh!" I screamed.

"Ben? What are you doing?"

Oh, it was her. Her voice demanded, sparkling with irritation. Like a powerful, angry bell, sounding through the windy silence, vibrating my entire heart and soul.

She was standing with her hands on her hips in the middle of the clearing.

"Bee! Hey!" I ran over and nearly slammed into her, stopping just short. She jumped, with sharp intake of breath, then relaxed and rolled her eyes. I quickly looked her over. She did seem a little grungy. . . . *She wasn't showering.*

"What are you—" She narrowed her eyes at me. "Whatever.

Never mind." She waved a hand. "They sent me up here to find you. Were you even hiding?"

I stared at her for a minute. I didn't know if I could talk.

Hiding? Why would I be hiding?

"Oh, yes!" I shouted, suddenly remembering, startling her again. "For the *game*. In that bush, for most of the night."

"Well, the game's over, Houdini." She sighed. "Nobody found the snitch. Hiding that well is kind of poor sportsmanship."

The game was over. I had no idea what else she said. "Thank you so much for coming to tell me." Why did my voice sound so formal?

She scrunched her brow. "You're welcome? I got *sent* to find you. You're, like, an hour late for s'mores."

"Oh, I see," I said. "Sorry about that—didn't mean to make you worry." I smiled at her and strode toward the trail.

She didn't follow. I looked back, and she was staring at me as if I had horns. Would she still like me if I had horns? From what Claudia said, probably. Cool.

"I wasn't *worried*," she said, and then stomped over. "It's not like I *care*. You're in trouble with everyone else."

Aha! "So you wanted to give me a heads-up?" I asked. "Thank you!" We came out at the bottom of the trail.

"What?" she snapped. "No. Why are you being so weird?"

"I'll grab extra supplies, to make up for it." Before she could protest, I jumped into Dam's kitchen to grab an exorbitant amount of marshmallows and chocolate. And some extra bug juice mix, just in case. I threw all of it into a cooler while Bee watched.

On our way out, I had a sudden thought and pointed to the bathroom. "Do you need to go before we head over?"

She looked at the door, then me, then the door, then me. Maybe

I shouldn't have suggested it—but I didn't want her to be in any sort of discomfort, and I *had* seen her eat a cheeseburger at lunch.

"Ben, if you're stoned," she said slowly, "I won't tell anyone, but you need to go lie down until you're sober."

"I am not stoned!" I laughed. "Just being considerate!"

She shook her head. "Fine. But I'm not a camper, and I don't need a bathroom reminder. Let's go."

We walked up toward Dam's front doors in perfect silence. I'd read somewhere that the best relationships are ones where you can be silent together. That was important. At the threshold, she paused to look at me.

"Fudge nuggets, Ben!" she hissed. "Stop smiling at me like that!"

"Like what?"

"You know what?" She lifted the cooler from my hands. "You're obviously high, and I don't know on what, but you should go to bed. I'll tell everyone you're puking or something."

"I'm fine," I assured her. "But okay."

"If you're fine," she said, rolling her eyes, "you're more of a weirdo than even I realized. Go to bed."

It was just as well. Though being around her was incredible, I knew I probably needed time to cool down before I did or said something stupid.

I lingered for a moment in the doorway, watching Bee trudge down the slope. I thought about how we'd been apart for a whole year. And now we'd finally be together again.

Just as long as I didn't screw this up.

CHAPTER 30

Bee

I FELL BACK ONTO the poofy brown love seat in Luna. "I thought that last round was never going to end."

"We can't pair those two up again." Raph gathered up the few slips of paper left on the floor. "Reading loves the spotlight too much, and Meredith doesn't know what to do when she starts screaming like that."

"Do we even know?" I asked. Raph had "turned down the volume" on the game, but Reading had a knack for whisper-screaming.

"And just once, I want Meredith to play something other than an inanimate object."

"I thought her salt shaker was very convincing."

"That's the problem."

I laughed. I'd spent day three of camp so blissfully busy I'd barely had time to think. Wake up, set up, CIT assignments, lunch, improv all afternoon, dinner, campfire, games, crash. The routine made me so happy I could burst. No way college was going to be this much fun.

Raph stayed for dinner, and I quietly filled him in on Ben's antics the night before. I was hoping he'd have ideas about what was going on, but neither one of us could explain it, so we chalked it up to boy PMS.

"See you tomorrow!" I smiled at him on our way out.

"Oh, hold up!" He grabbed my shoulders and steered me back toward Luna. "Kangaroo Court tonight."

"Oh shit!" I said, too loudly. I quickly looked around—no close-range campers. "I mean, oh shiitake mushrooms. I completely forgot!"

"No, you didn't," Raph assured me. "I didn't put it on the schedule in Luna."

"You didn't?"

Raph got a scary gleam in his eye. "No."

"Why?"

"Because then you'd've asked me who was on trial. . . ."

I stopped dead in my tracks in the grass. Are. You. Kidding me?

"Raph," I said, slowly. "This better not be about polar bear swim."

"Oh dear." Raph patted my shoulder. A swarm of kids poured out of the dining hall toward us, thrumming with excitement.

Kangaroo Court was one of the best traditions we had at Camp Dogberry, started by Raph when he worked here in college and had joined the mock trial club. We would squish the whole camp into Luna, which became the Dogberry courthouse. Raph was the judge, the campers sat as jury members, and the CITs served as lawyers. Every session a couple counselors were put on "trial" for various "crimes." Singing in the shower (Donald), irresponsible sunburning (Margo), sleeping late (Ben), and one year, flirting with the day lifeguard (Francis, the art assistant from last year).

The system was a little twisted, because anyone could suggest a case to Raph, and he usually picked whatever sounded the most hilarious.

He married people, too. Mom and Dad, Francis and Sam, and he'd *tried* to marry Ben and me when we'd "dated" in seventh grade, but I wouldn't let him. It occurred to me, sitting in my defendant chair that evening, trying not to pout, that maybe Claudia and Hana could get married this year.

I was practicing my pitch in my head, when I realized we were starting. Over dinner, the CITs had set up the courtroom. Campers were crowded in, doubling up on chairs or snuggled against pillows on the floor, and a special group of them were positioned to my right, at a long, narrow card table. These were the jury. I smiled at them. A little waved back at me. Then Maddie whispered to the kid urgently, and his expression went neutral.

How did *Maddie* get on this jury? She was so clearly biased.

"Order in the court!" Raph banged his gavel on his tiny folding table. The gavel's name was George, and it had a bowtie and googly eyes. The crowd hushed, except the rest of the counselors, who smirked at me from the back of the room. Ben waved, with this bizarre smile, and then winked. What the actual frick?

"This court is now in *session*!" Raph declared. We didn't have a judge's wig, so he wore our family's Santa beard. "We bring to trial the case of the People—"

He gestured to Wallace, the prosecutor, who waved at me cheerfully. Cheeky.

"Versus Beatrice Leonato."

I did a queen wave. Nessa, my lawyer, shifted in the chair next to mine.

Raph turned to Wallace. "What are the charges?"

Wallace stood confidently. He'd done this last year, too. "Your Honor, the defendant is charged with cowardice and hypocrisy."

"*Hypocrisy?* How dare you!" I cried out, slamming my fist on the table. The room shook with laughter.

Raph looked at Nessa. "Counsel, get your client under control."

My lawyer turned red but then looked at me, held a finger to her lips, and deliberately patted my knee. The room giggled again. She was good.

"Prosecution, please be more specific," Raph entreated.

"Specifically," Wallace declared dramatically, "she is charged with skipping out on polar bear swim *while* encouraging everyone to be a team player. *Constantly.*"

Laughs again, especially from the returning campers. Margo and Donald whistled in agreement at the back of the room. I mentally gave them the finger.

But okay, so I did use the term "team player" a lot—especially in improv class. Even if we explained the rules, there were always actions during games that Raph and I had to gently stop: campers would whip out guns and "shoot" the other campers in a scene, or one camper would be a dinosaur—"I'm a dinosaur"—and the other would say, "All the dinosaurs are dead." The best way to not shame the kids, but also let them know that wasn't okay, was to frame it under teamwork. *"Pause! Okay, let's start rewind a little, and everyone try to be a team player!"* Once I'd figured this out, it kind of became my catchphrase in class.

"So you see, by skipping out on a Camp Dogberry team-building activity, i.e., polar bear swim"—Wallace circled a hand thoughtfully—"Bee is being *cowardly* as well as *hypocritical*. The prosecution rests."

He sat to thundering applause.

Well, I was doomed.

CHAPTER 31

Hana

FIREFLY TAG. LIGHTS FLASHING, screams of joy, and definitely some actual crying. Somebody'd tripped on the other side of the field.

"Everyone okay?" I called out breathlessly.

"We got it!" I heard back from Ben.

I dropped back down to the ground. I'd been tagged for a while—I'd let a little catch me—and I was waiting for my opening to get back in the game. I heard footsteps approaching from behind, I turned in my awkward squat—

"Quick." She caught my hand and dragged me backward, into the trees. We stumbled through the brush and came out on the dirt road behind camp, the streetlamp illuminating our faces.

Claudia reached forward, grabbed my cheeks, pulled me in. Lips and tongues and breath. I felt light everywhere on my body.

"Sorry, I just couldn't—"

"I know." I smiled. "But we should go back."

She stared into my eyes, her forehead pinched in thought. There was something she wanted to say. My legs shook, just a little, from the anticipation. Or maybe from other things too.

"I don't want this to end," she said finally.

"Me neither," I agreed. Who would ever, ever want that?

"I mean," she breathed, "when we're together, I don't want *this* to end."

My turn to stare at her. I knew what she meant, but did I have the courage to say it back?

Instead, I ran my fingertips across her forehead, brushing her temple, down her face and neck. I pulled her T-shirt's neck down, kissed her collarbone, in a way I hoped—in a way I *knew*—was sexy. She shuddered. I pulled back.

"Me neither."

"So, then." She shuddered again when she spoke. Kind of a spasm. It was so hot. "Fourth of July is Friday."

I barely followed. My mind was so many places. "Yes."

"There's going to be a party."

"Yes."

"So let's get a tent, for after the party."

Suddenly, my mind was just one place: in a tent. With Claudia. And our clothes were off.

"Mmm . . ." I let out the tiniest moan. Maybe I should've been embarrassed, but she'd just shudder-spasmed, so I think I was okay? She smiled and pushed a loose curl behind my ear. I was okay.

"Sounds good?" she confirmed.

"Sounds perfect."

One more kiss that I felt down to my curling toes. She went back up to the game first so we wouldn't seem suspicious.

As I stood there in the dark, tingling all over, I realized:

A tent. Was I really going to have sex for the first time in a *tent*?

CHAPTER 32
John

DURING THE THIRD ROUND of Firefly Tag, I got my proof. Did I ever.

I'd tried to keep an eye on Hana and Claudia, where they were on the field. This game seemed like the perfect opportunity to slip off and hook up somewhere. That's what Margo and Bobby did.

My plan only faltered once, when I got too into the game and tagged, like, twenty campers in a row. I finally let Jay catch me because, you know, that kid was cool.

Crouched down in frozen mode was when I saw it: Hana hunched over in front of me, maybe twenty yards away. In one motion, Claudia approached, grabbed her, and they disappeared into the woods. I quickly switched off my light and followed them.

They retreated down the little hill, to the road that runs behind Camp Dogberry. The girls paused under a streetlamp. I followed and positioned myself behind a tree, far enough away that I couldn't quite hear their whispers. Then they kissed, and I could see this *thing* between them. My breathing felt sharp. Then, at the end of the conversation, before they made their way back toward the field, I actually heard Claudia say—

"So let's get a tent, for after the party."

And I realized: Claudia had completely forgotten about our conversation. The hangout that I was agonizing over wasn't even on her radar anymore.

Asshole.

I watched Claudia romp off into the game again. Just like that. Like I didn't matter in the slightest. I felt that familiar heat rising in my stomach.

"Where's John?" I heard a camper's voice call.

Firefly, I thought to myself. You're a *firefly*. Bzz. I switched on my flashlight, switched off my brain.

But I couldn't get back into it. After another round, I handed my flashlight off to a CIT who'd forgotten his and stalked back to my cabin, knowing Bobby and Connie would eventually turn up. They did. Good old lackies.

"Dude, sing-along?" Bobby poked his head in. Connie's appeared too, but the minute she saw me, she stopped smiling and looked concerned.

"You know, singing," Bobby reminded me. "It's like words that you say with your mouth, but you say them longer?" I didn't respond. "We say them around a campfire, because we get paid to. . . . Yeah, it's making less sense as I say it out loud." He sat down on a camper's bed.

"What's going on?" Connie asked.

"You guys were right. About Claudia and Hana," I said. I swung my legs around and leaned forward on my bunk. "I need to come up with a plan."

CHAPTER 33

Bee

I DIDN'T BREAK RULES, and this was a super obvious one: the sun was supposed to wake you up. Anything else was against nature.

Unless you were a nocturnal animal, like a bat. Most humans are *not* nocturnal, though, I thought to myself blearily. There's absolutely no reason for me to be awake for this activity invented by Satan. Or whoever came up with polar bear swim. The name made it sound cute. But we were *not* polar bears, and I bet polar bears would think we were insane for doing this.

Team player, Bee, you're a team player.

But my teammates were so evil! I vowed to get back at Raphael—maybe I'd take *him* to court for . . . being a jerk. Loving Lin-Manuel Miranda inordinately. Wait, that was impossible. My brain was too tired to think.

Stop. Just get up, Bee.

I took a deep breath and opened my eyes, which actually *hurt*—every blink felt heavier. I rubbed at them, flattening the puffy lids. I gritted my teeth and pushed back the sleeping bag and almost screamed from the cold. As I pulled on sweats and a sweatshirt, I checked Hana's bed: she was already gone. Probably down at the docks warming up. How did that girl wake up freezing every morning? I'm sure she thought it was invigorating or something ridiculous like that.

Only one other camper from our bunk had gone down with her. Though it pained me, I wrote on our little whiteboard that Hana and I were at polar bear swim, in case of an emergency. Little Bat was, blessedly, only a couple minutes from the waterfront, and we had the oldest girls, twelve-year-olds, so they'd be fine for an hour. I shoved my bathing suit and towel under my arm and headed to the bathrooms.

Gulls barked obnoxiously over the harbor. A breeze took a swipe at the back of my neck. The sky had just started to go from gray to a pink; the transition looked disgusting. Worm colored, as far as the eye could see.

That was mean. Margo loved worms.

The fluorescent lights of the bathroom hurt too. I punched open a stall door and sat down on the toilet lid. Where was *my* camp counselor to tell me not to sulk? I sulked a bunch.

Finally, I stood and stripped in the stall. My body immediately began shaking. My teeth started chattering, for real. As I pulled my *damp bathing suit* over my *shivering body*, I heard the swinging squeak of the door, and then Hana and Margo coming into the building. Laughing. Like the demon polar bears they were.

"Is she even up?" Margo asked. Margo didn't come to polar bear swim that often, so clearly she was just here to watch me die.

"I don't know," Hana replied. "Maybe we should go get her?"

I couldn't decide what to do. Should I scream and terrify them? Burst out of the stall and terrify them? Anything that ended in terrifying them.

"Are you going to tell her today?"

What?

Hana paused, then shook her head, I could hear it. "No, I don't think I'm going to tell her at all."

Tell me what? I leaned forward.

"Seriously? You're not going to tell Bee that Ben's in love with her?"

What?

My legs gave out. I wrapped my towel around me and sank back down onto the toilet seat, as softly as I could.

CHAPTER 34

Hana

I FELT BAD, THINKING about Bee, still mostly asleep, trying to understand all of this. We'd been waiting in the bushes outside and watched her fumble into the bathrooms, then followed her in after a minute or so. I knew Bee would take forever to change. We'd timed it right, at least.

Margo nodded at me. She had bags under her eyes that almost matched her purple hair. How late had she been up? Well, she had the littles this session.

"Yes, I'm sure." I nodded back. "I'm *not* going to tell her that Claudia told *me* that Ben told her and Donald that he's *in love* with Bee."

Keeping all of that straight felt like being a CIT again.

"Right, right." Margo eyed Bee's feet under the stall door. "And Claudia told *you* to *tell* Bee?" She'd decided beforehand that I should be the one with the info that Ben liked Bee. Because if this were actually *real*, Claudia might've told me. I got the reasoning, but I was afraid Bee would hear all the lies in my voice.

"Yeah," I confirmed. "*And* Claudia said Donald thought I should tell Bee, too. But I realized I couldn't."

"Really? Why?" Margo prompted, with a goofy grin that didn't match the fake sincerity in her voice. I had to look away and collect myself.

"Because," I said finally, "Bee doesn't *like* Ben." Well, she hadn't told me otherwise, had she?

"Are you *serious*?" Margo pealed laughter. "She totally likes him. She just won't admit it!" I swear I could hear Bee's breathing.

"Maybe you're right," I said, pretending to think about it. "It feels like something happened between them last year, but she won't tell me about it."

"Well, they can't have hooked up." Margo shook her head. "Because lord knows Bee doesn't think *anyone* should ever just hook up."

I froze. Had this just become about Margo and Bobby? And was it suddenly real? I glanced at the stall, and then back to Margo, indicating that she should keep going.

"But anyway, Ben!" She snapped back into the script, thank goodness. "He's not a hookup person, either. They could be dating snobs together, in snobby, snobby romance land."

"Totally." I laughed. "And he's definitely the kind of guy I could see Bee with."

We *almost* heard a snort. It was like a stifled snort. We paused. I didn't know what to say next.

Luckily, Margo had it covered. "Maybe you're right, though." She sighed. "I wouldn't want him throwing himself at someone who wasn't interested. He's, like, the sweetest guy."

This I could speak to. I really did think Ben was the best. "Totally. He's hard-working and *goal-oriented*, and he's so good with his little sisters. And he might be the nicest person at camp." When I said it out loud like this, I really did believe that Bee and Ben would be perfect for each other. I almost couldn't believe it hadn't happened already.

Margo nodded along, and then, as I finished, got that wicked grin on her face. "Wait, what about Claaaaudia?"

"Claudia's not nice like Ben's nice," I explained. But that sounded bad. Whoops. "I mean, she's nice, but she's also . . ."

"Dark? Brooding? Sexy?" Margo wiggled her eyebrows at me.

"Maaaybe." I giggled back. Sexy. Tents. Sexy tents.

"But, wait—why don't you just tell Bee all that about Ben?" Margo leveled suddenly. "I mean, you're her sister—wouldn't she listen to you?"

"To me?" I laughed. "No way. Ben's kind of an off-limits subject. She's never . . . She wouldn't let me, even if I tried to. She'd just change the topic or distract me." It was true. It usually worked on me, too, embarrassingly.

Margo nodded. "She hides those feels so well. . . ."

Did she?

". . . She can be tough."

"Very tough," I said, hoping Bee would like that. *Tough* was a Bee word.

"And besides, if she knew he liked her, she'd have so much more ammo to make fun of him," Margo pointed out.

"Oh yeah," I said, before I could stop myself. "I wouldn't want him to get hurt." That was true. I was terrified that Bee was going to hurt Ben—or vice versa—more than they already had. I knew what heartbreak was like. Suddenly, I super wanted this conversation to be over.

"That's real," Margo said. "I guess Ben'll just spend the summer hiding sad erections in his sleeping bag."

I choked on my own laughter.

Suddenly, the toilet in Bee's stall flushed.

"Ghost toilet!" Margo screamed, and we both burst out laughing and tore out of the bathroom, down to the waterfront, leaving my sister emotionally reeling in a toilet stall.

CHAPTER 35

Bee

I CAN'T MOVE. I can't breathe.

I'd climbed up onto the toilet back and accidentally stepped on the flush handle on the way down.

After Margo screamed and they ran out of the bathroom, the familiar whirring started in my ears. They pulsed hot. I stumbled out of the stall, yanked on a faucet—cold water—and splashed it on my face and ears.

Ben, telling Claudia and Donald that he's in love with me?

In *love* with me?

I heaved a breath, looked up at myself in the mirror. Early morning puffiness, braids flopping to one side, boobs kind of lopsided in my one-piece.

Me?

Seriously?

After all of that?

WHAT HAPPENED: PART 7

Bee

IT SHOULD'VE BEEN UNCOMFORTABLE to make out on a stack of tarps, but I barely noticed. Every once in a while I could feel them crinkling under us.

First I kissed him, and after a moment, he kissed me. And then I lost count, but it just seemed like we were kissing each other. Press, push, tongues, release, repeat. Passing breaths back and forth. Why did it feel so good?

Ben's arms held me close, and almost every part of me was touching every part of him. Maddening. I wondered which move, which kiss, brush, or graze, would strike and burst us both into flames?

Now his hands were on my neck, his lips on my ear. I shuddered. If I did the same thing back to his ear, was that copying? I tried it. He didn't seem to care if it was original.

His hand moved down; his fingers paused at the edge of my T-shirt hem.

"Yes," I whispered.

Then my shirt was off. Then his shirt was off. Skin against skin, I felt dizzy. It felt like I'd always wanted to touch him like this. Be touched like this.

But even with all the contact, it still didn't feel like enough. Because we needed to be closer than this. This was nowhere near close enough. Whatever that feeling was, it kept us going. . . .

Finally, after what felt like hours, we drifted off in each other's arms, shirtless with bruised lips.

And when we woke up, everything had changed.

CHAPTER 36

Bee

I DRIED THE COLD water off my face. Had Ben been feeling this way this whole year, just like me? Did he really want me? *Me?*

Of course you.

Because Ben's yours, too.

The thought popped into my head without warning, and I gasped. Actually gasped, by myself alone in the bathroom. But I'd been so harsh to him since he'd arrived. How could this be real?

But how could it not? Why would they all know otherwise? Did Hana and Margo really think I was too proud to admit I was in love with Ben?

Wasn't I?

I took deep breaths, but that just let in a suffocating rush of bathroom mildew and bubbly antibacterial soap.

I needed air.

I pushed open the bathroom door. Outside had changed. The sun was finally beginning to rise, now pink-and-gold. The grass, dew, cabins awash with yellow glow. My feet automatically steered me down to the waterfront.

"Hey, sleepyhead!" Margo called as I approached.

Margo. She clearly thought I'd judged her for hooking up with Bobby. Well, I had. And for the first time, I actually felt bad about it.

"Morning!" I replied, my voice somehow working without me.

A dozen campers swarmed me, and I gently led them back down to the water, patting heads and asking questions, not quite sure what I was saying. Maddie and Jay bragged to the group that they'd gotten me sent to Kangaroo Court. I managed to act put out.

"You missed the warm-up," Hana said, concerned. "Why don't you do some jumping jacks, and we'll wait?"

"Okay," I said. Because what else would I do. "Will you all count for me?"

My trusty, disloyal campers cheered me on, and once I was through, we went out to the dock and lined up all along it.

"Polar bears at the ready?" Hana called.

"Ready!!" The kids screeched, giggling.

"One . . . two . . . three . . . jump!"

I didn't jump immediately. The spray hit me, fiercely cold, and I balked. But there was no turning back now, particularly because I knew if I didn't jump, the campers would pull me in, waterfront safety be damned.

Instead, I sat on the edge of the dock and carefully lowered myself in. Torturous, but somehow more manageable than a plunge. When I was up to my waist, I let myself fall—icy liquid closed over my head, and I came up screaming, much to the delight of everyone around me.

That was the worst of it. I went under again and again. Partly because then no one could accuse me of half-assing polar bear swim and make a case for extending my sentence.

And one more reason.

When I dove under, I was alone, and if only for a few freezing seconds, I could think. The cold water cleared my head. Voices giggled and shouted above me, people who wanted my attention. But I wasn't really there. I was sinking, floating, feeling minuscule grains of salt pricking my skin in a million places.

And I knew I hadn't imagined or dreamed it.

Any of it.

Ben.

Every time before I submerged, I took a breath and held Ben with it, tightly suspended in my chest.

I loved him.

I loved him.

I loved him.

CHAPTER 37

Vanessa

I HAVE TO TELL you, I was totally relieved when we got to Pirate Day. Thursday Theme Days at Camp Dogberry were always fun—we dressed up, there were special activities—but as a camper, I never appreciated Pirate Day the way I did now.

Because the kids spend the second half of the day on boats, being all pirate-y. And those less waterfront-inclined counselors/CITs get the afternoon off. We made up for it by working on another theme. I'd signed up for Halloween Day in a few weeks. So today, Pirate Day, I got a whole afternoon. To myself. I dropped off the kids at the water and thought for a sec about going back to my cabin. I could spend the break catching up on sleep.

Well, as soon as I finished an extra dish shift. That was part of the price for my afternoon off. An extra chore during your break. Campy Dogberry's fairness felt a little annoying to me at this exact moment.

I dragged myself through Dam, into the back. Sophia and Wallace were already at work in the big sinks with the hoselike faucets. I grabbed a pair of dish gloves.

"Nessa!" Sophia shouted above the spray. "Did you hear about tomorrow?" She'd drawn on a blue beard to go with her outfit.

I flicked up my eye patch. "What's tomorrow?"

"The Fourth of July!" she reminded me. "It's a *party*, like, a real one."

"Reeeeeally?" A party sounded like heaven.

"Totally. With sparklers and beer and everything." Sophia smiled, despite the gross bean dip she was scrubbing out of a bowl. "I heard Donald talking about it at art today."

"Wow," I said. "We're going to a real party."

"I know—"

"Except that we're not invited."

Wallace, loading the industrial washing machine, in a skull and bones captain hat, looked at both of us like: duh.

"We're not?" Sophia shut off the water.

"No way." Wallace shook his head. "CITs don't get to go to those kinds of parties. Doug told me."

"How do you always know everything?" I wondered aloud.

Wallace shrugged.

"Well, that's the worst." I sighed, flipping a pot onto the drying rack. "But we can probably grab some sparklers and hang out together—"

"Is this the way the entire summer is going to be?" Sophia demanded. "We bust our butts, and we don't get any perks?

Wallace shrugged again. "We get weekends and some time off."

"To do what?" she replied. "Make more friendship bracelets??"

"It sounds like a cool party," Wallace agreed sadly. "It's up in Nest."

"The view from up there is so beautiful," I said, remembering that year Doc had taken us on a stargazing trip, when I was a little camper. I hadn't been there since.

"Too bad we won't get to see it," Wallace said.

"What if we go on strike?" Sophia suggested.

"Isn't a strike kind of hard to pull off when your parents are paying for you to work?" I said. "Plus, I don't think Nik and Andy would care too much about CITs not getting invited to parties that are probably *inappropriate*. And then the counselors would hate us for bringing it up."

"Good points," Sophia sighed. "Wait . . . What if we talked to one of the counselors about it? Ben?"

"Nah." I shook my head. "I don't think he'd be super sympathetic . . . but *maybe*—"

Suddenly, Bee's head appeared in the drive-thru window. "Hey, all, great teamwork!"

We startled and looked at one another, then at the kitchen around us. None of the faucets were even running. We looked back at her dubiously.

"Hint, hint." She smiled, knocked once on the doorway, and then disappeared again. The side door slammed. We quickly got back to work. I had an idea now.

After dishes, I ran and found Margo—I knew she'd be sunning herself outside our cabin.

"Hey, chickadee!" She smiled as I walked up. She was lying out on her beach towel, wearing a swimsuit and her big star-shaped sunglasses. No shoes. Scandalous.

"Hey." I sat down in the grass next to her. "Can I ask you a question?"

She smiled into the sun. "I know everything about birds, fungi, *and* periods. Ask away."

I laughed. "It's about the party on Friday."

"Ooooh." She sat up and slid her sunglasses back onto her head, pushing back her purple curls. "What about it?"

"Do you think that—"

"Aww, sweetie." Margo shook her head. "Sorry, but CITs totally can't come."

"Oh, okay." Margo'd been so nice and welcoming, and she was a lot less scary than Bee, and cooler than my brother (sorry, Ben). So I figured maybe . . . Now my ears were burning. I felt so juvenile for even asking.

"Hey." Margo snapped me out of it. I looked at her—she looked kind of pained. "I'm *really* sorry." She ducked her chin emphatically. "It's just, it's an older person kind of thing."

"But what if it was just me and Sophia and Wallace?" I ventured. "We wouldn't tell the others, and we'd be really cool there, I promise."

She smiled her dimply smile. "You're the coolest, Nessie. But if we brought you, we'd for sure all get fired."

"Oh." I hadn't even thought of that. Of course they'd get in trouble.

"You'll be able to go when you're older!" Margo slung an arm around me and squeezed.

"Right."

"*And* I'll totally sneak you guys some sparklers, if you'll be careful. You can have your own hoppin' Fourth!"

I grinned, the disappointment starting to fade. "That would be great! Really?"

"You got it. I'll make Donald get you some outside snacks from town, too."

After another hug, I went and found Sophia and Wallace in Luna. Neither of them had had any luck, either.

"I ran into Hana at the bathroom, but she totally blew me off," Sophia complained. "She just said, 'You won't be a CIT forever!' and then left. Probably to go make out with Claudia."

I was glad I'd got Margo, at least she was super nice about it. We both looked at Wallace.

"Oh, I chickened out," he said quickly. "I didn't ask anyone."

Neither one of us said anything, because we'd figured he wouldn't.

"Look," I said. "Margo's getting us snacks and sparklers. It'll still be good."

"I guess." Sophia sighed. "But we won't get to be in the middle of all of that action!"

A thought occurred to me. "But, Sophia"—I nudged her shoulder—"we'll be *around* it. . . ."

Her eyes widened. "We'll totally have to do some surveillance."

"Yes!" I agreed. "It'll be like a scavenger hunt. For *gossip*."

"Totally!" she squealed. "And, Wallace—"

"Yeah?" he said excitedly.

"You keep doing whatever you're doing," she finished. "Because somehow you always wander into it."

"Got it!" He saluted, beaming. Sometimes I wondered what Wallace thought about all of this gossip stuff, but looking at his smile, I realized he probably didn't care what we were talking about as long as he was talking to Sophia.

Then I told them I had to go check in at the waterfront, because Rudie never reapplied his sunscreen unless I sang to him during the process.

CHAPTER 38

Claudia

THURSDAY AFTERNOON, DONALD GRABBED Bee and me for a run into town for party supplies. Apparently, Donald had set up a contact to sell us a few fireworks, too. Bee claimed she just needed time out of the woods. I wanted to get a present for Hana, for the party. We piled into Donald's green Mercedes—Bee and Donald in the front, me in the back.

I clicked in my seat belt, lost in thought. A present. I wasn't sure what kind of present you bought for this kind of occasion—the we've-made-out-a-lot-but-we've-got-a-tent-now-so-we-both-know-this-is-going-to-go-further occasion.

Maybe chocolate?

A knock on my window startled me.

"AHH!" I yelled at Ben's face.

"AHH! is right," Bee snorted.

I rolled it down.

"What's up, creeper?" Donald said.

"Can I come?" Ben asked. "I need Capture the Flag stuff."

"Capture the Flag isn't till next Wednesday," Bee pointed out.

"Just planning ahead." Ben grinned.

She shook her head and turned back around.

The car went silent for a full three seconds. I looked at my knees, just in case Donald was looking back at me. I knew we'd both crack up.

No complaining from Ben about the Capture the Flag change. No "Oh, planning ahead for once in your life" from Bee. That was the most pleasant exchange between Ben and Bee that we'd seen this year.

"Makes sense," I said, finally. I opened the door for Ben and slid over.

"Thank you!" Ben said brightly, and climbed in. Since Counselor Hunt, being around Ben felt like hanging out with a cardboard cutout version of him who showered more. As I scooted toward the middle, suddenly the other door opened. John.

"Hey, guys, heard you're making a run?"

Before Donald could flip out, Ben said, "Sure, you need something?"

"I just want non-camp coffee," John explained, sliding in next to me.

I nodded at him. I missed real coffee too.

"Well, we can bring you some," Donald offered lightly. "Or not. Either way, you need to get out of my car."

John froze. "It's my car too, for the summer."

"Cool, you can have it when I'm done," Donald shot back. He was being stubborn. Whenever there was a town run, we took whoever.

Bee touched Donald's hand on the gearshift. "Hey, we all need a break from camp. Let's just go."

Donald took a breath, paused, then shifted into drive. "Fine. Let's go."

He pulled out of the lot at a speed most of us would find danger-ous, but Donald seemed completely comfortable with—in fact, he kept it up the entire way to downtown Paris, the closest actual town to Messina. When we finally found a parking spot and pulled over, I think everyone felt on the brink of puking.

"I vote John drives back" was all Bee said as we got out.

"It's only fair," Ben agreed, then after Donald's scowl, added, "Equal share of the car!"

"So, should we have a Maine Adventure?" Bee asked.

Reny's was this wild department store they had in Maine, and their tagline was "A Maine Adventure" because they stocked *every-thing*. Clothes, toys, household stuff, pet supplies, hunting gear, not to mention a wide variety of quality hiking socks. I knew I could find something for Hana there. A person could probably find their long-lost cousin there.

"Reny's!" Ben snapped his fingers in her direction. "That's a good place to go! Yes!"

I inwardly, not outwardly, groaned at Ben's weirdness, which took a lot of effort.

"Welcome to Reny's!" A woman in a green smock smiled at us as we came in. After weeks in the woods, the bright fluorescent lighting slapped my eyes in the face, and the AC felt like walking onto frozen tundra.

None of us knew what to say. What were real humans, again? It had been two weeks of nothing but camp. I felt the sense that we were all suddenly, painfully aware that we wore dirty T-shirts, athletic shorts, and sneakers. Oh wait, and pirate costumes. I don't know how we forgot we were wearing pirate costumes.

We split up. Donald took off to look for sparklers, Bee toward food, and who knew where Ben was going. I found myself in the swimming stuff aisle, looking at inner tubes printed to look like sprinkle donuts. Didn't feel exactly right, though.

In the next aisle over, I saw Ben studying a bottle of mouthwash. He shoved it in his basket the second he noticed me.

"Capture the Flag supplies?" I asked innocently, peeking into the basket. There were half a dozen deodorants in there.

"For our older campers," he explained quickly. "Next week's supposed to be hot, and they always smell."

Well, that was true.

"And the mouthwash?" I asked.

It was a gallon-size container of acidic teal. He looked down at it; his face went completely blank for one second. Then—

"Too much bug juice," he explained. "I'm gonna get cavities."

I made a mental note to tell Donald about this hilarity later. Emergency mouthwash, right before the sparkler party? Dude had plans. He then kind of sprinted away from me down the aisle. Maybe to pay and bag before anyone else could call him out. That's what I'd do.

Which brought me back to my task: try to find anything that looked like something Hana would want me to give her. I'd just made it to outdoor living, the bird section, when John showed up.

"Hey, they accidentally gave me two," he said, holding up two white coffee cups. "You want one?"

"Hell yeah." I grabbed it from him and immediately took a scalding sip. Black, not burnt, not instant . . . I hadn't wanted to spend the money, but damn. This was almost as good as kissing Hana. Was coffee-flavored lip gloss a thing? Should I buy it for her?

"Thaaaank you," I sighed, bringing it away from my lips.

"Sure thing." John nodded. "That's one of the perks at Yale—excellent coffee."

"Cool," I said.

"Hey, listen," he said, moving in toward me and the birdseed. "Can I talk to you about something?"

Did anything good ever start with that sentence? Was he going to want to talk about what happened on the island? I thought he'd probably taken the hint, given that . . . well, whatever.

"Yeah, sure, go."

"Okay." He leaned up against the shelves, lowered his voice. "I've heard this rumor you're hooking up with Hana."

He paused. I didn't say anything back.

"Okay," he continued. "I just wanted to bring it up because before I heard that, I'd heard she was hooking up with some townie who's sneaking into camp at night, after quiet hours."

Did he just say words? I must've looked shocked, because he took something I did as an invitation to keep going.

"Yeah, Connie told me she saw them down by the volleyball net." He nodded. "Like, a couple nights this past week. Hey, are you okay?"

I sipped my coffee. Stay calm, stay calm, stay calm. Was this even possible? "I'm . . . fine," I said. "Why . . . Why are you telling me this?"

John's pretty face pinched into some expression between anger and embarrassment.

"Because I like you," he said. "I know you're friends with Donald but . . . And I would want to know, if I didn't know. Did you know?"

I stared at him.

"Guess not," he said.

I was really done with this conversation.

"Well, thanks." I held up the coffee.

"No problem, I hope . . ." He turned away, then back again. "I hope I didn't fuck up by telling you?"

My brain caught up with my emotions for a split second. "No, no." I rubbed my cheek with one hand. "I . . . Yeah. Thanks."

He nodded, then disappeared at the end of the aisle.

I looked at the miniature bird feeder on the shelf, the red one, the one I'd just decided to get for Hana. I thought she could hang it outside her window in Little Bat. It seemed like something she'd love.

Could this really be a thing? What townie? I'd known, like, last year, there'd been a guy who'd messed her up. Was it him? What was his name? Chris?

"Christopher?" Bee's voice from the aisle next to me.

A spastic chill shot down my neck. What the hell? I turned around and walked slowly, quietly to the end of the aisle.

"Yeah, hey, Bee," said a dude's voice. "How you been?"

"Fine." She sounded tense. "How about you?"

"I'm doing good, busy summer."

"Really."

"How's your sister?"

"Why?"

"I just thought—"

"She's doing *great,* and she doesn't want to talk to you."

"Really?" This guy sounded like a total dick.

"Really. Stay away from her," Bee's voice growled. If I were this guy, I'd be retreating.

"If she doesn't want to talk to me, then why does she keep texting me in the middle of the night?"

A brief moment, which felt like the pause before Bee punched his lights out. I waited for it, because if she didn't, I felt like I needed to.

"You're lying," Bee said.

His voice sounded amused as he replied, "I can show you the texts right now."

But instead, she marched out of the aisle and walked right into me.

"Fudge nuggets!" she exclaimed. Camp swearing. "Claudia, the fuck?" Regular swearing.

"Sorry," I said, then held up a red bird feeder. "Do you think Hana would like this?"

Her harsh expression immediately softened. "Oh, that's so sweet." Her voice went from razor to butter knife. "She can hang it on the roof edge outside her window."

I smiled. "Yeah, that's what I was thinking." Out of the corner of my eye, I saw a guy pass by at the other end of the aisle. I turned, but only caught the back of his blond head, in a UMaine sweatshirt. I wanted to run after him and get a better look, but of course I didn't.

Bee frowned, then handed the bird feeder back to me. She searched my eyes for a half second, then said, "You're cool, Claudia."

"Thanks." I nodded. "What did you get?" I pointed to her bag.

She froze. "Um, deodorant."

I headed toward the counter to pay. Don't act weird, don't act weird. I bought the bird feeder, I didn't know what else to do. As the smiling woman rang it up and bagged it, I wished so much that this whole trip had never happened.

On the ride home, John drove at a much more normal pace, Donald glowering with sparklers, fireworks, and mysteriously obtained alcohol in the front, Ben under his massive pile of toiletries on my right, Bee lost in thought to my left. I felt suffocated in the middle.

I closed my eyes and retreated to the corner in my head where I kept everything shitty.

The confused look in my mom's eyes. My "friends'" mocking laughter. My uncle's sneers. Long strands of black hair.

I added the bird feeder to the pile, scattered a handful of paper stars. I couldn't bring myself to leave her smile there yet, though.

At dinner, I watched Hana from across the room—she always sat with the emptiest table. I usually snuck glances at her, but this was different. I looked for signs of anything, suspicious behavior of any sort.

Her dark curly hair hung damp and tousled.

But there it was: I saw her look down at her pocket, take out her cell phone under the table. She stuck it back in, then got up and went to the bathroom.

I felt like I might throw up.

Maybe she was just texting a friend.

I had to know for sure.

I grabbed Donald and dragged him out to the flagpole.

"I need your help," I said. "I need you to come with me to the volleyball court tonight."

"I'm flattered." Donald smiled and raised an eyebrow. "But I don't think I'm your type."

"Ha-ha," I said. "Your brother told me that Hana's hooking up with some guy from town, and when they get together, it's at the volleyball court."

I expected him to be shocked, but he just nodded, slowly. "Is his name Christopher?"

"You know him?" I gulped down a scream. *Donald* knew about this guy, too.

"No. Just of him." He ran a hand over his face in thought. "I don't think . . . I mean, I don't think Bee would let Hana get back together with Christopher."

"Well," I said, "contrary to popular belief, Bee doesn't actually have control over what her sister does."

Donald stared at me, puffed out his cheeks, let out a sigh of air. "I mean, John's the worst . . ." He trailed off. "But he doesn't usually lie. I don't think."

I looked at him sharply.

"I'm a virgin, so."

I nodded. "Right, so."

"But this *is* Camp Dogberry," Donald continued. "So he might just be repeating a rumor."

"Right, but . . . I heard Bee run into this guy, Chris, at Reny's. They talked about Hana—it sounded like she's still talking to him."

That brought Donald up short. "Maybe we should talk to Bee?"

"No way." I shook my head. "If Hana was hooking up with someone else, it's not like Bee would tell us."

"Maybe she doesn't know," he mused. "So talk to Hana?"

"I don't want to accuse her of anything until I know this is real," I explained. "If John's wrong about this . . . I can't risk it." Truthfully, I couldn't imagine asking her.

"Should we tell Ben?" He jerked a thumb in the direction of Snowshoe.

"No way. He'd throw a fit. They're like family. So are you in?"

Donald paused, then nodded in agreement. Say a lot of things about Donald, but he's a loyal friend.

"Oh, and speaking of Ben," I said. "Did you see that he bought a crap ton of mouthwash?"

CHAPTER 39

Bee

OWLS HOOTED, STARS DANCED, I wrestled out of my sleeping bag. Luckily, our twelve-year-olds in Little Bat slept like logs, and salty Hana had crashed right after sing-along, done in by five hours of swimming and the ten verses of "Princess Pat."

Normally, I would've been crashing too. Ever since polar bear swim, my head had been spinning like a wheel of fortune, landing randomly on a hundred different tasks: Were the CITs okay? Were they in their right spots, doing their work? Did Raph have everything he needed? Were the campers bored of pretending to be stuck in Jell-O? Would they remember how to improv for the parents performance? Please remember how to improv. Are the goats good? Did everyone look adequately like a pirate?

This evening, in moments of brief camp pause, the wheel sometimes landed on: Was Hana getting in over her head with Claudia? Why was she texting Christopher again? Was Donald still hurt that I'd shot him down?

But tonight, the wheel had spun and stuck on what I'd been avoiding, and I had to get out of the cabin.

I threw on my sandals, grabbed my Reny's bag, and tiptoed down the porch steps. The salt cut through my big, emotional breaths. My legs shook.

"Calm down," I whispered to them. *"Calm down."*

I thought about going to the art building. Maybe do some origami, like Hana did when she was feeling the feels. I couldn't sit still, though. I hiked forward.

I stopped in Dam, flicked on the lights, went into the bathroom, changed my shirt. I stared at myself in the mirror:

Wow.

Gross.

Wow.

Gross.

I mean, I looked good, really good, but I was simultaneously utterly disgusted with myself. I wanted to fist-bump the girl in the mirror, and tell her how gorgeous she was. Alternatively, I wanted to shake my head and dismiss her for being so naive.

I changed back into my pajama shirt.

Outside again, I followed the moonlight past Dam, past the garden, past Luna. I stopped briefly to look out at the ocean. Something was still wrong. Why could I barely breathe?

The moonlight led me to Stickleback. I stepped inside—the Bandytails had been there. It reeked of raccoon poop. I walked through the maze of rope and metal clips on the floor, made it to the old dinghy in the corner, sat down in it, and immediately began to sob.

Now my whole body shook from crying. Long, low moans and shrieks escaped me, vibrating my lips. I couldn't keep up with wiping the tears away. I curled into a ball, to try and suppress it, but whatever was in me forced its way out: I must've cried for an hour straight.

And then all at once, it was over, and I was whimpering. My head felt clearer. I could hear what I was thinking—

College. I don't want to. I don't want to leave.

Hana. I don't want to leave her. She's messed up still. My parents can't handle it. They don't get it.

Donald. I don't want to lose him. He feels further away now.

Raph. Could he please shut up about how the world is better somewhere else?

Everything's changing, no matter what knots I tie.

Ben.

I'd avoided Ben as much as I could today. Both in person and in my head. But then it rushed at me all at once:

Ben, I like you, too. Wanna, like, do stuff?

Ben, I heard you're, like, in love with me. Is that true? 'Cause ha-ha-ha-ha, me too.

Ben, PLEASE ACTUALLY END SPORTS ON TIME FOR ONCE.

Memories pushed forward. I couldn't stop them. Smiles, hikes, hands, inside jokes, text messages, video chats. There was so much, so much I had shoved down and away.

Last summer.

I thought about it. I *really* thought about it. Not just thought about not thinking about it. I remembered the whole thing, all the way through.

And then I remembered it again.

And again.

I played the memories over and over, and they hurt more each time, like biting down on chapped lips.

I tried to add the new information to them—that though these were painful things that had happened, we had liked, maybe loved, each other this whole time.

It was baffling.

Ben, you totally baffle me.

I started to cry again, softly this time. I drifted off, crying in a boat in a raccoon-pooped shed. And then, just as I lost consciousness, I felt a little better.

CHAPTER 40

Claudia

ONCE QUIET HOURS STARTED, around nine, Donald and I ditched our cabins, jumped on the trail, and made our way up to Monarch. As soon as we got to the edge of the clearing, I wished I had never come at all.

Illuminated by the moon, two figures. One a girl, with dark curly hair, splayed out in the sand. The other a blond guy, in a bright white UMaine sweatshirt, pressed on top of her. I watched as they rolled over. Donald's sharp intake of breath next to me confirmed that it wasn't one of my paranoid nightmares. This was actually happening, right now, in front of me.

Donald's hand reached for mine. "Claud, I'm so sorry—"

I turned and sprinted back to the path, back to the crossroads at the waterfront. I stopped there, bent over, heaved up giant bursts of air. Black dots splattered my vision. Every bad emotion shimmied up my spine, into my head, pounded in my skull.

"Claudia!" Donald caught up with me. He kneeled down so we were face-to-face. "Are you okay?"

I didn't respond. It was a pointless question.

"I need to . . ." I started. But then I realized I didn't know what I needed. I needed to have never fallen in love with Hana Leonato.

"Look," Donald started. "Did you two . . . Ah, did you ever say you were exclusive?"

I dropped to sit, right in the middle of the trail. I racked my brain.

"No," I eventually whispered. We hadn't. I'd just felt it. I'd just thought.

"So maybe she didn't realize it was a big deal to you," Donald's voice floated in through the storm clouds.

My heart clung to that idea—that she didn't know how much it would hurt me. If she had, she couldn't have done it, right?

But my brain latched on to another thought—that she hadn't told me. We talked about her depression, her sister, her school . . . and she hadn't told me Chris was still in the picture?

"I can't deal with this right now," I said.

"Let's go back to the cabins," Donald suggested, and held out a hand. "Maybe you should sleep on it."

"Good idea."

He helped me up and looked me in the eye. "It's going to be okay."

"Okay," I replied, even though I couldn't see how.

He squeezed my shoulder before we split up, walking back to our separate cabins.

I got in my sleeping bag but did absolutely no sleeping.

CHAPTER 41

Bee

I WOKE UP AT five a.m., and at first I thought I just felt gross because I'd been sleeping on a tarp all night. But as I trudged back onto the trail, my nose started to run. Bee's Midnight Romance Worries had clearly been a walloping success.

I diverted to Big Bat, AKA my house, and crawled onto the couch in the living room. An hour or so later, Mom woke me up and shepherded me to the dining hall for early morning pancakes, which were almost worth the terrible sleep. It was nice to spend some alone time with her—although she kept asking me if something was wrong. I pleaded lack of REM.

"You're sick?"

"I think just tired." I blew my nose. "It'll probably clear up on the weekend, when I can sleep forever."

She laughed and ran her hand over my hair. "Well, try to get a nap in this afternoon after checkout, or you'll be drifting off during the fireworks. Have you checked your mail? You got more stuff from EBU."

I shook my head.

"Well, you can take care of that this weekend, too," she said, like it was no big deal. College paperwork. It took the fun out of paperwork.

"Mom, is Hana . . . Do you think she's okay?"

Mom rolled her eyes but smiled. "Apart from coming *dangerously close* to breaking every PDA rule in the book, she's fine."

"Okay." I bit my lip. "But I think she might be talking to *him* again."

Mom paused as she chewed a bite of her pancakes. "Why do you think that?"

"I saw something on her phone. . . ."

"You two need to get off your phones." She pointed her fork at me.

"I'm not on my phone! This was her phone!"

"So get off hers, sweetie." She laughed at my defensiveness. "If she's still talking to him, she'll stop soon. I think Claudia will prove a good distraction." She kissed my forehead, cleared our dishes, and got back to being the person in charge of, like, a hundred children.

∾

That night, after the fireworks, Margo, Hana, and I piled into the Dam bathroom again to get ready for the party. In my case, that meant blowing my nose a lot in the corner. I had my new shirt with me but didn't have the guts to change into it yet.

"Bee, you don't look so good," Margo said. "Maybe you should talk to Ben."

I froze, mid nose-blow. Which was gross. I finished the nose-blow.

"What? Why should I talk to *him*?!" I said it louder than I meant to. Margo raised her eyebrows at me. Hana glanced over from the mirror, without moving her head.

I quickly blew my nose again.

"Well, he's going to be a doctor, right?" Margo went back to touching up her eyeliner. "Maybe he's got a cold cure-all or something?"

"I've got the keys to the first aid office," I protested. "I think I'm good." I checked my watch. "We should get going soon. We're already ten minutes late."

Hana *eeped!*, and Margo quickly piled her own curls into an inspired messy bun. I looked at them both, so glam. It was now or never. I ducked into the bathroom, flipped off my top, pulled the new one on, adjusted my boobs a little, took a breath, unlocked the stall door.

"Bee!" Margo immediately screamed. You could count on her for the big reaction. Hana turned from doing her mascara, and her whole face lit up.

I looked at myself in the mirror again, this time bolstered by my friends. A stretchy white halter, with a delicate green vine pattern moving up the straps.

"Do you like it? I got it at Reny's. You really can find anything there." I put in my big silver hoop earrings with silver dangly bits, all nonchalant.

"You look *gorgeous*," Margo gushed. Hana's big eyes shone, almost watery. I'd expected the squealing, but why was everyone so emotional suddenly?

"So let's go?" I asked, before everyone started crying about my halter top.

"Let's go!" Margo pushed us out the door.

My stomach zigzagged as we made our way up the steep path. What was really going on here? Was I sick, or just nervous? What could I possibly be nervous about? I didn't have to do anything about the Ben thing, if I didn't want to.

It's my last summer. Just friends. He'd said those words exactly one year ago. What was I supposed to believe?

When we were nearly at the top, I got outside of myself enough to pull Hana briefly to the side of the trail.

"Oh, I forgot matches!" Margo exclaimed, and ran back down the hill. She was such a good sport about sister moments.

Once we were alone, I brushed Hana's arm. "Hey, so you and Claudia?"

My beautiful little sister blushed in the twilight, hiking the tent strap over her shoulder. With her hair done, and that glow around her cheeks, she'd never looked cuter. "Yes?"

"Ahh, you know . . ."

"Bee, what?"

"Sex?" The word popped out. I was trying, but the dizzy feels and the Ben stuff took up so much of my mind, it was hard to find tactful words. "You're going to have sex, right? Tonight?"

"I don't, uh . . ." She looked down at her feet. "I think so?" she finished, finally. "Maybe? That's what I think we planned, but with the swimming demos and checkout, we haven't talked today."

My lips pursed automatically. "Okay, well, as your big sister, it is my duty to remind you that you *should* talk about it first."

"Okay."

"And about STDs and stuff."

"Okay." She nodded.

"*And* about how you feel."

She stopped nodding. "How I feel?"

"Look." I sighed. "I've never done this before, but I do know people who have, and it's *really* important that you talk about how you feel about it first."

I glanced pointedly in Margo's direction up the trail. "I mean, I have friends who have done this before they're ready. Before they know how they feel, and how the other person feels. And it *messes things up.*"

"Right."

"Oh, and also," I said, rushing this part. "If you have feelings for someone else, it's probably not a good idea to sleep with another person without talking about it."

Hana's eyes got wide. "Bee—"

"And *consent!*" I finished. "Yes means yes. Got it? Great, let's go!"

I pushed my baffled sister up the trail. I might have been weird and out of it, but I needed to make sure she knew how I felt. My mind kept flashing back to yesterday—running into that douchebag at Reny's. He made me feel so powerless. Well, fuck that, Christopher, you have no power here.

At the top of the clearing, I felt the extreme urge to run into the trees and throw up. It was all too familiar. If I just avoided Ben the whole night, though, it couldn't possibly go the same way.

Maybe, I thought to myself, I should not have worn this shirt.

CHAPTER 42

Hana

THE EDGE OF THE clearing felt like the end of the high dive. I paused, the tips of my toes clinging to the familiar surface.

Talk first, I reminded myself. Bee was right, of course—although I didn't know if she was right about Christopher. What did she know about Christopher?

Bee gave me a squeeze as she walked by. I saw Ben's eyes widen to moon-size as she made her way across the lawn. Maybe tonight, Bee and Ben would finally begin. My chest warmed at the thought, and then burst into wildfire at the sight of her—

Claudia, sitting on a picnic blanket that she probably brought for us. She wore a blue flannel. The silver in her hair flashed in the moonlight. She picked at the grass around her. Did she feel as nervous as I did? That felt comforting.

I vowed then, there, that I would never talk to Christopher again. Over the edge, there was something so much better.

I stepped out and fell toward her.

CHAPTER 43

Claudia

HANA RADIATED IN THE darkness. She appeared like a star growing brighter on the navy sky. A small beam of light, bringing all good things.

It wasn't fair. I hadn't even told her I was in love with her yet.

Slowly, she made her way over to me, through the sparklers and the beer and the others.

"Hi!" She sat down on the blanket next to me and set the little green tent bag behind us.

"Hi," I managed. This was so much harder than I thought it would be.

"How was your day?" She ran her fingers over the back of my hand. I flinched.

"It was . . ." Distracted. Torturous. Fine!

I didn't want to talk like this wasn't happening. I tried to remember how I'd rehearsed with Donald.

"Look, we need to talk about something." That was the first part.

"Yeah." She settled in, leaning on her right hip and putting a hand on my leg. "I think that's a good idea."

Stars shot up my body. *Stop, stop, stop, stars.* I took her hand off my leg. She looked confused.

"I need to ask you something."

"Okay."

I brought my eyes to meet hers. I almost wanted to lean in to kiss her—that's always what happened after we looked into each other's eyes. I forced myself not to. "Are you . . . Are you and Christopher back together?"

Her mouth dropped open, but she regained composure quickly. "No! No, no, I'm not. That was . . . That was over in March, remember?"

"So you're not talking to him?"

She bit her lip. "No."

Not convincing.

"And you're not hooking up with him?"

"What?!" Her voice got strained and high-pitched. "No! No way. Why are you asking me about this?"

"Please don't lie to me," I begged.

"I'm not lying, Claudia."

"Can I look at your phone?" I held out my hand. It was shaking.

Hana reached down to her front pocket but paused. "Actually, no." She looked back up at me. "You can't look at my phone."

The fierceness in her eyes startled me. I felt like I'd been slapped across the cheek.

"I need to go." I stood up, pulled at the blanket. Hana scrambled up. The tent rolled away.

"Wait, Claudia—"

I had to get away from her. I jogged across the clearing toward the trail. Who knew why I'd brought the picnic blanket with me. As I reached the edge, her hand touched my shoulder, I knew it was hers, and I spun around automatically.

Big mistake. Hana's enormous eyes bored into mine. Her perfectly braided hair was wisping out on either side, like static electricity.

"Claudia, who told you all of this?" she demanded. Loudly.

Behind her, I saw Donald break away from the group and start coming toward us. Good. I needed backup.

"Stop," I said quietly. "Just stop. You're a liar, Hana."

Her face crumpled in reply. I could feel people moving toward us. Whatever. Let them find out that Hana had a lot of growing up to do. That she didn't know how to treat people decently yet.

Besides, I couldn't really control myself.

She took a breath. "Claudia, I don't know why you're doing this, but I—"

"I saw you!" I cut her off. "I saw you last night, okay? You were hooking up with *Christopher* at the volleyball court."

"What are you talking about?" she gasped, but I caught an amber flicker of guilt in her eyes.

"Claudia," Donald said, appearing to my right. "Everything okay?"

Hana's hand went up to her mouth. "Claudia, no, I didn't—"

"Hana." Donald turned and calmly held out a hand. "I saw you there, too. Don't lie."

"*You* don't lie!" she sputtered.

Suddenly, Bee and Ben were there, too. My head reeled. I shouldn't have— This was too much—

"What's going on?" Bee's hands slid to her hips.

"Walk away, Bee." Donald shook his head. "You don't want to hear any of this."

"Like hell I don't!" Bee yelled at him. She glanced at me, then back to her sister. "Hana, what's going on?" Hana went to reply, but suddenly, the other counselors were in on this, too—Connie, John, Rachel, Ellie, Dave, and Doug all hovering around us. Thanks, Bee, that was helpful.

"Guys, calm down," Ben said, his voice low. "Why don't we take a deep breath, and someone can explain what's going on."

Bee ignored him and turned to me. "Why's my sister crying?"

So many times this year I'd been bullied. So many times I'd been blamed. But this one felt worse than all the others. This wasn't my fault. It was never my fault, but especially this.

In an instant, I became stony, hard, cold.

"What's going on," I said, "is that *Hana* was hooking up with *Christopher* without telling me."

Hana flung up her hands. "I would never, ever do that!" she cried.

"That's bullshit," Bee replied quickly. "Utter bullshit. How did you even come up with that?"

My voice and brain replied for me. "I *saw her.* Last night. At the volleyball court."

Bee looked at her sister—*doubt*—but Hana waved her hands around, shouting: "No, no, no, no, no! No, they didn't! I wasn't *there*!"

Bee pulled her in to her side. "There you go, idiots. She wasn't there. Did you even ask before you started accusing?"

Donald and I exchanged a look that the whole group took in.

"I don't want to get into this," he said. "But Hana was there. I saw it too."

"Why are you being an asshole?" Bee asked him.

"Really?" Donald fired back. "*We're* the assholes?"

In one swift motion, he grabbed Hana's cell phone out of her hand.

"Donald, *no!*" Ben yelled.

Too late.

Donald opened it, held it out in the middle of the group for everyone to see. There, in the recent messages—

Christopher.

Total silence. Then Hana: "I . . . We talked, but I didn't *do anything*—"

Hana sobbed and collapsed into Bee's shoulder. I could barely process everything that was happening, but of one thing I was sure: Hana didn't feel the same way about me that I did about her. Hana had been talking to Christopher. Hana had hooked up with Christopher. Hana didn't love me.

My whole body began to shake.

Bee snatched the phone out of Donald's hand and gave it to Hana calmly. Bee cradled her sister for the briefest moment, then looked up again. Her glare blazed like a comet aimed at me and Donald.

"Both of you"—she pointed at us—"stay away from my sister." She pushed past us and ushered Hana down the trail. Hana sobbed into her shoulder.

I immediately went to follow them. My heart still thought I cared about Hana. Donald put a hand on my shoulder and stopped me.

As soon as they disappeared, I took off into the woods.

CHAPTER 44

Bee

I HELPED HANA UP the porch stairs at Big Bat. She hadn't untucked from my armpit—still sobbing quietly, shaking, asking choked questions:

"Bee, you believe me, right?"

"Of course, Hana," I whispered.

"Why did she think I hooked up with him?"

"I don't know."

"Why doesn't she believe me?"

"It's okay; it'll be okay."

Of course, my idea of okay was probably vastly different from Hana's right now. It was relatively early, and when we barged inside, my parents were curled up watching a cheesy horror movie.

"What are you two doing here?" Dad paused the movie. He was slower on the uptake. Mom was already up and crossing the room.

"What happened?" She drew Hana out of my arms into hers. Hana just sobbed, finally wailing at full volume.

"Bee?" Mom looked at me wild-eyed.

I explained that Claudia thought Hana had cheated on her and that Donald had grabbed Hana's phone and shown all the counselors that she'd been talking to Christopher. Dad's eyes almost went black at Christopher's name.

"I *didn't* hook up with him again," Hana insisted, in between sobs, looking at Mom. "I promise Mom, I *didn't*."

"Okay, okay." Mom smoothed her hair. "I believe you, sweetie." But the glance my way told me otherwise.

"We both do." Dad hovered behind Hana and Mom.

"Good," I said forcefully. "I'm glad we all believe her. So you can fire Claudia and Donald tomorrow."

Mom pursed her lips at me. "Not now, Bee. I'm going to get Hana her pill and get her into bed."

"But—"

"We'll talk later. Stay up, we'll talk."

She directed Hana upstairs. I gave one of Hana's hands a squeeze, and she squeezed back. As I watched them go, Dad's arms wrapped around me for a big Dad hug.

"Hey, Bumblebee," he said, pulling back and resting a hand on my shoulder. "Everything'll be all right."

"Right." I nodded. "If we *fire* them."

"Bee," he sighed. "Like Mom said, we'll talk about that later. But I want to warn you: we don't typically fire people for romantic drama."

I broke away from him. *"Romantic drama?!"* I shouted, throwing up my hands. "Donald showed everyone her phone! That's a violation of privacy!"

"Right, and we'll give him a warning about privacy," Dad said calmly. "But this who-hooked-up-with-who isn't something we want to get into the middle of. Especially—"

"Don't say it." I held up a hand. "I don't want to know how deep in the pocket of King you guys are."

"Bee, that's not—"

"I'm going for a walk."

I stomped to the front door and yanked it open to find Ben there, hand in a fist, poised to knock. I felt tears in my eyes as soon as I saw him.

"Oh, hey!" His hand moved into an awkward wave. "I was just hoping to check on you and Hana. Is she—"

"Come on," I said, purposefully not looking back at my dad. Ben followed me down the porch stairs, onto the trail. We fell into a silent walk, side by side. I led the way to the right, toward Dam.

How could Claudia believe that Hana had cheated on her? I'd always thought she was insecure and whatever, but I didn't know it extended this far. How could she break up with Hana in front of everyone? What kind of person does that?

We reached Dam's veranda, and I sat on the wide bottom step of the stairs. I pulled my knees up to my chest and hugged them. Ben sat down, too, on the other side of the stair. I was vaguely aware that somewhere, far away and overhead, the second round of Messina fireworks were popping.

Boiling, angry tears seared down my cheeks. I had trusted Claudia with Hana's heart. How could she do this? She was *worse* than Christopher.

"Bee? Are you crying?"

"Uh, yup." I didn't look at him. "I'm probably going to be crying for a while."

He scooched closer to me, till our sides were touching. I was too tired and too confused to feel anything special.

"I'm so sorry." He hugged his legs up to his chest, too. "I don't know what happened back there."

I turned and glared at him through half-filled eyes. "Claudia and Donald went asshole rogue. Hana *did not* bring a guy to camp and hook up with him." Only the smallest part of me protested *She might've*, but I threw it in the trash. See, Claudia? Not that hard.

Ben flinched. "Oh I know, I know. I believe Hana. She wouldn't do that."

Relief flooded through me, and I nodded and snuffled a little, wiping at my nose with the back of my hand. I didn't care how gross that was.

"No, she wouldn't." It felt good to say. "And she didn't. And I'm never forgiving Claudia *or* Donald."

Ben scooted just a smidgen closer to me. "I get that."

"I want to fire them. And carve out their hearts with the gardening shears."

Ben laughed, kind of forced.

"I'm not joking."

"I know, it's just . . ." He trailed off.

I sighed, turned away, and stared out into the dark. I didn't care if Ben thought I was ruthless. I wasn't exaggerating. If he didn't get that those people had *hurt* my *sister,* and were therefore *scum,* then—

"Bee, I'm in love with you."

CHAPTER 45

Ben

THE WORDS LEFT MY mouth so effortlessly, I barely registered that I'd said them. Bee froze for, like, *seconds*, so I couldn't even tell if I *had* said them. Just silence, save for some ironic fireworks. If things had gone according to plan, we would've been *underneath* the fireworks when I'd said this, and then maybe she wouldn't be glaring into the night with her forehead perpetually pinched like that.

Finally, she spoke. "What . . ."

I held my breath.

"What the *fuck,* Ben?"

Shit. "Umm . . ." What if Donald and Claudia had been wrong somehow? Crap, crap, crap. "I'm into you, very into you, in like . . . a romantic and, uh . . . sexual way?"

She stood up immediately. "I can't deal with this," she announced. "I have to go." She took off down the trail.

"Wait!" I scrambled up to follow her. She was almost jogging. "Bee, please!"

She suddenly stopped at the waterfront and whipped around. "What do you want?"

I took a step toward her. "To know how you feel. Please."

She stuffed her hands in her shorts pockets. "What, so you can turn around and accuse *me* of being in love with *you*? I don't think so."

"What?" I sputtered.

She rolled her eyes so hard I was sure they'd gone all the way around. "Last summer."

Okay, so we were finally going to talk about this. "Yes."

"*Last summer*, Ben."

"I don't—"

"Do you not remember what happened last summer?!"

WHAT HAPPENED: PART 8

Ben

WHEN I WOKE UP, pain erupted in my back. *Where am I?* Someone asleep, hot and sweaty, was lying on top of me. It was Bee, half-naked, breathing steadily. My shirt was gone, too.

Sunlight poured into Stickleback. Shit. Then the back pain made sense. I'd been lying with Bee on top of me, with crinkled, pointy tarps underneath me, for hours.

I gently shook her. "Bee . . . Bee . . ."

"Mmmm . . ."

"Bee, morning meeting."

Her eyes flew open. "Crap!" She pushed herself off me and up—I looked away—and sprang into action, quicker than I'd ever seen Bee in the morning. She threw my shirt at me, and we both scrambled out the door.

"Have you heard the trumpet yet?" she asked, as we hurried (no running!) down the path.

"Wait." I reached into my pocket and pulled out my phone. It suddenly occurred to me I could check the time. "Oh. It's only six thirty."

We had an hour before we had to wake up the campers.

"God." She heaved a sigh of relief. "I thought—"

"I know."

"We should still hurry back."

"Definitely."

And that was it. We walked in silence along the trail together, and in some nonverbal agreement, back up to Nest. We grabbed the beer cooler and the sparkler bucket and dropped them off down at Dam, buried the beer bottles deep in the recycling.

There, in the grass behind the building, we paused, a few feet away from each other. I needed to go to the right, back to Snowshoe, and Bee would go left, to Little Bat. Disheveled and exhausted, yes, but neither one of us seemed to be able to move.

I felt acutely aware that if we didn't talk about this now, it could all disappear.

"So . . ." I began.

She raised her eyebrows. I almost gulped.

"So . . ." I pushed forward. "Last night?"

"Yeah." Her face went blank.

"I just wanted to say . . . umm . . ." I searched for the words. "Well, I guess what I want to know is . . . do you like me?"

"What?" she snapped.

"I mean, I think you like me?" I said again, glancing at her.

She went quiet for a moment, seemed to decide something, then looked up at me with blazing eyes. What had I done?!

"Yeah, I *like* you," she snapped. "We're friends."

"Just friends . . .?"

"Isn't that all we are?"

"Right." I swallowed. Tactile memories bombarded my brain. Fingers, mouths, tongues, ears, nipples—*friends*?

Bee

I stood there, behind Dam with Ben, furiously processing. It all made stupid sense now. We'd been drunk, it was late, it was after a party. Of course he didn't like me. Neither of us had really meant it. Alcohol and horniness meant it, clearly. And now he accused me of liking him! I could say the same thing! So how dare he pin all of this on me?

I needed to leave. To run the fuck away. I blabbed about us being friends, and then ended it.

"Okay, well, glad we worked that out," I said, cheerfully. "I gotta go."

"Me too . . ."

Strangely, we both went in for a small hug—a hug neither of us probably wanted—and after, he pulled back and did this weird thing. Our faces were close again, and it seemed for just one moment, faster than a second, that he was leaning down toward me. In a kissy way.

But I didn't want to kiss him again if he didn't like me. My hand automatically moved in between us and gently pushed him away.

"No." I half laughed. "No more of that."

"Oh." He laughed too. "Right."

"See you soon."

"Okay."

And with that, I turned and ran the fuck away.

CHAPTER 46

Ben

WAS THAT REALLY HOW it had happened? Bee's side of the story hung in the air, so vivid I could hardly catch my breath.

"And there I was, thinking I was pathetic for liking you, because you didn't like me back," she finished. "And what, now you're *in love* with me?" The pain in her voice screamed.

I tried to process everything I'd just heard.

"Bee." I took a step forward. "I'm sorry. If that's how you . . . I really fucked that up."

"Oh?" She didn't move.

"But I was scared." I scratched my nose. "I didn't know what I was saying . . . or what you were feeling . . . and I should've done what I'm doing now. I should've told you first. I was so scared you didn't feel the same way."

"And now?" she asked.

"Well . . ." I decided it was best *not* to bring up the Donald/Claudia conversation. That could come later. "Well, it's now or never. I like you. Love you. And if you don't feel that too, I guess tough shit for me."

She laughed, and when she stopped, her smile stayed. My heart leaped. I took another step forward. My sneaker snapped a twig. She stepped forward, too. One step at a time, till my arms were wrapped around her waist, her hands resting on my shoulders. We were at a middle school dance, swaying to "Stairway to Heaven." We were in space, floating between planets.

"Ummm . . ." she whispered, lips so close. "I don't know, okay?"

"What?" I whispered.

"I mean . . ." She looked away. It was physically painful not to be looking into her eyes. She turned back. Thank goodness. "I mean, of course I'm in love with you."

Adrenaline shot through my body, my grip on her tightened ever so slightly.

"But, like, I don't want to . . . I mean, I'm not in love with you, really. I don't even know how to explain this."

I tried not to smile. I must've failed, because she smiled back at me.

And suddenly we were kissing. So much kissing. All the kissing. Memories of kisses combining with current kisses. Pressed into each other, my hands grasping the back of her neck, her hands through my hair. Feeling, feeling, *feeling.* The most intense ten seconds of my life.

We broke away, each springing back a couple feet. I took a moment and caught my breath, tasting night sky and waves. Moment taken, I looked back at Bee. She felt me looking and met my eyes, like a deer in headlights. Crap, was this happening again?

Then she burst out laughing. Loud, magical Bee laughter, and I was afraid she would wake the whole camp.

She paused, wiped tears out of the corners of her eyes. "Ben, what just happened?"

I couldn't help laughing too. It was the most romantic moment of my life so far, with the girl I loved, with Bee Leonato, the greatest girl in the world. But also the girl who got the entire camp to call me Bunny. What even was life?! I kind of wanted to call my mom and ask her.

"Bee, I love you." I said it again, because we could now. "I love you more than anything."

She smiled, rushed forward, and threw her arms around me again. "Do you really?"

"Yes." I went to kiss her again, but when we pulled back a little, and I leaned in again, something broke. A shadow passed over her face. I stopped.

"What's wrong?"

"Ben, I just . . . I can't do this right now." She broke away again and pulled on her hair. "Hana—Hana's so upset."

"Right—I'm sorry." I shook my head. "I didn't mean for this to happen on the same night."

"Well, duh." Bee sighed, staring out at the water. "Who could've guessed Claudia and Donald would turn into assholes for Fourth of July?"

"Tell me about it," I agreed, inching over beside her at the shoreline. "But I'll talk to them in the morning. I'm sure it's just a big misunderstanding. We can work it out."

"Work it out?" Bee turned to me, eyes wide with surprise. "What are you talking about? Those two are dead to me. There's nothing to work out."

CHAPTER 47

Bee

"WHAT?" HE STAYED CLOSE, so close I could feel his breath on my lips when he spoke. *Concentrate.* "What do you mean?"

"Ben, I don't care what kind of misunderstanding this was," I said, feeling my stomach begin to twist in that familiar way it does when I have to set people straight. "Claudia just *dumped* Hana in front of *everyone*, and Donald showed everyone her *private messages.*"

Ben winced. That was good. He should wince. "Yeah, I know, that was real bad. He needs to apologize. I don't know what came over him."

"Apologize?" I sputtered. "They both need to leave camp. What they just did was unforgivable."

Ben's eyes got serious in the buzzing lights. They searched mine; I let them. He wasn't going to find what he was looking for.

"Bee, those are our friends, two of my best friends," Ben said, finally, slowly. "They fucked up, but we need to figure this out. We've all known each other for years."

"And?" I growled. "And who the fuck cares? You don't get to hurt people and then explain yourselves. You don't get to just apologize and move past humiliating someone."

He hesitated. *That* was bad. That was all I needed to see.

"We're not talking about this anymore," I explained. "We're done here. I have to go."

"Are you serious?"

I turned and walked away, calling back over my shoulder: "Are *you* serious?"

"Bee, not yet—we need to figure this out first. As friends, right?"

Friends. The word burned in my chest.

"Friends?" I whipped around and pointed at him. "We can't be friends if you're friends with my *enemies*!"

"Are Donald and Claudia your 'enemies'?" Ben demanded. I heard an eye roll in his voice. I hated it.

"Now they are!" I shouted. "They hurt someone I love! You of all people should understand this!"

He brought a hand up over his face. I instantly regretted saying it. I knew what Ben had been through. I knew because he had trusted me last year.

"I'm sorry, I didn't mean . . . I shouldn't have said that." I sighed. "But I'm done talking about this."

"Great," he said, his voice hollow. "Me too."

He stayed; I walked away. What a fucking mess. Maybe this fight was for the best. We didn't make sense. And now I could stop trying to make it make sense.

Now I *knew* this was over, 100 percent. And that was a relief.

CHAPTER 48

Hana

I WOKE UP AN hour after Mom tucked me in. Apparently, Xanax doesn't actually work through your life being *obliterated* in a ten-minute explosion of crap.

I sat up and immediately looked across the room—

Bee's bed was empty.

I grabbed my phone and texted Christopher.

> I hate life. You up?

I waited for half an hour before I gave up on a reply. Fireworks cracked outside my window. Right, it was Fourth of July, and it was only midnight. Christopher would be out partying. He was with someone else.

Text Claudia, my brain automatically proposed. You'll feel so much better.

But that's how it worked before, I thought, tears reemerging. It doesn't work that way now.

I hugged my pillow and screamed into it. I had to. The sadness— the big, angry one—ripped through me. When it was over, my throat felt as raw as the rest of me.

I must've fallen asleep again after that.

CHAPTER 49

Vanessa

"ANYTHING??" SOPHIA WHISPERED. I'd just taken my fourth trip to the bathrooms in Dam. I shook my head. Almost an entire night of bathroom trips and staking out Nest's trail entrance and . . . nothing.

"Maybe we should stop for now, I'm getting tired," I said. Which actually wasn't an excuse—I couldn't stop yawning. Was this what getting old was like?

Sophia sighed in agreement and sat back to watch the movie. We'd done the sparklers earlier, and now we were hanging out in the attic of Luna, the counselor chill spot. They'd abandoned it for the night, so us CITs got to use it to party. And by party I mean eat cheesy popcorn and watch this old movie *Clueless*, which only Wallace had voted against. Wallace explained he was a Jane Austen purist. I don't know what that had to do with Cher, but whatever, the movie was hilarious, and he came around.

Another makeover montage started, and my eyelids began to flutter, my head nodded forward. . . . This beanbag chair was so mushy and if I curled up like a cat . . .

Sophia shook me awake. "Nessa, you gotta go to bed."

"Merrrgh." I batted her hands away. "I'll sleep here."

"You're going to regret that in the morning."

"No, you will." I stuffed my face into the fluffy beanbag cover.

I woke up a few hours later, disoriented. Popcorn crumbs, paper cups. What a mess we'd made. No wonder the counselors didn't like us being up here.

With all my strength, I rolled like a pill bug out of the beanbag chair and pushed myself up. It was chilly. I wanted my sleeping bag now. Why was there so much space between me and my sleeping bag??

I walked back to Moose, too out of it to even swat at the mosquitoes. Okay, mosquitoes, eat me! You win this round!

I reached the cabin, poked my head in. Margo wasn't home, still partying probably, and it felt weird inside without her and the campers. I missed them already, even if they'd chewed me up and spit me out, kind of literally.

I didn't want to go inside yet. I turned around and sat on the little porch steps instead and decided to look wistfully up at the stars.

I missed home, too, wherever that was. Our new apartment, maybe. Camp usually felt like home, but being a CIT was different than I'd thought it would be. And I had to do it for the whole summer. I thought being part of the staff might mean I'd feel insider-y, finally a member of the cool group. But we were still once removed. Or three removed, maybe. The highest up, Ben's group, seemed to glow with royalty—constantly bickering and laughing about things only they could talk about.

I wondered if Sophia, Wallace, and I would ever be those counselors. Siiiiiiiigh.

My eyelids began to flutter again. Maybe I'd grab my sleeping bag and sleep out here. It might be nice to be woken up by the sun. . . .

Instead, whispered voices woke me. I sat up, disoriented, everything dark and blurry. I was still outside. How much time had passed? Instinctually, I lay back down. I didn't know who was there, maybe a serial killer, and I didn't want them to see me.

"I don't know, I feel kind of bad." I knew the voice, but my ears weren't awake enough yet to identify it.

"Like they were going to last anyway," another voice answered. A *pair* of serial killers! "Claudia's an idiot."

Hmm. Serial killers who knew Claudia. Unlikely.

"Ha! Well, that's true. Can you believe how she acted tonight?" Suddenly, I realized: that was Connie. "I just don't get what John sees in her."

"Boobs?" said a boy's voice.

"Maybe," she replied. "But other people have boobs. Do you think Margo's going to out you guys, if she puts it together?"

I peeked over. They were paused on the trail, near the bench.

"I fucking doubt it." Bobby. It was Bobby. "She's totally paranoid someone's going to find out about us this summer. Hook up with me, ignore me in the morning."

"Why do you keep hooking up with her, then?" Connie asked. I was blearily wondering that myself.

"Oh, you know." Bobby's voice sounded sad. " 'Cause I like her. And every year she's funnier, and prettier. . . ."

"All right, I get it." Connie snorted. "I don't need to hear a poem."

"And you know, I get laid. Are you getting laid?" Pause. "Didn't think so."

"You're disgusting."

"That's not what Margo said last night."

I heard a slight shuffle, a thump, and then a yelp.

"Fuck off, Connie!"

"Sorry, you absolutely had to be subdued."

"So, do you actually think this is going to work?"

"What do you mean?"

"Is John going to hook up with Claudia now?"

I held my breath, trying to remember everything. I wished I had my phone to write this down. Did one of the kids leave their dream journals?

"Ehh, I doubt it. Like, highly doubt it. But maybe . . ." Connie didn't sound pleased at the idea. "But maybe if he tries to, and she blows him off, he'll finally get over her."

"Oh, and you're counting on that?"

More shuffling, another louder yelp.

"OUCH! I'm going to bed before you do permanent damage."

"It's not my fault. Quit saying gross stuff."

Jeez, I'm glad I'm not their CIT. When their footsteps and grumbles sounded safely far away, I hopped onto the grass out front to pace. *Think, think, Vanessa!* So John likes . . . Claudia. Connie likes . . . John. But the bigger point: Connie, John, and Bobby had set up Claudia?

With Margo as a pawn? Maybe?

Somebody had to tell her.

I thought about sneaking to Sophia's cabin, but then I realized that waking up to the shock of all of this just might kill her.

CHAPTER 50

Ben

I WASN'T ALWAYS SURE that my mood controlled the weather, but that weekend was proof: Saturday morning rain pelted down. I spent the first few hours in my bed, in my cabin, just listening to the sound. Wallace and Doug both got up for brunch. Wallace asked if I was coming. I mumbled something about catching up on sleep. I hoped my face didn't look obviously puffy from crying. They left.

Fuck everything. Fuck it all to the moon.

My stomach started protesting the whole not-ever-moving-again thing I had going. I pulled myself out of my sleeping bag and shoved into a slicker.

On the weekends, when the kids went home, we usually hung out in Dam too long during meals, messing around, and then chilled upstairs in Luna. Watching movies, playing card or board games. If we had any leftover energy, sometimes we'd do ropes course teams, or go bowling in town.

Not this Saturday. The trails felt like the roads of a ghost town. No campers, no counselors, not even any squirrels or chipmunks. A couple snails. That helped, a little.

I opened the door to Dam quietly, just in case. I didn't want to draw attention to myself. But there was nobody in there, either, except Shane and a few CITs, finishing up pots and pans from brunch.

I grabbed blueberry pancakes and bacon, and sat right in the middle of the room, because why the fuck not? It was usually Donald's seat, but where the fuck was Donald?

My head cleared some after eating. Maple syrup can do that. I took out my phone and texted Donald:

Hey, where are you guys? In Dam.

. . . (typing)

. . . (typing)

Seriously? I thought. It's a simple question.

We're off campus.

Where?

I wanted to add *And what the fuck are you thinking?* But also: *Why wasn't I invited?*

I'm not gonna say, no offense.

I stared at his response. Why even bother texting back if you weren't gonna say. Just don't say anything back at all.

Look, I need to talk to both of you. What happened last night? This is messed up.

Not interested, sorry.

Another nothing response. They were freezing me out. I felt like throwing my phone in the harbor. I shut it off and shoved it in my pocket. Returned to my pancakes.

I was starting to get a creeping feeling that Bee was right about Donald and Claudia. And that really shouldn't have been surprising. She was always right.

CHAPTER 51

Vanessa

AS SOON AS I opened my eyes, alarms went off in my brain: *You need to talk to Ben!! And Margo??*

Right. Something totally messed up had gone down last night, and I might've been the only one who knew.

I flumped out of bed—still no Margo; maybe she was in Little Bat? Or maybe she'd been here and had actually gotten out of bed before noon.

I changed clothes, slid into rubber boots and my slicker, and charged through the rain to Dam. Luckily, Ben was in the corner, eating alone. I shook off and ran over to him.

"Ben—"

"You might want to get pancakes before they go cold."

He was correct; I did want that. I grabbed a plate and a mug of tea and squished in my boots back over to the table.

"Ben."

"Nessa."

He looked tired. Nothing new, Ben was tired a lot. But something else. The bags under his eyes were shiny and red. He'd been crying.

Mooooom! I wanted to yell behind me. *Ben's crying! Come help!*

Instead, I pushed the maple syrup toward him. He nodded at me and doused his pancakes again. The rain tapped at the windows. I grabbed an end of my hair and chewed it a little. How to bring this up?

"You excited about the girls coming on Monday?" he said.

"Ben, there's something I need to tell you," I said, at the same time.

He looked up startled. "Okay, Ness, what is it?"

"I overheard this thing, and I just want to know if—"

The door to Dam slammed open, surprising us both. We turned. There stood Sophia, in an orange poncho and rain boots to match.

"Nessa!" she yelled, and squelched over. She slammed down her hands at our table. Ben protectively scooped the small glass syrup pitcher away from her.

"Nessa, you'll *never. be. lieve* this," Sophia said, with huge breaths in between the words. She didn't even wait for me to prompt her, she kept going.

"Last night, at the sparkler party . . ." Did she even see my brother sitting there? Probably not. *"Claudia dumped Hana."*

"What?" I gasped. "That doesn't even make sense!"

"I *know*," she whispered. She didn't know the half of it. The third of it! "I can't believe we missed it! But yeah, turns out Hana was cheating on Claudia with some townie guy. Can you believe that? What a total slu—"

"Wait," Ben said quietly, startling us both. "Where did you hear this?"

Sophia glanced at me, I nodded. "Connie?" she said. "Well, I overheard her talking to Rachel about it this morning in the bathroom."

Ben nodded slowly. He set down his fork. I could tell a grown-up speech was coming.

"Ness, you're better than this," he said. Yup. "This isn't funny, and I don't expect either of you to tell anyone about it. And I don't want to hear gossip anymore." He looked at Sophia. "And I definitely don't want to hear that word you were about to use."

"Sorry," she muttered.

"Sorry, Ben," I added.

Ben shoved away from the table, grabbed his plate and put it away, then disappeared out the side door without another word. Sophia watched all of this silently, but the minute he was definitely gone, she made a face.

"Your brother's kind of a pain."

I smiled at her but felt sick inside, like rotten eggs were scrambling in my stomach. My brother was disappointed in me, and I had this enormous secret. I'd have to go to Margo.

Suddenly, I really, *really* missed being a camper.

CHAPTER 52

Bee

SLEEPING WELL SEEMED LIKE a thing of the past, so hauling myself out of bed for Monday morning when my body screamed at me it needed more sleep just felt totally normal.

Nothing else felt normal.

I poured cereal, milk, coffee like nothing was wrong. I sat down at a table with Margo, who rubbed my back, and continued listening to Ellie overanalyze her feelings for Doug. She knew I didn't want to talk, and I felt super grateful for that.

This weekend was the worst. The worst I could remember for a very, very long time. The cereal wouldn't fit down my throat. Its sharp edges caught and scraped. I let it get soggier.

Pull it together, pull it together, camp is in one hour. There's days when you're gonna have to teach through some bad shit, Bee, I reminded myself. When the president gives another craptastic address, or you actually go through a real breakup, or your dog might die. After you get a dog. And you're still gonna have to teach.

I forced myself to surface, finish my cereal, toss my dishes in the bins, and made my way out for setup. As I was leaving, though, little whispers reached out from tables by the door—

"Can you *believe* that? She brought some townie onto camp grounds."

"Well, if you're the director's daughter, I guess you can get away with anything."

"I just feel bad for Claudia. She was crying so hard."

"I haven't even seen any of them all weekend."

I blinked. Were they talking about . . . ? I turned to look, and both Rachel and Doug immediately shut up. Technically, I'd known there had been other witnesses on Friday, but I'd fled with Hana immediately. I hadn't even thought—I turned and looked out at the dining hall, usually a hubbub of singing and laughter.

Thirty faces looked back, blushing, curious. The face you made when you'd been talking about someone.

I turned and slammed the door behind me. Fuck. *Fuck.*

Even if my mom convinced Hana to get out of bed, she'd now have to deal with *this*? I thought about banging the gong in Dam and announcing that anyone who talked about my sister could fill out their resignation paperwork *immediately*, and I'd be *happy* to help them.

But I'd promised my parents I wouldn't do anything rash about this. I'd promised Hana.

Check-in went fine. How could I care? But I smiled and fist-bumped kids, inquired about their new siblings, their new schools. My heart ached through all of it. And then, two little faces stared up at me, and the sun came out.

"Ava, Layla!" I cried, and bent down to hug them both. They were arguably our cutest campers: *almost* identical—pale; freckly; big brown eyes, like Ben's and Nessa's; dark, shoulder-length hair; and adorable, pointy chins. The only way most people could tell them apart was that Layla had thick red glasses. By the time we'd finished our hug, Ben had appeared, and they both lit up. I tried not to light up too.

"BEN!" Ava threw herself into his gut. "I thought you were DEAD!"

"Well, she tried to convince Mom you were," Layla said, arms crossed, waiting her turn. "So she could have your PlayStation."

Ben scooped up Ava, twirled her around, switched to Layla, and did it again.

"Twice for Layla, since she didn't try to kill me off," he explained to them. Ava stuck out her tongue, grinning. "I missed you munchkins," he said. And he had. You could tell. His whole being glowed now that they were here. For a moment, I forgot how pissed I was at him.

"Missed you too, Bunny!" Ava cackled.

"He doesn't *like* that." Layla kicked her.

"Hey, babies!" Nessa called out from the lice check. They squealed and sprinted over to her.

Ben's mom, Colleen, appeared, kissed my cheek, and fussed about the weight Ben had lost in the last two weeks. He smiled and took it all good-naturedly, gently asking her how everything was at home, at work. I took a step back so they'd have some privacy.

I glanced at Nessa wrestling Ava into the folding chair while Layla chatted in her ear. Colleen, laughing easily at a joke Ben made. The Rosenthals. Their happy family, free. Tears welled in my eyes.

"I'm gonna go say hi to Nessie," Colleen said with a wave. I waved back, faintly. As she left, there stood Ben across from me. I couldn't hide. Our eyes met.

He registered the tears and quickly closed the distance between us. "Can we talk, later?"

I said nothing back. I had so many feelings, but nothing came before Hana.

"I know, okay?" he whispered. "I promise, I'm on your side."

His eyes flickered back and forth, searching mine. My side. That sounded like an improvement on last night.

"Okay." I gulped. "Later."

He nodded, then went and joined his sisters.

"Bee!" yelled a car pulling in. Three kids tumbled out, and I smiled brightly and showed them where to put their stuff.

CHAPTER 53

John

MONDAY MORNING, WE OFFERED mini activities while the new session's campers settled in. Claudia ran the knots elective again, and I volunteered to help. I found them at the campfire pit, sitting on logs. From the top of the trail, I could see Claudia explaining the basics with her low, calm voice.

But when I walked up and got close, her voice sounded raspy and on edge. She glanced up at me—her face paste pale, purple bags under her eyes like they'd been drawn on with a Magic Marker.

"This is John," she said to the campers. They nodded or said hi quietly. Claudia's mini sessions were always like this: chill as fuck. The kids knew, sensed not to mess with her.

I helped a couple kids through the basics of a fish tail till the session was over. They returned the ropes and then hightailed it to their next activity. The farther from the campfire they got, the louder their voices boomed. Spell broken.

I grabbed the ropes and threw them in the box, then finally looked at Claudia again. She was slumped on a log, staring at her phone.

"Hey, you okay?" I sat down next to her.

Her bronze eyes looked up at me, tears welling on her lower lids. Crap.

"What do you think?" she asked.

Shit.

"Uhh . . . no."

"You get a prize." She looked away again.

I'd meant, I thought—I thought I could maybe bring something up here. Movies this weekend. But her face, her eyes, her shoulders hunched, I didn't . . .

She sighed. "Sorry, but this was the worst weekend ever. Like, ever."

I froze.

She shifted, looking up at the trees above us. "I just feel like, what's the point of me being here anymore?"

"Seriously?" I laughed. "Hana's so . . . young. She was probably just messing around with a girl for fun. You don't need to throw away your summer 'cause of her."

She didn't reply, just stared up at the trees. I checked my watch: we both needed to go.

"I think it's time for—"

"John," Claudia said quietly. "Fuck. Off."

Everything stopped. The waves, the birds, the bugs, the air. I stared into the ashes of the fire pit. She stood up, grabbed the box of ropes from my hands, and walked away. I couldn't have moved if I tried.

How Claudia acted felt so familiar. But it felt familiar because I'd felt like that, acted like that, a hundred times in the last five years, ever since my "family" went public. But this time, it was me. It was my fault.

I'd kind of thought this before, but here it was, knotted in my face: I was an asshole. As big an asshole as my father.

CHAPTER 54

Hana

"IF YOU GO TO work today, we'll talk about whether you have to work tomorrow." My parents broke. "We'll talk" was code for "We'll cave."

"Fine, I'll go." I forced myself out of bed, brushed past them into the hallway to use the bathroom. I turned on the shower, but listened to them whisper about calling Louisa, my therapist, at the door. When I got like this, my family seemed so pathetic. So small in comparison to the wad of dark crap settling into my chest.

I changed into my swimsuit, pulled myself together for the waterfront. Smile, welcome, buddy board, don't let anyone drown. Swim tests, tests, tests. For the first time in a long time, the water felt frigid.

"Hana." Judy looked at me, eyebrows pinching in worry. "Your lips are turning blue. Sit the next one out and go warm up."

I nodded in reply, grabbed my big towel, and shivered into Dam for a snack and coffee. No, coffee made everything worse. But maybe I could talk to Shane into making me cocoa?

Dam bustled with counselors and CITs running in and out, grabbing food or forms from the paperwork corner. No sign of Donald or of . . . her.

I went to the counter to plead my blue-lipped case. Dave and Jen came out of the bathroom, walked by me, I guess not noticing I was there.

"Yeah, Claudia's so messed up about it."

"What a bitch."

"I don't know, man. I was hanging out with this girl last year, and then there was another girl I kind of liked, and so *I* broke up with the first one before I did anything with the second one. . . . It's the right thing to do. . . ."

Their whispers faded the closer they got to the whirring drink machine.

"Hey, Hana." Shane appeared behind the counter. Sweet, professional, older. Didn't know I was a bitch/slut or anything. What a relief. "Can I get you something warm?" he asked.

"Can I just have a packet of instant?"

He smiled and handed me a whole box of cocoa. "Sure thing."

"And can you tell my mom I feel sick and that I needed to go lie down?"

"Sure, but does Judy—"

"Judy knows. Thanks."

"Hana! Are you—"

The side door's slam cut him off. I clutched my box of cocoa and walked barefoot through the needles and ferns back to our house.

CHAPTER 55

Ben

FIRST DAY AGAIN, SPROUTBALL. Outline the rules, hand out a million rainbow squishy balls. And, screaming in three . . . two . . . one . . . go!

Claudia and I both went down fairly quickly, because half the fun of Sproutball was being tagged as a seed and getting to throw balls at people (both maniacally and helpfully). Claudia and I made a big pile in the middle of the field and crouched down.

"Hey. We need to talk after this," I whispered, tossing a few to Maddie. Session 2, she was vicious.

"No thanks." She lobbed one across the field that hit Ilse in the butt.

The freezing out continued all morning. When we finished our last session, Claudia disappeared with the final group, leaving me to put away the giant bag of sproutballs and cones by myself. Cool.

I'd now given both Donald and Claudia opportunities to explain their shitty-ass behavior. But neither one of them was interested. Which meant . . . I had no way forward to fix this.

"ARGH!" I said out loud on the field, to no one in particular. "Just ARGH!" And then: "I *told you* so!"

It wasn't that satisfying. *Whatever, Ben. Get to lunch, talk to Bee about what you heard at breakfast.* She'd know what to do.

But lunch was a nightmare.

If Camp Dogberry had a gossip magazine, then Claudia and Hana would've been on the front page. In line, Sophia and Wallace talked about Hana's mystery guy (guess she really took my outburst to heart). I passed Ellie, Dave, and Rachel whispering in hushed tones about Claudia's broken heart. Gossip happened at camp, but something about this seemed especially off.

This gossip had a slant: Claudia wronged, Hana the wronger. Amid the bustling, in the corner, Donald and Claudia sat at a table, purposefully not looking my way. A couple younger counselors and CITs surrounded them, talking in excited, hushed tones.

Those. Assholes.

They were doing this. They were not only feeding the gossip flame, but putting their own spin on it so that Hana was the bad guy.

The screen doors slammed open and in walked Bee and Margo, escorting a group of campers. They showed their kids where to get food, where to sit. Bee's single-minded concentration on the campers shouted her anger loud and clear. Margo looked around nervously, glancing at the evil table in the corner.

I tried to get near Bee, to warn her, but she artfully avoided me by offering to replenish the napkin baskets. I sat down with my sisters instead, for the Layla and Ava recap of life at home.

"And that's why Mom won't let us make a fourth cat elevator." Layla sighed.

"How are we going to be engineers?" Ava demanded. "Where's the support for the sciences in our house?"

Nessie jabbed a thumb at me. "Mom's paying for Ben to go to

doctor college, doofuses. Stop almost killing the cat and you'll get support."

I laughed; she shot me a small smile. I hoped she understood what I'd said earlier. I wasn't mad at her, I just didn't want her to forget that gossip could *hurt* people.

Lunch ended. I ran outside without staying to help clean up. There was too much on the line—I waited at the side entrance, nearest Luna, where like magic, Bee appeared, slamming open the door.

"Hey!"

"What!" she yelled, then saw it was me. "Fudge nuggets, Ben, what are you *doing*?"

"Can we talk now?"

"I need to get to class."

"Please?" I knew she was early. She was always early.

She sighed and threw up her hands. I motioned for her to follow me, toward the back of the building where we'd have some privacy. As soon as we got there, I realized this was the spot where everything had gone wrong between us last summer. *Don't let it happen again.*

Standing across from her, I saw she didn't look much better than I did. Sleepy eyelids, braids hastily bunched, no earrings. Not exactly typical Bee.

"Look, you were right," I explained. "Claudia and Donald shut me out all weekend, they're *still* shutting me out, and I think—"

"This isn't about you, Ben."

"Can you let me finish?"

"Fine." She crossed her arms. Clearly she was still skeptical.

"*Everyone* knows," I said, lowering my voice. "I've heard it all morning, all through lunch. The story's that Hana cheated on

Claudia, and Claudia's heartbroken, and Hana's an asshole. And *I'm* not telling them that, and I'm assuming *you* aren't."

Bee sighed a sigh so large I swear it blew my hair back. "I know . . . I heard some of it this morning." She paused, then raised her eyebrows at me. "But wait, aren't they your *friends*?"

"Not if they're doing this!" I tried not to yell. I gestured at Dam, at the general camp. "This is—*crap*. It's unforgivable."

"It's socially and morally reprehensible," she spat out in agreement.

The mutual anger brought us a step toward each other. Up closer, I saw in her eyes that something else was wrong.

Her face softened, her arms went from crossed to lightly intertwined. She started talking, on her own this time. "I've spent all weekend messed up about it. It feels like everything's . . ." She sighed. "Everything's fallen apart."

She looked so vacant, so tired. I wanted to hug her so badly. Turns out, she did, too, because suddenly she was pressed up against me, and my arms circled around her.

"I didn't want to write you off," she whispered.

"Please don't," I said, squeezing her. "I promise I'm on your side."

"Her side."

"Her side." As I said, I realized the thing I'd seen in her eyes, the other thing that was wrong. I pulled back. "Bee, where's Hana?"

Her chin quivered. "Emergency therapy session."

"Shit," I whispered. "I'm sorry. Those crapheads, if they had any idea—"

"Don't you dare say anything," she fired back.

"Of course not," I said, quietly. I felt my chin quivering back. "I'm just, I'm so sorry–"

"I have to get to class," she said, squeezed my hand, wiped her eyes, and took off.

∽

That evening, after evening games, for the first time, I used my activity leader privileges to skip the nighttime sing-along. I sprawled out in Luna, with a camp map and a notepad, planning out Wednesday's event. For a couple years, I'd had a secret idea for how to win Capture the Flag. It was dirty, it wasn't nice, and it didn't follow most of the rules. When last year was my *last year*, I'd put the idea away forever.

But plans change.

And Claudia was going down.

CHAPTER 56

Hana

TUESDAY MORNING SHONE THROUGH the window of my cabin. Mom had talked me into sleeping there. I know she thought I'd get up with everyone else, change, go down to the water early. I didn't. I slept in, and then I watched the campers get up with Bee, go to the shower, come back, grab their things. I couldn't imagine doing all of that, going to Dam, hearing their voices again.

"Hana cheated on Claudia." "Claudia's better off without her." "Thought she was nicer than that."

It sounded just like school.

"Do you actually think Chris was into her?" "It's just kind of pathetic and sad." "I didn't want to say anything but . . ."

It was back; it was back; it was back.

The sun warmed the cabin and soon the air became thick and stuffy. I sweated through my sleeping bag. Kamile, a CIT, came to find me—I knew I was missing my first class. I pretended to be asleep. She said my name a few times, loudly, but didn't have the guts to shake me. She left.

I fell half-asleep. The gray in-between sleep.

"Hana?"

I opened my eyes. Bee's face hovered so close to mine, I groaned.

"Let's go to the house, okay, sweets?"

I tugged sweats and a T-shirt on over my clammy skin. I felt like the third day of a terrible cold. Bee walked me around back, through the woods to get to Big Bat. I guess I wasn't fit for the campers' innocent eyes. I took some sick pleasure in that—*See, Mom? I can't go back to work.*

At the house, Bee led me up the stairs to the shower and handed me a towel.

This was all so familiar.

This time I actually showered, I think. I was wet, then I was slightly less wet, then I was back in my sweats and my Messina Squids swim team shirt.

I wandered downstairs, paused on the last step, around the corner from the living room.

"You *have to* fire them!" Bee's voice hissed.

"What I *have* to do is take care of your sister." Mom's voice, much calmer. "She needs to see Louisa again today."

"Yes, definitely," Bee replied. "*And* you have to fire Claudia and Donald."

"We've talked about this." They had? "I can't fire people over a romantic dispute, Bee. Especially if it happened at a nonexistent party."

"But, Mom, they're bullying her. They've got the whole camp talking about her. It's the Chris thing all over again."

"Sometimes people talk about you—"

"Preaching to the irate choir, here, Mom."

"—and then they stop. It'll pass. You know that, Hana knows that. Like you said, she's been through this before. Everyone'll get bored by the new session."

"She didn't get out of bed this morning."

"It's a breakup, Bee, that's kind of normal."

"It's *not* normal!"

"I know you're scared, but we'll get Hana in to see Louisa again this afternoon, and we'll talk to her about getting back on the water tomorrow."

Yeah, right.

"Aren't you even worried about what happened last time?"

I bit my fist to keep from screaming. I was causing so many problems. Again.

"Bee! That's enough! I think you know I love Hana, and I'm concerned for her."

They must've moved to a different room, because the conversation morphed into angry muffles. I tiptoed back to my room, pushed in earplugs, climbed into bed, and hoped I would dream of kissing Claudia.

CHAPTER 57

Vanessa

"VANESSA! HAVE YOU DECIDED?" Sophia demanded, as we deposited compost. "Are you Team Claudia or Team Hana?"

"Don't be gross!" I insisted, dumping oatmeal-french-fry-mayo mush onto the pile.

"I'm Team Claudia," she said. "Hana was such a jerk the other day about the party. She totally blew us off."

"But—"

"And if she cheated on Claudia, that's *super* crappy."

"Yeah," Wallace agreed.

Had she? I wanted to ask. How did we know that for sure?

Ben's comment had hit me hard. And I hadn't told anyone about that weird conversation I'd overheard on Friday night/Saturday morning. How many people might hate me if I did?

For once, this didn't seem like any of my business. Especially since I was just starting to get a handle on my CIT life. Get up ten minutes earlier than you want to, always keep extra Band-Aids in your pockets, and never let them see you flustered. My seven-year-olds felt a lot more manageable this week, which was good, because

Margo was super out to lunch. Like, more than usual. I felt like I was running our group without her.

I snuck up behind Layla and Ava on the way to campfire. Layla screamed, and Ava turned and hugged me. I'd missed them so much, the stinkers. This was a much better week.

On the way back to our cabins, though, I heard two girls from Connie's group, the eleven-year-olds, talking.

"Can you believe that?" one asked the other.

"At camp?" the other gasped.

"On the *volleyball court*."

"Wow, what a slut."

My mouth dropped open. I turned around and fell back with the little kids, grabbing the hands of the two who were already homesick. My heart pounded in my ears, I barely heard them singing "There Was a Great Big Moose." I felt my voice echo their verses, while my thoughts were decidedly un-mooselike.

A slut?

Really?

Campers knew about this???

The littles brushed their teeth, which was a massacre, we tucked them in, and Margo sang to them. Then we went out onto the porch, like usual, me with my book, and Margo with her phone. But I couldn't read.

Was it gossiping if you just went straight to the source?

"Margo?" I bit my lip.

"Mmm?" Margo asked, eyes glued to her screen.

"Can I talk to you about something?" I whispered.

"Give me a sec, darlin'. . . ." She sent another text and then looked up and smiled at me. "What's up?" Was I imagining things, or was her smile not reaching the freckles on her cheeks?

"I, umm, I heard a camp rumor."

"Okay, Nessa." Margo laughed. "You need to be a little more specific."

I must've looked stricken, because she gave me a pat on the knee. "Spill, sweetie!"

"I heard this thing about Hana."

Margo sighed as big as the moon. "Oh, that, yeah—don't listen to that. Hana's not a slut, or whatever. *Slut* is actually a not-real word, because women should be allowed to express their sexuality, too."

"Okay, thanks," I said quickly. "But what I need to tell you is that I overheard Bobby and Connie talking on Friday night."

Margo's head tilted.

"About that night?" I said. "They said a lot of things, but they kind of made it seem like . . . like they'd tricked people into thinking it was Hana and some guy on the volleyball court."

"The volleyball court."

"Yeah. They said that you and Bobby had been down there." I winced saying the words. "And I think that maybe John told Claudia it was Hana and someone else? Or something?"

Margo set her phone down. She paused. I held my breath, waiting for her to explain this.

"That's not true," she said, finally. "None of that is true. You must've heard wrong."

"But they said that John liked Claudia." I was determined to get it all out. "And he does, doesn't he? That's what Rachel said that Connie said last summer."

Margo's face went so pale, her freckles disappeared. "I need to go to the bathroom." She stood up and hopped off the porch. Then she turned back. "Just don't . . . don't repeat this, okay? I'll take care of it."

I paused, then nodded.

"Great." She turned back to her phone, her fingers moving like lightning across the screen.

I had done it. I'd told someone. Someone who could do something. But I didn't feel any better.

CHAPTER 58

Ben

I THOUGHT I KNEW what Hana was feeling. Well, not exactly, because nobody can exactly be in someone else's shoes. But I remembered feeling that stuck, and dark, and hopeless.

That January night that my mom took us all to Camp Dogberry wasn't the first time I'd gone there that year. My mom didn't know this, but I'd run away a few months earlier, Thanksgiving night two years ago. Tim's family came over—they're terrible, even compared to him—and they stressed him out so badly he roared at Ava at the dinner table, and the twins both burst into tears. Ava'd interrupted grace, or something stupid like that. I started to snap back, but my rotten "grandmother" said, *"Can't you just stop?"* Like it was my fault—like I had been the one who'd started this. But my mom caught my eye from across the table, and I knew whatever I did was going to make it worse for her. Head pounding, I'd apologized. The kids made it through dinner silently, and none of us stuck around for dessert.

It was late. I told my mom I'd take my sisters for a drive so they'd fall asleep. All the girls had been car babies, and the hum of the road could still conk them out. I whispered I had my phone with me. She clearly had her hands full with our charming extended Tim family.

I had a secret thought, though. What if I took them and drove away and never came back?

The girls blinked tears as Nessa and I wrestled them into their pj's and coats. I grabbed all our toothbrushes, just in case. I tucked the girls in the back seat of the car, and we pulled out of the driveway. After a couple rounds of camp songs, the twins fell asleep, and twenty minute later, Nessa fitfully drifted off to an audio book. And then I jumped on the highway.

I only stopped once, for gas—paid to fill the tank. A few hours later, we took the Messina exit, followed the brown signs with jaunty white lettering, and let the road slowly give way to dirt and gravel.

Camp Dogberry's parking lot looked strange in the off-season. Empty, no check-in tent. It didn't matter, though. The minute I pulled in, a sense of calm washed over me.

I thought about driving through and up to the main house, but seeing Bee felt like way too much. And though it would be great to see Nik and Andy, I couldn't have explained why we were there without someone getting suspicious, or getting in touch with my mom.

And it's Thanksgiving, duh. They might not even be there.

The parking lot it was, then. The girls were still fast asleep. I left the heat on and braced myself for the cold outside.

The air bit but didn't feel so bad. I jogged over and sat down on the ground, right where the white tent would have stood. Where I checked kids in and out every summer; where I got checked in and out every summer.

What if we just stayed here? Vanessa, Ava, Layla, and I could learn to adapt to the winter camp temperatures. We could grow long white hairs all over our bodies, sturdy paws, thick black noses, slowly transform into polar bears. Maybe my mom could, too, if she ever actually left Tim.

Tim couldn't turn into a polar bear. You knew just looking at him.

The water on my eyeballs got hard and sticky. I blinked. Was it really that cold? I tried to move my fingers; they creaked in protest.

But the block of ice in my chest had started melting. It didn't feel great, but it felt better than before. Despite the sharp air, I could breathe.

Eventually, I stood up and went back to the car. I turned around and drove straight home. Nessa and I carried in the little girls, tucked them in their beds. Tim yelled at me for being gone for so long. Once he finished and stormed off to watch TV, my mom thanked me and kissed me goodnight.

I'd gone to bed that night feeling something more than despair. Hope. Summer was only six months away. Surely we could exist until then.

CHAPTER 59

Bee

THIS WAS THE MOST dysfunctional week of camp, ever. Half our staff wouldn't speak to one another anymore. I had to squash a newsletter poll of "Team Hana or Team Claudia." I kept sending CITs to Monarch or Turtle instead of going myself. Claudia and Donald probably thought I was scared of them, but really, I was scared of my parents. I knew that they would kill me if I blew up.

They already wanted to kill me.

I woke up Wednesday morning: Capture the Flag. The air stuck to my skin. Scorcher in the making. I wrapped my blue bandanna over my braids and slipped out to Big Bat to check on Hana.

I walked in on a confrontation in the living room, my little sister in her sweats, snuggled defensively on the couch. Not dressed, curly hair matted. This was off to a good start.

"I'm leaving," she said, with the force of someone who's repeated themselves again and again.

"Pumpkin," Dad sighed, "I don't even know if Aunt Beth *can* take you for a whole summer."

"And you need to work," Mom reminded her.

"So I'll get a job at a café in Portland," Hana said, flapping her right hand. "None of this is a problem."

"It's a problem for me that you wouldn't be here," Mom said. "I'd need to hire a new instructor—"

"Call the Y."

"You're leaving?" I said.

Everyone turned and looked at me. Hana's normally warm brown eyes looked dusky and cold. I slid onto the couch next to her.

"I can't be here with her," she said softly. "Please tell them to let me go."

I stared up at my parents. They looked helpless. I didn't blame them, really. Hana like this was like . . . parallel-universe Hana. Angry, bitter, always sad.

Still, she was Hana. I smoothed her hair. "I just want you to feel better."

"I can't." Tears started. "Not here."

I hugged my sister and looked past her at my mom, who threw up her hands. I shook my head, just a little.

"Want to play Capture the Flag?" I asked Hana, just in case.

"No."

"Okay. I'll grab you some paper from the art building."

"Don't bother. I threw out all the stars this morning."

I gulped. None of this was good. "Okay. I'll see you later, sweetie." I stood up off the couch, and Mom took my place. Dad followed me to the entryway.

"She dumped out all her water vases too," he said, voice low, eyebrows furrowed together.

My poor dad. I hugged him.

My poor Hana.

CHAPTER 60

Ben

I WOKE UP AT five a.m. Wednesday morning. *Capture. The. Flag.*

I grabbed an orange and got out on the field before anyone else, map and pen in hand. Time to *get ruthless.*

The breezy, blue, warm day didn't feel very ruthless, but instead of clouds, there was *doom for my enemies* hanging in the sky.

Around eight a.m., the counselors shuffled the entire camp onto the field. Claudia and Donald, talking mostly to each other. Bee and Raph arrived in the same manner—no sign of Hana. My heart hurt. No Margo, either. Eventually, Claudia wordlessly helped me take out the two boxes of red and blue bandannas. Thanks so much, sports assistant.

We divided up the camp into colors. I picked all the new counselors. I made sure I got Vanessa this time, and that the twins got split down the middle. Nik came out on the field with her whistle and explained the rules:

- Capture the Flag would last until noon, lunchtime.
- Each side had a flag to hide somewhere in camp.
- Each team had to appoint at least one guard for the flag.

• Each team had a "caught zone" where they would guard the other team's captured players.

• No touching except for tagging, no inappropriate language, and everyone needed to wear closed-toe shoes.

• Nik and Andy would be walking around camp keeping an eye on things, so if anyone needed help, they could find them.

"Finally," Nik said. "Listen to your counselors. Except when their plan isn't a good one—then, I'd advise you to stage a mutiny."

A great cheer went up from the campers, and I smiled for real for the first time all day. It felt good.

I led the blues to our base camp: the garden/compost bin. It smelled, but there was no way to approach without someone seeing you. I would normally turn to Bee as my right hand, but she looked exhausted.

I grabbed Rachel instead, and we passed out the blue bandannas. Then I sat everyone down and laid out the plan. Layla giggled, Jay's face lit up, Nessa whooped, and everyone was generally super enthusiastic. Only Bee eyed me with a little bit of scorn, but I'd known she wouldn't like parts of it. I reminded everyone that, *technically*, trickery was in the rule book for Capture the Flag. She conceded.

I broke it down for the group.

"All right, here's how it's going to go." I laid out a camp map in front of them. It was a brochure, and kind of inaccurate, but I'd scribbled on it with red and blue markers, which got the team very excited.

"Ava is a double agent. Layla swaps out for her and grabs the flag, while you guys create a diversion—a fake base, on the island."

Giggles and gasps broke out. A few campers asked if this was allowed.

"You're on Team Ben now." I pointed at the map. "I run sports. Everything I say is allowed."

That got a big laugh. I broke everyone up into patrol, scout, and special ops groups. Then I assigned counselors and CITs.

"Hey," I whispered to Bee. "Do you just wanna guard?"

"Sure. Thanks."

I assigned the other guard positions to a handful of less adventurous campers. Then I grabbed special ops 1, led by Raph (I really liked that Raph always showed up for Capture the Flag).

"Head to the island, noisily, with a blue T-shirt," I explained. "You'll need to be good actors, though, because you have to pretend you're trying to be sneaky going out there, and you *have to* make sure someone from the red team sees you doing it."

"We got this," Raph assured me. He had football black stripes under his eyes. "Right, y'all?"

"And it's very possible," I continued, "that you'll get put in the caught zone, so you have to be okay with that."

"We're team players," Meredith replied.

"Excellent. Go around the back of the island, to the west end dock," I instructed. "And remember: pretend you're *trying* to be inconspicuous."

"We're the worst spies ever!" Raph clarified. *"Got it!"*

We all put our hands in the middle. "Go BLUE!"

Bee and company set up the base with our actual flag. Rachel, Dave, Vanessa, and Doug went on their scouting patrols. I took special ops 2 to get some cereal, because Layla hadn't eaten breakfast.

"It was too early," she complained. "My stomach hurts when I eat that early."

"I know," I said quickly. I loved the kid, but her voice was screechy and I was worried someone on red would hear. "But we can't have you, our star player, running around on an empty stomach."

I coaxed her into eating with Shane's secret stash of marshmallow cereal.

"So what do I have to do?" she asked, mouth full.

"Now, we wait for intel."

I didn't like the waiting part of the plan. It made me antsy, and then I had time to think. Like about how my enemies in this game were actually my enemies. And about how Bee's eyes seemed permanently lined with tears now.

Luckily, Vanessa's group returned quickly, handed off the info, and it was just as I'd hoped—

Ava had weaseled her way on to the red guard team.

"Let's move out, special ops two."

∽

Ah, classic. Team Red had hidden their flag on the hill behind the art building. The hill was always a great pick. Normally, it would mean it would be impossible to get there without strenuous activity.

My sister and I stayed low, approached the building from the right corner. They didn't have anyone guarding around the side, because the entrance was so narrow; they could tag anyone on our team the second they came through.

But I wasn't sending someone through from our team.

There they were: waiting for us, a flash of red hidden under a pile of leaves under the building's drain spot. Ava'd come through.

"You ready? You remember where to meet?"

"I got it."

I saluted. "Godspeed, shortcake."

Ava put on Layla's glasses, grinned, and went in.

Ten minutes later, red flag in hand, we were running for our lives.

☙

Halfway back to base, off trail, I heard leaves rustling. I knew two things.

"Layla," I whispered, and handed her the flag. "You need to run. Quietly. *Now.*"

Her eyes went wide, and she took off. I ran to the right, making a big effort to crash and stomp through big piles of underbrush. Soon, I was apprehended by a snickering Maddie. Sometimes you have to take one for the team.

She led me down to the waterfront, where they'd set up their caught zone. Waterfront was smart, because you'd have to somehow swim to get in and tag your caught teammates. Pathetic but unsurprising, I was the only one captured there.

"Where's the rest of your team?" I asked the guard, Claudia. Talk about hiding with her head in the sand.

"The island," Claudia said. "And out looking for our flag. We probably have yours by now."

"Thrilling," I said. And it was, but mostly because they'd fallen for the whole thing. We were minutes away from winning, I was sure.

"So the mastermind is caught!" Donald sauntered over. To Claudia, he said, "We got the flag." Then to me: "Didn't think I'd see you here, Rosenthal."

"Well, perhaps I'm still masterminding, *King.*" I stood up.

Claudia stood up too. "Hey, you're not allowed off the dock—"

"We need to talk."

Donald glanced at Claudia, then back at me. Claudia looked at her feet.

Maybe they felt guilty. Maybe I could actually get through to them.

I pulled off my bandanna and raked my fingers through my hair, pushing it back. So sweaty. The water actually looked pretty good right now, and running the length of the dock, jumping in, and swimming away and never returning would solve a lot of my problems.

But Hana was more important.

"Okay, look," I said finally. They both did. "Why haven't either of you actually asked Hana about that night?"

"I saw it," Claudia said simply. Her face was blank.

"I did, too." Donald sighed. "Look, Hana's a great kid"—I saw Claudia flinch—"but she was a real jerk. You can't blame Claudia for dumping her."

"No, I can't!" I said. "You can dump whoever you want. But why are you being such an asshole about it? Why not have a conversation with her?"

"I tried to!" Claudia fired back. "But then I saw her phone." She glanced at Donald, who looked at the ground. "She was using me, okay? She probably just wanted to make Christopher jealous. Or maybe I was, like, that girl fling everyone has, I don't know."

"Something's screwy here." I gestured at the general everything. "You know Hana's not the kind of person who would do this."

"I *thought* I knew her!" Claudia said.

"It was really bad," Donald said. "They were hooking up right out in the open."

"Fine." I threw my hands down. "Fine, but even if you think she did this, what excuse do you have for telling people about it? Why make everyone hate her?"

"Back off." Donald stepped forward, in front of Claudia. "Ben, buddy," he said, weirdly slowly. "Don't you think your judgment is kind of clouded on this one?"

I crossed my arms. "Meaning?"

He looked back at Claudia, then at me again. "Did Bee put you up to this?"

I was so taken aback, I couldn't reply. Donald sighed and nodded, taking this as an admission, which I guess it kind of was. But this wasn't *just* because of Bee.

"Seriously, Ben?" Donald rolled his eyes. "You spend all this time harping on people for 'creating drama' when they like someone, and it happens to you, and you do the same thing?"

"I'm not being dramatic."

"Then how do you explain this: you taking her side, just because you like her?" he asked. "You didn't even check to see if Claudia was okay on Friday. What happened to friends coming first?"

I looked at Claudia. She met my eyes briefly, then stared at her shoes.

Too many ideas flooded my head. Was that what I was doing? What was going on right now? I closed my eyes, and I immediately saw Hana's face, tears running down her cheeks. I saw her helping my sisters learn to swim, holding the nervous kids in her lap during campfire. This wasn't about Bee. Or it was, because she was right.

It had only been an instant, but it was clear now. I opened my eyes to Donald's.

I stared at him, and replied: "Bee *is* my friend."

"Are you serious?! After she totally screwed you up last summer?" Donald fumed. "Don't pretend she didn't!"

"I—"

"Besides," Donald fumed, "she didn't even *say* any of that stuff. We just—"

A cheer went up from somewhere over by Dam, then the victory horn. My team had done it. These two had lost. They were going to keep losing. Just then, one of our little windjammer sailboats pulled around the corner, Bee at the bow, my knight in shining armor.

"I think that's my cue." I backed up, pointing up toward my base. The look of disbelief on both of their faces, in the beautiful sunlight, was just completely priceless. I wished I had a camera so I could take a picture and commission Donald to make a mosaic of it later.

At the end of the dock, Bee held out a hand and steadied me onto the boat. Immediately, I felt nauseous, but I didn't really care.

"Ready to sail in to victory?" She smiled.

"In every way possible." I turned back, briefly, and called out: "You guys are being fucking douchebags! We're done! Got it?"

"Fuck you, Ben!" Donald called back.

On that melodious note, Bee sailed us around the beach, then into the old west dock. And I only puked once in the whole five minutes.

Victory.

CHAPTER 61

John

THE GOOD NEWS WAS, if you went to enough pointless, enormous events, you recognized them for what they were: opportunities. You could either make a scene and piss everyone off, *or* you could wait an hour and slip away, without anyone noticing.

CHAPTER 62

Bee

"I LOVE WINNING." Raph sighed happily. "It just makes me feel warm and fuzzy all over. It's the opposite of losing. Losing's the worst."

"That's an excellent example to set." I snorted. We'd taken our Jell-O and whipped cream desserts—and snuck away to the parking lot to sit under the white tent.

Not particularly comfortable, but outside, away from everyone else. Whenever I spent time in the dining hall this week, I'd come out reeling and internally swearing. Especially the last two days, without Hana.

"Hey, aren't we always telling kids to be themselves?" Raph quipped, smiling with a spoon between his teeth. "I'm just insanely competitive."

"Thank goodness you're not a gym teacher."

"Honey, improv *is* gym. Or at least, I sweat so much during class that it would be weird if it wasn't."

I snorted with laughter this time. "All right, all right. You really kicked butt today. You're the whole reason we won, and winning's the best."

"I wasn't fishing for compliments, but I'm not mad I caught some."

"Hey, Bee! I was looking for you."

I looked up. In the after-dinner Jell-O twilight stood the shadowy, stocky figure of Ben.

"Hey, you found me," I said, and smiled.

"That's my cue to exit," said Raph, standing up.

"Pursued by bears?" I asked.

Ben shuddered. I'd almost forgotten about his history with bears.

"I sure hope so!" Raph toasted at us with his Jell-O. "See you in the morning, Queen Bee." As he walked past Ben, he turned to wiggle his eyebrows at me. I tried not to make a face, but I think I failed, because Ben turned to look—by then, Raph was halfway to his car.

"Can I sit?" Ben asked.

I looked dubiously at the dirt patch beside me. "If you really want to," I said. "We could also go somewhere else?"

"Nah." Ben dropped down next to me. Raph's car started. The light blinded me for a moment. "This is one of my favorite spots at camp."

I laughed. "The dirt parking lot?"

"Yep." Ben looked across the lot, wistfully, as Raph's car pulled out, like we were standing on a cliff beholding the roaring ocean. "I love it here. Under this tent."

"You're kind of weird."

"You kind of like it."

"I thought we weren't accusing me of liking you anymore?" I fired back, straining my voice to sound lighter by the end of the sentence. Ha-ha-ha, just kidding, just kidding.

"But I've already said *I like you* now," Ben reasoned. "Isn't it official?"

I thought for a moment. "Well, I think I'd need it in writing." Then I had an idea: "Hey, can I see your phone?"

He handed it to me. I opened a text message, sent it off, and handed it back. He checked out the message, and then laughed and held out his hand. I gave him my phone. He typed, sent, handed it back.

Done. Official.

"So we're good?"

"We're good." I nodded, taking another spoonful of Jell-O.

"But for the record, again, you're right." Ben turned to me, his face closer to mine, looking me in the eyes. The light from our one parking lot lamp bounced back and forth between us. "I'm sorry. I won't accuse you at all, I promise. I like *you,* and I hope you like me, even if I'm weird."

I'd asked for honesty, I'd gotten honesty, and I felt like I might pee myself from it.

"So," he continued. "During Capture the Flag today, I had a few moments alone with the red team captains."

Donald and Claudia. They'd been sore losers. Aching losers. Throbbing losers. I'd have found the whole thing hysterical if it hadn't been so surreal, if Hana had been there laughing with me.

"Yeah, I think I barged in on that." I smiled.

"That was *the best*." He smiled, then sighed, ran a hand down his face. "It was a special conversation. I tried to talk it through with them, and ask them why they didn't just talk to Hana. And why they were telling everyone about it."

"And?"

"And they said a bunch of bullshit. Like that they hadn't told everyone, and they really . . . I don't know. They've cracked. They think they're right, and they're being dicks about it."

"Couldn't agree more," I said, wishing with every bone in my body we weren't talking about our friends right now.

"Yeah." Ben sighed again. "So you know how that ended. I told them they were being douchebags and that I was done with them."

"It was colorful." I nodded. "And very definitive."

He barely heard me. "I just don't get it. I tried to talk to them reasonably, and they just wanted to trash Hana. Something's wrong with them."

My calm, listening demeanor evaporated instantly. The Jell-O in my stomach turned into liquid fire. *Trash Hana.* Those losers. Those complete and absolute fuckers. I *would* tear out their hearts and eat them in the dining hall. I would—

"Hey." A hand rested on my knee. My bare knee. "I'm sorry, I didn't mean to upset you. I just want you to know I'm on your side, here, Bee."

My eyes followed his hand up to his wrist, his elbow, his T-shirt line, his neck, his face. His eyes.

"Our side," I corrected. "Hana's side."

"Hana's side," he said. "How is she?"

My nose immediately wrinkled in an effort not to sob. "Bad," I said, my throat choking. "She's really bad."

"Oh no."

"Yes." I preemptively wiped under my eyes. "It seems like this Claudia thing brought back her depression full force."

"I'm so sorry."

"She wants to leave camp and go stay with my aunt in Portland, but my parents don't love that idea."

"Why not?"

"They want her to stick it out." I bit my lip. "And they want to be able to keep track of where Hana's at."

"That kind of makes sense?"

"But the real solution is super clear to me," I said. "Hana shouldn't go, Claudia and Donald should."

Ben didn't hesitate this time. "I wish they would."

"She's sinking, Ben." I looked at him again. "She's sinking, and I don't know what to do—"

Without warning, for either of us, I ducked my head onto his shoulder. His arm went around me. I scrunched my face up really tight, trying to squeeze out tears and keep them in all at once. Ben smelled strangely refreshing and tropical.

"It'll be okay," he whispered, his voice touching my ear, sending shivers down my spine. "I promise, it'll be okay. She'll be okay."

I pulled my head up. A few stray tears fell from my eyes, but I didn't care—I pushed my lips into his. Then away, then back again. For a few moments, I only felt the kissing, the warm and fuzzies racing through all parts of me. This was better than winning.

We broke for air, and the pause became a halt. Ben's hands grasped my face, my hand lay on his stomach. We breathed like that, staring at each other, for maybe a whole minute.

I got up first, fighting the urge to rip his clothes off. Ugh. How could I be feeling so many things at once?

We walked back to the head of the entrance trail. Our hands found each other, intertwined. We hesitated at the opening.

"Maybe there's some way you can show her?" Ben said suddenly.

"What?"

"Maybe there's a way to show Hana you don't want her to go," he said.

"Like what?"

"I don't know. There must be something."

I closed my eyes, took a deep breath, and tried to imagine the big gesture. What would get through to Hana. How could I make her see?

The frogs peeped. The stars danced.

And an idea came to me.

WHAT ELSE HAPPENED

Bee

I KISSED BEN FOR the first time two years ago.

One night in January, Ben's mom brought him and his sisters over. It was after dinner, I remember, because it wasn't a normal time to have people over. That was confusing. There was something hushed about the whole thing, too.

Knowing what I know now, Mom was probably giving Colleen advice or help. Mom had gotten out of a bad relationship a long time ago that she sometimes talked about. Maybe Ben's mom was thinking about leaving his stepdad then.

So yeah, Maine, January, freezing, always snowing. Suddenly, Mom told us the Rosenthals were coming over. I remember running upstairs and changing into my favorite shirt at the time—my long-sleeved Ethiopian pro soccer shirt, striped green and yellow with red trim. I don't know why I thought wearing my favorite shirt was important.

They'd shown up a few minutes later. Colleen and Ben carried in the twins, both asleep in their big girl car seats. Nessa insisted we play a board game, so Hana and I set up Monopoly in the living room, while our parents "had coffee" in the kitchen. Ben kept getting up to check on the twins. I remember thinking it was so weird to see him in winter clothes—plaid flannel bottoms and this dorky argyle sweater.

All through the night I tried not to look at him. Eventually, Nessa ran out of steam, and Dad asked us to tuck her into Hana's bed. I remember exchanging an awkward glance with Ben, like we were thinking the same thing:

Were they really not going home yet?

After we settled Nessa, Hana said she was ready for bed, too, and went to sleep in my room. Ben and I wandered into the kitchen. Our parents were huddled around our small wooden kitchen table, heads bent forward. I got one brief look at Colleen's face, and I turned around and pushed Ben back with me, before he could see.

But my mom saw us and brightly asked if Ben and I would go get firewood.

Phew. Something to do.

We both grunted a yes, bundled up, and went out into the snow, neither of us saying a word. Which was a miracle in retrospect, because my hat was covered in pom-poms, and his pointy blue hat made him look an elf.

The air didn't nip—it *bit* at our cheeks. We stomped a trail through the crunchy snow, around the side of the house, grabbed a few logs, and shuffled back to the front door and set them down. We'd done our task, but for some reason, it seemed like we weren't going inside right away.

We looked at each other. Ben's cheeks were bright red, his nose had started to run. When looking at each other got too awkward, I glanced up.

There's nothing more beautiful than a Maine sky at night. You can see every single star, big or small, bright or fading. I loved it, and Ben was looking at it like he loved it too. For the first time that night, I let myself feel excited he was here, and that I got to see him in the middle of winter, like magic. I felt my heart rise up, up into the starry black sky. It floated up there, gently bouncing between the lights.

I glanced over at him; he was already looking at me. His kind, twinkly eyes, strands of floppy brown hair swooshed over his forehead, squished under his elf hat.

Suddenly, we were a foot apart. I pursed my lips. Kissing, right?

He reached out a hand, grabbed mine.

I fell closer, and our lips met. One second, one kiss: floating, starry.

When we drew back, I looked at him and quickly said, "Um, this never happened, okay?"

CHAPTER 63

Bee

I SAT WITH RACHEL and Ellie at evening campfire, with dozing littles in our laps. Apparently, Margo had been in Black Bear for a headache and was now asleep.

I tried not to enjoy seeing Ben across the flames too much.

Later, past bedtime, on my way back from another visit to the parking lot, I felt someone hovering behind me on the trail.

"Hey!" I called softly. "Do you need a buddy?"

Claudia stepped forward, out of the shadows.

"Ugh, not you," I said. "You've already got one." I turned around and started to march toward my cabin.

"Wait!" Claudia called out.

"I'll pass!" I called back.

"No, seriously, Bee—"

She caught up with me, face-to-face. I always forgot Claudia was taller than me. The bags under her eyes were as dark as squished blueberries. She wore boxer shorts and a black T-shirt. I crossed my arms over my chest.

"I don't want to talk to you," I said.

"Same," Claudia said quickly.

"Great." I went to turn around—

"But I want to know how Hana's doing?"

I turned back. Her face looked hopeful, in the way Claudia's face can. Not quite as serious, eyebrows slightly arched instead of a terrifying straight line across. What did Hana see in this asshole?

"Maybe you want to know that," I said slowly. "But you don't *get* to."

Her lips quivered ever so slightly. "I know, but . . . I heard she's leaving."

Ha! The Dogberry rumor mill. Hana hadn't shown up to work in three days, so I guessed that made sense. What did this girl want me to do, though? Tell her the location of the person she'd beaten up on? How dare she?

"Yeah, she's gone." I spat it out. "She left, because *you* made her life here miserable. You made up a shitty rumor, and she fell apart, and now she's gone. Are you happy?" The lie came out fast, and I didn't care that it wasn't all true. It was only not true *yet*.

"I—"

"You gigantic bully," I said, stabbing a finger at her. She winced and stepped back. "Do you get off on making other people feel bad?"

"Bully?" she sputtered. "I know all about bullying, believe me. The kids at my school—"

"Boo-hoo," I snapped. "So school's rough sometimes. You think it wasn't for me?"

"Umm, no, but—"

"So shut up!" I heard my voice getting too loud. "If you take it out on other people, you're just like them."

"That's not what I'm doing!" Claudia's voice almost matched mine. "Your sister cheated on me, Bee!"

I shook my head. "Bullshit. I hope all of this was worth it. And I hope you don't miss her. Because now she's gone, and she's going to miss the entire summer at camp, our last summer before I leave. So good on you for taking that away from her." I was done. I turned around and stomped away. When I got to my cabin, I glanced back—Claudia was sitting on the side of the trail, her face buried in her hands.

Fuck you, I thought.

And then I quietly burst into tears.

I zagged and went home to Big Bat. Rachel was in my cabin for the night, she could handle it.

CHAPTER 64

Hana

WAKING UP FROM MY dream—

I'm in her arms.

I'm touching her.

And then I'm drowning, gasping for air, choking on sharp gulps of water, the sunlight tries to reach me, but I'm already too deep—

My bed. The sheets, wrinkled and damp from sweat. It took me moments to understand where I was, who I was, why I was here.

"What can you do to help yourself feel better, Hana?" Louisa had asked me earlier, in our session.

"I can sleep," I'd said. "And pretend this never happened."

"What about work?" Louisa pressed. "You love swimming, teaching."

"It's a little hard to swim when your body feels like lead," I explained patiently.

It hadn't been the worst session. But I hadn't felt a whole lot better leaving it. She must've talked to my parents, because she didn't want me to leave camp, either. Why didn't they get it was killing me to stay?

I have to go. Now, I realized. *I can't wait. If I see her one more time, I'll drown.*

I had never been so miserable before. Well, in months. Being this miserable was impossible.

It was late. Really late. No one to keep tabs on me.

I changed into jeans and a sweatshirt and sneakers. I don't need to visit Aunt Beth, I thought. I can go somewhere else.

Christopher. Christopher wouldn't turn me away, if I showed up at his house. Christopher understands miserable. He would let me crash. Or we'd drive somewhere. And maybe he'd kiss me. . . .

My hands grabbed the car keys. I closed the front door quietly behind me.

It felt like ten miles to get to the parking lot, but I finally reached the blue hatchback. Dad's new car. I jumped in the passenger's seat, before realizing I was on the wrong side.

I settled behind the wheel, moving the seat up a few inches so my foot could safely reach the pedals. I was only just learning to drive, but I didn't intend to get pulled over. And if I did, what was the worst that would happen? I'd get arrested? The thought made me laugh inside, just a little.

I rotated the key carefully, feeling the engine wake up. I realized I needed to plug my phone in—I knew how to get to Christopher's, but I'd never driven there myself before. I flipped on the overhead lights and rummaged around for the phone charger in the glove compartment, but it wasn't there. I turned to check the back.

There, on the seat, was a pile of gear.

At first I sighed, thinking I would need to sneakily drop this off back at camp before I could go, in case they needed it tomorrow.

But then I saw whose gear it was: mine.

My old purple backpack with the daisies on it, monogrammed with my initials. The orange two-person tent my parents got us when we were little so Bee and I could camp out together. My mess kit and mini cooler, with my name written in all caps in black Sharpie: *HANA*.

I picked up the backpack and plunked it in the space between the front seats. Inside were a change of clothes, a pair of pajamas, a bathing suit, bug spray, sunscreen, a small thing of dry shampoo, and a toothbrush kit, all the kind we sell in the camp store. There was even a plastic bag with scissors and origami paper.

Only one person could've put this backpack together.

Heart pounding, I realized who it was.

Slowly, I unzipped the tiny top pocket, the one that didn't really fit anything. Except a small piece of paper, with a message, written in sloppy Magic Marker:

Hana. I love you. Please don't go. ♥

Under the overhead car lights, I reread the note four times, then folded it up and held it in my lap.

I could go. I could put the car in reverse, and back up, and follow the dirt road to the highway. I could go to Christopher's, where he'd probably make out with me. Or I could pull over on the highway instead, and sit in the dirty highway grass, and cry and cry and cry, and when I was soaked with tears, I could go find a river and wash it off.

But I loved Camp Dogberry. In a way, this note was from this place too.

But it was mostly from Bee.

I turned off the car. My feet found their way—down the dirt trail, up the front porch steps, up the stairs.

Bee was in her bedroom, waiting up, reading. She smiled when I came in.

"Hey, baby."

I crawled up into the bed, in between her and the window. I fell asleep with my back pressed against her.

CHAPTER 65

Vanessa

THURSDAY. WE'D ALMOST MADE it through another week. I was actually pretty sad to see this group go home. My silly, cranky peanuts.

They had even sort of distracted me from the terrible secret that had been taking over my brain, and from that terrible conversation with Margo. And now she was sick and MIA?

Sophia and I had our break at the same time Thursday morning, when we dropped the kids off at swim, right after breakfast. I helped them use the buddy board (most of them got it by now), moved their towels far enough away from the shoreline, and waved good-bye.

"Come hang out with me in Luna!" Sophia grabbed my arm. She'd been kind of obsessed with hanging out in the "counselor room" ever since Fourth of July. I didn't love how hot it got up there, but there were some video games, sooo . . .

As we walked away, I looked back one more time. No Hana, again. Just Judy with the sub instructor. I felt the creeping secret again. I turned and followed Sophia.

Luna's loft was empty. We fell back onto the couches, took out the old Nintendo console.

I'm usually awesome at the racing games. Ben made me learn

when I was little so he'd have competition at home. But the third time I came in last, Sophia paused the game.

"Okay." She shifted on the couch, bouncing to face me. She wore lime green today. "*What* is wrong with you?"

"What do you mean?"

"Why have you been weird all week?" she said. "You won't be on Team Claudia with us, you mope around, you spend all your free time with your campers—you're hardly taking breaks unless I make you!"

"I'm trying to get hired next year," I reminded her.

"It's not just that, though," Sophia insisted. "You're more lethargic than Gustavo."

"Can you not compare me to the camp turtle?" I asked. "And hey, Doc gave him some medicine. I think he's doing a lot better."

"Fine. So you're *more* lethargic than Gustavo!"

She waited for me to laugh. I managed a weak smile.

"Tell me what's wrong."

I bit my lip. "I can't?"

She grabbed my arm. "Now you're freaking me out, Nessa! You have to tell me!"

"I'm not freaking you out!" I complained. "You've done that to yourself!"

"Fine! So help me and tell me! What's the worst that could happen?"

You'll tell everyone, I said to myself. Then I realized: maybe that wasn't such a bad thing? But Margo might hate me forever. I liked *hearing* rumors. I didn't *start* them . . . but if I didn't tell someone, would that creeping sensation ever go away? It would feel so good to be done with it. . . .

"Hey." Wallace appeared over the railing, at the top of the stairs. "So I heard something, at Capture the Flag."

Sophia and I looked at each other. Wallace sat down and methodically explained the conversation he'd heard between Ben and Claudia and Donald. When he'd finished, my head was stuffed in a beanbag chair again.

"Okay," I groaned into the fabric, then sat up. "My turn."

And then I spilled my guts. I watched Sophia's jaw drop farther and farther. I almost stopped to laugh, but it felt so good to tell her, both of them. When I finished with Margo's reaction, she smacked her forehead.

"Nessa, why would you tell Margo?"

"I don't know!" I said. "It was about her?"

"She's obviously in the middle of this." Sophia shook her head. "You know who you need to tell."

"My brother."

"Yup. We've got lunch plans."

CHAPTER 66

Bee

HANA DIDN'T GO TO work on Thursday. But she didn't insist on leaving, either, so that was a win. Meanwhile, both my parents were pissed at me.

"Do you know anything about this?" Mom shook her phone in my direction.

"Yes, I can show you how to use a smartphone," I replied calmly. "But honestly, I'd ask Hana before me."

"Nooo." Mom shook the phone again. "I got a *call* from Senator King last night. John's back in New York City. As in, not at camp."

"Why would I know anything about that?"

Mom raised her brow at me. That brow, tho.

I held up my hands. "I seriously have no idea, Mom. Is someone covering for him?"

"Doug," she huffed. Then she grumbled something about camp drama, like she had any idea. She was living in a blissful bubble.

Hana left for therapy again around lunchtime. Which ended up working out well, because lunchtime, oh lunchtime, imploded in a way I'd never thought possible of lunch.

"Bee?" Ben approached my table, mid-conversation with Kamile and a few older campers.

"Ben?" I asked dramatically. The girls giggled. Ben turned red, which was satisfying.

"Can I talk to you?" he asked. I nodded, ignoring my table's escalating giggles.

He led me down the center of Dam, past all the tables. I felt Claudia and Donald watching us.

"Where are we—"

There, at the flagpole, stood Sophia, Vanessa, and Wallace, shifting and whispering to one another.

"What's going on? Do we need to get my mom?" I whispered on our way over to them.

"Not just yet," Ben said. "Hear this first."

∽

"Hey. How's your headache?"

Margo looked up. She was sitting on the little bench she'd put in the goat pen. Her phone sat next to her. The four kids crowded around her knees.

"Hey, Bee," she said. The goats turned and stared at me with their weird eyes. I eased into the pen, reached into the bucket, and scattered a handful of feed to clear a path to Margo.

I sat down on the bench next to her. "We need to talk."

"Are you breaking up with me?" she joked. But she wouldn't meet my eyes. It was only when I put my hand on her hand on the bench that she looked up at me.

"Never," I said. "But I do need to ask you something—have you been hooking up with Bobby this summer?"

Tears formed in her perfect twinkly eyes. "Bee, I promise, I didn't know."

"At the volleyball court?"

She nodded. "Bobby and I have been meeting up there."

"And so . . ."

"And I think Donald and Claudia must've seen us."

"Why didn't you say anything?"

"I didn't know what they were talking about that night!" she cried. "I thought they were talking about Christopher. And then I thought they meant that Hana had been hooking up with him at the volleyball court, too."

I raised my eyebrows.

Margo blushed. "Okay, but Hana *was* still texting him," she protested. "And with how things went last fall, I thought it might be a possibility. . . ."

Mushroom Fairy tried to eat the end of my shirt. I brushed him away.

"I only found out the other night what had actually happened, for sure," Margo admitted. "Vanessa told me that John had set me up, and Bobby had been in on it."

"Vanessa told Ben, who told me."

"Makes sense." Margo shrugged. "I knew she probably would. I just freaked out. I couldn't believe that I'd . . . That Hana had stopped coming to work . . . That this was all my fault."

"Not all your fault," I said quickly.

"Hugely my fault." Margo sniffed. "If I had been honest and

told you. Or if I'd been less pathetic, and just gotten over Max, or Donald . . ."

"Donald?" I gaped.

"Oh my God, you prude." Margo rolled her eyes. "Yes, I like Donald. And he asked *you* out."

"But he didn't really—"

"Darlin', you need to stop pretending people don't feel things." Margo stood up. "Camp is complicated, and we all feel stuff about it. Including you. That's part of why we like camp."

I crossed my arms and stared at the goat poop. Maybe she was right.

"But I *do* have an idea," she continued. "About a way we could fix this."

"That seems impossible." I sighed. "We're too far into it."

"It's only second session." She smiled. "Summer's only just started."

CHAPTER 67

Bee

I TOLD HANA ABOUT the misunderstanding, and about Margo's idea. Her whole face lit up for the first time in a week. After a quick conference with Raph, Margo released the news the next morning.

Kangaroo Court that evening, after camper pickup. Counselor and CIT–only edition.

Thus, camper pickup buzzed with tension. Yes, yes, here, take your child, right now, please. They had a good time, but we have a ton of shit to sort out.

Raph, Margo, and I walked over to Luna together, conferring on the stage directions.

Luna felt especially packed with all the adult-size people. Everyone was murmuring, and the crowd's eyes widened when I walked in.

No Bobby in sight. Connie sat at the front of the room with Ellie and Rachel.

At first, I didn't see Donald and Claudia, but Ben pointed out Claudia in one corner, and Donald in another, no longer united in their assholery. I nodded at Ben, walked to the back of the room, opened a window, and then sat down at the defense table. Ben sat down next to me, and Raph took his place front and center.

"Welcome to another round of Kangaroo Court," he announced. The room hushed. "Today, I present to you a personal case. We won't be needing a jury, no offense."

Ben called out: "Also, we're gonna have a dance party afterward."

A few tentative giggles from the crowd. "Yes, that too," Raph agreed. "Dance party in the dining hall after we're done here." He banged the gavel before continuing. "No doubt you have all heard rumors," Raph said, raising his voice slightly higher than the whispering, and they were quiet once more. "That our beloved Hana viciously betrayed Claudia." Audible gasps. Were we really going to address that *here*? "Bee, please present the rest of this case."

You bet we were. I tried to see Claudia's face in the back, but it was hidden in shadow.

I stood. "I don't know how many of you believed this absolute and total falsehood, but let me set the record straight: my sister did no such thing. She did not deserve your glares or gossip, and she left, humiliated, determined to spend the summer somewhere other than Camp Dogberry, for the first time *in ten years*!"

My crowd delivered a reaction with an appropriate amount of terror and excitement. I turned to look at Ben, whose face clearly said to me: Oh, Bee, *come on*.

Okay, okay.

"All right, so, I want to clear the air here for Hana. This week—"

"Wait, Bee!" Margo stood up.

"Oh right, your turn."

Margo marched to the front of the room and stood where the witness usually stands.

Raph smiled and gestured at her. "Ms. Margo, you have the floor."

"Thank you." Margo nodded back. Her purple hair flew out in

all directions. She glanced around the room until her eyes landed on me. I smiled at her, and she lifted her chin.

"I need to apologize," she said. "For what's happened here. Donald and Claudia made this assumption because they saw two people on the volleyball court . . . together."

The room murmured.

"I know you've all heard about that," Margo said, raising her hands up. "But what you didn't know was that was Bobby and me."

Gasps. But I couldn't take my eyes off Claudia, who flinched so hard it looked like she'd been punched.

"I didn't realize what had happened until it felt too late to tell the truth," she explained. Raph nodded encouragingly, Santa beard bobbing. "But Vanessa did, and she convinced me to do the right thing."

All eyes turned to Vanessa, whose cheeks flushed pink. She gave a small wave.

"And here's the thing: this was just an *enormous* waste of time!" Margo smiled, a little unconvincingly, but the room felt lighter when she did. "And really, the problem is: people need to stop making out at the volleyball court. It's not camp appropriate."

Everyone laughed, even Donald.

"I highly recommend any romantic endeavors happening in a less public spot." Margo shrugged, finishing the last line of her statement. "And I'm sorry for any part I played in this."

The audience murmured in what sounded like disapproval. But at the exact right moment—

"I forgive you!" Hana's beaming face appeared in the open window.

"She's aliiiiiive!" Margo shouted.

All the counselors burst out laughing and started shouting. Hana ran around the front, and walked through the door to an enormous cheer. Everyone crowded around her, hugging her, yelling their apologies. She hugged everyone and smiled. The laughter in the room sounded relieved, and my heart panged.

Hana pushed forward to me and slid under my arm, and the audience began to clap, but then another person took the stage, one who was definitely not included in my carefully planned script. Bobby had jumped up toward the front of the room, over by Raph.

"Hey, so, umm . . ." The happy action immediately paused. When did he get here? "Yeah." He sighed. "I need to come clean. John was really into Claudia—" He gestured at Claudia, who looked like she might dissolve instantly into bug juice. "And he thought they were gonna, um, go out. So he got really upset when he heard about her and Hana, and we planned this thing, and then things got out of hand. . . . I'm sorry, Margo."

The whole room went silent. I quickly looked at Ben, then Margo, who looked like she might stab Bobby with an improv'd knife. I wouldn't have blamed her at all.

"And to be fair"—he turned to Claudia and Donald—"*we* were the ones who helped spread all that Team Claudia stuff. I'm sorry about that, too."

"You're fired," I said firmly. I totally didn't have the authority to do that, but in that moment, it didn't matter to me at all. I was sure what he'd done crossed professional lines.

Bobby shrugged. "Yeah, that makes sense." And he hightailed it out of the room. Nobody had any idea what to make of all of this, so I went into teacher mode.

"Another lesson needs to be learned here—we need to be careful with gossip at this camp."

I was met with dubious stares.

"Look at where these rumors got us!" I gestured at Hana. "It's one thing to buzz for fun, another to believe everything we hear and pass it along as if it's truth."

The room was absolutely silent, but then Connie raised a fist in the air. "Yeah!"

"Hear, hear!" called out Raph, banging his gavel. The crowd began to disperse, in a giant, rumbling cloud of excitement. "Dance party in Dam!" Raph shouted over everyone, and began leading the staff out the door, still wearing his puffy white beard. He turned and winked at me. Thank goodness for Raph.

Hana turned to give me a full-on hug. I was so happy to have her back from the edge that I almost starting crying right there. Then I saw someone approach from the corner of my eye. It was Connie, with Donald and Claudia hovering behind. I nudged Hana and she released me.

"I'm sorry," Connie said. "I knew what John was doing, and I didn't stop him." Her eyes were watery, too. She looked genuinely ashamed.

"That's okay," Hana said. "We all get confused sometimes." My benevolent sister pulled her in for a hug.

"But, um . . ." Connie glanced between us nervously. "Do you know where John is? I haven't seen him."

"John's left camp," Donald cut in, his voice flat. "My dad's gonna be so pleased."

Connie smiled tightly. "Thanks. Good to know." She turned and caught up with Rachel and Ellie on her way out. Donald, after shooting Ben and me a rueful, apologetic glance, followed.

But Claudia stayed, eyes locked on one person.

CHAPTER 68

Hana

CLAUDIA GLOWED FAINTLY, LIKE the sorriest star in the sky. She walked toward me, past Bee and Margo, as if right out of a dream. I walked toward her, and we met in the middle of the room.

"I'm sorry," she whispered. "I can't believe I thought—"

"It's okay. You were tricked," I said. "This whole thing was unreal."

Tears were falling on the floor, pattering quickly, like rain.

She took my face in her hands. "I'm so sorry. I'm so, so, sorry."

"I'm sorry, too." I gently reached out for her waist. "I'm sorry that I texted Christopher back, and that I didn't tell you." When I said this, her gaze never faltered. "I wasn't hooking up with him," I explained, my voice low. "He just messaged me a couple times, and I messaged him back . . . and then realized I needed to shut it down. I promise, I'm done with him."

It's you forever and forever.

"I believe you," she said, so seriously I almost laughed, but I didn't. "I shouldn't have assumed. I was just afraid, I just thought—I thought you didn't love me like I love you."

I blinked, then smiled. "I think I love you exactly like that."

CHAPTER 69

Ben

CLAUDIA RAN OFF AS soon as the group got to Dam. She made Hana wait outside on the porch while she sprinted to her cabin and inside the dining hall. About fifteen awkward minutes later, Hana was allowed to enter.

Strung in the entryway, across rows and rows of garlands, were a million little paper stars.

"I got them out of the compost," Claudia explained. "The less gross ones, anyway. I was going to apologize, but then you left, and now . . . Here." She gestured, spastically, romantically, above her head. "I'm sorry."

Hana cried, and they kissed. It was pretty freakin' cute.

And then the dance party finally started. Raph had dimmed the lights, moved the table, and happily DJed from the kitchen counter.

It felt like a fog had finally lifted from camp. Nessa talked and laughed with her friends. Rachel, Ellie, Connie, Jen, and Margo led the Macarena and Electric Slide. Maybe the drama had just exploded early in the summer, and we'd be done now!

One could only fucking hope.

Eventually, a slow song came on. Couples immediately formed, pulling each other out on the floor. Bee and I automatically didn't look at each other. No matter how much I wanted to sweep her into the music, I wanted her to be comfortable. And she clearly wasn't.

I offered her a baby carrot instead. She smiled, like she knew the carrot was really a dance.

Suddenly, a shout from our left startled me.

"Ben, Bee!" Donald stepped forward. "Aren't you two going to dance?"

Suddenly, we'd attracted our entire group's attention. Even Hana and Claudia wandered over.

"Oh yeah," Margo chimed in. "I think they really should."

"What?!" Bee shouted, looking like a deer in headlights again.

Everyone burst out laughing. I leaned over and whispered, "Umm, maybe they know?"

"They can't know anything—we have nothing to tell them!" she hissed back.

Maybe before that would've hurt, but I knew Bee now in a way I didn't before. I squeezed her hand again. "Bee—"

"Okay, listen up." Donald laughed. "It's time for us to reveal our plot."

"Yes!" Margo squealed. "It's the best thing we've done all summer."

"By far." Claudia rolled her eyes. Hana kissed her cheek.

"What?" Bee demanded.

"Cupid Donald's plan," Margo explained. "Hana and I—"

"And Claudia and I—"

"Set you two up!" Margo finished proudly. "We tricked you into liking each other!"

I thought back to what had started this—the conversation in Dam, Claudia and Donald saying she liked me. It all dawned on me at once.

They must've have seen that on my face, because everyone burst out laughing.

Bee looked at me, in a mix of emotions I'd never quite seen on her before. She was half laughing, watching everyone shout, half crying, for, like, four thousand reasons, and one part of her looked at me in the way I wished for every second I was awake, and in every dream I had.

Bee

Did everyone seriously know? Was this entire camp shipping us the whole time?

My knees shook forcefully, knocking and rubbing together under the table. I looked at Ben—he seemed okay, smiling, laughing at their reactions. Why couldn't I be so relaxed?

And yeah, I was happy we'd all united again, in the name of humiliating me. I felt anger bubble up inside me, and then the truth along with it—

"You didn't trick us," I said, my voice cutting like the adult scissors in the art building. "We're—we're not—"

"Before you say anything," Ben said, "can I see your phone?"

What? But I pulled it out of my pocket and handed it to him.

"Ahh, yes, here it is. Here's mine." He handed it back to me. "Open up the texts from me."

I did and immediately burst out laughing.

> Hey, girl. I like you so much. I'm actually in love with you. I worship the ground you walk on. I think you're funny and fiery and gorgeous and ambitious. Please go to college prom with me

Ben showed me the text on his phone that I'd apparently written.

> Hey, I like you so much Ben. Really, I love you. You're super hot, and hilarious, and you're premed, which is devastatingly attractive, and I think it's really sexy that you sleep in late

"In writing, remember?" Ben said gently. My heart warbled, and then sang out long, clear notes.

And then we both cracked up, but nobody knew what we were cracking up about. When I finally recovered, I replied to their amused stares.

"Fine, fine," I said. "You didn't trick us, because Ben and I have liked each other for *years*."

That sent up a big cheer from all of our friends.

Including Ben. He grinned. "Years and years."

"And I'll have you know—"

"Bee." Hana put an arm on my shoulder. "Babe, just dance with Ben, okay?"

I looked at her in disbelief. My baby sister had never condescended to me, ever. I was going to say that, when Ben grabbed both of my hands and placed them around his neck. I heard a whistle from the back. *Raph.*

I'd fantasized about bringing Ben to every school dance. About everyone watching us. About his laughing eyes meeting mine as we swayed to some cheesy love song. And now that was exactly what we were doing.

We danced far enough apart, on purpose, so we could stare at each other. Disgusting but true, and it felt so good.

After a minute, Ben pulled me closer and leaned to whisper in my ear, "Bee, I'm in love with you."

My vision got blurry. My heart tripped up its beat.

"But aren't we just friends?" I whispered back.

℃ℂ

After the dance was over, we flew out of Dam—*flew*—down to the trail, to the water. He pulled me so close, while the waves lapped. And just like that, I forgot everything else, the last few weeks, the last year. We kissed, again and again and again, and it all made perfect sense.

CHAPTER 70
John

SUMMER IN NEW YORK CITY smelled like hot dogs and pigeon poop, but man, oh man, had I missed it. My mom had a million questions, and I'd felt bad she'd looked so worried when I'd shown up. I told her not to answer her phone if King called—I'd handle it. And I did, by ignoring him. Maybe he'd cut me off. Maybe Yale wouldn't take me back. I didn't care anymore. I watered the plants and got back my old job at the café down the street. I smoked and wandered blocks at night with friends who knew me.

A few weeks after I'd ditched Dogberry, Bobby came to visit for a night. I had to hand it to him—I didn't think that kid could hang in the city with my friends here. But they liked him, and I didn't mind having him around.

After a couple beers at a friend's house party, I finally got the balls to ask, "So, what happened with Claudia?"

Bobby smiled, and popped the collar on his terrible acid-washed jean jacket. "I knew you'd ask, eventually."

"And?"

"It's all good. She and Hana got back together."

That night, under the lights, on the road behind camp, their hands in each other's hair, flashed in my mind.

"Okay, good."

"Good?"

"Yeah." I finished my beer. "I'm glad."

Bobby cackled and shook his head. "Seriously? You pull all this crap, and then you're just, like, 'Good'?"

I shook my head. "You don't get it."

Bobby shrugged. "Nah, I don't. But the whole thing got me fired."

I got him another beer.

WHAT HAPPENED NEXT

Ben

THE SKY IN MAINE has the best stars, and everyone knows that, but Boston's streetlamps were beginning to look more beautiful every day. And while snow in Maine fell in sparkling, trustworthy heaps, these city-scattered flakes had their own look about them. I could barely remember what it felt like to hate living here. Especially when a figure hustled toward me from the subway stop, and when she got close enough, her smile beamed as bright as any summer star. She wore her Dogberry-green beanie all slouchy and perfect.

"Can you believe this?" She laughed, holding up a mittened hand. "It's not even Thanksgiving! Isn't Massachusetts supposed to be warmer?"

"It's still New England." I grinned, reaching for her other hand to pull her closer. Our lips touched. "That's the second time we've kissed in the snow," I whispered, when we pulled back.

She only rolled her eyes a little, which was how I knew she loved me.

We grabbed coffees and started our usual routine—loops and loops around Boston Common, catching up. We were both so busy

with classes, and Bee's part in *West Side Story*, that sometimes we only saw each other once a week.

"So, what's the news on Hana and Claudia?" I asked.

"Back together." Bee sighed. "That's three times since this summer."

"That's ridiculous," I sputtered. "Can you imagine if we broke up and got back together that many times?"

She laughed, lighting up the snowflakes. "Yeah, because we kind of did."

"Oh, right."

Bee

Ben's hand in mine felt like the sun—constant, even in the cold. I couldn't imagine a time when we wouldn't be together. Although I never told him that. Some secrets you keep to yourself. They make you glow inside.

Ben was talking about class, the snow was falling, his eyes were twinkling in the fading, hazy city lights. When I was with Ben, I felt . . . myself. Relaxed. At home. My dorm, my classes, and rehearsals—my new life was exhilarating, and sometimes confusing and overwhelming. A kind of free fall.

But with Ben, I felt like I was standing on solid ground. Our hands, together, made sense.

"Hey, did you know it's our three-month-and-three-day anniversary?"

I looked up from our hands—his eyes smiling at me from behind his hair smooshed on his forehead from his dorky elf winter hat.

"I did know that!" I said. "I have it marked on my calendar, next to *remind Ben to get a hobby.*"

"So since it's our anniversary," he continued, "I was wondering if you'd tell me: When did you first fall in love with me?"

I tried to tell my EBU friends that my boyfriend was a sap, but they just didn't get to what extent. I pulled him down to sit on a bench, just in case I was going to pass out from his cheesiness.

"Well, it had to be when you puked at the lobster fest," I reasoned. "When we were nine."

"Yeah, that must've been pretty attractive." Ben nodded. "I remember feeling very bold, throwing up right there in the middle of the sing-along."

"Exactly." I nodded back. "When did you first fall in love with me?"

"Same." He shrugged. "When I was puking."

We both cracked up, and he reached over and wrapped a glove around my neck and pulled me in for a kiss. And then another.

"You're so weird," I whispered.

"Mmmm," he countered, nuzzling my nose with his.

"But the world is full of weird things," I continued, my lips touching his to form the words.

"Yeah?"

"And you're my favorite," I said.

He pulled back, his eyes twinkling into mine. "I'm your favorite?"

"Yeah." I smiled, pushing his hat back. "You're my favorite weird thing in the world."

ACKNOWLEDGMENTS

Book two! Here we go! I have so many people to thank, again. I swore it'd be shorter this time, but . . .

Thank you, Gus, Nellie, Tory, and Jenny, for being such wonderful, witty siblings. Thank you, Mom, Vicki Horton, for believing in me and believing in yourself. And happy sixtieth birthday!! Thank you, Aunt Lynn, for all of your help and for Suzie.

Thank you to my agent, Alex Slater, for your keen eye and never-ending enthusiasm. Brainstorming with you is like the best kind of summer camp. Thank you, everyone at Trident Media Group, for believing in and supporting my career.

Thank you to my editor, Kieran Viola, for, oh gosh, everything. But a lot for infusing power and friendship in everything we do, and for sharing my vision of this Much Ado. Thank you, Cassie McGinty, and every lovely person at Hyperion I've had the pleasure of working with.

Thank you to Shadae Mallory for your thoughtful feedback.

Thank you, Girl Scouts, specifically Camp Runels in New Hampshire and Camp Pennacook in Massachusetts, for making me love summer camp. Thank you, Camp Blueberry Cove in Maine, for the inspiration, especially for Counselor Hunt and Sproutball.

Thank you to Deborah Cooper and Samrawit Silva for sharing with me your adoption stories.

Thank you, Tower counselors: Rachel Gianatasio, Jen Locke, Shane Mulcahy, Doug Pass, Sam Stratton, David Thibodeau, and Nellie Booth (again, it's fine, it bears repeating). Thank you, CITs: Ilana DeAngelo, Nick Hurley, Eric Krouss, Joe McKeever, Liam Norton, Chris Shepard, Nate Shepard, Danielle Shiloh, and Matthew Wallace. Obviously also, big thank-yous to Judy Locke, Ginny Morton, and Janine.

Thank you, Elisabeth Joffe, for being you and helping me be me.

Thank you, Rosie Kahan, for listening to me cry, cry, cry, and for being *Saving Hamlet*'s bookstore champion. Thank you, Jen Locke (Jewelry Ken), for being there when no one else could and also for playing Buckbeak in Video Production at camp. Thank you, Megan Reed, for our friendship, which includes clarification on split infinitives and many doggo Snapchat messages. Thank you, Ellie Roark, for endless Gchats and love.

Thank you, Julia Perlowski, the Beatrice to my Beatrice. Thank you, Brian Mooney and Vaune Trachtman—you two make me feel like I can do anything. Congratulations, Geraldine Pittman de Batlle and T. Wilson, on years of extraordinary teaching at Marlboro College.

Thank you, Betsy Klimasmith and the University of Massachusetts Boston, for a new, lovely academic home.

Thank you, Bridget Hodder and Dana Langer—your friendship got this book written.

Thank you to Doug and Lise Pass for being so supportive of my books. You truly make this world a better place.

Thank you, All the World's a Stage Players, for renewing my love of theatre and Shakespeare. Thank you especially to Jenny, for helping me create Margo.

Thank you, Lin-Manuel Miranda. Thank you, Griffin and Rachel McElroy. Thank you, Tegan and Sara.

Thank you, Paul Nelsen, for taking me to the Globe, and for showing me Shakespeare's Globe's *Much Ado About Nothing*, my most favorite production. Thank you, Eve Best and Charles Edwards, for your glorious performances that so much inspired Bee and Ben.

Thank you, Harriet and Suzie. You don't know why I stare at a screen so much, but you accept me and love me anyway, and trust that I'll come out of my trance and feed/walk/pet you soon.

Thank you to past me, summer 2016. I don't know how you wrote

this book. From now on, when I doubt that I'm a writer, I'll look to you, and this book, as proof.

Thank you, William Shakespeare, for Don John, Don Pedro, Margaret, Claudio, Hero, and Benedick, whom I love so much and felt inspired to explore.

But most of all, thank you for Beatrice, forever dancing in the stars of my heart.